BABES IN TOMORROWLAND

BABES IN

Tomorrowland

WALT DISNEY AND THE MAKING OF THE AMERICAN CHILD, 1930–1960

Nicholas Sammond

DUKE UNIVERSITY PRESS

DURHAM AND LONDON 2005

PRINTED IN THE UNITED STATES
OF AMERICA ON ACID-FREE PAPER ∞
DESIGNED BY AMY RUTH BUCHANAN
TYPESET IN DANTE AND BERTHOLD
BODONI BY TSENG INFORMATION
SYSTEMS, INC.
LIBRARY OF CONGRESS CATALOGING-
IN-PUBLICATION DATA APPEAR ON THE
LAST PRINTED PAGE OF THIS BOOK.

It is the nightly custom of every good mother after her children are asleep to rummage in their minds and put things straight for next morning, repacking into their proper places the many articles that have wandered during the day. If you could keep awake (but of course you can't) you would see your own mother doing this, and you would find it very interesting to watch her. It is quite like tidying up drawers. You would see her on her knees, I expect, lingering humorously over some of your contents, wondering where on earth you had picked this thing up, making discoveries sweet and not so sweet, pressing this to her cheek as if it were as nice as a kitten, and hurriedly stowing that out of sight. When you wake in the morning, the naughtiness and evil passions with which you went to bed have been folded up small and placed at the bottom of your mind and on the top, beautifully aired, are spread out your prettier thoughts, ready for you to put on.

—J. M. BARRIE, *Peter Pan*

Contents

Acknowledgments

This book has benefited enormously from the careful reading, insightful criticism, and thoughtful comments of many colleagues and friends, and the few words offered here can only begin to repay them. Thanks go first to Chandra Mukerji, who has been for many years an unfailing mentor and critic, and my first inspiration for this project. I also owe a debt of gratitude to Eric Smoodin, who gave unselfishly of his knowledge of cinema history in general, and of Disney in particular. The Critical Studies writing group at the University of California, San Diego, listened carefully to various versions of this work and pushed me to make more of it. In particular, group members Patrick Carroll and Corynne McSherry questioned weak points and celebrated strong ones, and I have suffered their criticism quite happily. Howard Brick, Margaret Garb, Timothy Parsons, Mark Pegg, and Robert Vinson at Washington University, St. Louis, also provided much-needed direction, close reading, and constructive suggestions. At different and crucial moments, Henry Jenkins at MIT and Charles McGovern, first at the Smithsonian and later at William and Mary College, acted with unstinting generosity as critics and editors, and I will always be grateful to them. Shelley Stamp in the Department of Film and Digital Media at the University of California, Santa Cruz, also offered valuable support and encouragement.

My deep and sincere thanks go to my editor Ken Wissoker for having faith in me as an author, and for his seemingly endless patience, humor, and goodwill, which saw me through doubt and hesitation on more than one occasion. Courtney Berger and Kate Lothman at Duke University Press were also unflagging in their support and guidance, for which I am very grateful.

I offer my warm appreciation to Yrjo Engestrom and Carol Padden in the Communication Department at the University of California, San Diego, who taught me much about Marx and about the history of childhood, respectively. At various times, Alison Schapker, Mark Sussman, Mark Frankel, Jon Nichols, Anthony Freitas, and Susan Sterne each offered insights and critique for which I remain indebted. Thanks are also due to Erik Knutzen, Kelly Coyne, Pat Kelly, and Caroline Clerc for making of my time in San Diego an experience in the ironic and brilliant surface that is Southern California; and to Dave Landau, Melissa Ehn, Shay Braun, Neon Weiss, and Emanuella Bianchi in San Francisco for meeting my perpetual crankiness head-on with unflappable whimsy. Thanks to my brother, Christopher, for his love and consideration.

Above all, I am deeply grateful to Amy Greenstadt—whose intelligence, insight, wit, wisdom, and craft are exceeded only by her patience and love—for teaching me by example the proper ratio of sweat to faith. "This thing of darkness I acknowledge mine."

Portions of this work were supported by the Communication Department at the University of California, San Diego; the Spencer Foundation (under the auspices of the Laboratory of Comparative Human Cognition, under the supervision of Michael Cole); and the National Museum of American History at the Smithsonian Institution. Revisions were supported by the Andrew W. Mellon Foundation and the Modeling Interdisciplinary Inquiry program at Washington University, St. Louis, under the able direction of Steven Zwicker, Gerry Izenberg, and Derek Hirst. I am particularly indebted to Professors Hirst and Zwicker for their encouragement and support. My thanks also to Dave Smith and Becky Cohen at the Disney Archives for opening both the archives and their own stores of knowledge to me. Kay Peterson in the archives at the National Museum of American History at the Smithsonian Institution, and the staff of the SUNY Center at the Rochester Public Library, generously helped with image research. The Library of Congress and National Archives also provided research assistance. The National Science Foundation provided ten hours of supercomputing, which remain unused.

Introduction THE CHILD

By now we have begun to forget the story. On April 20, 1999, Eric Harris and Dylan Klebold walked into Columbine High School in Littleton, Colorado, and went on a shooting spree that left fifteen people dead, including themselves. It was, by all accounts, a tragedy.

In the aftermath of that tragedy, a wide range of social actors—from the police, to local, state, and federal politicians, to pundits, to child advocacy groups, to the families of the victims—began to reach for answers. What led these boys to this act of insanity? In national media reports that followed, as well as in hearings in the U.S. Senate, one culprit repeatedly rose above the rest: the media. Harris and Klebold had listened to heavy metal music, played violent video games, and watched violent movies. Like the people who had supplied the boys with their weapons, media producers became accomplices in the death of so many innocents. The boys who pulled the trigger were, in a sense, victims themselves, unable to resist mass culture's siren call to kill. While the boys' home life and friendships were examined in the soul-searching that followed (sometimes sincere, sometimes hyperbolic and self-serving), media influence soon loomed larger as an explanation than, say, their easy access to nine-millimeter pistols, an assault rifle, and sawed-off shotguns. It provided a relatively simple answer to a complex and deeply troubling question: *why* would they do such a thing? What *made* them do it?

The idea that Harris and Klebold—and the other white, suburban children (almost all boys) who attempted to kill their peers and teachers in the late 1990s—were themselves victims of media influence also foreclosed a number of other, related questions and observations. What was the relationship between this tragedy and the epidemic of gun-related deaths in poor and working-class neighborhoods in American cities? What were the larger social and material causes—beyond family trouble and peer pressure—for their acts? If Klebold and Harris had all of the advantages that are supposed to make an act like this so unthinkable—a middle-class upbringing in safe, suburban surroundings, good schools, and the prospect of a bright economic future—if all of those things were true, did this mean that we, as a society, expected and accepted that children denied these advantages were more likely to commit such acts of mayhem? Did we signify by our silence that this was somehow OK?

What could such a grim and haunting topic possibly have to do with something as wholesome and happy as Walt Disney? They are linked by the notion that if bad media create bad kids, then surely good media will create good ones. If violent children such as Klebold and Harris—or Lionel Tate, who at age twelve beat his six-year-old friend to death and blamed it on televised professional wrestling—had grown up on a steady diet of Disney products, perhaps more than one tragedy might have been averted.[1] For over seventy years Walt Disney Productions has made a name for itself by offering products that are ostensibly an alternative to unsavory popular media and a prophylactic against their negative effects.[2] Thus, arguments about the role of popular media in producing violent and delinquent children not only mask other discussions of social cause and effect, they also open up market opportunities for savvy producers. This is one of the two objects of this book: to understand how arguments about regulating harmful media gave rise to arguments for media beneficial to the development of children into socially productive adults, and how Walt Disney Productions benefited from those debates.

These arguments have required a stable and widely held understanding of what a child is, and what its place is in the production of American social and cultural life. This constitutes the second object of this book: examining the origins of a "generic child" against which parents judge their efforts in raising their real children, which marketers of educational products mobilize to inspire the anxiety that leads to sales, or which social critics invoke as in need of protection from the excesses of American public and commercial culture. Is that child comprised of a set of universally recognized qualities, or is its nature contingent upon historically specific understandings of the relationship between nature, culture, and society? If Walt Disney products are good for the child, how does the company imagine that child, and from whence does it draw that description?

This project has its origins in twenty years of teaching in public schools, museums, community centers, juvenile detention facilities, and universities. Yet I call upon this experience not to lay claim to authority or essential wisdom, but to deny it. Having taught many different children in a range of institutional settings, I find myself less able to say what a child truly is than when I began teaching twenty years ago. Indeed, the variety of my experience is what led me to question the meaning(s) of childhood in the United States. Over and over, I have been struck by the distance between the rhetoric deployed about the importance of children and childhood to our nation's future—by candidates for national office, or by the makers of new technology, or by media watchdogs on the left and right who fear the corrupting influences of mass media on youth—and the conditions under which most children grow up. The recent shootings by white suburban teens have raised a question long asked by those concerned with the welfare of the urban poor and their children to a level at which it may be heard by all: whether the youth who are ostensibly so important to our national future are receiving the attention and resources they need to grow into a mature and meaningful humanity. As they have been at similar historical junctures, the responses to this question have ranged from calls to censor popular media and install prisonlike security in schools, to return working women to the home, to post the Ten Commandments in study halls and cafeterias, or to lower the age at which young people may be tried as adults. Correct the way children are raised, the reasoning goes, and you will eliminate a number of social ills. In all of this furor, however, few have asked why it is that we expect children to solve the social, moral, and political problems of our age, or how we arrived at that position.

The term *child* is broadly generic and sometimes serves to erase or obscure important social differences and similarities between persons, some of whom are children, some of whom are not. Beyond this primarily negative function, the term is also enlisted in the service of programs, organizations, or campaigns within which a better or worse future plays a significant role. The most obvious of these is the political campaign in which a contender invokes the well-being of children as a necessary component for maintaining the community's (town's, city's, nation's) well-being. Another might be the organization that attempts to impose regulatory limitations on media—particularly television, movies, and the Web—by arguing that unrestricted access to those media will bring about permanent changes in the child that will affect its ability to function as a worker or a citizen in adult life—as a "productive member of society." Though grounded in the real bodies and the real lives of actual children, the term *child* is a highly potent discursive tool that is invoked to shape, limit, or foreclose arguments about social and material relations between individuals and classes of people in this country. More so than the terms *adult*, *senior citizen*, or *working-class person*, the term *child* performs specific operations that shape the possible understandings available when we attempt to speak of those relations. What I hope to demonstrate during the course of this work are some of the specific operations by which the current popular concept of a generic child came about during the twentieth century, and the different functions that concept has served at historically specific moments and in relation to specific classes of people. For the real strength of the concept of the child resides in its transcendent nature, its potentiality, its susceptibility to an environment of which it is not yet a fully active part, its state of being more sinned against than sinning. In a clientist liberal state such as the United States of America, the child is the ultimate client: its requirements are generally defined according to its condition of becoming, and unlike the adult it will become, its status as citizen-in-the-making means that it can be invoked without immediate recompense. The benefits accorded to it are assigned in trust to others, and the loss of those benefits by other client groups is unassailable, so potent and virtuous is the child's social function. To make an argument for the children, for the future, is to invoke a constituency not yet arrived, the common good of which cannot be questioned.

The important thing here, then, is not *whether* the child is socially constructed, but *how* it is socially constructed. What are the specific processes through which the terms surrounding childhood have taken on their operative meanings? The examples above offer a small sample of the current uses of those terms, but they do so without sufficient grounding in the sociohistorical circumstances that give rise to them. More simply put: how is it that when the child's welfare is invoked, other more immediate claims appear to transgress a greater social good? How does the child so often trump the homeless, the poor, the destitute, persons of color, and so on in social and political discourse? Wendy Brown has argued that "liberal discourse itself . . . continuously recolonizes political identity as political interest—a conversion that recasts politicized identity's substantive and often deconstructive cultural claims and critiques as generic claims of particularism endemic to universalist political culture" (Brown 1993). As a constituent group, children straddle the line between the particular and the universal, occupying a unique position in which they are simultaneously the creatures of their parents and of the state, but not yet individuals unto themselves. What I hope to demonstrate here is one particular discursive operation that makes that conversion possible, that posits in the generic child an embodied potential subject which has the power to reduce identities to interest groups and to defer claims for immediate redress to a relatively uncertain future.[3]

The future of "America's children," hence America, is a potent social and political lever. Each of the classes of persons trumped by "the child" may or may not have children, and each may have needs that conflict with another, but the presence of children and *their* needs serves to override those distinctions. For example, in the late 1980s, I worked as a substitute teacher in the public schools in rural Vermont. At that time, one of the schools in which I occasionally taught was in serious need of repair and expansion, and the matter was put to a vote in town meeting. On the surface, the matter seemed simple: the school was in disrepair and too small for its growing population; it should be fixed. Unfortunately, the cost of the repairs would require the town to float a bond, which the townsfolk would finance from property taxes. Here, the town divided. Many of the poorer townspeople, whose families had lived there for generations and had earned their living in rapidly failing rural professions such as logging and dairy farming, argued that the increase in taxes would force them to leave the land and the area. The newer arrivals, many of whom made their living in more metropolitan and larger nearby communities and commuted to and from town, argued that to forgo the repairs would doom all of the town's children (including theirs) to a substandard education and a limited future. The vote was close, but the repair bond passed. The school was repaired and the town became even more attractive to commuters. Within a few years, some of the poorer residents were indeed forced to sell their land and move, and their children no longer benefited from the improvements. But the repairs had been made for "the children" and for the future.

The child has not always occupied this privileged position in the social hierarchy, nor, obviously, do all real children today.[4] There is a contradiction between the lived experience of children today and the generic concept of "the child." This book traces the history of the *concept* of the child in twentieth-century America, as opposed to an historical account of lived childhood in the United States. Rather than examine accounts of the living conditions of actual children in different historical, geographic, class, and racial locations, in order to map changes to a "children's culture" or a "children's market," I will follow the general notion of childhood as it operates in arguments in which children are considered to have a significant stake. More specifically, I will map out changes to the notion of childhood as it has operated in several distinct discursive locations: (1) in popular literatures on child-rearing; (2) in an emerging literature of popular sociology that purported to represent a unified American culture to its readers; and (3) in arguments about the effects of mass media on children and the responses of media corporations (particularly Walt Disney Productions) to those arguments. I have chosen these three locations from a larger universe of discourses about children and childhood because each shares a common understanding of the child as an object producing and produced by American culture, and because each of the three imagines child-rearing as more than simply the immediate practice of feeding, clothing, and disciplining children, but as constituting through those actions the nascent form of a future society. The child is understood as a marker for a set of assumptions about the nature of personhood and citizenship, rather than simply as a definition that sets basic maximum and minimum age limits. Beginning at the turn of this century and working forward until the beginning of the 1960s, I will examine how these three discourses interacted with each other, and how in that interaction they contributed to the production of the abstract and generic notion of the child that carries so much currency today.

The Twentieth Century: Children of Science, Children of the Market

Although Western theorizing about the nature of childhood and the practice of child-rearing dates back to classical Greece, the child of the twentieth century is historically unique for two reasons. First, unlike preceding generations, it was the object of rigorous empirical study by an organized network of researchers: it was the product of the quantification, validation, and circulation of physical and behavioral norms against which the progress of individual children was to be measured. Although the foundations for this study had been laid by the moral and natural philosophy of Montaigne, Locke, and (particularly) Rousseau, students of childhood in the late nineteenth and early twentieth centuries, such as G. Stanley Hall and Arnold Gesell, broke the rhetorical chain of arguing from and against one's predecessors, choosing instead to rely more directly upon clinical observation.[5] Second, the child of the twentieth century was the first child consumer of mass culture—of dime novels, pulp magazines, movies, radio, and eventually television. By the late 1910s the child was emerging as the distinct target of advertisers and marketers, a valuable commodity in its own right.[6]

These developments are not unrelated. As the twentieth century progressed and the empirical data of child development was translated for a popular audience, it increasingly addressed the question of the effect of mass consumer culture on the child. As mass culture had an appeal that crossed the lines of class and race, and as many of its early producers were immigrants and from the working class, it represented a potential threat to a child's uniform development, particularly for those children of early adherents to the scientific study of childhood. Most of these enthusiasts were from a primarily white and Protestant middle class that imagined itself as the backbone of an inherently American culture that had been, until that moment, considered distinct from an increasingly threatening commercial culture. At the same time, as children's markets became more clearly defined, marketers increasingly turned to popular developmental theory to isolate different age markets and to bolster arguments for their products by triggering and assuaging parental anxieties about the child's increasing presence in public space. As the emerging generic child became the inevitably consuming child, regulating consumption became integral to regulating development. As mass consumer culture increasingly came into conflict with an ideal American culture, the child became a focal point in the struggle to preserve those American ideals and enforce their inclusion in mass-mediated products.

Thus, science and the market are inextricably interwoven in the figure of the child. The beginning of the century saw in Child Study, Child Guidance, and pediatrics the outlines of emergent disciplinary boundaries for the scientific study of the physiology and psychology of childhood. The coincident rise of mass-market books and periodicals engendered a plethora of child-rearing books, and of magazines dedicated to women's issues in general and child-rearing in particular.[7] The dominant presence of members of the white, Protestant, progressive middle class in the study of childhood ensured that certain fundamental assumptions about the inherent nature of the child and its environment (based on observations of their own children) would find their way into baseline descriptions of normal childhood. These assumptions were then linked to a larger progressive program through which immigrants and the working class were to be assimilated into American culture through exposure to and involvement in naturalized middle-class habits.[8] The emergence of the generic child, then, began from a specific location of class and race and proceeded outward from the scientific community and into popular understandings of the nature of the child, so that in a very real sense twentieth-century child-rearing manuals may also be read as manuals for entering the middle class.[9]

Similar assumptions were built into an emergent American sociology, which counted as its major participants people of the same social location. Figures such as Robert Park, Charles Ogburn, and F. S. Chapin, to name but a few, forged a discipline that from its beginnings struggled to balance a dispassionate empirical study of American lifeways with a reformist drive to improve the living conditions of immigrants and the working poor, particularly through assimilation.[10] As American sociology stabilized as a discipline, it subdivided into an agglomeration of smaller sociologies—of work, of leisure, of sport, of the family, of the rural environment and the urban. Yet even as this specialization developed, there emerged a popular sociology that attempted to isolate and portray a unified American culture in all the myriad details of its being. Beginning with *Middletown* (Lynd and Lynd 1929) and continuing through *The Lonely*

Crowd (Riesman, Denney, and Glazer 1950) and *The Organization Man* (Whyte 1956), American middle-class readers avidly absorbed ostensibly sociological accounts of the nature of American character and culture, turning to them for holistic accounts of the meaning of their lives. These too were (often anxious) manuals for a new middle class, offering cautionary tales of what middle-class behavior ought not be rather than what it should be, disciplining their readers by mirroring back to them their excesses and missteps. Each of these books devoted considerable space to the place of child-rearing in the project of repairing and refining the ongoing development of a unified American culture. As such, these texts deployed concepts of childhood in arguments about the evolving nature of American culture and society, borrowing understandings about the meaning of childhood from popular and professional child-rearing discourses, further enshrining a notion of the generic child in the imagination of an American future.

Children of the Movies

The beginning of the twentieth century was also the dawn of the movies, and the emerging generic child was to become the child who was the victim or beneficiary of this popular medium. From film's earliest days, those who tried to reform or regulate movies based their arguments around the need to protect susceptible populations, initially women, children, immigrants, and the working class, but eventually simply children. Although by the 1930s the Catholic Church had developed a powerful national voice in the movement to censor the movies, during the early part of the century the primarily Protestant, progressive middle class (always a vocal and highly organized minority) formed the vanguard of movie reformers, and those reformers in turn drew a model of a child affected by the movies from the emerging sciences of child study.[11] In the early part of the century, when progressive reformers decried the deleterious effect the new medium was having on efforts to Americanize immigrants and the working class, they did so by invoking the ideal values of the white middle class, which movies contravened, and particularly invoked immigrant children as a prime example of their effects on impressionable minds. In arguments about the effects of movies, perhaps as much as anywhere else, the implicitly white, middle-class generic child met immigrant and working-class children and was written over their more clearly marked bodies and behaviors.

As the movies became more popular and children of various classes mixed in movie theaters more frequently, arguments about the effect of movies further erased class as a significant element in the production of a child threatened by popular culture. It wasn't just immigrant children being threatened by the output of immigrant and working-class movie producers, but *all* children. As the movies became a truly national medium, the working-class and immigrant child was subsumed within the form of the naturalized middle-class child threatened with infection by the immigrant and working-class ethos the movie industry transmitted through its products. In effects arguments, especially those of the 1920s and 1930s, the generic American child circulated out from the pages of child-rearing literatures and into the wider public domain.

Histories of this situation have tended to focus on arguments about the *negative* effects of popular culture in general, and movies in particular. Those arguments have been constrained by forces of regulation whose vested interest has been in maintaining control over the extent and meaning of American culture, and who have mobilized the figure of the child in that effort. As Richard Maltby put it in his excellent discussion of the Motion Picture Production Code,

> . . . different sites and forms of popular cultural expression in the twentieth century have derived their innovative energies from culturally and socially disreputable sources, but they have also operated under systems of convention and regulation that keep contained the subversive potential of their origins and that ensure that they endorse, rather than challenge, the existing distribution of social, political, and economic power. The issue has seldom been expressed in such overt terms: more commonly, it has been articulated as an anxiety about the effects of entertainment on children, and specifically on the criminal behavior of adolescent males and the sexual behavior of adolescent females. Partially concealed by the concern for youth has been a deeper, class-based anxiety about the extent to which sites of entertainment provide opportunities for the heterogeneous mixing of classes. (Maltby 1995, 41)

While this is undoubtedly true, and an important point to remember in marshaling arguments against the attempts to curtail free speech that are a regular feature of today's social and political landscape, too much emphasis on the negative and limiting aspects of regulation may overshadow a detailed examination of its *productive* aspects. To the point, efforts to describe the effects of movies (and later television) on a generic American child, and to regulate movies and other media accordingly, involved not only prescriptions about what was bad for children, but prescriptions for which media products would be *good* for children (such as the Production Code). Thus, the reform movement that culminated in the code (and its successors) also produced a set of guidelines by which the enterprising media producer could tailor its public relations address and its products in such a way that those products would appear to be beneficial to that child. More than any other movie producer, Disney succeeded in doing just that. Beginning in the 1920s and continuing through the succeeding decades, the company gradually refined its public presence, in particular the persona of its eponymous founder, to align itself with popular conceptions of what was good for the child. Besides winning the company immense popular acclaim and (eventually) substantial profits, Disney's efforts to appear beneficial to the generic American child substantially assisted in the process of naturalizing the white (largely male), Protestant, middle-class origins of that child.

Histories

Walt Disney and the child are mutually constitutive objects, and the narrative produced here is neither one in which Disney's use of the child determines its ultimate meaning, nor one in which the meaning of the child at the moment when Disney appears determines the nature of the company. Properly speaking, this is neither a history of childhood through the lens of Disney, nor a history of Disney through the lens of the child. Rather, it is an attempt to chart the interrelation of seemingly disparate discourses in the production of a common object, and to denature that object by locating it within the social, cultural, and historical moments within which it has undergone significant changes, revealing both the continuities and discontinuities in its meaning. In a very real sense, the figure of Walt Disney and that of the child are two aspects of the same object, and that is why their histories are so interwoven. Both represent an effort to embody the ideal qualities of a democratic capitalist society, a fantasy through which contradictions in the social and material relations of a given moment are resolved through the reinscription of those relations in a hiatus between a determining past and an indeterminate future. Disney and the child represent the moment at which American culture and society could be apprehended and worked upon before they rushed into the future. (For a discussion of the theoretical tools used to parse the relationship between Disney and the child, please see the conclusion.)

The idea of the child as plastic, and as the point at which a culture, arising from its natural foundation, is susceptible to intervention, has been very much a central element in the post-Enlightenment rhetoric of child nurture, its most famous example being Rousseau's *Emile* (1979 [1762]). As Bernard Wishy (1968, viii) points out in his survey of American child-rearing,

> Child nurture has undoubtedly aroused so much debate and enthusiasm because it relates to essential creeds of modern enlightened men: the ability of reason to analyze the world and the power of ideas in creating any desirable mutation of human nature. The child's nurture is one important key to a more controlled and rational future and, presumably, parents with the right kind of ideas will assure him the best possible nurture.

The child, then, is a transhistorical object, linking a precultural (if not prehistoric) raw "human nature" to a future in which problems obtaining in the social and material relations of the moment are resolved through adjustments to the culture as it is impressed into the malleable material of the child's psyche. As Wishy further points out, however, this operation rarely occurs in the isolated country estate that Rousseau had imagined for the ideal upbringing of his little Emile. Adjustments to culture and to society through the child generally are understood to occur first by way of its parents—who are no longer simply biological progenitors, but representatives of the state and society responsible for shaping that child in ways acceptable to those organs—and second by its peers and social milieu. In like fashion, the child is not simply the product of the reproductive activities of its parents, but a means by which a culture or a society asserts its prerogatives to persons who have become constituted as parents through child-rearing (Donzelot 1979).[12] Although generally applicable as a model of societies that deploy these modern understandings of relations between persons and the state, this operation is not uniform across different societies and historical moments, but specific to the sociocultural moment in which it is observed.

This final point is what distinguishes histories of childhood that treat the condition of childhood at a given historical moment as indicative of the overall progress of human cultural evolution—such as that of Aries (1965)—from those that understand the child as a contingent object useful for the analysis of a particular set of social and material relations at a specific historical moment. A notable example of the latter is Viviana Zelizer's *Pricing the Priceless Child* (1985), a study of the conflict between the Victorian sentimental version of childhood and the mechanisms by which insurance companies calculated compensation for the wrongful death of children in turn-of-the-century America. Also important is David Nasaw's *Children of the City* (1985), which examines the lifeways of working-class children in early twentieth-century New York. Another is Barbara Hanawalt's *Growing Up in Medieval London* (1993), a catalogue of the different meanings of the concept of the child in different class locations and occupations in late medieval London. Recent useful examinations of American childhood have included Peter Stearns's *Anxious Parents* (2003) and Joseph Illick's *American Childhoods* (2002); for a more general survey of the topic, see Anne Hulbert's *Raising America* (2003). More specifically related to the topic at hand is Chandra Mukerji's "Monsters and Muppets" (1997a), a close reading of "Muppet Babies," juvenile versions of characters specifically designed to be beneficial for children. This analysis offers important insights into the reinscription and naturalization of historically and culturally specific concepts of the child through media designed to spontaneously evoke that creature.[13] While Phillipe Aries's *Centuries of Childhood*, perhaps the most famous history of childhood, performed a valuable function in opening up childhood to serious historical analysis, the text's dependence on elite representations of the child—and its attempt to enlist a universal child unmarked by class, race, or gender in the project of delineating the progress of an equally unmarked universal human cultural evolution—limits the work's value in the contemporary study of childhood.[14]

In what sense, though, is Walt Disney simply another aspect of this socio-historical creature, the child? Just as the answer to that question in relation to the child is answered not in a history of actual children, but in a study of the concept of childhood, so Disney's role in the production of an imaginary ideal American culture lies not so much in a review of the man's life and works, but more in a history of the social construction of "Walt Disney." Eric Smoodin (1993) has laid the groundwork for this endeavor, arguing that from the late 1930s onward, Disney as a public figure was in part produced by his critics and fans as they policed the company's output and debated which of the company's films were and were not properly "Disney." Even today, some thirty-odd years after the man's death, his social reproduction continues, in the company's public relations, in the autobiography of its current CEO (Eisner 1998), and in a right-wing backlash against the corporation post-Walt, which finds in the company today a betrayal of its founder's principles (see Schweizer and Schweizer 1998). A recent biography of Disney, Steven Watts's *The Magic Kingdom* (1997), describes Disney as so embodying the American zeitgeist that his name is one of the first words out of an infant's mouth, along with "mommy" and "eat." Watts asks, "How and when did Walt Disney become such a powerful, pervasive presence in our culture that he exists at the level of language itself? What explains this entertainer's enormous popularity and enduring impact on generations of modern Americans, young and old alike? Why has 'Disney' become so influential that . . . it is something to be imbibed along with mother's milk?" (Watts 1997, xv). The answer, he tells his readers, resides in an unconscious coincidence in which Walt Disney simply happened, time and again, to touch upon themes essential to an American character and to the trajectory of an unfolding national enterprise: "Walt Disney operated not only as an entertainer but as a historical mediator. His creations helped Americans come to terms with the unsettling transformations of the twentieth century. This role was unintentional but decisive. Disney entertainment projects were consistently nourished by connections to mainstream American culture—its aesthetics, political ideology, social structures, economic framework, moral principles—as it took shape from the late 1920s through the late 1960s" (xvi).

Watts's very able and thorough hagiography is part of a longstanding discursive tradition that celebrates Walt Disney as a spontaneous expression of an essential American character the physical and social landscape of the United States produced to mirror back to its people its most basic qualities—a tradition that the company has from its earliest days had no small part in producing. Through its public relations—including press books, articles attributed to or written by Walt, interviews, and the company's trademark studio tours (produced on film, for example, as the 1942 release *The Reluctant Dragon*)—Disney represented its products as each invested with the essential character of Walt, a character the company took pains to paint as inherently middle-American.

To suggest that Walt Disney was discursively produced is not to deny the man agency in the creation of a wide range of films and other media properties. There is no doubt that Walter Elias Disney was an entrepreneur of incredible energy, a showman profoundly invested in making entertainments that appealed to a wide segment of the population, and a businessman able to exercise an almost superhuman control over the form and content of those entertainments. However, our experience of Disney as the source of those products (many of which were, ideology aside, quite beautiful and often innovative) was and is mediated by a complex of discursive apparatuses, many of which the man and the company were quite willing to deploy to locate both Walt and his products as close to the ideal American child as possible.

Discourse and Circulation

Although Disney's animated features from the 1930s through the 1950s (and even today) repeat a formulaic narrative of generational succession in which the parent is left behind and the child discovers its own inner resources as it overcomes seemingly insurmountable obstacles, Disney tales never refer directly to the life story of Walter Elias Disney.[15] The process by which his biography appeared to become available to children happened offscreen in a complex of arguments about the nature of childhood in a modern, mass-mediated society. Throughout this text, I have chosen to describe this complex as a "discursive matrix" because it is comprised of several distinct but mutually constitutive discourses. The most obvious of these is that of the effect of movies (and later television) on children. This particular discourse, which laid claim to knowledge of the harmful and beneficial effects of movies on a child's development, depended upon regimes that defined the nature of childhood, a concept that underwent several significant changes during the first half of the century. The child produced by these regimes was, in turn, important to arguments about the nature of American culture and its role in the production of American citizens—citizens who, it was believed, would eventually shape the direction of that culture.

Each of these discursive areas—media effects, the nature of the child, and an ideal American culture—are here further divided into the professional and the popular. As the twentieth century progressed and the disciplinary outlines of the social sciences, particularly pediatrics, psychology, and sociology, became more clearly delineated, popular journalists and reformers turned with increasing frequency to professionals for support in arguments for social change. General circulation magazines such as *Harpers'*, women's magazines such as *Ladies' Home Journal*, and child-rearing publications such as *Parents' Magazine* printed articles from researchers in leading university laboratories. Some of these experts also moved between those institutions, reform organizations, and state and federal government bodies; a number sat on the *Parents'* editorial board. As Carmen Luke put it in describing the discursive production of the child imagined to be viewing mass media: "The historically varying concepts of the child that have emanated from the social sciences are the product of discursive practices which are rooted in social and political interests and relations. Academic social science does not function outside of such constraints, but rather functions within social and political . . . relations and interests that are institutionalized and highly ritualized" (Luke 1990, 9). Institutions constraining and directing the construction of the child included not only universities and social-reform organizations, but also the producers of mass media such as newspapers, magazines, and mass-market books, which looked to the social sciences for validation, and which in turn supplied much-needed exposure for the theories and methods of different and sometimes competing institutional actors, sometimes helping to forge their public careers. This was certainly the case for John B. Watson in the 1920s and for Benjamin Spock in the 1940s and 1950s.

This does not mean, however, that these different discursive locations have shared a common language. While it is true, as Joan Scott has argued in her gloss on the work of Foucault, that "discursive fields overlap, influence, and compete with one another; they appeal to one another's 'truths' for authority and legitimation," it is also true that "[a] discourse is not a language or a text but a historically, socially, and institutionally specific structure of statements, terms, categories, and beliefs" (Scott 1988a, 759–760). A 1930s study of children's galvanic responses to movies that relied upon behaviorist understandings of childhood, for example, may have supported popular arguments for the regulation of film production, but those arguments rarely referred directly to behaviorism.[16] Or, in the case of the relationship between popular and professional discourses on child-rearing, a common pose of popular periodicals and manuals was to serve as interlocutor between the professional and his or her audience, explaining in lay terms the psychological and sociological mechanisms at play in the child's development. These texts often deployed a tone of address that asked readers to indulge the academic in his or her inability to state plainly what the case was. Thus, although both discourses claimed the child as a common object, they deployed distinct means of describing that object and approached the language of that description from complementary but not identical positions.[17] One used the scientifically produced child to firm up its arguments; the other attempted to humanize the methods that produced that child in order to present them to a popular audience. In spite of significant institutional interpenetration, the prerogatives of specific discursive practices produced distinct versions of the child for their respective audiences—and different facets of the same object for the sociohistorical researcher.

For Disney, it was not important that its employees be well versed in the current research on child development, only that they be aware of contemporary understandings about the nature of childhood. Then as now, such arguments circulated freely in popular periodicals and were easily available, if not unavoidable. More to the point, it is not my purpose here to establish a vector of direct influence, either from child-rearing to Disney, or vice versa. Rather, I am interested in understanding Disney and child-rearing as two sites mutually involved in the refinement and production of the ideal, generic child deployed in a wide range of social arguments today. In Disney's case, that work occurred as much in the company's public relations as in its films. While Disney's movies may have played out "timeless" childhood fantasies of separation, abandonment, and empowerment, the frame the company provided its *adult* viewers—parents who were told that they ought to be concerned about the fare their children watched—proposed a metaphysics of consumption in which the means of production were inherent, invisible, and available in those products. Because they bore the imprimatur of Walt Disney, they contained his character, forged in an ideal fantasy of self-making. A close reading of Disney's public relations, done through the lens of popular and professional representations of the child, illustrates the varied and complex interactions that contributed to the production of the child as a public commodity. It is not so much that Disney, Spock, or Watson constructed a version of the child that parents then absorbed unthinkingly. Rather, it is that each of those men, and everyone who thought of themselves as a parent, entered into a complex set of historically specific relations centered around and reproducing the child as a varied but common object of discourse. As Scott has argued, one enters into this close analysis of texts not to locate the hegemonic lever that moves the parent toward false consciousness, but to trace the (uneven and contingent) circulation of embedded social relations: "Language is not assumed to be a representation of ideas that either cause material relations or from which such relations follow; indeed, idealist/materialist opposition is a false one to impose on this approach. Rather, the analysis of language provides a crucial point for understanding how social relations are conceived, and therefore . . . how institutions are organized, how relations of production are experienced, and how collective identity is established" (Scott 1988b, 34).

The concept of the generic American child threatened by commodities that took shape during the twentieth century was not, as some have argued, a result of Disney's colonization of childhood.[18] Nor was it strictly the product of the social sciences, or of popular child-rearing media. As Raymond Williams said, "A lived hegemony is always a process. It is not, except analytically, a system or a structure. It is a realized complex of experiences, relationships, and activities, with specific and changing pressures and limits" (Williams 1977, 112). Walt Disney Productions may have realized more benefit from this emerging idea of the child than any other institutional or individual actor, but it cannot be credited with (or indicted for) the production of that child.[19] Indeed, any attempt to do so entails a reduction of a complex of social and material relations to the influence of a single actor, which denies agency (and responsibility) to a consuming public, casting them as victims of cynical ideological manipulation. Ultimately, this sort of argument reproduces the very construction of the (child) viewer as susceptible to media influence and reinforces a sense of Disney (and other media entities) as productive of the social relations they mediate. In the final analysis, it is more useful to view Disney as one of a set of actors with mutually constitutive interests, contributing to a set of discourses that interact as a carrier wave, along which tacit assumptions about the nature of the child are transmitted in the midst of conversations about the potential disposition of that child in an imagined American future.

Method

This work examines a variety of different primary documents produced between the years 1890 and 1966, with the preponderance of material falling between 1930 and 1960. This material includes popular child-rearing manuals and periodicals; texts by sociologists that found a mainstream audience; advertisements and advertising trade journals that discussed an emerging youth market; the products of Walt Disney Studios, including short and feature films, television programs, and ancillary products such as watches, clothing, and toiletries, as well as public relations materials, fan letters, and annual reports. Much of the popular child-rearing and sociological materials are widely available in the public domain, through university and public library systems. The advertising materials were obtained with the assistance of the N. W. Ayers and Warshaw collections of the National Museum of American History in the Smithsonian Institution, as were a variety of Disney ephemera not available through the Disney Archive. The records of the United States Children's Bureau—also used here—are held in the United States National Archives.

The primary focus of this research was to trace conceptions of the child across different discursive domains, charting continuities and discontinuities in the meanings and uses of the term over time.[20] Within professional discourses of child-rearing, this required noting at which points significant changes in the practice of studying children occurred—from those based around behaviorism in the 1920s and early 1930s, for instance, to the child-centered approaches of the 1950s—and which assumptions about the place of the child in society continued from one model to the next.[21] This involved overlooking certain specific methodological or theoretical differences—say, between an increasingly popular psychoanalytic model, Individual Psychology, and behaviorism in the 1920s—in favor of overarching similarities such as the common deployment of a language based around concepts of management. This common language also appeared in related social sciences, as well as in popular discourses such as arguments about the effects of movies on children.

This is also a book about the emergence and circulation of the notion of an ideal American child in popular mass culture, and of the role of that culture in naturalizing and obscuring formations of class, race, and gender through that child. While some of that work happened in child-rearing manuals and periodicals, it also happened in the commercial address of producers such as Walt

Disney Productions. Since Walter Elias Disney was born in 1901, at roughly the same time that the movies emerged as a mass medium, and since his life story formed the backbone of the company's appeal to parents, chapter 1 begins with a comparison of Disney's hagiography to the emergence of arguments about the effect of movies on the consuming child. These early arguments were rife with fears of an ethnic and working-class movie industry polluting an inherently white and middle-class American culture, and of its interference in the process of Americanizing new immigrants. By the time Disney had established its corporate persona in the early 1930s, the tale of Walt's humble origins and his rise to a successful adulthood—a theme that would be recapitulated in a number of Disney features such as *Pinocchio* (1940), *Dumbo* (1941), and *Cinderella* (1950)—offered to parents the appealing prospect of an ideal American childhood distilled into products for their children. Comparing the company's public relations to discourses about movie effects, and reading *Pinocchio* through the lens of both, this chapter charts one part of the circuit through which this ideal child would emerge.

Chapter 2 examines the other side of this coin, detailing the stabilization and professionalization of the study of childhood in the early twentieth century, and its production of an increasingly standardized child threatened by the mass culture into which it had to enter. It discusses how the early child-study movement, by using the children of its members as subjects, naturalized white, middle-class assumptions about normal behavior and development, and how progressive social reformers (largely from the same social location) furthered that process by using those norms as goals in the Americanization of European immigrant and working-class children. Thus, children from a range of social locations (largely excluding African American, Asian, and Latino children) were subsumed under the sign of the child as bearer of a nascent *and* threatened ideal American culture. By the late 1920s and early 1930s, popular discourses on how to produce this child centered on the concepts of "management" and "efficiency," both as a means for organizing that production, and as behavioral virtues the child was expected to internalize. During the same period, Disney's public relations wove into the story of Walt's life a celebration of the organization and efficiency of its studios as an industrial concern, demonstrating Walt's humanized efficiency and presenting his workers as virtual children under his highly organized and humane direction.

Enthusiasm for tropes of management and efficiency wasn't limited to child-rearing, however. Taking as its frame Helen and Robert Lynd's surprisingly popular sociological study of American culture and character, *Middletown* (1929)—which also located those concepts in the white middle class—

and Lillian Gilbreth's manuals for industrial efficiency in the home, chapter 3 considers how efficiency and management were linked to ideal Americanism in everyday life. In the realm of the everyday, the child became less an abstract vessel for the production of an ideal American future, and more a conduit between the private sphere of the home and the public sphere, particularly school and a commons increasingly built around mass entertainments. Disney's response to this change in social relations extended well beyond its short films and features; the company also marketed a wide range of ancillary products—everything from handkerchiefs to notebooks to wristwatches—meant to insure its presence in everyday life. At the vanguard of this occupying force, was, of course, Mickey Mouse—the ostensible child of Walt's mind and spirit. Through such vehicles as a brief early incarnation of its Mickey Mouse Club or a *Mickey Mouse Magazine* delivered with the morning milk, the company worked to extend its discourse of humane efficiency into the most mundane aspects of everyday life. Especially with the onset of the Great Depression, there it met a public anxious to maintain order (particularly control over children whose involvement in rapidly changing popular culture was alienating to their parents), and to ensure a viable and successful future for their children in a highly competitive environment.

The Great Depression and the encounter with totalitarianism in World War II would serve to dampen popular enthusiasm for discourses of efficiency and management. World War II would also force Disney to diversify its operations, moving the company beyond animation into industrial training films, live action drama, and nature documentaries, and establishing the conditions for the themed approach to differentiating its products that would find its apotheosis in Disneyland. However, just as Disney's decision to diversify was a strategic response to historical conditions, the shift in popular discourses of American culture away from tropes of industrial efficiency, and toward those of the natural evolution of culture and society, resulted (at least in part) from the reasoned response of a number of social actors. Chapter 4 outlines the efforts of popular social thinkers, such as Margaret Mead and David Riesman, to attenuate the enthusiasm for efficiency, suggesting that concepts of scientific management contained the seeds of an American totalitarianism. Combining the psychoanalytic theories of Sigmund and Anna Freud with the cultural anthropology of Franz Boas and Ruth Benedict, a growing collection of scholars and popular social theorists in the late 1940s and early 1950s warned against the dangers of an overly managed society, arguing for a view of American character as the interaction of a vital American culture rooted in a white, Protestant past with the natural world—both in the landscape from which the nation was carved, and in the immediate meeting point of nature and culture, child-rearing. Within this shifting social landscape, Walt Disney Productions would describe itself less and less as an efficient industrial concern, and more as expert in locating and representing the natural world, both in its animated features and its surprisingly popular nature documentaries, the True Life Adventures. These films rendered nature recognizable by building narratives of animal life that appeared to mirror the trials and tribulations and hopes and anxieties of daily life in the United States. Examining them in relation to arguments about the promulgation of American character provides a means of understanding the rapid postwar shift in thinking about the relationship between nature and culture embodied in the growing child.

The postwar period also marked an important turning point in the life of Mickey Mouse. In 1949, Mickey turned twenty-one, leaving the realm of childhood behind for a more placid existence as an adult. Being the mature mouse that he was, Mickey stepped aside and shared the spotlight with Donald Duck, who, though ostensibly also an adult, was by far the more immature of the two. If Mickey had been childlike, Donald was childish: frenetic, anxious, narcissistic—in short, a bit of a neurotic. But perhaps the most significant difference was that Donald was far more sexual than Mickey, somewhat of a skirt-chaser. Donald's ascendance coincided with the rise of a discourse of childhood that admitted (albeit uneasily) to the presence of childhood sexuality, and to its importance in the development of character. Perhaps the single most important person to introduce parents to their children's sexuality was, of course, Dr. Benjamin Spock. Drawing upon the work of Mead and other theorists of childhood (particularly Erik Erikson), Spock gently coached parents on how to manage their children less and observe them more, allowing them to develop their behaviors and characters through the encounter between their natural selves and the cultural world they were entering. Spock had more in common with Walt Disney, though, than a gentle and avuncular manner. Both presented the world as highly and naturally gendered. For Spock, parents could help ensure that their children would grow to be happy and well adjusted if they performed *their* genders properly for their children, helping them to understand how sexuality operated in American culture. In his True Life Adventures, Disney presented an apparently natural expression of gender in the sexual and familial habits of the animals it portrayed. Chapter 5 details the role of gender and sexuality in the new child-rearing of the 1950s, its importance in the formation of a character resistant to the totalitarian impulse, and how the anxieties produced by this new regime were met by the nature documentaries and public relations of Walt Disney Productions.

The child was not the only significant point of contact between nature and culture in the postwar United States. Chapter 6 returns to popular sociological descriptions of suburban American culture and the encounter with technologies of modernization. If the Lynds had located the center of American culture in the small-town Midwest of Walt Disney's childhood, postwar social theorists found it in the burgeoning suburbs, describing them as a frontier region at which nature and culture met. The suburbs became a contact zone between the past and the future, and between a fragile American individualism represented by the child and a mass society and culture represented by suburban conformity and its spate of mass-produced goods, including the new technology of television. In this final chapter, the thematic organization through which Disney presented itself to its public in its television programming and Disneyland, and by which we know it so well today, appears as more than simply clever marketing, a way to manage diversification. The cosmos that Disney constructed on the ground and on the airwaves in the 1950s carefully ordered the relationship between an idealized natural prehistory, a fantasy of frontier life, and an ideal future and presented them as products that would deliver the individualism of the nineteenth-century United States through the very technologies of modernization and rationalization that seemed to threaten it. Through its efforts to involve itself in education and in local institutions, and through public relations that stressed its expertise in locating the real and natural through its True Life Adventures—as well as in delivering visions of a utopian tomorrow through "science factual" programming such as *Our Friend the Atom* (1957)—Disney moved beyond offering products that were generally beneficial to children, to ones that were ostensibly edifying. What Disney offered was what chroniclers of American character suggested children sorely needed: a natural understanding of themselves that would allow them to compete in a highly rationalized and rapidly changing democratic capitalist society without sacrificing their individuality and humanity. As it had when it addressed the parents of the managed child in the 1930s, Disney offered up products that recapitulated popular understandings of the child's role of mediating between nature and culture, of remedying excesses of conformity and potential failings of democratic action through the very process of its enculturation.

If there is an overarching principle to this research and analysis, it is not whether a given scientific theory of child development, or of American social organization, ultimately proved valid, but whether it was popular—and what meanings and practices arose during its tenure. Rather than follow Thomas Kuhn (1962) and chart significant paradigmatic shifts in understandings of the child and practices of child-rearing within the confines of institutional practice, I have attempted to locate those movements within larger epistemic fields. Thus, the fall of behaviorism in child-rearing takes place within the popular rejection of scientific management as a principle for ordering society, and the eventual rise of child-centered philosophies (epitomized by Spock) is accompanied by a rhetoric which treats behaviorism as the handmaiden of totalitarianism. Adherence to this principle in the ordering of this work has caused the omission of certain schools and texts that others might include. The works of C. Wright Mills, for instance, are largely absent from discussions of conformity and totalitarianism during the 1950s, not because they are not germane to the discussion, but because they were not particularly well received by the mass middle-class audience upon which this research has focused. Thus, arguably inferior works by William Whyte or Geoffrey Gorer are analyzed in detail, because they circulated more widely in popular discussions about the nature of American culture and society.

In charting these epistemic shifts, I have made frequent reference to a "democratic capitalist society" that finds its apotheosis in the middle class. The blending of the economic and the political in these terms is intentional. The basic premise of democratic political organization in the United States is that "all men [*sic*] are created equal." Yet the basic premise of capitalist organization is that value is created by taking advantage of inequality—whether between two products, or between wages in two locations—that economic power is not and should not be evenly distributed. A reasonable observer might comment that democratic equality extends only to the right to participate in political activity, and to have unfettered access to compete in inherently unequal markets. Yet one of the fundamental concerns of the twentieth century was that newcomers to the democratic process lacked the necessary values and behaviors to make political choices that would ensure the health of the American capitalist economic system. The contradictory compulsion that newcomers to this system were to be guaranteed the freedom of thought and of choice necessary to a healthy democracy, yet were to make their choices according to the dictates and expectations of others, formed the engine behind the movements for social reform and organization discussed herein.

Thus, as the imagined seat of an ideal American culture—one outside of but contributing fundamental ethics and behaviors to both capitalist practice and democratic politics—the middle class has been essential to managing this contradiction. For example, the massive influx of immigrants from southern and eastern Europe at the end of the nineteenth century and beginning of the twentieth century gave rise to anxieties about the destabilization of

American social, political, and economic life. Once "naturalized," these immigrants—who might have been anarchists, socialists, Bolsheviks, syndicalists, or simply primitive agrarian traditionalists—would have had the right to vote and might have elected individuals hostile to capitalism as the organizing principle of American economic life. The solution to this problem was to inculcate those newcomers into an inherently American middle-class (white and Protestant) culture, one that stressed self-denial and deferred gratification, and which favored the individual over the collective as the fundamental unit of socialization and social activity. Similar fears arose after World War II, when many in the white working class were catapulted into the middle class (in terms of earning capacity, home ownership, and access to managerial positions). Having made the leap in class standing without necessarily having finished the process of assimilation, those new members might have lacked the fundamental values of the class into which they were entering. With their massive buying power, they might have disrupted American cultural life through their plebian tastes, turning the middle class into a "mass class" that would ultimately undermine American social and political life.

At both of these junctures, the generic child played a critical role in managing social relations. Immigrant children were considered more malleable than their hidebound parents and so would serve as better agents of assimilation. Since they couldn't be shielded from mass culture, the children of the postwar mass middle class—whose parents were told they were alienated from and confused by rapidly modernizing American life—required mass products imbued with the essential middle-class values necessary to continue its orderly existence. The degree to which the adult that each of these children was to become would accrue social, political, and economic power, then, was not to be determined by larger social and economic forces, but by the patterns of their consumption.

Like Walt Disney, the child at the center of this complex operation is anything but a natural creature. Yet it does continue to *naturalize* a set of values and social markers that privileges certain identities and modes of social organization over others and forecloses solutions to immediate pressing social and economic problems—such as institutionalized racism or gendered economic inequality—by deferring them to the next generation.[22] The impulse behind the production and reproduction of this child is benign and well-intentioned: to correct through its small imagined body pervasive social, political, and economic inequalities (say, through Head Start) while preserving an idealized American culture and character predicated upon its ability to reconcile the values of democracy and capitalism. And like Walt Disney, this child exists everywhere and nowhere, its essence present to some degree in everything that bears its name. Though each appears universal, each has a history, and it is by unraveling those histories that we may come to understand how it is that we assign to the chairman of a media enterprise, or to a child, significant responsibility for organizing how we live.[23]

1 DISNEY MAKES DISNEY

Introduction: Walt Disney and the Celebration of the Self-Made Man

There is an urban legend that when Walt Disney died in 1966, he had his body frozen until medical science could progress to the point that it could cure what had killed him. Disney is also reported to have made a series of short films for his employees shortly before he died. Every five years, they were to play the next film in the series, in which Walt would issue instructions for the company's next five years of operation. In this way, the company that bears his name could remain on the path he had set for it, forever enacting his dreams.

The durability of these legends derives from an intimate association between the man and his corporation, the idea that the company was nothing more or less than the physical manifestation of his innermost desires and dreams, a fantasy he made real and shared with the world. In the space of about ten years, the company that bore Walt Disney's name went from a one-room operation in Kansas City to a global enterprise that has become today one of the most powerful corporations on the planet. In the hagiography of Walt Disney, this happened because one man with a clear vision, a good heart, and sound, middle-class Protestant values struggled through hard times in a single-minded effort to make the world laugh and cry. Walt Disney Productions was not simply an industrial concern; it was the vehicle through which the man imprinted himself on the landscape that produced him. Walt Disney, it has been said over and over, embodied America, and in doing so gave America back to itself, and eventually to the world.

This is the way that stories about Walt Disney, be they laudatory or critical, inevitably begin: with the man. What I hope to demonstrate here is that the Walt Disney of hagiography and demonology alike was the creation of his own corporation (in collusion with its consumers). As much as Mickey Mouse, Donald Duck, Bambi, or Pinocchio, the Walt Disney that circulated in the American public imaginary—in newspapers, in magazines and books, and on television—was produced in the studios alongside the other creations nominally credited to him. However based in the facts of the man's history it may be, the saga of Walt Disney's life that has been told over and over since the company's inception—a story of humble beginnings and hard times, of aspiration and perspiration—is the company's most enduring tale, and its most important.

I wish to reverse-engineer Walt Disney the self-made man—but not because I want to reveal that he was a fraud or that the company was putting something over on its public. He was a talented entrepreneur with a brilliant head for business, good organizational skills, and a keen sense of the currents of American culture. No, ultimately I wish to explore the discursive and social construction of Walt Disney because I am interested in its relation to the social construction of the twentieth-century American child, because that child was created in conjunction with the fantastic figure of Walt Disney. The man's life story, which his company repeated and refined, and which journalists, reviewers, and biographers placed at the center of Disney's ability to create products ostensibly good for children, is ultimately a celebration of his own commodification. As Walt Disney gradually transformed into Walt Disney Productions and Walt Disney Enterprises, the man and the company became the mutually sustaining embodiments of a fantasy of capitalist self-control, one in which the proper management of one's personal resources promised a near-absolute control over the disposition of one's life as an adult. This was (and is) the middle-class American fantasy of personal development, one in which the child so masters its attitudes and behaviors that in its adult life it becomes the master of its own fate, rather than a worker in the production of the social and material capital of others.

This fantasy is deeply interwoven with longstanding ideas about the primacy and sovereignty of the individual in American social and cultural discourse, and in one form or another it certainly predates the twentieth century. Yet the shape it has taken, and the importance of mass media in that process, are unique to the century and to the emergence of producers such as Disney. The past century marked the emergence of a specifically scientific conception of the child, one that drew upon prior moral and sentimental notions of childhood as an ideal period within which to structure the eventual adulthood of a person, but which increasingly subsumed the moral and sentimental within rubrics of empirical observation and controlled experimentation. The isolation and verification of standards by which to chart the normal physical and behavioral development of children, the circulation and discussion of those standards in mass-market programs for child-rearing, and their importance in emerging discussions of the regulation of consumption of mass media signaled a shift in the way that members of an expanding middle class imagined the role of childhood in the production and regulation of shared cultural and social relations. While the story of Walt Disney partook of sentimental fantasies of self-making, its framing in the tale of the rise of a major media concern intersected with, naturalized, and recirculated assumptions about the nature of the child involved in the fantasy of self-making in twentieth-century mass culture. If the child is the father to the man, Walt Disney was the fantastic father to that child.

The Man

The figure of Walt Disney is chimerical—part man, part corporation, part myth, created between fans, critics, columnists, reviewers, and, of course, the company's public relations department itself. That Walt reportedly couldn't reproduce the trademark signature that to this day magically appears at the beginning of each Disney animated feature, or that he set up a corporation named Retlaw—"Walter" spelled backward—in the 1950s to regulate the use of that name are both emblematic of the difficulty of speaking of Walt Disney as a self-determining, unified subject.[1] This is the first obstacle that must be overcome, the powerful synecdoche in which the man stands in for the studio, and the symmetrical metonymy in which the studio appears as nothing more than an extension of the man. Beyond that, however, ranges a complex of determinations in which the man and the corporation stand for an ideal American past and its continuation into an ideal future, the meeting of artisanal practice and scientific management, the elevation (or corruption) of the fairy tale, and the realistic portrayal of nature.[2] Yet the assumption behind each of these discursive operations, whether positive or negative, has been that the man embodies the corporation as its generative and regenerative principle, and that the corporation embodies the man as the highly coordinated physical realization of his mental processes. This has been true since the early days of the corporation: "Walt Disney has not drawn his own pictures for nine years. To turn out the mass production issued nowadays under his name, he would have to have 650 hands. And 650 hands he has. With slim, 36-year-old Walt Disney as the guiding intelligence, his smooth-working cinema factory produces an average of twelve *Mickey Mouse* films and six *Silly Symphonies* every year," reported *Time* magazine in 1937 ("Mouse and Man" 1937, 19).

In this public fantasy, Walt Disney sat like Shiva at the center of a well-oiled Fordist fun factory, his innate intellect virtually animating his employees to produce films that simultaneously informed and entertained the masses. This was possible, the public was told, because Disney was uncommon, a native

American genius, a born tinkerer and inventor, like Henry Ford or Thomas Edison. The conflation of the man with his eponymous corporation was a reflection of an actual physical (and perhaps metaphysical) situation: Disney's imagination was so vast that his own two hands were inadequate to the task. Walt Disney Productions was the tool that the man fashioned to incorporate his vision, just as Ford had done. One popular profiler claimed that "it can never be said that Disney is inarticulate, but he seeks to avoid, by refusing to put his thoughts and ideas into words, the impression that he's a genius" (Churchill 1938, 9). Yet even if Disney demurred, the company, in its public relations, wasn't shy about touting the man's abilities:

> Walt Disney has pioneered every forward step in the history of present-day animated pictures. . . . The first animated sound picture . . . "Steamboat Willie" . . . The first [cartoon] in color . . . "Flowers and Trees," which raked in awards both in the United States and abroad. . . . The first animated picture to show an illusion of third dimension [*sic*] . . . "The Old Mill." . . . All of these developments have taken place within the last ten years, since Disney started his now-extensive studio in the back of a garage. (Walt Disney Productions 1938, 37)

In a sense, this claim was true. Disney rarely blew his own horn in his own voice. But his corporation, an extension of his being, did praise him as a genius.

And as is so often the case with invention, many of those innovations were not his, but those of his workers and associates. Credited with bringing sound to animation, Disney applied an existing system that he had recently purchased to a cartoon he had already produced—*Steamboat Willie* (1928). The same is true for the multiplane camera, which Disney was lauded as having introduced; the device was designed and built by animator Ub Iwerks (once Disney's partner) and William Garrity, another worker in the studios (D. Smith 1987). And although Disney was for many years the voice of Mickey Mouse, he couldn't really draw his most famous creation, nor could he easily reproduce his own hallmark signature during autograph sessions. In both cases, he had to rely on junior animators for lessons (Wallace 1949; Schickel 1968). As with other famous American inventors such as Edison or Ford, Disney's talent and drive were amplified by convention into genius, the acceptance of which converted his considerable skills at industrial management into generative creativity and reduced his employees to mere factota.

Even if Walt Disney's abilities as an animator and inventor were to some degree invented, they were not the only facets of his public construction as a genius. As the studios grew, both feature stories and public-relations releases lauded the corporation's industrial techniques and praised Disney's ability to create a family atmosphere in a highly regulated workplace, as in this piece from a 1940 issue of the *Atlantic Monthly* (written one year before Disney employees went out on strike):

> Somebody has made a successful effort not to festoon the place with the lambrequins and trappings of business pomposity. Walt is the president. Roy is the executive vice president. The rest of the official titles you can put in Mickey's eye. . . . When a boy or a girl who just hasn't made the grade is recommended to Walt for dismissal, Walt is more likely to maintain that the suspect hasn't been used right. . . . "We have never found Walt's judgment lacking," his playmates say . . . "The only employee that's against Walt is the electric elevator," they say. The staff voted not to unionize. (Hollister 1940, 38–39)

Depictions such as this marked a significant departure from previous presentations of the craft of animation. Earlier animators, such as James Stuart Blackton or Winsor McCay, had presented themselves as magicians who brought inert drawings to life. The next generation of animators, the first to truly industrialize the form, had downplayed the celebration of production in favor of a focus on developing popular characters.[3] Disney, on the other hand, presented himself as an entrepreneur, a hard-working manager who organized first a few, then scores, then hundreds of workers who then brought his ideas to life (Merritt and Kaufman 1993). Yet what ostensibly permitted that organization was not the iron hand of corporate control, but the casual atmosphere that Walt Disney himself created in his facilities. "He is little interested in books, but fond of sleight-of-hand tricks and mimicry. Often he regales his workers with some new trick or impersonation learned the night before," reported Douglas Churchill (1934, 13), one of the journalists responsible for the popular production of Disney's hagiography (as opposed to that flowing from his own corporation). Disney was represented as a benevolent patriarch, often referred to as "Uncle Walt," who tirelessly and selflessly oversaw the entire operation, from the creation of individual characters, to the development of specific scenes, to the choice of color schemes, to the final product: "Through the production pattern of every picture Walt threads in and out like a guiding outline. Having done single-handed, at one time or another, nearly everything that is being done in the studio, and having designed every functional fraction of the plant, Walt knifes into the most minute step of the most microscopic element in an effort to help, help, help" (Hollister 1940, 700).

Even though the work was performed by his employees—after 1938 sometimes compared to the happy dwarfs of *Snow White*—it was his all-seeing eye that stamped the ineffable Disney character on every product. In 1934, *Fortune* magazine described that character as combining the qualities of Horatio Alger (entrepreneurial determination), Henry Ford (industrial efficiency and management), and Abraham Lincoln (humble origins and hard work) ("The Big Bad Wolf" 1934). In short, the public persona of Walt Disney embodied the very behaviors that parents of the 1930s were expected to engender in their children—industry, modesty, and thrift—and spoke more of upright, middle America than of the morally questionable Hollywood where his studios were located. Inasmuch as those studios were described as a family operation, Walt Disney was the model of what every parent hoped to be, a manager who encouraged obedience and excellence through kindness and inspiration. As Churchill (1934, 12), praising Disney's modest genius in the *New York Times Magazine*, put it: "He doesn't pose or put up a front. He has seen too much of hard struggle to be very deeply impressed by the to-do over him or by the tributes he receives in every mail. His attitude toward the public, his 175 employees and his product conflicts with every traditional attitude of the 'practical' cinema."

In direct contrast to other Hollywood producers, who were often portrayed as immodest, spendthrift, and immoral, Disney's genius as a manager and a creator was depicted as deriving from his basic American-ness. The image of Walt Disney presented over and over again during the course of his life was that of the archetypal American rags-to-riches story. Born at the turn of the century, Disney was raised on farms and in cities in the Midwest and was put to work at a very young age to help support his family. After leaving home in his late teens to serve as an ambulance driver in World War I, he suffered through years of hardship to realize his dream of making cartoons—becoming rich and famous in the process. Disney's was the sort of inspirational story quite popular in a period that suffered through cycles of severe economic depression.[4]

Ironically, what was most significant about Disney's story was its banality. It wasn't so much that he had overcome hardship during his childhood: rather, it was the plainness of his experience that the company offered as the core of what made him (and his products) so American, so good, and so good for children. As Gregory Waller (1980, 53–55) puts it: "Seen through the rose-tinted prism of popular journalism, Disney's life story became a homespun mythic saga and a reassuring affirmation of the American Dream. [He was described] in the *New York Times Magazine* as 'the Horatio Alger of the cinema . . . who through industry, courage and all the other Algerian virtues attained international recognition.' He was . . . praised by the *Ladies' Home Journal* as a 'living testimonial to the importance of moderation in education.' " Douglas Churchill suggested in 1934 that "perhaps it was Disney's early life that gave him the understanding needed to appeal to world audiences. Born in Chicago, he grew up in rural Missouri among down-to-earth, middle-class people" (Churchill 1934, 12). That very middleness, Churchill and other chroniclers such as Paul Hollister or Irving Wallace suggested, allowed Disney to direct his employees in the production of movies that appealed to the better angels of American mass audiences. Particularly for Depression-era consumers, this mythology of homespun genius derived from hardship offered a compelling back story to Disney's products.

Yet the idea that Disney's genius was shaped by his early years was not limited to the virtue of his humble beginnings. As late as 1980, Leonard Maltin offered a more Oedipal interpretation, though one that still posited Disney's childhood as crucial to his story: "He learned to work—and work hard—from the time he was a child. He never knew luxury. Drawing was more than just a pastime for him; it was an escape from the harsher realities of life. Disney's father was an itinerant ne'er-do-well. One could say that Disney's adult life was a reaction to these childhood experiences and situations" (30). Was his art (or his skill as a manager) a defense mechanism to ward off the pain of a difficult childhood under the poor stewardship of a neglectful father? Were his virtue and talent the result of simple middle-class living? Such sentimental biographical pastiche—in which more than one biographer has noted significant alterations by Disney from time to time—directed Disney's Depression-era audiences to his humble origins as both the burden he overcame and the root source of his genius. More than just a success story, Disney's life was presented as that of an Everyman. He was described as an ordinary, middle-class man, "with Irish, Canadian, German, and American blood in his veins" (Hollister 1940, 690). In short, Disney was absolutely normal, so much so that his body could be simultaneously ethnically specific (German and Irish) and unmarked (Canadian and American). Like the American child, he was a transitional object, moving from poverty to the middle class (and beyond) and from ethnicity into whiteness, embodying the direction of American cinema as its ethnic roots paled, and the contradictory end of every American childhood, a success by virtue of being uniquely average.

Thus it is far from simply a natural consequence of the content of its products that Disney has long been the nexus for arguments about what it means to be American, to produce American culture, and to produce Americans. Eric Smoodin (1993) has aptly demonstrated how the figure of Walt Disney was discursively produced in popular American periodicals of the 1940s—both through praise of his life and products and through criticism of his work in relation to earlier efforts. Richard deCordova (1994) has argued that Disney's success must be understood in terms of the conception of childhood prevalent in the late 1920s and early 1930s, and of the company's ability to market to that conception. These two important observations meet in Disney's willingness to offer Walt up as a public commodity, to celebrate his own desire to trade on his history, to share of himself through the act of consumption. Just as Mickey was reproduced on watches, tiepins, and handkerchiefs, so Walt's story was told and retold, in newspapers and magazines, year after year. That telling and retelling positioned Walt Disney as an average American who made good by dint of perseverance and simple middle-class virtue. It further suggested that his corporation and his products were direct extensions of an essentially American self, and that they were the means by which that self was propagated in American public culture and made available for consumption. This begs a question: How was it that the life story of Walt Disney added value to products marketed for children? The answer to this question begins with a look at the history of movie effects, continues with an examination of the movie industry's role in that history, and ends with Disney's choice to weave the personal history of its founder into larger historical narratives of the fantastic and of the fantasy of America. Although the company's public relations and the popular recreation of Walt Disney suggests that the circulation of that story was widely valued, perhaps its importance in discourses of the child will begin to become clearer through an examination of its circulation through a Disney product from the period, the 1940 hit feature *Pinocchio*.

Becoming a Real Boy: Pinocchio and the Anxiety of the Public Child

In many ways, Disney's *Pinocchio* (1940) is emblematic of Depression-era anxieties around child-rearing. It is a movie with a deceptively simple plot: Gepetto, an old toy maker, creates a puppet he names Pinocchio. Before going to sleep, Gepetto wishes that his puppet were a real boy. A fairy hears his wish and animates Pinocchio, but doesn't make him flesh and blood. Instead, she makes him a living puppet with the potential to become real:

> *Pinocchio*: Am I a real boy?
>
> *Blue Fairy*: No, Pinocchio. To make Gepetto's wish come true will be entirely up to you. Prove yourself brave, truthful, and unselfish, and someday you will be a real boy.

The world in which Pinocchio must be brave, truthful, and unselfish lies between his front door and school, along the path that every child must follow. Gepetto, his creator, can only see him out the door and hope for the best; the possibility that the old man will become a real father depends on Pinocchio's character and on the puppet's conscience, which, embodied by Jiminy Cricket, is the size of a bug.

The movie was a fitting parable for the world faced by Depression-era parents and their children. In an economy barely stood on its feet by the New Deal, the idea that a middle-class child would grow to be a middle-class adult, or that a working-class child could leave its humble roots behind, was not a given. The easy road to a better life seemed narrower; in the popular imagination, personal initiative and hard work were still the best bet for improving one's tighter odds of getting through, but relative scarcity made that passage a less certain proposition. Though ultimately the child's success would hinge on its own hard work, its ability to do that work would depend on the tools a parent gave the child. With the ongoing promulgation of compulsory universal education and the refinement of scientific methods of child-rearing purportedly able to improve a child's chances for success, a youth's failure was often viewed as that of its parents, so much so that in April of 1931 *Parents' Magazine* informed its readers about the new field of "parent education," the purpose of which was to create a standardized system of instruction for parents that dovetailed with efforts by major child-study institutions to promulgate more scientifically grounded methods for child-rearing (L. Meek 1931). Likewise, in June of the same year, developmental researchers William Blatz and Helen Bott asked *Parents'* readers, "Are You Fit to Be a Father?" and offered up a quiz by which fathers could rate their parenting skills (Blatz and Bott 1931). In these and similar articles, the magazine (the most popular child-rearing periodical of the period) suggested that a parent's ability to impart the proper values and behaviors to a child would shape the child's future.

While Gepetto eventually proves a good father, much happens in the interim. Pinocchio doesn't make a beeline for school and a better future. Instead, he falls into one misadventure after another and never makes it to class. Yet in the end he does become real. The outcome is never really in doubt: even when Pinocchio eagerly hands himself over to an unemployed con artist, Honest John Foulfellow, and when it becomes obvious that his conscience holds almost no sway over him, the film's melodramatic tone makes it clear that ultimately he will escape every scrape. Indeed, at almost every rough turn, the Blue Fairy returns to help Pinocchio out, even raising him from the dead. As Jiminy Cricket puts it, "Gee, what they can't do these days."

Where was a parent to find such strong magic in real life? In the products of manufacturers such as Disney, perhaps. Yet while *Pinocchio* certainly trumpeted the middle-class virtues of hard work and deferred gratification over easy pleasure, one movie was hardly a prophylactic against the vicissitudes of a staggering economy or the allure of unwholesome amusements such as standard Hollywood fare.[5] Yet Disney offered much more than movies alone. In a sense, each Disney movie was not the first but the last stage in a complex system of imbrication through which the company occupied a central place in an imagined future in which children's lives seemed secure. That system began with Disney's public relations apparatus, which went to great lengths to place its products in settings perceived as virtuous and appropriate. It continued in reviews (often derived directly from Disney PR) that portrayed Disney the man as the embodiment of essentially American virtues, which were transmitted directly through the films to his audiences. This notion was reinforced in periodical articles about children and children's products that held up the man, the company, and its products as paradigmatic of what was best for children. It entered the bedroom, the bathroom, the kitchen, and the schoolroom through the myriad licensed products the company distributed with each release. Finally, Disney found a secure place between parents and children because it arrived on the scene at a moment when arguments about the importance of children's development to the nation's continued well-being, and about the role of popular amusements in influencing that development (either positively or negatively), were exerting a significant influence on both the production of movies and the meaning of childhood.

Disney offers the perfect example of marketing as something far more than simple advertising: marketing truly was (and is) the means by which commercial products became part of the cultural fabric of everyday life (Lears 1994). In what Michael Schudson (1984) has described as the "capitalist realism" of advertising, marketing encourages consumers to imagine a world in which they live an ideal lifestyle made possible by commercial products. Needless to say, this is somewhat difficult to do with animated characters. Yet Disney's solution to this problem was simply to try to make its products integral to domestic life. The objects on which Disney imprinted its cute and cuddly characters were themselves mostly banal and linked to the homely business of daily life. When Disney premiered *Pinocchio* in 1940, for example, it offered over forty licensed products, including "Sweaters . . . Handkerchiefs . . . Tableware . . . Candles . . . Tumblers . . . Boy's Hats . . . China Figures . . . Mufflers . . . [and] Milk Bottles" (Walt Disney Productions, 1940). (See figure 1.) The basic utility of most of the items referred back to the film's focus on hearth and home, and

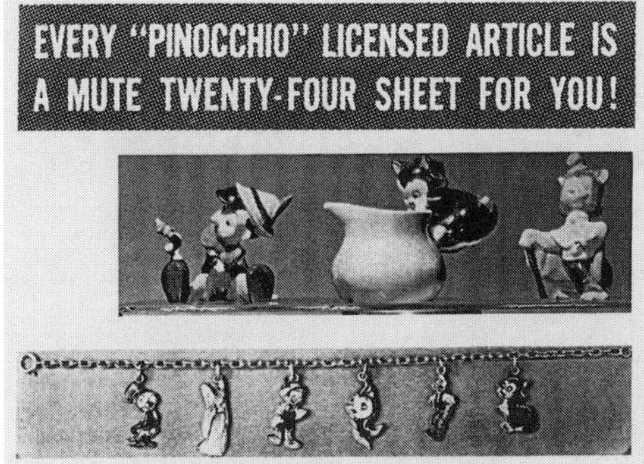

EVERY "PINOCCHIO" LICENSED ARTICLE IS
A MUTE TWENTY-FOUR SHEET FOR YOU!

Art Galleries in Over 50 Cities Are Now Displaying And Selling Original Paintings from PINOCCHIO!

1. A small sampling of promotional products for *Pinocchio* (1940) that Walt Disney Productions offered through licensed retailers. Disney worked for maximum exposure by offering everyday items such as milk bottles and glasses and by making cels and original artwork available for sale in gallery settings.

increased trademark visibility through their daily use. Disney's ancillary products increased its market presence *and* associated its characters, not with the glamour and excess of Hollywood, but with day-to-day mundane practices.

Nor was Disney's use of self-promotion and product tie-ins to increase the visibility of *Pinocchio* anything new, either to Hollywood public-relations practices, nor to the company itself. Richard deCordova (1994) has outlined in detail Disney's first forays into character licensing and marketing with Mickey Mouse in the late 1920s and early 1930s. From its beginnings, Disney understood that the production, promulgation, and control of its corporate image were as important as the images it put on film, and that product tie-ins served the double purpose of generating extra income and increasing visibility.[6] According to deCordova, by 1932 children "could, with enough money, have the image of the mouse on almost all of their possessions—their brushes, hot water bottles, and bathroom accessories; their silverware and china; their toys and games; and their school supplies" (205).

The company's marketing and public relations thus linked its cuddly and wholesome characters to the family, and to the genius, drive, and Americanness of Walt Disney himself. It routinely trumpeted Disney's awards and accomplishments, including special Academy Awards and testimonials from international art institutes, with each film (Walt Disney Productions 1934a). (See figure 2.) The company touted Disney as both the creator of Mickey and as his voice, describing that voice as speaking to "that deathless, precious, ageless,

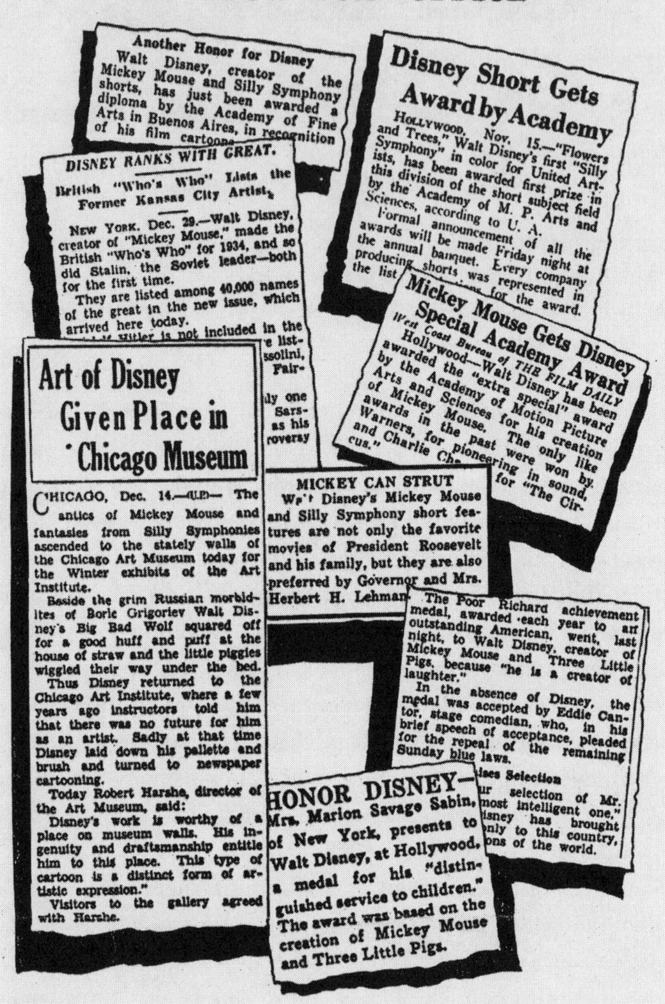

WALT DISNEY IS BIG NEWS!

HEADLINES THAT MEAN BUY - LINES AT YOUR BOX - OFFICE

Another Honor for Disney

Walt Disney, creator of the Mickey Mouse and Silly Symphony shorts, has just been awarded a diploma by the Academy of Fine Arts in Buenos Aires, in recognition of his film cartoons.

Disney Short Gets Award by Academy

HOLLYWOOD, Nov. 15.—"Flowers and Trees," Walt Disney's first "Silly Symphony" in color for United Artists, has been awarded first prize in this division of the short subject field by the Academy of M. P. Arts and Sciences, according to U. A.

Formal announcement of all the awards will be made Friday night at the annual banquet. Every company producing shorts was represented in the list ... for the award.

DISNEY RANKS WITH GREAT.

British "Who's Who" Lists the Former Kansas City Artist.

NEW YORK. Dec. 29.—Walt Disney, creator of "Mickey Mouse," made the British "Who's Who" for 1934, and so did Stalin, the Soviet leader—both for the first time.

They are listed among 40,000 names of the great in the new issue, which arrived here today.

... Hitler is not included in the ... e list- ... ssolini, ... Fair- ... ly one ... Sars- ... as his ... roversy

Mickey Mouse Gets Disney Special Academy Award

West Coast Bureau of THE FILM DAILY

Hollywood—Walt Disney has been awarded the "extra special" award by the Academy of Motion Picture Arts and Sciences for his creation of Mickey Mouse. The only like awards in the past were won by Warners, for pioneering in sound, and Charlie Ch... for "The Circus."

Art of Disney Given Place in Chicago Museum

CHICAGO, Dec. 14.—(U.P.)— The antics of Mickey Mouse and fantasies from Silly Symphonies ascended to the stately walls of the Chicago Art Museum today for the Winter exhibits of the Art Institute.

Beside the grim Russian morbidities of Boris Grigoriev Walt Disney's Big Bad Wolf squared off for a good huff and puff at the house of straw and the little piggies wiggled their way under the bed.

Thus Disney returned to the Chicago Art Institute, where a few years ago instructors told him that there was no future for him as an artist. Sadly at that time Disney laid down his pallette and brush and turned to newspaper cartooning.

Today Robert Harshe, director of the Art Museum, said:

Disney's work is worthy of a place on museum walls. His ingenuity and draftsmanship entitle him to this place. This type of cartoon is a distinct form of artistic expression."

Visitors to the gallery agreed with Harshe.

MICKEY CAN STRUT

Walt Disney's Mickey Mouse and Silly Symphony short features are not only the favorite movies of President Roosevelt and his family, but they are also preferred by Governor and Mrs. Herbert H. Lehman.

The Poor Richard achievement medal, awarded each year to an outstanding American, went, last night, to Walt Disney, creator of Mickey Mouse and Three Little Pigs, because "he is a creator of laughter."

In the absence of Disney, the medal was accepted by Eddie Cantor, stage comedian, who, in his brief speech of acceptance, pleaded for the repeal of the remaining Sunday blue laws.

...ises Selection

...r selection of Mr. ...most intelligent one," ...isney has brought ...nly to this country, ...ons of the world.

HONOR DISNEY—

Mrs. Marion Savage Sabin, of New York, presents to Walt Disney, at Hollywood, a medal for his "distinguished service to children." The award was based on the creation of Mickey Mouse and Three Little Pigs.

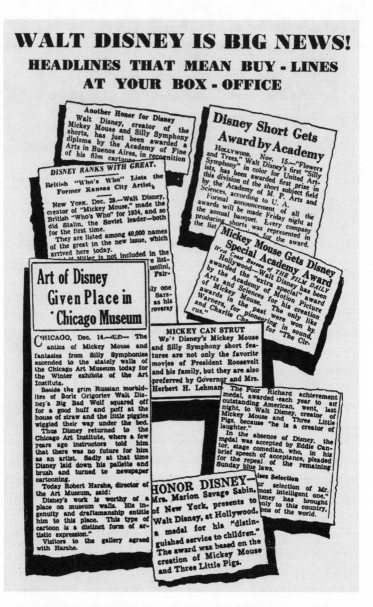

2. The press book for Disney's *The China Shop* (1934) encouraged exhibitors to feature Walt's celebrity as a draw, focusing specifically on his many awards and linking the cartoon short to his essentialized genius.

absolutely primitive remnant of something in every world-wracked human being" (Herring [1931], in Waller 1980; Walt Disney Productions 1934b). What was true for Mickey held true for other Disney products: Disney the man embodied the best and humblest human virtues and was manifest in every product.

Evidence such as this indicates that from its early years, Disney was developing a complex understanding of the market that it was soon to capture. Yet it is important to understand that, in the 1920s and 1930s, the mass children's market was a relatively new phenomenon, shaped by and shaping converging and sometimes contradictory discourses about the meaning of childhood and its place in rapidly changing networks of social relations. Since before the beginning of the century, children increasingly had been viewed as proper objects for scientific study, organisms affected by and affecting their environment. As G. Stanley Hall put it in a 1915 issue of *Woman's World*, "I should be inclined, if I were formulating a declaration of children's rights, to lay down as one of the first their right to be studied right from their birth" (5). At the same time, however, childhood had come to be sentimentalized as a special realm that needed to be protected from the vicissitudes of adult life. Middle-class children in particular occupied simultaneously contradictory subject positions as cherished family pets and as laboratory animals whose behaviors could be shaped through application of proper stimuli.[7]

Significant among these stimuli were, of course, toys, games, furnishings, and clothing—and particularly entertainments such as movies. Although arguments over the effects of movies on morals and behaviors were as old as the medium itself, by the 1920s the nature of those debates had changed significantly. In the early part of the century, reformers concerned with the effects of movies had focused their concerns primarily on immigrant and working-class children and adults (whom they considered to be childlike in their understanding of the world) and had often been as concerned about the spaces in which they viewed movies as they were about the films' content. Movies and moviegoing were depicted as distractions that could potentially limit the ability of people in these groups to assimilate into an American culture that was implicitly white, middle-class, and Protestant—they were a little too violent, a little too sexual, and perhaps too ethnic.

Yet even as these arguments took shape, popular concerns about children and childhood were changing. During the same period, popular discourses concerned with child saving, rescuing poor and immigrant children from the dangers of ghetto life, began to share space with an increasingly articulated set of concerns about the well-being of children in general. In this model, the excesses of the lower classes became available to the children of the upper classes through mass entertainments and the spaces in which they were consumed. Since emerging professional discourses about the nature of childhood were predicated around the bodies and behaviors of white, middle-class children (as norms), arguments about the effects of movies on children extended those terms to immigrant and working-class children, while the moral imperatives underpinning progressive efforts to protect poor children increasingly informed the study of child-rearing and development. (For a more complete description of early-twentieth-century child-rearing, see chapter 2.)

Debates about the effects of movies intersected with arguments about the nature of childhood in a shared emphasis on the importance of a properly defined and regulated American culture—as that which produced good Americans *and* as that which required proper Americans in order to be reproduced. As the century progressed and children of the lower and middle classes mixed more on playgrounds, in schools, and at the movies, both discourses increasingly imagined the child as an abstract object, one that subsumed and erased troubling markers of race, class, and ethnicity. By the 1920s, the need to save the immigrant or working-class child (or adult) was rapidly giving ground to the need to regulate the environment of a generic child—to articulate and control the practices and products that would convert all children into proper Americans. By the onset of the Depression, middle-class children were considered almost as much in need as their inferiors, and almost as much at risk.

So, while it would be accurate to say that the young Walt Disney adroitly read a market in formation, an emphasis on the agency of one man and his corporation underplays the circuit of anxiety and desire that produced and drove that market. Disney was as much produced by that market as crucial to shaping it. To start to understand how Disney became synonymous with the best of childhood entertainment, then, a good place to begin is to examine how and why movies came to be considered important to childhood development.

Early Movie Effects

> *The intensity with the which the plays take hold of the audience cannot remain without social effects. . . . The associations become as vivid as realties, because the mind is so given up to the moving pictures.*
>
> —HUGO MUNSTERBERG (1916), IN JOWETT, JARVIE, AND FULLER 1996, 21

In general, from the birth of the medium in the 1890s to the early 1920s, debate over the effects of movies shifted gradually but steadily from a concern about both the content of motion pictures and the physical spaces in which they were viewed, to one that focused increasingly on content alone.[8] Before about 1915, the American movie scene was highly localized, often chaotic, and given to rapid and uneven changes in technology and modes of display. Patrons could view moving pictures in elaborate arcades, in cramped storefront parlors, as curtain-raisers at vaudeville shows, or as "visual aids" at traveling lectures. (In poorer rural locations, traveling cinemas would continue well into the Depression.) While some early upscale establishments catered to middle-class shoppers and white-collar workers on lunch break, many were situated in working-class neighborhoods and were often crowded, poorly ventilated, and dirty. Urban reformers (both those concerned with the effects of movies, and those concerned with the general welfare of the poor) feared that these conditions would lead to the spread of infectious diseases such as influenza, tuberculosis, and diphtheria, and to sexual predation upon single women and children (Nasaw 1993; Peiss 1986, 158–62).[9]

From the earliest calls for the reform and regulation of moviegoing practices, the regulation and production of class boundaries were at issue. In major metropolitan areas such as New York, Boston, and Chicago, violations of health and fire-safety codes at poorer venues provided a foot in the door for reformers concerned about controlling the moral and behavioral effects of movies upon the poor and ignorant, particularly children. Early metropolitan crusaders against vice and physical and moral corruption in immigrant and working-class communities were usually from the white, Protestant middle class, and they applied the metaphor of contagion equally to diseases of the mind and spirit as to the body. Motion picture houses were often described as closed and overheated, filled with both unwholesome vapors and unhealthy images, and not places in which the poor would be inspired to lift themselves above the squalid conditions of their daily lives. As Richard Maltby (1995, 41–42) points out in his description of early regulation: "Since the first motion picture censorship ordinance was introduced in Chicago in 1907, public debate has revolved around the question of whether the motion-picture industry was morally fit to control the manufacture of its own products. The terms of this debate were established by progressive reformers who regarded 'commercialized amusements' as an ameliorated form of 'commercialized vice' rather than an acceptable mode of recreation."

This particular configuration was to mark the construction of movie-effects arguments throughout their early history: excesses in the behaviors of moviegoing publics were laid at the feet of the producers, distributors, and exhibitors of motion pictures, as if the public practice itself were encouraging those behaviors. Even the National Board of Review of Motion Pictures, which had begun in 1909 as the National Board of Censorship and by the Depression had evolved into a voluntary regulatory agency, described its own beginnings as deriving from a (well-meaning) assault on the recreations of the poor. In its 1935 pamphlet "What Started the National Board," the organization described how "On Christmas Eve, in 1908, all five cent motion picture houses in New York City were closed at midnight by the police, under orders of the Mayor" (National Board of Review 1935, 3). Citing equal concern about the content of pictures shown and the conditions under which they appeared, urban reformers pressured Mayor George McClellan to close New York's movie houses. Even to regulators of the 1930s, this Scrooge-like gesture on the part of their predecessors seemed a somewhat mean-spirited attempt to control the few pleasures of the working class: "The chief attack was against the nickelodeons, which had become the poor man's theatre. They housed a new, growing, inexpensive form of entertainment for a mass of people who never went to theatres where plays were acted on the stage because they could not afford to. Into the lives of the toilers, weary after their day's labors, mentally and spiritually starved, the magic screen with its moving shadows brought glimpses of romance they had never dreamed of before" (ibid).

Although the National Board of Review's retrospective description of turn-of-the-century working-class leisure practices was perhaps shaded by its own interests, it reveals a sort of tolerant romanticism, a nostalgic fantasy that posited workers drawing spiritual sustenance from the screen and overzealous reformers as failing to acknowledge the value of that simple nourishment.[10] Perhaps even more telling, the board referred to early motion pictures as "a lusty infant growing miraculously fast with no guidance at all, any way it could; looked down on by most people of taste and intelligence" (National Board of Review, 4). By describing the early cinema as a sort of unruly natural child and early censors as prudish and cruel parents, the board created a revisionist history in which sensible, well-meaning regulators such as themselves would eventually push aside the overzealous and counterproductive reformers to take in hand an industry in need of gentle, wholesome direction.[11] Unlike their enlightened successors, though, those early censors were tight-lipped, Victorian, undemocratic, and self-interested: "There were the repressors, of dour puritanical calibre, who found in the motion picture machine . . . a new object for their fears and intolerances. . . . There were the professional reformers who made their living out of policing the morals of other people—in the movies they found a new evil . . . and a new branch, with salaries attached, for their blessed work of purifying and saving the world" (National Board of Review, 5).

On the other side of the equation were immigrant and working-class audiences and the businessmen who supplied them with entertainment, all of whose interest in the medium was in immediate gain, whether of pleasure or of profit, rather than in the cinema's potential as a vehicle for personal and collective edification: "Aside from the inarticulate masses and the confused men whose business was to make and distribute films, the only friends the young industry had were the people who perceived . . . a new form of art" (National Board of Review, 5). Those "only friends" were, of course, people of the ilk of the National Board of Censorship—whose only interest in regulating the medium was in realizing its inherent potential for good.[12]

While this was only one perspective on a complex and diverse situation—and one that favored regulation of content at the national level over complex struggles around censorship and the control of moviegoing venues at a local level—it represented the view of one of the most significant players in the regulation of American cinema before the 1930s (Czitrom 1996, Couvares 1996, Maltby 1995). This self-interested retrospective placed perhaps an inordinate amount of responsibility on the actions of reformers and censors in the emergence of a (relatively) coherent national cinema in the United States, but it paints a reasonably accurate picture of some of the key struggles that shaped discourses around the regulation of movies. Ultimately, it would be more accurate to say that the large regulatory groups that evolved out of early struggles over the practice of moviegoing—particularly the National Board of Review and, later, the Catholic Legion of Decency—derived their strength from the willingness of an increasingly limited and coherent group of producers to shape their production standards in ways that forestalled the possibility of censorship, either at the local or national level, and to enlist their critics in that process. This became particularly true as local reformers gradually succeeded in forcing municipal governments to enforce health and safety codes, causing poorer venues to improve or to close.[13]

By the late teens, with the ongoing consolidation of distribution and exhibition, arguments over the regulation of movie spaces began to recede and were largely overtaken by ongoing struggles over the content of motion pictures.[14] Like attempts to regulate venues, arguments about the content of movies had originally been couched in terms of a concern over the medium's effect on immigrants and the working class. In these early arguments, children and adults alike were seen as in need of moral uplift and examples of elementary Americanism to improve their station in life and to make a positive contribution to an emerging American mass culture. In these early assimilationist arguments, if one adopted the behaviors of one's middle-class betters—particularly those of thrift, hard work, self-denial, and deferred gratification—one was more likely to succeed as an individual and to contribute to the betterment of society as a citizen. For progressive-era urban reformers, moviegoing was one symptom in a complex of social and moral behaviors that condemned immigrants and the working class to conditions of crushing poverty, disease, and death by diverting them from experiences that would expose them to those more upright behaviors. Movies that offered the promise of sexual titillation or glamorized crime, and movie houses or parlors that encouraged physical proximity and the squandering of precious resources on frivolous amusements, were a threat to moral decency, to immigrant and working-class uplift, and thus to society as a whole. By the late teens and early twenties, these arguments would expand to include the suggestion that violent and salacious film programming encouraged crime, particularly delinquency (Koszarski 1990, 166).

At the same time, however, some progressive reformers, such as Jane Addams and Florence Kelly, were aware that the movies represented an opportunity for immigrant and working-class children (and adults) to escape the oppressive and unhealthy living conditions in tenements (for at least short periods of time), that the cinema provided business opportunities for a small minority of immigrant entrepreneurs, and that movies had the potential to serve as a means for immigrant and working-class patrons to reflect on their experience (E. Ewen 1985; R. Sklar 1975; Peiss 1986, 139–62; Alexander 1992; Hansen 1991, 63; Nasaw 1993, 178–79; Stamp 2004, 140–69).[15]

So, as the movies left small parlors and nickelodeons behind, a discourse about the potential benefits of moviegoing developed alongside arguments about its deleterious effects. If watching a movie could arouse illicit desires and habits, perhaps it could also impart more socially beneficial behaviors. As they fought the negative effects of movies, progressive reformers also argued for the *positive* effects that a well-regulated movie industry could have on American society and culture. In 1910, *Moving Picture World* declared that movies were the "Working Man's College," and progressive reformers claimed that movies could inculcate immigrants into American life (Ross 1990). In large urban centers, some settlement workers offered films they hoped would lure young boys and girls away from more lurid commercial offerings, while progressive labor reformers made movies to sway recalcitrant capitalists from the excesses of the sweatshop and to turn workers away from radicalism (Addams 1926, Nasaw 1992, Ross 1990).

In the progressive imagination, children were susceptible to either the positive or negative effects of movies simply because the movies formed such a substantial portion of their experience of a world to which they were relatively new. Immigrant and working-class adults were likewise vulnerable because they were relatively childlike in their approach to the world: because their formative experiences within their native cultures had not prepared them for American culture, they were in some ways more disadvantaged than their children (Addams 1926). The right kind of movie, then, viewed in the proper environment, would help immigrant and working-class children (and perhaps their parents) assimilate into American culture. When a 1915 pamphlet titled *Motion Pictures in Religious and Educational Work* noted that 8.5 million people, many of them children, attended the movies every night, it did so not with alarm, but with a cautious optimism (McConoughey 1915). The author of this Methodist tract suggested that pressures for beneficial children's films had grown so great that "special films are being manufactured for them."[16] In describing the status of efforts to regulate the children's viewing, he depicted a situation in which nascent market research blended with public policy in an effort to understand what children enjoyed and whether it should be permitted. He informed his readers that a "study of the kind of pictures best liked by the children has been made, particularly in Providence, R.I.; Springfield, Ill.; South Bend, Ind.; Cleveland, Ohio; San Francisco, Cal.; Portland, Ore.; and the Horace Mann School, New York City. In the lower grades both boys and girls prefer pictures of rapid action, of adventure and excitement, in particular the Wild West, cowboys and Indians, the percentage running from forty to sixty" (22).

In one instance, he related, the Investigating Committee of Cleveland reported that upward of ten thousand children a night attended motion pictures unaccompanied. Yet, rather than expressing alarm, "the Committee recommended not the prohibiting of children from attending in the evening, but to have the motion picture exhibitions places of wholesome entertainment" (McConoughey 1915, 23). Far from being the dens of iniquity that they had been considered fewer than ten years earlier, at least to some urban reformers, movie houses were potential sites for the edification of young children.

This did not mean, however, that a nascent national movie industry began an organized effort to produce films explicitly beneficial for children. Rather, a variety of social forces converged to create an environment in which it seemed as if some films might benefit children. These included a progressive reform movement willing to work with the new medium rather than against it, (eventually) a wartime environment that allowed for gestures of patriotism and

Americanism on the part of filmmakers, and, as the industry became consolidated in Hollywood, an effort on the part of major producers to address reformist concerns through public relations.

One means of doing this was for individual producers to print their own magazines, which appeared similar to (ostensibly) disinterested or independent publications such as *Photoplay* or *Motion Picture Herald*. Although these publications had a decidedly limited circulation, they allowed producers and distributors some marginal control over discourse. Thus, Fox printed in its *Exhibitor's Bulletin* a ridiculously angry letter from a vaudeville manager in Iowa, claiming: "Since the introduction of the moving pictures juvenile delinquency and criminality have increased many thousand percent, making necessary the establishment of juvenile courts in large cities. . . . Furthermore, since the introduction of moving pictures the use of morphine, heroin, cocaine and other . . . drugs has increased many thousand percent." It then paired that letter with a reasonable reply from a minimally identified Fox employee:

> There has been no such effort made to keep the speaking stage as clean and wholesome as is the silent screen. There are no vile pictures in the sense that there are and have been vile books. . . . The moving pictures are guarded at the fountain head by the decent men who absolutely control the industry. . . . [and] by the leading citizens in every community, who constitute themselves self-appointed boards of censors. . . . There has been no force for moral uplift or educational advance since the invention of printing so mighty and so speedy in its effect as motion pictures. . . . The foremost educators approve and use the moving pictures in schools and colleges. (McCardell 1915, 13)

Even independent film magazines such as *Photoplay*, dependent as they were on a fan base, helped promulgate public-relations discourses that positioned the studios as aware of the effect of movies on young minds and bodies, and as actively addressing the problem. One such issue was the contention that the movies could lead to "premature sophistication" in children, in which they became too knowledgeable about adult mannerisms and mores at too tender an age. The exchange above suggests one approach producers took to the problem. Another was to demonstrate that child actors, far from sacrificing their innocence for the silver screen, actually benefited from the experience. In "Photoplay Children at the Big Studios" (Streeter 1916), an author evoked the fear of adults at witnessing child actors in compromising situations, and then addressed that fear:

> What appears to be a prematurely acquired store of worldly wisdom is merely a combination of skill on the part of the directors, many of whom have specialized in this field, and another demonstration of all children's love of, and ability to imitate, their elders. . . . It has often been said of stage children that they become artificial, knowing beyond their years, unreal. But this is not the case with the children of the studios. Here . . . it is just one big game and the play spirit must be kept up and everything made into one big game, for nothing is so quick to detect artificialities as the eye of the all-seeing camera. (10)

Not only did the children never really realize that they were working, taking part in a serious enterprise, the author suggested, but if they had been adversely effected by being forced to act beyond their years, the camera would have detected it (and the viewer seen it). While arguments such as these were far from seamless, and often met stiff resistance from child-labor reform advocates and movie-effects reformers, they indicate nonetheless an early effort on the part of producers to address and shape arguments concerning the nature of the relationship between children and movies.

In a way, then, arguments about the negative effects of movies on American culture provided movie producers, distributors, and exhibitors with avenues into that culture, openings through which they could argue that they were actually making a positive contribution to society. Both David Nasaw (1993) and Robert Sklar (1975) point out that while the early years of movie making were heavily indebted to immigrant and working-class culture (and to vaudeville in particular), by the early teens, producers such as Adolph Zukor and William Fox were looking for ways to more consistently reach a broader, middle-class audience (Aronson 2002). By the mid-teens, larger producers were constructing a network of cleaner, more elaborate movie houses (and later palaces), and the issue of regulating viewing spaces receded, leading to an increased focus on motion-picture content. With the advent of the star system and the development of national distribution networks, the medium became accepted as an important element in an emerging national mass culture (Moley 1945, 20; deCordova 1990).

The arrival of this national culture wasn't altogether smooth, though. Since before the turn of the century, the United States had been troubled by periods of severe socioeconomic instability, class conflict, and racial strife. Much of the discord of the period had helped foster nativist and eugenicist movements, anti-immigration efforts, and red purges (Montgomery 1987, Bennett 1988, Appel 1971, Chambers 2000). Throughout these struggles ran a pervasive discourse that centered on what it meant to be American, and why Americanness was important to the well-being and unity of the nation. Even as progressives attempted to counter the more virulent eugenicist and nativist arguments against immigration with programs for assimilation through education, they inadvertently contributed to this discourse by positing an extant American culture into which immigrants and the working class could assimilate that was ostensibly unmarked but implicitly white, middle-class, and Protestant (Omi and Winant 1994, Burnham 1977).[17] This reasoning effectively blunted arguments against "racial pollution" and for natural hierarchies based on racial and national origin, but in the process created a set of mechanisms through which ethnic and racial others were expected to pass as they became "Americanized," and by which they could be judged as properly or improperly assimilating, or properly or improperly affecting the assimilation of others.[18]

Motion-picture producers and distributors, many of whom were Jews of Eastern European descent, were quite aware of this atmosphere. Some, such as Samuel Goldwyn and the Warner brothers, anglicized their names and positioned immigrant stars such as Rudolph Valentino, or American ethnics such as Theda Bara (Theodosia Goodman of Cincinnati), as imported foreign exotics.[19] Even these efforts to pass did not promise an escape from pointed calls to regulate ethnic and racial formations, as in this 1922 letter to *Photoplay* (the cover of which was adorned with a picture of Nita Naldi, "Mrs. Valentino"):

> In present day films, often the majority of the cast is of Jewish extraction. We all enjoy seeing Jewish actors in plays representative of Jewish life, such as east side dramas. . . . But it is impossible for an intelligent public to ignore such glaring inconsistencies as we saw in Jackie Coogan's "Peck's Bad Boy"[.] There in a typical American family, a Jewess is cast as the mother, while in the church scene, the minister (a most repulsive type, and an insult to the clergy) preaches to a congregation made up for the most part of Jewish extras. . . . We thoroughly approve of the campaign for new faces but—*please select typical American faces*! ("Miscasting—A Misdemeanor" 1922, emphasis original, 17)

Motion-picture practices maintained the color bar, both in the theaters and in the perpetuation of the minstrel tradition—through the use of blackface actors or in the reiteration of the minstrel caricature by black supporting characters (Nasaw 1993, 202; Rogin 1992).[20] In the process of fending off anti-Semitic and anti-metropolitan attacks, Hollywood slowly divorced vaudeville, with its explicit ethnic, racial, and working-class associations, from the movies (R. Sklar

1975, 148; Hansen 1991, 60–68; Rogin 1992; Jenkins 1992). In short, the birth of American cinema as a national form was deeply interwoven with struggles over what it meant to be American, to represent and to be representative of America.

The Birth of the Production Code, and of Walt Disney

> *It seems strange that the masters of the motion-picture industry, as they emerged from the World War years, should have been almost completely unaware of the complex nature of public opinion in the United States. . . . when their audience spread from the nickelodeon to the urban palace and then to the crossroads of the nation, their personal knowledge faltered. . . . This America . . . with its manifold prejudices and ideals, its innumerable traditions . . . an industry with a national market had to know. And theirs was at last a national business . . . with a highly developed public interest.*
> —MOLEY 1945, 23–24

Though veiled in polite language, Raymond Moley's assessment of the atmosphere that led to the establishment of the Motion Picture Producers and Distributors Association (the MPPDA, or "Hays Office") in 1922 speaks volumes about the social and political conditions that surrounded the emergent mass medium. In his adulatory retrospective on the Hays Office, Moley was recounting a moment in which a relatively small group of Hollywood producers were well on their way to establishing a uniform national network of distribution and exhibition. By the late teens, Hollywood had replaced the metropolitan New York area as the primary site of movie production. With consolidation came both the focusing of attacks on the industry as injurious to American culture, and to youth in particular, and the coordination and regulation of arguments about film's beneficial effects. A successful and concentrated industry with roots in New York and studios in Hollywood became a target for anti-Semitic and antimetropolitan attacks and a willing participant in the coordination and production of Americanism.[21]

World War I only intensified these conditions. During the war, the film industry developed a closer working relationship with the federal government. Filmmakers distributed movies sponsored by the government's Committee on Public Information (CPI) and also produced their own patriotic films, which often featured xenophobic depictions of Germans as monsters. Yet this relationship required negotiation: the CPI refused to allow the exportation of films that dealt with poverty, class conflict, or internal strife on the grounds that they offered a poor portrayal of American democracy. This relationship, while it allowed the film industry to avoid federal restriction, committed the medium to a rather specific patriotism and Americanism (Ross 1990, Nasaw 1993). Following the war, the relationship continued, with domestic enemies replacing those on the foreign front. When it came to melodramatic villains, the "Hun" was replaced by the "Bolshevik" or "outside agitator," who often looked like a southern or eastern European immigrant. In the wake of the Red Scare of 1919, producers even went so far as to clear scripts that dealt with issues of labor strife or social unrest with officials in the Labor Department (Ross 1990). Attempting to capture a middle-American audience, the movie industry worked hard to shed its image as a haven for immigrant peddlers of cheap amusements for the working class and to avoid criticism and censorship (R. Sklar 1975, Nasaw 1993).[22] Although dramas that dealt with cross-generational difficulties brought on by assimilation and comedies with broadly drawn ethnic characters continued to be made, by the 1920s the motion-picture industry was gradually subordinating the medium's ethnic and working-class roots for the sake of promoting patriotic Americanism.

While Raymond Moley may have been somewhat disingenuous in describing the movie moguls' response to these conflicts as a rude awakening, he did depict real social pressures.[23] As the movie industry became national, producers and distributors increasingly had to deal with state and local censors, and, increasingly, with persistent calls for censorship at the federal level. State and local censors were particularly sensitive to sex and the glamorization of crime, but also to themes that promoted political agitation, class struggle, or anti-Americanism (Ross 1990, R. Sklar 1975). As major motion pictures became more "American," concerns about movies were phrased more and more as about what they were doing to *average* Americans—particularly the average American child. More specifically, arguments about the effects of movies continued to shift from fears of what the medium was doing to the working class to fears about what the ethnic, working-class underbelly of the medium was doing to American values. In 1922, the Better Films Committee of Atlanta could expect of a program of "Boys and Girls Matineés" that it combine "clean, wholesome entertainment . . . [and] elementary Americanism" (*Moving Pictures Forward* 1922, 3). In that same year, in the wake of the Fatty Arbuckle scandal, a U.S. senator fulminated on the Senate floor that

> Hollywood is a colony . . . where debauchery, riotous living, drunkenness, ribaldry, dissipation, free love seem to be conspicuous. Many . . . "stars" . . .

were formerly bartenders, butcher boys, sopers, swampers, variety actors and actresses, who may have earned $10 or $20 a week. Some of them are now paid, it is said, salaries of something like $5000 a month or more. . . . These are some of the characters from whom the young people of today are deriving a large part of their education, views of life, and character forming habits. (*Congressional Record* 1922, 9657)

By the 1920s, moviegoing had become a social activity that crossed class lines, and any effects that movies had on the working classes might extend to other classes as well. The more a common American culture became possible and accessible, the more necessary it became to police that culture, to ensure that it remained an inoculant against base qualities, rather than their carrier. Hollywood responded by forming the MPPDA, which was headed by prominent Republican and former U.S. Postmaster General Will Hays. The organization's ostensible purpose was to clean up the industry, although it was widely understood that its primary function was to regulate public opinion about the industry in order to avoid state and federal censorship (Maltby 1995). Attempting to seize the moment and shape public opinion around the Arbuckle incident, Hays declared in *Photoplay* that "ours is a duty to youth. We are not so much interested in the millions of dollars invested in the industry as we are in the millions of children whose morals and education are invested in it" (Hays, quoted in Quirk 1922b, 19). This was an important moment in the development of discourses about the effect of movies on children. Hays's willingness, as the head of the national regulatory organization established by the movie industry, to aver not only that movies contributed to the morals and education of children, but that the industry was facing that problem in a responsible fashion, added a level of legitimacy and coherence to those assumptions that had previously existed primarily at a local level.

Hays was by no means alone in clarifying and regulating the terms of the discussion, however. His appointment set off a flurry of articles and letters in *Photoplay*, one of the primary outlets for motion-picture fans, in which the magazine and its readers discussed the nature of films, the proper regulation of the industry, and the MPPDA's role in that regulation. When Hays was appointed, publisher James Quirk demanded that he "call on producers to discharge all persons whose private lives and habits make them a menace to the industry" (Quirk 1922a, 53). A month later, the magazine profiled Hays in glowing terms, repeatedly describing him as a man who loved his country, who viewed America as "one vast assemblage" and saw the movies as "the greatest of all mediums for increasing the enlightenment and promoting the happiness of the millions" (Nicholson 1922, 31). For movie fans at the very least, and in public discourse concerning Hollywood, motion pictures had arrived as a national medium.

For *Photoplay*'s staff and readers, however, the establishment of the movies as American culture's national medium did not require federal censorship to protect that culture. In the magazine's September issue, one letter writer inveighed against censors, finally asking, "Where has our traditional freedom of thought disappeared to?" (Billings 1922, 115). Another wondered if Hollywood could make wholesome movies if it employed people like Fatty Arbuckle, while Billie Bobbink of St. Louis, Missouri, a self-described "flapper," declared,

> I would like to write a true story for the movies of actual events in the lives of my high school friends, but if I did, the censors would be so horrified that their clipping scissors would be worn out before they finished censoring it; which only proves that the movies are giving us angelic products compared to realities! No older person will agree with me, I am sure, but then these older people are not living in the world of their sons and daughters. So how can they understand? (Bobbink 1922, 115)

In the magazine's October issue, publisher Quirk declared, "PHOTOPLAY believes the morals of the young should be guarded. But censorship or suppression is not the right road. It believes that parents should use discretion and a sane discrimination about pictures they permit their children to attend. If this does not work out, an official regulation regarding the attendance of children would protect both the youthful imagination and the photoplay" (Quirk 1922b, 19). In a companion article, "Foolish Censors" (Smith 1922), a *Photoplay* writer stated, "There is no excuse for censorship and it will never be anything but intolerance. It savors tyranny, fear, and bigotry—it is the spirit of the Inquisition rekindled and rampant in our land. Censorship is the hooded Ku Klux Klan of art" (F. Smith 1922). (See figure 3.) In the magazine's November issue, a reader declared, "There should be separate theaters for children, so that adults would not have to see baby-stuff; and adolescents and children would not have to see the sophisticated dramas" (Arnold 1922). And finally, one wag who signed off as "Mrs. Grundy" bitterly mocked the whole question:

> And then this Arbuckle case. True he was exonerated on the extraordinary charge, but it seems to me it is the duty of all respectable people to voice their disapproval. It is quite apparent that his mind had been poisoned by seeing too many motion pictures in which the heroine is pursued around the table by a person who plainly means her no good. Which somehow

When these people finish with what little the censors have left, the movies will be about as entertaining as an old tintype of grandpa in his brown derby

3. An editorial cartoon in the October 1922 issue of *Photoplay* lambasted censors, whom the author of the accompanying article described as "Self-righteous, self-appointed, ignorant, [and] holier-than-thou." Many movie fans feared that the establishment of the Hays office and more aggressive policing of Hollywood pictures might encourage the infantilization of films to protect child patrons.

brings us to Mr. Will Hays, an estimable person, whose training as a postmaster and politician has admirably, no doubt, fitted him to be the high cleanser of the movies. I am sure that under his gentle guidance they will not make films that would tax the intelligence and powers of assimilation of a child of five. This will be a great day for the art. Many authorities have said that the movies are still in their infancy; and now with a concerted effort of the censors—both professional and amateur—they will succeed in keeping them there. . . . Hoping to have your support in our new slogan for the films, "Nothing that will hurt the moron," I am, Mrs. Grundy (Grundy 1922, 17)

Although it is difficult to determine whether letters such as these were actually written by fans, or if some or all were penned by *Photoplay* staff, they reveal a steadily stabilizing discourse around movie effects and censorship in the early 1920s.[24] Presenting a very different take on the effect of movies on the public in general (and on children in particular) than did reformers, fans and fan media such as *Photoplay* nonetheless reproduced and reinforced a number of tropes about moviegoing. In an effort to beat back the threat of censorship, editorial writers and fans alike reproduced a generic child in need of some sort of protection from movies that might produce premature and excessive sophistication. While admitting that this was a very real possibility, both groups suggested that it was the responsibility of parents to regulate the child's viewing habits. This marked a significant shift from earlier, more class-based arguments about the regulation of movies, in which it was often assumed that both parents were working, and that there was not necessarily a regulatory agency or extended family network to watch over the child. Beyond shifting responsibility for the potential effects of movies from producers to parents, discourses such as these assumed as normal a middle-class family structure in which at least one parent (usually the mother) was present to regulate children's behavior.[25] This assumption around movie-effects arguments circulated through popular media, reinforcing a notion of a generic child with implicitly middle-class characteristics at risk of infection by the movies. Although the basis for this version of childhood had its primary location in an emerging discourse of developmental theory (see chapter 2), it found wide public circulation in arguments about media effects.

Perhaps more significant, however, to young producers such as Disney (who began making films in 1921, moved to Hollywood in 1923, and hit it big with *Steamboat Willie* in 1928) was the circulation of the idea that the values of producers, directors, stars, and so on actually filtered through the movies and into the lives of audience members. In the responses of apologists for the movies, the irate senator's sentiment that the working-class roots of the entertainment industry presented a threat to innocent children, or the idea that movies could breed unnatural sophistication in child stars and patrons alike, provided further basis for the argument for the positive persuasive effects of movies, and for the idea that good moral character could be delivered via the screen. For established Hollywood producers, who had as often as not been associated with the negative effects of movies, this argument could best be made around certain stars, such as Douglas Fairbanks or Mary Pickford. But neither Fox, nor Zukor, nor Goldwyn could easily make an argument that *all* of their products were beneficial for children when, for instance, a leading author of child-rearing books and articles declared:

> Why do the "movies" make such a strong appeal to youth? Mainly because they indulge the passion for stirring, exciting, hazardous adventure . . . through scenes that are gruesome and fearful. . . . they usually portray sex relations and the . . . struggles and tragedies that arise out of them. . . . Those who produce moving pictures are keen students of the primitive impulses and interests in childhood and youth, and even in mature life. They know . . . they can bring crowds into their theaters if they will display scenes which the law would not tolerate on the street. . . . For its own protection society should prohibit the display of scenes in public places which would not be tolerated on the street or in the school or the church or the home. (O'Shea 1920, 146–150)

Nor did those producers want to make that argument. As much as the Hollywood majors made good money off of child audiences, they also traded on sex, glamour, excitement, and danger. It was more in their interest to argue for a partition of moviegoing practices and the promulgation of parental regulation. At the same time, however, these discursive shifts created an opening in which it became possible to speak about a producer of unimpeachable character turning out equally unsullied entertainments for an audience of children in need of that type of influence. In the same breath as he condemned the current crop of Hollywood producers for their cynical manipulation of their audiences, the same author intoned: "While moving pictures can make so strong an appeal to what is primitive and degenerate in human nature, they can make an equally strong appeal to what is exalted, courageous, heroic, and chivalric. . . . every other person who has the interest of the young and society at heart should insist on having scenes of wholesome, decent life in the moving picture shows. That which is brutal and lewd should be rigorously suppressed"

(151–152). Whether for good or for evil, the movies themselves were seen as able to directly influence children, and by extension, the society they would form as adults. While Disney would make much of the positive side of this equation, during the 1920s, for the most part major Hollywood producers (by way of the MPPDA) could only create an elaborate public-relations system designed to address and limit the damage caused by criticism of the industry's apparent excesses.

One public-relations effort that would become useful to Disney was the MPPDA's support for Saturday-morning matinees. A practice that had grown spontaneously in the late teens, organized primarily by theater owners and better-film committees, children's matinees were seen as a means of providing children with a steady flow of movies that were considered beneficial. This not only relieved exhibitors of criticism but also eased the burden of regulation on parents (deCordova 1983). Even by the early 1920s, the limitations of parental regulation as a solution to movie effects were becoming painfully evident: for whatever reason, all but the most vigilant parents seemed unable or unwilling to do the proper research necessary for the selection process. Writing in *Photoplay* in 1922, one former exhibitor described the system she had developed to aid parents:

> I wanted my hometown youngsters to see pictures they would understand and enjoy, and I figured it was up to the parents to co-operate with me and select the pictures that were suitable. . . . To make this selection possible, I issued each week a 16-page booklet, containing pictures of each production and a complete story. I . . . advertised heavily, so that I could carry out this same idea. I called the public's attention to the pictures most suitable for the children, and urged the parents to read the synopsis of each picture carefully so they would KNOW what their boys and girls were seeing. (Spurr 1922, 88)

Even though she claimed to have found over one hundred pictures she deemed suitable for children, for an average of two a week, she eventually abandoned her system because "after keeping at it for more than five years I grew disgusted and discouraged. A few of the parents saw the wisdom of selecting their children's amusements, but the majority . . . wouldn't take the time to find out, or didn't care whether the picture was suitable or not."

Saturday-matinee clubs were a partial solution to this problem, offering a prepackaged slate of films and delivering them in a guaranteed time slot so that parents wouldn't have to read previews. By the mid-1920s, the MPPDA had developed a list of films for use in Saturday matinees, and had even reedited some films to make them appropriate for children. But critics of the program claimed that the organization was simply trying to get children to watch more movies, rather than to create more selective viewers. By 1926, the MPPDA had abandoned the project (deCordova 1983).

To say that the MPPDA's efforts were a failure, however, would be a mistake. Hays's sentiments of 1922 aside, the association had little interest in improving the lot of children through movies. It was interested in maintaining a relatively unfettered production process, and to the degree that it could demonstrate even a debatable will to benefit the nation through its children, its efforts were a success. An unintended consequence of this work, however, was the further refinement of the notion of an unmarked American child affected by the movies. The MPPDA's efforts to create a national program of Saturday matinees took a set of local practices and attempted to standardize them for an ideal child, and, as similar efforts had done ten years earlier, created a stream of marketing data about the purported tastes of that child. As Richard deCordova (1983, 102–103) put it in his study of those matinees:

> Through the selection and editing of films [the MPPDA] tried to produce a particular kind of textual subject, a symbolic position and mode of address that would ideally produce the spectator as a true child. . . . through essay contests, organizers tried to gauge the actual response of real children to the films of the week. . . . [and] the matinées exerted power over the child's body, both through the ways in which it worked systematically to separate the child from the adult and through the ways it placed the child in a system of surveillance within the theater itself.

The bodies of the real children watching the movies, then, were in a sense transit points in the circulation of ideas about the ideal child in relation to the movies. As movies were selected with that child in mind, and the responses of real children to those movies gauged in relation to what that ideal child might be expected to obtain from the experience, the discursive positions of those children were highly regulated long before they took their seats in the actual theaters.

And notions of those ideal children positively affected by proper moviegoing continued to circulate in the popular imaginary, just as images of children suffering from the negative effects of moviegoing did. Writing to *Photoplay* in 1928, a self-described "minister's son" shared his own experience:

> From cradle days I have heard the movies and actors condemned as tools of Hell and the Devil. . . . [but] . . . Time and again I have sat and watched

> the faces of young America change expression with the actor's. . . . Every picture adds expressive power to our own personalities. . . . Hollywood and its movie stars are the creators of personality for the American future. . . . Of every group of children I know those who have come under the influence of the great movie personalities soon outdistance the children of the narrow minded neighbors in the mix-up of life. . . . Hats off!! to the movies—We owe them much. (Darling 1928, 10)

Replicating the idea that children could absorb the behaviors and morals of the stars directly from their characters, this movie fan suggested that the movies even offered an edge to those children, broadening their experience and understanding of the world. Another fan, writing to *Photoplay* in 1932, suggested that whole communities could benefit from the effects of the movies. Visiting a cousin who was a small-town mayor, the writer noticed that they went to the movies every night. When he asked his cousin why, he was told: "Back before we had this theater the parents of this town came to me day and night complaining of their children's behavior, saying they were getting into all kinds of mischief. . . . I was helpless, but by good fortune the theater was established and from then on I have had very few complaints. I owe to the movies more than I shall ever be able to pay, so I show my gratitude by attendance" (Patterson 1932, 6). Far from the corrupter of children or the cause of juvenile delinquency that reformers imagined the movies to be, in the eyes of fans the films had equal potential to do good in the world as they did to cause trouble.[26]

The Arrival of Disney and the Regulation of Children

At the same time that it instituted its Saturday morning matinee program, the MPPDA undertook a much larger, and ultimately more significant, public-relations project—the promulgation of a series of sets of guidelines for producers by which they could guarantee the delivery of wholesome films to their public, which would culminate in the Motion Picture Production Code. In 1924, two years after he was hired by the MPPDA, Hays put out the "Formula," a set of procedures by which producers were meant to select the proper stories for realization as motion pictures. This was followed in 1927 by the "Don'ts and Be Carefuls," which was based on standing rules of foreign, state, and local censorship offices that the studios had to deal with in any case (Moley 1945, Maltby 1995). Since this code was designed to counter the demands of censors before movies went into production, its public-relations value aside, it was a cost-effective method for streamlining postproduction costs due to reshooting and reediting (Maltby 1995). Compliance with this code was largely voluntary, and a number of civic organizations, censorship boards, and religious groups often objected to films that supposedly passed muster under the industry standards. In this sense, the standard was as much a public-relations liability as it was an asset. Although it demonstrated the industry's commitment to producing films that met a common set of goals, the Formula also became a standard by which individual organizations could criticize films, studios, or the industry in general. And, since it lacked an articulated enforcement mechanism, it laid the MPPDA open to accusations of hypocrisy and insincerity.

By the late 1920s, complaints against the ineffectiveness of MPPDA self-regulation were growing—particularly with the advent of sound, which made the postproduction alteration of movies by local censors a much more difficult affair than it had been during the silent era.[27] In general, state censors were acting more aggressively, and some reform groups were still attempting to establish federal regulation. In response, in March 1930, the MPPDA released the Motion Picture Production Code—soon to be known simply as "the Code"—a detailed list of production standards covering the depiction of crime, sex, dancing, religion, and so on, by which the movie industry promised to abide. Although the Code is remembered primarily for its more stringent rules—particularly its ban on representations of miscegenation and its absurd requirement that even married couples appear to sleep in separate beds—its most profound effect on the movies, and by extension American popular culture, was in the involvement (or, some would say, the co-optation) of religious and civic groups in its promulgation and enforcement. In writing and rewriting the Code, the Hays Office sought out representatives of a wide range of groups, from the Catholic Church to the American Red Cross, developing an enforcement regime that included outside reviewers. By 1934, Hays would report to the MPPDA that "socially-minded civic leaders in increasing numbers are accepting responsibility for aiding the industry by constructive criticism of motion pictures; in the education of public taste for pictures of the better kind; for the adjustment as far as possible of the theatre program to the entertainment needs of children; and for enhancing the positive constructive value of entertainment pictures dealing with social problems" (Hays 1934a, 6).

The list of those leaders that Hays involved (or attempted to involve) in the process of regulating the movies was extensive and included representatives from the General Federation of Women's Clubs, National Council of Teachers of English, California Committee of National Council of Catholic Women, Young Men's Christian Association, National Council of Jewish Women, American Library Association, National Society Daughters of the

American Revolution, and the United Church Brotherhood (Hays 1934a). Perhaps as much as the producers themselves, who were supposed to police themselves and each other in the enforcement of the Code, these groups encouraged a sense that the industry was actually doing something to improve the content of motion pictures. In 1934, Hays reported that "for [1933], 477 feature pictures and 602 short subjects were previewed by these organizations. . . . It is particularly significant that last year 72 pictures were endorsed by these previewing groups as suitable for children between the ages of 8 and 12 years, as against the endorsement of 51 such pictures in the year 1932" (Hays 1934a, 7). By agreeing to act as previewers, these organizations lent an air of legitimacy to the Code and to the MPPDA that both needed. Even as they appeared to increase their output of "family" films, the studios continued to make films that ran afoul of the Code and of state censors.[28] But beyond legitimizing the industry's efforts at self-regulation, the involvement of civic and religious groups in the previewing of movies was meant to create a set of practices by which representatives of those groups, and by extension their members, became invested in the production of motion pictures as acts of civic duty, if not as contributions to national culture. As part of the process of legitimization, Hollywood producers had to accept, in some degree, discourses that suggested that movies shaped character, particularly in children, and that character determined the well-being of society. Although too much emphasis on the ability of movies to create or shape behavior could leave them open to more severe forms of regulation, the validation afforded by those outside groups made some acknowledgment necessary. The preamble to the Code reflects this tension, in one breath suggesting that movies were merely entertainments, in the next admitting that they might serve a greater purpose:

> Motion picture producers. . . . recognize their responsibility to the public because of this trust and because entertainment and art are important influences in the life of a nation . . . Hence, though regarding motion pictures primarily as entertainment without any explicit purpose of teaching or propaganda, they know that the motion picture within its own field of entertainment may be directly responsible for spiritual or moral progress, for higher types of social life, and for much correct thinking. (Motion Picture Production Code, in Moley 1945, 241)

This connection was made even more explicit in another section of the Code, the "Reasons." Although this section was not included in the first version of the Code released in 1930, it did appear in subsequent versions.[29] Written by Martin Quigley, a Catholic reformer and publisher of the *Motion Picture Herald* who had been included in the process of drafting the Code in an effort to win Catholic support, the "Reasons" more clearly capture the sentiments of many reform groups of the late 1920s and early 1930s. Far from seeing movies as simple entertainment, the stricken portion of the Code suggested that "correct entertainment raises the whole standard of the nation. . . . Wrong entertainment lowers the whole living conditions and moral ideals of a race" (Motion Picture Production Code, in Quigley 1937, 57). Also, codifying a notion in wide circulation in the 1920s, the document declared:

> The motion pictures, which are the most popular of modern arts for the masses, have their moral quality from the intention of the minds which produce them and from their efforts on the moral lives and reactions of the audiences. This gives them a most important morality. *1. They reproduce the morality of the men who use the picture as a medium for the expression of their ideas and ideals. 2. They affect the moral standards of those who through the screen take in these ideas and ideals.* (Motion Picture Production Code, in Quigley 1937; emphasis original, 59)

Whether a firmly held belief or hyperbole meant to raise support for the regulation of movies, this discourse, which moved easily from the popular press into a code designed to guide movie production, made commonplace the idea that movies formed a direct conduit from the minds of producers to those of their audiences—particularly those of children.[30] Although the MPPDA generally tried to qualify this claim, even it contributed to this discourse. For several years in the 1930s, the association distributed copies of a "newspaper" titled *The Motion Picture and the Family* in theater lobbies. The paper was meant to encourage the sense that Hollywood was deeply concerned with producing family entertainment, and in it Will Hays declared, "The motion picture, and even more emphatically when presented in neighborhood theater, is a family institution" (Hays 1934b). The monthly paper offered tips on how to choose movies, news about movies good for children, and news of local movie appreciation courses and clubs, and in one announcement for the movie *Wednesday's Child* (Robertson 1934) it declared, "Motion pictures are giving the public excellent hints in the psychology of childhood" ("Wednesday's Child" 1934, 3). Thus, by the early 1930s, as much as it might have wanted to stress the entertainment quality of its product, the MPPDA was also caught up in reproducing notions of (positive) movie effects, and of ideas of a generic child who could benefit from those effects (see figures 4 and 5).

In some instances, these efforts paid off. In a radio talk in January of 1933, for example, a representative of the Erie County, New York, Children's Aid Society

A Bulletin for All who are Interested in Better Motion Pictures

The Motion Picture *and* The Family

Comment on Current Films by Teachers, Educators, Community Leaders

VOL. 1 | MAY 15, 1935 | No. 8

Teen Age Group Shows Its Scorn Of Sexy Films

Whatever other occasion it may have for concern, the Better Films Council of Green Bay, Wisconsin, need not worry about the motion picture tastes of the "younger generation." 'Teen age boys and girls in the Franklin Junior High School, who participated in a survey conducted by the Council, betrayed a healthy scorn of "sexy" films. Gangster pictures were also on their taboo or near taboo list.

Otherwise the pupils' film preferences varied according to age. Seventh and eighth graders had a liking for westerns, mysteries and slapstick comedy. Ninth graders, having achieved greater maturity of viewpoint, were enthusiastic about musical comedy, historical and political films as well as those which placed emphasis upon social values.

For all pupils, of whatever grade, the four most popular films were *Bright Eyes* and *Little Colonel*, both starring Shirley Temple, *Little Women*, with Katharine

(*Continued on Page* 4)

Managers Help Youth to College

As a result of the civic-minded-

Studios Throw Doors Wide For Envoy Of Catholic Alumnae

Mrs. James F. Looram, Chairman Motion Picture Bureau, is feted by M-G-M. Center: Louis B. Mayer; right: Bishop John J. Cantwell of Los Angeles.

"Ten million children can't be wronged by pictures if the present standard of motion picture production is kept up" was the encouraging message brought back from Los Angeles by Mrs. James F. Looram, Chairman of the Motion Picture Bureau of the International Federation of Catholic Alumnae when she returned from a trip to the West Coast to plan for a wider

(*Continued on Page* 3)

4,500 Pupils In N. Y. City See Character Film

Character education films made their official debut as a factor in the visual education program of New York City public schools on May 10 when 4,500 school children from Manhattan and the Bronx saw a one-reel cutting from *Sooky* and afterwards debated whether Skippy should have told his father before he charged groceries to the latter's account in an endeavor to save Sooky's family from the poorhouse.

Small heads nodded and foreheads wrinkled with concentration as the boys and girls tried to figure out for themselves whether it was wrong for Skippy to march in Dr. Saunders' pre-election parade when his father was a rival candidate for Mayor in order to get Sooky into the Boone Boys, and whether Dr. Skinner was to blame for his son's reluctance to confide in him.

The program was a prelude to the showing in New York City of a series of films prepared under the direction of the Committee on Social Values in Motion Pictures, of

(*Continued on page* 2)

Plan To Make Peace Films Pay

4. Even as the Motion Picture Production Code was promulgated, the MPPDA distributed *The Motion Picture and the Family* in theater lobbies as a means of deflecting criticism that the industry was insensitive to the needs of children. Like other efforts to avoid censorship, this short-lived organ shifted responsibility from producers to consuming families.

and Society for Prevention of Cruelty to Children reported to her listeners that "each year . . . critics find a larger proportion of the studios' output which they can heartily approve. Today about one-third of all pictures produced are approved, as the expression is, 'for family audiences.'" Still, she warned, the stakes were quite high: "From the movie [*sic*] these children, in their most impressionable years, receive impressions which influence them deeply—impressions which will have power in moulding their whole future lives, either for good or ill. Studies made on thousands of children leave the fact of such influence beyond a doubt."

The studies to which she referred were undoubtedly those of the Payne Fund (named for their sponsor). Comprising twelve different research programs conducted between 1928 and 1932, these studies were the most systematic attempt to date to locate, describe, and quantify the effects of movies on

Fox West Coast Adopts Audience Suitability Seal for Ads

By such devices Fred Wehrenberg, St. Louis theatre owner, coaxes the kiddies to family night shows

5. Two advertisements from *Motion Picture and the Family* (November 1934). Top: Fox indicates its willingness to police its product and demonstrates to patrons its imbrication in a rating system that is "family friendly." Bottom: A St. Louis exhibitor signals family friendliness by deploying Disney characters.

children. As Henry James Forman, the author of a popular summary of the studies that appeared in *McCall's Magazine* in 1932, put it: "It is very hard to believe that anything very harmful lurks behind the glittering portals where Mickey Mouse cavorts, where the news reels are shown, and where handsome actors and actresses walk through romances that bring diversion and recreation to both children and adults. Let us look inside for a moment, however" (Forman 1932b). It was as if the studies promised to take the reader through the screen and into the world in which the values of producers were imprinted on celluloid, to turn and look back at an audience of children and see, objectively, how their attitudes and behaviors were shaped by moviegoing. After thirty-odd years of movies, the medium had gone from a local phenomenon primarily of social concern for its influence on the bodies and behaviors of immigrant and working-class children, to a national art form consumed uniformly by children from different class, gender, and racial positions. More than any other preceding discursive formation, discussions of the Payne Fund Studies would cement the notion of a generic child engaged in a uniform practice of viewing and deriving effects from that practice applicable to any other child, regardless of race, class, or gender.

The Payne Fund Studies

> *Do the pictures really influence children . . . ? Are their conduct, ideals, and attitudes affected by the movies . . . ? [T]he investigators who cooperated to make this [Payne Fund] series of studies . . . set up individual studies to ascertain the answer to the questions and to provide a composite answer to the central question of the nature and the extent of these influences. . . . Parents, educators, and physicians will have little difficulty in fitting concrete details of their own into the outlines which these studies supply.*
>
> —W. W. CHARTERS, IN DALE 1935, V–VI

So begins the preface to *The Content of Motion Pictures*, one of the Payne Fund studies, couching alarmist questions in a tone of reassuring scientism. The studies were highly controversial within the movie industry, among procensorship groups, and even within the social scientific community that produced them. Many of the studies were contested—by both social scientists and the motion-picture industry—as poor science that relied upon hearsay, opinion, poor sampling methods, and an insufficient regard for history and culture.[31] As has been the case with virtually every subsequent study on media effects, they were ultimately deemed inconclusive. Yet the construction of the studies and subsequent debate about them marks the intersection of discourses about the nature of childhood and of movie effects at a time when Hollywood studios—including Disney—were consolidating their position as the purveyors of a truly national medium. Even though the studies were inconclusive, they produced a great deal of heat and light about the effects of movies on children, influenced the activities of the Hays Office and groups pressing for reform—such as the Catholic Legion of Decency and the Federal Council of Churches—and added significantly to a growing range of discourses that imagined a normal American child involved in a life of increasingly standardized practices. The result of a complex of institutional and political forces, the studies were meant to serve a variety of purposes. For some participants, they were to prove that movies could harm children and should be more strictly regulated. For others, the research was an honest intellectual enterprise to determine *whether* movies did affect children. For others, they were meant to put pressure on the industry to stop practices such as block booking that forced exhibitors to show substandard fare (Jowett, Jarvie, and Fuller 1996). Whatever the motivation of individual actors in the studies, however, they seemed to promise to a concerned public concrete information about whether and how movies shaped children.

The studies ran the gamut of social-science techniques, from the tabulation of audience attendance patterns, to questionnaires, interviews, autobiography, and galvanic-response testing. Although each of the studies but one was released as an independent volume, a popular overview of the series was written by Forman and published first as a series of articles in *McCall's Magazine* in 1932 and later as the book *Our Movie Made Children* (Forman 1932a, 1932b, 1932c, 1934). Although the individual studies attempted to present their findings in an even-handed manner, Forman's popular summaries (much to the dismay of some individual researchers) were heavily biased toward the assumption that the movies in the late 1920s and early 1930s had a profoundly negative effect on children.[32] In "Movie Madness" (Forman 1932b), the second installment in the *McCall's* series, Forman informed his audience that in 1929, "almost 23,000,000 minors were weekly movie fans and nearly 12,000,000 were fourteen years old or younger. . . . more than 6,000,000 were seven years old or less" (15). Accusing MPPDA president Will Hays of grossly underestimating children's movie attendance, Forman warned that "over 6,000,000 young children, according to the Payne Fund statistics, go to matineé [*sic*] performances weekly. They spend from two to four hours doing nothing except absorb the shadows which flit before them and the dialogue which comes forth from the sound apparatus.

6. Illustration for Henry James Forman's "Movie Madness" (*McCall's*, October 1932) places the (male) child at the center of a maelstrom of "bad" movies, praying for rescue.

It may be this group, denied the exercise and play essential to healthy growth, which grows jittery and nervous and far too excited" (Forman 1932b, 30). Describing showings of *The Phantom of the Opera* (Julian 1925), he depicted concerned mothers running from the theater with frightened children clinging to their skirts and movie-house nurses treating children who had vomited from sheer terror. Quoting a "noted neurologist," he suggested that repeated viewing of horror movies might sow "the seeds in the system for future neuroses and psychoses—nervous disorders" (Forman 1932b, 15).[33]

Moving from the particular—horror films—to films in general, Forman suggested that although it had been disproven that the flickering of movies damaged children's eyesight, there were far more serious consequences to consider. The millions of children, young and old, attending movies weekly were like frontline troops suffering a continuous bombardment of excessive and harmful cultural stimulation (see figure 6). The result, he warned, could be more than simple "oversophistication." Conjuring images of World War I, he painted a picture of shell-shocked psychotics staggering out of the theater and into adulthood, more a burden than a benefit to the nation. The persons responsible, of course, would be the commanders who sent them out into the trenches—their parents: "The average parent, although faintly alarmed by certain traits and characteristics which appear to have been derived from pictures, comforts himself with the thought that Johnny does not understand very much of what he sees, that no enduring harm can be done. It now appears that this was rather a complacent view of the situation" (Forman 1932b, 15, 28).[34]

Fearmongering aside, Forman's articles brought home the idea that the question of motion pictures' effects on children bridged the local concerns of parents to national concerns about citizenship and social well-being. The studies were organized for the express purpose of determining the effects of movies on *children in general*, not—as might have been the case two decades earlier—on working-class or immigrant children (nor on equally susceptible adults).[35] Designed and implemented by many of the same researchers who were in the process of analyzing, isolating, and creating technologies for the production of the normal child, the studies took it as a given that a universal model of the effects of movies on the normal child could be extrapolated from local and individual microsocial experiences of moviegoing.[36] The researchers applied the same rigorous analysis to movies that they did to the bodies and behaviors of the children they studied, bringing to bear a variety of clinical, experimental, and ethnographic methods in search of a definitive answer. That answer was to elude them, as a brief description of a few of the studies will make clear.[37]

In his series for *McCall's*, Forman summarized the findings of several of the Payne Fund studies, including *Children's Sleep* (Renshaw, Miller, and Marquis 1933), a study of the effect of movies on children's sleep patterns, and *The Emotional Responses of Children to the Motion Picture Situation* (Dysinger and Ruckmick 1933), which charted physiognomic responses to movies. In both studies, investigators attempted to avoid inconsistencies that might have arisen due to the subjective nature of self-reporting or of participant observation by deploying electromechanical devices to chart children's reactions to movies. In the sleep study, Forman reported, researchers used "an inconspicuous electrical device called a hypnograph. . . . attached to ten beds in the boys dormitory and ten . . . where the girls slept. . . . Wires from each of the hypnographs led to an adjoining room. Here were located batteries, motors, and revolving drums around which passed long strips of paper. The device might be compared to a seismograph. Each juvenile earthquake or tremor during the night was recorded" (Forman 1932a, 58).

Even though the researchers used a "hypnograph" as a means of producing reliable data, they felt compelled to further standardize their procedures in hope of guaranteeing a broadly applicable result. Forman told his readers that Renshaw and Miller "were less interested in special cases than in averages" and believed that a sample of 170 children "would give a fair idea of the effect of movies upon the sleep of children in the normal American home" (Forman 1932a, 58). However, since the use of private family homes would introduce too many variables into the experiment, "it was decided to carry on the work at a home maintained at Columbus by the Ohio State Bureau of Juvenile Research. The routine of institutional life offered the regularity and uniformity necessary for scientific investigation" (13).

This home was not a juvenile detention facility or an orphanage, and the children were, the reader was reassured, perfectly normal. Thus, in order to obtain results applicable to the normal American home, Renshaw and Miller conducted their research in an institution, the regimentation of which could more easily provide verifiable results. As peculiar in its logic as this situation was, it was perhaps no less notable than Forman's care in detailing it in his article. The researchers' requirement that their subjects be normal was of a piece with popular assumptions about the importance of "normal" or "typical" Americans to the production of transferable social knowledge (see chapter 3). Thus, a study designed to measure effects of movies on children, hence on the future of American culture, discursively produced that culture in its baseline assumptions, and the popular representation of those assumptions as essential to the study's verisimilitude propagated them in the popular imagination it was meant to gauge. Although he would later criticize Forman for sensationalizing his group's findings, like many of the other Payne Fund researchers, Renshaw drew overly broad conclusions from relatively inconclusive data.[38] Movies, it seemed, made children toss and turn at night, unless they didn't—in some cases children slept more soundly. The researchers' conclusion, said Forman, was that "[a]ny deviation from normal, whether greater or less tossing at night, is bad. The movies cause such deviation" (Forman 1932a).

In *Emotional Responses of Children to the Motion Picture Situation* (Dysinger and Ruckmick 1933), Payne Fund researchers in Iowa also sought out children who were "in every way average" (Forman 1932b, 28). These researchers also attached an electromechanical device to children in the hopes of deriving the most accurate data possible. In this case, the investigators had children watch movies while attached to a "Wechsler psychogalvanograph" (which monitored galvanic response) to "make a quantitative study of the emotional and affective experiences aroused by . . . motion pictures" (Dysinger and Ruckmick 1933, 11). (See figure 7.) Although the authors cautiously suggested that any effect movies might have on children appeared rather short-lived and difficult

PLATE III
THE EXPERIMENT IN THE THEATER
O is shown holding the fingers of his left hand in the electrodes. The wrist-band of the pneumo-cardiograph is seen around the right wrist. The control board is seen at *E*'s position, with the psychogalvanograph and other apparatus under the control of the assistant.

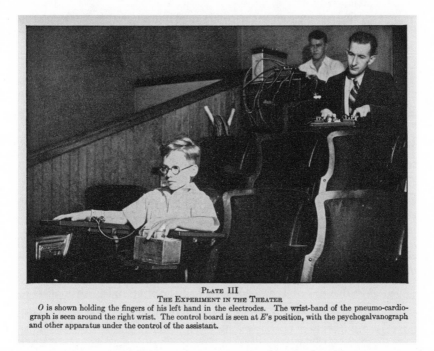

7. A child's reactions to a movie are tested using the Wechsler psychogalvanograph in Dysinger and Ruckmick's *The Emotional Responses of Children to the Motion Picture Situation* (1933).

to quantify, they nonetheless concluded that "profound mental and physiological effects of an emotional order are produced [by movies]. The stimulus is inherently strong and undiluted by post-adolescent critical attitudes and accumulated and modifying experiences. Unnatural sophistication and premature bodily stimulation . . . [can] result" (119).

In spite of the evanescent quality of movie effects, then, the real danger that Dysinger and Ruckmick pointed to was that even with subsequent proper socialization, the damage could not necessarily be undone: no matter how salubrious the influences children might receive in the home or at school, the prior shock of moviegoing would remain like a scar. In short, *children in particular* were vulnerable to the effects of movies, which could leave them prematurely stimulated, and as a result too soon sophisticated—even though those effects would soon be undetectable.[39]

To address the methodological problems inherent in attempting to extrapolate data on the effects of movies from single viewings, Frank Shuttleworth and Mark May (1933) designed a study that would "determine the influence, not of a single motion picture, but of the child's total motion-picture experience on a wide variety of conducts and a wide range of attitudes. . . . [by] surveying a wide range of conducts and attitudes . . . [and] . . . determining the differences between children who attend the movies very frequently and children who attend only infrequently" (1–2).

In other words, the authors surveyed children as to the frequency of their attendance at the movies, and cross-referenced that against a set of questions about their behavior and their beliefs on certain issues. "This method [of surveying]," they cautioned their readers, "leaves us without precise experimental controls so . . . it is difficult to say definitely what part of the observed differences can be attributed to the movies" (Shuttleworth and May 1933, 1–2). The hesitation they expressed in their opening chapter didn't result in an ultimate report of a negative outcome, yet it did lead to a bit of further hedging in their conclusion. The most definitive answer Shuttleworth and May could give in *The Social Conduct and Attitudes of Movie Fans* (1933) was that there were types of behaviors that *seemed* to be associated with the *sort of children* who went to movies—behaviors that might have been described as less wholesome or ambitious—but that there was no way to say whether the movies created those behaviors, or that children of that type were drawn to movies, or that perhaps there was some other explanation (Jowett, Jarvie, and Fuller 1996, 112–13).[40] With a few exceptions, the other Payne Fund studies followed this pattern, developing a rigorous methodology that turned up ambiguous results that researchers interpreted cautiously as suggesting that movies had some sort of effect on children. The few exceptions to this rule that made more definitive claims about the harmful effects of moviegoing on children, particularly the work of Herbert Blumer, were the most soundly criticized on methodological grounds.[41]

Underlying the whole process were the linked assumptions that moviegoing had become a uniform national experience, and that there were nationally uniform children who could well undergo some sort of transformation as a result of that experience.[42] Edgar Dale's *Children's Attendance at Motion Pictures* (1935), for instance, closed with the observation that "data have been presented in this report to show that children and youth the country over are regular patrons of motion-picture theaters. . . . [and that they constitute] a proportion of the audience that is far greater than we have commonly been led to believe. The effect of motion pictures, therefore, is universal and this fact must be faced in a statesmanlike manner by exhibitors, by teachers, and by parents" (Dale 1935, 73). This rather modest suggestion, and those of the other studies, was bent by Forman in the popular summary of the Payne Fund series, *Our Movie Made Children* (Forman 1934), to support the definitive claim that movies were a serious, tangible force in the production of American children. Beyond the objections of researchers, the strongest reaction to the summary came from the Hays Office, which was justifiably concerned that procensorship forces—particularly the Catholic Church—would seize upon the report in their efforts to establish a national system of censorship (Moley 1945, Maltby 1995).[43]

While federal censorship never came to pass, the studies did have significant impact: during hearings in the House of Representatives in 1936, proregulation forces relied heavily on the studies in making their arguments. In reply, the Hays Office touted methodological criticisms of the studies in an effort to discredit them and simultaneously took action to appear more rigorous in its efforts at self-policing. Even though the studies were eventually repudiated—by their opponents, and even by some of their creators—their popular circulation furthered the idea of an average, normal child that could be affected by the products it consumed. Even as they attempted to support critiques that discredited the studies on methodological grounds, however, the Hays Office and other anticensorship forces did not question the existence and nature of this child. Rather, they argued that industrial self-regulation and diligent parental management were the best prophylactics against any potentially deleterious effects from motion pictures. Certainly movies had effects on children, but they were just as likely to be beneficial as detrimental—provided that the child's viewing was properly regulated.

Thus, while the studies were gradually discredited in professional circles, the circulation of popular discourse on the subject stabilized the notion of a generic American child that could be negatively or positively affected by the movies. At this level of discourse, that child became a given, and the debate that naturalized its existence was whether it was the responsibility of parents, producers, or the government to regulate the consumption (or production) that delivered those effects to it. For the public, the question of movie effects had left the realm of moral speculation and entered that of science. In a two-part recapitulation of the Payne Fund studies in *Parents' Magazine*, James Rorty declared that it was finally possible to say definitively whether movies had an effect on children, and what that effect was:[44]

> whatever accusations have been made against motion pictures as affecting children, it has always been possible to question their validity on the ground that there was not an adequate body of facts to substantiate them. True enough, there was not. And so it became plainly a public duty to

get the facts. This tremendous task . . . has just been completed by The Payne Fund. Under their direction, a score of sociologists, psychologists, and educators . . . spent four years in discovering and analyzing data. (Rorty 1933b, 18)

Taking up the celebration of social scientists as true mirrors of social and material relations that would become a common trope in public discourse in the coming two decades (Herman 1995), Rorty delivered to the middle-class readers of *Parents'* a picture of their children as far more susceptible to the effects of movies than they had ever imagined. Repeating the studies' attendance figures, Rorty suggested that children were consuming movies far more often than parents imagined, and that serious things were happening to them as they watched. Summarizing George Stoddard and Perry Holaday's *Getting Ideas from the Movies* (1933), Rorty warned parents that children "saw everything and remembered practically everything, and what they didn't remember the next morning after seeing the film they remembered a month later at another testing. Their powers of absorption were amazing. Which serves to prove beyond the shadow of a doubt what a power for good or bad education these movies are" (Rorty 1933b, 19).

The message was clear and simple: depending on the types of movies they saw, children could either improve or damage themselves. Either outcome was possible. To drive the point home, however, Rorty reiterated a much more disturbing (and quite dubious) finding from the study—that bad movies could actually drain children of positive effects they had gained elsewhere:

> When a child goes to a movie and there learns things that aren't so, his stock of true knowledge is thereby decreased. After seeing a movie which was heavily loaded with misinformation, it was found that the children from eight to nine years old had reduced their stock of correct information in the field covered by the movie, 8%; the children from eleven to twelve lost 19%; the high school children lost 34%. Some adults were also tested: they lost 37%. (Rorty 1933b, 19)

The more misinformed a child became, of course, the harder it would be for it to make sensible choices later in its life. The findings could also be read as hopeful, however. It was possible, with proper supervision, that a child could reverse the detrimental effects of movies through the consumption of beneficial cinema.

The magazine's second installment began by asking, "Do gangster movies help to make gangsters? Are sex pictures a factor in promoting sexual delinquency . . . ?" In answer to its own question, the article replied, "The answers of The Payne Fund investigators are, with certain qualifications, definitely affirmative with respect to these questions: the movies do help make criminals and sexual delinquents" (Rorty 1933a, 18). Citing some of the most widely criticized of the Payne Fund studies, *Movies and Conduct* (Blumer 1933) and *Movies, Delinquency, and Crime* (Blumer and Hauser 1933), Rorty warned his readers that at the very least, 10 percent of the boys and 25 percent of the girls who had become criminals or sexual delinquents had done so because of the movies (Rorty 1933a, 18). In a rare nod to the possibility of other operant conditions playing a role in the children's development, he did acknowledge, "It is, of course, true that the slum movie is only one factor in a complex of conditions each one of which is anti-social, and no one of which is the sole cause of crime, delinquency, disease and misery which such districts generate. The Payne Fund study makes it clear, however, that the gangster and sex films do play an important part in inciting crime and delinquency in those neighborhoods" (Rorty 1933a, 19).

This was the Depression-era precipice upon which Pinocchio would soon teeter, and a recapitulation of progressive arguments about uplift reframed in terms of the social science of the late 1920s and 1930s. For many Depression-era parents, their hold on middle-class status was (or seemed) tenuous, and the possibility that their children would experience negative class mobility appeared quite real. The democratic mixing that was supposed to occur in movie houses carried with it the promise of uplift for working-class and immigrant youth through contact with their betters, and with a better sort of film (L. May 1980). Yet at the same time it threatened the infection of middle-class children with values and behaviors that would be detrimental to them later in life. Rorty made it clear that a parent could not depend on Hollywood producers to do anything about it:

> Of course, Hollywood is not interested in influencing minors toward a delinquent or criminal career; neither is it particularly interested in deterring minors from such careers. It is interested in billings, in box-office receipts, in profits. They have found that pictures which treat sex pornographically and pictures which treat crime sensationally yield profits. These are cold business facts. But balance against them the fact, established by the Payne Fund study, that the movies also yield a by-product of young criminals and sex delinquents. (Rorty 1933a, 19)

What was the solution to the movies' deleterious effects on American youth? In the first article of the series, Rorty suggested that "parents, educators, all those concerned with the care and training of children will wish to go to Mr. Forman's book or to the actual reports to be issued in many volumes to get the whole picture of movies and their effect on children" (Rorty 1933b, 57). In other words, parents' first line of defense was neither censorship nor industrial regulation, but self-education and the better regulation of their own children. In the second article, Rorty echoed a call by William Short, founder of the Motion Picture Research Council and a major force behind the studies, for a library of classic movies appropriate for children.[45] He further suggested that the Depression itself might ease the production of delinquents by reducing the number of fans from the lower classes in attendance at the movies, thus forcing the studios to produce material for a more discerning elite audience (Rorty 1933a). That audience would still have to be led by informed adults, however, and Rorty's prescription, which more or less recapitulated the best possible outcome for industry in terms of regulation, placed the responsibility on parents to regulate their children's consumption. As Ellen Seiter (1993) has pointed out, this requirement, which has persisted through the development of a variety of other mass media, translated into a requirement that the mother be responsible both for regulating her children's consumption and for any misbehavior that could be attributed to that consumption.

Ultimately, the weight of public discourse and the concerted efforts of the motion-picture industry shaped the outcome of the studies more than did the research itself. When the dust settled after the last parts of the Payne Fund studies had been published, the MPPDA was not appreciably more or less encumbered than it had been five years earlier. Although it still had to accommodate a number of civic and religious organizations in its review process, its willingness to do so made the industry look as if it were concerned about movies' effects on national character, and the participation of those organizations provided a network that generated further discourse about movies in general and about specific movies reviewed. The Production Code would continue to operate for some time to come, satisfying neither its proponents nor its detractors and creating a number of cinematic and rhetorical tropes as writers and directors learned to circumvent it.

Perhaps the most lasting effect of the Payne Fund studies, then, was the naturalization as fact-via-premise of a number of assumptions that had arisen long before the studies commenced. First and foremost, the studies' dogged attempt to construct a normal American child affected by movies continued to effectively displace the immigrant and working-class child as an object of study and correction in regard to social action around the movies. Second, the progressive-era notion that the character of motion-picture producers (broadly defined) was directly transmitted to consumers by way of their products was reinscribed as a given precondition in a number of the studies. Finally, popular summaries of the studies affirmed the necessity of parental regulation as the best mechanism for directing children to those products most likely to improve their behaviors and values. What the discourses that ran through and around the Payne Fund studies produced, then, was a relatively stable matrix in which notions of childhood, of consumption, and of family relations could be deployed both by those interested in the regulation of practices of production and consumption, and those interested in using that regulation to generate productive public perceptions. As Richard deCordova (1983, 93–94) puts it: "Studies on the cinema and children in the 1920s and 1930s provide ample evidence with which to question . . . claims to transparency. Audience research of the day hardly existed in the realm of disinterested knowledge; it was connected to broader social and political imperatives, ones which in fact depended upon a certain conceptualization of the (child) audience as a necessary support."

Simply put, the Payne Fund studies greatly stabilized discursive formations useful to producers like Disney, who could profit from a conception of a generic child audience in need of products beneficial to their development. The broad outlines of the nature of those beneficial products, their qualities and their operations, derived directly from arguments about detrimental products and carried with them a set of assumptions about social and material relations that not only favored the type of product that Disney increasingly turned out, but the type of man that Walt Disney purported to be. For this reason, the nature of Walt Disney and of the industrial process through which his character was imparted to his company's products became a central element in the company's public relations. Walt Disney was the man that the child might become by consuming the products that he made. Thus, the depiction of Disney's studios as a tightly managed facility over which Walt maintained an absolute but benevolent control spoke to the expectation that parents be able to identify in motion-picture products qualities good for their children. The process of animation, as metaphor for the creation of life, would serve well for this.

The Manager in the Garden: Walt Disney Studios

The Payne Fund studies were not entirely without prescriptions for the concerned parent. In their own summary of the findings of the studies, researchers W. W. Charters and Edgar Dale suggested that parents "must first familiarize themselves thoroughly with what is shown on the screen. They ought to formulate in their own minds the deficiencies of such pictures, and make every attempt to see that motion pictures which do not have such deficiencies are made available to all children. Next, they should see . . . that antidotes be supplied the child if they still think it desirable for him to attend, knowing that harmful effects may accrue" (Forman 1932b, 30).

This sensible advice raised as many problems as it solved. During the 1920s and early 1930s, periodicals such as *Parents' Magazine*, *Christian Century*, and *The Rotarian* began supplying family-friendly reviews to their readers, but the parent faced with children asking to go to a particular movie at a given moment required knowledge and abilities not so easily obtained. This was especially true in regard to the major studios, each of which issued a broad range of products, from the innocuous to the morally and behaviorally infectious. Admonitions to regulate children's viewing that were meant to encourage parents to assume a more active role in their children's consumption habits, then, also had the potential to produce in them anxiety about their ability to successfully meet those expectations. A parent who chose her children's movies poorly risked raising delinquents, social malcontents, or simply people poorly equipped to compete in a society troubled by a scarcity of opportunity.

Viewed in this light, Disney's move during the 1930s to develop a public-relations address based not only around individual productions, but also around a company gestalt deriving from its eponymous founder, had the potential to provide to parents brand recognition that did not require assessment of individual products. To be sure, many of the products, which were of high quality and generated their own buzz, contributed to this overall strategy. The immense popularity of *The Three Little Pigs* (1934) and its catchy theme song led Will Hays to praise it as paradigmatic of Hollywood's contribution to the national recovery effort, stating that "historians of the future will not ignore the interesting and significant fact that the movies literally laughed the big bad wolf of depression out of the public mind through the protagonism [*sic*] of *Three Little Pigs*—a screen feature that overflowed to the radio, the public press and to millions of homes" (Hays 1934a). In the same year, *Fortune* magazine argued that unlike other Hollywood productions, a Disney Silly Symphony such as *The Three Little Pigs* was truly art, because "it is moral: with a deft touch that gives no offense, it builds its themes upon the basic distinctions in human behavior which have guided the common man since he emerged from savagery. Courage overcomes wickedness and fear; industry triumphs over dalliance; false ambition gives way to resignation" ("The Big Bad Wolf" 1934, 88).

While these themes appeared in some of Disney's Silly Symphonies, the company equally aggressively represented them in its oft-repeated hagiographic rags-to-riches accounts of Disney's life, and in its suggestions that its products (and their consumers) benefited from the morals and behaviors that the man had developed through that experience. (The implication that a Disney product bears with it a certain set of inherent values has become such a commonplace that the formation of this idea at a sociohistorically specific moment—and its appeal to an emerging class of parent-regulators—easily disappears.) If anything, the atmosphere of anxiety engendered by the Depression and by the enforcement of the Production Code allowed Disney to demonstrate its willingness to participate in a program of uplift for children. The two widely documented moments when the company ran afoul of censors in the early 1930s, and its willingness to celebrate one of them, speak to its self-construction as a morally responsible institution. In February of 1931, the *Motion Picture Herald* reported that Mickey was perhaps a bit too ribald for a child audience: "Mickey Mouse, the artistic offspring of Walt Disney, has fallen afoul of the censors in a big way, largely because of his amazing success. Papas and mamas, especially mamas, have spoken vigorously to censor boards and elsewhere about what a devilish, naughty little mouse Mickey turned out to be. Now we find that Mickey is not to drink, smoke, or tease the stock in the barnyard. Mickey has been spanked" (Ramsaye, quoted in Maltin 1980, 37). A year later, and one month before it would begin Henry Forman's series on the Payne Fund studies, *McCall's Magazine* ran a light piece titled "Mickey Mouse's Father" (Pringle 1932). The "Dear Reader" column for that issue, placed alongside its table of contents, and which summarized the magazine's offerings and upcoming features, followed its brief summary of Pringle's article with a warning to parents:

> If you are the kind of parent who gives his child a coin and sends him to the local motion picture theater with the fond hope that he will be entertained for an evening . . . You will be concerned to know that McCall's is, in its next issue, publishing a revealing picture of the consequences. For the past four years the Motion Picture Research Council, an independent group of noted psychologists, has been gathering information about the influences of the movies upon the sleep, health and conduct of children from five to eighteen years of age. The eloquent report of their findings will be vital reading for all movie-goers and all parents. (2)

Inside *that* issue, however, things were not so ominous. Reporting on Mickey, and on the goings-on inside the walls of Walt Disney Studios, Pringle described the mouse as the four-year-old "child of Walt Disney's brain . . . which is a proper age since his parent is only thirty-one" (7, 21). Comparing Mickey to Charlie Chaplin, Douglas Fairbanks, Mary Pickford, and Ronald Colman, Pringle declared that "Walt Disney is the envy and the despair of his fellow producers in Hollywood. . . . He does not have to supply ornate dressing rooms and personal press agents for his stars. They receive no salaries and therefore do not strike for raises just when the industry is least able to afford them. They do not have fits of temperament, sulk over story situations, or become jealous if some other player is given too many close-ups" (21).

If Mickey's behavior had been a bit troublesome before, he was maturing nicely, and not a moment before the Payne Fund's critique of Hollywood issued from the same organ that celebrated his fourth birthday. The description of Walt Disney as father to Mickey, and his company as an idyllic alternative to the other contentious, petty, and immoral major Hollywood studios, would become a leitmotif in the many profiles of Walt and his company that would follow over the years. While there is no doubt that this trope fit well with the tone of determined optimism adopted by many Depression-era periodicals, it also depended on Disney's skillful presentation of itself as responsive to the needs of its audience and systematically consistent in its approach. On a studio tour two years later, Douglas Churchill (1934, 13) would note, "There has not been a censorship cut in a Disney film in four years. The last was over a cow. Since then, all Disney cows have worn skirts [to hide their udders]. . . . Previews are held for the entire Disney organization, and written criticisms are required. The wolf [in *The Three Little Pigs*] said 'lousy.' The wife an employee questioned the word, and it was removed." The tone of the piece simultaneously poked fun at the idea that anyone would have to censor a Disney cartoon and suggested that Disney worked hard to address criticisms of its work. Beyond that, its mention of the studio's use of survey techniques revealed an organization willing to use the tools of social science to better meet its audience's needs, and one that employed a demographic like its intended audience, that average American so important to the popular social science of the day. Disney's approach seemed to respond to the call of Payne Fund researcher Charles Peters in *Motion Picture Standards of Morality* (1933) for "a small group of highly competent social-science workers . . . [who] could do as much to set up the motion-picture industry on a high plane as agricultural research has done for scientific farming or research in engineering for the improvement of the radio and refrigerator" (165).

Pinocchio Redux

> *What with his books, his records, his gadgets, and his toys, no less than with his films, there was scarcely a nursery he had not invaded or a small mind he did not occupy . . . Almost all children, and grown-ups, were babes in Mr. Disney's toyland.*
>
> —J. BROWN 1945, 23

In this description (meant to be positive), Walt Disney appeared as a combination of two of the characters from *Pinocchio* (1940), Gepetto and Jiminy Cricket. He was part good-natured toy-maker, providing simple amusements and asking only that the children he helped to make become real boys and girls. And he was part conscience, through his many products the voice that encouraged the child to do the right thing, or, as Jiminy Cricket—speaking in the voice of parental anxiety—defined the term, "that still, small voice that nobody listens to."

Like the child in a fearful parent's imagination, Pinocchio doesn't listen to his conscience—at first. No sooner does he walk out his front door than the two grifters he has befriended sell him to the grotesquely ethnic and unscrupulous theater manager, Stromboli. He is rescued by Jiminy Cricket, and by the magic being that invested that conscience, the Blue Fairy, but immediately returns to his vagrant friends, who once again sell him into slavery. This time he is ensnared by free passage to Pleasure Island, where young boys (most of whom look Irish and decidedly working class) indulge in the pleasures of public amusements: pool halls, carnivals, and bars. At the entrance to this amusement park, gigantic cigar-store Indians spew cigars and cigarettes into the crowd of boys, encouraging them to light up. Down the midway is a tent in which the boys can fight each other to their hearts' content: its entrance is framed by the legs of a giant statue of a thug with the posture and face of an ape, who barks a come-along in a thick Brooklyn accent. The camera (and J. Cricket) finds Pinocchio with his friend, Lampwick (who lights a match for his cigar on the Mona Lisa, already defaced) in a bar, drinking beer, smoking cigars, and shooting pool.

The ultimate price for this indulgence is steep, though: Pinocchio watches in horror as Lampwick turns into a jackass, his cries for his mother melting into incoherent braying. All the boys devolve into donkeys and are sold into slavery in salt mines and circuses, their captor crying, "You boys have had your fun, now pay for it!" Pinocchio, too, begins to change but escapes before his transformation is complete. Yet he retains his ears and tail even in death—until the end of the film, when he is resurrected as a real boy by the Blue Fairy for the brave and selfless act of saving Gepetto from Monstro the whale.

The message of the movie was clear: indulgence in the pleasures of the working class, of vaudeville, or of pool halls and amusement parks, led to a life as a beast of burden. Ultimately, one was either a manager or managed, and the choices one made determined the outcome. Although Pinocchio's "father," a simple craftsman from a bygone era, could craft the puppet from inert material, he could not protect him from the unsavory influences filling the deceptively short distance between home and school. Nor could Depression-era parents. Though they could create their children, they couldn't invest them with reality. To do that, they needed help, a conscience to whisper to the child from his notepad, her lunch box, his milk bottle—someone to help steer him past the wrong pleasures (like bad movies) and on his way to school and the right pleasures: the rewards of hard work, deferred gratification, and self-control. Walt Disney was that someone: simultaneously the tinkering old father and the conscience on the child's shoulder that could be there when the parent could not. If anyone could help to make a child real, a real American, it was Uncle Walt: father, scientist, manager—in short, a normal parent, just like any other.

Conclusion

In his relentless and compulsive celebration of his rise to commodity status, Walt Disney promised to confer upon children who consumed his products the distillation of that ascendance, the behaviors and attitudes through which he incorporated the sentimental, animal, and human qualities of his childhood into the act of his perpetual commodification. In a fantasy in which the qualities of the producer appeared to pass directly through his product to the consumer, Disney offered through his/its public relations the distinctly (and specifically) middle-class virtues of deferred gratification, self-denial, thrift, and perseverance naturalized as the experience of the most average American alive, and distilled through the rigorous and highly regulated process of animation. Without the discourse of movie effects in circulation at that moment, Disney would not have had recourse to this form of address. The idea that Walt Disney's essential being became available through the films that he produced required an ongoing discourse in which the lives, habits, and behaviors of other Hollywood producers were represented as damaging to children.[46] Walt Disney was the inoculant against infection by the working-class and immigrant roots of Hollywood producers, a prophylactic against the vices they could not help but transmit through their films.

If one considers that the primary consumers of Disney products were small children largely uninterested in the finer points of Disney's public career, the company's aggressive marketing of the man in conjunction with its products is best understood as aimed at their parents. The ritual repetition of his life and accomplishments as a marketing strategy for its entertainment products functioned successfully because it operated within a commonplace that posited—repeatedly, and against any substantial proof—that children's consumption habits (particularly around media and media-related products) played a determining role in their subsequent development. This notion was predicated on the assumption that media producers in particular infused their products with their own morals, beliefs, and behaviors, and that parents (particularly mothers) were ultimately responsible for regulating the consumption of those products. In this invention, children who consumed Walt Disney products were consuming the embodied life of Walt Disney, and in doing so, were increasing the odds that their lives might follow a trajectory similar to his.

This modern metaphysical turn begins to resolve the contradiction that Alan Bryman (1995, 192–93) observes between Disney's celebration of its founder's individualism and its aggressive protection of its corporate interests: "Walt's life-story may be a paean to individualism, an Horatio Alger story of overcoming all odds to achieve success . . . but it also represents a story of the building of a corporation which, through its control over copyrights, land and contracts, celebrates an individualism that it keeps at bay." This contradiction has not been a problem for Disney but has operated as a means through which the corporation has made use of the tensions and anxieties that accompany child-rearing in America. It begins to come into focus when one understands Walt Disney as a subsidiary product of the corporation and his individualism as a trademarked quality of that product. Furthermore, it represents the tension inherent in the very concept of American individualism, in which each person attempts to fashion him- or herself as simultaneously unique and clearly recognizable as a commodity. Thus, the individualism that Walt Disney represented was not that of the rebel or outsider, but one of marginal differentiation: the company billed him as special by dint of being the most average American possible. In this light, the company's infamous defense of its trademarks and copyrights is a fight to maintain the cohesion of Disney as an entity. Given its profoundly average origins, without that defense the company and its founder might diffuse quite rapidly into the American landscape from which they both derived. But more important, the contradictory nature of Walt Disney's epic individualism and his corporation's equally epic regulation of its representations is but another example of the totemic quality of Walt as the ur-child. Walt

Disney's ability to celebrate and to regulate his commodity identity in all of its far-flung parts, far from being an example of excessive repression, represents the victory of the individual in embracing its commodity nature with no loss of control over the particulars of its personal life.

The circumstances that positioned Walt Disney to take advantage of his life's story did not derive entirely from popular efforts to regulate the movies, however. Especially as they came to center on children—and eventually on a generic American child largely unmarked by class, race, or gender—discussions about the effects of movies and other commodities drew upon an emerging matrix of professional and popular discourses that was producing that generic child as an object of scientific study. This child was a benchmark by which parents (both those of the middle class and those aspiring to that class) were expected to evaluate the development of their own children, and a centerpiece in scientific programs for the efficient and proper production of children designed to succeed in American democratic capitalism. The counterpart to Walt Disney, this generic child was the homunculus of an American future: produced by and eventually reproducing an emerging mass culture of which Disney products were but one element, the child was figured in popular and professional child-rearing discourses as a creature profoundly susceptible to external stimuli (especially in its early years) and extremely likely to replicate the moral and behavioral impulses embedded in those stimuli in its adult social life. This was the child of the Payne Fund studies and its popular renditions, and the regulation of its moviegoing was but one part in a larger schema concerning the control of its environment and its entry into culture. As the century progressed, this child became the means by which problems in social and material relations between adults were deferred from one generation to the next, and its acts of consumption became determinate not only of its own future, but of larger social and political conditions in that future. If one is to fully understand how Walt Disney emerged as the leading producer of entertainments considered beneficial for this generic American child, and to grasp the affective weight behind the idea of consumption as a social and political act, then one must examine more closely the arrival of this child.

2 MAKING A MANAGEABLE CHILD

> *If hard times last much longer and nothing is done for these boys, things will be pretty bad for them. They won't get an education. They'll form the habit of getting by without working. They'll get used to going for days without taking their clothes off, and they'll learn stealing and vice from the old bums that are always on the road. Take it from me, an awful lot of young people in America are growing up to be criminals.*
>
> —K. DAVIS 1935, 6

Some five years before Walt Disney would release *Pinocchio* (1940), the University of Chicago Press, under the auspices of the New Deal, put out *Youth in the Depression* (K. Davis 1935), an account of the effect of the country's economic crisis on its young people. In words that echoed the plot of *Pinocchio*, a railroad policeman described to the author a generation of criminals and vagabonds in the making. Cut loose from their familial and social moorings, with little reason to attend school, these boys were changing from a precious national resource to a national burden. By this account, by 1933 "one out of every twenty young men in the United States was wandering aimlessly around the country. . . . Just as many young men, and probably more, were at home, idle. They needed only a little more want and suffering to push them, too, out on the road" (K. Davis 1935, 7–8). Like grim versions of Pinocchio, these teenage boys were setting out on the road to become real, and like the animated character, they would form their reality based on the influences they encountered along the way.

While the Great Depression profoundly informed the anxieties of parents concerned for the future of their children, and of a society worried about youth in general, the terms used to voice these concerns were shaped well before the 1930s. Beginning in the late nineteenth century, progressive social reformers such as Jane Addams, Florence Kelley, or Jacob Riis fought to improve the lives of the urban poor, many of whom were recent European immigrants.[1] Much of this struggle involved immediate efforts to ease the effects of crushing poverty—such as the reform of housing laws and rehabilitation of tenements, or the improvement of working conditions and hours. But the language reformers used to make their case to the public often invoked the rhetoric and images of child-saving and assimilation: the idea that the working poor and immigrants could best improve their lives by internalizing the values and behaviors of that same middle class to which reformers spoke. Since children were pliable and adaptable, they were the key to that enterprise. As progressive-era social reformers appealed for support, they invoked an ideal childhood into which poor children would assimilate, one which was being produced in the emerging fields that comprised child development.[2] This child, modeled on the bodies and behaviors of the white, middle-class children of researchers and the communities they served, was a benchmark against which middle-class parents were to gauge their own children's progress, and toward which social reformers could direct their efforts to improve the material and social lives of the poor (Cravens 1985). In the discourses of both development and uplift, this generic child—a complex of specific behaviors and bodily norms—was an endpoint, a fulcrum in the ordering of relations between culture and society. What had changed between the turn of the century and the 1930s was that children in need of protection and uplift were no longer simply those of the poor; they were increasingly referred to generically, as "children" or "youth." As a depression-era ad placed by Encyclopedia Britannica in *Child Life* and *Parents' Magazine* put it to middle-class parents, "Are you preparing your children for FAME OF FAILURE? The average child in the fifth grade, according to government statistics, has *only one chance* in 50 to complete a college education—*one chance* in 50, really, to avoid failure."[3] (See figure 8.)

If this ideal child isolated through empirical research comprised a set of physical and behavioral norms, though, the children gauged against it were anything but abstract: in public discourse about the well-being of children, they were understood as members of a new mass consumer culture. These were the children affected by the movies in the Payne Fund studies, as well as by books, toys, and other articles they consumed, who, as they entered the hurly-burly of daily mass culture, might well deviate from the parameters set by the ideal child. This normal child, on the other hand, was the result of decades of research and data correlation, the aggregate of thousands of measurements and observations of weight, height, posture, smiling, laughing, speaking, eating, defecating, aggression, cooperation, understanding, misunderstanding, etc. Whether applied to middle-class children whose parents (i.e., mothers)

8. An advertisement for *Encyclopedia Britannica* destined to appear in *Parents' Magazine*. Like many ads of the period, its fulcrum was a mother's anxiety that she was responsible for her child's future success. Ayers Collection, Archives Center, National Museum of American History, Smithsonian Institution.

were to regulate their consumption, or to poorer children whose consumption was to be regulated by social reformers (in the stead of absent, working parents), this child was imagined as the product of that which it consumed. The adult it would become would be the aggregate of the behaviors and values that mass-cultural producers had built into their products, a reproduction of the social relations inherent in that which it consumed. In essence, then, this abstraction of a child was a sort of time machine, a historically transitional object through which adults could imagine themselves able to reach into the next generation and determine, in some part, its terrain. And, as the author of *Youth in the Depression* warned his readers, if adults did not avail themselves of this opportunity, they were, in effect, leaving the future in the unsteady hands of that child: "If the older people do nothing to help the young, they may take matters into their own hands and do things . . . for themselves. Crimes committed by young people increase; revolution is not improbable" (K. Davis 1935, 12). In short, the child improperly raised would at least form the nucleus for a criminal future, and at most contribute to the eventual overthrow of a democratic capitalist society weakened by the faltering of its underlying economic system.[4]

So, while it was important that Pinocchio get to school, an education alone couldn't guarantee his future. A child's public life as a consumer—in the very commercial space between home and school (and increasingly within both)—would shape it long before it set foot in the classroom. Of humble origins—made of wood by a poor, ethnic craftsman—Pinocchio had to internalize the values of the life Gepetto wanted him to have. If Pinocchio represented every child, he embodied a very specific set of social and cultural assumptions (and anxieties) about the nature of that child. Acting "brave, truthful, and unselfish," he had to actively repudiate his cultural origins in favor of the ideal that would make him real. In this model, working-class and immigrant children (and, to some extent, adults) were to be assimilated into American culture through social and educational programs that inculcated in them white, Protestant, middle-class values such as self-denial and deferred gratification. The discursive circuit through which this naturalization occurred was mutually constitutive. On the one hand, the social scientists conducting research into the nature of childhood were themselves generally white and of the middle class, as were their research subjects. On the other, progressive reformers used that child-study research to argue for a baseline American culture into which every child entered during development that was modeled on progressive, middle-class virtues. The background against which students of child development in the late nineteenth and early twentieth century observed their subjects were often middle-class homes (or modeled on them), and the habits and environments that obtained therein—from eating to conversing, hygiene, and personal and collective property relations—were taken with little exception as a natural milieu for the child's entry into human society.[5] By the 1920s and 1930s, data on the eating and defecation, speech and mobility, and so on, of supposedly normal children that had originally been derived under very culturally specific circumstances were widely accepted as a baseline for the observation and regulation of *all* children. These assumptions about the nature of childhood were further woven into popular discourse by their deployment in arguments about the effects of an increasingly shared popular culture on children of all classes (see chapter 1).

By 1940, then, Pinocchio could become a "real boy" by mastering the middle-class virtues of "truthfulness" and "unselfishness" (as well as deferred gratification and self-denial) and through a rejection of (working-class) modes of instant gratification. Actual Depression-era children could consume the absolute American-ness of Walt Disney by using his products, both because it was commonly assumed that the uptake of consumer goods translated directly into uplift (or downfall), and because the "averageness" of the man that the company trumpeted and its public accepted was actually the profile of the white, Protestant middle class that made the natural basis for American culture. The normal American child for whom Disney products were widely considered beneficial derived from the gradual interweaving of two distinct discourses of childhood during the early twentieth century: that of the immigrant child in need of saving and uplift, and that of the middle-class child as the subject of the study of normal child development. This circuit, however, was some thirty years in the making, and a more detailed mapping of its development may make clearer the process by which it produced a generic normal child susceptible to both the negative and positive effects of movies and movie-related products.

However, to do so involves more than simply noting how progressive-era reformers used the terminology of the emerging field of child development (and its popular corollary, child-rearing) in their public address, or how both reformers and middle-class parents tacitly accepted a notion of the white, middle-class child as a baseline for normality. Proponents of child-saving regularly couched their arguments for the assimilation of poor and immigrant children in broader terms of its benefit to American social and cultural well-being. As these children became citizens (voters and social actors) in American democratic capitalist society, it was essential that they belonged to the American culture which had purportedly produced that society. And as that elite ideal of American culture came increasingly in conflict with mass popular culture in the teens and twenties, discourses of child-protection expanded to include children of the middle class. The popular middle-class and elite view was that popular culture—such as movies, radio, or dime novels—was produced for and by the very immigrants and working-class people who were supposed to assimilate into an older and more refined American culture, and it seemed possible that children (poor or otherwise) who consumed popular culture might unwittingly absorb the very values that reformers and middle-class parents were trying to erase or avoid. Even as the children of the poor and immigrants were to be assimilated into that ideal American culture, the children of the middle class were increasingly seen as in need of protection from a popular culture associated with the immigrants and working class.

Already increasingly joined around the figure of the normal child, discourses of child-saving and child development were further fused around a common concern for children as consumers. If immigrant and poor children had to be Americanized, the "native" children of the middle class had to avoid being alienated from their own culture—de-Americanized, as it were. So, even as progressive-era reformers drew upon the terms of child development and popular child-rearing increasingly adopted the Americanization arguments of the reform movement, media producers such as Disney could present themselves as inherently American to access the common hopes and anxieties centered around the emerging figure of the generic American child, drawing on arguments for the regulation of popular culture and its delivery of inherently American values. By pulling at these three threads, these three interwoven discourses of childhood, we may begin to see how the figure of the normal child circulated in popular discussions of the regulation of American culture, becoming by the 1930s and the rise of Disney a commonplace within which a complex matrix of very specific social and material relations lay embedded.

Boys in the Streets: The Rhetoric of Child-Saving

In the eyes of turn-of-the-century progressive reformers, the movies were just one element in a complex of vices and distractions that threatened to divert poor children from the path of sobriety, hard work, and thrift that would lead them out of the teeming ghettoes and the folkways of their parents' homelands and into a middle-class American life. Thirty-odd years before *Youth in the Depression*, the author of *Boys in the Streets* (Stelzle 1904) painted a slightly different picture of the world that awaited the teenage boy outside the home:

> The boy in the city usually starts to work at fourteen. If he is large and strong for his age, he goes to the factory just as soon as he can pass for that age. His evenings are now open to him, since he has no school lessons to prepare. He has more money to spend than he ever had before. . . . and it is only a matter of time before the slender tie that binds him to his humble home is broken, and he falls into the clutches of the manager of the cheap theatre, the saloon keeper, and the keeper of the downtown dive. (14)

This, again, was the plot of *Pinocchio*, but with an important difference: the boy who would have to fend off the temptations of the streets was not a generic child, but a working-class urban youth whose childhood was ostensibly over at fourteen when he (or she) went to work in the factories (E. Ewen 1985; Nasaw 1985, 1992). This was a child marked by class, and often by ethnicity, a child linked to poverty, dissolution, and squalor. For progressive reformers, it was also a child that stood on the brink between the Old World and the New. The child's desire to join and to belong (which Walt Disney would make much of in the formation of its first Mickey Mouse Clubs in the early 1930s) could lead the urban child into social clubs and benevolent societies which at best encouraged a backward-looking allegiance to ethnicities and nationalisms at odds with Americanization, or to join the newly forming Boys Clubs, Boy Scout troops, and settlement youth groups (Stelzle 1904, Addams 1926).[6] Even the desire for entertainment, if not properly managed, led to detrimental amusements:

> If he has a love for music, he cannot indulge that most elevating taste, unless he can afford to spend as much for the concert as he has earned in a whole day. The only alternative is to resort to the vaudeville, where he may hear fairly good music, but where he must take with it so much of evil that the good is usually more than over-balanced. Where else could he go in the average city if he would see the "moving pictures" which have become so popular? (Stelzle 1904, 16–17)

For immigrant and working-class children growing up in ghettoes, home offered no respite from the temptations of the streets. Living conditions in tenements were often horribly overcrowded, and if both parents weren't working, the child's living space might well function as a piecework factory in which children as young as four (particularly girls) worked alongside their older siblings and mothers (Youcha 1995). In reformers' pleas for charity (and in no small part, in reality), children who weren't pressed into labor in the home roamed the streets, abandoned by their mothers and prey not only to amusements, but

9. Like the *New York Times'* Fresh Air Fund today, this pamphlet for a summer camp for poor children played upon the sympathies of the well-to-do and on their sense of responsibility for the uplift of immigrants and the poor. Warshaw Collection, Archives Center, National Museum of American History, Smithsonian Institution.

to the day-to-day danger of urban living. As author and reformer Charlotte Perkins Gilman put it in 1900, "The accidents to little children from electric and cable cars are pitifully numerous. What mother has taken any steps to prevent these accidents? Individually, each tries to protect her own, as does the animal or savage. Collectively, they do nothing; yet it is the lack of this collective motherhood which makes our cities so unsafe for children" (284–285).

The spectacle of poor waifs at the mercy of a cruel urban environment was a repeating trope in religious appeals for funds and calls for the support of progressive urban reform programs (see figure 9). But it was not the only appeal used. While reformers offered up the image of the starving and generally imperiled child as a plea to the sentiments of their middle- and upper-class sponsors, they also presented a specter designed to touch those more concerned with hard-headed issues of business and politics: the undermining of American society through immigrant profligacy. Theodore Roosevelt, arguably the most famous of the progressives, described the problem in 1907 by claiming that "we shall never achieve true greatness . . . unless we are Americans in heart and soul, in spirit and purpose, keenly alive to the responsibility implied in the very name of American" (18). For Roosevelt (and other progressives), the sheer number of immigrants who were fueling the Industrial Revolution represented a potential threat to a white, Protestant ruling class that considered itself the center of a national American cultural, social, and political life.[7] Thus it was important that immigrants, who would vote, and who would, through their consumption habits, play a role in the development of popular culture, be fully "naturalized." "The mighty tide of immigration to our shores has brought in its train much of good and much of evil," Roosevelt warned in the book *American Ideals*,

> and whether the good or the evil shall predominate depends mainly on whether these newcomers do or do not throw themselves heartily into our national life, cease to be European, and become Americans like the rest of us. . . . But where immigrants, or the sons of immigrants, do not heartily and in good faith throw in their lot with us, but cling to the speech, the customs, the ways of life, and the habits of the Old World which they have left, they thereby harm both themselves and us. If they remain alien elements, unassimilated, and with interests separate from ours, they are mere obstructions to the current of our national life, and, moreover, can get no good from it themselves. (28)

Whether in response to nativist calls to curtail or end immigration, or as a matter of profound unease with the undermining of American values, progressives pushed for the implementation of universal public schooling, and of settlement houses and neighborhood associations in poor neighborhoods—in a general policy of moral, spiritual, and behavioral uplift designed to Americanize newly arrived immigrants.

Although progressives invested a great deal of energy in adult education programs for newly arrived immigrants, the natural location for beginning this work of Americanizing immigrant populations was with their children (Addams 1926; 1930, 231–58; 1960, 145–55). Charlotte Perkins Gilman put the matter quite bluntly, stating that "the way to make people better is to have them born better. The way to have them born better is to make all possible improvement in the individual before parentage. That is why youth is holy and august: it is the fountain of human progress. Not only that 'the child is the father to the man,' but the child is father to the state—and mother" (Gilman 1900, 21).[8]

In the progressive address, conditions obtaining in urban ghettoes contributed to what late-twentieth-century reformers would refer to as a "culture of poverty," and they had the potential to spread throughout the nation. Simply put, bad habits and behaviors were passed on from one generation to the next, either through the parent, or through the associations, clubs, and entertainments that made the lives of the working poor minimally bearable. The progressive program of "uplift" involved the gradual replacement of immigrant and working-class behaviors and habits with those of a primarily Protestant middle class. Given that this middle class was meant to represent American culture at its purest, the child (or adult) would be more likely to succeed should it learn to conform to societal norms of thrift, deferred gratification, self-denial, and sexual restraint or abstinence.[9]

The progressive program to accomplish this replacement of behaviors and habits involved compulsory public schooling, home visits by social workers, and settlement houses and other community centers where progressive workers (most often women) could expose immigrant children and adults to those virtues.[10] The settlement houses, of which Jane Addams's Hull House was the most renowned, were the central locations for this work, offering practical services and moral education in one package (Clement 1985, K. Sklar 1993, 1995). "The University Settlements do an enormous amount of work," declared Teddy Roosevelt. "They help people help themselves, not only in work and self-support but in the right thinking and right living. . . . [They have] offered to the people of the neighborhood educational and social opportunities ranging from a dancing academy and musical classes, to literary clubs, a library, and a children's bank—the clubs being administered on the principle of self-management and self-government" (Roosevelt 1907, 350–351).

Although perhaps the most significant work the settlement houses performed was in providing very basic (and necessary) services such as child care and tutoring, public depictions of their efforts stressed their work to train young minds and bodies in the rigors of "self-management." That small phrase, taken as a given by middle-class parents at the turn of the century, was meant to stand as a marker between the lives of immigrant children and their parents, an ontological boundary marker between the Old World and the New. If one learned to successfully manage one's self, then one increased the odds that one would not later be managed by others. Within the model of progressive uplift, the child that successfully internalized the authority of (the middle-class, Protestant version of) American culture was less likely to require the attention or largesse of state authority and was more likely to become an independent contributor to the state, rather than its dependent. More than simply self-control, "self-management" required of the immigrant and working-class child that it develop a relationship to itself in which it observed, regulated, and evaluated its own behavior with an eye to self-improvement.[11] Unlike its immigrant and working-class parents, who sold their labor and the control of their selves to industrial managers, poor children involved in the progressive program of uplift constituted a step both toward becoming more fully American, and toward an American-ness located in an individuality that preceded and preempted associations of ethnicity or nationality.[12]

The failure to properly integrate immigrant and working-class children meant more than simply the continuation of poverty and immiseration; it threatened the diminution of the social and political power of a white middle class that was producing fewer children than were the poor. The specter of "race suicide"—whether raised by anti-immigrant nativists or more conservative progressives—became a powerful incentive for assimilating poor and ethnic children into regimes of whiteness.[13] (See figure 10.) The popular commonplace that the white middle class represented an evolutionary advance guard converted assimilation from a charitable act to one of social preservation. And although the preferred method for this reformation was through public education and the restructuring of immigrant life through social work, American culture in general could also have a salutary effect. In 1911, Franz Boas, writing for the U.S. Immigration Commission, reported that in his examinations of immigrant children he had discovered that "the head form, which has always been considered one of the stable and permanent characteristics of human races, undergoes far-reaching changes coincident with the transfer of the people from European to American soil. . . . We are compelled to conclude that when [body parts] change, the whole bodily and mental makeup of the immigrants may change" (5).[14] Speaking the language of anthropometrics, Boas claimed nothing less than that the American landscape, American culture, and American lifestyle could physically change immigrants into Americans within one generation.[15]

Boas's words sum up nicely the enthusiasm, the anxiety, and the contradictions of the progressive enterprise at the beginning of the twentieth century. Reading through progressive writings of the period, it is often difficult to tell when a writer is beating back nativist attacks (such as efforts to end the flow of immigrants from southern and eastern Europe to which Boas was responding) or when he or she is actually espousing some attenuated version of the eugenicist science popular at the time. Boas, for instance, is commonly regarded as responsible (with his protégés, Alfred Kroeber and Ruth Benedict) for

31 C 1924

Is our native stock slowly committing suicide?

IMAGINE this country of ours, one hundred years hence, teeming with millions of foreign-born men and women and their progeny, and only here and there a last surviving member of a native family. This is the picture of the decadence of our native stock drawn with a warning pen by Edward A. Ross, Professor of Sociology in the University of Wisconsin.

"At least a third more babies should be born if the native middle class is to replace itself," writes Professor Ross. "It is now committing slow suicide. In a century it will have shrunken to a mere half of its present numbers, while contained in a nation twice as populous. Figures show that only the family with four or more births can count on producing a father and a mother from among the children. The right remedy for family suicide is to correct our philosophy of success. When the public rates success more in terms of offspring, more couples will consent to rear a real family."

Read Professor Ross' amazing article, "Slow Suicide Among Our Native Stock," in the February Century Magazine. The shocking facts presented there with outspoken frankness are an arraignment of the shameful complacency of our middle class.

Besides Professor Ross' article, the February Century presents five other articles that reflect the *liberal, literary* and *aggressive* policy of the Century. If you are not reading the Century, you are missing some of the most conspicuous magazine literature of today. Begin with the February number. Buy it at the better class newsstands or send in your subscription on the coupon printed below for your convenience.

Eight Big Features in the February Century

Slow Suicide Among Our Native Stock, *by Professor E. A. Ross.*

Uncle Sam and the Statue of Liberty, *by Ralph Barton Perry.*

The Mexican Renaissance, *by Ernest Gruening.*

Is America Fit to Join the League? *by Francis Hackett.*

The Wondering Jew, *by M. E. Ravage.*

The Age of Experiment, *by Henry Seidel Canby.*

The Kitten and the Masterpiece, *a story, by Floyd Dell.*

Margaret Blake, *a story, by Chester T. Crowell.*

The CENTURY MAGAZINE

Liberal - Literary - Aggressive

THE CENTURY COMPANY, 353 Fourth Avenue, New York City

For the $5 enclosed, please send the Century for one year to

Name...

Address...

10. An advertisement for the *Christian Century Magazine* (February 1924) citing University of Wisconsin sociologist Edward Ross's warning to ostensibly white or "native" Americans that their falling reproductive rates were tantamount to "race suicide." Not only was this rhetoric meant to encourage reproduction, it also fed arguments for contraception as a eugenic practice by reformers such as Margaret Sanger and Charlotte Perkins Gilman. Ayers Collection, Archives Center, National Museum of American History, Smithsonian Institution.

purging the nascent field of anthropology of excesses in racialism and pseudo-evolutionary thinking by stressing the distinction between the biological and the cultural (Stocking 1968). Although Boas would continue to refine his position over the coming years, the project of replacing the racial hierarchies of hard-line eugenicists apparently required a moderate position in which a quasi-Darwinian notion of uplift made permeable supposedly inviolable barriers of heredity. Indeed, the term *progressive* was (and is) so vague as to admit a variety of positions, even in individuals. For example, Charlotte Perkins Gilman could frame a quite earnest and modern call for the improvement of the living conditions of the poor, immigrant family in outwardly racist terms:

> The nearer we are to the animals, the more capable and bright the very little ones. In the South it was common to set a little black child to take care of an older white one: the pickaninny matures much more rapidly. So, again, in our own lower social grades the little children of the poor are sharper, better able to care for themselves, than children of the same age in more developed classes. It is no proof of greater intelligence in the adult. It is retrogression,—a mark of bad social conditions. (Gilman 1900, 294)

In the mind of this sincere progressive reformer, the contradiction between the racism of one sentiment and the social radicalism of the other disappeared into the body of the immigrant child. Children of other races were evolutionarily previous to their white peers, but only temporarily so. The doctrine of uplift allowed for the advancement of the backward races through cultural and social enlightenment while maintaining the immediate reinforcement of racial difference by forestalling evolutionary parity (if only slightly) to an indeterminate future that was meant to become determinate with further research. Thus Boas's position in 1911 seems a significant improvement over that of Charles Ellwood (who would eventually become president of the American Sociological Society) in 1901 that "natural selection" separated the races by heredity, and that this selection could be only attenuated, not wholly erased:[16]

> The negro child, even when reared in a white family under the most favorable condition, fails to take on the mental and moral characteristics of the Caucasian race. His mental attitudes toward persons and things, toward organized society, toward life, and toward religion never become quite the same as those of the white. His natural instincts, it is true, may be modified by training, and perhaps indefinitely in the course of generations; but the race habit of a thousand generations or more is not lightly set aside by

the voluntary or enforced imitation of visible models. (Ellwood, quoted in Stocking 1968)

Although by the 1920s the American social sciences would, in the course of disciplinary formation, largely purge themselves of such excess, the public progressive project of uplift during the first two decades of the twentieth century espoused a view of the world in which heredity and environment both played a role in shaping people, but within which only the environment could (and should) be altered (Hall 1965).[17] And while adult immigrants could be trained in American ways of living—through adult education and home visits by social workers—their children could actually be *made* into full-fledged Americans if they had the proper social and cultural exposure. If the nation were to survive and prosper, it would be because the children of Poles and Italians, of Romanians and Russians—and the working-class "American" children growing up alongside them—were being raised in an "American" environment engineered to speed the process of assimilation.

That engineering was not limited to regulating child-rearing practices, however, and many other social policies instigated and promulgated by progressive reformers in the late nineteenth and early twentieth centuries are taken as givens today. Viviana Zelizer (1985) reports that although efforts to enact federal bans and constitutional amendments outlawing child labor failed repeatedly well into the 1920s, the number of children in heavy industry declined during the period nonetheless. Ironically, the influx of cheap immigrant labor and several agricultural depressions made the work of state societies for the prevention of cruelty to children (and animals) easier, and as reformers lobbied at the state and local level, heavy industries began to curtail their use of child labor (see United States Department of Labor, Children's Bureau 1930). Increasingly, the only jobs thought acceptable for children were in agriculture, domestic work, and in services such as newspaper delivery. (Roediger 1991 points out that the lack of reform in these industries meant that working conditions for black, Asian, and Latino children—and many adults—remained largely unchanged.)[18]

Even if progressive-era social reformers were unable to pass a comprehensive ban on child labor, however, progressive efforts for social uplift by regulating the life of the child succeeded in generating limited federal action. In 1909, the first in a series of White House conferences on children that would continue into the 1960s convened, and by 1912 a federal Children's Bureau had been established within the Department of Labor. Two members of Jane Addams's Hull House, Julia Lathrop and Grace Abbott, would serve as directors of the bureau, and under Abbott in particular it would expand its ambit from an initial focus on the living conditions of poor rural and urban mothers, to advocacy for a more generalized child study that benefited all children, regardless of class, race, or ethnicity.[19] As the century progressed, the confluence of these various social and economic changes created a condition in which children were perceived as occupying a social sphere increasingly different than that of adults. Hamilton Cravens (1985) suggests that from the 1890s onward, children increasingly constituted a social group different from adults, and Zelizer (1985) argues that the gradual removal of children from the labor market forced a reconsideration of their value to parents and to society in which the labor value of children was converted to "preciousness," and childhood became a "sacralized" time prior to the harsh realities of adult economic life.[20] Thus, efforts to protect the children of the poor, and to convert their values and behaviors to those of their betters, discursively positioned those children as culturally and socially distinct from their parents, operating in the liminal and malleable sphere of childhood that they shared with children of the middle class. This convergence had the effect of facilitating the application of discourses of protection to middle-class children, and of extending developmental parameters to poor children—provided that they were raised in the proper environment. The emergence of this sacred child set the preconditions for a mass children's market by imagining the child as having psychic and material needs entirely different than those of adults, and as being susceptible to the environmental influences of culture, whether "American" or mass-produced. For progressive social reformers, the idea of a distinct child's environment would focus efforts to define both the proper nature of that environment and the development of the child within it.

To do this work, however, progressive-era social workers required a methodology that delivered to the child the necessary attitudes and behaviors, as well as a set of guidelines for gauging that child's progress. As Geraldine Youcha put it (1995, 133–135), settlement houses such as Hull House imagined themselves as a form of "scientific charity" in which middle-class norms were extended to immigrants and the working-class through "scientific child-rearing principles." As a condition of the social location of most social scientists at the turn of the century, the scientific principles that reformers such as Jane Addams, Florence Kelly, or Grace Abbott deployed in these operations were derived from data gathered and collated by amateurs and professionals in child-study societies made up of people from middle- and upper-class backgrounds such as their own, studying the behaviors and habits of their own children, often within their own homes. Beginning in the last decade or so of the nineteenth century, these societies, and a growing number of professional researchers, collected and collated an impressive array of data on child development that purported to apprehend the child in its natural state, but which (even in early laboratory work) assumed that the conditions obtaining in middle-class households (or in the behaviors of middle-class laboratory workers) were so appropriate to "the race" that the middle-class child appeared to be operating in a natural environment, and the data collected from its observation was culturally untainted. Thus, the scientific language that progressive reformers used to describe a generic childhood emerged not only from the pens of early developmental researchers such as G. Stanley Hall or Arnold Gesell, but initially from their collaborators in amateur child-study associations And in that collaboration we find the naturalization of the middle-class home and child that would form the basis for the generic child and environment that Disney would target in the coming decades.

From Child Study to the Study of Childhood

In the letters column 1893 annual *Childhood* magazine, an organ of the Parents' Association of America, association member B. O. Flower argued that

> [Parents] are the moulders of a new civilization, and as such, it is all important that the grave responsibilities devolving upon parenthood be brought home to the conscience of every enlightened man and woman. . . . There are three lines of investigation or research which . . . should be carefully followed:
>
> I. Hereditary.
>
> II. Pre-natal Influence.
>
> III. Influences of Early Environment. . . .
>
> The quickest way to accomplish great reforms is . . . through the presentation of carefully arranged data resting upon authenticated facts. . . . [and through such reforms] we will have such a marked change in the children coming into the civilized homes that an entirely new era will ensue. (254–255)

The concerns of members such as Flower, in an organization so firmly rooted in the upper and middle classes that many of its members apologized for missing its summer meeting because they were on the Continent, were with the development of a scientific program for the study and improvement of their own children—and by extension, all children. The rhetoric employed here differed from that of progressive reformers on several counts. First, it assumed an educated and concerned parent with sufficient leisure time to collect and collate data, as well as the financial wherewithal to adjust her living conditions to best suit the prepartum "child" and infant in its "environment." Next, it linked individual parents (rather than the state, or social reformers) with the future of "civilization," the natural assumption being that in the proper dyadic or triadic relationship between parent and child, the particulars of culture were most effectively transmitted from one generation to the next. Finally, in contrast to the Galtonian excesses of extreme eugenicists and nativists, it sought to lend equal weight to heredity, environment, and prenatal conditions, backhandedly offering a program that promised *some* uplift (by way of proper prenatal care and early environment), but which hewed to a milder eugenicist position in which, no matter what advantages obtained, heredity could limit the ultimate effect of uplift.[21]

As it is difficult to locate in the term *progressive* a single, coherent political or social philosophy, it is equally difficult to ascribe to the proponents of child study in the late nineteenth and early twentieth centuries a unified theoretical or methodological base. Early child study was a cottage industry, a loose fellowship that comprised matrons, mothers, college students, doctors, and psychologists (G. Stanley Hall was ostensibly a member of the Parents' Association of America). This fellowship shared the common goal of obtaining useful data on the behavior and development of infants and children. And although the methodological discussions carried on by the likes of William James, Wilhelm Wundt, John Dewey, or Hall himself may have filtered down to amateur members, as a whole the movement, like many scientific enterprises in their infancy, did not until the late teens or early twenties develop clear disciplinary boundaries or apparatuses for the discursive policing of its adherents.[22] What members shared, were they professional or amateur (if indeed one can clearly make that distinction in the absence of a clearly formed profession), was a belief in a broad concept of "progress" based loosely on a Darwinism that, at its most optimistic, was often shaded with Lamarckian overtones, and at its most pessimistic assumed that members of immigrant and working-class groups, should they multiply, might well pollute an imagined American race with genetic weaknesses such as idiocy, alcoholism, and sexual deviation.[23] This basic belief that some form of Darwinism operated in both the production and correction of long-term social problems bound a wide range of amateur and professional researchers in child development. Far from fatalistic, this shared approach assumed that knowledge of evolutionary theory compelled the researcher and the reformer alike to strive toward the betterment of the race as one's personal contribution to the regulation of the process of a nonetheless inevitable natural selection.

As has been noted elsewhere, the Darwinian bent of child-study adherents crossed over into Lamarckism for those who assumed that changes in culture translated into changes in biology, and that the regulation of culture through environment was the most effective way to direct the process of selection.[24] Thus, an author writing on character development in *Childhood* began her article with a brief description of evolution as a biological process, stressing nature's inexorable urge to move from the primitive to the advanced: "From the beginning, all history of nature, from the story of a coral reef to the tragedy of humanity, has been a record of development. There has always been progress from less to greater, with many lapses, it is true, with many missing links in the sequence, but, looked at from age to age, the movement has been onward" (J. Smith 1893, 347).

Citing basic work conducted on cats, in which feline motor and reflex centers were successfully isolated, the author then blended those results with phrenology to suggest that if "the brain can be mapped out, and if, as seems not impossible, science can, by careful investigation and experiment, say in which ganglia love sits enthroned, where reverence, where hate, may it not be that, knowing the possibilities of a given organization and the hereditary traits, one can abort evil and cultivate the good?" (J. Smith 1893, 350). Even if it weren't possible to surgically suppress and encourage sentiments and behaviors, the author suggested, the research of the day promised that it might well be possible to regulate the child's environment to the point that the same effect was achieved, causing noble qualities to flourish through exercise and baser ones to atrophy until they simply weren't strong enough to express themselves in subsequent generations. Confronted with the inexorable nature of evolution, Smith asked her readers, "Where, then, is our refuge from . . . fatalism?" (351) In reply she quoted a contemporary evolutionary theorist (Théodule Ribot), who suggested, "Evolution produces physiological and psychological modifications. Habit fixes these in the individual. Heredity fixes them in the race" (Smith 1893, 352). Through a tidy sleight of hand, evolution's programmatic imperative was turned from a handicap to an advantage: even as the child expressed both negative and positive evolutionary changes, proper regulation of its habits would allow for the selection of beneficial qualities for transmission to future generations and the suppression of the detrimental.

Much as the introduction of electricity to the domestic environment in the turn-of-the-century United States encouraged flights of fancy such as galvanic belts, rectal thermeators, and low-voltage baths—devices which would miraculously cure ailments both physiological and psychological—enthusiasm for a universal Darwinism led to a few such excesses in the emerging field of child study. Yet at the same time, efforts to catalogue the child's basic range of developmental and behavioral markers, as well as its relationship to its environment, also resulted in the assembly of impressive amounts of data on child development, and in the formation of broad disciplinary boundaries. Beginning in roughly the 1880s and extending well into the next century, psychologists, sociologists, and philosophers such as Dewey, James, Thorndike, and Hall (to name but a few) traced the outlines of a discipline that would first be called Child Study and would eventually form a broad umbrella of developmental studies that would include specialties in psychology, pediatrics, the domestic economy, and education.[25]

During this formative period, relations between parent and child, between child and environment, and between child and researcher were the topic of some debate. Some researchers insisted that mothers be separated from their children during research because they would exert undue emotional influence on the child, corrupting observational data; others argued the opposite, claiming that only the mother, given her close natural bond with the child, could properly interpret its gestures, movements, and cries (Sully 1902, 21–52; G. Hall 1965). The ideal researcher (for some) would be a mother who was also a trained research scientist. This appeared to be the case with Kathleen Carter Moore, whose monograph "The Mental Development of a Child" (1896) appeared in *The Psychological Review*, a professional journal that listed Alfred Binet, John Dewey, William James, Hugo Munsterberg, and other leading social scientists on its board.[26] Deploying a highly articulated and rigorous observational apparatus that differentiated child-rearing activities from the conditions under which they occurred, and changes in behavior from the conditions under which they were observed to occur, Moore studied her own child from birth, recording reams of data on his physical, mental, emotional, and sensory development (see figure 11).

To guarantee the reliability of her data, and in conformity with contemporary thought on observational technique, Moore established a relationship between herself and her child/subject that encapsulated arguments about the mother's influence on the child (as mother, or as researcher) and about the child's relationship to its environment:

> The course of my child's development has, I believe, been a normal one. He suffered little from interference, and was never stimulated to premature action. He was accustomed to playing alone. Especial care was taken

TABLE IX.

Ninety-Sixth Week.					One-Hundred-and-Second Week.				
124 sentences containing 384 words.					138 sentences containing 570 words.				
Vocabulary = 118 words.					Vocabulary = 150 words.				
Number and Percentage of Words of a Class Contained in:									
	The Sentences.		The Vocabulary.			The Sentences.		The Vocabulary.	
	No.	Percentage.	Number.	Percentage.		No.	Percentage.	Number.	Percentage.
Nouns and Pronouns.	200	52.0 + %	72	61.5 + %	Nouns and Pronouns.	267	46.8 + %	78	52. %
Verbs.	82	21.3 + %	22	18.6 + %	Verbs	131	22.9 + %	40	26.6 + %
Adjectives	29	7.5 + %	11	9.3 + %	Adjectives	37	6.4 + %	13	8.6 + %
Adverbs	26	6.7 + %	5	4.2 + %	Adverbs	46	8.0 + %	11	7.3 + %
Prepositions	13	3.3 + %	5	4.2 + %	Prepositions	21	3.6 + %	5	3.3 + %
Others	34	8.8 + %	3 (art. 1, interj. 2)	2.5 + %	Others	68	11.9 + %	3(art. 1, interj. 2)	2.0 + %

Ninety-Sixth Week.		One-Hundred-and-Second Week.	
Average number of words to a sentence	= 3.02 +	Average number of words to a sentence	= 4.1 +
" " nouns and pronouns[1]	= 1.6 +	" " nouns and pronouns*	= 1.9 +
" " verbs	= 0.6 +	" " verbs	= 0.9 +
" " Adjectives	= 0.23 +	" " adjectives	= 0.27 +
" " Adverbs	= 0.2 +	" " adverbs	= 0.3 +
" " Prepositions	= 0.10 +	" " prepositions	= 0.15 +
Percentage of sentences containing no verb	= 33.8 + %	Percentage of sentences containing no verb	= 7.2 + %

[1] Read " to a sentence " after all but first and last lines.

11. Tabulation of Katherine Carter Moore's systematic observation of her son's development in the October 1896 issue of *Psychological Review* (whose contributing editors included Alfred Binet, John Dewey, and William James). Moore's research was conducted in the home rather than the laboratory, and her maternal position ostensibly made her a more environmentally appropriate observer than a man.

> not to teach him the tricks which are commonly taught to babies. . . . When it was necessary that he should be taught habits essential to his welfare, no pains were spared. Regular hours of feeding, sleeping, etc., were maintained. Good health and rapid growth have uniformly been his. (Moore 1896, 3–4)

This representation of the child's early life suggests a complex ontological schema in which the child was treated as a natural creature subjected to the minimum of "interference" in order to obtain the purest observational data possible. The idea that it not be "stimulated to premature action" suggests further a regular timetable for the expression of certain abilities and a scientific detachment related to their elicitation. Where the child by (almost unfortunate) necessity had to be enculturated, that process was regulated, as were its eating and sleeping patterns, in an effort to maximize useful observational data before uncontrolled variables became too prevalent. Far from the victim of abuse or neglect, the child raised in isolation was considered the perfect test subject, and the fortunate beneficiary of the latest in regulated, scientific guidance in its development.[27] Thus, although the child was isolated from contact with other children (and presumably other adults) and unregulated contact, play, feeding, and so on were strictly avoided, Moore described his development as "normal." The meaning of "normal" implied in this work meant "standardized"—the child's upbringing was regulated to the point that abnormal or irregular influences were minimized, its environment carefully monitored, its bodily functions entrained within a set schedule. This did not mean, however, that the term *normal* bore *no* relation to later usages: the data generated in experiments such as this would become the foundation for setting the acceptable parameters for the physical, mental, and behavioral development of average American children in generations to come. The use of normalized conditions to raise the turn-of-the-century white, middle-class child within optimal parameters thus also generated data through which conditions that today might be called cultural were incorporated into a natural environment that in turn naturalized a set of developmental and behavioral curves as inherent to any child.[28]

Understood in this fashion, the child has been, at least since the turn of the century, a fantastic object, a device that translated social and material relations into natural phenomena, and that converted natural stimuli back into social relations when it became an adult.[29] This idea of the child was not, however, simply the byproduct of neo-Darwinian faddism. The child formed a strange exception, a site where the time frame of natural selection violated an ever more widely accepted schema that understood evolutionary change as happening over many successive generations, rather than within a single generation. What made this exception possible was the widely held belief that "ontogeny recapitulates phylogeny" (that the development of the individual child encapsulates the evolution of the entire species). While in its strictest sense this little commonplace was meant to refer only to the fetus in utero, its meaning soon expanded to include the social and cultural development of the infant and child. If the fetus recapitulated the prehistory of the species—from invertebrate, to fish, to amphibian, and so forth—then the developing infant and child recapitulated the march of human civilization, from the primitive to the modern. This child-as-homunculus, then, provided an exceptional window into a maddeningly slow evolutionary process, a fulcrum against which to apply pressure in efforts to direct the seemingly natural evolution of American social and cultural life. As John B. Watson suggested in an article for the educated, middle-class readers of *Harper's Magazine*, it seemed possible to shape the future in the crucible of the laboratory (domestic or otherwise), by treating children as experimental animals whose natural instincts could be scientifically separated from cultural influences:

> The students of experimental evolution . . . becoming more and more dissatisfied with the Darwinian conception of instinct—calling as it does for

> a belief in "fitness" or "adaptiveness" of all forms of instinctive action—are asking the comparative psychologists to re-examine the forms of animal activity in the light of recent data which have been gathered by experimentally controlling the process of evolution—data which I may say in passing are revolutionizing our present theory of evolution. Both to bring the work in animal behavior in line with these newer facts on evolution, and to assist the child psychologist in his problems, we need to have more exact knowledge of the different types of "native" or "untutored" activity in child and animal. (Watson 1912, 376)

While progressive-era social reformers would adopt this reasoning to argue for programs of uplift for the poor and working classes, the audience for those arguments were familiar with them through calls to shape their own children's environments to regulate their development and, by extension, the evolution of American culture.[30]

To properly produce that environment for their own children, the progressive middle class had access to an array of increasingly scientific child-rearing manuals, the most popular of which was pediatrician Luther Emmett Holt's *The Care and Feeding of Children* (1894), which employed the question-and-answer form that Benjamin Spock would adopt some fifty years later, and which encouraged rigor in the regulation of the child's eating, sleeping, and even crying: "*How many* [bowel] *movements daily should an infant have during the first few weeks of life?* . . . Usually three of four a day for the first week, and then two or three each day. . . . *How much crying is normal for a very young baby?* . . . From fifteen to thirty minutes a day" (Holt 1894, 49–52).

Texts such as Holt's assumed, of course, that the child would have sufficient food to fuel three or four bowel movements a day, and to satisfy needs it expressed through crying. They also assumed a literate public with leisure time sufficient not only for reading, but for developing and maintaining a regime of observation that would permit proper control of the child's environment. For poor families, literacy and leisure time were hardly guaranteed, nor were sufficient quantities of food or the relative isolation of the child's environment of which Moore had spoken. *The Care and Feeding of Children* also marked a trend that would only become more pronounced as the twentieth century progressed: the emergence of child-rearing literature for a popular audience written by experts in child development. For while members of the hybrid domestic/clinical child-study associations of the late nineteenth and early twentieth centuries may have framed their discourse in a Darwinian rhetoric of the advancement of the species, their immediate means of accomplishing that goal was the actual raising of children, and this required the translation of theoretical discussions into practical advice.

By the mid-1910s, psychologists such as G. Stanley Hall at Clarke University and Arnold Gesell at Yale, operating from the progressive premise that the environment was at least as significant as heredity in shaping children, had established clinics and were conducting research into how best to produce a normal child.[31] By the 1920s, a network of research facilities devoted to what was increasingly referred to as "child training" or "child management" had developed between such diverse research institutions as Yale; Columbia; the University of Iowa; Ohio State University; the University of California, Berkeley; and the University of Minnesota. Although the theoretical orientations and methods of individual labs varied, from Adler's Child Guidance, to Gesell's Child Development, to John B. Watson's behaviorism, all shared the common goals of isolating the characteristics of the normal child and of creating child-rearing programs that deployed that data in helping the child to develop to its fullest potential. And all were committed to using the latest observational technologies—particularly new methods of sequential photography and extended longitudinal and latitudinal studies—to isolate and analyze their subjects. Echoing the theory of recapitulation in an argument for detailed serial observation of development, Gesell stated, even as late as 1930:

> Inasmuch as behavior can be seen, described, and photographed, we are justified in saying that mental growth can be formulated and in a sense measured. The growth of the mind, scientifically conceived, is essentially the development of a sequence of behavior values which are correlated with the maturation of the nervous system. The structural problems of developmental psychology are not unlike those of embryology; a serial cross sectioning of the stream of behavior leads to an understanding of its genetic relations and its laws of emergence. (138–39)

Although this emerging network of experts would continue to invoke the language of evolution in professional discourse, it is more significant in this instance that experts also used it in their popular address. Although the United States had a tradition of moral instruction to parents dating back to its earliest days (Wishy 1968), the move to regulate the home and family through distinctly scientific principles was very much a phenomenon of the twentieth century, and the role of regulating national culture through evolutionary advancement (and vice versa) was central to that change. By the 1920s, the research laboratory would supplant the home as the site for gathering empirical data on the nature of childhood, and the middle-class home would become the primary location for the application and verification of that data. If settlement houses had been places for conducting large-scale experiments in social engineering, the middle-class home became the site for testing and applying empirical data at a microsocial level, and parents became research assistants in that process.

Between the Professional and the Popular

> *The most far-reaching influence that the progressives had upon the development of scientific management was their bringing the notions of democracy* [sic] *that prevailed in the progressive era to bear upon the doctrines of Taylorism. . . . Taylorism, in turn, had a significant influence upon progressive thought. It had carried the ethics of professionalism, so appealing to the middle class of the progressive era, into the heartland of "commercialism."*
>
> —HABER 1964, 166–67

Ideally, what would permit parents to properly order the domestic environment, and their children's behaviors and consumption, was a clearly defined set of norms against which to evaluate the child's development, and well-defined regimes with which to "manage" that development. A network of professional research facilities in the United States and abroad emerged during the 1910s and 1920s to supply those normative standards. In Vienna, Charlotte Buhler studied children's behavior through a glass wall; at Yale, Arnold Gesell recorded children on film; at Columbia Teacher's College, Ruth Andrus deployed squads of graduate students to observe children in kindergartens and nursery schools to produce an "inventory" of behaviors against which parents could compare their children's development (Beekman 1977, Andrus 1928). While it is not surprising that investigators in an increasingly well-established discipline (or group of disciplines) used similar research techniques, what was significant about the work of many child-rearing experts of the period is the degree to which they celebrated those techniques in popular versions of their published findings. Andrus published a voluminous compilation of charts and graphs along with her inventory, and Gesell not only printed photos from the Yale Psycho-Clinic, he even published the floor plan of the clinic in *The Guidance of Mental Growth in Infant and Child* (1930), and it was common in popular child-rearing books of the 1920s and 1930s to offer a wide array of tabulated data to the parent against which (one may suppose) they would rank their child.

Just as the data were important, so were the techniques by which they were derived. Child-development experts speaking to a popular audience stressed methods of isolation, observation, and transparency to validate the scientific production of data—and to naturalize techniques of detached observation begun in child-study associations in previous decades—as an integral part of a more standardized child-rearing practice. In a sense, they attempted to shift child-rearing from an artisanal or cottage industry model to one of standard clinical practice integrated into a rapidly rationalizing and nationalizing domestic economy.

This discursive approach was meant to involve middle-class parents (and those aspiring to the middle class) in the scientific enterprise of disseminating norms and of regulating the development of children to conform to those norms, the techniques of which were similar to those being deployed by scientific-management labor engineers in industry. By observing and recording workers' motions and behaviors—in some cases using stop-action photography to break down those motions into discrete units—and subjecting that raw data to statistical analysis, industrial researchers were trying to determine and design working environments for maximum efficiency and worker comfort. Far from accidental, this rigorous empiricism played on a widespread enthusiasm for Taylorist management techniques that extended beyond the industrial world into a popular fantasy of daily life in which efficiency was linked to social order and to the regulation of the excesses of popular democracy. Indeed, efficiency and Americanism were officially linked in the Progressive party platform of 1912, in a campaign which suggested that efficiency was an inherently American quality. Scientific management also found its way into the social sciences, with some sociologists arguing over the possibility of an "objective standard of social control," and into progressive social work, where Charles Stelzle (whose work opened this chapter) argued for the application of efficiency to church work, and Charlotte Perkins Gilman published an article on "The Waste of Private Housekeeping" in the *Annals of the American Academy of Political and Social Science* (Haber 1964, 61–62, 160–62; Nelson 1980).[32] Although Haber argues that by the 1920s the craze for scientific management as an expression of social control was fading (along with the progressive movement), it continued in work on domestic economy, and in child development, the discipline of which had experienced a substantial portion of its organization during efficiency's heyday (Haber 1964, 134–38). As late as 1927, Lillian Gilbreth issued a manual for the scientific management of the home, *The Home-Maker and Her Job*, under the same publisher's imprint as Douglas Thom's *Everyday Problems of the Everyday Child* (Thom 1928). (See chapter 3.)[33]

As had been the case in previous decades, the popular presentation of different professional child-rearing techniques in books and periodicals shared the idea that producing normal children remained a matter of national security and well-being. This notion, rooted in earlier progressive programs of assimilation for the sake of social harmony, retained in the form of behaviors the progressive virtues of self-control, deferred gratification, and hard work. Yet even as progressive theories of child-saving gave way to professional programs of child management, the idea that the health of the nation was tied to that of its children remained, and a popular author of child-rearing manuals reminded his readers, "the indications are that we are just entering an era when the welfare of the child will be the chief concern of the home, the community, and the nation. Throughout the civilized world to-day, the subject . . . that is receiving the most serious attention of statesmen as well as of teachers and parents is probably the child" (O'Shea 1929, 5).

Yet even as (primarily middle-class) parents were encouraged to sign up for the national enterprise of producing normal children, they still had to choose which techniques to use. Just as F. W. Taylor had competed with Lillian and Frank Gilbreth for market share in the scientific management of industrial operations, so were there competing programs for how best to train children in the business of childhood. From Yale University to the Iowa Research Station, each institution offered a program for the management and training of children. While there were significant differences between these models, there were also important similarities, and it was not uncommon to mix and match different developmental philosophies. For example, *Child Care and Training* (Faegre and Anderson 1929), put out by the Institute of Child Welfare at the University of Minnesota, listed in its references for parents works by Watson, Gesell, and Thom, each of whom favored an ostensibly different approach to child-rearing. What the works shared, though, was a commitment to scientific methods and a language based around the concept of management.[34] Books about children and child-rearing from the early part of the century had favored titles such as *Youth and the Race* (Swift 1912) or *What Grandmother Did Not Know* (Fisher 1922), relied heavily upon the wisdom of their authors and upon common sense, and were often without illustrations. As the century progressed, titles such as *Child Management* (Thom 1925), *Psychological Care of Infant and Child* (Watson 1928), or *An Inventory of the Habits of Children from Two to Five Years of Age* (Andrus 1928) became more common. The authors of these later books replaced wisdom with credentials, common sense with research, and larded their pages with photographs, charts, graphs, and sample surveys for parents to use in assessing the development and behaviors of their children. And, as the central focus of public discourse about children expanded from the aberrant child produced by macrosocial conditions of class and ethnicity to include the normal child produced by microsocial conditions of its immediate environment, the burden of responsibility for the production of a socially useful child gradually shifted from the state or community to the individual home and parent.[35] Normalcy was a given beginning point for most children, and the actions of its parents determined whether the child would be able to maintain it.

Many of these institutions—especially those located at state universities, such as the Institute of Child Welfare at the University of Minnesota or the Iowa Research Station—also distributed courses in child management to parents, as did the Children's Bureau. Although some historians of childhood consider these efforts largely unsuccessful due to a failure to achieve wide dissemination, they underestimate the overwhelming impact that this work had on ongoing popular discourses about children. By the 1920s, discussions of childhood in popular women's magazines and in periodicals devoted to child-rearing recapitulated the professional emphasis on the need for parents to construct an environment appropriate to the production of the normal child. At the same time, professionals such as Gesell and Watson published popular books that disseminated their ideas about childhood and its management beyond professional circles. One need only examine the masthead of *Parents' Magazine*, an exceptionally popular child-rearing periodical begun in 1926, to find that many of the leading lights in the field—such as Grace Abbott (director of the U.S. Children's Bureau), Arnold Gesell (director of Yale's Psycho-Clinic), Lillian Gilbreth (industrial efficiency expert), and Douglas Thom—sat on its board of advisory editors.[36]

Child advice thus became less and less simply a matter of offering homilies to help parents smooth over the inevitable rough spots that arose in dealing with their children. In the late 1910s and 1920s, popular child-rearing literatures paradoxically insisted that a child's successful development depended on its parents' ability to supply and regulate a beneficial environment for the child, and that raising a child was no longer an exclusively private matter between parent and child. Children were precious natural (and national) resources, and their proper management and deployment required—no less than any other rapidly modernizing industry—the expert assistance of trained scientists who could offer a full range of techniques and technologies that could be applied (as *Parents'* put it on its cover) "from crib to college." In 1920, the introduction of one child-rearing manual stated:

> The author has constantly kept in mind that most parents and teachers are neither familiar with nor interested in technical psychology, biology,

> or hygiene. . . . They wish to understand why children act in certain ways and how they can most effectively divert them from wrong action. . . . [I] have used terms which can be understood by those who have had little or no study of [these] sciences, though the suggestions for child training given herein are based upon data derived from [them]. (O'Shea 1920, 8)

In 1923, a popular child-training manual offered parents a complete system for evaluating and regulating the child, and warned the parent in stark terms that

> It is now evident that certain acts of standardized value must be given parents . . . that they may teach them to their children with the purpose of scoring the proficiency with which the child performs them. . . . Whatever the result of the tests the values of the acts should be recognized and recorded on the score sheet for the purpose of giving the child his social or character grade. . . . for the day is not far distant when society, and schools, as well as professional and business interests, will ask for a standardized and verified character score. (Clark 1923, 9)

In order that the parent could score her child on its development, this author broke down the child's actions and behaviors into "acts of standardized value" graded by age, such as "*At eighteen months* he should help set and clear off the table; wipe a selected dish or two; paste strips of paper to make squares and crosses; unpin safety-pins in clothing; unbutton and pull off shoes and stockings; use handkerchief and replace it in his pocket" (13, emphasis original). The text also encouraged the parent to take notes on the child's development and provided space for those notes following the description of each developmental stage.

As the decade progressed, the message delivered to parents in child-rearing manuals and periodicals was that the analogy between them and industrial efficiency experts wasn't casual: they were professionals with a job to do. A 1927 manual for a correspondence course in parenting published by the Institute of Child Welfare at the University of Minnesota put the matter quite bluntly: "It is only recently that we have come to recognize parenthood as a profession— to see that merely becoming a mother or father does not bring the knowledge and ability necessary for a good parent. By reading, studying, by acquaintance with the experiences of others, we may gain much that will help us in our task of bringing out the best there is in the child" (Faegre and Anderson 1927, n.p.). Like the professions of developmental psychology, pediatrics, and home economics that supported it, parenting had (at least in its popular representation) attained all the markers of professionalism, including a literature, study groups, and data sharing practices. In his popular 1928 manual *Psychological Care of Infant and Child*, John B. Watson, the leading proponent of behaviorism, would warn:

> The oldest profession of the race to-day is facing failure. This profession is parenthood. Many thousands of mothers do not even know that parenthood should be numbered among the professions. They do not realize that there are any special problems involved in rearing children. . . . In happy contrast [to these mothers] . . . the modern mother . . . is beginning to find that the rearing of children is the most difficult of all professions, more difficult than engineering, than law, or even than medicine itself. (Watson 1928, 15–16)

During the 1920s, then, professional and popular literatures began to describe parents as virtual middle managers in what was imagined as a national child-rearing project. It was their job to use the tools provided by professionals in the proper upbringing of their children, and those children would in turn grow up to be evidence of how well they had performed their managerial duties. "Parents slant their children from the very moment of birth," Watson warned his readers (1928, 39), "nor does the slanting process ever end. The old, threadbare adage, 'As the twig is bent so is the tree inclined,' takes on a fresh meaning. You daily slant your children; you continue the process until they leave you. . . . It has become so fixed in their modes of behaviour, and even in their very thoughts, that nothing can ever wholly eradicate it. Truly do we inevitably create our young in our own image."

Given the public and professional enthusiasm for imagining child care as a quasi-Taylorist enterprise in which parents played the part of middle managers—applying techniques provided for them by experts and gathering data on their child's development—Walt Disney Productions' decision to link its founder's middle-class, middle-American childhood to his passion for modernizing and rationalizing animation fit well with contemporary ideals in child-rearing. Yet what made this public-relations address particularly effective was an increasing concern for the effect of mass-cultural products on children. Disney's address wasn't simply analogous to that of child-rearing; it participated in the social and cultural construction of the generic child as a worker in the production of itself as an adult, drawing its raw materials from popular culture.

Consuming (in) the Middle Class

While the expansion of the progressive project from the local to the national played a significant role in the production of a generic American child, there were, however, other forces at work over which reformers had relatively little control. As efforts to expand public education and child-safe common spaces such as playgrounds succeeded, and as moviegoing spaces and practices became standardized, the children of the middle class were more likely to mix with their counterparts from the working class than they had been in decades previous. If the early years of the century had centered on assimilating immigrant and working-class children (and adults) into an American culture that was implicitly middle class and Anglo Saxon, by the 1910s and 1920s that project was expanded to ensure that the children of the middle class, who were beginning to participate in an emerging mass culture, didn't slip their class moorings and drift into the profligate ways from which their new working-class peers were being rescued. Even as it encouraged a democratic mixing that was beneficial to the lower classes, an emerging American mass culture threatened to undermine the basic progressive values deemed essential to the nation's future. As popular child-rearing author Dorothy Canfield Fisher put it in *Self Reliance* (1916):

> The whole trend in American life is away from the old, plainly visible, individual responsibility. . . . it is apparent that to muddle-headed people, and to unformed minds like children's minds, the fact that so often in modern America one may press a button and be served, seems to relieve one of any responsibility about what goes on behind the button. It is also apparent that for the naturally indolent mass of humanity, and for children with no experience in life, there is a great danger of coming to rely so entirely on the electric button and its slaves that the wheels of initiative will be broken. (Fisher 1916, 3)

Although the child of which Fisher wrote was implicitly of the middle class, and the looming threat of "slavery" seemed to suggest an indolence that led to downward class mobility, she still deployed the generic sign of "child." As the discourse of child-saving expanded to embrace a general project of protecting all children from society's excesses, appeals once based on ethnicity, assimilation, and uplift became more broadly applicable, and childhood became both an actual and an imaginary location for rewriting the boundaries of class and ethnicity. (In the era of *Plessy* and immigrant exclusion acts, the bounds of race remained far less fluid.)[37] Appeals for uplift, which had made use of middle-class fears about the effects of unwashed newcomers on American culture, were increasingly subsumed within a more generalized conception that the fate of the nation now hinged on the well-being of all children. This gradual reinscription of the meaning of the child in social discourse would work to overwrite the very terms that had recently been so important to it and would produce a generic American child which would require entrepreneurs such as Walt Disney to supply it with the products necessary to preserve and nurture it.

For the concerned parent of the 1920s and 1930s, then, a parent's hard work to regulate the domestic environment for optimal effect could in principle easily be undone by the child's consumption of items from a popular culture in which values based in class and ethnicity were often hopelessly jumbled. Although they extended to radio, cheap pulp publications, and even public education, these fears often coalesced, sometimes to the point of hysteria, around the practice of moviegoing. This activity not only took the child out of the home and into the socially unregulated (except for the small matter of Jim Crow color lines) public space of a theater in which it watched movies capable of transmitting any number of values, but which also encouraged the child to purchase ancillary products with which it might disrupt the moral efficiency of the domestic economy. Thus an important part of the parent's training as middle manager in her child's upbringing involved obtaining practical tools for regulating her child's consumption—in particular, its viewing practices. Popular child-management books offered advice on how to select movies, which ranged from a few paragraphs in sections on socializing or consumption to whole chapters devoted to the subject. Even the Payne Fund weighed in with help, publishing a book for parents and teachers to use in teaching children proper viewing tastes and habits, *How to Appreciate Motion Pictures* (Dale 1938 [1933]).[38]

For the most part, though, child-rearing books of the period discussed the possible consequences of lax parental regulation of media consumption in broad terms but offered little concrete advice on how that regulation was to operate. As manuals for managing the domestic environment, the texts devoted the bulk of their advice and parent-training to the particulars of managing the child's behaviors and development as they occurred in the home. For practical advice on how best to regulate the child's life as a public being and nascent consumer, women's magazines such as *McCalls*, *Good Housekeeping*, the *Ladies' Home Journal*, and *Parents'* offered features designed to teach parents what to look for in movies and how to influence the regulation of movie production. These articles encouraged the parent to attend movies with her child and to practice choosing movies that, far from being a detriment, might actually benefit the child, as did a feature in *Parents'* which suggested that "haphazard attendance, on the part of parents and children, at the local movie theatre is of little value, but careful selection of the pictures boys and girls see can be of real benefit in helping them to consider life values and right attitudes. It can prove a thoroughly educational experience" (Lasch 1937, 26).

It wasn't the city, the state, the nation, or some other associational group that was to be responsible for regulating the child's consumption habits, but the parent. This type of reasoning—with its implicit assumption of a middle-class, single-income household in which the mother was free to either attend movies with children or to closely monitor their public life—furthered the idea of the normal American child as developing out of a naturally middle-class environment. More than that, it also encouraged parents to develop a conception of movies and their producers that would contribute positive elements to the normal child's environment. And, in an article that offered to help parents in that task, and around the margins of which Mickey and Minnie Mouse and Donald Duck cavorted, Disney was singled out as providing the antithesis of the detrimental film:[39]

> The motion picture producers are not as much to blame as we if our children see such pictures. They say frankly they are in the business of making pictures for adults, not children. Ours is the responsibility of keeping our youngsters away from sex-filled pictures, eternal triangle and adultery themes, horror films. . . . Instead we should see that the youngsters see other types of feature films, plus the Mickey Mouse, Silly Symphony, newsreels, travelogues, nature films, and so on. (Lasch 1937, 112)

By the mid-1930s, Disney had developed a distinct advantage in this regard through the licensing of an incredible array of products—from pajamas to milk bottles, notebooks, wristwatches, handkerchiefs, and more—that could properly and completely fill the natural, middle-class environment of the normal child. Even the working-class parent who hoped for more for her child could purchase a piece of this domestic fantasy, so wide was the range of products that bore the company's imprimatur.

Yet since new movies appeared weekly, parents could find more practical and immediate information in popular periodicals. Beginning in the late 1920s, *Parents' Magazine* published a monthly guide to movies, which rated movies according to whether they were appropriate for adults, youths, or small children; included capsule descriptions of new releases; and urged parents to save each issue for future reference. (See figure 12.) This guide, *Parents'* assured its readers, was based on not "the views of one person, but the composite judgment of a number of leading women's organizations . . . and of certain other well-qualified reviewers" ("Family Movie Guide" 1939, 62). Nor was *Parents'* alone in this service; other family-oriented periodicals such as *The Rotarian* and *Christian Century* also produced guides for their readers along similar lines. *Parents'* in particular, though, went out of its way to recommend movies to parents, awarding one or more movies a month a medal of honor, as well as conferring special silver and gold medals on particularly deserving fare. (By the late 1930s, Disney won several of these a year, and the magazine awarded Walt Disney a special medal for "outstanding service to children.") The U.S. Children's Bureau even recommended the *Parents'* guide to concerned parents.[40]

At the height of struggles around the enforcement of the Motion Picture Production Code, during which the Payne Fund studies reproduced the normal child as the site for determining movie effects (and as susceptible to those effects), *Parents'* movie guide was emblematic of a number of locations where family audiences took shape. The guide was important enough in this regard that major studios often ran advertisements alongside it and featured its awards in their public relations. The guide was particularly well-disposed to Disney, forgiving the company, for instance, for rewriting *Pinocchio* because "the spirit of the tale is always enhanced by [Walt Disney's] imaginative treatment" and announcing that "The Parents' Magazine, desiring to encourage the production of motion pictures suitable for whole-family audiences, is giving recognition to outstanding films of this kind. It is pleased to announce that a medal has been awarded to 'Pinocchio,' the December, 1939, movie-of-the-month for family audiences" ("Family Movie Guide" 1939, 65). Given that *Parents'* presented itself as a reporter of the most scientific and effective approaches to child-rearing, endorsements such as these improved Disney's image as producing media beneficial for children.

Only one example of the operation of the idea of childhood during the 1930s, Pinocchio's achievement of the status of "real boy" at the end of Disney's film was supported by a matrix which reinscribed the class and racial underpinnings of that reality in a web of discourses and practices that linked the scientific process of isolating the characteristics of the normal American child to those of reproducing that child in the bodies and behaviors of real children. The popular assumption regarding children and movies at the time was that every child in the theater would partake not only of Pinocchio's triumph, but of Walt Disney as the motive force behind that triumph. To watch *Pinocchio* was to consume Pinocchio; to consume Pinocchio was to consume Walt Disney. To consume Walt Disney was to ingest the qualities essential to Americanness that were required for its reproduction in subsequent generations. In the

FAMILY MOVIE GUIDE

RELIABLE APPRAISALS FOR ADULTS, YOUNG FOLKS AND CHILDREN

ffice Hours (AY). Fast-
mystery solved by a
per editor. Good com-
or A—Good. For Y—
For C—Unsuitable.
(MGM.)

King's Horses (AY).
comedy in which a
star substitutes for a
For A and Y—Amusing.
-Little interest. 6.

Face Harrington (AY).
ding family man is in-
involved with gang-
For A and Y—Amusing
For C—No interest. 2-3.

the Green Lights
Intelligently produced
ma in which a girl
is torn between a shy-
yer and a young de-
For A—Good. For Y
ng. For C—Doubtful.
ot.)

Fury (AY). Realistic
l of labor troubles in
vania. For A—Strong
For Y—Grimly in-
. For C—Mature. 7.
at'l.)

er's Millions (WF).
nan struggles to spend
nillion dollars in order
it six million. For A
-Entertaining. For C—
sted. 7. (Un. Art.)

Melody, The (AO).
cant film with pleas-
ic. For A—Fair. For
C—No. 2-3. (Olympic.)

All Cars (AO). Fast
gangster melodrama.
-Fair. For Y and C—
ing ethics. 7. (Syndi-

Hurricane (WF).
character study of
d folks. For A—Mild-
taining. For Y—Good.
-Mature. 6. (RKO.)

(WF). Exciting melo-
about the adventures of
in the Michigan State
For A—Very good. For
C—Thrilling. 1-2-3-4.

al Richelieu (AY). His-
drama about the
uncrowned ruler of
For A and Y—Ex-
For C—Mature. 7.

THE BIRTH OF AMBITION

This poster, designed by M. Leone Bracker, expresses graphically the influence that good movies may have upon a child

Death Flies East (AY).
tery surrounds murder
passenger plane. For
Y—Fair. For C—Little
est. 1-2-3. (Col.)

Devil Dogs of the Air
Rivalry of two flyers at
air base, featuring
stunt flying. For A
Very good. For C—
exciting. 1-2-3-4.

Devil Is a Woman
Sophisticated drama
Spain. For A—Bizarre
credible. For Y and
interest. 3. (Para.)

Dog of Flanders, A.
Ouida's story with a
plot. For A—Interesting
Y and C—Entertaining.
(RKO.)

†Eight Bells (AY).
portrayal of human
to danger in a typhoon
For A—Great sea drama
Y—Stirring. For C—
citing. 6. (Col.)

End of the World, The
Propaganda for world
For A—Amazing. For Y
ture. For C—No. 3.

Farewell to Love (AY).
teenth century court
Sweden and Denmark.
—Good. For Y—Sophist
For C—Too mature.
mont-Brit.)

†Florentine Dagger, The
Young Italian believes
Caesar Borgia and
himself in murder
For A and Y—Horror
drama. For C—No.
ner.)

Folies Bergere (AY).
Chevalier plays a dual
this musical comedy.
—Amusing. For Y—
cated. For C—Little
1-2-3-4. (Un. Art.)

†Four Hours to Kill
Cross section of life
atre lounge. For A—
melodrama. For Y—
ethics. For C—No
(Para.)

†George White's
1935 (AY). Glittering
podge. For A and Y—
of time. For C—No
1. (Fox.)

Ghost Walks, The (AY).

12. The Family Movie Guide from *Parents' Magazine* (June 1935), complete with an accompanying graphic that depicts "the influence that good movies may have upon a child." A caption below admonishes parents, "Don't run the risk of letting your sons and daughters see movies that are harmful."

figure of Walt Disney, that essential Americanness joined naturalized markers of middle-class American culture with principles of industrial efficiency to suggest that the impact of industrialization and modernization (that is, mass culture) could be regulated by providing the child with a material environment and popular media infused with the values and behaviors needed for it to efficiently reproduce that culture in its development. For it was not enough that Disney's own childhood recapitulated that ideal development; it was also necessary to demonstrate that the many workers involved in the industrial process of animation would not dilute it, that the spirit of Disney himself was present in every phase of manufacture.

Disney and Efficiently Engineered Entertainment

Needless to say, the child's environment was composed of more than simply the furnishings in its home. It also included clothing, toys, games, toiletries, books, music, and movies. If parents were to efficiently manage their children's development, then even the products of popular culture, particularly of the mass media, had to be taken into account. By the 1930s a well-defined popular discourse around the potentially detrimental or beneficial effects of the movies operated in the United States—one that suggested that the means of producing mass entertainments could determine the nature of the children who consumed them. In the case of the Payne Fund Studies, it was not only the means by which those effects were studied—by electrical measuring devices, sociological surveys, and psychological profiles; a broader complex of discourses argued for the benefits of regulating the industry through scientific management.

Disney, it seemed, had just such an operation. By the middle of the 1930s, not only was the company distributing under its name a wide range of products for children's domestic consumption as ancillaries to its films, it was also working to link the efficiency of its industrial operation to the beneficial nature of those products. Depicting itself as an industrial facility in the business of producing children's entertainment, Disney let it be known that, like parenting, animation was a difficult and extremely labor-intensive art. By the 1930s, the Disney studios had grown from its beginnings as a relatively collective operation in which a small group of men shared responsibility for the various tasks involved in making a cartoon to become a highly complex and diversified industrial organization.[41] Between 1928 and 1939, the studios released 198 short cartoons, as well as the feature-length *Snow White*. A ten-minute film required roughly

14,400 drawings; *Snow White* consisted of over 2 million (Walt Disney Productions 1938, 36–37; Hollister 1940). In 1942, Disney himself told *Time* that it would have taken one man 250 years to have produced *Snow White* (Smoodin 1993). The company broke up its facilities into divisions that thought up and wrote stories, created initial and final drawings for those stories, inked and painted the drawings, created music and visual and sound effects, and shot and produced film—as well as departments of administration, housekeeping, and a school where artists learned Disney techniques (Hollister 1940, De Roos 1963).[42] In its studio tours and press releases, the company touted this division of labor as exemplary of its modernity, and as proof of its commitment to a Fordist imaginary of efficiency as humanized industrial practice:

> Walt Disney's rambling, Spanish studio in Hollywood, California, is a factory for making myths. A factory, because there the technical problem of producing the 10,000 or so separate drawings that go into a one-reel animated cartoon (some eight minutes of entertainment) is solved with the utmost speed and efficiency which modern industrial methods will permit. . . . In Disney's studio a twentieth-century miracle is achieved: by a system as truly of the machine age as Henry Ford's plant at Dearborn, true art is produced. ("The Big Bad Wolf" 1934, 88)

In a fetishistic celebration of repetition and standardization that recalled Futurism in its boyish optimism about the ultimate good embodied in the rapid and regular output of mass production, Disney encouraged depictions of its plant as a hypermodern industrial concern, as if perhaps the very regularity of the operation were a component in the guarantee that its products were beneficial.[43] "If a privileged investigator could stay around for the six months it takes to complete a typical cartoon short," an anonymous reporter for *Time* reported after taking a tour, "he would find it a highly efficient, if occasionally cockeyed, procedure."

> First step in the making of any Disney picture is the story conference, at which the Disney story staff gathers to sort out ideas. . . . [then] the story is adapted into sequences, scenes, shots, and the main action illustrated . . . with a series of rough sketches. A director is then assigned to conduct the picture through to its conclusion. He and subordinate music, art, sound effects and dialogue directors decide on timing. In a typical Disney cartoon, the action and sound move according to an intricate schedule in which the frames of the film are synchronized with the musical beat or sound effects. . . . While the musical staff prepares the score, the dia-

logue director collects his cast of voices. . . . The sound effects department records a third track. In the recording room, sound engineers then synchronize the three sound tracks on one. Meanwhile background artists have been sketching out scenes. . . . [and] the story is now ready for the animation. ("Mouse and Man" 1937, 20)

More than simply factories, however, Disney's facilities were often compared to scientific laboratories and were described in such obsessive detail in the company's public relations, from a state-of-the-art air-conditioning system that filtered out cel-damaging dust, right down to its paint-mixing operation. In its press book for *Snow White* (1937), Disney depicted the color scheme of the movie as deriving from "months of research . . . by the chemists in the paint laboratory" in which they developed "secret formulas" for the Disney artists to use (Walt Disney Productions 1938, 37). This public-relations language—whether lifted from PR releases or gathered on studio tours—was picked up by magazine writers and circulated freely, as in this piece from the *Atlantic Monthly*: "The pigments are made in the Disney laboratory. They are issued to the painters in numbered and sealed and inspected china jars, each containing just enough paint to cover the specific task—not for parsimony so much as to ensure uniformity and permanence of color tone" (Hollister 1940, 29).

Neither a motley collection of pouty, unreliable, and egotistical stars and directors, nor a slapdash collection of artists, Disney billed itself as a high-tech assembly line, a scientifically regulated industrial concern that required no external oversight because its own internal regulation was so meticulous. This very regularity, this scientific approach to the production of cartoons, placed the studio apart from those of the immigrants, petulant Europeans, and working-class hedonists who produced films of questionable value to American children. Disney's operation was apparently so well regulated that when the United States entered World War II, the studios had little trouble retooling their operation to produce technical-instruction and industrial-safety films. As independent producer Walter Wanger crowed (1943, 19), "If every American could visit the studio, he would have a new admiration for his country. There is nothing comparable to it in all the world. More experts, scientists, and technicians operate under Disney's roofs than in any other one organization in the universe."

That a company that was becoming synonymous with beneficial children's entertainments would have showcased its industrial techniques and employee relations might seem a bit odd. There is, after all, nothing cute and cuddly about assembly-line production or high-tech air conditioning. Yet the company's facilities played a substantial role in its public relations, and although its workers were touted as models of industrial efficiency, they were also depicted as members of one big, happy family, with Walt as their avuncular leader. For a corporation that was attempting to corner a substantial part of an emerging market aimed at children and families, this was an intelligent choice. Although until recently cartoons have been commonly considered children's fare, at the time this wasn't necessarily so. Certainly, other major animated works of that era—say, Betty Boop or the Merrie Melodies—weren't strictly "children's fare": they were often filled with sexual innuendo, cross-dressing, political satire, and explosive violence (see, for example, Sandler 1998). And, as part of the larger Hollywood movie-making industry, cartoons produced at the larger studios always ran the risk of being associated with a culture and a lifestyle that were often vilified as decadent and corrosive to American values. In the metaphysical fantasy in which the character of a producer was transmitted directly to the consumer through its products, to mark the activity of one's production as wholesome was to set one's product apart as wholesome, too. Thus, a rhetoric that stressed the industrial nature of Disney's plant was balanced with one that focused on the family nature of the business. The entrance to the studio was adorned with an image of Disney's "son," and its public facade suggested an environment given over to (well-regulated) play:

> Mickey himself, his hand outstretched in welcome, is perched on top of an electric sign which announces that this is the Walt Disney studio. The courtyard is divided, California style, into little sections of green grass. There is a ping-pong table in one corner. . . . At the extreme right is a two-car garage; a miniature garage in which two very small cars are kept. Name-plates proclaim that Mickey owns one of the cars and Minnie, his playmate and leading woman, the other. (Pringle 1932, 7)

At the center of this world was Walt Disney himself. Although Disney was little older than most of his employees, he was regularly depicted as a compassionate and wise father figure and his workers as playful and imaginative children for whom he wanted only the best: "Knowing that incessant tension also is fatal to work calling for intelligence, imagination and humor, Disney tries to give his artists and writers two days a week for play. His ambition is to pay his employees well enough for them to save for old age and still enjoy living as they go along. Success is worthless, he says, if health is gone at middle age" (Churchill 1934, 13).

At the same time, however, Disney was portrayed as having maintained a childlike spirit, one that informed his workplace management practices, hence his company's products. Referring to the new multiplane camera that his workers had developed for him, a gleefully childlike Disney was quoted in *Time* as saying, "It was always my ambition to own a swell camera . . . and now, godammit, I got one. I get a kick just watching the boys operate it, and remembering how I used to have to make 'em out of baling wire" ("Mouse and Man" 1937, 20). And even though Disney's facilities were industrial laboratories, this down-home attitude apparently made the official regulation of those facilities unnecessary: "With a staff of 1,000, there is not a time clock in the place. Disney does not want his men to feel that they are in a factory; rather he prefers a natural sense of obligation that goes with a professional calling" (Churchill 1938, 23).

In spite of the absence of time clocks, however, according to another journalist who took the studio tour, Walt Disney still noticed when some of his employees showed up late and left early, and he threatened punitive action. The author speculated that "such drastic measures would probably have taken the form of, say, closing the men's clubroom, free massage parlor, and squash court for half a day" (Hollister 1940). In other words, Walt was a father whose tendency to indulgence derived from his identification with his childlike workers, and whose impulse to discipline his employees consisted of temporarily suspending luxuries unheard of in most industrial facilities. (This article appeared just before the Disney animators went out on strike, complaining primarily that they were not being properly credited for their work or receiving a fair share of the company's profits.) Walt Disney was depicted as the ideal parent of his workers, one who ameliorated the rigors of a highly regulated industrial environment by investing it with his spirit of play and invention, and through the achievement of workplace efficiency by way of the careful deployment and utilization of his facilities, resources, and workers: "To discover in each artist the caprice he likes best to draw, then to harness that specialty, is just one more example of Walt's determination to use the best available person for every task, even if he has to make that person the best" (Hollister 1940, 699).[44]

The depiction of Walt Disney Productions as an industrial facility dedicated to the production of children's amusements, then, maintained a tension between industrial efficiency and artistic abandon, between regimentation and carefree play, not unlike that of the Seven Dwarfs in *Snow White* (1938). In this fantasy, personal growth was achieved by the subordination of one's self to regulation by a benevolent mechanism, as did the Algeresque, down-at-the-heels, damaged commercial playthings in the public relations for Disney's *Broken Toys* (1935): "In these modern days of mass production and super speed you can rely on the Walt Disney characters to keep their mode of motion and living right up to the minute. . . . In 'Broken Toys' the doll characters, in an effort to rehabilitate themselves, construct an assembly line on a par with those to be found in our automobile factories" (Walt Disney Productions 1935).

The guarantee of the benevolence of the machine was its inspiration by Walt Disney's ineffably American character, and by his paternal vigilance. The Disney studios were represented as a well-oiled machine that turned out products which were not only beneficial for children but designed for the growth and personal improvement of Disney employees. This was the channel through which Walt Disney's character made its way from his body to those of the children who consumed Disney products: the inspiration and regulation of Disney workers made them into conduits for his vision, less artisans than fabricators, or eternally apprentices, practicing the master's craft in a tightly controlled environment.

Disney's choice to capture the children's market by foregrounding its industrial practices, and even investing its characters with "up to the minute" Fordist impulses, speaks to the popularity of the discourse of scientific management in the quasi-professional, management-oriented child-rearing programs that were popular at the time. In addition, the company's willingness to appear a perfectly regulated entity spoke to prevailing concerns about the effects of movies on children. Hollywood during the 1930s was often depicted by its critics as an industry out of control, its producers unable to properly regulate the productive or personal activities of its writers, directors, and stars, and its products tainted by that permissive environment. Finally, Disney's exclusive focus on animation during the 1930s added to the company's aura of absolute control over its subjects. In an emerging children's media market in which concerned adult consumers were attempting to locate products beneficial for their children, animation offered an apt metaphor for child-rearing, in which parents attempted to invest their children with the proper values and behaviors so that they would develop the well-rounded character needed to compete in a competitive and rapidly changing labor market. Like Disney's studios, the ideal home was imagined as an industrial facility dedicated to the efficient production of well-regulated (and ultimately self-regulating) subjects, yet still grounded in the warmth and sentimentality of family life. Like Disney's workers, parents would apply the scientific methods supplied by child-rearing experts, tempering them with love and warmth, laboring to animate their children through a process in which regimes of efficiency would guarantee a product imbued with values and behaviors that would enable it to become a successful member of a democratic capitalist society.

Professionalization and the Production of the Managed Child

At the beginning of the twentieth century, the application of scientific discourses to child-rearing occurred largely in the colloquies of child-study organizations, and subsequently in the public appeals of child-saving. By the 1920s and the rise of Walt Disney Productions, however, the application of scientific regimes of child-rearing dominated popular discourse. A comparison of two passages separated by about twenty-five years illustrates this gradual but profound change in discourse about childhood. The first, from 1902, is by progressive reformer Jane Addams:

> The family as well as the state we are all called upon to maintain as the highest institutions which the race has evolved for its safeguard and protection. But merely to preserve these institutions is not enough. There come periods of reconstruction, during which the task is laid upon a passing generation, to enlarge the function and carry forward the ideal of a long-established institution. . . . The family in its entirety must be carried out into the larger life. Its various members together must recognize and acknowledge the validity of the social obligation. (Addams 1960, 144–45)

Deploying forceful rhetoric such as this in tracts and in the many public lectures she gave, Addams argued for the assimilation of immigrants and the working class through the education of their children, their "uplift" into a social consciousness taken for granted by their betters. Hers was part of a call for programs at the local, state, and national levels that would save poor children from conditions that affected them as a group. Needless to say, this rhetoric was addressed not to the people it wished to improve, but to a middle-class audience that was meant to feel responsible for its inferiors, and which was supposed to take action on their behalf.[45] The discourse of child-saving produced an immigrant child for consumption by a concerned middle class that was distinctly other than its middle-class peers. It was a child marked by its ethnic origins, by its class position, and even occasionally by its gender. That it would attend school was not a given, nor that it would derive any moral or intellectual benefit from it. This child's potential was primarily as a problem: either as a burden to society or as a potential criminal or revolutionary.

The second piece, written in 1928 by a leading expert in the emerging field of child development (with an introduction by Grace Abbott, chief of the U.S. Children's Bureau, alumna of Hull House, and herself an author of child-rearing guides) offered practical advice to the parents of *any* child, (ostensibly) regardless of its race, class, or ethnicity:

> Normality in the field of the child's mental life is concerned with his ability to live up to an arbitrary standard, set for his chronological age, in his intellectual achievements and his social adjustments. . . . The normal child is capable of meeting and adjusting to the everyday problems of life as found in the social, racial, and economic level to which he has been born, under what might be termed average conditions. . . . Our interest is in helping parents to understand why the problem child is often only a symptom of a problem environment, or that perhaps [the child's problem] is a common problem of the phase through which he is passing. (Thom 1928, viii)

This child-rearing manual, *Everyday Problems of the Everyday Child*, was essentially an expanded version of *Child Management* (Thom 1925), a pamphlet that the author, Douglas Thom, had issued three years earlier under the auspices of the Institute of Child Welfare at the University of Minnesota, with the support of the Children's Bureau. In both, the emphasis was on giving *individual* parents practical tools (from advice on how to design the home environment, to methods for observing the child, to charts and graphs for recording and understanding those observations) for ensuring that they were producing a *normal* child. And both are examples of how, in the space of twenty-odd years, the center of discourses and practices surrounding children and childhood in the United States shifted from a concern with the protection and salvation of children of certain class and ethnic positions to one devoted to the production of the individual child using norms ostensibly unmarked by race or class. (Although Thom referred to race and class in his introduction, the rest of his text outlined an environment available only to middle-class parents. Where photographic evidence was used in such manuals, the children featured were inevitably white, fair-complected, and usually male.) Although the discourse of child-saving continued in an ever smaller measure, child-rearing had grown from a cottage industry to a fully articulated social scientific enterprise that encompassed both child-rearing manuals for the middle class and an abstracted public child. Most significant in this change was the development and scientific elaboration of the concept of the normal child, and the shift in responsibility for the well-being of that child from social groups or institutions onto its individual parents. In this new discourse, the American child was no longer the product and responsibility of its macrosocial environment, but the handiwork of individual parents: "The home is a workshop which, unfortunately, often spoils much good material. The parents are the ones who control the destiny of the child and make his environment to a large extent. Their mental ability, their control of their emotions, their interests, particularly their interest in the child, their ambitions or lack of them, their moral standards—these all determine what the child shall make out of the endowment nature has given him" (Thom 1925, 34).

This new discourse did not replace the progressive paradigm, however. Rather, it reproduced the progressive argument for uplift within the scientific guidelines for producing the normal child. At both a professional and public level, the discourse of child-rearing in the 1920s and 1930s was essentially progressivism writ small: the middle-class home that had been both the ideal of reformers and the backdrop for early child study became the natural environment of the normal child, while the middle-class, Protestant values of deferred gratification, self-control, and thrift continued on as behaviors which were to be developed by regulating that child's relationship to its natural environment:

> Conforming to rules and regulations, obeying customs and traditions, being well mannered and properly groomed, all contribute to what we call adjustment to life; but one may be very unhappy and inefficient if, while acquiring these habits of conformity, he fails to develop a broader view of life, which embraces happiness, peace, contentment, love, sympathy, and the finer sentiments. These attitudes are absorbed by the child from the atmosphere in which he lives, and are not acquired through training. . . . The conduct of the child is simply his [instinctive] reaction to his environment. (Thom 1928, 39)

In this model, the environment itself carried those "finer sentiments" and the child absorbed them through its interaction with that environment. Like the immigrant child who might have received an education but returned home each day to the street and tenement life that formed its substantial behavioral matrix, the child of the 1920s and 1930s could be trained to act properly, but if the environment its parents provided for it were emotionally and behaviorally impoverished, that training would benefit the child little. Worse than that, it would be "inefficient"—the child's training would put it at odds with its environment, forcing it to use valuable personal resources to resolve the contradictions it encountered. In language that hinted at the concepts of equilibrium and harmony that Piaget was developing in Europe, and which would have a significant influence on the postwar notion of a natural child promoted by Benjamin Spock, authors such as Thom blended progressive notions of uplift with industrial methods and imagery of management and efficiency in which the normal child was an efficient child, and its environment a space designed to maximize that efficiency.[46]

Nowhere was this blending of the progressive idea of uplift—with its embedded assumptions about the natural and evolutionarily proper quality of white, middle-class culture—with the rigors of empirical observation associated with scientific management clearer than in the First Berkeley Growth Study. Conducted at the University of California, Berkeley, in 1928, the study was intended to do no less than chart "the mental development and physical growth of normal individuals, observed from birth to maturity" (Institute of Child Welfare 1938). This task would be accomplished by monitoring the development of children "from month to month and year to year" (Bayley 1940, 2). Tracking would include laboratory observation and measurement; home visits and the recording of parents' income, occupation, and education; photographs and X-rays; motion pictures of creeping and walking; and "observations of behavior in standardized social situations . . . [and] at eight and one-half years the Rorschach ink blot test" (Institute of Child Welfare 1938, 4; Bayley 1940). As significant as this array of observational technologies, however, were the parameters by which the researchers chose their subjects:

> In the group are 30 girls and 31 boys, nearly all of North European or early American stock. All the children were born in hospitals; this made possible the scientific measurement of each child from the first days of his life. The parents of the children were white, English-speaking residents of Berkeley. . . . Colored races were excluded in order to eliminate the complications of gross racial differences; parents not speaking English were excluded because of [language difficulties] . . . transient cases . . . were excluded, because it was our aim . . . to study these children from birth to maturity. (Bayley 1940, 2)

Framed as simple commonsense choices made to limit the statistical noise of too many independent variables, the study's guidelines reproduced, in a longitudinal study meant to locate norms, progressive-era notions of whiteness and of middle-class life as representative of the natural environment within which those norms occurred. The decision had a perverse logic: conscious decisions to practice racial exclusion were justified by the requirements of scientific sampling and the production of latitudinally verifiable results. At a strictly visual level, conformity in the sample allowed for the presentation of images of norms in which changes in age could be presented without "complications" produced by race for each gender. Far from exceptional, this was standard practice (see, for example, figure 13). And in terms of the production of scientific knowledge, it fit long-standing assumptions that norms generated by these methods—which were designed to set benchmarks for parents and researchers alike—would be applicable across race, ethnicity, and class. The

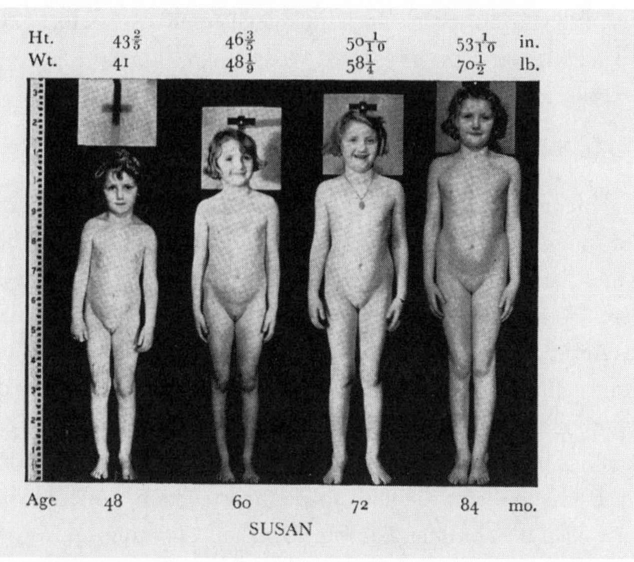

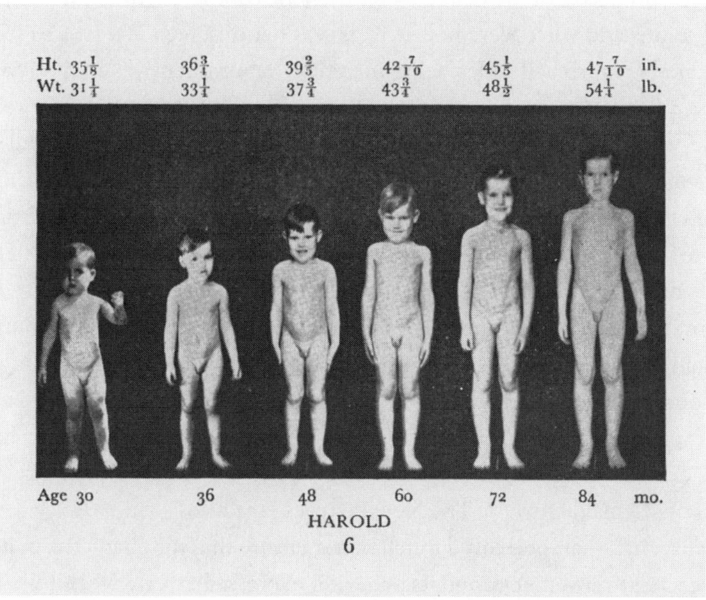

13. Two images from Lois Meek's *Your Child's Development and Guidance Told in Pictures* (1940). This guide for normal development were accompanied by differential growth charts (boys versus girls) and standard weights and heights.

supposition in the 1920s, and into the 1930s, was that parents were to use information generated in such studies to adjust their child-rearing practices, as well as the environment in which the management of the child's development took place.

Bodies and Behaviors

Management-based child-rearing discourses overlapped with Disney's celebration of its own industrial techniques in the particularization of the child's environment and the serial segmentation of its physical and behavioral development. Both addressed the parent anxious to manage her child's entry into (mass) American culture, and both emphasized regimes of management, control, and efficiency as a means of reproducing that ideal American culture. Film production in general—and animation in particular—offered a compelling analogy to the anxieties and expectations of parenting.[47] Even in live-action film, the director had the ability, through instruction, camera work, and editing, as well as the command of sound, makeup, lighting, and so on, to master the presentation of the actor and the visual field. Ultimately, though, the actor's expressions and voice were her own, as was her offscreen life. Not so for the animated character. Besides being incredibly labor-intensive, animation also allowed for nearly absolute control over character and setting. The very shape of the body, the face, the clothing, every movement and background—all were created by the animators, all were subject to review and revision. And the animated character had no life of its own off camera through which to bring ill repute to its studio. In an era in which the public was both enamored of child stars and concerned for their welfare (Eckert 1974), this may well have been a comfort, enough that one could even crack wise about taking advantage of an animated character: "*The New Spirit* (Disney) reveals the astonishing fact that one of the world's most beloved cinema actors earns less than $50 a week. That miserable retainer not only has to support himself . . . but also has to feed, clothe and house his three adopted nephews. This underpaid box-office paragon: Donald Duck" ("The New Pictures" 1942, 36).

More than that, one could much better ensure that the character, in its appearance, its movements, and its behavior, expressed exactly what it was supposed to, exactly what would be most beneficial to the child viewer. As the 1930s progressed, Disney made much of this ability, extending its discourse of industrial control beyond the bodies of its workers, to include those of its characters. As it had depicted Walt watching over and making best use of his employees, Disney represented its studios as laboratories in which its artists were busy observing, analyzing, cataloging, and reproducing the gestures, mannerisms, behaviors, and bodies of humans and animals alike.[48] Following its success with *Snow White* (1937), Disney expanded its representations of its studios as scientific industrial facilities to include images of its workers using photographic techniques as well as naked-eye observation: Walt was photographed sketching deer, and animators were depicted in word and image as watching live-action films and nature footage in order to better understand human and animal movement and behavior. This was particularly true as Disney features moved from a focus on human characters to films with animal protagonists, especially *Dumbo* (1941) and *Bambi* (1942), about which Walt explained in *National Geographic*: " 'In *Bambi*, we had to get closer to nature. So we had to train our artists in animal locomotion and anatomy.' Walt introduced live animals into the studio, deer and rabbits and skunks. 'But they were no good,' he says. 'They were just pets. So we sent artists out to zoos, and all we got were animals in captivity. Finally I sent out some naturalist-cameramen to photograph the animals in their natural environment' " (De Roos 1963, 178).[49] Even though Disney was producing animated fables, this public compulsion toward verisimilitude, specifically represented as a need to get "closer to nature," carried as its unvoiced Other cinematic practices that delivered the unreal and the unnatural to their audiences. Disney's complex public-relations address produced the claim that animation, as practiced by Disney, was an exacting industrial process that distilled and delivered essential qualities to its patrons largely unadulterated by creative interpretation other than Disney's. (In subsequent decades, as tropes of regulation and industry lost value in public discourse, Disney would couch its mastery over nature by dwelling less on its physical plant and more on figures such as the "naturalist cameramen" mentioned above, as an extension of its founder's will. See chapters 4 and 5.)

The company also publicized an in-house school in which newly hired cartoonists were trained to do the same—in much the same way that teachers at Columbia University or parents taking a correspondence course in child-management techniques were being trained—by learning to apply categorical systems of behavior and attitude to acute observation of living models to produce "real" and "natural" animated characters.[50] Indeed, Disney animators have even claimed to have borrowed from studies of child behavior in the production of their animated characters. Speaking in a "making-of" video that Disney released with its fifty-fifth-anniversary reissue of *Bambi* (1942), Marc Davis, one of the animators responsible for the title character, stated, "I took a huge book on baby behavior and every interesting child's face . . . I would interpret it into the mask of this young deer. And I think that this was the turning point for this character" (*Bambi*, 55th Anniversary Limited Edition, 1997).

In this case, then, the original work in which a researcher isolated and categorized a set of infantile behaviors was taken up and transferred to an animated character meant for a children's market, designed (at least as far as the company's public persona intimated) to deliver to the child information essential for its own proper character formation. And while in this instance the information was retrospective, at the time Disney quite proudly displayed its artists as they broke down and reassembled the particulars of movement and behavior. In a celebration of the panoptic, the company offered concentric rings of observation in which the public observed Walt Disney observing his workers, who observed the world around them in order to deliver it back to the public in its real and natural form. Sometimes, though, as *Time* happily noted ("Mickey Mouse on Parade" 1941, 32), Disney's workers were put on display all by themselves as they particularized bodies and movements like their counterparts in the industrial practice of scientific management, breaking their work into component parts that might be missed by the naked eye, as when "the Los Angeles County Museum . . . put on an exhibition [of] . . . a Disney animator at work, tracing the successive movements of animal arms and legs."

Disney represented its work, then, as the deployment of the latest scientific techniques of management, observation, and production to create the full range of human (and anthropomorphic) emotions and behaviors—from the wholesome goodness of its protagonists to the (attenuated) evil of its villains. For the middle-class parent attempting to regulate the attitudes and behaviors of her own children, Disney's success was comforting, as this fan letter suggests: "Bambi was to my children a beautiful experience, and subconsciously they must have absorbed a lesson which will make them better human beings. . . . You have proved by this kind of picture you not only can entertain but you can mold the character of people" (Corken 1942). For the ever larger number of parents enrolling their children in compulsory public school systems that would deploy observation, categorization, and management to produce hierarchies determinative of their future success, the studios' ability to turn the cold and calculating technologies of science and observation to the production of warm, generous, intelligent, and successful creatures offered an added appeal to its entertainment value.[51]

This last point is important: while Disney increasingly aimed its films at a children's market, their public relations in the 1930s and into the 1940s targeted adults. When pegged with the label of producing children's movies, Walt

Disney invariably replied that he produced "family entertainment." This was quite true: the movies were for children, but the PR was for their parents—who were expected to regulate their children's consumption of popular media.

Conclusion: The Production of Anxiety and Its Cure

> *All of [Disney's products] are aimed at the most vulnerable portion of the adult's psyche—his feelings for his children. If you have a child, you cannot escape a Disney character or story even if you loathe it. . . . The machine's voice is so pervasive and persuasive that it forces first the child, then the parent to pay it heed—and money. In essence, Disney's machine was designed to shatter the two most valuable things about childhood—its secrets and its silences—thus forcing everyone to share the same formative dreams.*
>
> —SCHICKEL 1968, 18

Richard Schickel's observation that the Disney corporation's web of marketing and product tie-ins created a cultural landscape in which the company's products were (and are) absolutely unavoidable is undoubtedly true—but it is incomplete. Like most critics of Disney, Schickel is too ready to assign to the man (and the company) credit for having woven this web all by himself. What Schickel ascribes to the corporation—the inimical purpose of colonizing childhood—aptly describes the social and cultural conditions surrounding parents and children in the late 1920s and early 1930s. At that time, childhood was considered a terra incognita that had to be (and was being) charted, analyzed, and categorized, with all of "its secrets and its silences" exposed, explored, and explained. It wasn't Disney who began this process, but the contemporary professional and popular programs of child-training and management. The "playthings" that children made use of in the act of self-production which their parents managed had to come from somewhere, of course, and had to pass some sort of scrutiny. Child-rearing experts such as Gesell, Thom, and Watson, and popular magazines such as *Parents'*, formed a popular/professional matrix for the evaluation, promotion, and distribution of the elements proper for a child's environment—while companies such as Disney produced the materials to be judged and passed. While this was certainly a boon for companies such as Disney, it was no less so for the men and women who were building careers and reputations by mapping the contours of the normal child, or for publishers who printed their work. There was a profound interdependence between the three: the experts needed exposure; the publishers needed both content and advertising revenue; and competitors in the children's market needed access to consumers.

If the child was at the center of this matrix, however, that didn't mean that the parent had been shoved aside. Child-rearing programs didn't insert themselves between parent and child. Rather, they enlisted parents as native informants and amateur researchers who were participate in a collective process of child-rearing that ultimately extended beyond the family. To be a parent at that time ideally involved the semiprofessional micromanagement of a child's environment, from clothes, to toys, to furniture, to books, to movies, right down to the tone of one's voice—all of which could determine (for ill or for good) the child's future as an adult and as an American. Even the parent who didn't subscribe to such programs had to deal with their influence in defining the nature of childhood at the time. And, as the nation moved toward universal public education, exposure to this attitude began to filter into the home as parents came into contact with a growing class of professionally trained teachers, guidance counselors, and school administrators. The terms of address made the stakes clear: if a child faltered in its development, the responsibility lay with the parents (most likely with the mother). This sense of the potential for failure and its redress in the assistance of experts informed the tone of both the advertising and the articles in magazines such as *Parents'* or *Ladies' Home Journal*, and in child-rearing pamphlets and books. Mothers were represented, both in images and in words, as living in a terrorized state of anxiety for their children's safety, well-being, and future, and as relieved of that anxiety by the advice and products offered to them (see figure 14).

Central to both the production of this anxiety and its assuagement was the notion that consumption was itself productive—that children in particular distilled in their emerging selves the values and behaviors inherent in the mass-produced items they enjoyed and would reproduce them in their adult lives. As Marshall Sahlins (1991) has noted, the "modern totemism" of twentieth-century middle-class thought has come to imagine consumption as "an exchange of meanings, a discourse" unto itself. When Sahlins suggests that use-values and virtues are attached to objects only *after* they have been consumed, he refers to the personal status of the consumer, the "cultural capital" gained (or lost) through acts of consumption (Sahlins 1991, 286; Bourdieu and Passeron 1977). Alongside this very personalized and individuating notion of a consumption that produces marginal differentiation in status hierarchies, there has developed, in the past century, an idea of consumption as a direct conduit between producer and consumer, in which the virtues and values of the producer are transmitted directly to the consumer. This has been evident in ongoing

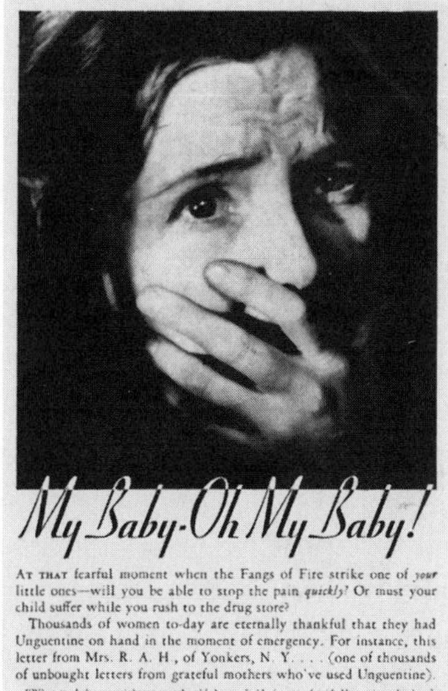

My Baby-Oh My Baby!
At that fearful moment when the Fangs of Fire strike one of *your* little ones—will you be able to stop the pain *quickly?* Or must your child suffer while you rush to the drug store?
Thousands of women to-day are eternally thankful that they had Unguentine on hand in the moment of emergency. For instance, this letter from Mrs. R. A. H., of Yonkers, N. Y. . . . (one of thousands of unbought letters from grateful mothers who've used Unguentine).
"When my baby was eighteen months old, he got hold of a can of acid. He got it on his hand, and when it began to smart he rubbed it right across his face and mouth! His face was like fire and little holes began to pit his cheeks. I literally smeared it with Unguentine. The baby's face is perfect to-day. Not a scar!"
Unguentine stops the pain—quickly! It helps Nature to heal more rapidly. Rarely ever is a scar left. And, being a *true antiseptic*—Unguentine guards against the danger of blood poisoning.
It is a duty you owe your family to have Unguentine on hand—ready to apply *immediately*. Be sure to get a tube from your druggist—to-day!

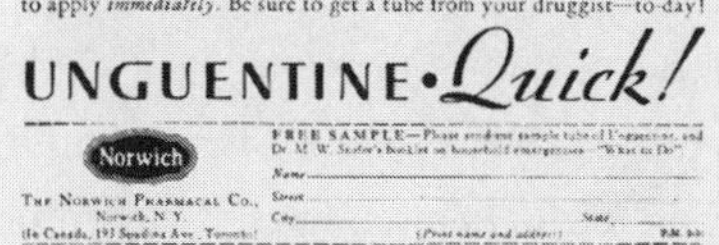

14. An advertisement for the topical antiseptic Unguentine, from *Parents' Magazine* (1931), stresses parental responsibility and anxiety.

discourses of media effects, in which either the noble or base qualities of a producer were (and are) imagined as delivered directly to media consumers. This idea has always depended upon the notion of classes of individuals—children, the poor, racial and ethnic others—who, by dint of their primitive natures, are particularly susceptible to the power of media commodities. In the quasi-Darwinian perspective of progressive-era child-study, as well as in its subsequent professional instantiation, the child's evolutionary recapitulation of the development of civilization—from its primitive origins in infancy, to its arrival at absolute modernity as a middle-class adult—configured acts of consumption as determining the outside limits of that development, the telos of that arrival. More simply put, a child that consumed products imbued with the sensibilities of the working class or of the Old World, would, upon achieving adulthood, reproduce in its worldview and behaviors the values and virtues inherent in those products. A child provided with an environment produced by modern middle-class sensibilities, on the other hand, would absorb them and would have the tools necessary to (re)create a modern, middle-class world for itself and those around it. Inasmuch as the working-class sensibility (ostensibly) concerned itself only with immediate needs and pleasures—the getting of money in exchange for labor and the spending of that money in immediate gratification of wants and needs—while the middle-class, progressive sensibility imagined the ongoing perfection of self and surroundings through the deferment of pleasure, the latter was widely considered more evolved. The child who consumed products imbued with middle-class virtues represented "the race's" best hope, a creature made aware of its own place in the evolutionary chain of being and of its responsibility to the evolution of its national culture through proper consumption.

Child-rearing, then, was far more than a personal affair. Parents were often reminded that they had a responsibility, both to their children (that they should have the best possible chance at success) and to the nation as a whole (that it should continue to stand at the vanguard of human civilization, and that the republic be peopled by as many self-sufficient citizens as possible). As the epigraph at the bottom of *Parents'* editorial page reminded its readers, "The future of the race marches forward on the feet of little children." Recapping the findings of the 1930 White House conference on the child, *Parents'* editor Clara Savage Littledale reminded her readers (1931, 9): "In the annals of the child study and parent education movement, 1930 will be remembered as the year of the White House Conference on Child Health and Protection. . . . Out of that conference must come . . . a deep realization on the part of mothers and fathers that the bringing up of their children is not an isolated affair in which they alone are concerned but one on which the life of the nation depends."

These observations went beyond the obvious fact that children grew to become adults, and adults were citizens. The suggestion of child-management advocates during the 1920s and 1930s was that everything a parent did in private—every word spoken; every purchase of clothing, books, toys, movies; every meal—had consequences that were ultimately public and national. The choices parents made about how to raise their children, and the technologies they deployed in that activity, were interwoven with discourses about what constituted normal life in America: "Observers and students of human life have come to realize that 'environment' has a deeper meaning than mere neighborhood. . . . This environment, so important for character and personality making, includes very subtle things as the amount of love and understanding or its lack, the co-operation and maladjustments of the parents, even such trivial things as playthings or the tone of voice in which the child is addressed" (*Child Care and Training* 1927).

At an ontological level, the child constituted a signal problem in the constitution of personhood in a mass society formed around democratic capitalism. Not only was the child transhistorical—delivering a nascent future into the present—it also acted as a bridge between the public and the private (Donzelot 1979, Gordon 1990). Where the immigrant child, as threat to and promise for an emerging American mass culture, had provided access to tenements and family relations for progressive reformers, the generic, normal American child invited, if not the actual regulatory gaze of the state, its perpetual potential presence. As Hamilton Cravens put it, "Presumably popular attitudes had not absorbed or digested all of the ramifications of the normal child. . . . If most children were normal, if, in other words there was no wide gap separating the children of the white middle class from those of other groups in the national population, then possibly the sons and daughters of white middle class might go astray if care were not taken that they were correctly and carefully reared" (1985, 438). In short, efforts to extend the domestic sphere into the public for certain classes through childhood had created the unintended effect of extending the public sphere into the domestic for all classes.

In the midst of reconfiguring and regulating this normal child, Disney was almost universally presented—either explicitly or implicitly—as making that "better type of picture" or book, or record, or doll that would help the child along. Still, although the company made much of its acclaim as the paradigm of beneficial children's entertainment, it didn't draw the discursive boundaries that positioned it as paradigmatic. The corporation's emphasis on its Fordist production principles helped align it with the prevailing rhetoric in childrearing, and that focus gained its affective hook from the representation of the company as a scientifically engineered family fathered and run by a man whose archetypal American trajectory inspired and directed the actions of each of his children/employees. His was the human face put on the image of science, and his life story—which the company told and retold almost compulsively—was the parable of the path to success for every Depression-era child. Walt Disney embodied a faith in the power of science and a paean to the purity and power of the normal that countered anxieties that the child's entry into popular culture necessarily sacrificed its future as a successful individual and a productive member of society.

In the 1920s and 1930s, the moral underpinnings of this middle-class sensibility were condensed into the more modern and scientific concepts of "efficiency" and "management." An efficiently managed environment reduced the possibility of unwanted social and cultural noise. The more perfectly the child's environment was constituted—from its furnishings, to clothing, toys, books, and even movies—the less distracted that child would be by the noise of other cultural messages, and the more able it would be to fully and efficiently integrate a middle-class sensibility into its worldview. For parents raising children who had far more leisure time and access to a growing consumer market for mass-produced wares than had previous generations, the problem was with how to provide an environment most likely to consistently provide products imbued with proper virtues, such as hard work and deferred gratification.[52] Disney provided products suitable to that environment, and child-rearing experts offered tools for managing it. What remained was to link that process to sustaining an ideal American culture, an "American character." The generic or normal child would play a key role in this regenerative logic, acting as a mechanism by which to reliably reproduce that character, the point at which to make the ideal real. To witness the social reproduction of that child, we will travel next to Middletown, a sociological fantasy of an ideal America that captured the popular middle-class imagination of the Depression-era United States.

3 IN MIDDLETOWN

Would you be interested in visiting a studio which has no sets, no paid actors, a studio whose assets are the creative minds of the artists plus plenty of ink, drawing pens, and cameras? Shall we drop in at the Walt Disney Studios, which in 1933 will produce twenty-six cartoons, thirteen of which will be Mickey Mouse, and thirteen Silly Symphonies in Technicolor? Perhaps you have seen "Babes in the Wood" and "Three Little Pigs" which have just appeared.

The first question that you will ask . . . is, Where do you get your stories? Does one man actually furnish all the ideas? The guide will tell you that the Story Department is one of their most important divisions. . . . Here, for example, is a tentative story outline for "Santa's Workshop":

> *. . . Story opens showing exterior of Santa's workshop at the North Pole—beautiful scene, snow falling, etc., Santa's factory buildings.*
>
> *. . . This dissolves to the interior of the workshop, showing happy gnomes busily operating the quaint machinery; all gnomes whistle as they work. Show various closeups of individual elves making toys. Everything is run in the manner of the Ford factory. . . .*
>
> *Santa is the big boss who "okays" all the toys. He is happy and very good natured, and gets a big kick out of the various things the toys do. Santa could teach the dolls to speak and say "mama." . . . Walt [Disney].*

—DALE 1938, 53–54

This Fordist fantasy of production, reproduction, and child-rearing, in which Santa Claus is a "big boss" who usurps the mother's job of teaching her children to say "mama," is a story treatment for *Santa's Workshop*, a 1932 Silly Symphony that was released, as one might expect, shortly before Christmas. The treatment found its way into Edgar Dale's *How to Appreciate Motion Pictures* (1938), a Payne Fund manual for teachers, parents, and children on the finer points of moviegoing. Beyond its obvious interest as an example of Disney's celebration of scientific management in both its production and its public relations, the passage offers several insights into the discursive matrix operating around childhood in the 1930s. In the first paragraph, the reader is treated to a catalog of the company's output for 1933, a demonstration that even in the midst of the Depression, Disney was highly productive. Given a question to ask her invisible guide (in much the same way the dolls were taught to say "mama"), the child is informed that an entire department produces the stories that she sees on the screen. It is collective production in action. Yet when the child reads down to the bottom of the passage, she discovers that the treatment is "signed" by Walt Disney. Perhaps one man furnishes all the ideas after all, and the story department exists merely to make sure that they are realized. Finally, Santa's "workshop" turns out to be anything but: rather than craftsmen involved in hand manufacture, as the term implies, we find the precursors to the Seven Dwarfs operating automated machinery in a factory. Finally there is Santa, a "big boss" who is good-natured and willing to assist mothers in training their children—supplying wholesome toys and investing them with his inherently good nature.

The treatment—provided as an example of upright movie production that yielded films good for children—is richest in its embedded assumptions about how the world properly operates. The passage gives a sense of the significance of metaphors of production and management, not only in the rearing of children, but in life in general in the 1920s and 1930s. At a historical moment when the nation's productive capacities were in question, when the destinies of individuals, families, and communities seemed increasingly linked to an ever more rationalized national economy, productivity and efficiency were often synonymous with right behavior and good citizenship. In the mid-1920s, before the Depression, when the economy wavered between boom and bust, new mass-production techniques and economies of scale generated an enthusiasm on the part of producers for industrial efficiency and scientific management, and an anxiety on the part of workers who feared that established hierarchies of skilled labor were being replaced by interchangeable, automated piecework. By the 1930s, the faltering economy began to produce similar anxieties in the middle class. This threat helped tarnish the luster of tropes of efficiency and gave rise to transitional discourses that sought to humanize the more mechanistic elements of management-oriented practices in home and in industry. The enthusiasm for locating and regulating the normal child—and attendant anxieties around those regimes—that marked child-rearing discourses of the late 1920s and early 1930s were not exceptional; they were part of a larger concern surrounding the development and potential collapse of new systems of production, distribution, and consumption. In a social and cultural milieu in which the immigrant (or the nonwhite in general) was associated with interchangeability and a willingness to undertake degrading and depersonalizing labor, and the "native" American with individualism and upward mobility, the tension resolved as "manage or be managed." If efficiency was the rule, the question remained whether one would be the object of that managerial gaze, or its subject. In this atmosphere, the white, Protestant, middle-class virtues embodied in the "normal" and "average" American (such as Walt Disney) became boundary markers through which individuals could hope to achieve marginal differentiation in a larger mass society. Disney products provided one avenue through which people could engage in the fetishistic practice of directly absorbing essential Americanism through consumption.

While the application of principles of scientific management in the factory was fairly straightforward—a matter of retooling machinery and adjusting worker practices—in society at large the project became more vague and difficult. Ideally, an efficient and well-ordered society would witness a reduction in antisocial and immoral behaviors—less crime and dissipation in its citizens—and an increase in social harmony by way of the common enactment of behavioral norms. This was the hope behind management-oriented child-rearing programs: the policing of potential social problems through the internalization of those norms in regimes of self-regulation. In the logic of scientific management, people who properly regulated their own behaviors in relation to accepted norms increased their odds for personal fulfillment while reducing the common social burden of external regulation. Efficiency benefited both the individual and society.

This was the theory. How was it to work in practice? Child-rearing manuals and periodicals in the 1920s and early 1930s provided models instilling a normal and regulated American culture in the nursery, and producers such as Disney promised to extend that process through beneficial media consumption, but participants in the program also needed practical examples of how that culture was enacted in daily life.[1] In the 1920s and 1930s, this requirement found an outlet in sociological surveys that attempted to isolate and catalog typical

American culture and behavior, the most famous being *Middletown* (1929), by Helen and Robert Lynd, and its follow-up volume, *Middletown in Transition* (1937). *Middletown* (a chronicle of four years of daily life in Muncie, Indiana) was meant to present a recognizable picture of what it meant to be an average, normal American, and what real American culture was. The Middletown books, as well as other popular contemporary tracts on the nature of average American culture and society, then, offer both an image of how social scientists imagined the where, how, and who of Americanness, and a sense of the willingness of literate Americans to embrace those parameters. If popular child-rearing texts of the period attempted to create regimens for the production of the normal child—and through that child a regulated American culture—popular sociological assessments of American culture provided an ideal landscape for that child to inhabit. And if Walt Disney was presented as the archetypal American, Middletown was the figurative ground upon which he stood, a schematic by which to read the civic and social fabric with which the company associated itself through its products and public relations. Where Disney offered to resolve the contradictions between the rational and the human, the unique and the average, Middletown provided a massed performance of the working out of that resolution, a dioramic exposition of the American heartland that had (ostensibly) produced Disney. For in the production of the public persona of Walt Disney, it was the landscape of middle America itself that generated the man.[2]

Middletown and *Middletown in Transition* did more than represent an ideal American landscape. These two popular sociological texts charted the transformation of that culture from its nineteenth-century roots in an individualism based in agrarian and small industrial practices into a rationalized and increasingly centralized mass culture and society. They detailed both the enthusiasm for and anxieties about this change as they were expressed in the daily lives of ideally average Americans. Central to that examination were efforts to understand the relationship between economic and cultural life, particularly the increased role of consumption in the relation between self and society (Lears 1994, Marchand 1985). With the rise of mass production—and mass culture—came the apparent loss of local control over the production of daily necessities, and with it a seeming loss of control over patterns of consumption. Particularly in regard to cultural production and consumption—of entertainment and social mores—local meanings and practices were being replaced with mass meanings and practices. As the ability to control the means of producing and reproducing an idealized culture slipped away, the focus on regulating that culture through consumption increased. In short, consumption—especially by children—became seen as a productive act, one that needed constant regulation, in the home and in public life.[3]

By closely reading the Middletown texts, as well as other popular works that dealt with the question of productive consumption—particularly Lillian Gilbreth's works on domestic scientific management, such as *The Home-Maker and Her Job* (1927) and *Living with Our Children* (1928)—we may chart that transition. This opens up an examination of how a discourse of productive consumption centered on the child and its environment transposed ideas of scientific management created for the industrial workplace onto domestic life.[4] As in the industrial psychology that Gilbreth practiced before focusing on the home, this discourse of productive consumption centered on the idea of efficiency as a means of reducing wasted effort and increasing individual satisfaction and social harmony (Graham 1997, 1998). Even as the Middletown texts were themselves self-reflexive—revealing an ideal American culture to an American audience—so was the discourse of efficiently productive consumption: efficient consumers were expected to reflect upon their own consumption and its effect on their individual and social lives, and to eliminate those products and practices that produced or introduced unwanted cultural noise.[5] The requirement to consume efficiently and (particularly for children) to consume representations of efficiency created a common ground between the microsocial process of raising children and the macrosocial process of mass-producing America that Disney offered.

Finding Middletown

Researched between 1920 and 1925 and published in 1929, *Middletown* (Lynd and Lynd 1929) is widely considered a milestone in American social science: it was the most famous "whole life" study of a community, and, as anthropologist Clark Wissler put it in the book's forward, the opening of the new field of the "social anthropology of everyday life." Before the Lynds' study, "no one had ever subjected an American community to such scrutiny," Wissler claimed.[6]

Funded by the Institute for Social Research (ISR), the study had its origins in plans by John D. Rockefeller to ease tensions between labor and capital by developing a national network of Protestant relief organizations (Hoover 1990). As part of that effort, the institute attempted to assay the social and cultural landscape within which that network would take shape. *Middletown* was just one of the institute's research projects, but it struck an unexpected chord with a literate American public. When the ISR found the Lynds' data too diffuse and unfocused and refused to publish their findings, the study ended up with the popular publisher Harcourt Brace. The book was immediately successful with a popular audience and received front-page reviews in the *New York Times* and the *Herald Tribune* (Hoover 1990). In years to come, it would set the standard for studies of communities, so much so that by 1948, in his popular survey of the social sciences, *The Proper Study of Mankind* (1948), Stuart Chase would devote an entire chapter to them, boasting, "In my library I have a 'Middletown' shelf of a score of volumes, which I enjoy collecting as others collect ship models" (141). Among those titles he would list *Plainville, USA* (Withers 1945); *Deep South* (A. Davis, B. Gardner, and M. Gardner 1941); *Preface to Peasantry* (Raper 1936); *Arctic Village* (Marshall 1936); *Small-Town Stuff* (Blumenthal 1932); *Home Town* (S. Anderson 1940); and *Yankee City* (Warner and Lunt 1941). On the occasion of the publication of the Lynds' second volume, *Middletown in Transition* (1937), Margaret Bourke-White photographed Muncie for *Life Magazine* (Hoover 1990).[7]

Basing their methodology on recent developments in cultural anthropology, the Lynds assembled a small team of investigators and moved to Muncie, Indiana, in 1920.[8] They depicted the idealized middle-American denizens of Middletown as American "natives," and the visiting researcher as anthropological other whose alienation provided him with the perspective necessary to interpret local folkways:[9]

> Having one's accustomed ways scrutinized by an outsider may be disconcerting at best. . . . many of us are prone to view the process of evolution as the ascent from the nasty amoeba to Uncle Frederick. . . . To many of us who might be quite willing to discuss dispassionately the quaintly patterned ways of behaving that make up the customs of uncivilized peoples, it is distinctly distasteful to turn with equal candor to the life of which we are a local ornament. Yet nothing can be more enlightening than to gain precisely that degree of objectivity and perspective with which we view "savage" peoples. (1929, 4–5)

Like anthropologists in remote tribal lands, the researchers attempted to join in the lifeways of their subjects; they became participant-observers in town life, renting apartments, attending civic functions, interviewing different members of the community. Their goal was "to study synchronously the interwoven trends that are the life of a small American city" (3). Following W. H. R. Rivers, the Lynds divided these "interwoven trends" into six categories: getting a living, making a home, training the young, leisure activities, religious practices, and community organization. They reviewed the census, town and state records, and the records of local colleges, newspapers, and business inventories. Muncie happily yielded itself up to analysis. City administrators provided data, as did local business people. Housewives supplied information on magazine subscriptions and domestic practices, and children replied to surveys about a range of topics, from school life, to patriotism, to sexual awakening.[10] In the preface to *Middletown in Transition* (1937), the authors reported that "Middletown" largely and gladly accepted the Lynds' interpretation of their lives. The editor of one local paper informed his readers, "If you have not read *Middletown*, you have not taken proper stock of yourself. . . . Lynd endeavors to take the bunk out of our social conditions, not as meaning [Middletown] but meaning America, and he does it rather thoroughly" (Lynd and Lynd 1937, xi). If the Lynds' reporting of the town's reaction was honest, the citizens of Muncie took *Middletown* as a fair assessment of who they were, not only as locals, but as Americans.

Contrasting their study to those that attempted to address a single social problem, or which took up a small social subgroup, the Lynds and their colleagues delivered to their public an ostensibly complete picture of life in Middletown, one from which those readers could (and did) draw parallels with their own lives. "A typical city, strictly speaking, does not exist," they claimed, "but the city studied was selected as having many features common to a wide group of communities" (Lynd and Lynd 1929, 3). (They would offer this last disclaimer repeatedly, just as often referring to Middletown as the archetypal American city.)[11] In a neat round of logic, they seemed to suggest that the lives of Middletown residents were applicable to Americans in general because they lived such generically American lives:

> Middletown can be lived and described only because of the presence of large elements of repetition and coherence in the culture. As one moves about the city one encounters in the city government, in the church, the press, and the civic clubs . . . and about family dinner tables points of view so familiar and so commonly taken for granted that they represent the intellectual and emotional shorthands of understanding and agreement among a large share of people. . . . Those persons who most nearly exemplify the local stereotypes thrive, are "successful" and "belong"; while dropping away behind them are others who embody less adequately the values by which Middletown lives. (Lynd and Lynd 1937, 402)

The ambiguity of this passage typified Middletown's drift from the specific to the general, from the local to the national. Were the "points of view" to which the authors referred as so "familiar" and "taken for granted" specific only to the other residents of Middletown, or applicable to anyone participating in the production of a generic Americanness? On the whole, both volumes suggested the latter: Middletown's citizens exhibited such uniform behaviors because their lives were largely untouched by the sorts of alternative (that is, "foreign") versions of life and of culture that they might have encountered in a larger metropolis. This made them more easily readable as typically American—both to the researchers and to their readers. Thus, *Middletown* became a sort of manual of Americanness—or a diagnostic gauge of that condition—and those who best typified its local stereotypes (or those who did not conform) could have just as easily resided elsewhere as in Muncie. Although later readers would find in the Lynds' second volume an implicit critique of the narrowness and repression of Muncie's social life, the very ambiguity that made the study seem to its readers so applicable to America as a whole (as either critique or celebration) undermined such a reading.[12]

Where the study was not ambiguous, however, was in the construction of its sample—and that construction provides important insights into the assumptions underlying the common understanding of the nature of Americanness in the 1920s and 1930s. The Lynds had chosen Muncie, they claimed, because of its "small Negro and foreign-born population," arguing that "in a difficult study of this sort it seemed a distinct advantage to deal with a homogeneous, native-born population, even though such a population is unusual in an American industrial city." This allowed them to concentrate, they claimed, on "cultural change" as it was experienced by a "constant native American stock" interacting with a "changing environment" (Lynd and Lynd 1929, 8).

In short, they chose Muncie to serve as Middletown because the city was largely white and well segregated (see figure 15). Like the researchers in the Berkeley Growth Study (see chapter 2), the Middletown team focused almost exclusively on the "native" white population of Muncie for its data because that population promised a cleaner sample.[13] More than a matter of mere circumstance during the course of the investigation, this was a significant element in the research design, and it carried on into the Lynds' second volume. In fact, in *Middletown in Transition* (1937), they emphasized the applicability of their findings to the (white) general public, informing their readers that "the median size of Middletown's native white 'private families' was, in 1930, 3.15 persons, a size identical with that of the median native white family of the urban United States" (Lynd and Lynd 1937, 165). In the interim between the first study and the second, Middletown had maintained its integrity as a bellwether of conditions obtaining in America in general—if one understood "America" to carry a rather specific meaning. And even though this condition of relatively absolute whiteness was "unusual in an American industrial city," the researchers

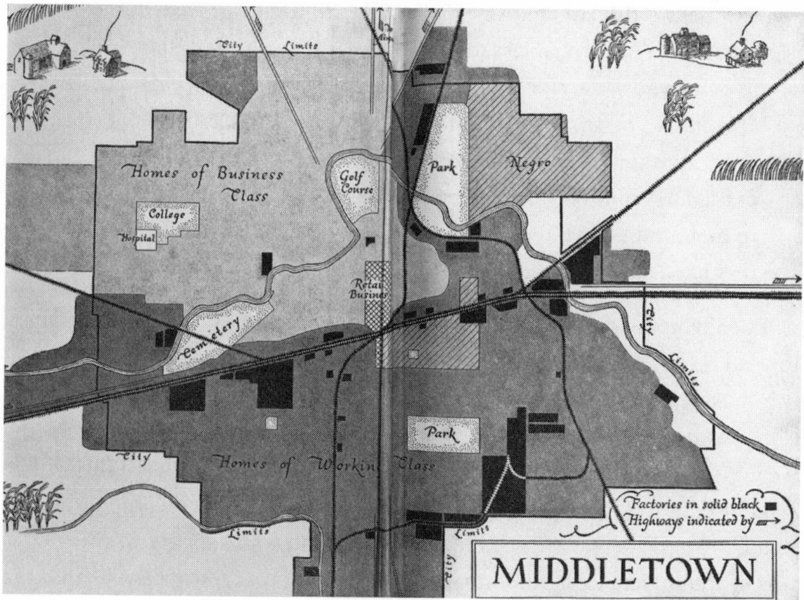

15. The frontispiece to *Middletown in Transition* (1937), which specifically depicts Muncie's African American neighborhood even as the book, and its precursor *Middletown* (1929), excludes nonwhites from its analysis of American character.

felt that it was beneficial to a study of cultural change in the United States occasioned by industrialization.

Not surprisingly, when race was specifically at issue, the Lynds' respondents tended to confirm the importance of whiteness to a generic Americanness. When the researchers asked high school students whether it was true that the "white race is the best race on earth," 66 percent of the boys and 75 percent of the girls answered in the affirmative (Lynd and Lynd 1929, 200).[14] While it might be argued that the Lynds' willingness to so starkly outline the white supremacist culture of mainstream Muncie was evidence of a critical distance from that culture, they offered no commentary to support that position. Rather, the researchers maintained a position of objective reportage in which their readers were left to determine whether the contours of Americanness they offered up were commendable or objectionable. In its essence, "Middletown" was white, and its culture was white culture. If race was an issue, it was so because of the blurring of racial and ethnic boundaries:

> Racial lines, according to the old residents, were less felt in the days before the Jews had come so largely to dominate the retail life of the city

> and before the latest incarnation of the Klan. Jewish merchants mingle freely with other business men in the smaller clubs, but there are no Jews in Rotary; Jews are accepted socially . . . [but] . . . they do not entirely "belong." The small group of foreign-born mingle little with the rest of the community. Negroes are allowed under protest in the schools but not in the larger motion picture houses or in Y.M.C.A. or Y.W.C.A.; they are not to be found in "white" churches; Negro children must play in their own restricted corner of the Park. (Lynd and Lynd 1929, 479)

Equally noteworthy was the Lynds' depiction of class relations in Middletown. The Lynds divided Middletown into two classes: the working class and the "business class" (1–23). Arguing that vocationally the meaningful distinction was between manual labor and bourgeois accumulation, and that the wealthy constituted such a small minority as to be indistinct from the middle class in either work habits or social practices, *Middletown* offered a view of middle-American culture in which everyone who wasn't of the working class was of the middle class, and in which the common expectation was that the children of the first group would find their way eventually into the second. In short, Middletown was a middle-class city, so much so (the Lynds informed their readers) that in 1936 a local paper would declare, in an editorial titled "The Middle Class Rules America":

> The United States never was a feudal nation. . . . As a result, while some became very rich and others very poor, the sovereign authority rested with a great middle class, whom we like to term the typical Americans. . . . It is from the children of these middle-class families that our industrial and political leaders have come. They have been neither revolutionists nor class baiters. They have held the government on an even keel. That is why the radicals have hated them so—the Reds well know that this middle class is the great obstacle to revolution. (Lynd and Lynd 1937, 446)

Thus, paradoxically, Middletown's anomalous class structure was part of what marked it as an archetypal American city. The absence of discernible class conflict, and a common belief in the inherent goodness of the middle class and its central place in the production and maintenance of a national culture, both of which were lacking in larger, more metropolitan settings, made of Middletown an idyll of consensus and cooperation considered essentially American.

What made this fantastic situation possible was, according to the authors, Middletown's profound middleness. The Lynds chose Muncie because of "the absence of any outstanding peculiarities of acute local problems which would mark it off from the mid-channel sort of American community." The ideal city should, they declared, "be in that common-denominator of America, the Middle West" (1929, 7–8).[15] The nature of the Midwestern landscape in general, and Middletown in particular, was such, the authors argued, that it produced in its citizens the bourgeois fantasy of a classless society embodied in a universal middle class:

> The Middletown workingman is American born of American parents. He lives on a Middle Western farm, has moved in from the farm, or his father's family moved to town from a farm. . . . He has not worked with masses of big-city men, many of them foreign born, where he has lost his personal identity and learned to substitute as symbols of his "belonging" the traditions and ideologies of massed proletarians concerning the "class struggle" and similar amalgamating concepts. He is an individualist in an individualistic culture. (Lynd and Lynd 1937, 453)

In essence, the average resident of Middletown was someone quite similar to Walt Disney. In contrast to the large cities of the East Coast, into which immigrants poured with foreign and alienating ideas about class struggle and common cultural affiliation, Middletown was the first stop off the farm, the place where rural individualism alloyed the cosmopolitanism of a rapidly industrializing society.[16] If—with mass production, mass media, and mass consumption—an American mass society was becoming an ineluctable reality, then a mass middle class forming in the Midwest presented an American alternative to the vaguely foreign "massed proletarians" of the big cities.[17] In Middletown, then, an extreme class position was virtually un-American. Neither extreme poverty nor extreme wealth, nor an overt identification with a class position, was acceptable.

Ostensibly caught between the nineteenth-century world of the farmer, small craftsman, and merchant, and the twentieth-century world of the middle manager or the line worker at the Ford plant (a Model A assembly factory operated in Muncie), Middletown appeared a perfect site for determining the evolutionary potential and direction of American culture. Its parochialism and racial exclusiveness made it appear a sort of natural laboratory in which to chart the response of a homogenous population to the arrival of mass culture. Positioning Middletown's residents as modern primitives in a contact zone of modernization contributed to a notion of the middle class as representing a "native" American culture affected by, rather than involved in the production of, a mass culture that was both subsequent to and distinct from it. In Middletown, the natural evolution of human culture, of which American culture was the pinnacle, offered itself up for examination and hived itself off from a metropolitan culture associated with an apparently decadent European civilization.[18]

More than simply one of many cultures evolving in parallel, the American culture of Middletown marked the vanguard of human development by always remaining firmly at the mean of existence.[19] "Every culture instills, whether by intent or inadvertently, some rationale of time into its members," they told their readers, "and this tends in the case of a given culture to constitute a normal pattern of attitudes and behavior, around which individuals, age groups, and sexes may exhibit variations. . . . In the main Middletown's culture teaches its members to live *at* the future rather than *in* the present or past" (Lynd and Lynd 1937, 468–69; emphasis original).

The "rationale of time" that the Lynds described was implicitly progressive, an ideal of deferred pleasure that a generation later would be celebrated (and mourned) in popular social theory as the (fading Weberian) Protestant work ethic. It also fit well with the conception of the child as a historically transitional object that existed in the present as an embodiment of a future as yet unrealized. To live *at* the future did not mean to live in a future as yet unrealized as much as it did to perfect one's self (or one's child) for that future, so that the person one would become would shape a better tomorrow. The Lynds' protestations aside, Middletown's status as an archetypal American city—the Muncie Chamber of Commerce printed "Selected as the Ideal American City" on its literature (xii)—meant that for the primarily middle-class readers who took *Middletown* as a blueprint for American culture, the progressive ideal of a perfectible future became a reality within an evolutionary rhetoric that celebrated an absolute normativity as indicative of natural behaviors. To be ideally American required ongoing reflection on what it meant to be American, and the elimination of those habits and behaviors that impeded the refinement and stabilization of an ideal American culture.

Observation and Efficiency

Of particular importance in working out that ideal were popular fascination and uneasiness with regimes of efficiency and observation, in which the home was sometimes likened to an industrial facility, the efficiency of which promised benefits extending back into the larger economy. An efficiently run home, the reasoning went, made for a more efficient and productive life for each of its inhabitants, the benefits of which were then felt in industry, the schools—wherever family members went. The most substantial example of this idea was scientific-management expert Lillian Moller Gilbreth's *The Home-Maker and Her Job* (1927), a fictional version of which appeared as her children's semi-autobiographical celebration of domestic scientific management, *Cheaper by the Dozen*. The book applied efficiency regimes designed by Gilbreth and her late husband, Frank, converting industrial time and motion study to the day-to-day business of running a home.[20] In *The Home-Maker and Her Job*, Gilbreth informed her readers that the homemaker had to detach from her surroundings, to see them as constituting an environment that she could analyze and, if necessary, alter, and which housed a social group—the family—the actions and behaviors of which she could also regulate. Indeed, Gilbreth argued, the home was the ideal setting for conducting an in-depth study of domestic lifeways because the wife and mother was uniquely suited to gain intimate access to all of her subjects. "Where can one find a group so accessible," she asked her readers, "offering such opportunities for observation under many circumstances many hours a day, often so varied in ages as well as temperaments?" (22). Gilbreth, as much as any other social researcher of the period, celebrated the technologies of observation—particularly the use of still and motion picture cameras—in regimes for streamlining social and material relations between "workers" (broadly defined).

Gilbreth urged homemakers to develop a database cross-referenced by task and individual by which they could monitor and refine a domestic environment specifically modeled on the factory floor. (See figure 16.) "Records and charts may act as . . . incentives," she told her readers, "and also are most important maintaining devices. They tell each member of the household where he and all the rest stand" (L. Gilbreth 1927, 48). More than simply a tracking device for the housewife, a proper domestic database became a mirror and lens for each member of the family, informing the child of its performance relative to its siblings, as well as to itself at different moments. For the home without a motion-picture camera, this was as close as one could get to an observational system that would allow the individual to adjust and improve her performance over time. The home that had a camera, of course, was at a distinct advantage: "If a film were taken . . . of you washing dishes, you could see yourself doing the work at the actual speed at which you did it and thus notice what rhythm and ease you had developed, or you could see yourself making the same motions very slowly, detect your slightest awkwardness, and find out just why you succeeded or failed at the work" (114–16).

Yet her enthusiasm would have been for naught had she not found a public interested in deploying those regimes. It is understandable, within the logic of capitalist production, that early-twentieth-century industrialists would view

THE *HOW* IN THE HOME

SYMBOLS FOR THE ELEMENTS OF THE MOTION CYCLE

Symbol	*Name*	*Color*
	Search	Black
	Find	Gray
	Select	Light Gray
	Grasp	Lake Red
	Transport Loaded	Green
	Position	Blue
	Assemble	Violet
	Use	Purple
	Dis-assemble	Light Violet
	Inspect	Burnt Ochre
	Pre-position for Next Operation	Sky Blue
	Release Load	Carmine Red
	Transport Empty	Olive Green
	Rest for Over-coming Fatigue	Orange
	Unavoidable Delay	Yellow Ochre
	Avoidable Delay	Lemon Yellow
	Plan	Brown

16. In *The Homemaker and Her Job* (1927), Lillian Gilbreth laid out symbols and colors for organizing a domestic time and motion study. The up-to-date wife and mother was expected to enter into a regime of self-observation in which she was both a time and motion expert and an experimental subject.

the introduction of scientific-management engineers into the workplace not as an intrusion, but as merely an operational refinement. It is less immediately understandable, however, that Gilbreth (among others) would publish popular books and articles extolling the same sort of regimes in the home. Yet regimes of observation and reporting were already well established and widely accepted in middle-class child-rearing by the mid-1920s. By the 1930s, in a *Parents' Magazine* article that purported to measure empirically a father's parenting ability, the author suggested that "this age of ours is an age of testing, of measuring, of determining. We want to know how much we have of this, how strong that is, how hot or how cold the other may be. The schools are attempting to ascertain with meticulous care the exact quantum of intelligence possessed by my girl and your boy" (Richardson 1935, 36).

Not only was there a newfound enthusiasm for empiricism, there was also a sense that it was one's responsibility to participate, and that perhaps there was no choice involved. "It is only natural and inevitable," the author continued, "that parents should suddenly awake to the fact that *we ourselves* are being subjected to the universal testing that has become the vogue" (Richardson 1935, 36; italics original).[21] Knowing that the eyes of social science were upon them might serve to encourage in fathers the activation of an internalized mechanism of self-regulation: "If taking this test stimulates honest, thoughtful concentration on the subject of fatherhood, it will have achieved a very valuable purpose" (77). At the same time, as Richardson suggested, children were being placed in a nationwide diagnostic grid by which the intelligence of each could be compared to that of any other child in the country. The same was true in Middletown, the Lynds informed their readers, where the comparative intelligence of a "cross-section of the white population was secured in the form of scores (Intelligence Quotients) of all white first-grade . . . children in the public schools, according to . . . the Binet-Simon Intelligence Tests, administered by the professional school psychologist" (Lynd and Lynd 1929, 36–37).[22]

While it may not always have been clear why so much data was being gathered, it seemed that the nation was engaged in an information-gathering project that permeated every aspect of American daily life. It was not so much that every American was gathering data for some implicit central authority, but that the act of gathering and correlating information was becoming part of the project of being American. This was true in the workplace, in the community, and in the home. In an article justifying the addition of a home-improvement section to her child-rearing magazine in 1937, editor Clara Savage Littledale of *Parents'* informed her readers that the term *child study* no longer meant the examination of environmental influences *on* the child. Now, she claimed, the purpose of child study was to "see the child whole," "to consider in studying him his home, his school, the community in which he lives, all the many interacting forces that affect his personality" (Littledale 1937, 11). From the perspective of child-rearing, then, the collection of data in the larger world cohered in a more profound understanding of the individual child. From the perspective of the sociologist—or the advertiser, or the merchandiser—the home itself offered a node for data collection that would have been largely absent in a society less centered around the single-family dwelling.[23] *Parents'* decision to include a regular home-improvement section opened the homes of *Parents'* readers to the manufacturers of domestic products even as it contributed to arguments for a "whole-culture" perspective on the child that contributed to a number of observational regimes.[24] Finally, it linked, by way of the child, discourses of scientific management with those of domestic economy. "The mother who enjoys her job as homemaker," Littledale told her readers, "who wants her home to express her family's interests, esthetic appreciations, ideals, is the kind of mother who makes home a vital, growing, beautiful place. This mother is no drudge but an executive in charge of a well-equipped, efficiently run plant" (Littledale 1937, 11).

Far from a private domain in opposition to the hurly-burly of the public sphere, the American home was a semitransparent realm that revealed to the community at large—particularly through the child—the talents of the wife and mother as homemaker. A source of anxiety and hope, in the 1920s and 1930s the metaphor of efficiency served as a means by which a home and a family could be compared to the American mean. The very idea of a "domestic economy," as much as it served a metaphoric function of structuring relations within the home, also linked that home as an entity to larger local and national economies via its consumption practices (which were imagined as productive of the behaviors and bodies of its children). As an organizational principle, it validated a conception of the home as part of a larger matrix of data collection and distribution (through advertising) in which production and consumption acted simultaneously as personal and civic activities. The Lynds observed in *Middletown* that following Coolidge's election in 1924 and the failure of an anticipated subsequent economic upturn, Muncie's local papers argued that the responsibility for correcting the problem lay in the community: "Within a year the leading paper offered the following prescriptions for local prosperity: 'The first duty of a citizen is to produce'; and later, 'The American citizen's first importance to his country is no longer that of a citizen but that of a consumer. Consumption is a new necessity' " (Lynd and Lynd 1929, 88). In this new America, consumption challenged citizenship as a central fact of public life, and economic activity overshadowed political and social effort.[25] Roughly ten years later, in *Middletown in Transition*, the authors would report that Muncie's press blamed "underconsumption" for the local effects of the Depression and urged its citizens to do more buying as an act of civic responsibility (Lynd and Lynd 1937, 17–18).

Efficiency, Community, and Anxiety

In Gilbreth's model (1927, 20), written for an audience of housewives, methods designed for the shop floor were directly applicable to the home because "housekeeping is an industrial process. Industry has reduced much of its procedure to standard practice, and this is equally applicable to and available to housekeeping." Application of industrial techniques in the home could only serve to further refine them, Gilbreth argued, after which Dad could bring them back to the shop. "He will find that not only does he transfer from industry to the home, but that often he will transfer methods of home to industry," she claimed (149), "for the laws of management are the same everywhere, and the success or failure in a home application may send one back to industry with a new slant on plant problems. Dad becomes a more understanding person. He comes to know not only what Mother and the children do, but what they think and feel. And this understanding helps him in understanding the rest of the world."

This approach imagined the housewife as both worker and manager, and the home as a potential backwater in an increasingly seamless industrial landscape. The ostensible purpose of applying industrial engineering in the workplace, from the turn of the century on, had been to improve the workers' relationship to an increasingly machine-oriented and rationalized production process. The Lynds (1929, 39–40) described this shift as the gradual disappearance of craft in Middletown's industrial life between 1890 and 1925: "Inventions and technology continue rapidly to supplant muscle and the cunning hand of the master craftsman by batteries of tireless iron men doing narrowly specialized things over and over and merely 'operated' or 'tended' in their orderly clangorous repetitive processes by the human worker." "The shift from a system in which length of service, craftsmanship, and authority in the shop and social prestige among one's peers tended to go together," they further noted, "to one which, in the main, demands little of a worker's personality save rapid, habitual reactions and an ability to submerge himself in the performance of a few routinized easily learned movements seems to have wiped out many of the satisfactions that formerly accompanied the job" (75–76).

This potential loss of prestige and satisfaction, however, could ideally be ameliorated by a circuit of intelligence and reflection operating between the home and the shop floor. Not only could the husband import standards and techniques of efficiency into the home, but the management-savvy wife could refine them for return to the plant. If scientific management entailed the loss of satisfaction in the mastery of craft (as the Lynds suggested), efficiency might ideally make up for that loss through an increase in harmony within and between the workplace and home.

Between home and the factory, though, lay the school. In Middletown (as elsewhere), "the 1920's were years of educational 'efficiency' in American public education and of yardstick making by which to measure this efficiency. . . . Education was becoming 'scientific' with a vengeance; 'measurement' was in the saddle in all departments, from teaching to administration; and administration ceased to be the business of veteran teachers and became a series of specialties, its offices increasingly filled by specially trained persons" (Lynd and Lynd 1937, 205). The 1920s witnessed the arrival of the guidance counselor and the school psychologist in public schools, and the beginnings of mandatory intelligence and aptitude testing for children.[26] While this entailed a loss of craft for the teacher (as it had for the industrial worker), and purportedly imbued the schools with a more regimented and industrial atmosphere, it also involved the more rigorous and particular tracking of the development of individual children. According to the Lynds, this was not coincidental:

> In 1927–28 the Middletown schools embarked upon a ten-year program of school planning and reorganization. Taking off squarely from the platform of industrial "planning" ardently sponsored in those pre-New Deal days by . . . Hoover . . . and commending the "many startling results" being accomplished by engineering intelligence applied to industrial problems. . . . Central to this ten-year planning and reorganization program was the redefinition of the philosophy of education in Middletown, and central to the latter was the emphasis on the individual child. (220)

Far from a mere vogue, in the 1920s scientific management was considered rational civic planning, and its most basic unit was the individual child. In Middletown, celebrated as a nexus of American culture, management described a way of life, and the application of scientific principles to the particulars of daily existence was simply common sense.[27]

In a similar fashion, Lillian Gilbreth (1927, 42–43) could reasonably suggest that mothers were integral elements in an evaluative network operating between the home and school, informing women that they could use academic data to improve their domestic operations and to develop their own testing programs: "In these days . . . when school children have examinations frequently and inspection daily, the home-maker can get all the necessary data without much trouble. . . . As for mental tests. . . . certain of the home force are apt to have been tested in industry or the schools. It is possible to give psychological tests at home and make a game of it with results of some value." From Gilbreth's perspective, this was merely respectful of women's capacities and responsibilities.[28] Describing child-rearing in Middletown, the Lynds (1929, 149–50) suggested that this approach was widely accepted:

> One cannot talk with Middletown mothers without being continually impressed by the eagerness of many to lay hold of every available resource for help in training their children: one business-class mother took a course in the Montessori method in a near-by city before the birth of her daughter; another reads regularly the pamphlets of the Massachusetts Society for Mental Hygiene and such books as a *System of Character Training for*

> *Children*; a few get formal help from the head of the Home Economics Department of the schools and from occasional state demonstrations on child care; a handful get hold of government bulletins.

In some instances, they added, that enthusiasm extended beyond the middle class, to women who were encouraged to hope for more for their children: "Forty mothers, many of them from the working class, paid over forty dollars for an installment set of ten volumes on child-training entitled *Foundation Stones for Success*; with the purchase went membership in a mothers' club where child-training programs were to have been studied, had not the club died after a meeting or two" (150). At the same time, *Parents' Magazine* sponsored parents' reading groups, devoting a section of the magazine to synopses of readings and study questions. As much as it was supposedly a private institution, inviolate and independent, the family was considered a primary site for the production of citizens and of public culture (Donzelot 1979). The benefits of this arrangement, although they did not necessarily accrue to the individual household, were imagined to be realized in the society as a whole: "With secondary education become a mass experience, the feeling has grown that education must not only be good but must be good for something—to the individual and to society" (Lynd and Lynd 1937, 222).

Personally, however, the Lynds were less enthusiastic about the application of industrial models of efficiency to realms outside the factory. The standardization required by the application of principles of scientific management, while intended by industrial engineers such as the Gilbreths to increase the number of "happiness minutes" of free time for anyone engaged in tasks that could be called "work," seemed too regimented, too great a price to pay for an incremental increase in deferred freedom.[29] This was especially true for children, whose ambiguous status as both family pet and laboratory animal made them both fitting subjects for the latest advances and the potential victims of anything that smacked of cruelty. Describing education in mid-1920s Muncie, the Lynds (1929, 188) painted a grim picture reminiscent of the darker days of child labor:

> The school, like the factory, is a thoroughly regimented world. Immovable seats in orderly rows fix the sphere of activity of each child. For all, from the timid six-year-old entering for the first time to the most assured high school senior, the general routine is much the same. Bells divide the day into periods. . . . by the third or fourth year practically all movement is forbidden except marching from one set of seats to another between

periods, a brief interval of prescribed exercise daily, and periods of manual training or home economics once or twice a week.

Given the relatively pro-labor sentiments underpinning *Middletown*, the apparent distaste with which the authors viewed these educational practices seems to reflect a personal concern with the loss of working-class autonomy due to automation, as much or more, perhaps, than a wider discontent with those practices. In the spirit of scientific objectivity and fairness to the sentiments of their subjects, however, they reported that "all this ordered industry of imparting and learning facts and skills represents an effort on the part of this matter-of-fact community immersed in its daily activities to endow its young with certain essential supplements to the training received in the home" (188–89).

The application of management principals in the home was not quite as simple as it was in the school. Scientific management applied to the industrial facility took as its goal maximizing productivity through efficiency. In the home, efficiency, applied with the rigor and consistency that Gilbreth proposed, might increase the aggregate free time in the household, allowing for more collective leisure activity, more time for self-improvement through hobbies, or for capital improvements. But potential benefits created by increased leisure time could as easily be wasted in counterproductive activities, such as going to the wrong movies. Quite simply, in regard to the moral uplift and ongoing Americanization of the child, efficiency as a device could work only when applied assiduously to *every* aspect of the child's life. Thus, leisure time and consumption had to be reconceived as a sort of work unto themselves, one that yielded the product of a child more likely to succeed, prosper, and be happy in an America to come. Gilbreth was quite clear on this point (1927, 150–51), suggesting to her middle-class female audience that

> Every contribution toward the laws of work and rest can be applied to the child's field. Johnny must have freedom—freedom from restriction but not from responsibilities. . . . Johnny needs to work. We can see that the work is of such a nature that it will develop him both mentally and physically as well as test his aptitudes and increase his abilities. . . . We cannot let him use the wrong tools or use the right tools in the wrong way. . . . And here again, it is our responsibility to see that he learns the right habits, for only by doing so is he really free. One may be a slave of wrong habits but he is surely the master of right ones.

Foreshadowing Pinocchio's brush with the salt mines, Gilbreth threatened her readers with the possibility that the child poorly managed would become a "slave of wrong habits" even as the child properly raised would benefit from diligent management leading to self-mastery.[30]

The ultimate benefit of successfully applied management regimes, beyond a more efficient household (hence social approbation), was the preparation of children for places in the new managerial middle class. As the Lynds pointed out in both Middletown studies, scientific management, more than increasing the wages of individual workers or producing more contentment among them, was producing a new middle class in the town. In 1929 they informed their readers that "the 'general manager' of the glass factory of a generation ago has been succeeded by a 'production manager,' a 'sales manager,' an 'advertising manager,' a 'personnel manager,' and an 'office manager.' The whole business structure is dominated by the necessity of keeping costly machines busy" (44). By 1937 and the Depression, they were more specific, and perhaps more critical in their assessment:

> The work of management engineers like Frederick Taylor in the early years of the present century inaugurated a trend toward functionalized management. . . . [and] the ratio of foremen to working force was somewhat higher in Middletown plants in 1925 than in 1890. But in recent years this specialization of managerial function has tended to move up into . . . specialized departments—technical staff, scheduling and routing department, personnel and training department, and so on—increasingly staffed by technically trained personnel rather than by men who have come up from operating machines and punching the time clock. (Lynd and Lynd 1937, 67)

While industrial facilities might adjust for a more efficient and complicated operation by expanding vertically and adding layers of management, however, in the home the extra duties that evolved out of a more complex regime of observation and regulation became the primary responsibility of the mother. Besides her regular duties of cooking, cleaning, and managing supplies, she was expected to manage the labor of her charges, in regard to both household duties and leisure.

Middletown housewives and mothers who answered the call to serve as managers in the standardization of the domestic economy often turned to periodicals to locate themselves in that project. "Most important of all new sources of information," the Lynds reported (1929, 150–51), "are the widely-read women's magazines. 'There was only one weak magazine thirty-five years ago from which we got help in child-training,' according to one mother, 'and it was nothing like the fine women's magazines we have today.' Such 'baby books' as Holt's *Care and Feeding of Children* are also supplanting the family 'recipe book' of 1890."[31] Although many mothers were glad for the increase in information, the authors warned their readers, they were also bewildered by the choices they now faced: " 'Life was simpler for my mother,' said a thoughtful mother. 'In those days one did not realize that there was so much to be known about the care of children. I realize that I ought to be half a dozen experts, but I am afraid of making mistakes and usually do not know where to go for advice' " (151). The idea that a parent should embody "half a dozen experts," and that she would become paralyzed by the possibility of erring in her domestic duties, not only suggested that the new web of information offered by mass periodicals was a mixed blessing, it also described the modern home in general, and the modern child in particular, as objects so new and delicate that simple errors could have profound consequences. Concepts of scientific management, and the trope of efficiency, were in principle supposed to generate for the mother and child previously unavailable leisure time that could be diverted into valuable self-improvement. That was the progressive paradigm of uplift operationalized, and the sincere goal of domestic engineers such as Lillian Gilbreth. In the hands of merchants and advertisers, however, the scientifically managed domestic economy became a specter of potential social evaluation:

> The advertisement of an electrical company reads, "This is the test of a successful mother—she puts first things first. She does not give to sweeping the time that belongs to her children. . . . Men are judged successful according to their power to delegate work. Similarly the wise woman delegates to electricity all that electricity can do. She cannot delegate the one task most important. Human lives are in her keeping; their future is molded by her hands and heart." (Lynd and Lynd 1929, 173)

Pressed to act as supervising managers in the scientific management of a fluid public/private space that spanned the home, school, and workplace, mothers were expected to regulate production, consumption, and the leisure time of their children. The message was reinforced in child-rearing manuals, periodicals, and advertising: the family was a productive unit. It produced future citizens and workers (or managers), and it produced social harmony through the integration of habits of efficiency into all aspects of daily life. The child who did poorly in school or the husband who slipped up on the job threatened not only their own futures, but also those of the family and society at large.

Both the anxiety and the enthusiasm deriving from modernized regimes

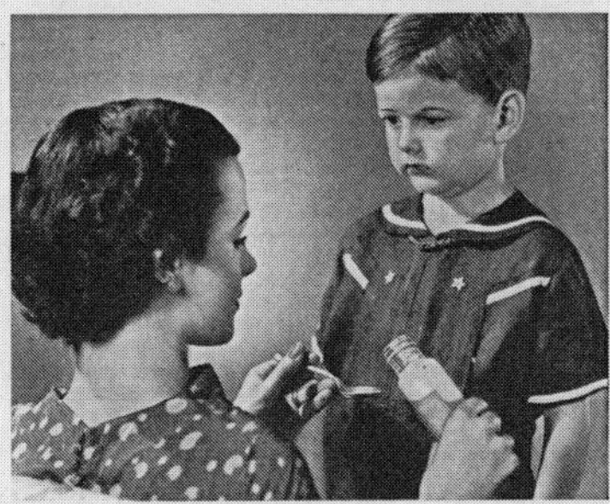

A Grave Mistake For
A Mother to Make
Giving Child Unknown Remedies without Asking Doctor First
No matter how limited a family's income, there's one "bargain counter purchase" no mother can afford to make — *without asking her family doctor first.* That's in remedies for her child to take.
Any doctor, any child authority will tell you this. Tell you to know all there is to know about any medicine your child takes internally.
Do this about *any drugs* you buy for your child. And do it, too, for your sake as well as ours, about the frequently used "milk of magnesia" given children.
Ask Him About "Phillips'"
Ask particularly about Phillips' Milk of Magnesia. He will tell you, we know, that for over 60 years doctors have endorsed it as SAFE for your child. One of the finest that men of science know. *The kind of remedy you feel secure in giving to your child.*
Now Also In Tablet Form
Phillips' Milk of Magnesia is now made in two forms. Liquid and *tablet.* Each tablet contains the exact equivalent of a teaspoonful of the liquid form, tastes like peppermint, easy to get children to take.
A big, convenient box that you can carry in your purse or pocket costs only 25c at drug stores. But — see that the words "GENUINE PHILLIPS' MILK OF MAGNESIA" are printed on any box or bottle you accept.
Safety for You and Yours

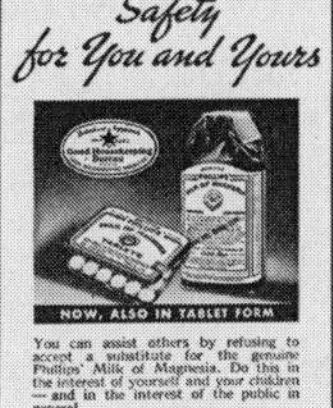

NOW, ALSO IN TABLET FORM
You can assist others by refusing to accept a substitute for the genuine Phillips' Milk of Magnesia. Do this in the interest of yourself and your children — and in the interest of the public in general.
PHILLIPS' MILK OF MAGNESIA

17. An ad for Phillips' Milk of Magnesia in *Parents' Magazine* (1934) stresses a mother's culpability in choosing outdated or inferior products while caring for her children.

of domestic economy worked to involve middle-class households in a complex matrix of regulation and evaluation in which acts of consumption became measures of the quality of the household's productive processes. Commonly imagined in the sociological gaze as indicating status hierarchies, consumption practices also signaled to the community the parent's commitment to her charges, her willingness to invest in quality raw materials and to apply them wisely.[32] (See figure 17.) Advertising played on the evaluative nature of consumption hierarchies, suggesting to the parent that the community always judged the rectitude of her management practices. "Each Middletown household stands an isolated unit in the midst of a baffling battery of diffusion from personally interested agencies," the Lynds reported (1929, 175n), "the manufacturers of laundry machinery spray the thinking of the housewife through her magazines with a shower of 'educational' copy about the mistake of a woman's neglecting her own children for mere laundry work, and she lays down her magazine to answer the door-bell and finds there the suave installment payment salesman ready to install a $155 washer on trial."

In the main, the Middletown home was "isolated" only in that the parent and homemaker was made to feel that she was being watched, and that her child-rearing and consumption practices were the object of community scrutiny. Deviation from normative practices—which would manifest itself in a cascade of inefficiency that would spill out of the home in the persons of family members—would be remarked upon, and it seemed that privacy could be purchased through conformity. Improper management of domestic production and consumption was construed as a personal choice with public consequences. In this light, the family was as much a public institution as it was a private one, and the mother, far more than the father, was its responsible administrator.

The commonly understood function for the American family, the Lynds told their readers, was to manage the primary formation of the child's behaviors and attitudes, which occurred in the first five or so years, during which its parents (i.e., its mother) constituted the central authority in its life. After that point, authority over the child and responsibility for its well-being gradually transferred to the community (Lynd and Lynd 1929, 132–34). Assuming that the "American" trajectory was from the nineteenth-century farm to the twentieth-century middle-class urban home (rather than, say, from the boat, to the tenement, to the apartment), the authors described a parallel path in which the child's movement from home to society recapitulated a historical shift from a more traditional culture to a public mass culture:

> New cultural demands pressing upon . . . [the nineteenth-century] . . . compact home and family are altering its form: geographical vicinage and permanence of abode apparently play a weaker part in family life; there are fewer children and other dependents in the home . . . activities adapted to the age, sex, and temperament of its members are replacing many whole-family activities. . . . the impetus toward higher education, sending an increasing proportion of boys into lines of work not shared by their fathers, is likewise tending to widen the gap between the generations in standards of living and habits of thought. (176–77)

In this model American community, parents were becoming semipublic functionaries as the family as a social institution evolved along with the culture within which it operated. Rather than petty capitalists who would hand over their meager holdings to their young upon retiring to the hearth, parents were facilitators of the domestic phase of the child's training before it entered a public life increasingly alien to the older generation. For the enthusiasts of scientific management in Middletown, the end product of the proper management of children, the increase in efficiency in their care, would be personality types most likely to be viable in the culture, rather than dissonant types that would impose a burden on that culture, impeding its evolution.

For those less certain about the benefits of efficiency applied to the child, or of their ability to properly apply its regimes, discourses of scientific management represented the possibility of a failure with both personal and social consequences. In the early 1930s, the concept still carried currency in the domestic arena (see figure 18). By 1937, however, one writer for *Parents'* would argue for a reaction against "the cult which believed that a cool and scientific objectivity provided the best environment for children" and that "parenthood is not 'just another kind of profession.' It is a relationship springing from instinctive needs and physical experiences as deep as life and which, before any other approach can become effective, must be accepted on this level" (Wolf 1937, 88). In a tone which suggested that management-oriented approaches to child-rearing were more popular than they should have been, the author demanded of her readers, "Which is the more important for four-year-old Billy, that he should get to bed punctually at six o'clock as the book says or that he should remain up awhile longer and so have a few minutes in which to make his father's acquaintance?" (21). Transitional discourses such as this signaled both the continued dominance of management-oriented methods, and the willingness of publishers and editors to countenance alternative or oppositional approaches. Quite simply, while the 1920s marked the heyday of popular and professional discourses of efficiency—both within and outside child-rearing—during the 1930s those discourses, though still widely deployed, increasingly were called into question.

Hence the aptness of the title of the Lynds' second volume: *Middletown in Transition* (1937). Beyond the stresses caused by industrialization and the ongoing implementation of technologies of mass production during the first three decades of the century, the introduction of the mass media of radio and the movies and the implementation of compulsory mass education, the Depression promised a massive reorganization of the day-to-day lives of the people of the United States. The social and cultural life of the country seemed precariously balanced between excesses of control and chaos. The overall trend—in economics, in technology, in politics—appeared to tend toward increased rationalization, but the ability of any one entity to control or comprehend that change seemed far less certain. Outside the workplace, the metaphor of efficiency was invoked as a talisman against the irrationality of rapid change, a

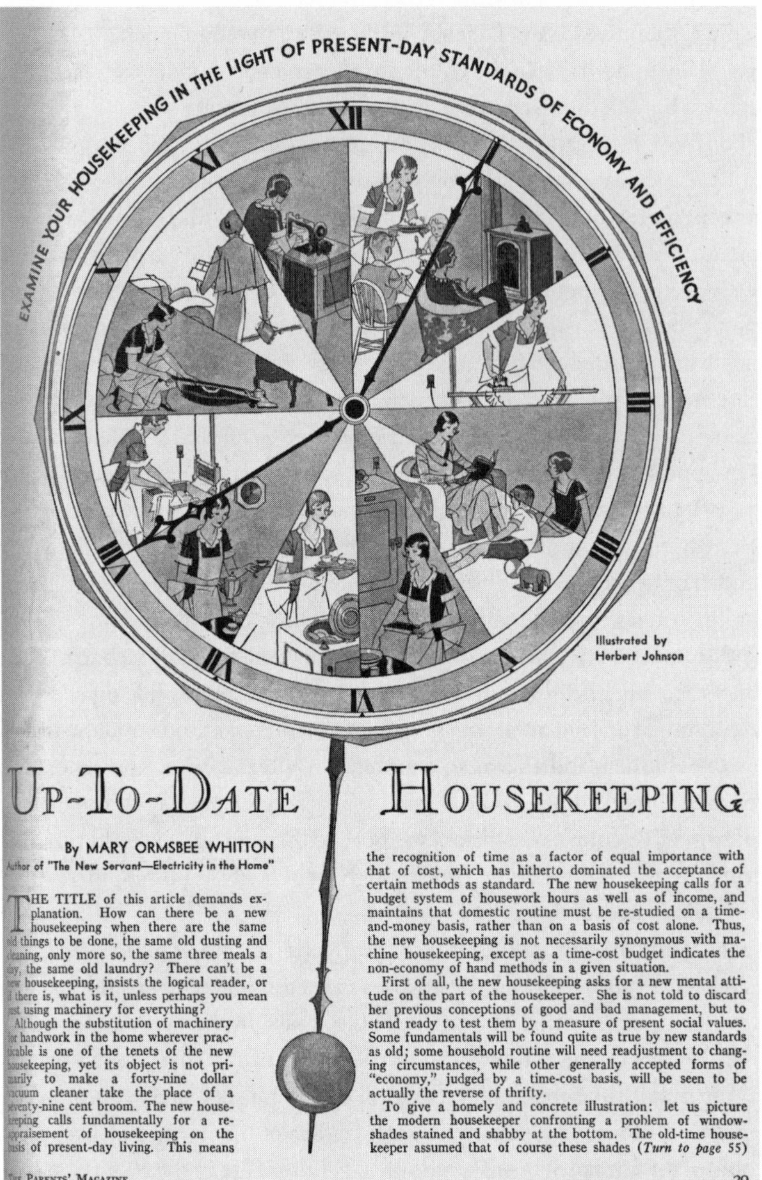

EXAMINE YOUR HOUSEKEEPING IN THE LIGHT OF PRESENT-DAY STANDARDS OF ECONOMY AND EFFICIENCY

Illustrated by Herbert Johnson

Up-To-Date Housekeeping

By MARY ORMSBEE WHITTON
Author of "The New Servant—Electricity in the Home"

THE TITLE of this article demands explanation. How can there be a new housekeeping when there are the same old things to be done, the same old dusting and cleaning, only more so, the same three meals a day, the same old laundry? There can't be a new housekeeping, insists the logical reader, or if there is, what is it, unless perhaps you mean just using machinery for everything?

Although the substitution of machinery for handwork in the home wherever practicable is one of the tenets of the new housekeeping, yet its object is not primarily to make a forty-nine dollar vacuum cleaner take the place of a seventy-nine cent broom. The new housekeeping calls fundamentally for a reappraisement of housekeeping on the basis of present-day living. This means the recognition of time as a factor of equal importance with that of cost, which has hitherto dominated the acceptance of certain methods as standard. The new housekeeping calls for a budget system of housework hours as well as of income, and maintains that domestic routine must be re-studied on a time-and-money basis, rather than on a basis of cost alone. Thus, the new housekeeping is not necessarily synonymous with machine housekeeping, except as a time-cost budget indicates the non-economy of hand methods in a given situation.

First of all, the new housekeeping asks for a new mental attitude on the part of the housekeeper. She is not told to discard her previous conceptions of good and bad management, but to stand ready to test them by a measure of present social values. Some fundamentals will be found quite as true by new standards as old; some household routine will need readjustment to changing circumstances, while other generally accepted forms of "economy," judged by a time-cost basis, will be seen to be actually the reverse of thrifty.

To give a homely and concrete illustration: let us picture the modern housekeeper confronting a problem of window-shades stained and shabby at the bottom. The old-time housekeeper assumed that of course these shades (*Turn to page 55*)

THE PARENTS' MAGAZINE 29

18. A *Parents' Magazine* article from June 1931 outlines practices of domestic scientific management and the benefits that accrue to the woman in charge of a more efficient home.

means of stabilizing communities and households in flux. And yet, too much scientific management seemed only to encourage the baffling process of rationalization, while too little threatened exclusion from the ongoing (if faltering) national socioeconomic enterprise.

Far from offering an impediment to producers such as Disney, however, the anxieties and contradictions that arose as people attempted to practice that contradictory Americanness did not entirely dampen their receptiveness to appeals based around management and efficiency. Rather, like Santa Walt, who taught the dolls that would teach the daughters to say "mama," appeals to efficiency by advertisers and in public relations suggested a burden shared by producers whose expertise could provide a packaged, ideal Americanness, an aid for a parent whose success as a middle manager would be gauged by the quality of her output—her children. Coupled with a program of weaving its products into the social relations and practices that signified civic engagement, this approach yielded both material success and social prestige for Disney. The many links between the public and the private, between citizenship and personhood, provided affective and practical avenues into the lives of citizen consumers.

Though the actuality of a seamless social network extending from the home, through school, and into the workplace—or temporally from birth, through childhood, and into a distant adulthood—was tenuous, the approximation of that matrix obtained signal importance in the 1930s, both for consumers seeking to engage in efficient domestic management and for producers attempting to insert themselves into the fabric of daily life. According to the Lynds (1929, 285–86), the overall tendency in Middletown was toward increasing organization and participation: "While the city has grown less than three and one-half fold [since 1890], adult social clubs have increased from twenty-one to 129, church adult social clubs have increased from eight to 101, adult benevolent groups, trade unions, and the group of literary, artistic, and musical clubs have each doubled, business and professional groups have increased from one to nine and civic clubs . . . from one to eleven." In particular, they informed their readers, "the current of organization has apparently run even more rapidly in the . . . juvenile clubs, as national organizations such as the Boy Scouts and Girl Reserves have increased in Middletown from zero to ten groups. . . . Organized juvenile clubs of all kinds have increased from six . . . in 1890 to ninety five . . . [in 1925]" (286). For producers such as Disney, a middle-class investment in an Americanness linked to belonging, a tempered efficiency, and normality provided not only a set of sites for the promotion of their products, but also a set of discourses and practices within which to frame those products. For Disney, that location (which Disneyland's Main Street,

U.S.A., would reprise) bore a striking resemblance to Main Street, Middletown; and its address suggested a transitional discourse of scientific management tempered by the humanizing force of Walt Disney, whose essential Americanness and love of things natural provided him with the sort of holistic vision that the parent of the 1930s was expected to cultivate. Although Disney would not take full advantage of it until the 1950s, the loosely knit matrix of schools, clubs, and social organizations provided an orderly terrain within which to create an apparent local presence for the company, and a way to further encourage a practice of benign social engineering through consumption.

Disney Comes to Middletown

The transition that Middletown was experiencing was not simply one of adjusting to new regimes of efficiency at work in the home. It was, the Lynds suggested, integrating into an ever more organized American mass society—and one of the significant forces behind that integration was the rapid expansion of mass media. Even in 1929, they reported that radio (for instance) was operating, "with national advertising, syndicated newspapers, and other means of large-scale diffusion, as yet another means of standardizing many of Middletown's habits. Indeed at no point is one brought up more sharply against the impossibility of studying Middletown as a self-contained, self-starting community than when one watches these space-binding leisure-time inventions imported from without—automobile, motion picture, and radio—reshaping the city" (Lynd and Lynd 1929, 271).

Through its integration into a rapidly coalescing national network of mass media, they argued, the ideal American middle class was confronting a loss of control over the means of enculturating its children. "Some high-school teachers are convinced that the movies are a powerful factor in bringing about the 'early sophistication' of the young and the relaxing of social taboos," the Lynds (1929, 267) informed their readers. More specifically, they suggested, the movies, among other media, were shaping children negatively, directing them away from middle-class norms:

> One working class mother frankly welcomes the movies as an aid in child-rearing, saying, "I send my daughter because a girl has to learn the ways of the world somehow and the movies are a good safe way." The judge of the juvenile court lists the movies as one of the "big four" causes of local juvenile delinquency, believing that the disregard of group mores by the young is definitely related to the witnessing week after week of fictitious

behavior sequences that habitually link the taking of long chances and the happy ending. (267–68)

In Middletown (as elsewhere), parents and other concerned members of the middle class organized as a countervailing force against the creeping influence of the lower classes through those media. A working-class mother might have been willing to allow the movies to indiscriminately educate her daughter, but the guiding lights of the community—its teachers and judges—saw unregulated movie consumption as a potential path to ruin. As others had suggested, the movies were a medium through which the very nature of its makers were transmitted to its consumers: "While the community attempts to safeguard its schools from commercially intent private hands, this powerful new educational instrument, which has taken Middletown unawares, remains in the hands of a group of men—an ex-peanut-stand proprietor, an ex-bicycle racer and race promoter, and so on—whose primary concern is making money" (1929, 268). At the same time, the Lynds observed, movie houses were locations in which the classes mixed, and which reduced the amount of time families spent together in meaningful interaction. "The decentralizing tendency of the movies upon the family," they argued, "is further indicated by the fact that only 21 per cent. of 337 boys and 33 per cent. of 423 girls in the three upper years of high school go to the movies more often with their parents than without them" (264–65).

In other words, the movies—both as a social event and as a means of understanding the world—were encroaching on the family as the locus for the socialization and enculturation of children.[33] Nor were the people of the Middletown of the 1920s likely to counter this situation through the screening of more edifying fare. In Middletown in the late 1920s, they informed their readers, "the program of the five cheaper houses is usually a 'Wild West' feature, and a comedy; of the four better houses, one feature film, usually a 'society' film but frequently Wild West or comedy, one short comedy, or if the feature is a comedy, an educational film . . . and a news film. In general, people do not go to the movies to be instructed; the Yale Press series of historical films . . . were a flat failure and the local exhibitor discontinued them after the second picture" (265).

The only possible benefit that the movies might have had on Middletown's denizens, the Lynds suggested, was in exposing the working class to the culture of their betters, as "week after week at the movies people in all walks of life enter, often with an intensity of emotion that is apparently one of the most potent means of reconditioning habits, into the intimacies of Fifth Avenue drawing rooms and English country houses, watching the habitual activities of a different cultural level" (1929, 82n). Whether this would have any effect other than to create a desire for more consumer goods was open to question, but at least those working-class individuals who desired to assimilate into the "business class" might obtain some edification through "classier" pictures. All in all, the portrait of middle-American movie watching that the Lynds delivered to their public reproduced and recirculated as fact common assumptions about movie effects.

As Richard deCordova (1983, 1994) has pointed out, Disney was not the only Hollywood producer attempting to make itself a part of American daily life through demonstrations of its value to American culture. By the early 1930s, the motion picture industry attempted to convince its critics that it was making real efforts to enforce the Motion Picture Code and to involve middle-American social and civic organizations in that process. In his annual report to the MPPDA in 1934, Will Hays announced to his Hollywood employers that "in the past year contact was established with more than 10,000 additional local leaders, including 6,000 teachers, editors and club group leaders; 1,200 librarians; 800 clergymen, directors of religious education and Y.M.C.A. secretaries, as well as 2,000 theatre managers, cooperating in the movement to focus public support upon the socially desirable elements of screen entertainment" (6). By the mid-1930s, producers understood that they had to associate their industry as best as possible with the local and the civic, especially in communities outside of New York and Los Angeles, where antimetropolitan feelings were sometimes directed against the movies. Writing on the history of the Code, Richard Maltby (1995, 63) has shown that the "wave of Hollywood adaptations of literary classics and historical biographies designed to appeal to middle-class readers of *Parents' Magazine* and *Ladies' Home Journal* resulted directly from the industry's public relations."[34]

To a certain extent, historical epics and literary adaptations did please the American middle class. In 1936, *Parents' Magazine* ran a feature-length addition to its regular movie guide, "What's Ahead in the Movies?" which praised Hollywood's efforts to produce uplifting films. The author suggested, though, that the ultimate responsibility for this change lay with the concerned parents and citizens who had recognized movies as a major social and cultural force, and had actively and vocally intervened in their production and distribution: "Not the least of these influences responsible for better pictures is the conscious effort of the enlightened members of the public, and of parents in particular. Parents have been working more successfully in relation to films because they realize increasingly their responsibility toward them. They cease to view pictures as belonging exclusively to the industry—to producers, officials and directors, and have recognized the fact that, in quite as true a sense, they are the property of the audience" (Benedict 1936, 31). This meant that parents had to reconceptualize their place in the social order. No longer were they merely individuals engaged in the difficult task of raising children; they were civic functionaries operating in a larger social matrix that linked different organizations and communities in a common project. "Parents are speaking no longer as Mr. and Mrs. Smith or Mr. and Mrs. Jones," she insisted, "but as Mr. and Mrs. Main Street, Mr. and Mrs. East Side, or Mr. and Mrs. Community. They are tending to unite in their efforts—locally, nationally. They are combining with various civic and educational groups throughout the country, and are mobilizing solidly behind the forward-looking elements of the industry" (52). Just as the Lynds suggested, middle-class Americans were encouraged to orient themselves toward the future and were imagining themselves as integral elements in networks of organizations whose primary purpose was to ensure that future.

For Disney, the increased scrutiny brought about by arguments about the effect of movies on children and on the nation's well-being was a boon. Not only did those arguments provide a set of discursive tools through which the company could differentiate its products from those of its competitors, they also played an integral part in a larger process of social integration that served both to produce and circulate that discourse and to direct consumers to products associated with its proper negotiation. In the early 1930s, before *Snow White* (1937) and subsequent features, Mickey Mouse was Disney's front man, doing a large portion of the work of establishing the company's presence in the community. By 1932 Disney was using Mickey on a stunning variety of licensed products, many of which were common household items—such as notebooks, handkerchiefs, and glassware—to maintain an ongoing Disney presence within the home (deCordova 1994). Outside the home, Disney briefly attempted to join the network of clubs and organizations to which children belonged, creating the Mickey Mouse Club, precursor to the company's famous television program two decades later. Through talent shows, dancing lessons, or holiday-related activities such as Easter-egg hunts—all linked to Mickey Mouse shorts—the club was designed to draw the children into theaters and to link in parents' minds the image of Mickey Mouse, healthy and productive entertainment, and elementary Americanism. As the 1930 guidebook for establishing a chapter of the club put it:

> The primary purpose of the [Mickey Mouse] Club is twofold:
>
> a) It provides an easily arranged and inexpensive method of getting and holding the patronage of youngsters and
>
> b) Thru [sic] inspirational, patriotic and character-building phases it aids children in learning good citizenship, which, in turn, fosters good will in parents.
>
> . . . Everyone knows how strong the "gang" instinct is in children. The Mickey Mouse Club is unique in that it furnishes entertainment of the most popular nature (stage and screen) and at the same time, implants beneficial principles, the latter so completely shorn of any suggestions of "lessons" or lecturing, that children absorb them almost unconsciously. (Disney 1930, 1)

Thus, within two years of its success with *Steamboat Willie* (1928), the company had already begun the process of associating itself with community activities, and with beneficial social practices and patriotic sentiments.[35]

It is important to note that from this early time, Disney (and its exhibitors) understood that the objects of their address were not solely the children they hoped to draw into the theaters, but also their parents. In an issue of the *Mickey Mouse Club Bulletin*, a newspaper distributed to theater managers, Disney offered an example of how to address local mothers:

> Is Saturday one of those hard mornings for you, Betty gets into this, Bob falls down and skins his knee, the cake falls; oh, well, in fact, everything goes wrong . . . ? Do you know that for 10 cents—maybe 20 or 30—you can be relieved of all this . . . ? Send Betty, Billy, and little John down to the Metropolitan Theatre to the Mickey Mouse Club, where they will meet with the other boys and girls in supervised Club work. . . . We'll take care of them for almost three hours. They see the best and hear the best; they have a chance to appear before other children, to gain self-confidence, which means so much. (Walt Disney Productions 1932, 2)

Disney also encouraged theater owners to associate the club with major domestic holidays. As it would with its practice of releasing and rereleasing its features around the Thanksgiving and Christmas holidays, the company's decision to encourage a Mothers' Day event clearly linked the company with the family, and with the domestic. In the same issue, the company suggested to exhibitors, "In celebration of Mothers' Day, issue a general invitation to the Mothers of all members to attend the meeting. Plan your program to include as many stage activities as possible, as the Mothers will all enjoy seeing their

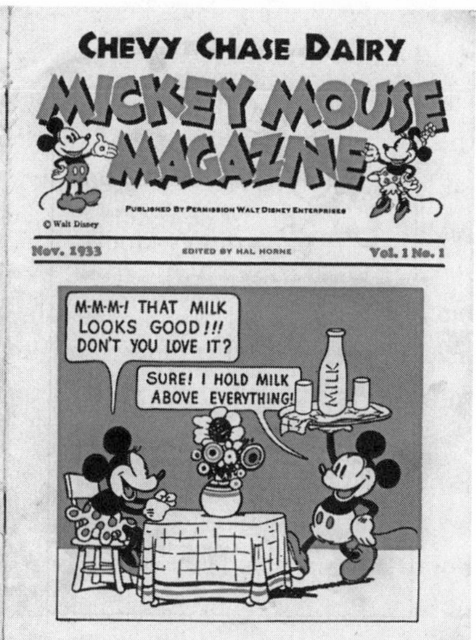

19. A *Mickey Mouse Magazine* distributed by a dairy in Chevy Chase, Maryland, in 1933. Part of a larger campaign orchestrated by Disney, the magazine linked the wholesomeness of drinking milk to Mickey and Minnie, as well as to other distinctly American institutions such as the Boy Scouts. Articles also featured Walt Disney as the foundation of Mickey's wholesomeness. Warshaw Collection, Archives Center, National Museum of American History, Smithsonian Institution.

children perform. . . . Your members' Mothers will appreciate the courtesy shown them, and by securing their good will as well as that of their children, you will certainly have gained more than the nominal loss at the box office for that one day" (2).

As he did through licensed-product appearances in venues other than theaters, Mickey aided Disney's efforts to maximize its presence in the daily practices of average people. In the mid-1930s, for instance, the company distributed its *Mickey Mouse Magazine* through local dairies. (See figure 19.) Each dairy would print its company name at the top of the magazine and deliver it with the milk (D. Smith 1996). The magazine offered articles by Walt and by Mickey, profiles of the company and its products, and contests that featured Disney products as prizes.[36] Not surprisingly, in the first issue, Walt Disney issued "An Important Message to Parents from Mickey Mouse," in which he admonished them: "Parents at times find it difficult to educate their children to the importance of milk so that the child will really desire it and voluntarily drink its requirements. Each growing child requires a minimum of one quart or four glasses of milk every day" (Disney 1933, 2). In February of 1934, Mickey interviewed Dan Beard, the head of the Boy Scouts of America, in an article titled, "Boys Will Be Boy Scouts," which celebrated National Boy Scout Week. In the process of encouraging boys to become scouts, he reminded them in capital letters that they needed to drink a quart of milk a day (Disney 1934). A month later, Minnie Mouse announced that "It's Great to Be a Girl Scout" (Disney 1934b) and told her readers that a steady diet of milk was an important part of scouting. Not only did these messages help dairies sell milk, they linked Disney with children's health. Because children represented the nation's future, this was an issue both local and national, as a *New York Times Magazine* article from April 1934 (purportedly repeating the sentiments of Franklin Roosevelt) reminded its readers: "The problem of the future, so far as child health and milk are concerned, is not to crusade for a better or bigger supply but to increase the demand. We hear a great deal about the overproduction of milk. There is no overproduction, according to our health authorities. . . . We have never brought the country up to the point of consuming a quart a day a child, which is considered essential for health" (Ripperger 1934, 16). As was the case in Middletown, consumption was a civic duty because it would stimulate the economy while it stimulated the proper growth of young Boy and Girl Scouts everywhere.

Given the class (and coded racial and ethnic) antagonism endemic to 1920s film-effects arguments, it is hardly surprising that Disney would attenuate the rags-to-riches trajectory of the classic Horatio Alger myth to stress Walt Disney's middle-class, middle-American origins. Nor is it surprising that Disney would have attempted to claim a segment of the Saturday matinee market that the MPPDA had created in an attempt to profit from concerns about the availability of acceptable fare for children. By the mid-1930s, those matinees were a fixture in Middletown's landscape, providing for parents just the sort of respite Disney had offered to mothers in 1932: "Saturday matinees for young children have become a marked feature of the movies. The morning paper reported in February 1936: 'Yesterday's children played at home on Saturdays in the family kitchen to be out of the way while mother cleaned the rest of the house. Today's attend the children's matinees at the local theaters [while] mother . . . is shopping, visiting, or playing bridge.'" (Lynd and Lynd 1937, 261–62). The child audience of the 1930s, the Middletown newspaper reported, were a mass of waifs abandoned to their own devices, and to those of Hollywood producers. Even though Hollywood attempted to provide the matinee fare purportedly good for children, the newspaper of record for ideal middle America was unimpressed, the Lynds observed, commenting that the films "were 'satisfactory,' but no educational reels were offered during the period of observation. . . . They were exciting recreational films. The report did take exception to one of the adult features. This was a 'murder-mystery drama featuring drinking rowdiness and a series of horrible murders' " (262).[37] Even if educational films had been available, the children would not have watched them, though. This was where the stealthy education that Disney offered to parents through devices like the Mickey Mouse Club would come in—the uplift masked in mouse's ears, backed up by the humanized industrial efficiency of the Disney plant and the inherent middle-class goodness of Disney the producer, would form a prophylactic against the negative consequences of going to the movies.

As the above examples suggest, newspapers and magazines were particularly complex and useful locations for linking movies to day-to-day life. Newspapers in particular provided a discursive environment that both constrained and permitted the construction of arguments and identities, covering the movies in advertising, reportage, reviews, letters columns, and editorials. Producers and exhibitors advertised in the same venue that reviewed their work, while editorialists commented on the nature of moviegoing in general, or upon one movie in particular, and readers offered their own commentary. Letter writers responded to arguments already in circulation, taking up terms and ideas—of movie effects or of a normal child subject to them—and reinforcing them through uncritical redeployment. Editorialists claimed to articulate commonly held beliefs, or to speak for a common good, and so on. Together, in a relatively brief period, each form contributed to a larger public sense of the meaning of moviegoing in the larger formation of an imagined American culture. The producer that placed itself in several of these locations simultaneously, then, benefited from an appearance of spontaneous enthusiasm or interest. Public-relations press books were built on this premise, more commonly referred to as "creating a buzz" about a product. Thus, a journalist could ingenuously suggest to his readers that "Disney believes that good films create all the publicity necessary" (Churchill 1934, 13), while the company sent to its exhibitors prepackaged articles, sample advertisements, and instructions in how to place both: "Note to Exhibitors—*Below is a five-column tabloid-page newspaper feature which is suitable not only for use in tabloid publications but also as part of a full page newspaper feature. Submit it to your editor in advance of your 'Snow White and the Seven Dwarfs' play date*" (Walt Disney Productions 1938, 36; emphasis original). (See figure 20.) The producer that could generate simultaneous advertisements, features, and reviews in local papers created the impression that its product was circulating on its own merits, having won a place in

Note to Exhibitors—*Below is a five-column tabloid-page newspaper feature which is suitable not only for use in tabloid publications but also as part of a full page newspaper feature. Submit it to your editor in advance of your "Snow White and the Seven Dwarfs" play date.*

AT LAST COMES INTO HER OW
AS LATEST WONDER C
THE PICTURE SCREE

By GEORGE T. PARDY

An event, surely not the least of those marking the incessant progress of motion picture entertainment, is the current advent to the screen of the sumptuously produced full-length animated feature, "Snow White and the Seven Dwarfs" in Technicolor, with music and dialogue, a challenge to the major dramatic features of Hollywood. This remarkable example of the work of Walt Disney—creator of "Mickey Mouse" and the "Silly Symphonies"—as an evolution from the half-reel, one-reel and two-reel subjects, has struck the amusement world with a force parallel to the effect made by the transition of pictures from "silent" to sound.

"Snow White and the Seven Dwarfs," three years in the making, had its origin between the covers of one of the most widely circulated and popular books known to civilization — the Grimms' tales. This compilation of legendary folk lore and the madcap, magical doings of sprites, goblins, and other mysterious Little People, first appeared in print

The heroine of "Snow White and the Seven Dwarfs" has been devised to appear the "ideal girl," for she has been given the qualities which most appealed to Walt Disney's corps of talented young men who pooled their efforts to create her.

In general she had to follow the description in the fairy tale—"hair black as ebony, skin white as snow, lips red as the rose." But, as to her personality, facial expressions and so on, the artists had the freedom of invention. The Snow White of the film is an adorable girl, with her sweetness enhanced by vivacity, a free play of emotion and a definite sense of humor.

Disney took care to assign to artists who were fond of drawing pretty girls the task of turning the basic sketch of the character into a lifelike young woman for the screen.

the climax of all animated screen treatment of fanciful characters.

of virile drama among the audience-pleasing attributes of such a flight into the realms of fancy as "Snow White and the Seven Dwarfs." Yet it is there in generous quantity, carrying a double appeal to juveniles and adults. The rare feat has been accomplished of combining dramatic thrills and infinite pathos with the exquisite, delicately enchanting atmosphere of fabled Gnomeland, lilting tunes, merry, catchy songs and bewilderingly graceful dances.

An essential factor in successful drama is the early arousing of audience sympathy for hero or heroine. Snow White, the little Princess, gets that much-desired sympathy because she is from first, almost to the last, a victim of undeserved persecution, a sympathy heightened and sustained by her innocent charm.

You see her under the iron rule of the wicked Queen, degraded from her royal state to that of a scullery maid, dressed in ragged garments. For the Queen is jealous of the fast budding beauty of Snow White which she fears will some day surpass her own imperial loveliness.

WALT
DISNEY

the diamond mine. She wins th
men's hearts with her sweetness,
and good cooking, and they adopt
their pet and housekeeper.

Meanwhile the Queen learns fr
magic mirror that Snow White stil
With arts of sorcery she changes
into an old witch, finds her rival, a
suades the little Princess to take a
an apple which is supposed to gr

20. A press book distributed by RKO Pictures in 1938 provides a print-ready newspaper feature on Walt Disney and *Snow White* in anticipation of its exhibition. The inset box describes Snow White as an "ideal girl" and Walt Disney carefully choosing the artists most likely to be able to make that ideal lifelike.

a network of common experience articulated in apparently separate locations within the community.

When the buzz caught, Disney could, like other companies, recirculate independent public commentary, acting as a sort of amplifier for common sentiment. One early example of this was the popularity of its *Three Little Pigs* (1933). The movie's theme song "Who's Afraid of the Big Bad Wolf?" became an overnight sensation and was quickly declared an anthem for the Depression. During the same period, it became a common journalistic trope that Americans were turning to the movies to escape the mental anguish brought on by economic hardship. When journalists such as the author of "Movies Reflect Our Moods" (Hager 1934) offered examples of this phenomenon, Disney came to mind. Writing in the *New York Times Magazine*, she reminded her readers that

> the average American, as life became increasingly difficult under the clouds of the depression, turned once more for escape to a search for that which did not constantly remind him of every-day disasters.

> "The Three Little Pigs" came tootling across the threshold with Mickey and Minnie Mouse, to be welcomed by a laughter starved nation. Any one could sing "Who's Afraid of the Big Bad Wolf" and make it mean his own particular wolf, and, like the little boy in the dark cellar, whistle back his own courage in so doing. (Hager 1934, 22)

Optimistically deploying the past tense as if to suggest that the Depression were over, the author performed the optimism that the Disney films were meant to represent, suggesting a positive effect even in the retelling. Like any savvy corporation, Disney noted the common perception and tucked it into its growing corporate cosmology, redeploying it in the press releases it pretended not to use, as in this one for a 1934 Silly Symphony:

> Walt Disney has produced another anti-depression story in his latest Silly Symphony "Grasshopper and the Ants." Just as the timely philosophy of "The Three Little Pigs" was judged to be one of the outstanding for its phenomenal popularity . . . Disney has again hit upon an angle that will have an equally strong appeal for the "man in the street." In it the advantage of industry over indolence is cleverly and humorously portrayed in the inimitable style which has made Disney's name a household word. (United Artists 1934)

This made Disney no different from any other Hollywood producer; it was (and is) common practice.[38] But behind the company's skill at producing popular, well-made cartoons, it also demonstrated an impressive ability to align itself, its founder, and its products with prevailing discourses about an ideal American culture, and to suggest that Disney was actually purposely contributing to the national good. On Main Street and in the heart of the "man in the street," good business sense dovetailed with a sensible, middle-class American culture, each reinforcing the other. Thus, *Fortune* magazine could reveal to its "business class" readers, in an article titled "The Big Bad Wolf," that "as with all films, and most plays, the Silly Symphony goes first to a tryout in some obscure theatre where the reactions of an average audience can be observed. Sometimes, but rarely, the audience is so pleased that the Symphony can be safely released to the public. More often the audience (by failing to laugh) will show signs of boredom at one spot or another. That means further cutting and arranging" ("The Big Bad Wolf" 1934, 146).

According to *Fortune*, Disney pretested its cartoons on the average audience as a matter of practice, keeping a circuit of reflection and observation open between producer and consumer. For the business historian, or for the average businessperson, this would appear simply sensible strategy, nothing particularly unusual. Yet for Disney, more than for the other Hollywood studios, the circulation of its films through middle-American preview audiences, and the circulation of representations of its founder and of its business practices, took the form of a celebration of production, and of the investment of that production with the spirit of its ultimate manager. Disney differed from other producers in that while other studios emphasized products, Disney also promoted its *process* and strove to create a sense that its audience was involved in that process. More than that, it celebrated that process as deriving from one source (Walt), and any number of popular commentators joined gladly in that celebration, even intellectuals such as Walter Benjamin or the poet Mark Van Doren, who told readers of the *Nation* that Walt Disney "lives somewhere near the human center and knows innumerable truths that cannot be taught. . . . With him . . . we feel that we are in good hands; we trust him with our hearts and wits" (Van Doren 1938, 93).[39]

Over and over, reviews of Disney's films and features on the studios created what amounted to a hagiographic depiction of the man, his life, and his work (see chapter 1). In an extreme version of the way that reading Middletown provided a road map to middle-American culture, consuming a Disney product became a mystical ritual by which one could consume the essence of middle America. It formed an exact counter to the tropes of infection in which harmful movies were described as delivering the ethnic, urban, proletarian past of their producers, and of distracting youthful consumers from the efficient and productive utilization of their leisure time. Through the figures of Walt Disney and Mickey Mouse, the company offered up a means of communion with the "human center" of an American culture attempting to locate itself in an ostensibly generic American landscape and set of practices.

Belonging

In *Middletown in Transition*, the Lynds reported that by the early 1930s, enthusiasm for scientific management had begun to wane. In an editorial in a Middletown newspaper titled "Machines and the Human Equation," a newspaper editor admonished his readers that "we have been making society mechanical instead of making machinery social. We have to humanize our mechanized industries by putting human values and the real welfare of all above the false welfare of the few. . . . What is needed here is social engineering" (quoted in Lynd and Lynd 1937, 496).

This "social engineering" was to be different than the regulation of workspaces and work habits experts in scientific management had imagined. Scientific management, it was becoming apparent, was not necessarily ushering in a new age in which jobs became satisfying, relations between management and labor more amicable, and the fruits of increased productivity returned to the worker. The social engineering referred to in the editorial was more akin to Clara Savage Littledale's call to "see the child whole." Whether speaking of the child or the factory worker, these transitional discourses attempted to understand the individual as a whole person whose social environment was to be integrated between home, school, workplace, and community. Combining elements of scientific management with individual psychology and psychiatry, efforts at "social engineering" in the 1930s (the largest, perhaps, being the New Deal) attempted to ameliorate the more exacting requirements of mass production through attempts to address the worker (or child) as a whole person, to develop in management an awareness of both physical and psychic needs (Cravens 1985). As the Lynds noted, one significant effect of this shift was a diversification and specialization of management functions on the shop floor, in the schools, and in public administration. Of equal significance, however, was the proliferation of discourses of the psychological in a variety of social locations, from the home, to schools, to the workplace, and an increase of popular and professional discussions about how to integrate the psychological well-being of individuals and communities.

Expressed in terms of efficiency or in a rhetoric of industrial relations that sought to supplant or augment it, discourses that posited an ideal American future did so by imagining a rational and ordered society in which discord and contradiction were resolved through administrative fiat. Whether this ideal arose in response to the economic and social chaos brought on by the Depression, to a fear of the erasure of social, regional, and racial distinctions by mass culture (including media), or to a fantasy of social cohesion arising from the naturalization of progressive notions of uplift, it remained an important element in arguments about the production and protection of American culture in the 1930s. As an embodiment of the future manifest in the present, the child loomed large in these fantasies, and the need to order the society around it was described not so much as an immediate good and an end in itself, but as a means for better regulating that future. The model from which to imagine this future, Middletown, was described by its chroniclers as forward looking and as dedicated to realizing that future in its children. In the Lynds' ideal American town, if one weren't yet of the middle class, one's children would be, and there the story ended. In Lillian Gilbreth's world, the line between the domestic and the industrial economy narrowed as children were trained as workers and managers from infancy.

In the era of Middletown, however—before the American encounter with European fascism and the onset of the cold war, and in the midst of the New Deal—the notion of "social engineering" offered the possibility of providing the operationalized means of extending the middle-class, progressive ideals of uplift, assimilation, and harmony into every part of society. In *Middletown in Transition* (1937), the Lynds invoked James Plant, psychologist and author of *Personality and Cultural Pattern* (1937), to describe the importance of that harmony: "One of man's deepest emotional needs is for a sense of 'belonging.' While some adults may lull this need through extreme preoccupation with work or variety of interests, even active adults ordinarily shun the experience of being socially 'lost in the shuffle.' Dr. James Plant has emphasized the constant and urgent need in the child for an answer to the fundamental question, 'Who am I?'—an answer patently related to the child's established relationships in the neighborhood and community" (Lynd and Lynd 1937, 188–89).

As it had been in the previous generation, the place to begin this work of social engineering was in the home, in the raising of children. In the October 1937 "Books for Parents" column in *Parents' Magazine*, Helen Lynd favorably reviewed *Personality and Cultural Pattern*, reporting to her readers that Plant "stresses adjustment *to* problems that are inherent in family life rather than *of* problems; the necessity of looking at children's behavior in terms of why they do what they do rather than of what they do, of meeting them on their own emotional level rather than forcing them to a more mature one" (128). (An anonymous review of *Middletown in Transition* in the same column claimed, "The book presents a fascinating picture of how we everyday Americans work and play and bring up our children," 128.)[40]

By the 1950s, the United States would have a booming economy, be flush from a victory in World War II, and face an ideological nemesis in the Soviet Union. To postwar social theorists, American culture and society would appear *too* organized, *too* conformist, *too* uniform and regulated. "Belonging" would seem a problem rather than a solution (see chapter 4). In the 1930s, however, the problem for the middle class was not the fear of an overly engineered society, but how much engineering was required to restore order and stability to American society. The move from the laboratory to the broader environment, from the home to the community, and from separate domestic and industrial spheres to a more unified social fabric represented in the minds of its proponents a humanizing of the social sciences and of the social practices associated with them. This move entailed not the abandonment of the trope of efficiency—nor of conformity to norms and standards—but its augmentation by expanding it to encompass that which was *naturally* efficient in the whole person's response to its environment and in the whole community's response to its social, material, and historical circumstances.

Middletown offered neither a ringing endorsement of scientific management, nor its repudiation. Nor did *Middletown in Transition* fully reject arguments for social efficiency. The circulation of discourses of efficiency and its discontents between subjects and researchers, or between the moment represented by one volume and that of the next, were not so tidy. While there was a growing sense that perhaps rationalization and management were ideologically incompatible with notions of individual freedom and personal responsibility, this did not yet necessarily cohere in a widely shared repudiation of efficiency. Instead, there emerged hesitations and amendments, and these were echoed elsewhere in popular discourse, including Walt Disney Productions' celebration of its mastery of nature in the late 1930s and 1940s.[41]

The Transition to Natural Production

There is a scene in Disney's *Fantasia* (1940) that captures perfectly the hope and anxiety parents faced in applying techniques of scientific management to their children. It involves Disney's own cinematic child, Mickey Mouse. In the "Sorcerer's Apprentice" sequence, Mickey plays an apprentice to a powerful wizard. "The Sorcerer's Apprentice" opens with a shot of the orchestra in silhouette, while the narrator sets the scene. "It's a very old story," he announces, "one that goes back about two thousand years." In its usual style, then, Disney represents the story it is about to tell as something out of a distant, traditional past. It is a "classic" tale, authorless and cultureless, raw material to be refashioned. The very old story, continues the narrator, is a "legend about a sorcerer who had an apprentice. He was a bright young lad, very anxious to learn the business. As a matter of fact he was a little bit too bright, because he started practicing some of the boss's best magic tricks before learning how to control them."

The scene crossfades to the sorcerer's lair, in which Mickey totes water while his master conjures beautiful illusions from thin air. (This sorcerer, the credits will eventually announce, is named Yen Sid, which is "Disney" spelled backward.) The sorcerer grows tired, lays down his magic hat, and leaves the room. After a moment, Mickey dons the hat and animates a broom resting in the corner. He gives the broom arms and legs and teaches it to carry water from a well outside to a cistern in his master's chambers, a task he had formerly been performing. The broom briskly carrying water, Mickey settles into a chair and drifts off to sleep.

Once asleep, Mickey dreams, and as he dreams his soul (a slightly transparent copy of himself) departs from his body and drifts upward into space, where he becomes master of the cosmos. He commands comets to streak across the sky and to crash into one another. The sparkling fragments of the comets fall into the waters below him, which he commands to rise in mighty waves that crash at his feet. He commands the clouds to roar with thunder and lightning, and as the waves rise higher about him, the clouds let loose a torrent. . . .

Below, of course, his dreaming body is lapped by waves as the overflowing cistern fills the room. The broom will not stop. Mickey wakes when his chair, almost afloat, tips. Failing to stop the broom, he grabs an ax and brutally chops it to flinders. A moment of calm descends on the workshop. Then the splinters of the broom animate, each becoming an exact copy of the original, each already with full bucket of water in hand, each with the same single purpose: to fill the overflowing cistern. The brooms march on the workshop in time to the music, their numbers doubled by shadows cast on the wall that recall wartime propaganda posters. They tromp over Mickey, so relentless that when the room is submerged they continue to march under water and empty their buckets at the appointed spot. Mickey swims to the sorcerer's magic book and desperately searches for a spell to end the madness. Clinging to the book, he is swept away and dragged down into a whirlpool. At this moment, Yen Sid appears on the stairs above the flood. With a couple of imperious gestures he disperses the flood and finds Mickey lying like a drowned rat on the floor. Mickey hands the sorcerer his hat (after restoring its limp tip to its fully erect state) and the broom. He picks up the buckets and grins at Yen Sid, who frowns. As Mickey makes his way to the door, a hint of a fatherly smile alloys the sorcerer's grimace—as he takes the broom and swats the mouse out the door.

It is not hard to read in "The Sorcerer's Apprentice" a tale about the anxiety attendant on regimes of scientific management, and the resolution of that anxiety through their mastery. In the hands of the master, the magic derived from the book created illusions of beauty, which took the natural shape of butterflies. Left to his child—and Mickey was discursively constructed as Disney's child—that magic became a dangerous, uncontrollable force that threatened to destroy the master's work and everything with it. More specifically, though, the child who took up the tools of management before it had done its stint as an apprentice ran the risk of management run amok, of unleashing an inhuman, unstoppable efficiency. Taking up the master's tools,

Mickey animates the broom and sets it to work doing a simple, repetitive task. He dreams that he has control over the machinery of the universe but awakes to discover that he has set in motion a juggernaut of automation. Unable to locate the stop button, he commits violence against the machine/worker he has set in motion. But his rash and unthoughtful action only exacerbates the problem: automation becomes the force of mass production, a complex but utterly orderly system that replicates the actions of the individual worker on a grand scale, multiplying its results exponentially. Mickey's management fantasy has now fully become a nightmare, for the worker/machines (which industrial efficiency experts treated as a continuum) have begun to pursue their task with a ruthless efficiency. These automatons are vaguely human in form—they have arms and legs and four fingers, like Mickey—but they are soullessly singleminded and frighteningly powerful. They literally flood the workshop and overwhelm their feeble, self-appointed manager with their mindless productivity. Only the return of the master can restore order—which includes reminding the apprentice of his place. The upstart returns to the master his tools, and the punishment is firm, but forgiving. Order is restored, but it is a humanized order.

How many ideal subject positions could a parent watching *Fantasia* occupy? If one discounts the various brooms, the parent would most likely occupy Mickey's position, or Yen Sid's. Certainly any parent attempting to raise a child using the precepts of scientific management had experienced the anxiety of deploying expert systems in which they were positioned as functionaries, applying observational and regulatory regimes and attempting to locate their children within a matrix of data. Like Mickey, they weren't necessarily masters of the method, but only middle managers. The ideal outcome was a child who ascended beyond the parent's control, to a higher-class position or a better job. But by the mid-1930s, child-rearing discourses had begun to admit the possibility that, were those regimes applied too rigidly, the child might end up dehumanized, damaged by the very process that was designed to optimize its chances for success and happiness, an automaton without the will to think for itself. All that Mickey could do with the magic at hand was to create soulless drones which were efficient but inhuman.

Yen Sid, on the other hand, could use the same magic to create miracles. More specifically, he created butterflies, creatures that transformed from earthbound, leaf-munching larvae into beautiful creatures able to fly. Applied to Mickey, this magic of management, and the sorcerer's private amusement at the mouse's attempt at mastery, suggested the humanization of developmental regimes. Likewise, the seeming horror of the child's failure at mastery was ultimately resolved through the timely intervention of the parental figure. Where the moviegoing parent might feel anxiety at the social weight placed on the act of child-rearing, Disney offered up the figure of Walt and the "Disney magic" as a resource in the process. This was social engineering by proxy: Disney engineered and managed the work environment in his studios, and the absolute expertise of that engineering imbued each of its products with the balance of science and humanity necessary to conform to the difficult requirements of 1930s parenting. To increase the possibility of producing the humanly efficient child, then, one could focus on managing its consumption.

This discursive construction began in the early 1930s but took off with Disney's entry into feature-film production, beginning with *Snow White* in 1937–38. With the exception of its early Alice shorts,[42] Disney had always favored animals as its main characters. In its shorts, however, these creatures tended toward human caricature. With *Snow White* (1937), Disney would lay a larger claim to the natural, celebrating in its public relations the "realistic" birds and animals that fluttered around Snow White even as the dwarfs performed their Fordist production number, "Whistle While You Work." By the time of *Dumbo* (1941) and *Bambi* (1942), those two worlds would fuse, and both films would start with "naturalistic" sequences that gave way to a process of birth and child-rearing as an attenuated fantasy of scientific management made natural. In *Dumbo*, squadrons of storks delivered infants in formation on a single night.[43] Likewise, in the opening scenes of *Bambi* the forest floor was a giant nursery in which the young of various species, all of precisely the same age, acted in a confederation of young animal belonging.[44] As had been the case with *Snow White* and *Pinocchio* (1940), and as would be the case with many later Disney features, each of these movies took as its central theme the question of generational succession—how one generation would pass on its collected wisdom to the next, and whether the younger generation would make proper use of that wisdom in its inevitable ascension to adulthood. As Disney refined its message, it created a natural fantasy in which all good creatures, of whatever species, acted in absolute harmony, while its evil creatures stumbled through a graceless sideshow of error and petty rancor that doomed them to failure. Disney's natural world was a unified environment that was (as an animated cosmos should be) seamlessly engineered.

As the 1930s gave way to the 1940s, Disney would make more and more of this access to nature, both in its public relations and in its feature interviews. In 1938, one interviewer would inform his *New York Times Magazine* audience that Disney's focus on the animal world derived from shame over killing an owl when he was seven (Churchill 1938). This formative trauma only strengthened Disney's character, the article implied, committing him to expiation for his cruelty through the depiction of the gentle beauty of natural creatures. Unlike, perhaps, Bugs Bunny or Daffy Duck, Disney's creatures were (by the late 1930s) "natural." "We don't want our animals to ape human beings in an illogical way," Disney told his interlocutor. "We want them to caricature humans in a way that is natural for them to act" (Churchill 1938, 23). Paradoxically, then, Disney's creatures were to be anthropomorphic, but in a way that would not violate their essential animal nature. Beyond furthering the company's claim to expert knowledge, this sort of reasoning forged a link between the human and the animal worlds in which it was possible (indeed, natural) to locate corollaries for human behavioral traits in animals and vice versa. In circumstances in which it was important to see the "whole creature"—whether child or chipmunk—in the context of its natural environment, this sort of claim was valuable. By 1940, another Disney profiler would extend this logic further, claiming, "Article I of the Disney constitution stipulates that every possible element of a picture shall be not a mere pictorial representation of the character or an element of scenery, but an individual, with clearly defined characteristics. . . . So your story crew will psychoanalyze every character, and from each man's suggestion will evolve on paper a character with defined proportions and mannerisms" (Hollister 1940, 691).[45]

In a clear explication of the power of animation as a metaphor for "social engineering," the author informed his readers that Disney was involved in the creation of real, whole (animal) persons, and that the company even psychoanalyzed its characters to ensure that the collective process of the story department would create a creature in tune with its environment. To guarantee that this world would remain consistent throughout, Disney built a database that fulfilled the fantasy of a perfect administrative control over a nonetheless natural environment: "The files of the model department are packed high with photostats of sketch sheets each containing dozens of character notes on each personage in each picture: one such here before me outlines the personality of a baby rabbit, M-9-B, *Snow White*—a character of the utmost triviality in the action of that extravaganza—and on this sheet are forty-three sketches of that single obscure rabbit" (Hollister 1940, 692).

Disney found a public quite receptive to this mutation in its Fordist fantasy of production, and the circulation of arguments about its/his intent and ability with regard to the animal world served the company well. When an editor at *Outdoor Life* decried *Bambi* as antihunter propaganda that abetted the

BAMBI GETS A SPANKING

RECENTLY the editor of a leading sportsmen's magazine, Outdoor Life, sent Walt Disney a telegram stating that he, the editor, did not like Mr. Disney's movie, "Bambi." The editor did not like it in his capacity as a hunter nor as a protagonist of hunters (he did not disclose his attitude toward the movie in the capacity of a moviegoer). "Bambi," the editor pointed out, showed a deer being killed by an unseen hunter in spring, which was something no hunter would do "and which of course would be unlawful anywhere in North America."

After saying that the movie was an "insult to American sportsmen" and using other similarly strong language to express several varieties of resentment, the editor then cautioned Mr. Disney:

"I urge you strongly to insert a foreword stating plainly that the picture is a fantasy and that its locale is not in North America."

Well, this Disney fellow, appar-

BAMBI A NAZI?....AN AUSTRIAN CREATED HIM, DISNEY NATURALIZED HIM, A MAGAZINE EDITOR WOULD PURGE HIM.

cute little animals Disney makes so lifelike and so appealing, will carry

such things as hunters, that they sometimes go into our forests and shoot wild and semi-wild game (Sporting Life, page 8). Three will get you five that if Dad took Junior along on one of his deer treks, Junior would be a lot more impressed by actuality than by any water-color scene Disney puts on the screen. We may as well admit it, such things do happen in North America, and in a single season a great many Bambis (maybe does included) fare no better than Bambi's mother (Sporting Life, page 19).

The difference between Mr. Disney and the editor is, I should say, quite marked. Mr. Disney creates animal life; he does not destroy it. He gives these little creatures a voice and, being a creator in an artistic sense, the breath of life, which means feelings, tears and laughter. He instills in them the touch of humanity and sensibility which a lot of folk will assure you on solemn oath exists in their little breasts. Anyone who has roughly seized a rabbit and noted the fear in its eyes and felt the wild beating of its heart may understand a little of what that means.

21. A newspaper editorial rebuts charges by the editor of *Outdoor Life* that Walt Disney is abetting the Nazis because *Bambi* (1942) has turned children against guns and hunting. Regulating Walt's inherent American-ness, the article describes Disney as able to give the creatures "he" depicts a voice and a "touch of humanity."

Nazis, a newspaper columnist defended Disney in no uncertain terms, claiming that "the difference between Mr. Disney and the editor is . . . quite marked. Mr. Disney creates animal life; he does not destroy it. He gives these little creatures a voice and, being a creator in an artistic sense, the breath of life, which means feelings, tears and laughter. He instills in them the touch of humanity and sensibility which a lot of folk will assure you on solemn oath exists in their rough little breasts" (Koury 1942). (See figure 21.) In simpler and more folksy terms, the writer reiterated the idea that Disney (the man) had the actual ability to locate the human personalities and behaviors inherent in animals that made them "real" to its audience. Because Walt Disney was so absolutely American, and because he existed on a plane of consciousness somewhere near the "human center," the life he breathed into those animals (by way of his employees) was both accurate and inspirational.

Unless the Disney Archive has been selective in its practices, the many letters that Walt Disney received seem to support this impression. Besides ordinary folk, antivivisectionists, humane societies, Theosophical societies, and

SPCAs praised *Bambi* as an animal-rights picture.[46] A member of a group called the Poets of the Pacific declared,

> Bambi is an unforgetable [*sic*] experience. . . . The understanding love of nature which permeates it could not but bring to every spectator some echo of childhood joyousness and innocency [*sic*]; some revelation of the blood-brotherhood uniting all life. . . . you have made a greater contribution to humane education, and a stronger appeal for the preservation of wild life, than all the years of organized effort have done. No one with normal human instincts could come away from a showing of Bambi without forever after feeling some kinship with all living creatures. (New 1942)

For this writer, the animal and human worlds formed the very continuum that Disney represented. Echoing Victorian sentimentalism, she imagined children as particularly open to this experience through their innocence. For two women from Madison, Wisconsin, Disney had created in *Bambi* the necessary environment for fostering the normal child's inherent connection to the animal world, producing through that action a prophylactic against world war, declaring that "the normal child is a natural animal lover and were this trait cultivated through life with pictures like 'Bambi' which instills a humane respect even for our forest creatures, less conflagration would be likely to spread in the war camps" (Bergheger and Wilson 1942). Finally, one fan found in Disney's characterizations something beyond either animal or human, describing the characters as "wonderful—more human than humans" (Eckelberry 1943).

Are these letters a spontaneous outpouring of localized interpretation that indicate a common reading of Disney films, evidence of the effectiveness of Disney's public relations, indicative of the selective practice of the clipping service, or some combination thereof? At minimum, they would seem to demonstrate that Disney maintained a feedback circuit with its public that allowed it to refine its address and to gauge responses to its messages—both those delivered on-screen and those offered through other media. While public-relations blitzes, celebrity interviews, and the use of clipping services and other feedback vehicles were (and are) common industry practices, Disney coordinated each of these elements with a rigor and an attention to the consistency of its internal logic that no other studio matched. Although the circuit of public relations and fan reaction may have constituted standard industrial practice, it also served to join producer and consumer as (extremely unequal) partners in the production of social and cultural meanings that accreted around Disney's films and its ancillary products. What set Disney apart was its celebration of that relationship, its production of a fantasy of a cycle of production and consumption that ran parallel to the generational cycle it repeated in its feature narratives. In this fantasy, the investment of Disney's characters with essential human and animal qualities was laid bare, and parents were provided with an imaginary world in which they appeared able to participate in the production of the commodities their children consumed, and through which their children produced themselves as nascent adults.

Viewed in this light, Disney's increasingly aggressive protection of its copyright and trademark properties may be viewed as more than simply the hypervigilant patrolling of corporate borders. It also served to signal to Disney's consumers that the company would do everything in its power to maintain the purity of the meanings traveling the fetishistic circuit between producer and consumer, meanings deployed in other contexts with significant consequences. As Eric Smoodin (1993) has pointed out, by the 1940s, Disney's patrons and reviewers were more than happy to return the favor by policing Disney's forays into new media—or into experiments combining animation and live action, such as *Three Caballeros* (1944) or *Song of the South* (1946)—making it clear which of the company's efforts they found properly Disney, and which they did not. For Disney, the celebration of its production practices and the family atmosphere of its facilities produced in miniature an ideal world in which the spheres of social relations and of production shared a seamless logic that flowed through them effortlessly. The inclusion of nature in that process merely extended the sense that Disney's world was that whole world in which Clara Savage Littledale told parents they had to locate their child. The apparent transparency of Disney's operations, and of Walt's life, appeared the epitome of the ideal American culture envisioned as the end product of evolving regimes of child-rearing and other regimes of domestic observation and regulation.

So potent was that epitome that it extended into professional realms one might expect to be immune from public relations. Robert M. Yerkes, head of Yale's Primate Research Facility and one of the leading figures in primatology, wrote to Walt Disney after viewing *Pinocchio*, asking Disney to invent a cinematic device that would relieve the strain of "visual fatigue" (Yerkes 1941). Louise Bates Ames, a researcher in Arnold Gesell's Child Development Clinic (also at Yale) wrote to Disney to compliment him on *Bambi*, calling it "the most beautiful cinema I have ever seen" (Ames 1942, 1). But, she suggested, Disney (and his child viewers) might benefit from the input of a professional child psychologist "who presumably has a knowledge and understanding of the manner in which children in general (not just one particular child, as in the case of the average parent) respond, that the few minor changes which would probably result would greatly improve the picture from the point of view of audience reaction" (1). Although letters such as these were few in comparison to those of adoring fans, they indicate a willingness among at least some professionals to view Disney as holding a position of authority in relation to beneficial amusements for children. Discussing Disney's contribution to the war effort, Walter Wanger (1943, 18–19) told his *Saturday Review of Literature* readers that Disney's command of efficiency — as appropriate as it was to making cartoons and to imparting efficiency to children through those cartoons — was equally useful in training soldiers: "Disney has been close to this war. More than ninety percent of the facilities of his studio have been devoted — since Pearl Harbor — to the making of films for our armed services and other governmental agencies. These are pictures that for the most part will never be seen by civilian audiences. They are making pictures there which in many instances have helped cut down the training period of our boys as much as forty-five percent."

Disney's expertise, then, extended from the observation of the behaviors of bunny rabbits to the efficient training of soldiers and workers. This was, in an odd sense, an enactment of the seamless, socially engineered society called for in Middletown, or what Lillian Gilbreth had imagined as the result of the adoption of regimes of domestic efficiency. "Another great aid to satisfied home-making is a belief in the newer economics," Gilbreth declared (1927, 144–45). "Labor is no longer a commodity. The relation of production to life and to consumption can make the home-maker feel the essential part of the community that she is. Economists have not only recognized her to be such, but are writing of her status in such a way that soon no one will underrate what she does or her contribution to social welfare." What did it mean to make the startling claim that labor was "no longer a commodity"? In an engineered ideal democratic capitalist future, work was not compelled in relations of unequal exchange, and the wife and mother was not merely a middle manager in the business of growing children, but an engineer herself, responsible for a segment of socially ordered production. Children's labor would not be for others, and their consumption would not doom them to commodity status. Like the homemaker contributing to social harmony by enacting and monitoring regimes of domestic scientific management, Disney modeled a humanized efficiency in which regimes of observation and adjustment were applied with equal facility to the reproduction of lifelike behaviors in animals and training American soldiers. Suggesting that it imbued its products with the essential

American character of its founder, Disney's efficiency linked production and consumption through the guarantee of the delivery of ideal character undiluted by haphazard production practices—providing the mother at home (or the drill sergeant) tools by which she could further regulate her children's self-productive environment.

"Middletown" caught the popular imagination in the late 1920s and 1930s because it filled an unanticipated desire to locate and comprehend the nature of a "native" American culture through which one could evaluate one's self, one's peers, and perhaps most important, one's children. In Middletown, contradictions between rationalization and individualism, between the attractions of modern cosmopolitan life and fading rural traditions, met and were resolved. Yet while Middletown revealed itself as a template laid gingerly over Muncie, Indiana—one that defined itself by its rapid fusion with a future both desired and feared—Walt Disney offered the possibility of a Middletown internalized through the consumption of his products. In the fetishistic logic of movie effects, those products were imbued with Disney's ineffable Midwestern character and delivered as an inoculant to unsuspecting child consumers. And even as the public's understanding of the child changed, requiring less celebration of the joys of management and more appreciation for the child's inherent relationship to nature, Disney's reflexive relationship to its public allowed it to adjust the meanings of its founder and his products to suit those changes. This was social engineering naturalized, the willingness of the producer and consumer to relate to each other as if joined through the commodity in a seamless chain of being.

World War II would further cement this relationship, as mandatory and voluntary wartime adjustments to social relations, such as rationing and scrap drives, would make clear. Efficiency and the mutual interdependence of home, industry, and government would become patriotic tropes during the war, so much so that the National Association of Manufacturers would consider it a patriotic duty to celebrate that relationship in public-relations pieces such as "Management—1942 Model":

> changing diapers and changing shifts are part and parcel of the same picture. . . . Acknowledging this, industrialists are closeted hours each day with nutritionists, child psychologists, kindergarten experts. . . . In Southern California one plane manufacturer wearied of waiting for State and Federal solution of the problem of what to do with young children of mothers working in his plant. So . . . he purchased a large estate adjacent to his factory; installed the area's most distinguished experts in the field

> of child care; and now operates a nursery and progressive school on a 24-hour-a-day basis. . . . This, according to the manufacturer, is not a generous gesture, feebly executed to pacify discontented workers. The nursery school, he feels, is an insurance policy, not alone for himself, nor for his workers, but for democracy. (Anspacher 1942, 9)

Walt Disney was, of course, one of the first of those "new industrialists," understanding that in and ideal democratic capitalist society, the child was itself a commodity in the making, the commodity nature of which would disappear into the orderly regulation of the relationship between production and consumption. Here, the nursery was next door to the factory, and Santa met the toys as they came down the assembly line, teaching each one to say "mama." This seamless society would create a new set of anxieties for postwar social scientists and social critics who feared the inception of an American totalitarianism (see chapter 4). But in the 1930s and into the 1940s, the possibility of that society offered as much promise as threat, and Walt Disney embodied the difference between the two.

This was exactly the discursive position that Disney had hoped to occupy ten years earlier when it established, briefly, its Mickey Mouse Clubs: to be viewed as a conduit to the child's formative unconscious experience of the world, and to be praised for that role. For the ever larger number of parents enrolling their children in compulsory public school systems that deployed observation, categorization, and management to produce hierarchies determinative of their future success, the studios' ability to turn the cold and calculating technologies of science and observation to the production of warm, generous, intelligent, and successful creatures offered an added appeal to its entertainment value.[47]

Conclusion: The Transformation of the Normal Child

> *The American craze for standardization has given us, among thousands of other standardized objects, the standardized child. . . . who at the moment of its birth weighs exactly 7 ½ pounds and measures, from the tip of its straight black hair to the sole of its curled pink foot, precisely 20 ½ inches. . . . It is a child who must have its didies changed thirteen times a day when it is three weeks old, twenty times a day when it is three months old, and its panties unloosed nine times a day when it is three years old. . . . It is a child who until it is six cannot tell its right hand from its left, or its left ear from its right, but who after that year never makes a*

single mistake in this direction. . . . It is a child, presumably, though we know far less about its desires and predilections than about its capacities and capabilities, who likes spinach, carrots, early bedtimes and fawning strangers.

—ADAMS 1934, 13–15

Even as Walt Disney Productions associated itself with technologies used in the production of the normal child, that child was showing its first signs of fatigue. The quote above is excerpted from a much longer catalog of the dimensions and tolerances of the "standardized" child that opens Grace Adams's *Your Child Is Normal* (Adams 1934), a child-rearing manual designed to counter the dominant discourse of scientific management (particularly of behaviorism) in child-rearing discourse. Describing the book as "the result of my somewhat varied work with children . . . which has included social work among the mill children of the South, and psychiatric work with the problem children of wealthy parents in New York City," she promised her readers to provide a picture of children "not as sociological products, laboratory subjects, or psychiatric problems, but as a unique, interesting class of human beings. . . . [based on] observations through which children retain their characteristically human qualities . . . [rather than] those which make them appear as stereotyped subjects of impersonal laboratory experiments" (vii–viii).[48]

The generic, standardized American child Adams wanted to replace with a more nuanced and human child was somewhere between a statistical fiction and a marketing gimmick. "And who . . . is this child?" she asked. "To supply the answer we must search the lore of child study which teachers, doctors and psychologists have been compiling during the last forty years. . . . This child whom psychologists, physicians, school teachers and the manufacturers of 'Kute Klothes for Kiddies' regard as the normal child is one they have constructed, painstakingly and after many years of toil, not from human flesh and blood, but by means of pencils and paper" (Adams 1934, 15–16). Adams claimed that the normal American child was a social construction, and that its deployment—far from helping to ensure the happiness and success of children modeled in its image, or to guarantee the security of the republic by producing a well-regulated and uniformly content citizenry—was an outrage against the unique and delicate creature that each child was. Focusing her critique on behaviorism in general, and on its chief proponent John B. Watson in particular, Adams argued for a more personalized and individual model of child-rearing that eschewed slavish obedience to normative practices. "The young child's mind," she argued, "is a more mysterious and intricate phenomenon than its pancreas or thyroid or any other organ in its body. And the means by which it can be affected and modified are too subtle and various to admit of any universal formula" (66–67).

This particular program offered a popular version of the Piagetian model of childhood: rigid timetables and developmental benchmarks were replaced with a gentler set of developmental stages in which a child's progress was not measured against precise weekly or monthly markers, but which offered broad spans of many months and even years within which the child could evince behaviors and aptitudes.[49] Furthermore, the child's eventual capabilities and temperament would depend as much on its inherited characteristics as on the proper regulation of its environment. This return to the genetic was meant not to signal a reinvestment in eugenics (which by the late twenties had lost many of its adherents), but to encourage parents to accept their child's strengths and limitations as expressions of its unique character, rather than its failure to perform within established tolerances.

As sensible in its critique of management-oriented child-rearing as *Your Child Is Normal* was, it did not signal the immediate collapse of that paradigm. During the 1930s, and into the early 1940s, arguments for efficiency and scientific management in the domestic economy coexisted with a growing number of child-rearing manuals based around a more holistic and interactive depiction of the child and its relationship to its environment. This was true from one text to the next, and even within individual works. In *Babies Are Human Beings* (Aldrich and Aldrich 1938), a (self-described) pediatrician-and-wife team, combined thinking from G. S. Hall, Gesell, and a sprinkling of carefully camouflaged Freud to produce a picture of the child as a natural creature of a higher order than Watson's reflex-directed child. It was a creature whose early years still replicated the dawn of human civilization and its primitive animal roots (which required orderly regulation to be properly enculturated), but whose inherent humanity would be stifled by an excess of regulation. The child's development still recapitulated the evolution of human society, and the regulation of that development was still considered capable of directing the future of that evolution, but the transition from animal to human primitive, and from primitive to modern, became a much more wrenching and spectacular event, one much more likely to suffer from an excess of tampering:

> The period since man began to record his acts is only a moment compared to his evolutionary antiquity. For this reason, newly born babies would probably fit in more acceptably with a cruder society where their violence would be necessary for survival than they do in our sophisticated and

> protecting environment. If we remember how ancient our baby's behavior really is, we can be more understanding of the forceful characteristics which he shows from birth and can better appreciate his amazing powers of adaptability as he is absorbed into our complex life. (Aldrich and Aldrich 1938, 11)

Without naming names, this shift in thinking replaced Watson with Freud and recast natural instinct as perverted by management rather than shaped by it. "The crude behavior of a baby," they continued (Aldrich and Aldrich 1938, 11), "is vitally important for his survival and is a part of his mechanism for growth. His violent protests against restraint and his compulsive demands for gratification, whether they concern hunger, warmth, or muscular exercise, are so fundamental for his protection that they are prominent in his behavior long before he is able to act on a voluntary basis." This child was less reflexive and more instinctive than its discursive predecessor, its relationship to its environment less a matter of mechanical reaction and more of spontaneous feeling. As a result, its responses to the regulation of its environment were inherently less predictable, and attempts to enforce a rigid regime that would generate expected responses was considered stifling to the natural creature that lay at the core of every civilized being.

That did not mean, however, that the child was not to be regulated, or that the trope of management had vanished altogether. Rather, the acknowledged need for regulation, and the recourse to the terminology of scientific management, was undercut by a concern that the imposition of rigid standards of care and behavior on the developing child before its particular temperament, bodily habits, and aptitudes were known would damage it emotionally and socially. The problem was not with the application of management techniques per se, but with their *misapplication*. "As a rule this training is given in a conscientious and kindly manner," the authors assured their readers (Aldrich and Aldrich 1938, 21). "Its misfortune is that without adequate understanding of his development and its accompanying growth changes, our standards are often too heavily imposed and conformity is expected of him before he is ready for it." The results were likely to be a sort of robot, a person who was obedient and responsive, but not fully human.

This emphasis on the child's humanity marked the beginning of a critical reappraisal of the normal child that would reach its fullest expression in the work of Benjamin Spock and would begin to gain wider popular acceptance a decade later. In its earlier stages, it took the form of a cautious reassessment of the shortcomings of applying an industrial template to child-rearing. "If [babies] were always entirely alike, however, and if they always grew at approximately the same rate, their care would be comparatively simple but infinitely dull," the Aldriches cautioned would-be parents (1938, 51). "We might, in that case, use the mass production methods of the chick industry and bring them up in huge infant incubators." This was more or less a parody of Watson's call to replace mothers with professionals, which would produce a malleable society, but one without dynamic humanity. "It is the differences between individuals which make the care of children so interesting and difficult. . . . the developmental attitude toward babies must be tempered by a deep-seated recognition of the importance of individual differences. . . . For these very difficulties make it impractical to adhere entirely to any one plan of management, no matter how well-founded, in our dealings with children" (51–58).

This shift toward understanding the child as an individual, however, did not extend to complete repudiation of the concept of the ideally normal child, or of expert information on the subject. Although the consolidation of this trend under the banner of "child-centered" (or, in the pejorative, "permissive") child-rearing in the late 1940s and early 1950s would involve the deployment of anti-expert rhetoric in popular discourse (see chapter 5), in the late 1930s, it merely signaled a rethinking of the concept of normalcy. Rather than being that creature that fit within acceptable parameters of mental and physical growth and behavioral development, and which operated properly in its environment, the normal child was increasingly viewed as a budding primitive that needed the tools to adapt to the highly structured nature of twentieth-century life. "Competent observers suggest that part of the trouble, at least, lies in the inability of human beings to adjust satisfactorily the differences between their own natural trends and the pressure of the regimented life they have built up for themselves," the Aldriches (1938, 63) suggested. Fortunately, though, the significant quantities of data on child development gathered in the previous decades were being reinterpreted to accommodate this new understanding of the child: "Efforts are being made to sift out the various physical, mental and emotional factors in the early environment, to determine which are healthful and which are unduly obstructive and therefore disturbing. Research being carried out along these lines in many schools and clinics and by individual students is being reported monthly in technical journals." Following a trajectory quite similar to that of theorist of human industrial engineering Elton Mayo (see chapter 4)—which critiqued scientific management not for its attempt to improve the lot of workers (and owners) through efficiency, but for its belief in a single method to achieve that end—this version of child-rearing still treated the child as both a valuable source of data and the beneficiary of efficient modes of environmental regulation. Being normal was still important; the meaning of that normality was changing.

Though at the end of the 1930s popular discourses of child-rearing, especially in periodicals, still discussed scientific management in measurably favorable terms, a large part of this may be put down to institutional inertia. The strong ties between the major developmental research units and *Parents' Magazine*, for example, coupled with the multiyear design of many research programs, meant that broad institutional changes took place gradually (Cravens 1985). In addition, the onset of World War II complicated the matter, both encouraging new perspectives on child-rearing and limiting both their dissemination and the amount of public attention they could command. Just as Disney's contribution to the war effort limited the number of significant innovations or releases the company could engage in, so substantial alterations in the dominant mode of child-rearing were postponed during the hostilities.[50]

For some wartime child-rearing manuals, though, the conditions of privation and social control brought on by the war provided an object lesson on the dangers of over-regulation to a democratic capitalist society. In *You, Your Children, and War*, Dorothy Baruch painted what was meant to be a grim-but-realistic picture of wartime domestic life. "We are fighting to preserve the democratic way of life. And yet, as an inevitable by-product of war, there has come to our existence the tightening of authoritarian reins," she cautioned parents. "No longer does individual liberty function as freely as in pre-war days. We may not use as much gasoline as we desire, nor as much sugar, or wool, or rubber. We may not charge what prices we wish to our customers. . . . We may soon be deprived of choosing whether to work or not, as have the people of England where labor is conscripted. More and more, our cherished freedoms are being tabled" (Baruch 1942, 89). While adults might understand this as a temporary necessity, for children it would constitute their formative experience of the world: "Our children see in the world about them no very true picture of democratic living. They see, instead, a kind of autocracy in action. And yet, if they are to live democratically, they should know what constitutes democracy. . . . They should have a warm, expansive feeling about democracy, and sure knowledge of the principles on which it rests" (89–90).

As citizens in the making, this relative absence of democracy left children open to developing a worldview in which obedience to authority seemed a normal part of social intercourse. Parents were thus encouraged to think of their interactions with their children as opportunities to express and experience democracy, and thus as inoculants against authoritarianism. Practically, this meant imagining the domestic environment as a democracy-in-miniature in which the child could participate in as many decisions as were reasonably possible. (The absence of the father, though depriving children of an important role model and emotional support, also provided greater opportunities for democracy, as mothers and children restructured domestic life around his absence.) These practical conditions, however, provided Baruch (and others) with an opportunity to mount a critique of management-oriented child-rearing methods on the grounds that they dangerously deprived the young child of an environment in which the practice of democracy seemed possible, if not natural. "Too many hardships and deprivations, too many blockings and frustrations, create defeatism," she claimed. "A child must learn first and early that life can be good. He then continues to search for the good. . . . Once having found this conviction, he can hold to it when hardships do come. He can see his way to better things" (76). The child too strictly regulated in its early life would not be predisposed to democracy later, even if presented with examples of its operation. The rigid schedules for feeding, elimination, and so on that the scientific-management model of child-rearing espoused—all intended to produce an orderly and efficient democratic society—were actually antidemocratic. Before a child learned that it is occasionally good for it to yield its individual liberty for the good of the group, it should have a fully articulated experience of that liberty. That experience, Baruch argued, began in infancy, when the child's basic needs and wants were met with cooperation and encouragement, rather than restriction and denial, providing it with an "awareness that people can be mutually helpful; that one can participate in society, working with and for others—such knowledge arises out of having had people *with* one, not *against*. . . . on the fulfillment of basic satisfactions, not on their lack" (77).

Keep Them Human (Dixon 1942) adopted a similar stance in questioning the previous generation's approach to child-rearing. Offering a picture of the Hitler-Jugend (Hitler Youth) as soulless automatons in children's bodies produced by the state, the author suggested that, even as the United States fought for democracy, it could accidentally produce fascists:

> [The Hitler Jugend] seems a far picture from anything we could imagine as a future for our children. . . . But something comparable to it can happen to any generation of children who are biased to thinking in war terms during the most plastic years of their growth. . . . the way the child lives in these early years determines to a great extent the kind of adult he will be. While we are making the world safe for democracy we must preserve

> in the children readiness for democracy—these are the people in whose hands the new world order will be moulded. (Dixon 1942, 15–16)

The implication was that children subjected to rigid systems of regulation in their early years would become compliant and unthinking pawns of the totalitarian state tomorrow—unless the parent acted to instill in the child a sense of freedom of choice. In this case, this did not mean abjuring the use of management-oriented techniques; it simply required more finesse. "Charts are fine for reference," Dixon assured her readers. "We suddenly find that Jimmy is difficult. What shall we do? We look on the chart and see that at five o'clock a drink of water is in order. . . . We look at the chart anyway, but if Jimmy is deep in a play interest, we use it very differently. We don't yank him away for a drink of water. We say, Here, Mr. Bus-man, perhaps you'd like a cup of coffee. We learn to sell our wares, learn to sell our program" (37).

Using charts and other observational apparatuses remained a valid exercise in middle-class child-rearing, as did activity schedules. The parent, however, was to refine her management skills, locating less repressive means by which to accomplish the same end of producing a well-regulated (but more independent and individual) child. It was still important to track the child, to determine its relation to established norms, and to regulate its developmental environment so that it might mature efficiently.[51] Yet that model of efficiency required not a rigid adherence to the "one best way" to raise the child, but a more individualized program designed to produce regulation the child would be most likely to follow.[52]

The American Youth Commission of the American Council on Education offered a somewhat more compassionate assessment of parental responsibilities during the war years. In *Youth and the Future* (1942), it asserted that parents were obliged to "apply modern scientific knowledge to child-rearing as completely as their limitations permit. They should encourage and support the agencies through which this knowledge is discovered and disseminated, such as the United States Children's Bureau and the federal and state public health services and similar agencies at the community level" (American Youth Commission 1942, 171). Harkening back to the more statist progressive model of child-rearing, the Youth Commission represented parenthood as a collaborative effort undertaken with state agencies, the desired outcome of which was to produce a useful and productive citizen. To do so, parents were to work with the state, in particular with organizations such as the Children's Bureau and the public schools, to foster in the child the two necessary and complementary components of citizenship: "conforming" and "contributing" citizenship.

"Contributing citizenship" was a willingness to actively participate in democracy through respect for the opinions of others, a desire to contribute to the general welfare, as well as "familiarity with major social problems and issues which must ultimately be solved through informed public opinion." "Conforming citizenship" involved developing the behavioral skills necessary to live and work with others, to a "willingness to understand and carry out simple instructions, both oral and written, under circumstances when coordinated action is required for the public health, safety, and welfare." This conformity, however, was not to be confused with that of mindless obedience: "The conforming citizenship with which we are here concerned is not the total conformity of the totalitarian state, but rather the irreducible minimum of conformity that is necessary even in a democracy under the complex and crowded conditions of modern life" (206).

Deriving in part from the United States' encounter with fascism, and from the limitations placed on social and personal freedom during wartime, the commission's version of childhood described the central dilemma that would define child-rearing for the next two decades: how to balance the needs of an orderly and rational society against those of individual freedom in the production of future generations. As the embodiment of future social relations, the child was the most important location for working out this contradiction. In a society that, following the New Deal and the regimentation of World War II, was far more rationalized than any that had preceded it, and in which the child had access to a popular mass culture distinct from its domestic life, the child's body would become a site where profound ideological differences would be converted into productive social practices. The normal child of the 1920s and 1930s—itself a place marker for progressive notions of the behaviors necessary for the production of a society based on ideals of Protestant, middle-class whiteness—created a profound uneasiness with the idea of social engineering and control, and a need to locate and produce a natural conformity to democratic capitalist principles.

Even as this newer version of the American child was in formation, however, parents were still encouraged to understand that the production of the normal child increasingly occurred in the act of consumption, that parenting involved the regulation of that consumption, and that efficiency was creating a harmonious relationship between the means of production and those of consumption. As Americanness was increasingly considered a quality produced at the interstices of the public and the private (as opposed to within the sanctity of the Victorian home), the location of normality in the middle class required a reassessment of the location and nature of that middle class outside of the home. While the child retained its discursive status as a crucial site for the production of an American future, the terms by which the production process was regulated were changing. A portrait of the daily life of average Americans, against which other Americans could compare their lives, had emerged in Middletown—Muncie, Indiana—site of the most extensive sociological portrait of American living ever conducted, some 150 miles from the Chicago where Walt Disney was born, and 350 miles from Marceline, Missouri, his childhood home. Purportedly mirroring back to Americans the nature of their day-to-day life, Middletown offered to producers such as Disney a template for locating their products in the center of an ideal American landscape and gave consumer/citizens a model for gauging their position in that terrain. The years following World War II would see an outpouring of popular sociological, anthropological, and psychological texts that attempted to locate that ideal American character in a historical landscape that extended before and beyond Middletown—from the puritans and the pioneers toward a potential future—and which treated the child as central to its preservation. At the same time, Disney would turn to its mastery of nature and of science, presenting Main Street, U.S.A., as stretching from America's prehistoric past into its ideal future, passing through the hearts and homes of the average American child.

4 AMERICA'S TRUE-LIFE ADVENTURE

For family devotion and parental care, the beaver, the bear, and many other animals and birds can teach us lessons. The antics of courtship, male rivalry, the training and feeding of the young provide movie plots, and prove that the animals can and do solve problems of family life much like our own. Animal behavior often reveals the instinctive beginnings of the deepest, most basic human emotions.

—DISNEY 1953

Walt Disney's allusion to the natural family—from "What I've Learned From the Animals," a public-relations piece for the studio's True-Life Adventure nature films in the *American Magazine* —gestures toward a significant shift in ideas of the family, child rearing, and American culture that occurred in the wake of World War II. The formerly popular cult of domestic efficiency had fallen into disfavor during the war, becoming associated with an unwarranted intrusion of the public sphere into the home—a regulation of family life not unlike that of Nazi Germany or the Soviet Union. Its scientific-management regimes were replaced with ones that stressed a hands-off approach that converted management to monitoring and expected the child's social being to spring naturally from its instinctual base.

These new regimes still required close observation of the child and its environment but would do away with correlating those observations to rigid developmental timetables and behavioral benchmarks. Parents and children alike were expected to become more self-aware and to apply that self-awareness to their integration into new social environments, such as the growing suburbs or the multiple layers of management appearing in U.S. businesses. Likewise, as they consumed the myriad products issuing from a booming postwar mass market, these new families had to have the inner resources to recognize which of those mass products aligned with an inherently American culture, and which detracted from its reproduction, encouraging instead blind and slavish conformist impulses that could signal the first stages of a slip toward a totalitarian obedience to culturally hollow norms.

In essence, the members of this new family had two tasks distinctly different from those of the previous generation. They had first to learn to discern between a naturally occurring American culture—that is, the one that had evolved out of the efforts of earlier generations to mold the American nation—and a mass culture at odds with that ideal past. Second, and equally important, they had to unlearn modes of observation and regulation that disrupted the course of that natural evolution, that attempted on a mass basis to impose standards of behavior that had seemed so important only a generation ago.

This change in the conception of the relationship between nature and culture in family life was not limited to child-rearing texts. It also played a significant role in the circulation of popular theories of American culture and character, which argued, across a relatively broad ideological and theoretical spectrum, for intervention into American social and domestic practices as a prophylactic against totalitarian tendencies latent in an emerging mass society. This chapter will examine those theories of culture and character—and the regimes of observation and social control that spurred their creation—while the next chapter will consider their promulgation in new postwar regimes of child-rearing.

These far-reaching changes weren't limited to anthropological, sociological, and psychological texts, however. They also circulated widely in popular culture. Following World War II, Walt Disney Productions parlayed its reputation for creating "natural" and "lifelike" animated characters, presenting itself through its products and public relations as a popular translator of the natural and scientific. Particularly in its popular True-Life Adventure nature documentaries—but also in short films on everything from the people of foreign lands to atomic power and space travel—Disney produced popular guides for translating the natural and the scientific into familiar terms. Even before its television programs aired or its theme park opened, Disney used its public relations for such films to expand upon the substantial reputation it had developed for the accurate depiction of natural behaviors during the making of films such as *Bambi* (1942) and *Dumbo* (1941). Playing upon the notion that for over a decade Disney had been training its employees to scientifically observe the movements and behaviors of animals, in 1948 the company released its first nature documentary, *Seal Island*, which would be the first of thirteen films it made under its True-Life banner. Not only did these films fare far better critically than many of the company's other forays outside of animation during this difficult period—winning Disney eight Academy Awards—they also were very well received by the viewing public. Disney produced no fewer than eight True-Life Adventures before the television program *Disneyland* premiered—*Seal Island* (1948), *Beaver Valley* (1950), *Nature's Half Acre* (1951), *The Olympic Elk* (1952), *Water Birds* (1952), *Bear Country* (1953), *Prowlers of the Everglades* (1953), and *The Living Desert* (1953)—all of which received critical acclaim and profited in their theatrical runs before being recycled whole and in part on Disney television programs.[1] While part of this was no doubt due to the company's self-promotion and aggressive efforts to associate itself with the daily life of its patrons, the films obviously resonated with a public for whom the dispassionate scientific observation of natural behavior—a bay window that revealed the natural and uncompelled sociality of undomesticated animals—was important. Disney's True-Life Adventures resonated not only with a postwar shift in ideas about child-rearing, but with larger concerns about American culture and character that sprang from fears of a burgeoning "mass society" and its relationship to the totalitarian regimes the country had encountered during the war. By examining how theories of American character and culture—particularly in popular sociological and anthropological texts—and Disney's films and public relations circulated notions of natural development, we may better see how this shift in thinking joined quotidian anxieties about raising children to concerns about national well-being.

Observation on the Home Front

> *Give a suburban housewife a map of the area, and she is likely to show herself a very shrewd social analyst. After a few remarks about what a bunch of cows we all are, she will cheerfully explain how funny it is she doesn't pal around with the Clarks any more because she is using the new supermarket now and doesn't stop by Eleanor Clark's for coffee like she used to. . . . I believe this awareness is the significant phenomenon. . . . [Suburbanites] know full well why they do as they do, and they think about it often.*
>
> —WHYTE 1956, 331

What the nature documentary and child-rearing shared was an anxious fascination with regimes of observation. In its advertising, its television programs, its movies, and its intellectual discussions, mainstream 1950s America was preoccupied with observation and self-reporting: the self-reflexive spectacle of a culture watching itself. The red-baiting of Joseph McCarthy and the House Un-American Activities Committe and the generally popular anticommunist hysteria remain the most resonant examples, but their excesses make them seem more historically aberrant than they actually were. This culture of observation had derived from a wartime environment in which citizens were encouraged to watch themselves and others, especially in casual conversation, to avoid spilling sensitive information that might be overheard by spies. It was reinforced in the transition from a wartime economy in which the federal government had urged individuals and industries alike to police themselves and others in order to minimize waste, and in arguments by advertisers and industry groups that consumption was an act of citizenship, and failure to consume, either by one's self or by others, might undermine the new prosperity.[2] Campaigns encouraging workers to cut waste, to report potential sabotage, and to avoid talking about war-related work also taught housewives to monitor their consumption habits and those of others.[3]

Although World War II played a significant role in making the scrutiny of self and others a part of daily practices, the basis for such behavior-modification campaigns had been laid long before the war. Though both market research and the social survey date back to the turn of the century (Strasser, McGovern, and Judt 1998), Lynd and Lynd's *Middletown*, first published in 1929, established self-reflexive social data as a popular form, useful to social researchers and to a consuming public looking to understand its own lifeways. By the 1950s, it was widely understood that the purpose of such work was no longer strictly the improvement of social knowledge or the addressing of social problems. Work such as Elihu Katz and Paul Lazarsfeld's landmark "Decatur study" (1955) provided methods that charted variables such as "taste" and "opinion," information that was as useful to politicians as it was to advertisers. The data collected in these studies were more than intellectually fascinating; they were practically useful. They showed people in the business of influencing people, such as advertisers, more effective means of doing so. And, as techniques developed from such studies—such as refined methods of opinion polling—filtered out into popular media, they intensified a sense that observation was very much a part of American daily life. By the 1950s, a generation after the publication of *Middletown*, it was quite normal to assume that the American experience was quantifiable, one which required a steady stream of data, and which found its most reliable expression in a rapidly expanding middle class. The advertising and marketing agency J. Walter Thompson, for instance, could promise its customers monthly reports from "5,000 families under glass!" (1949). These families, claimed Thompson, were "America's great new middle class . . . the millions of families who have moved up several notches in income without changing their buying habits" and who were quite willing to keep and turn over detailed logs of their consumption habits (9). The middle class, as psychologist Martha Wolfenstein put it, was the de facto center of an emerging American cultural gestalt, and the willingness of that burgeoning middle class to describe itself to any interested parties "testifie[d] to the extension of the domain of science into human affairs" (1955, 345). The success of this enterprise was so extensive that by 1954, sociologist David Riesman could complain, "This very readiness to talk, this availability of a critical vocabulary, may hinder as well as help the researcher; words about words may screen rather than reveal underlying meanings" (183). The average middle-class respondent, it seemed, had become so good at responding, so willing to submit and reveal, that her responses were no longer wholly true, no longer reliable, no longer natural.

This problem of self-reflexivity was only intensified by the increasing presence of marketing in interpersonal relations. From the mid-twenties on, advertisers and marketers had increasingly come to recognize youth as not only as a market in its own right, but an entryway into other markets. The advertising trade journal *Printers' Ink* imagined middle-class children and teens as salespeople in the home, pitching products to their parents.[4] Even if parents still controlled the purse strings (which they did, in large part, until after the war), children could be used to tug on those purse strings—via the heartstrings. "The enthusiasm with which young people accept a new product," an expert in youth marketing suggested to interested advertisers, "kindles in parents a sympathetic warmth and paves the way for family acceptance" (E. Gilbert 1957, 28).[5]

But children weren't only useful as live advertisers in the home (much like radio, and later television), they also were excellent sources of information. Since answering questions truthfully and filling out forms were a child's means of gaining praise in public schooling, it seemed reasonable that children would eagerly provide useful marketing information if asked. In the late 1940s, the publishers of *Seventeen* magazine began selling *Life with Teena*, a compilation of "interviews with 2,516 girls and 799 of their mothers," in which women and girls gladly yielded up for manufacturers and advertisers valuable information about teenage female preferences and buying habits ("Importance of Youth Market" 1947, 78). At the same time, *Scholastic* magazine, under the guise of the "Institute of Student Opinion," surveyed "15,932 boys and 17,964 girls, ranging in age from 13 to 19 years" in forty-four schools in forty-four states to determine the students' brand consciousness and relationship to advertising and to offer that data to interested buyers (78).[6]

It was expected that children would develop brand loyalties, which, if properly cultivated, they would carry throughout their lives. This was a matter of concern for advertisers and educators alike, though in very different ways. The advantage of the Baby Boom to marketers was that it supplied plenty of fresh recruits and more potential lifetime customers for whom "brand consciousness" was a part of the formation of consciousness in general: "Where else on earth . . . is brand consciousness fixed so firmly in the minds of four-year-old tots? . . . What is it worth to a manufacturer who can close in on this juvenile audience and continue to sell it under controlled conditions year after year, right up to its attainment of adulthood and full-fledged buyer status? It CAN be done," read one trade journal ad for television (quoted in Packard 1957, 159).

By the middle of the 1950s this trend had become a widespread matter of public concern. As Vance Packard warned middle-class readers in his best-selling book *The Hidden Persuaders* (1957), "large-scale efforts are being made, often with impressive success, to channel our unthinking habits, our purchasing decisions, and our thought processes" (3). What made these new admen so much more dangerous than their predecessors, said Packard, was that they had enlisted the forces of science in those efforts: "Many of the nation's leading public-relations experts have been indoctrinating themselves in the lore of psychiatry and the social sciences in order to increase their skill at 'engineering' our consent. . . . [and in] many of their attempts to work over the fabric of our minds the professional persuaders are receiving direct help and guidance from respected social scientists" (4–6). The social sciences, the ostensible purpose of which had been to explain social conditions and to suggest solutions to social ills, suddenly seemed to also be in the business of explaining the inner workings of people's minds to advertisers.[7]

For the burgeoning managerial class, an object of scientific scrutiny since a largely unionized postwar workforce had successfully rejected the rigors of scientific management, what was true in the home was also true on the job.[8] The likelihood that a new middle manager would fit in—increasing social harmony in the workplace—depended upon latent tendencies and potentials the revelation of which required extensive batteries of predictive tests. These tests, such as the Thematic Apperception Test (TAT), Rorshach, and Minnesota Multiphasic Personality Index (MMPI), were meant to read below the surface, to locate the true person that lurked under an increasingly untrustworthy surface. The assumption behind these tests was that they could and would locate essential qualities in the individual which, if not acknowledged, could lead to maladjustment if he or she were forced into life decisions incommensurate with his or her true nature. But if these qualities were properly understood and fit to the proper job, the individual could expect to lead a well-adjusted and socially harmonious life. The challenge, then—for parents, human relations experts, and social theorists alike—was to create observational regimes that isolated those latent qualities, as well as to create environments that would foster them in a relatively nondirective fashion. Like the "naturalist photographers" that Disney used to create its nature documentaries, they had to observe without creating an awareness of the mechanisms of observation—or at the very least, without engendering behaviors produced in direct response to the observational apparatus. In short, the contradictory solution to the problem of producing conditions for a harmonious social environment was to provide the means by which people would learn to behave naturally. The catch was, of course, what "natural" meant in an emerging mass society and culture.

The response to this problem was complex and contradictory, particularly for those members of the middle class who found themselves and their children simultaneously the subjects and objects of scrutiny, and who imagined their consciousness as representative of the commonweal. On the one hand, personality tests and marketing data were comforting, providing a sense of commonality, of making choices based not on mere whims or impulsive desires, but upon a common sense shared by a statistically significant number of like-minded people.[9] On the other hand, there was a fear of disappearing into the crowd, of becoming just one of many "men in gray flannel suits," of having no individual will or opinion that was not prepackaged and delivered via predictive testing or market persuasion. Caught under the lenses of commercial and scientific scrutiny, a self-conscious public engaged in a search for a means of behaving naturally, of responding to social pressures in ways that constituted neither a blind acceptance of those pressures nor an unthinking rejection of them. This need to "act naturally," to find a mean between excesses of conformity and anarchic rebelliousness, engendered an interest in observational mechanisms—from surveys of American character to nature films that found that character enacted at a primal level—and in participating in that observation as its subject rather than its object.[10] What sociological surveys of American culture and character offered Americans in the 1950s was a model for balancing the needs and behaviors of the individual against those of the mass, and an argument about how that model sprang from the landscape from which the United States had arisen.

Visiting Nature at Home: Disney's White Wilderness

> *There are very few villains in wild nature—only an occasional renegade who is wantonly cruel or guilty of a "crime" against his own species. The vast majority of nature's children, often referred to as the lower orders, are irreproachably "moral." But among themselves, in their interrelated*

behavior and destiny, no creatures are "bad" who obey the laws of their nature, as instinct commands. This is thematic in "The Living Desert."
—OREGONIAN 1953

The structure of Disney's True-Life Adventure nature documentaries was as reassuringly invariable as nature itself. The films always began with an animated segment and voice-over that placed viewers firmly in the realm of natural history (as opposed to human history) by locating the opening of the narrative in a time before humans appeared in the landscape. What followed was what the narration (and Disney's public relations) called "nature's never-ending drama": a series of vignettes that centered on survival (battles over territory or hunting for food) and reproduction (mating and the rearing of young). Through a rhetoric of observation and revelation, the narrative would locate an unusual animal or a behavior and reveal the natural logic that informed its existence.

Almost invariably, that logic mirrored that of midcentury suburban America. Calling many animal characters "mom," "dad," and "the kids," and representing a variety of nesting and mating habits in terms that referred specifically to suburban middle-class domesticity, the films reconfigured as natural and universal a place and a set of practices that were taxonomically and historically specific. Disney didn't simply provide the familiar to its viewers as it revealed nature's suburban underbelly: it reinscribed the unfamiliar in terms that preserved its peculiarity while demonstrating its surprising underlying resemblance to middle-class American daily life. The True-Life Adventures revealed a strange natural landscape—a tundra, desert, or prairie—that reproduced the social world of the American suburb in its animal life. Thus, nature appeared exotic, independent, and distant, yet familiar and comforting. Disney provided a natural world simultaneously strange and predictable, invoking and calming anxieties that suburban America's built environment might produce in its future generations unnatural social relations—particularly excessive conformity.

A case in point is the aptly named *White Wilderness* (1958), Disney's penultimate True-Life Adventure, and the last to win an Academy Award (D. Smith 1996, 511).[11] Like each of its predecessors, the film begins with an animated segment that traces the emergence of an environment (in this case, the Arctic tundra) from the dawn of time through human prehistory (represented by the cave paintings at Lascaux) into the present. As the image dissolves from animation into live action, narrator Winston Hibler tells viewers, "the Arctic has always been a legendary land. And even today there exist here living legends, creatures about which man knows so little, they seem a blend of myth and mystery. In this True-Life Adventure, we shall find them continuing their Ice Age existence."

In *White Wilderness* (as in every other True-Life Adventure), the camera operates as a sort of time machine, revealing the continuity of animal behaviors over millennia and their applicability to modern situations. The single longest segment of the film—12 of its 102 minutes—is devoted to the phenomenon of the periodic mass suicide of lemmings. A study in mass behavior in nature, the episode offers viewers a detailed analysis of the structure of lemming society, and of why that society occasionally approaches the brink of mass destruction. As such, it reads as a compelling response to cold-war anxieties around mass behavior in general, and nuclear annihilation ("mutually assured destruction") in particular.

The episode begins with a "mother" lemming foraging for food, to be able to better nurse her young. In a nightmarish sequence, the hungry lemming becomes disoriented in an ice field soon after leaving her "home." The narrator comments, "It's like being lost in a hall of mirrors. In a moment you can't decide which is you, and which is your reflection." Like a postwar suburban mother desperately trying to understand which parts of her personality are natural, and which parts the result of her own unhealthy childhood conditioning, the lemming struggles to locate herself in a confusing white world in which the apparent sameness of every part of the landscape threatens disorientation. Just as her confusion deepens and threatens to be her undoing, the lemming escapes the ice field, regains her bearings, and "finds herself back at her own front door."

Safely "at home," the camera offers the audience an interior shot of her burrow as if seen through a bay window. Yet as the lemming feeds her young, the "family" is deluged by runoff from the spring thaw (because "the roof leaks"), and they are forced to abandon the den. At this moment, the narrative leaps from the individual to the mass and from the present to a future in which all of the young are grown. The lemmings are all forced out by the same leaky roof, and a society of adults begins to denude the landscape. The narrator explains that overpopulation has set in, and that it has caused a food shortage. "So Nature herself takes a hand," he explains. "A lemming migration is about to begin." The compression of time in the narrative sequence evokes the rootless and reactive behavior occasioned by the mass migration to white-collar suburbia that disturbed David Riesman in *The Lonely Crowd* (1950), as well as the specter of a future in which the grown children of the Baby Boom might have to compete for scarce jobs. "A time of tremendous reproduction generally means a time of famine," the film warns. "Lemmings literally eat themselves out of house and home. Whenever this happens they find it necessary to move to a new feeding ground." More than simply the result of prosperity and upward mobility, the audience is told, the lemmings' unthinking mass behavior quickly evolves into mass panic: "It would appear that the lemmings are a lot like sheep. Let one or two go somewhere, and the rest are determined to go, too. Once in motion, none stops to ask why. A kind of compulsion seizes each tiny rodent. And carried along by an unreasoning hysteria, each falls into step for a march that will take them to a strange destiny."

Here, the anxiety surrounding the production of natural conformity that was so important to many 1950s sociologists and developmental researchers comes to a point. Group identification is natural, but excessive identification is potentially fatal. While the need to belong permits the mobilization of individual impulses as mass action, the lemmings' problem, the film suggests, is that they are lemmings: as a group, they are naturally inclined to mass behavior. Although nature directs that behavior, just as it does that of other creatures, every now and then it requires that they compulsively march to the sea and to their deaths. The frenzy the lemmings undergo is so intense that they lose all sense of propriety and, during the course of their death march, repeatedly walk right into the clutches of predators. As they rush on toward their fate, the music builds, a galloping, wagon-trail theme.[12] The film recapitulates the anxiety and uncertainty of new suburbanites: pushing toward an uncertain future in an unknown terrain, suburban families aggressively followed paths of upward mobility in career, consumption, and leisure practices. As had their symbolic forebears, suburban homesteaders felt as if they were entering a new wilderness, one which promised a better life, but which also threatened an unknown future. Even those of the "new middle class" who hadn't yet set out for the suburbs could imagine their children some day making that move. Yet in the desire to conform, to get along, lay the possibility of following that group into oblivion: as the narrator of *White Wilderness* warns his audience, "They reach the final precipice. This is the last chance to turn back. Yet over they go, casting themselves bodily into space."

Driving home the results of unmoderated mass action, the segment's final sequence is shot from many angles. The audience watches from below as lemmings fall toward the water; it hovers above the edge of the cliff and, godlike, gazes down as they hurtle toward oblivion; it stands on a ledge and watches them bounce off the rocks and into the sea below. The consequences are brutal and nature is unsparing in its logic. But in Disney's neo-Darwinian world, the individual's drive to seek its own destiny ultimately serves the group. If nature drives the masses toward suicide, it is only so those few individuals whose enlightened self-interest marks them as superior may further the good of the species, and this tale of mass suicide ends not with death, but with life, as nature "in her infinite wisdom, has spared a few. Back on the Arctic plain there remains this small handful that did not make this fatal journey. And in time, new generations will take the place of those that have been lost." Reprising themes of individual restraint versus mass panic, the wisdom of the bomb shelter and civil defense association instead of the hunger-induced mania of the unprepared monistic mob, the scene neatly accommodates the ideal of individualism against the collective health of the group (the species).

If acknowledging nature as the ultimate arbiter of the child's future provided the parent with some degree of absolution around certain child-rearing decisions, it by no means delivered her from anxiety. The very same nature that held back that lucky few lemmings also drove the majority to their deaths. The lemming "mother" so confused by her natural landscape did everything she could to provide for her "children," yet that was no guarantee that they would be spared in the final frenzy. Maternal instinct by itself was no guarantee of success. How, then, was one to maximize the possibility that one's young would make the right choices, those that led to individual and species survival? A parent's clear performance of her relationship to her own emotions and behaviors, and the provision of further examples through instructive media, were the best guarantee that nature's inevitable process of selection would favor her child, but by no means a sure bet. The best a parent could hope for was that, by behaving "naturally," she would give her child the behavioral base necessary to move into culture with a sense of autonomous self-consciousness, a detached awareness of how natural impulses informed its cultural choices. As in its animated features, the Disney nature film played into this tension perfectly: its scenarios recapitulated parental anxieties, while appearing to offer children instructive examples of how to resist both pressures to conform and the unreasoning impulses that made them susceptible to those pressures.

Mass Culture and Mass Society

This ambivalence and uncertainty was recapitulated at the level of critical social commentary. The 1950s marked a point of arrival for the ideal American culture that progressive social reformers had thought so necessary to the well-being of the United States . . . and not everyone was sure it was a good thing. American mass culture—as it was dubbed to differentiate it from elite high culture—seemed to hold the potential for both good and evil. The relatively highly rationalized nature of post-Depression, postwar American middle-class society allowed for cohesive social activity and infrastructural development of a scale and pace never before imagined—from the introduction of the interstate highway system, to the standardization and expansion of public education, to the rapid development and expansion of communication technologies such as television.[13] At the same time, this apparent national unity, following so closely on the heels of the encounter with Nazi Germany, and contemporaneous with the specter of the Soviet Union, gave rise to fears of the onset of an American totalitarian mentality in this new mass society. The pleasure of participating in a robust national economy and a thriving mass culture was tinged with an uneasiness about the loss of individual identity and the dangers of demagoguery. These competing impulses could simultaneously give rise to the mass hysteria of the Red Scare and blacklists, and to popular warnings against unthinking mass behavior, from *The Fountainhead* (Vidor 1949) to *A Face in the Crowd* (Kazan 1957) or *The Manchurian Candidate* (Frankenheimer 1962).

As Henry Steele Commager put it in a 1950 New Year's Day prospectus in the *New York Times Magazine*, the United States that straddled the postwar world was a radically different place than it had been even a decade earlier:

> The past half-century has witnessed, everywhere in the Western world, a steady, perhaps an irresistible, expansion of government activities and enlargement of governmental authority. The felt necessities of the time—the rise of giant corporations, swift advances in technology, the shift from rural to urban life, the increasing complexity and sensitivity of economy, the compulsions of war and of international relations—all these have enlarged governmental activities and strengthened governmental power far beyond what was imagined possible in most Western countries in the nineteenth century. (30)

As Commager and many others pointed out, the traditional boundaries that had separated the home from business, civic organizations, and government appeared to be rapidly disappearing, and although this reorganization of social and material relations might have been the natural consequence of technological and rational advances in social organization, an accounting of their effects was in order. The alternative was an increasingly totalized existence that could easily shade into totalitarianism, the state control of every aspect of social and cultural life. This concern was particularly acute following World War II, when a minor intellectual industry erupted around the definition and analysis of authoritarian societies, including Hannah Arendt's *The Origins of Totalitarianism* (1945), Theodor Adorno et al.'s *The Authoritarian Personality* (1950), Erich

Fromm's *The Sane Society*, and Carl Friedrich and Zbigniew Brzezinski's *Totalitarian Dictatorship and Autocracy* (1956). More than simply performing an autopsy on the Nazi regime or anatomizing Soviet communism, these works also stood as warning posts about the etiology of totalitarian or authoritarian sentiment in purportedly free societies, arguments for a self-reflexive awareness of such tendencies in American society.

While such works aimed at changing social and political thought, others took aim more directly at popular culture. For example, Dwight MacDonald's acerbic jeremiad "A Theory of Mass Culture" (1953) epitomized midcentury elite and critical concerns about the influence of mass production and consumption on an ideal American culture and spoke to the producers and consumers of cultural objects high and low.[14] Drawing on diverse sources, from Clement Greenberg's "Avante-Garde and Kitsch" (1939) to the critiques of the Frankfurt School, MacDonald depicted American mass culture as a carbuncle on the face of modern civilization, one that threatened to become cancerous. MacDonald's essay was perhaps most significant in that it made explicit a point implied in many other midcentury discussions of mass culture: that the U.S.A. and Soviet Union shared a historical moment in which each had developed a mass culture. "The U.S.S.R. is even more a land of Mass Culture than is the U.S.A.," MacDonald wrote (1953, 60). "This is less easily recognizable because their Mass Culture is in form just the opposite of ours, being one of propaganda and pedagogy rather than that of entertainment. . . . [Yet like American Mass Culture] it is manufactured for mass consumption by technicians employed by the ruling class and is not an expression of either the individual artist or the common people themselves."

MacDonald's anxiety, like that of many of his contemporaries, was that mass culture in the United States and the Soviet Union, while formally different, were instrumentally identical. In either society, he argued, mass culture wasn't something produced by the masses—a modern folk culture—but something visited upon them by technocrats who played on their ignorance and instilled in them a blind need to consume. Even though he contrasted American entertainment with Soviet propaganda, he expressed a profound dismay that it was producing a populace that believed it was engaged in the reproduction of culture, when it was really merely consuming the shabby output of mass industries. As the American middle class grew in size and cultural influence, its confusion of its passive and mediocre tastes with critical aesthetic engagement replaced orderly regimes of discernment with "a tepid, flaccid Middlebrow Culture that threatens to engulf everything in its spreading ooze" (MacDonald 1953, 63–64).

In many ways, MacDonald's critique was no different than many from the previous generation.[15] While largely stripped of racial and ethnic overtones and forthright in its discussion of class, the essay laid blame for the disruption of American culture, not at the feet of immigrant producers, nor with the consumer, but with a technocratic class that produced the masses as a useful construct for the effective delivery of mass-produced goods. In his view, social scientists ("questionnaire sociologists") had deluded the mass public into mistaking its tastes and opinions for reality, while cultural producers (the "Lords of *kitsch*") debased that public by offering it, not what was best for it, but what it wanted (MacDonald 1953, 70). According to MacDonald, these technocrats were creating an infantile society in which the distinctions between the adult and the child collapsed in the face of demographic models that treated both as primitives to be stimulated into a consuming response. This produced infantilized adults who refused the intellectual work of consuming serious cultural objects, and prematurely sophisticated children with access to an adult world for which they weren't prepared (66). (See figures 22 and 23.)

Since MacDonald was long on diagnosis and short on prescription, "A Theory of Mass Culture" has often been dismissed as the fatalistic grumblings of a disaffected Trotskyite.[16] MacDonald agreed with neither the calls of conservatives such as T. S. Eliot or José Ortega y Gasset to reinvest a faltering class structure nor with those of Marxists such as Max Horkheimer and Theodor Adorno to reinvent the means of cultural production. Yet if one considers MacDonald's influential essay part of a discursive matrix involved in the education of a new middle class, then its implicit call for a reinvestment in individualism attained through the practice of discernment—and its emphasis on culture as a relationship between producers and consumers—becomes understandable as expressing a common concern with the negative effects of the growing rationalization of American social and cultural life. To whom was MacDonald speaking? Equally dismissive of the upper classes, whom he held responsible for the production of mass-cultural commodities as mechanisms of social domination, and of the masses consuming those products, MacDonald directed his tirade toward his fellow cultural and social critics, whose job it would be to shape a popular, middle-class understanding of the importance of cultural consumption to the health of the American social body.[17] As parents would facilitate their children's entrance into culture, critics such as those to whom MacDonald spoke would have the responsibility of explaining the proper shape of that culture to those parents, and to other adults increasingly inclined to act like children.

22. As part of a "Family Fashion Section," *Parents' Magazine* (February 1955) offered a series of style suggestions that reproduced sons as miniature versions of their fathers, or perhaps fathers as larger versions of their sons.

23. Blue Bell Jeans also used the father-and-son motif in an ad campaign in the mid-1950s. Ayers Collection, Archives Center, National Museum of American History, Smithsonian Institution.

American Character: The Nature of American Culture

During and following World War II, there was no shortage of descriptions of American character and culture and prescriptions for how best to maintain it. Some, like the follow-up volume to *Middletown*, *Middletown in Transition* (Lynd and Lynd 1937), or *Yankee City* (Warner and Lunt 1941), operated from a primarily sociological perspective, conducting latitudinal surveys of the social practices and attitudes of specific locales. Others—eventually called the "culture and personality" school—such as Margaret Mead's *American Character* (1944) or Geoffrey Gorer's *The American People* (1948)—proceeded from a more anthropological premise, attempting to locate common cultural traits across a wide variety of social classes and locations. These texts were themselves anticipated by works such as James Plant's *Personality and the Cultural Pattern* (1937), which applied Benedict's notion of "patterns of culture" to the analysis of the relationship of personality to the production of culture; or Elton Mayo's *The Human Problems of an Industrial Civilization* (1933), which argued that the application of Freudian analytic techniques to management could humanize industrial relations, increase productivity, and produce social harmony.[18] Similarly, in works such as *Characteristically American* (Perry 1949), *The Next America: Prophecy and Faith* (Bryson 1952), *People of Plenty* (Potter 1954), or *The Achieving Society* (McClelland 1961), psychologists, sociologists, historians, marketing consultants, and economists attempted to explain how a rapidly integrating network of domestic, social, working, and governmental spheres could remain human and socially viable.[19] Many also attempted to locate qualities that contributed to an essential and sustainable American character.[20]

Whether critical or celebratory, all of these texts were concerned with the rapid rationalization and integration of social, cultural, and economic life in the United States following the New Deal and the transition from a wartime to a postwar economy. Many framed this concern by comparing American mass culture to the regulation of cultural life in Nazi Germany, or in the Soviet Union. Taking the rationalization of social life as a historical inevitability, these discussions of American culture and character produced models that differentiated that process from its counterparts in authoritarian or totalitarian regimes, and in particular worked to isolate those elements of the American psyche—whether individual or cultural—that were resistant to excesses of obedience and self-regulation. The American middle class had to understand how the standardization of daily life—in the use of normative testing in public schooling, in the psychological regulation of the burgeoning managerial class, and in the built environment of the suburbs—was qualitatively different from that of its ideological opponents (but still worthy of a healthy suspicion). More important, it had to have the necessary tools for ensuring that this difference did not disappear in the ongoing rush of mass society and culture.

Delineating the proper relationship between nature and culture was key to this project. If there were essential qualities in American culture that made it resistant to authoritarianism and totalitarianism, and if it were susceptible to positive or negative social influences, then understanding what exactly culture was, and how it was produced and maintained in human beings, became vital. In a widely shared neo-Freudian perspective, the child, a being that began life outside of culture—a natural creature functioning solely at the level of primal desires for food, comfort, shelter, companionship—was the point at which one could most successfully intercede in the evolution of a national culture. The type of culture the child would encounter during the process of domestication and socialization would shape not only its behaviors and life choices but also the culture it would produce and then reproduce in its own offspring.

In this sense, these studies of "American character" shared a common ancestor in the efforts of Progressive Era social reformers to name and deliver a common and stable American culture into which immigrants could assimilate. Figuratively describing twentieth-century American culture as a cultural-evolutionary child fathered by European civilization, many of these later studies argued that child-rearing practices in the United States recapitulated this relationship, and that the careful study and reinvention of those practices would provide the best prophylactic against further propagating decadent European tendencies toward fascism or totalitarianism. Because children traversed the gulf between animal nature and its expression in culture, between an imperfect past and an improvable future, the facilitation of that transit offered an essential point of intervention into the direction of an emerging global civilization of which the United States was at the forefront. For this reason, almost all of these studies of American character moved beyond *Middletown*'s modest goal of describing middle America to itself, to discussing how best to shape American culture through its children.

Two studies in particular achieved widespread popular acclaim on the order that *Middletown* had before them: *The Lonely Crowd* (1950), by David Riesman, Reuel Denney, and Nathan Glazer, and *The Organization Man* (1956), by William H. Whyte. Although each took a significantly different approach to the question—Riesman's work derived from the "culture and personality" school, while Whyte's was more traditionally sociological (and hostile to intervention)—both expressed a common concern with the problem of conformity in

American society and culture, with the tendency of Americans to observe and regulate themselves and others, and both emphasized the role of child-rearing in both compounding and correcting that problem. Yet, as both were written in response to a number of their antecedents, a moment's consideration of two of those works—Margaret Mead's *American Character* (1944) and Geoffrey Gorer's *The American People* (1948)—will help situate their contribution to the circulation of conceptions of the child in midcentury popular American culture.

Originally released as *And Keep Your Powder Dry* (1942), Margaret Mead's *American Character* (1944) placed the study of American character in the service of the war effort. A student of Ruth Benedict, Mead had leapt to public prominence with the publication of *Coming of Age in Samoa* (1928), which sought to demonstrate for a popular middle-class audience the practical applicability of comparative anthropology to immediate social problems by contrasting American adolescence to the life of Samoan teens (see chapter 5). Imagining a world "on the verge of social self-consciousness," Mead argued for a shift in the role of the social scientist from that of neutral observer, to that of active participant in the restructuring of society (3). "To the investigation of social materials to the end that we may know more," she argued, "has to be added the organization of social materials that we may *do* more . . . to attack the problem of reorganizing the world" (4).

Mead's premise in *American Character* was that national character derived from the social environment in which one was raised, not from inherent racial characteristics, and that as such it was malleable. Written during the war, this argument was meant to counter sentiments sympathetic to Nazi eugenic arguments. It was also intended to contribute to the construction of unified domestic front by overcoming irrational interracial and interethnic hostilities by arguing that differences ascribed to race or ethnicity were actually social and cultural. For Mead, cultures experienced evolutionary change, just as species did. Unlike the blind determinism of natural selection, however, which unfolded incrementally over many generations, cultural evolution was susceptible to direction and regulation. Such direction required an understanding of the beliefs and behaviors of previous generations, and an appreciation for the importance of child-rearing as the moment at which a culture was most open to reinvention. Imagining an audience of young parents (particularly young mothers), Mead described the process by which parents' responses to historical circumstances shaped American culture. "The behavior of those of us who live today carries traces of other behaviors, themes developed under other stresses," she suggested (1944, 120–21). "Our behavior, good or bad, our strengths and our weaknesses are the resultant of the choices, voluntary and involuntary, of those who have gone before us. Americans are what they are because they have been reared in America by parents with certain ways of behaving."

As the United States entered a protracted world war, Mead warned that Americans were in danger of passing to their children behaviors developed in response to the rapid rationalization of daily life, and to the hardships of the Depression. The current generation of parents, she argued, had learned to view their lives through the lenses of failure and victimization by social forces too large to be confronted as individuals. The crushing hardships of the Depression, the rapid industrial consolidation that had helped engender it, and a dependence on government intervention had engendered in Americans a passivity in dealing with their circumstances, a sense of fatalism. At that crucial historical juncture, these behavioral responses to historical circumstances had to be countered by a conscious effort to instill in children values and behaviors by which they could rise to the challenges they now faced.[21]

What Mead suggested as a corrective was nothing less than "social engineering," the purposeful regulation of behaviors and practices (176). The problem for Mead, and for the popular audience she addressed, was the similarity of her project to the state regulation of culture by the Nazis (who used "Dr. Goebbels' methods"). "Wherein lies the difference," she asked, "between the streamlined Nazi state and a state in which we, as Americans, analyze and use the strengths and weaknesses of the American character?" (176–77). Would we produce our own version of the Hitler Jugend? This would be a fundamental question for proponents of the regulation of American character throughout the postwar period. The difference, she argued, was one of intent and methods. The totalitarian state proceeded by developing a comprehensive plan and then bending the lives and wills of its people to that plan. The democratic social planner studied the relationship between nature and culture in her society—the refraction of natural human behaviors by the sociocultural moment in which they developed—and provided that data to an informed populace so that it could *adjust itself* to meet the challenges it would face (183–92).

The association between the immediate concerns of child-rearing and the history of national character that Mead outlined were further explored in British expatriate anthropologist Geoffrey Gorer's *The American People: A Study in National Character* (1948). A friend and protégé of Mead, Gorer made much more explicit the expression of the Freudian architecture of the psyche in an evolving American character. For Gorer, the structure and operation of the middle-class American family was metonymic for the relationship of the American state to the rest of the world. The United States was the wayward son of Anglo-European civilization, perpetually repeating through immigration an Oedipal struggle with an increasingly distant European father that had begun with the American Revolution, and at the mercy of a domineering, high-strung mother (actual American mothers) (Gorer 1948, 27, 55–60). In this scenario, the American character was inherently white and male, more advanced than its tradition-bound European father, and more vulnerable for its lack of an immediate and strong father figure against which to rebel. American culture and society were an evolutionary step forward from European civilization, containing the promise of an emerging new species and the danger of an unsustainable adaptation.[22]

The relationship between the parent and the child was essential to Gorer's story. A nation of immigrants, the United States had a transformative effect on new arrivals. While new immigrants had rejected their European father, they remained culturally linked through their own upbringing. Their children, however, were transformed by the institutions of American public culture, particularly its schools and public entertainments. For boys in particular, this created both possibilities and limitations. In the Oedipal struggle with the father, rejecting his European traditions was easy; finding a masculine figure with which to identify was a problem. Rejecting their own tradition-bound fathers as an object of either rebellion or identification, American boys were likely to look to public role models and to each other for information about their identities, making them vulnerable to manipulation. Likewise, American girls were likely to reject the European child-rearing traditions of their mothers and turn to fads and experts in a desperate search for an authoritative version of how to behave. In the era of scientifically managed child-rearing, he argued, this charged the domestic environment with maternal anxiety, the fear of improper management. The advent of "permissive" regimes of child-rearing offered no respite from this problem, as mothers anxiously absented themselves from the role of disciplinarian, leaving the child to seek guidance from peers and adults outside the home (Gorer 1948, 70–89).

The debilitating potentials of this pattern of culture, Gorer argued, were exacerbated—whether by the paternalism of the New Deal state or by the military requirements of World War II—by the moral or physical absence of the father in the home and in civic life. Lacking a male role model to emulate (or a male barrier to their mothers' excesses of affection and attention), American boys were growing up insecure and uncertain about their masculinity. Anxious to please their mothers or their female schoolteachers, boys shaped their behaviors and personalities in order to gain feminine praise. Conversely, if they rebelled against this predominantly feminine authority, they did so without a positive masculine role model to emulate. They transferred this behavior to relations with their peers, looking to others (and to media) for validation of their character and expressive choices. This could lead to a society of men who lacked a masculine core, and who were overly dependent on the opinions of others — either in accepting or rejecting them — and to a social milieu in which feminine values dominated (Gorer 1948, 50–69). The presence of men in the domestic sphere offered no corrective for this imbalance if men deferred to the dominant feminine organizing principle, acting like older masculine siblings with their sons. Although far less prescriptive than Mead, Gorer's psychohistorical sketch of midcentury American character offered its middle-class readers a persuasive argument for the reinvestment of masculine authority in domestic and civic life. His application of Freud to the history of American culture and to the immediate problem of safeguarding the national future through its children appealed to anxieties about the role of management-based child-rearing in undermining the positive aspects of American individualism and encouraging totalitarianism (28–31).[23]

Mead and Gorer thus both favored intervening in the evolution of American culture through adjustments to the enculturation of its children. This intervention could not be direct; that was the Soviet model. Instead, the child's enculturation had to proceed from those naturally responsible for the task: its parents. This required that American parents understand the culture into which they were introducing their children, how their own upbringing had distorted certain essential qualities in that culture, and how they could best correct for those distortions in their own lifestyles and methods of child-rearing. The problem, of course, was in being able to discern what was an inherent American culture or character, and what was the distortion. Of the broad range of works that attempted to address this problem, two in particular reached a substantial popular audience, tapping into broadly held fears about the increasing rationalization of American social and cultural life. While Riesman's *The Lonely Crowd* (1950) and Whyte's *The Organization Man* (1956) were significantly different in theoretical orientation and in prescription, both works addressed profound concerns about the problem of excesses of conformity, observation, and belonging in 1950s society, and both found a broad middle-class audience interested in coming to terms with them.[24]

David Riesman Addresses a Lonely Crowd

A conventional reading of popular expressions of fear of mass behavior in the 1950s is that they were a manifestation of cold-war anxieties about Soviet domination or invasion. This reading ignores, however, the emergence of a widespread concern that the United States itself harbored latent totalitarian impulses not entirely unlike those that held sway in the Soviet Union. Those concerns were not solely the province of an intellectual elite uneasy about the spread of mass popular culture. Sloan Wilson's novel *The Man in the Gray Flannel Suit* (1955) was an overwhelming sensation among the very middle-American types it depicted, and *The Lonely Crowd* and *The Organization Man* were both quite popular with the very same managerial class in which they saw the potential for totalitarian behavior. If sales and popularity are any indicators, the new middle class was just as worried about its own propensity for totalitarian behavior as were its elite betters, and desired guidance in the practice of being truly and naturally American.

Of all of the works discussed thus far, Riesman's *The Lonely Crowd* (1950), as well as his subsequent *Individualism Reconsidered* (1954), provided a theory of American culture and character as just such a manual for social practice.[25] Attempting to explain changes in the social and cultural landscape of middle America, Riesman's research took as the object of its study the same group that found in *The Lonely Crowd* a means of explaining those changes to themselves and each other—the rapidly expanding professional middle class: "*The Lonely Crowd* did not move outward from individuals toward society, but rather the other way around; we started with society and with particular historical developments within society. We concerned ourselves, moreover, with the upper social strata, particularly with what has been called the 'new middle class' of salaried professionals and managers" (Riesman and Glazer 1961, 427).

The Lonely Crowd was immensely successful, attracting both a general audience and many social theorists attempting to explain and instruct this new middle class. If Margaret Mead's increasing stature as a public figure, and the popular reception of Geoffrey Gorer's work (positively reviewed in *Time* magazine), marked a new wave of explaining America to itself, *The Lonely Crowd* was the first such book since *Middletown* (Lynd and Lynd 1929) that found a mass audience looking for instruction in how best to translate itself into the (nation's) future. Aided by circulation in the Reader's Subscription Book Club—a self-styled intellectual alternative to the middlebrow Book of the Month Club—and by glowing reviews in mass periodicals (and a cover story in *Time* in 1954), the concept of an "other-directed" American middle class struggling to understand and moderate its tendencies toward conformity that Riesman sketched in *The Lonely Crowd* became the lingua franca of collective self-reflection, "the common coin of the new cocktail-and-breezeway Bohemia" (Aldridge 1955).[26] The sociological study of suburban living and managerial culture gave voice and form to popular concerns about the contradictory impulses toward harmony and social cohesion, and a fear of excessive conformity and a loss of an inherently American individualism.

A law professor turned sociologist, Riesman borrowed from Malthusian economics, Weberian sociology, and Erich Fromm's psychoanalytic approach to history to create a complex sociohistorical model that attempted to explain why 1950s America had developed such a profound culture of conformity and self-observation.[27] First, Riesman divided all cultures into three rough groups: the tradition-directed, the inner-directed, and the other-directed. *Tradition-directed* types (primitives) derived their impetus for social action from collectively maintained and unchanging traditions in which the group's will superseded that of the individual (Riesman, Denney, and Glazer 1950, 10–13). *Inner-directed* persons navigated social life by using moral codes internalized in childhood instead of external social codes enforced by the collective (16). These figures emerged during and after the Renaissance, he argued, as European society became more mobile and enabled individuals to follow the flexible dictates of labor and take advantage of the potential to accrue capital.[28] Like the individual in the Protestant ethic, this inner-directed person had a relatively well-defined social role but was personally responsible for success or failure in that role (13–17). Finally, Riesman argued, the twentieth-century iteration of the sociocultural individual, the *other-directed* person, lacked the "internal compass" of the inner-directed, or the clear boundary markers of the tradition-directed, depending instead on feedback from its peer group to determine its course of action (17–25). This person was the member of the "new middle class" of the 1950s, the problem to be addressed and the subject of that address. The other-directed individual had no internalized moral code, no rigid set of external beliefs; instead, it relied upon a constant reading of its own choices "through an exceptional sensitivity to the actions and wishes of others" (22).

Riesman then suggested a relationship between these modes of social practice and certain conditions of population and economic development.[29] He associated tradition-directed societies with "high growth potential," a high birth rate that, if coupled with a declining death rate, would lead to a rapid and destabilizing population increase. These were societies likely to have complex cultural operations around birth and death designed to keep each in check

(10–11). Inner-directed societies were associated with "transitional growth," in which a sudden shift in population dynamics was usually accompanied by a change in labor relations away from a feudal model and toward a mercantile capitalist model (13–14). Finally, Riesman described the other-directed social character as arising in periods of "incipient decline," in which population began to taper off as agriculture gave way to industrialization and child labor gradually became superfluous (17–19). (Obviously, Riesman had overlooked the Baby Boom, which was already under way when *The Lonely Crowd* went to press, an oversight for which he was later criticized.)[30] Riesman's complicated heuristic participated in the general enthusiasm for things scientific or scientistic that marked the decade and represented a trend in American social science toward more empiricist and scientistic modeling (D. Ross 1991).[31] A discussion of neo-Malthusian concepts such as "incipient population decline" seemed to blend the hard science of Darwinian biology with economics to create an understanding of the mechanisms of cultural evolution. Yet in popular and professional discussions of *The Lonely Crowd*, this complex interplay of demographics, cultural theory, and political economy largely disappeared in favor of Riesman's three basic character types—the tradition-, inner- and other-directed—and indeed it was those types that Riesman focused on in the majority of both *The Lonely Crowd* and *Individualism Reconsidered* (1954).

Yet there was another compelling reason for the work's complex modeling of social relations. Riesman's model offered a means for differentiating between U.S. and Soviet rationalization and conformity: the Soviet Union was still involved in "transitional growth," and its people still locked between "tradition-direction" and "inner-direction." Hence its social conformity arose from state imposition, rather than from a properly evolving social psychology (Riesman, Denney, and Glazer 1950, 17; see also Riesman 1954, 32 and Riesman and Glazer 1961, 448). The distinction was crucial: if a tendency toward conformity in the United States arose because its other-directed people were experiencing economic and social conditions associated with abundance and "incipient decline," then one could understand it as deriving from individual responses to social and cultural conditions and possibly responsive to their modification. Conformity in the Soviet Union, however, was out of sync with its characterological profile, deriving from totalitarian state action rather than from the spontaneous responses of individual Soviet citizens to sociocultural conditions.[32]

The ability to illustrate the relationship between sociocultural behaviors and material conditions, then, allowed one to understand and describe those behaviors as a relatively natural response or—in the case of state-enforced communalism—as an unnatural, externally imposed mechanism doomed to fail in its collision with immutable circumstance. While every society demanded typological conformity from its citizens according to its place on the cultural evolutionary ladder, Riesman argued, that demand derived from the intersection of material necessity and cultural pattern. Even though residual character types from previous epochs, or types that suggested the next evolutionary adaptation, might be present in a given society, it was not possible to change an entire society simultaneously. Only the natural interplay between cultural form and material circumstance could accomplish that change, and then only over generations. This was true in every culture, including that of the United States:

> In America, it is still possible to find southern rural groups, Negro and poor white, in the phase of high growth potential—and it is here that we look for the remnants of tradition-directed types. Similarly, immigrants to America who came from rural and small-town areas in Europe carried their fertility rates and character patterns with them to our major cities . . . [and were] forced to make . . . the jump from a society in which tradition-direction was the dominant mode of insuring conformity to one in which other-direction is the dominant mode. (Riesman, Denney, and Glazer 1950, 32)[33]

While some could make this leap in character type in a single lifetime, Riesman was quick to assert, more often the change took place between generations, with the children of backward types bringing a cultural subgroup into sync with the majority culture. Here, a Boasian rhetoric of assimilation and race was subsumed under the sign of character, configured as a neo-Darwinian model that described cultural evolution as an ineluctable natural progression indifferent to social and political resistance.[34] In a similar fashion, class struggle was naturalized as "a struggle among different characterological adaptations to the situation created by the dominance of a given mode of insuring conformity" (Riesman, Denney, and Glazer 1950, 31). In this formulation, conflict and tension between social groups—whether defined by race, ethnicity, class, or even gender—derived not from the discourses, structures, or practices of subjugation and resistance, but from the necessary clash of outmoded cultural imperatives with their evolutionary descendants.[35] This formulation was an effort to differentiate between *coercive* "social engineering" and *instructive* social science—the scientific process of providing to a people knowledge of themselves necessary to further their ability to make and remake their society in ways they saw fit.[36] Even though the neo-Malthusian part of Riesman's thesis was quickly called to question, the rest of his work remained fundamental to many other projects and was cited in popular works into the next decade.[37]

Having laid out this complicated schematic for the interplay of nature and culture in the production of personality, Riesman spent the bulk of *The Lonely Crowd* describing in simple terms how "other-direction" had developed in American society, how the social and cultural practices of an emerging mass society reinforced the character trait, and how, perhaps, members of this society might act to attenuate the excessive tendencies toward conformity inherent in other-direction. Important to both comprehending and acting upon this situation was a clear understanding of the function and importance of child-rearing in the (re)production of culture and character. For Riesman, the best model for understanding the centrality of child-rearing was the process of reaction-formation that Margaret Mead (1942) had outlined as the method by which members of one generation attempted to forge their culture, by accepting or rejecting their parents' behavioral responses to their own sociocultural circumstances. In order to properly respond to the changing social conditions that so concerned them, parents of (or aspiring to) the new middle class had first to understand that the conditions under which they had entered culture were significantly different from those under which their children would make the same journey: "It is largely as the socializing agents are affected by these life conditions that there is a break in the genealogical succession of more or less identical character types. . . . changes in general social conditions can alter the competitive position, and therefore the influence, of competing agencies of socialization. . . . the peer group and school now take over some of the functions previously performed by the family alone" (Riesman, Denney, and Glazer 1950, 37).

There was a distinctive gap, Riesman argued, between the social world of fifties parents and that of their children. Although middle-class parents, especially those of the new managerial class, worked in environments designed to encourage other-direction—regulated by personality and aptitude testing, as well as by management techniques that favored group dynamics over individual achievement—they had been raised on the cusp between inner-direction and other-direction (138–41). Raised under rigid, management-based child-rearing regimes during the Depression, on the one hand, and subsuming their personal aspirations and desires to the common good in wartime society on the other, they had experienced firsthand the contradiction between these two characterological modes. Yet if they understood and rejected the methods by which their parents had raised them, they didn't necessarily understand which means were applicable to the new social organization in which they found themselves.

In short, 1950s parents knew enough to fear repeating the child-rearing mistakes of their parents, but not enough to know what to do in their stead. If they attempted to raise their children the way they had been raised, they risked producing a person unable to fit into a culture and society that favored either harmony and belonging or individual competition. "Under the new conditions of social and economic life," Riesman warned, "parents who try, in inner-directed fashion, to compel the internalization of discipline run the risk of having their children styled clear out of the personality market" (Riesman, Denney, and Glazer 1950, 48). On the other hand, if they backed away from the systems that had guided their own development, parents seemed to have little choice but to leave the process in the hands of others: "Inhibited from presenting their children with sharply silhouetted images of self and society, parents in our era can only equip the child to do his best, whatever that may turn out to be. What is best is not in their control but in the hands of the school and peer group that will help locate the child eventually in the hierarchy" (48).

Yet the impulse to turn over the child's socialization to others was fraught with pitfalls. (Nor did it address the problem of how parents were to handle the child's enculturation in its infancy and early childhood, before it developed a peer group or entered school. See chapter 5.) Leaving the process in the hands of others was itself a lesson that collective organizations were more important than individuals and might sway the child toward excessive conformity. Even if parents demonstrated confusion or concern over achieving the proper balance between teaching their children internalized discipline and allowing them to learn in and through other groups, Riesman argued, they could not "help but show their children, by their own anxiety, how little they depend on themselves and how much on others. Whatever they may seem to be teaching the child in terms of content, they are passing on to him their own contagious, highly diffuse anxiety" (49). It wasn't simply what parents *did* that facilitated or hindered children's proper entry into culture; the process also hinged on how comfortable they were with themselves, no matter what they did. Just as important was how they *appeared* to their child, a higher-order creature that could sense emotional states and would adjust itself accordingly—whether the way they interacted with that child was natural and consonant with their own relationship to society.

While Riesman considered the peer group the most potent childhood socializing agent for children, that group's common currency was that of consumption, taste, and style, which were supplied by the mass media. Perhaps most disturbing to him, mass media not only provided children with the stuff of taste and consumption, they even instructed them in what it meant to be a child:[38]

> While the educator in earlier eras might use the child's language to put across an adult message, today the child's language may be used to put across the advertiser's and storyteller's idea of what children are like. No longer is it the child's job to see the adult world as the adult sees it. . . . Instead, the mass media ask the child to see the world as "the" child—that is, the *other* child—sees it. . . . The media have created a picture of what boyhood and girlhood are like . . . and they force children either to accept or aggressively to resist this picture of themselves. (Riesman, Denney, and Glazer 1950, 100–101)

In a form of infinite regress, the child modeled itself on the media's image of what a child (as consumer) should be, while the media polled children as to what they wanted and what they thought their world looked like in order to produce that image. At the same time, parents looked on helplessly or encouraged their children to get along, to adjust, to fit in, to refine their marginal differentiation just enough that they would stand out as unique without seeming strange or antisocial (46–47).

Thus it was important—perhaps too important—to blend into one's surroundings, to carefully observe the behaviors of others without having one's own behavior overly scrutinized. What resulted, Riesman claimed, was a society with a dangerously flat power structure. Children, noting in their parents a profound uncertainty, and consuming very different mass-media models of what proper parenting should look like, turned away from their families as sources of guidance and socialization (Riesman, Denney, and Glazer 1950, 51). Likewise, to better fit in parents gave authority over their children to other agents and indeed allowed children an equal or even dominant role in the structuring of the family's social life (53–55). As children grew into adulthood, they would internalize a model of living in which their choices and direction were dictated by others, in which it was safer and wiser to react than to act. While this approach to life might have been culturally appropriate, it had the potential to become socially disastrous. It could lead to the production of adults so devoted to group harmony that they were uncomfortable with risking the possibility of confrontation that would come with a desire to lead, either in their own social circles, or in the larger arena of political life (184–90).

Even if other-directedness were a predictable cultural adaptation to circumstances of plenty and an increasingly rationalized society, it contained the seeds for undermining the very conditions that created it. Yielding too much to systems of external validation left open the possibility that those systems would become formally sedimented, freezing the culture's ongoing evolution. In Riesman's view, the roots of a totalitarian society began with this excess need to get along and belong, which could lead to a dependence on what Erik Erikson (1961, xii) would refer to as the "technicians of adjustment." These people—school guidance counselors, market-research analysts, and industrial psychologists—responding to the problematic tendency of the other-directed toward self-reporting and adjustment, would deploy the personality tests, opinion polls, and consumer surveys to determine the latent desires and potentials of the masses and, when necessary, to realign them to increase consumption or obedience to social and cultural dictates.[39] The very impulses that provided Riesman with the data necessary to define the other-directed personality—the urge to self-report and to treat social research as social fact—were both markers for a quality of American culture and a symptom of the flight from that culture, the extreme version of which was capitulation to the totalitarian impulse, the willful refusal to attempt to set the terms of one's own existence (Riesman, Denney, and Glazer 1950, 160–74, 307–24). Even as it became a matter of some urgency that social researchers provide the new middle class with the tools for regulating and altering that culture (and hence their society) it was also important that those people have some means for limiting their dependence on those researchers and resistance to any inappropriate attempts toward "adjustment."

This meant much more than simply calling for a return to an idealized, nineteenth-century individualism.[40] Other-direction was an evolutionary cultural adaptation to conditions in mid-twentieth-century America—conditions to which simple individualism no longer applied. Rather than returning to the storied days of inner-directed individualism, Riesman argued, Americans ought to work to foster the notion of autonomy in their cultural products and social lives.[41] This idea, properly understood and promulgated, would allow American culture to gradually transcend the excesses of other-direction and adjustment. Where the individualist always weighed personal benefit against social norms, the autonomous individual would have the tools to choose whether to conform to each given set of circumstances, rather than opting into or out of a culture of conformity and observation on a wholesale basis:

> The autonomous person, living like everyone else in a given cultural setting, employs the reserves of his character and station to move away from

> the adjusteds of the same setting. Thus, we cannot properly speak of an "autonomous other-directed man . . ." but only of an autonomous man emerging from an era or group depending on other-direction. . . . For autonomy . . . is a deviation from the adjusted patterns, though a deviation controlled in its range and meaning by the existence of those patterns. (Riesman, Denney, and Glazer 1950, 294–95)

This "autonomous person" would be neither a conformist nor a rebel, nor so disaffected that she imagined herself outside of culture but forcibly subject to it. She would, Riesman suggested, be able to see her culture as historically evolving, rather than as either an inherently natural set of preconditions for existence or an arbitrary set of strictures set up to thwart her own desires. At the same time, she would be able to understand the latent motives and structures driving her choices as directive, but not determinative. In short, the autonomous person would be an evolutionary adaptation in the American character induced through limited "social engineering" in order to direct that character past other-direction and into a phase in which it used systems of evaluation to regulate its social environment, rather than allowing itself to be regulated by them.

Of course, to influence the evolution of American culture required introducing this adaptation at the point at which it was most likely to take hold. Since adults, and even older children, were already participants in the culture, with other-directed investments in their status and location in it, they were poor candidates.[42] In that moment before children fully entered into culture, their vectors could be affected and a trajectory plotted toward relative autonomy rather than toward excessive other-direction. For Riesman, this redirection could take many forms. Parents could, for instance, strive to create a family leisure life in which their children had play time that was unstructured, not part of the complex of social integration and career formation that marked such activities as music lessons, sports, and theatrics (Riesman 1954, 209–11). In this way, children would have time to encounter themselves—to learn what their own interests and tastes were—and to encounter their families, free from the call of the peer group or the school. In similar fashion, parents could train children to understand the difference between freely chosen peer groups and those dictated by social convention (Riesman 1954, 269–70; Riesman, Denney, and Glazer 1950, 342–44). In this way, they would learn that social interaction, or "belonging," was not a mandate to be anxiously followed, but a choice.[43]

In part, Riesman's prescriptions echoed those offered to parents (i.e., mothers) of the previous generation: they were expected to monitor and direct their children's behavior and development with the understanding that what was at stake wasn't merely the individual child's future, but that of the entire nation. Yet Riesman required more than simple regulation. He suggested that parents present to their children the appearance that they were quite certain of what they were doing, that they demonstrate no anxiety and appear to need no direction in their child-rearing efforts—that they act *naturally*.[44] To do less would be to suggest to the child that its parents lacked the internal resources to raise it, that they were themselves too other-directed to do other than to turn to outsiders for help—encouraging the child to do the same (Riesman, Denney, and Glazer 1950, 48–51). Riesman's manual for a new middle class shared with child-rearing manuals of the previous generation, and with popular child-rearing magazines, the trap of producing anxiety even as it attempted to end it. If child-rearing regimes of the previous generation had raised the specter of the evaluation of one's family through one's children, this generation had to contend with the idea that children themselves, canny and wary, observed their parents and evaluated whether they were fitting facilitators for their own enculturation.

What had changed from one generation to the next, however, was the metaphorical role that parents were meant to take in the practice of raising their children. The idea that parents were meant to disguise the use of any methodology in raising their children, that they were to simultaneously facilitate their children's entrance into culture *and* allow the children to find their way naturally, meant that they had to observe both themselves and their children. If parents were to create the conditions necessary for inducing autonomy, they had to make sure that they appeared to be behaving naturally, and that their children were reacting naturally to that behavior. Where the previous generation of parents ideally had been industrial managers, clearly and obviously monitoring and regulating their children's self-production, this generation of parents were *naturalists*. They were meant to blend into the domestic scenery, to watch without being observed watching, to appear natural. This contradictory injunction—that parents observe themselves in order to determine whether they were acting as if they had no doubts about what they were doing—aptly captured the very impulse that created a mass audience for *The Lonely Crowd* Fortunately, experts specifically devoted to child development and child-rearing would supply many more practical solutions in manuals and periodicals (see chapter 5). And another source parents could turn to—and would be encouraged to turn to by popular periodicals—was Disney, particularly its True-Life Adventures. There they could find the culture of suburban America mirrored back to them in the lives and habits of animals, mothers and fathers just like themselves.

Interlude: Mrs. Rat's Bomb Shelter

One of the vignettes in Disney's *The Living Desert* (1953) neatly captures the company's postwar construction of a domesticated, suburban nature. The scene opens with an impossible view: we are peering into the den of a kangaroo rat, as if through a living room window. The camera takes us inside, and we watch a kangaroo rat tend to her newborn offspring. The narrator refers to her as "Mrs. Rat," who is "a nurse, housekeeper, and provider." As the rat forages for food outside the burrow, the action cuts away to a king snake making its way across the sand. The narrator tells us that the snake has caught wind of the rats and is hunting them down. To increase the tension, we see the snake strike at the camera in extreme close-up, presumably from the point of view of "Mrs. Rat." She has only moments to return to her burrow and rescue her young before the snake devours them. Fortunately, the narrator assures us, "for emergencies, every family of kangaroo rats has an emergency burrow." This is indeed fortunate, as the voice-over converts the snake to "the enemy," who has just entered the burrow through "the front door." To music recalling the chase scenes of westerns, the snake slithers through the burrow as the mother transfers her two offspring, one by one, from home to an "emergency shelter." As she transports the first, the snake closes in on the second, which, still blind, is lost in the burrow. The "mother" arrives just in time to save the second babe from a certain death. The music becomes whimsical as "an innocent bystander" (a gecko) distracts the snake, sparing the rat family (for the moment).

In this short scene, narratives of suburban domesticity, cold-war survivalism, and frontier adventure flow in and out of each other. The voice-over begins with a depiction of kangaroo rat behavior identical to suburban mothering while the cutting and music gradually move us into a western chase scene. As this happens, the voice-over shifts to something resembling a bomb-shelter training film, one in which a well-trained mother demonstrates how to remove children to safety according to a well-established family emergency plan. Where is "Mr. Rat"? No doubt he is still at the office, or riding the express train home.

Scenes such as this were more than simply a crystallization of a set of common hopes and anxieties; they were interwoven with other discourses about what properly constituted an American culture considered essential to the production of a healthy American society. Was the rapidly expanding, prepackaged mass culture of television, comic books, and suburban tract housing equivalent to that ideal American culture, or an aberration?[45] Would consumption of mass cultural products create viable citizens, or tractable servants of the state? Had Americans become too willing to obey governmental and social regulation of their behavior? Concerns such as these charged popular and professional discourses alike, positioning depictions of the natural as immune from the suspect productions of culture and society. If a kangaroo rat behaved like a suburban wife and mother, then perhaps women in the new suburbs weren't merely conforming to artificially imposed behaviors. When, for example, Disney's press book for *The Vanishing Prairie* (1954) claimed that "producer Disney tells a story as big as America itself," and that "the film deals with the vanishing wildlife of the American scene" the terms *American* and *wildlife* positioned Disney within that complex of concerns (Walt Disney Productions 1954b, 1). The metonymic process in which the prairie became America, and the "American scene" one in which America was a disappearing wilderness, recapitulated a set of concerns about increased rationalization in the United States, and the concomitant loss of spontaneity in its citizens. The same text described Disney's workers as "trespassing cameramen, naturalists all," who revealed "nature's most closely guarded secrets" (1). In short, they were interlopers whose actions were validated by the name *naturalist*, a term that drew a firm boundary between the cultural and the natural by suggesting that, unlike normal people ("culturalists"?) Disney's workers were researchers sent out from American culture into nature to bring back information by which to better determine its natural basis. In its public relations and in its nature films, Disney performed exactly the sort of work that Mead or Riesman were attempting: it located and described the boundary between nature and culture, apparently revealing through idealized methods of benign observation a matrix of behaviors (nothing more than "instincts" and "drives") that neatly presaged the lives of its patrons. The suburbs, Disney seemed to suggest, were not an intrusion on the natural landscape of the United States; they were simply an expression of its ongoing evolution.

Against Nature: William Whyte Confronts the Organization Man

> *As the middle class has expanded, the hereditary advantages of the upper strata have declined drastically. The spread of American education, the growing accessibility to culture, have so ironed out regional and social*

differences that a vastly greater number of Americans now compete on even terms in what might be called a national society.

—WHYTE 1956, 278

Not everyone considered the rise of suburban America a virtually natural phenomenon. Like *The Lonely Crowd* and other studies of American character, journalist-cum-sociologist William H. Whyte's best-selling *The Organization Man* (1956) also took up the problem of conformity in American "national society."[46] However, unlike Riesman, Whyte had little use for parsing the relationship between nature and culture in the production of national character. Although he was interested in tracing the place and function of individualism in American culture, he found in the efforts to articulate a theory of cultural evolution by Progressive Era social theorists and their descendants in the culture-and-personality school an unhealthy scientism which encouraged a dependence on experts. For Whyte, the problem of conformity that faced the middle class was social in origin, not cultural or natural.

Based on a series of articles on management culture for *Fortune* magazine, and on a study of the social life of a new Chicago suburb, *The Organization Man* was an attempt to explain to a popular audience their place in an emerging national society (Whyte 1951a, 1951b). Whyte's instruction manual for the new middle class was more than a set of casual observations. Rather, it was a defense of the individual against the rise of a "secular faith" in the power of the masses:

> The organization man seeks a redefinition of his place on earth—a faith that will satisfy him that what he must endure has deeper meaning than appears on the surface. He needs, in short, something that will do for him what the Protestant Ethic did once. And slowly, almost imperceptibly, a body of thought has been coalescing that does that. . . . [one] which makes morally legitimate the pressures of society against the individual. Its major propositions are three: a belief in the group as the source of creativity; a belief in "belongingness" as the ultimate need of the individual; and a belief in the application of science to achieve the belongingness. (Whyte 1956, 6–7)

Whyte alternately referred to this new religion as a "Social Ethic," an "organizational ethic," or a "bureaucratic ethic" (6). Each of these characterizations expressed a profound unease with the rapid rationalization of American daily life, with its standardization in education and in mass popular culture, and with the naturalization of those tendencies in scientistic arguments about the drives and desires of normal Americans. The "organization man," like Riesman's other-directed personality, was a creature that found definition only in and from groups, that found its identity in affiliation and in the markers provided by the organizations to which it belonged, rather than from the internal process of coming to know itself through its own successes and failures.

With the rise of the Social Ethic, Whyte argued, there was a decline in Weber's Protestant work ethic (Whyte 1956, 13–15; Weber 2001). This shift was more than just a change in values, he claimed; it constituted a profound alteration in ontology. Where the Protestant Ethic had imagined an individual perpetually striving *against* its environment, the Social Ethic imagined the individual as derived *from* that environment. (Thus, the legacy of the progressive program of assimilation was nothing less than the undermining of the very value system—that of the white, Protestant middle class—that naturalizing aliens were supposed to absorb and to be absorbed into.) To Whyte, this type of thinking represented a dangerous utopianism in which "social engineering" was imagined as able to eliminate conflict—conflict that he felt was absolutely necessary to a healthy society (32). In an early chapter, "Belongingness," he parodied calls by Elton Mayo and W. Lloyd Warner to establish centralized programs to engineer the social and material environment:

> What with the mischief caused by the philosophers of individualism, most contemporary leaders are untrained in the necessary social skill to bring the adaptive society to pass. What is needed is an administrative elite, people trained to recognize that what man really wants most is group solidarity even if he doesn't realize it himself. . . . unfettered as they will be of "prejudice and emotion," they won't have any philosophy, other than cooperation. . . . They will adjust him. Through the scientific application of human relations, these neutralist technicians will guide him into satisfying solidarity with the group so skillfully and unobtrusively that he will scarcely realize how the benefaction has been accomplished. (Whyte 1956, 36)

The Social Ethic and its creature, the Organization Man, derived not from cultural adaptations to historical and material circumstances, but from the well-meaning but wrong-headed ministrations of social scientists bent on creating a more harmonious society—and from quiescent individuals unwilling to question the purposes of that organized restructuring, ready to accept rationalization as a form of cultural evolution:

> Some critics of social engineering are sure that what is being cooked up for us is a socialistic paradise, a radically new, if not brave, world, alien to every tradition of man. This is wrong. . . . Boiled down, what they ask for is an environment in which everyone is knit into belongingness with one another; one in which there is no restless wandering but rather the deep emotional security that comes from total integration with the group. Radical? It is like nothing so much as the Middle Ages. (32)

In Whyte's view, this profound ontological shift—from being a subject acting against one's environment, to one created by and operating within that environment—derived from an intense loyalty on the part of the many beneficiaries of paternalistic government social programs that evolved during the New Deal and World War II (395). But where Gorer might have located this problem in a collective symbolic search for an absent father, Whyte placed the responsibility (and the possibility for change) at the individual level, arguing that "the fault is not in the organization . . . it is in our worship of it. It is in our vain quest for a utopian equilibrium, which would be horrible if it ever did come to pass; it is in the soft-minded denial that there is a conflict between the individual and society" (13).

The socially engineered spaces where Whyte saw this happening most were the workplace and the rapidly developing suburbs. He so despised the culture of observation and accommodation in the workplace that in his book he appended instructions on how to cheat on personality tests (1956, 405–10). These spaces shared, in his view, what today might be called a panoptic organization in which individuals willingly subjected themselves to the observational dictates of the environment, rather than taking an active role in ordering it. The two spaces, however, were not identical. If the workplace was a location for externalizing the lessons of managing self and others learned in childhood (171–201), the suburbs were sites in which notions of "group awareness" and adaptation to the needs of others were more than a response to a new-built environment, becoming internalized social virtues (393). For it was in the suburbs that those people entering the "lower limits of the middle class" (299) could learn how to subject themselves to social practices of observation and management: "The suburbs have become the second great melting pot," Whyte claimed. "The organization man furnishes the model, and even in suburbs where he is a minority he is influential out of all proportion to his numbers. As the newcomers to the middle class enter suburbia, they must discard old values, and their sensitivity to those of the organization man is almost statistically demonstrable" (300).

The means for interpellation ranged from going to church and volunteering for its various social and organizational committees, to joining the PTA, to taking one's place in a very clearly defined circuit of parties and other social gatherings (see figure 24). *What* one participated in wasn't as important, Whyte claimed, as that one *just participated* in some way. The idea that one was a "joiner," a person who was willing to be a part of the group rather than an outsider, indicated a commitment to social cohesion:

> Most potential [community] leaders hold the same view of man as a social animal, and though they say it much more intelligently [than the average suburbanite]—and know that they are saying it—they, too, tend to equate the lone individual with psychic disorder. "We have learned not to be so introverted," one junior executive, and a very thoughtful and successful one, told me. . . . The point he was trying to make was that for him doing things with and for other people was ultimately more fulfilling. . . . the basis for the Social Ethic is not conformity, but a sense of moral imperative. (394)

For Whyte, the problem of the middle manager's or suburbanite's tendency to subsume the self into the group was one not of surrendering one's will to the collective, but of deriving one's will from it. In particular, the error was in imagining that the Social Ethic naturally evolved from a certain necessity, a will to ingather, a need of the "social animal" to be in the group.

An equally troubling quality of the Social Ethic was its willful erasure of established social boundaries and their replacement with an imagined harmony. Rather than recognize the inherent struggles that social categories produced, adherents to the Social Ethic treated them as vestigial and unimportant. Discussing the fantasy of a classless society, Whyte reported that "suburban residents like to maintain that their suburbia not only looks classless but is classless. That is, they are apt to add on second thought, there are no extremes, and if the place isn't exactly without class, it is at least a one-class society—identified as the middle or upper middle" (1956, 299). To Whyte, this was mediocracy in action, a relentless drive toward an undifferentiated normality.

Nor was this compulsion to ignore useful and difficult social boundaries limited simply to a denial of class; distinctions between the social worlds of adults and children were breaking down as well. As the economy boomed, so did the birthrate, and more young families were leaving cities for the expanding new suburbs. This dislocated adults from older social networks and made their children the advance scouts on the new social frontier.[47] "It begins with the children," Whyte complained (1956, 342). "There are so many of them and

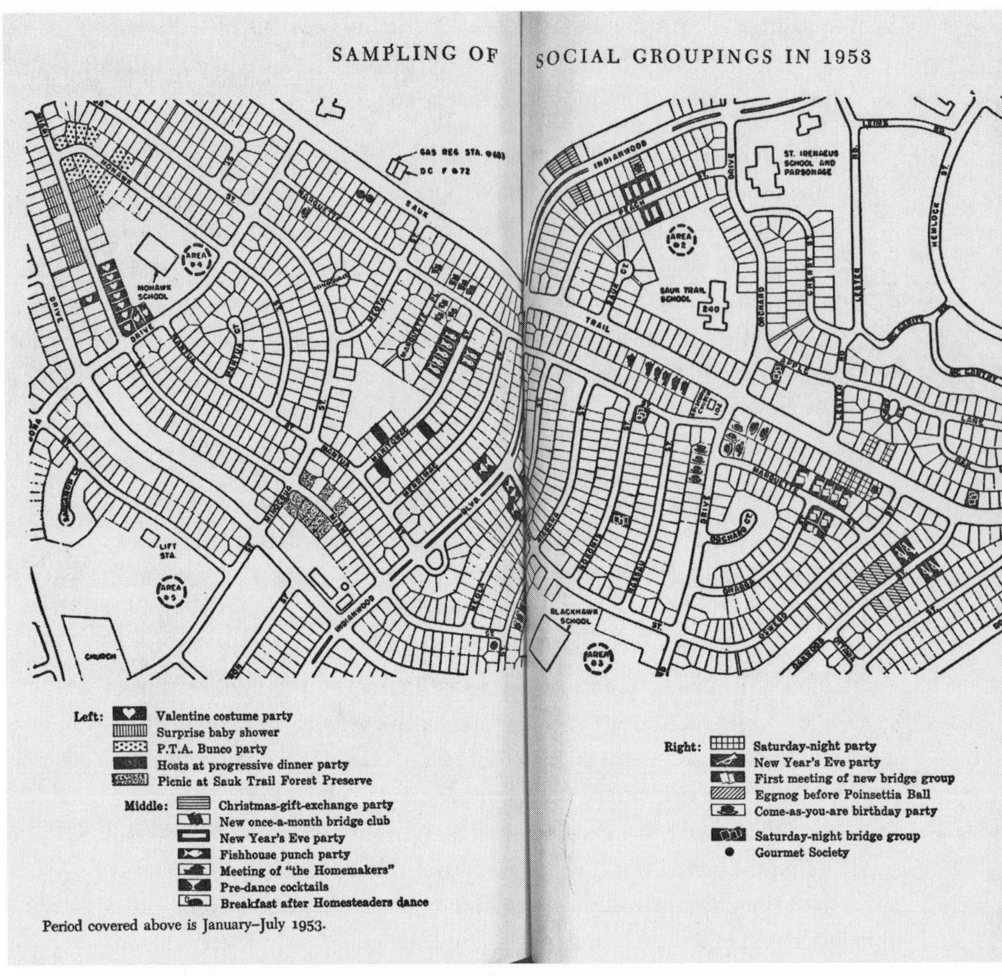

24. In *The Organization Man* (1956), William H. Whyte mapped the "relatedness" and social adjustment of a new middle-class neighborhood outside of Chicago, noting in particular how adults were bound by a pervasive "filarchy" in which children became primarily responsible for forming social bonds.

they are so dictatorial in effect that a term like *filarchy* would not be entirely facetious. It is the children who set the basic design; their friendships are translated into the mother's friendships, and these, in turn, to the family's."[48] In this inverted social order, the parent followed the child's lead, and the child, in turn, received formal instruction on how to socialize from schools overseen by parent-teacher associations. According to Whyte, suburban parents firmly believed that "the primary job of the high school . . . should be to teach students how to be citizens and how to get along with other people" (392).[49] So much had adults subjected themselves to a synthesized environment that they designed their schools to take over the socialization of their children and then relied upon those children to structure the social life of the family.[50] The school in the Chicago suburb Whyte examined offered a "Family Living" curriculum for both boys and girls, which included the study of "money management, everyday social relationships . . . nutrition and food . . . [and] preparation for marriage," and in which "the accent is on 'shared responsibility' in building a successful happy home" (390). Also, he observed, "the testing program is extensive. In addition to a battery of achievement tests, such as the Iowa tests, and intelligence tests, the school has given students the Kuder Vocational Preference Record, the Bell Adjustment Inventory, and the California Personal Adjustment Test" (390).

In other words, working with educators and school guidance counselors trained in the latest techniques of observation and assessment, parents had effectively handed over the socialization process to state institutions and had also come to depend on the products of that process to direct their own social interaction. The system approximated a closed circuit between the state and the home in which domestic relations, and relations between homes, were guided by social engineering practices centered around the management of personality and interaction. Surprisingly, Whyte made little comparison between this system and the regulation of social life in the Soviet Union (1956, 90–91). Rather, the message was implicit: the United States was constructing for itself, in the form of a national society, a system of state control of social relations that was more insidious than that of the Soviet Union. In the United States, systems of control, what Whyte called "social engineering," were naturalized as latent behaviors and aptitudes located through standardized tests and then further developed in schools, workplaces, and suburban communities, rather than acknowledged as conscious social choices made by free individuals. The state needed to do nothing overtly coercive, as the people were willingly yielding their social autonomy and self-determination.

This search for an environment of belongingness, in Whyte's view, engendered a profound sense of social unease, a compulsive need to fit in, to add to social harmony and equilibrium. Rather than producing a sense of comfort and assurance, it encouraged a paranoid state in which Americans felt compelled to watch themselves and others for telltale signs of aberration, for the potential to disrupt a delicate balance and puncture the bubble of postwar American prosperity and tranquillity. Beyond creating a slavish dependence on experts for self-definition, the impulse toward adjustment to norms produced not only a suspicion of difference in others, but a fear of difference in one's self:

> The quest for normalcy, as we have seen in suburbia, is one of the great breeders of neuroses, and the Social Ethic only serves to exacerbate them. What is normalcy? We practice a great mutual deception. Everyone knows that they themselves are different—that they are shy in company, perhaps, or dislike many things most people seem to like—but they are not sure that other people are different, too. Like the norms of personality testing, they see about them the sum of efforts of people like themselves to seem as normal as others and possibly a little more so. It is hard enough to learn to live with our inadequacies, and we need not make ourselves more miserable by a spurious ideal of middle-class adjustment. Adjustment to what? Nobody really knows—and the tragedy is that they don't realize that the so-confident-seeming other people don't know either. (Whyte 1956, 398)

What Whyte recommended as a partial antidote to the Social Ethic was a reinvestment in the individual opposed to, rather than deriving from, the environment. The solution wasn't revolution, the dismantling of the Organization, but principled opposition to unthinking acquiescence to its dictates (1956, 399–400). Nor could Americans return to the Protestant Ethic; it was impossible to wish away the profound structural changes wrought by the Depression and the war. Ultimately, there was no perfect response to the Social Ethic, the very idea of a perfect response was itself part of the utopian fantasy of harmony against which one was to guard. Mimicking his audience, Whyte inveighed against perfection: "But what is the '*solution*'? many ask. There is no solution. The conflict between the individual and society has always involved dilemma; it always will, and it is intellectual arrogance to think a program would solve it" (400, emphasis original).

Like *The Lonely Crowd* (Riesman, Denney, and Glazer 1950) before it, *The Organization Man* was a manual for social relations aimed at the very members of the new middle class who were its research subjects. Whyte began the project in 1951 for *Fortune*, a mass-circulation periodical favored by the middle managers he critiqued. His ability to gather data for that critique depended upon their willingness to yield up the intimate details of their lives to social researchers. The 1951 study, which explored the regulation of "corporate wives" in a managerial culture that evaluated husbands' career potential by examining how they managed their personal lives, was meant to encourage the questioning of that corporate intrusion into the domestic sphere (Whyte 1951b).[51] Rather than encourage a clearer separation between the two spheres, he complained, the ideas he had expressed in the series circulated through popular culture and were used by corporate wives to better adjust to the demands of their husbands' employers, and by corporations that refined their approaches to the problem (Whyte 1956, 259). In spite of his previous experience, Whyte seemed to expect that *The Organization Man* would escape the same fate. The book garnered a sizable middle-class readership and went through a number of reprintings in its first year. While Whyte had intended it for a popular audience, he seemed unreasonably optimistic about the impossibility that the book might end up as yet another tool in systems of self-regulation in which, for instance, one might want to guard against appearing *too* conformist, too much the Organization Man or the *Man in the Gray Flannel Suit* (Wilson 1955).[52] Looking back at the results of his work in 1986, Whyte declared the Organization Man "very much alive" (Kaufman 1999, A23).[53] In this sense, Riesman's solution of writing off the other-direction of the current generation and working to produce autonomy in the next offered a more practicable solution to the problem.

What the popular reception of both texts revealed, though, was a profound ambivalence toward the place of science—particularly social science—in the regulation of daily life. Riesman's efforts to articulate an evolutionary model of cultural change, and Whyte's dismissal of such modeling as empty scientism, spoke to both the power of scientific explanation in 1950s culture and society and a desire to be exempt from that explanation. Social science offered possible solutions to excess conformity and also contributed to its production. How was one to parse the difference, to make intelligent choices without disrupting the flow of everyday life? As had the hesitations around management-based models of child-rearing, this ambivalence created opportunities for companies such as Disney, in products like its True-Life Adventures, to act as popular interpreters, to explain science from the outside, to place it in its proper perspective.

Disney's Science, Disney's Landscape

> *The bourgeoisie . . . think of science as their familiar instrument. The masses are less confident, more awed in their approach to science. . . . science gives man mastery over his environment and is beneficent. But science itself is not understood, therefore not mastered, therefore terrifying.*
> —MACDONALD 1953, 68

One may forgive Dwight MacDonald's compression of mid-twentieth-century social and material relations in "A Theory of Mass Culture" as a product of the social criticism of the time. Yet even in its misapprehension it points to important social and cultural phenomena. Far from terrified of science, members of the new American middle class of the 1950s (many of whom were closely associated with the nation's industrial base) understood at least the physical sciences in a practical fashion as well as, if not better than, members of the previous generation's middle class. It wasn't science per se that was frightening in the 1950s, as much as were certain applications of it—particularly the testing and deployment of atomic weapons and the quantification and rationalization of daily life through the proliferation of psychological testing and "managerial culture." Alongside this rather reasonable anxiety about the destructive and intrusive capabilities of recently developed material and social technologies, there operated an equally powerful fascination with science and technology that found its expression in magazines such as *Popular Mechanics* or *Popular Science*, in the dawn of the space race, in a fetishism of the automobile that celebrated missile motifs in body design, and in an enthusiasm for consumer appliances in the home.[54]

While MacDonald found in the spate of science-fiction movies of the 1950s an example of the mass fear of the scientific, he might just as easily have found in cinematic monstrosities a mass fascination with the unknown, one that extended to the reassuring narrative voice of Disney's scientific documentaries. In those films, Disney provided a science humanized and explained by a patient and often paternally amused narrative voice. The voice behind Disney's documentaries, particularly behind its True-Life Adventures, seemed unfazed by nature's mysteries and conveyed a calm wonder, a sense of familiarity with the unfamiliar, and a folksy simplicity of description that suggested that what was being observed was obvious to the properly trained eye. This was a science that may well have been troubling in its excesses, but which also appeared an increasingly inescapable part of daily life and could be tamed through patient and thorough explanation.

In its nature films, Disney achieved that explanatory voice through a sort of reverse prolepsis, producing a narrative that began in an animated version of the past, then purposefully erased that past to reveal an underlying logic of nature lying just beneath, one that had predetermined the course of human development that led to the moment in which the film was projected onto the screen. Outside the theater, Disney's public relations reinforced the idea that the narrative it produced was really nature's own. It wasn't Disney that drew parallels between the animal and human worlds, but the animals themselves. Disney merely provided a portal into the animal kingdom, an eyepiece through which Americans could exercise their penchant for observation and reflect (for both their amusement and edification) on the relationship between nature and culture in their own lives.

At the same time, however, the truly natural world was far away, both in time and in space. The visual device of cross-fading from animation to live action created a sense of spatial distance by moving from map to landscape, and temporal distance by moving from graphic representations of the past to live sequences of the present-as-past. Voice-overs described the environments revealed as physically isolated, and as lineally descendant from prehistoric times: "There was once a time when all of North America was a great, green wilderness . . . nature's undisputed domain. . . . Today, the rocky wall of the Continental Divide is one of her few remaining strongholds. There are many hidden valleys here, almost inaccessible to man . . . where time is still measured by the passing seasons and only nature's law prevails. Such a place is Beaver Valley, the setting for another True-Life Adventure" (*Beaver Valley* 1950).

The animal communities Disney represented collectively and individually embodied a natural world unpolluted by human culture and performed unselfconsciously behaviors uninflected by higher motive or taboo. This was a prelapsarian fantasy in which any set of actions that resembled human behavior were that behavior's point of origin, a fantasy that provided the unadulterated absolution of natural compulsion. Disney's nature provided an unbroken chain of being from the prehistoric past into an implicitly suburban American present: "The survivors are unchanged in habit and behavior. As in all the TRUE-LIFE films, the animals are completely unaware that they are being spied upon. No human being is ever shown—nor any of his works. Neither are bird nor beast ever romanticized or distorted with super-imposed human vice or virtue. They are always strictly as the camera finds them in their home place and in relation to their creature neighbors" (Walt Disney Productions 1954c).

The idea of presenting a perfectly bracketed nature, and of appearing to possess the expertise to do so, was extremely important to Disney and extended beyond the films and their promotion. In order to reveal to its audiences the startling similarities between the animal and human worlds—and thus to link them at a primal level—the company insisted on exerting as much control over the depiction of nature as it did over the mass-production of its animated characters. True-Life Adventure director James Algar explained the ground rules for capturing that nature to amateur cinematographers submitting unsolicited footage to Disney: "All evidence of human beings is carefully left out," he cautioned. "Man's relationship to his lesser neighbors is never indicated. It is not permitted to disturb the completely detached inspection of animal and bird life in its free state. Animals are not even aware that they are being photographed. Hence their behavior is dictated only by their own nature" (Algar 1952).

The relationship between man and beast was, of course, added in public relations, editing, and voice-over. Disney presented its viewers to themselves as middle-class philosopher kings able to experience the seemingly unmediated spectacle of "wild" nature with perfect detachment. Strangely, those viewers could apparently attain this detachment only if the animals were unaware that they were being watched—as if an awareness of observation would create in them a set of false behaviors, a self-conscious mugging for the camera that would disrupt the viewers' platonic experience and undermine the object lessons of the films. It seemed a fragile arrangement in which either animals or humans could easily flee the sympathetic bond created for them through the camera, thrust back into an awareness of their separation. Neither humans nor animals could stand to be aware of the presence of artifacts of human civilization, to be alienated by the historical, specific, and manufactured world that threatened to sever the ahistoric bond nature provided—a bond which redeemed some of the quotidian practices of that manufactured world as rooted in instinctive behaviors.

The "scientific" portrayal of nature posed a particular problem for Disney. On the one hand, the company needed to appear authoritative in its descriptions of the natural world. On the other, it had to avoid alienating its audiences by appearing too aloof from its subject. It resolved part of this dilemma through its choice of narrative voice—both within its films and in the larger, ongoing metanarrative of its corporate history. In its public relations it invoked authority by, for instance, referring back to the making of earlier animated features—particularly *Bambi* (1942)—as the moment when Walt Disney and his workers began to study animal behavior in earnest. It then softened and "humanized" this authority by discussing how it translated those behaviors into the recognizable and comforting patterns of its animated features. Although the corporation publicly claimed the opposite, one method of achieving this effect in its nature films was to pattern them after its cartoons. In its manual for cinematographers, Disney explained, "In approaching the problem of story telling [in True-Life Adventures], once we have the basic footage, we use the same technique to be found in Disney cartoons. We look for personality, and we do this for a reason. If audiences can identify themselves with the seeming personality of an animal, they can sympathize with it and understand its problems better" (Algar 1952). In a deft turn of phrase, Disney claimed only to "look for" personality, not to create it. Not only did this protect the narrative from the appearance of construction; it also suggested that Disney's animated features were nothing more than an elaboration of traits latent in the animated creatures it produced.

This brief technical schema suggests a complicated interplay of forces and constituencies behind the production of an ostensibly transparent nature documentary. Patterning its wildlife narratives after those of its cartoons, the company generated a tautological harmony between the natural and the cultural, between the animated and the real. Disney's creative staff imagined a personality for each animal "character" likely to elicit a sympathetic reaction from its audience. To do so, however, involved imagining that audience—its problems and its sense of which animals would be likely to share those problems. Having made those determinations, it checked its results through in-house screenings in which both production and nonproduction (janitorial, secretarial, accounting, etc.) staff offered their reactions to rough cuts of the films.[55] Although these ostensibly amateur reviewers were meant to give immediate, personal reactions to the films, they filtered some of their observations through what they imagined an audience like themselves would require. As one anonymous Disney staffer put it in response to a survey, "I believe that the animal life in Beaver Valley was probably better suited to the cameras than the birds and bugs in Nature's Half Acre. However, I believe that the public will accept this picture very well" (Walt Disney Productions 1950b, 8).

Here, complex regimes of introspection and outward observation overlapped in a referential matrix for the location and representation of types of natural behavior involving real and imagined humans and (other) animals. Staff comments fed back into the production process, as Disney's crews determined which personality types resonated between animal characters and an audience already well versed in the cosmology of Disney's animated world. Thus, a supposedly scientifically accurate representation of nature began with a mediational process in which an imaginary animal met an imagined audience to produce a version of the real most likely to resonate in the larger popular imagination.

Beyond determining the personality of individual animal characters, Disney also constructed the dramatic narratives in which they appeared according to strict formulas. In its animated features, Disney had developed a system of tension and release in which dramatic and comical scenes alternated in a regular pattern, building fear and discharging it in laughter. Over this Disney laid a larger schema of emplotment—which it termed the "classic fairy tale"—in which its young protagonists, through a series of accidents and willful acts, placed themselves in danger and out of the reach of parental figures. The youthful protagonists then had to save themselves, realizing that their limitations had placed them in harm's way and understanding that only a combination of their talent and the help of allies attracted by their inherent good nature could resolve the situation. Offering adventure for younger viewers and anxiety and its resolution for parental audience members, this formula had proved very effective.[56]

Disney changed this structure slightly for the True-Life Adventures. The narrative spine of the documentaries replaced animated protagonists with a more diffuse "drama of nature"—a very Darwinian battle for species survival in which all animals were compelled to play their parts by Nature itself—in which a succession of vignettes was meant to illustrate the absolute pervasiveness of that drama. These vignettes took two distinct forms: scenes of intraspecies mating competition, or of interspecies life-and-death struggles. The former were generally more comical than the latter, which tended to stress a scarcity of resources or inbred enmity as the reason for competition between certain species (a trope that fit nicely with cold-war narratives). Except in the case of those animals with which identification would have been difficult—such as spiders or wasps—death and defeat were largely absent from the screen, most often referred to obliquely or narratively deferred until another inevitable offscreen encounter.

Unlike the alternating "classical" cycle of comedy and pathos in its features, though, the nature films suggested that this cycle of birth, struggle, and (implicit) death was natural, a process that began long before the film (even before humanity itself) and would continue long afterward. The company suggested a temporal continuity between the distant past and an unspecified future that ran directly through the film, which recapitulated continuity along a taxonomic axis, demonstrating a shared behavioral matrix, a set of personalities derived from a common instinctual base that extended from simple invertebrates up into the suburbs. And although *New York Times* critic Bosley Crowther (1953, 38) would complain about Disney's cyclic repetition of life and death struggles, and about its anthropomorphizing, he would also concede that his was a minority view: "[Beyond the repetition of life-and-death struggles] . . . there is another weakness of the Disney boys evidenced in this film. The general public will not object to it, but the studious naturalists may. That is their playful disposition to edit and arrange certain scenes so that it appears the wild life in them is behaving in human and civilized ways. . . . [It is] all very humorous and beguiling. But it isn't true to life." Disney's version may not have been true to the life that Crowther lived, but it resonated with Disney's audiences. However inaccurate this version of nature was, it wasn't merely unobjectionable to the public, it was popular—first in the theaters and later on television—and that popularity lay in the very inaccuracy to which Crowther objected, the specific human behaviors that Disney imputed to its animal subjects. Crowther was, of course, ignoring a strong desire on the part of audiences to see their lives replicated in the natural world.

Conclusion

> *America is a middle-class country and . . . middle class values and political styles of perception reach into all levels except the fringes at the very top and the very bottom. But it must be added that America is increasingly a country of the "new" middle class, bureaucratized in situation and other-directed in character . . . a country in which, perhaps, people will soon wake up to the fact that there is no longer a "we" who run things and a "they" who don't, or a "we" who don't run things and a "they" who do; but rather that all "we's" are "they's" and all "they's" are "we's."*
>
> —RIESMAN, DENNEY, AND GLAZER 1950, 260

David Riesman's naturalization of the new middle class as representative of an evolving American character and culture did more than contribute to the ongoing erasure of class conflict as a meaningful category in midcentury social discourse. Just as his description of the behaviors of southern European immigrants and poor rural blacks as the regressive sociocultural adaptations of the tradition-directed subsumed ethnic or racial difference under the master sign of cultural evolution, his attempt to produce in this new middle class a prophylactic self-conscious autonomy helped to discursively position the values of the white, Protestant middle class of the previous generation as evolutionarily antecedent, yet because of their natural sociocultural necessity, unburdened by those very markers of race and class (Riesman, Denney, and Glazer 1950, 32). As had been the case for the progressive social reformers before him, his intent was noble: to ensure the orderly development of a sturdy democratic society through the regulation of character. For the progressives, this goal had been shaped by the need to fend off nativist and eugenicist arguments for the racial inferiority of nonwhites and their detrimental influence on American culture. For Riesman (and others), the need to describe that culture as evolving independently of the racial and class markers of its members flowed from the imperative of developing a model of a national culture that was amenable to alteration, but resistant to co-optation or direction by the state or market forces. In both instances, the child was a pivotal element in arguments about the nature, purpose, and direction of American character and culture, and both further circulated and naturalized a notion of the generic child that sublimated the racially and socially specific location of its origins.

The function of culture was more than an academic question. For social critics concerned about the dangers of mass movements, the new mass society was a strange and unusual thing: the masses, the product of an extremely successful, increasingly rationalized postwar economy, were like an irrational beast, subject to the whim of the moment, easy to mobilize but hard to predict.[57] For the advertising agency trying to ensure a steady customer base for its clients, or for the researcher trying to understand voting patterns or civic participation, the problem seemed the same: to what degree, and how, was the average person susceptible to persuasion? Had the rationalized postwar society given birth to an irrational and dangerous animal, the mindless, gullible consumer?

While most social researchers were ostensibly interested in these questions for the strictly academic reason of furthering public knowledge, those in the employ of the persuasive industries were interested in developing mechanisms for maximizing control over consumer behavior. This blurring of purpose was a matter of alarm for social critics, from the journalist Vance Packard to William Whyte and C. Wright Mills. What all of these approaches shared, regardless of their intent, was a sense that a singular American mass culture had arrived and had to be made sense of: it had become too powerful an entity to be ignored. It became important to describe the historical and social position of that culture, from whence it derived and where it was taking American society, in order to properly distinguish between it and an ideal American culture that preceded it. This was an unintended consequence of the progressive project: that the unwashed immigrant masses assimilated into the new middle class would outnumber their predecessors and would effectively dictate the direction of middle-class culture and society.

With the exception of more radical critiques, such as Mills's *The Power Elite* (1957), or Horkheimer and Adorno's *Dialectic of Enlightenment* (1944), or even

MacDonald's "A Theory of Mass Culture" (1953), explications of the nature of American middle-class culture were in essence users' manuals for a new middle class, and as such, each contained significant discussion of the importance of children in the reproduction of that culture. Earlier depictions of childhood had also stressed the importance of the proper enculturation of children to the well-being of the nation. Yet what was distinct about these works, and the works devoted specifically to child-rearing covered in the next chapter, is that they inflected this concern as a need to achieve a balance between the influences of nature and culture. The child was thus homunculus for the masses, an unstable combination of the human and the animal in need of moderation.

Many of these analyses of American character, then, were a means of explaining to a new middle class what its newfound culture was (and was not). This began with a discussion of the relationship between culture and nature. For adherents of the culture-and-personality school, such as Mead, Gorer, or Riesman, the question of the relationship between nature and culture derived from their use of Freud to model the universal motive forces behind cultural change. By positing the child as a creature with innate drives and instincts that became legible—both to itself and others—only as it entered into culture, culture-and-personality theorists offered a quasi-Lamarckian solution to the problem of how American culture could be directed without being hijacked by the forces of totalitarian control. Only at the point of the individual child entering into culture could one hope to direct that culture; attempts made at other locations were at best misdirected, and at worst dangerously manipulative. For Whyte or MacDonald, on the other hand, this recourse to nature was part of the problem, an abnegation of the personal responsibility of shaping one's cultural and social life through individual choice and action. For marketers, Freudian models of infantile development and adult psychology offered new tools in their fight to claim the attention and direct the desires of consumers.[58] For industrial human relations experts, psychological testing, psychoanalytic or otherwise, offered an array of methods for determining and adjusting the aptitudes and tendencies of the managerial workforce. Yet regardless of variation, opposition, or agreement, the very circulation of the terms *nature* and *culture* in relation to the child made their proper negotiation a matter of popular concern.

Yet while sociologists such as Riesman and Whyte were concerned with grand social theory, middle-class parents were worried about practice. The immediate problem was to raise a child who could stand outside of the Social Ethic, of other-directedness, of a culture of observation arising from an increasingly centralized and rationalized social and economic system, without being cut off from its bounty. The problem for parents, and for the media they used in that process, was to strike that balance between the cultural and the natural that had seemed missing in the previous generation's management-based child-rearing literatures.

The figure of Walter Elias Disney underwent analogous changes at the same time. Following the war, the public-relations persona of the man shifted gradually from that of avuncular Taylorist manager to that of a senior scientist leading an immense research team. At the same time, the company's output expanded beyond animation to include nature documentaries, travelogues, and a collection of frontier epics that involved the meeting of culture and nature at society's furthest boundary. Yet, as before, it would be a mistake to explain this shift solely as the result of adroit market research. The company's cultural currency continued to appreciate because it addressed issues of public significance, such as the role of science in daily life, or the line between culture and nature. The short, cynical reading of this might be that Disney provided the benign face science and rationality so desperately needed. A longer view would acknowledge that even as the company moved to claim available discursive ground, it provided a space for a new middle class to work out the important ideological and ontological problems represented in these manuals.[59]

Historian of science Gregg Mitman has argued that the True-Life Adventures were "moral tales of the family, the Aesop's fables of 1950s television culture," and that in

> a period when parenthood, domesticity, and traditional gender roles were idealized as routes to personal fulfillment, social norms came to be reinforced through animal behavior stories. . . . The important point about these 1950s natural history tales was that the natural family was an identifiable and universal category throughout the animal kingdom. This ideal of universality conformed precisely to the marketing needs of national television advertisers, who sought to project an image of the white, middle-class American family audience in which ethnic and class differences were homogenized. (1993, 660)

While this take on Disney's use of nature documentaries in its 1950s television programs is certainly accurate, it only begins to tell the story of the place of its representations of nature and science in 1950s popular culture.[60] Long before the True-Life Adventures came to television, they enjoyed success in theaters. They spoke not just of canniness on the part of television advertisers, but of a desire on the part of postwar American audiences to observe and understand nature. That desire was itself part and parcel of a larger set of anxieties and desires that surrounded observing and being observed and the relationship of nature to culture. The work of Disney's True-Life Adventures—isolating, revealing, displaying, and explaining nature—was part of the sociocultural landscape of the moment, in which Americans worked to understand the new massive, rationalized, national capitalist system of the postwar United States as a natural landscape, in sharp contradistinction to the artificial landscapes of other nations and societies. The nature film, which celebrated the power of the scientific gaze to explain the seemingly irrational quality of the natural world, also celebrated that irrationality, the "wildness" that gave up information to the scientist without yielding its innate spirit to regulation and domestication.

Disney offered one answer to the problem of the proper relationship of nature to culture, ascribing through its narrative voice higher social motives to creatures ostensibly directed only by instinct. By positioning these narratives within a past-is-present/present-is-past frame of eternal natural logic, the company created a virtual evolutionary continuum that began in human prehistory, stretched through the American frontier, and ended in the suburban living room (either figuratively in the narrative, or literally on the TV screen). In Disney's suburban natural fantasy, the American pioneers who struck the template for the "settling" of the suburbs had their own predecessors in the animals that occupied the landscape before their arrival. In *Beaver Valley* (1950), for instance, the beaver is depicted as a "homesteader" of a particularly libertarian bent whose enlightened self-interest serves everyone: "The valley's number one citizen. . . . he builds not in the interest of public welfare, but solely for his own protection." More than a homesteader, the narrator informs the viewer, "The beaver is a true pioneer. . . . For wherever he fashions his dams, others follow."

In the trajectory of this narrative, the eventual arrival of human settlers in the landscape was virtually inevitable. They were simply the next wave of pioneers in nature's grand design. The American landscape produced families and stable communities by dint of its very nature. It taught them how to build for their own protection out of necessity. It could even authorize cold-war panoptic practices, as when the animals in *Beaver Valley* (1950) band together to protect the neighborhood:[61]

> Beaver country is fine country . . . settlers are pouring in . . . and whenever you have a land rush, there's sure to be at least one unsavory character among them. . . . Like this coyote who has strayed a long way from his native plains. . . . Beaver Valley should be easy pickin's . . . ! What makes it

hard is the vigilance committee. It seems that a coyote can't make a move these days . . . without somebody giving the alarm!

Disney's anthropomorphic landscape wasn't merely overwritten with human qualities. It discursively (re)generated a naturalized humanity with very specific social relations as a necessary iteration of species interaction within that landscape. Disney's animals merely clarified a 1950s commonplace that the frontier encounter with nature had infused the development of Euroamerican civilization with a much-needed pragmatism, a distinctly American quality that transformed the immigrant into the native. As Disney described it in its public relations, humans and animals shared the same foibles, the same dramas, the same petty personality traits: "In their tumultuous polygamous herd life, the seals draw their own parallels with elemental human behavior for an amazing amount of suspense, instruction and amusing reflection" (Walt Disney Productions 1948).

Disney was merely the go-between. It was the seals who drew the parallels between their lives and basic human behavior, and the audience that would learn and reflect. Yet as this brief quote from Disney's public relations for *Seal Island* (1948) indicates, that audience would have help in making sense of the lessons the seals offered. The following two chapters examine in detail how shifting arguments about the nature of childhood and its relation to media—particularly to television—provided Disney with the discursive matrix within which to market these narratives, and how that marketing in turn stabilized conceptions of childhood circulating in those arguments.

5 RAISING THE NATURAL CHILD

Mickey Becomes a Man

> *Mickey Mouse, either by name or by image, is better known in more places on this mud-ball earth than any human being in all history. In their day neither Caesar nor Napoleon were half so widely known.*
>
> —WALLACE 1949, 21

Shortly after World War II, Walt Disney Productions began releasing press material announcing the approach of Mickey Mouse's twenty-first birthday (in 1949). When Mickey became twenty-one, Disney glibly asked, would he be a man or a mouse? Mickey stood poised at several boundaries. Was he properly animal, or quasi-human? Was he about to become an adult, or perpetually remain a child? Beneath the light-hearted banter, the celebration of Mickey's pending transformation was an apt metaphor for changes in the popular conception of American child-rearing, which increasingly viewed the transition from childhood to adulthood as the proper domestication of healthy natural impulses into civilized behavior. Yet Mickey's rite of passage also described the maturation of Walt Disney Productions itself—from a popular animation house to a complex, multifaceted concern that produced and distributed a growing array of products for an international market. "The worlds that Alexander the Great conquered and Julius Caesar ruled," crowed one journalist, "were nutshell microcosms compared with that over which Mickey holds sway. His sovereignty is all but universal, yet he is as American as Kansas City" (Nugent 1947, 22). Articles celebrating the coming of age of an Imperial Mickey captured this tension, linking it to the United States' rising status as an international power (and a U.S. concern with an inherent American-ness).

Indeed, the mouse and the country were closely linked. As Disney was quick to remind its public, Mickey had graced the sides of bombers during the war, and his name was a code word on D-Day. Following a standing tradition of associating Disney with America, the company joined in postwar triumphal discourse, and journalists passed the material along virtually verbatim, trusting, perhaps, in public fascination with the sudden American presence on the world stage:

> Now he's Mikki Maus in Russia, Miki Kuchi in Japan, Miguel Ratocinto in Spanish-speaking countries, Michel Souris in France and Topolino in Italy. (Nugent 1947, 22)

> The sun never set on Mickey Mouse. In Japan he performed as Miki Kuchi, in France he was Michel Souris, in Spain he was Miguel Ratocinto, in Italy he was Topolino. (Wallace 1949, 35)

> By 1930 Mickey Mouse had become as international as chewing gum. From Mexico, where he became known as *Miguel Ratocinto*, to Italy which called him *Topolino*, and even in Japan, where slant-eyed youngsters talked about "*Miki Kuchi*," he became as popular in children's eyes as the local equivalent of Santa Claus. ("Money from Mice" 1950, 88)

Disney's association with the new national image also had practical roots in the company's activities in World War II. During the war, the company had made ends meet while its overseas assets were frozen and its film stock rationed by doing government work, producing propaganda such as *Victory Through Airpower* (1943), training films on the Norden bomb sight, and industrial safety films ("Money from Mice" 1950; D. Smith 1996). Besides cultivating valuable contacts in the federal government, this work allowed the corporation to develop a voice of scientific authority that it would deploy in nature films and educational shorts in the 1950s and to practice combining live and cartoon footage.[1] Transitioning from wartime production, the company wisely chose to diversify around strengths that it had developed over the years, and which the public had willingly imputed to the company—a grasp of the natural world and an ability to translate the complex and the scientific into lay terms. Immediately following the war, the studios made the most of connections in the State Department and produced a series of health-education films for South America (Cartwright and Goldfarb 1994). In the process, it also created a series of films—such as *Saludos Amigos* (1943) and *The Three Caballeros* (1944)—that combined live footage of Latin America with animated characters (particularly the company's rising star, Donald Duck). Along with its modern minstrel show, *Song of the South* (1946), these films met heavy critical resistance for their commingling of live and animated characters, and for, among other things, a certain un-Disneylike salaciousness in Donald's enthusiasm for live Latinas. As Eric Smoodin (1993) has pointed out, the company found itself discursively policed by its public, told what it was and what it wasn't, what properly counted as "Disney" and what did not.

In essence, as the corporation, its founder, and its products became more clearly associated with American-ness, and as they expanded into other areas of expertise, they faced a form of semiotic confusion related to debates about whether mass culture and an ideal American culture were synonymous. Mickey's proliferation and his association with wholesome goodness, which the company had worked so hard to achieve by insinuating Mouse-related products into the mundane practices of American daily life, began to sound a dissonant note with other of the company's creations. The development of a multiplicity of voices within Disney flowed out of a set of historical circumstances that directed its discursive production, both in its self-representation and in the content of its products. Making the most of the external (public) components in that process, Disney's celebration of Mickey's passage into adulthood was simultaneously an acknowledgment of his (temporary) demotion: "Some of the heretics at Disney's will confide that they have more fun working with the duck than with the mouse . . . and hint that the public's current preference for Donald over Mickey (the Gallup Audience Research Institute puts Donald first, Bugs Bunny second and Mickey third) is a vote for human fallibility" (Nugent 1947, 61).

The company spun Mickey's passage into adulthood as the passing of an era.[2] Mickey symbolized the discipline and obedience associated with children of the 1930s. Indeed, he had been disciplined as such as early as 1931, when Disney yielded to parents' requests that the mouse refrain from vices associated with adult behavior (Maltin 1980, 37). Donald Duck was much more the child of the "permissive" postwar era, much more "human," acting impulsively on his feelings and instincts. Asked in 1949 why the company was making very few Mickey Mouse movies, Disney replied, "Mickey's decline was due to his heroic nature. He grew into such a legend that we couldn't gag around with him. He acquired as many taboos as a Western hero—no smoking, no drinking, no violence" (Wallace 1949, 21).[3] In the same article, a "Disney writer" completed this thought, explaining that "public idealization has turned him into a Boy Scout. Every time we put him into a trick, a temper, a joke, thousands of people would belabor us with nasty letters. That's what made Donald Duck so easy. He was our outlet" (21). Basically, Walt explained, Mickey had discursively relocated to the suburbs: "The Mouse's private life isn't especially colorful. He's never been the type that would go in for swimming pools and night club; more the simple country boy at heart. Lives on a quiet residential street, has occasional dates with his girlfriend, Minnie, doesn't drink or smoke, likes the movies and band concerts, things like that" (Walt Disney, quoted in Nugent 1947, 22).

At the same time that Mickey was making the difficult transition to adulthood, the men and women who had grown up with him were becoming the new mothers and fathers of the postwar Baby Boom. With this new generation of parents came a repudiation of the child-rearing techniques of the 1920s and 1930s in favor of the more "natural" or "child-centered" methods epitomized by the immensely popular work of Dr. Benjamin Spock. Thus, a major shift in Disney's production practices and self-representation corresponded with a significant change in the conception of the child in popular and professional discourse. Circulating through both of these discursive realms was a concern about the proper negotiation of the relationship between nature and culture in a rapidly rationalizing American society. In Disney's public relations during the postwar period, particularly for its True-Life Adventures and television programming, tropes of the family, child-rearing, and their relation to naturalized social relations provided fertile ground for working out anxieties about what constituted a genuine conformity to the dictates of natural impulses. In Disney's products and public relations, and in child-rearing manuals and periodicals, the child continued to be a locus for invoking anxiety around individual success, reframing that anxiety in terms of the regulation of American culture and society and providing palliatives for its resolution. While ideas about both child-rearing and Disney's self-representation underwent radical transformations in the postwar period, the notion of the child as the embodiment of nascent future social and material relations remained a constant and productive location for imaginary interventions into an evolving human civilization represented by American society. The production of a naturalized white, middle-class life as American culture, and of that culture arising from the American landscape, invested in the figure of the child expectations for a more durable and vital democratic capitalist society.

The 1950s: The Decade of the Child

In 1950, George Hecht, publisher of *Parents' Magazine* (as well as *Humpty Dumpty's*, *Children's Digest*, *Calling All Girls*, and *Compact: The Teen Digest*), declared the 1950s the "Children's Decade" (Hecht 1950; see figure 25). Statistics were on Hecht's side: the Baby Boom had been building since 1945 and was considered by many a central fact in American life. In 1940, 2.5 million children were born in the United States. By 1956, over 4 million children a year were being born, with some optimistic demographers predicting a birth rate

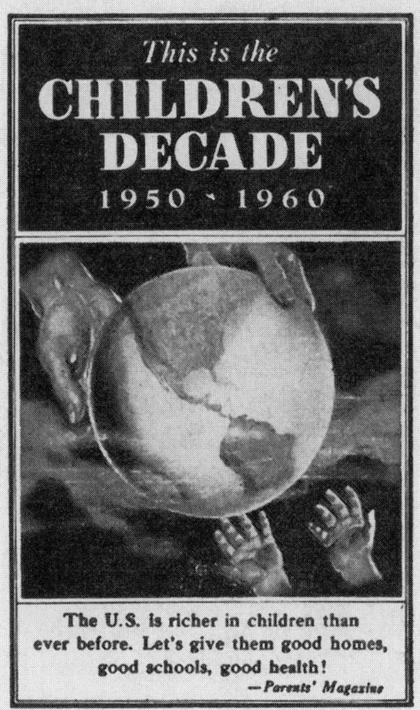

25. The January 1950 issue of *Parents' Magazine* led off with an editorial by publisher George Hecht, which declared the 1950s the "Children's Decade" and featured an image of adult hands delivering the globe to the next generation, signaling the imagined role of child-rearing in postwar international relations.

of 6 million a year by 1970 (Gould 1956). Spock's *Common Sense Book of Baby and Child Care* ([1946] 1957) was a national best seller, as was David Riesman's analysis of American culture, *The Lonely Crowd*, which devoted several chapters to the central place of children in middle-class life.[4] For Hecht, as for others, child-rearing was an issue of national infrastructural planning; he equated the need to care for children with building airports and the construction of the interstate highway system.

While Hecht's desire to promote the best interests of children may seem somewhat self-interested, he was not alone. Social commentators concerned with the nation's future considered an understanding of the increasing centrality of children (particularly middle-class white boys) in social life absolutely necessary to any description of America's future—regardless of whether they saw this focus on youth as beneficial or detrimental. Yet as the graphic that accompanied Hecht's essay suggests, by 1950 the importance of child-rearing was no longer limited to safeguarding the future interests of the United States. Godlike parental hands offered the entire world to the aspiring, desiring child: at the dawn of the Atomic Era, the fate of the planet would soon rest in those small hands.

The postwar boom in births also marked a radical shift in the meaning of childhood and the means by which children were raised (Strathman 1984). The previous generation—many of whom had recently become parents themselves—had grown up under a regime of "scientific" child-rearing that had imagined the child as a laboratory animal, the parent as a managing technician in the child's development, and the home as a domestic laboratory. As a counter to this, new American child-rearing regimes of the 1950s reimagined the child as a higher-order animal that needed to be encouraged to grow in harmony with its aptitudes, an untamed creature whose proper domestication would not only act as a prophylactic against totalitarianism but would demonstrate both the evolutionary necessity of American democratic capitalism and the ontological fallacy of Soviet communism. This new child was a significant element in a cold-war project to articulate midcentury American nation-building—particularly the rationalization and standardization of its infrastructure, educational systems, and economy—as distinct from similar operations by its ideological opponents, and as capable of producing future generations inherently resistant to the inducements of those opponents, or to any antidemocratic undercurrents in capitalist mass culture. This child had more in common with Donald than with Mickey and was more a creature of the True-Life Adventures—untamed without being too wild—than of *Snow White* or *Bambi*. The efficiently managed child of the 1920s and 1930s had acted as a prophylactic against uncertainty and instability during the Depression; this new natural child would serve a similar function, moderating the conformist excesses of postwar American mass culture and society. Ironically, the way to achieve that nonconformity was to help the child conform to its gender—to provide an environment in which it could harmonize its sensual impulses with its role in a tightly gendered culture. In the postwar years, child-rearing experts would explain the benefits and pitfalls of leading the natural child to its culturally sanctioned place in life, and Disney's version of nature would model that place, creating a matrix of both anxiety and its relief that parents would navigate as they attempted to insure the success and stability of their children, and of the nation.

Margaret Mead and the Child as a Cold-War Weapon

As the discussion of American character in chapter 4 suggests, the theoretical underpinnings for the shift in child-rearing theory and practice in the postwar United States had their roots in wartime concerns about engendering democratic behaviors in children. Following the war, these arguments continued in the articulation of a cold-war project to demonstrate the superiority of American social organization over that of the Soviet Union, a sort of precursor to the Nixon-Khrushchev "kitchen" debates later in the decade (Tyler May 1988, Marling 1994). The cold war may have been a war of technology and of clientism, but it was also very much an ideological struggle played out in discourses about everyday practices. As she had been during the war, one of the key figures in those discourses was the anthropologist Margaret Mead. A friend and colleague of Benjamin Spock (he filmed the birth of her daughter and was her pediatrician) and associate of child psychoanalyst Erik Erikson, Mead saw in the articulation of a culturally based model of child development a tool for studying the practice of socialization in diverse cultures and a means for refuting the state control of that process by Nazi Germany and, later, the Soviet Union. She would derive that model from Freud and articulate it through the comparative anthropology of her mentors and colleagues, Franz Boas and Ruth Benedict.[5] The ostensible purpose of this comparative anthropology was to isolate those behaviors and attitudes that were specific to a given culture and those that crossed cultural lines, which therefore could be rightfully called universal human traits.

What makes Mead significant in this instance is that her project involved not only developing a model of enculturation that simultaneously located universal developmental principles and respected a given culture's practices, but that she also believed that the popularization of that work was necessary to the creation of an informed democratic society. With *Coming of Age in Samoa* in 1928, Mead began a lifelong project of making anthropological concepts accessible to the American lay middle class, with the express purpose of giving that group a broader perspective on its own life ways and an appreciation of the value of cultural difference.[6] This would allow them to see their child-rearing practices as cultural responses to the natural process of development. The first step in this project was to alienate that middle class from its own culture by presenting in detail the lifeways of primitive Others and then comparing those lifeways to those of her readers. "We choose primitive groups who have had thousands of years of historical development along completely different lines from our own," she explained, ". . . whose social organization is not only simpler but very different from our own. From these contrasts, which are vivid enough to startle and enlighten those accustomed to our own way of life and simple enough to be grasped quickly, it is possible to learn many things about the effect of civilisation upon the individuals within it" (Mead 1928, 5). Through popular anthropology, Mead hoped to demonstrate to her American readers the specificity of their own social practices, and the possibility of their revision. Here, the implicit assumption was that there were potential — but not immutable — similarities and differences between American culture and those of other nations that could be revealed only by going native and experiencing firsthand (like any parent) the consonances and dissonances between practices in the everyday life in radically different social and cultural settings.[7] She had gone to Samoa, she claimed, to answer the question of whether "the disturbances which vex our adolescents [are] due to the nature of adolescence itself or to the civilisation" (6–7).

This wasn't merely an academic exercise. Mead's 1928 text marked an important moment in the rise of thinking about childhood that ran counter to the management-oriented and behaviorist theories then in vogue. Although it would take almost twenty years for this response to achieve widespread popularity, Mead in particular was laying a theoretical and practical groundwork for imagining the child as a primary site wherein a stable human nature could be separated from a malleable human culture. And although the idea that the child was the proper site for this investigation dated back to the work of G. Stanley Hall and other turn-of-the-century child researchers, the anthropological turn suggested by Mead represents an effort to replace the image of the child as laboratory animal with a more holistic image that required the study of the child in its own natural environment.[8]

By the time she edited *Childhood in Contemporary Culture* in 1955, Mead would frame the question more specifically, suggesting that "we are coming to a new appreciation of the relationship between 'culture' and 'nature,' of the ways in which our systems of learned behavior are safer than a reliance upon biological equipment, as well as to an appreciation of the hazard in the denial of the biologically given" (Mead 1955a, 451). For Mead, the rejection of behaviorism (and of other management-based approaches to child-rearing) did not require the abandonment of the rigorous study of the child's development.[9] What had to be lost was the notion of the child as a laboratory animal that could be exposed to rigidly controlled doses of culture with relatively quantifiable results (Mead 1928, 3–4). It wasn't that management-based methods of child-rearing had denied the animal origins of childhood, but that they had imagined developing techniques for the management of the child's environment as a clinical scientific enterprise distinct from its cultural underpinnings (Mead 1955a, 452–53). In Mead's view, one had first to develop a historical and cultural understanding of the meaning of childhood and child-rearing in midcentury American society, which could then be mapped against the already considerable and growing body of data about the physiological and psychological development of children, American and otherwise, in order to give both developmental researchers and parents information about the most useful methods of enculturation in those specific circumstances. The parsing of American child development into natural and cultural components required a careful survey of expectations for child-rearing in American culture, the hopes and desires that people brought to the task, which would produce "an adequate patterned representation of what parental ideals would 'predictably' be in the middle-class culture of the United States in the mid-twentieth century" (Mead 1955b, 16). An analysis of those often contradictory ideals would eventually reveal a "pattern of culture," a matrix of expectations that the child confronted as it was taught fundamental tasks such as walking, talking, and controlling its bowels. The image of a universal, natural child entering into midcentury American society was to resolve against the patterns of an identifiable middle-class American culture revealed and understood by anthropological, psychological, and sociological enterprises.

The purpose of this imagined project was neither to suggest that white, middle-class American children embodied the universal ideal of the child (although that was an unintended effect) nor to denature American mass culture. Rather, it was meant to suggest to social scientists involved with childhood, child-rearing, and education—and to their popular translators—a program of study and a praxis that could attenuate a tendency to conflate the natural and the cultural inherent in "authoritarian" programs of the past. The child, properly studied and raised in its natural environment, would be a cold-war tool for the promotion of a healthy democratic capitalism, with the power to defuse international hostilities, see past petty nationalisms, and resist psychological persuasion.[10] The association of stimulus-response conditioning and other rigid child-rearing methods such as schedules for feeding, diaper-changing, toilet-training, and so on, with the inculcation of mindless obedience and state control of the subconscious suggested unsettling parallels between a rapidly rationalizing United States and its ideological opponents, particularly the Soviet Union and later China. In some cases, such as a 1955 study by Else Frenkel-Brunswick (coauthor with Theodor Adorno of *The Authoritarian Personality* [1950]) on the relationship of excessive discipline in child-rearing to political consciousness, the correlation was quite literal. "The intimidating, punitive, and paralyzing influence of an overdisciplined, totalitarian home atmosphere may well exert a decisive influence upon the thinking and creativity of the growing child," she warned her readers (Frenkel-Brunswik 1955, 383). "The impoverishment of imagination seems to be analogous to that apparent under totalitarian social and political regimes."

Simultaneously looking back at the horrors of Nazi Germany and forward to the specter of totalitarianism lurking in mass culture, researchers such as Frenkel-Brunswik treated child-rearing as an important element in the production of future political formations. The need to understand and regulate child-rearing was not simply a matter of faddishness or marketing; it concerned the course of history. For sociologists, anthropologists, and psychologists charting the place of the new middle-class family in rapidly changing national and international social formations, the United States at midcentury was a focal point for studying and intervening in the social and cultural evolution of the species. As Margaret Mead put it, "The last half-century has been a period of insight into the dynamic processes of growth and character development, into the involvement of the whole organism in any particular activity or expression. . . . Gradually also our thinking about the way in which character was formed expanded from the immediate influences of parents face to face with an intractable organism, to a realization that these parents were themselves part of larger wholes, which could be analyzed into neighborhoods, communities, the wider society" (Mead 1955b, 449).

American society was evolving, learning to regulate its own development. The downside of this self-referential matrix, though, was that in the rush to correct perceived ills, social theorists could make overly directive suggestions that a society eager for improvement might be inclined to act upon without considering the long-term consequences: "The first response to any of these new insights is often crude and wholesale. . . . There were even . . . suggestions . . . that, as parental upbringing was obviously the cause of most of the trouble in human character, the less there was of it, the better—a point of view . . . adopted as a revolutionary tactic in totalitarian countries seeking artificially to hasten the development of a generation with a different character structure" (Mead 1955b, 450–51). Mead's ominous reference to the removal of the parent linked Soviet child-rearing practices to just such a suggestion by behaviorist John Watson, who in a popular child-rearing text in 1928 intimated that children were probably better raised by developmental professionals than by parents (Watson 1928). Yet Mead raised a difficult point that had to be faced: in a rapidly changing social structure in which the home appeared to be losing ground in child-rearing, what place would the parent have in the process and how would she be integrated? More important, perhaps, what was the correct way to intervene in child-rearing in a way that respected the primacy of the parent but protected the larger social good? The truth was that, be they Soviet or American, developmental researchers were interested in bringing about "a generation with a different character structure." The key distinction was that this process could not be "artificially hastened." Evolution had to be monitored and directed, but it could not be rushed. What was needed, then, was a way of understanding how culture related to nature, and how one could intervene in that process naturally.[11]

The boundary that Mead and others were to draw made a distinction between impulses to conform to mass authority and a natural desire to belong to a social group. The experts would help teach the parent the difference between the two, and the parent would guide the child. To do so, the parent had to learn to differentiate between a natural desire to see her child conform based on wishing it properly socialized (able to "get along"), and a desire that was based on an irrational need for obedience. The parent was imagined as the culture's representative in the home. Although she was to facilitate the child's encounter with culture rather than micromanage its development, she still had to impart to it some sense of common standards. If the parent understood herself as mediator between the culture at large and the child, rather than as the final arbiter of absolute values, then the possibility that her disciplinary decisions were the result of capriciousness or of defects incurred in her own upbringing might be reduced. Imagining the presence of the community in the acts of child-rearing was meant to both comfort and caution the parent.

Although it was important to show how a child raised "naturally" could be inherently resistant to totalitarianism and authoritarian manipulation, it was also important to demonstrate the unfortunate teleology of Soviet child-rearing practices. In "Child-Training Ideals in Soviet Russia" (Mead and Calas 1955), Mead and her Soviet expatriate coauthor painted a picture of Soviet child-rearing as a regulated enterprise in which the needs of the family and the individual were subordinated to those of the state, producing creatures who placed the dictates of local and national governments ahead of those of family and parents.[12] Inasmuch as the Soviet approach Mead described echoed calls by the previous generation of American child-rearing experts to regulate the production of good citizens, the task of differentiating between American and Soviet methods required the depiction of the former as spontaneous and the latter as overdetermined. "Instead of a series of partially related efforts designed to assist parents, educate teachers, and incorporate new bodies of scientific findings on child development," Mead and Calas warned, "Soviet laws of learning, child psychiatry, nutrition [and] child rearing may become a conscious instrument of the revolutionary regime" (179).

The difference was one of *compulsion*. According to Mead, the Soviet family was required by the state to follow a coordinated plan for child-rearing. The

Soviet child was not meant to be a free-thinking and freely acting participant in a democratic state. Describing the attitude of Soviet developmental theorists toward family life, Mead parodied the Party line: "When we realize that children are important because of their future usefulness to the state, then the role of the family as a state agency for the protection of human raw material is clear" (Mead and Calas 1955, 183). Unlike the American family, which was imagined as a private haven from which economic and governmental regulation were supposedly excluded, the Soviet family was nothing more than a workshop for the production of pliant citizens. Mead suggested that the end product of this type of approach were children who, like the Hitler Youth before them, would report on their own parents if their upbringing diverged from accepted state practice (183). Even after postwar reforms to the Soviet system, she reported, parents were still answerable to their children and to the state for their domestic practices.[13] If American families were accountable to the state through the public school system, and to the dictates of a rationalized economy through workplace "human relations," it was important that the formation of the child represent a point of resistance to the excesses of the rational and that the home form a boundary between the personal and the collective.

The Soviet model respected no such boundary. In this, its purported programs resembled the more extreme citizen-making rhetoric of the American scientific-management model of the 1920s and 1930s, in its calls for engineering social relations. More disturbing, though, was the intended product of this process, which bore a striking resemblance to the worst fears of Riesman and Whyte: the "other-directed" adult who enforced the "social ethic" on its peers. The Soviet parent was responsible for "the task of unremittingly forming the 'moral countenance' of the child, so that the child will learn to take control over itself and join the group of authorities who help maintain external controls on other people" (Mead and Calas 1955, 186). According to Mead and Calas, the Soviet child was socialized to mistake the ideological seamlessness of Soviet life for a natural system, to assume that the family was simply the most local instantiation of the Soviet government, and that all social life was inherently ideological. In this cautionary tale, the Soviets, historical materialists though they were, had not learned from history. They continued to make the mistake that American practitioners of the 1920s and 1930s had made: they treated child-rearing as a rationalized means of producing (national) citizens. Their approach limited the natural to a set of unconscious mechanical processes—such as reflexes, growth patterns, and behavioral stages—which responded in a predictable fashion to stimuli applied from without. It assumed that culture existed to serve the rational needs of the larger society by converting the (mechanistically) natural child into a citizen, and that cultural practices could be regulated in an orderly fashion to meet new social needs.

This false sense of nature could lead to an equally false sense of culture, Mead suggested in the conclusion to *Childhood in Contemporary Culture*, one which actually impeded a people's social evolution by depriving them of a creative role in adjusting their traditions and practices to new ideas about social relations, creating in them a reflexive need to follow the regimens they were given without consideration for whether they were appropriate. In this situation, parents and other caregivers would anxiously respond to direction (governmental or otherwise) by blindly attempting to adjust their previous child-rearing techniques to what they perceived as the "one best way" to raise the child. Yet these attempts to ignore or rewrite the relationship between nature and culture represented by the child, which could be facilitated but not programmed, were ultimately ignorant, misdirected, and outside of the general flow of human evolution: "There is, on the whole, less sophistication about the relationship between child-rearing practice and character formation in the published literature of the Soviet Union than there is in the present-day Admiralty Islands, among a people who twenty-five years ago were in the Stone Age" (Mead 1955, 181–82).

In sharp contrast to the Soviet Child, the American child of the 1950s had the potential to be more natural by virtue of its parents' willingness to allow it to develop in its own way, and by the family's collective ability to discern between things natural, cultural, and social. It was the job of theorists and researchers such as Mead to determine where each of these realms began and ended, and to provide that information for popular dissemination. The cold war was more than a struggle between two ideologies (or one ideology and one naturally occurring socioeconomic system); it was figured as a battle for the future viability of the species. Properly reared children were imagined as a potential prophylactic against the prospect of mass conformity and would also serve as a natural buffer against the next generation of Soviets, who were being raised to resist and disrupt the natural course of human evolution.[14] In "The Coming International Brains Race" (1956), *Parents'* publisher George Hecht imagined a Soviet expansion on the order of *Invasion of the Body Snatchers* (Siegel 1956):

> Rapidly replacing the present international arms race is an international brains race which the United States is in danger of losing unless we act decisively and promptly. . . . Shortly, if not already, the Soviet Union will have more engineers, doctors, and scientists than it requires, and its surplus supply of such indoctrinated specialists will doubtless be sent to the

underdeveloped and as yet neutral countries in Southeast Asia, the Middle East, and Africa, where they will be winning friends and influencing people for Communism. (Hecht 1956)

The image of a horde of minions of a Soviet Dale Carnegie fanning out through Africa, Southeast Asia, and South America was meant to inspire Americans to properly fund their public schools. At the same time, though, it linked a need to foster in children an inherent individualism resistant to mass behavior to the commonly held belief in the need to coordinate a counter-hegemonic force against Soviet expansion. In the postcolonial battle for the hearts and minds of the evolutionarily previous, the untutored and childlike postcolonials would be unable to distinguish a Soviet doctor from an American one, a helpful U.S. engineer from an equally solicitous Russian one.[15] The paradigms and programs of the latter would lead a people a step further along in their social and cultural evolution—simply by dint of allowing them to develop naturally—while the former would inhibit them. Like the people of the Admiralty Islands, they could either advance rapidly from the Stone Age into the twentieth century or be left worse off than before.

Practically, this move to the natural would entail, to a certain degree, a shift from the clinical to the pediatric and the psychoanalytic—from the child as a fixed point on a curve of normality, to the child as an individual organism arising at a unique historical and social moment.[16] As an eventual corrective to immediate social problems, the child not only acted as the crystallization of a set of historical and spatial conditions, it also located the solutions to those problems in its small (implicitly white and explicitly middle-class) body. The United States could resist totalitarianism not so much by collective political or economic action, but by eschewing rigid feeding schedules and unmotivated spankings. Though delicate and unreliable, the child was an adjustable homunculus of future social relations. That was the theory: it just required some translation.

Dr. Spock Explains It All

> *If you are an old reader of this book, you'll see a lot has been added and changed. . . . When I was writing the first edition, between 1943 and 1946, the attitude of a majority of people toward infant feeding, toilet training, and general child management was still fairly strict and inflexible. However, the need for greater understanding of children and for flexibility in their care had been made clear by educators, psychoanalysts, and*

pediatricians, and I was trying to encourage this. Since then a great change in attitude has occurred, and nowadays there seems to be more chance of a conscientious parent's getting into trouble with permissiveness than with strictness. So I have been trying to give a more balanced view.
—SPOCK 1957, 1–2

So began the third edition of the immensely popular *Common Sense Book of Baby and Child Care*, by Dr. Benjamin Spock. Dr. Spock began publishing advice on child-rearing in the early 1940s, and by the 1950s his name had become synonymous with the topic.[17] When *Baby and Child Care* premiered in 1946, it sold 750,000 copies and became only more popular after that.[18] Within a relatively short time, it was known as the child care "bible" and the standard signifier for enlightened parenting. References to it appeared in popular sources, from *I Love Lucy* to the *New Yorker* (Maier 1998). Depending on who was speaking it, the name "Spock" signified either the best and most modern approach to child-rearing, or the most faddish and absurd. Spock and his adherents referred to this approach as "child-centered"; his detractors described it as "permissive," and the child raised using Spock's method was often parodied as a petty tyrant whose meek and submissive parents bowed to its every wish (see figure 26).

In opening the revised edition, and in apologizing for his past mistakes, Dr. Spock offered a succinct history of recent changes in early-twentieth-century child care. The child-rearing practices of the 1920s and 1930s had been built around the rigid principles of behaviorists such as John B. Watson, or around softer versions of child psychology that still advocated the strict management of children along guidelines for the isolation and standardization of norms. Dr. Spock's "child-centered" philosophies favored allowing the child to develop at its own natural pace, letting it lead the process of child-rearing. Instead of regulating the child's physical, intellectual, and behavioral growth and charting it against established norms, the 1950s parent was to take a more hands-off approach. By allowing the child to develop naturally, observing its behavior rather than directing it, she would eventually be able to read in the child's actions its latent aptitudes and inclinations and to encourage the child to explore and develop them. The child, learning it inhabited a free environment within which to explore itself and its world, would be more likely to follow its natural inclinations and less likely to relinquish control over its life to an external authority.[19]

The need to enculturate the child was a given for both generations. Yet the problem with "scientific" child-rearing was that experts and parents had

"Parents expect too much of a child"

Drawn for Newsweek
by Marc Simont
"Some early aggression is simply exploratory"

26. *Newsweek's* 1956 cover story on new modes of child-rearing poked fun at the excesses of child-centered approaches in both word and image. In these images, stereotypical "permissive" attitudes were depicted as a form of indulgence unacceptable to adherents of older and stricter modes of discipline.

confused the sociocultural—the tabulation and deployment of data about the child—with the natural (the child's development itself) and had abused the child's nature through the rigorous application of that misconception. What was needed was a means for giving the 1950s parent the information necessary to discern between nature and culture, and the tools for improving the relationship between the two. Their parents had turned to experts and to management systems, standing between the child and the researcher, acting as middle managers in their children's upbringing. Rather than managers, 1950s parents were to be naturalists, studying their children for clues to their natural inclinations and abilities, and for most the primary text for this operation was Spock's.[20]

Avuncular, kind, and folksy, and far more popular than any other author on the subject, Spock sought to allay parents' fears that they would unwittingly continue the system of regulation and domination that had produced in them an excessive degree of conformity. He was to walk parents through the paradigm shift, encouraging them to trust in nature, and in themselves and their children as natural beings. Spock admonished his readers (1957, 47):

> You may have changed your theories because of something you've studied or read or heard, but when your child does something that would have been considered bad in your own childhood, you'll probably find yourself becoming more tense, or anxious, or angry than you imagined possible. This is nothing to be ashamed of. This is the way Nature expects human

> beings to learn child care—from their own childhood. This is how different civilizations have managed to remain stable and carry on their ideals from generation to generation.

Even as he sought to ease parents' fears about damaging their children, Spock invoked the responsibility of parent and child alike to carry civilization forward. If anything, the recent course of history had increased that burden. The child of the 1920s had represented a protocitizen, an investment in the nation's future; by the 1950s, its imaginary mandate had expanded to include the entire globe. As the decade opened, the child represented both a bulwark against impending world catastrophe and the next logical step in the evolution of the species—a fulcrum of anxiety and desire. It was the job of men and women like Benjamin Spock to guide and support parents in a voyage of self-discovery that would lead them to the resources needed to mediate between the forces of nature and culture in their child's development. With the advent of the atomic bomb, the Soviets' apparent determination to foment world revolution, and the United States' increased interests in that same world, nothing less than the future of humanity hung in the balance.[21]

In spite of its revered status, Spock's text was hardly revolutionary. Like its most direct antecedent, Holt's *The Care and Feeding of Children* (1894), most of *Baby and Child Care*'s six-hundred-odd pages delivered practical pediatric information—particularly on feeding, diapering, toilet training, and development—broken down by age and task. Spock differed from Holt, and from many other popular authors in the intervening years, in the inflection of that information. His purpose, he informed young parents, was to correct the damage done by the overly zealous application of strict regulation that had characterized the child-rearing regimes of previous generations. "Strictness was preached and practiced everywhere," he reminded parents (1957, 52). "Doctors and nurses feared irregular feeding so strongly that they . . . taught mothers that it would lead to spoiling the child. In the general enthusiasm for strictness, mothers were usually advised to ignore their baby except at feeding time. Even kissing was frowned on by a few."

Yet Benjamin Spock was more than just a pediatrician or the creator of the latest fad in child-rearing. He was also a phenomenon of American mass culture. A sort of liberal version of Walt Disney, Spock existed simultaneously as an author and the embodiment of a set of arguments about the nature of childhood and of raising children—arguments that were themselves displaced debates about proper social relations in the 1950s. Spock occupied the contradictory positions of a pediatrician attempting to naturalize relations between parents and children through a simplified psychoanalytic model; a child-rearing expert trying to disabuse parents of the need for experts; and a popular author promoting domestic intimacy via mass culture. As such, he became the focal point for arguments about children as public objects—citizens and consumers in the making—and childhood as a period of enculturation. Although Benjamin Spock and Walt Disney eventually occupied very different positions on the political spectrum, in the 1950s both played a significant role—as men and as symbols—in the formulation and propagation of ideas about the relationship between nature and culture, and the role of that relationship in the production of national and international citizens.

However, working out the difference between the natural and the cultural raised an unsettling question: who was to determine which was which? Were mutual observation and self-reporting the result of coercive social engineering or merely an expression of midcentury human sociocultural evolution? How was one to determine what was truly natural and what was cultural in human behavior? In sociology, David Riesman attempted to answer these questions by correlating population and economic development. Margaret Mead compared child-rearing practices in disparate cultures. Erik Erikson charted the difficult terrain of infantile sexuality. And Spock (and others) translated this research into practical advice for young parents.[22]

In short, Spock provided his generation another manual for the middle class, and this one was meant to teach its readers how to act naturally, and how to encourage the natural development of their children. Of course, a parent raising an infant in the 1950s thought little about the proper relationship between nature and culture, and a great deal more about feeding, diapering, and socializing the child. Child-rearing programs such as Spock's also served as a membrane between the professional and the popular, translating contemporary concerns in psychology, anthropology, and sociology into understandable domestic practices.[23]

Her Mother's Child

> *Among anxious fathers and mothers, the fear that even the most innocent appearing act or carelessly spoken word may "harm" the child or "damage" his future happiness has become a mass phobia. Example: One professional child-care expert suggested that pulling loose a dangling button from a little boy's coat might rouse "castration fears." . . . Then, too, there is the character of the educated modern mother. Fascinated by the*

behavior of children, Mrs. Norm, the enquiring type, wants to find out why they act that way. If she can't get a satisfactory answer to the question, she grows less and less certain about how to raise them.

—"BRINGING UP BABY ON BOOKS" 1956, 65

Between its parody of popular Freudian terrors and its caricatured victim of management-oriented child-rearing, *Newsweek*'s survey of the state of child care circa 1956 accurately (if snidely) depicted middle-class America's fumbling grasp on the new regime. Desperate for reliable information, surrounded by dubious "experts," and educated out of her common sense, the parody of the 1950s mother—like the lemming mother in Disney's *White Wilderness* (1958)—was of someone virtually incapacitated by the regime shift.[24] The child-centered approach replaced a model of child-as-amoeba—responding predictably to regulated external stimuli with one in which the child expressed its nature as raw drives and desires . . . for food, sensual pleasure, and even for sex. Yet if the occasionally incautious or insincere popularizer of Freud frightened a public ill-prepared for the notion of infantile sexuality,[25] there existed a broad network of researchers who took the idea quite seriously and provided a wealth of material for popular authors such as Spock.

One of the most significant figures in the application of Freud to child-rearing methodologies was Erik Erikson. A student and analysand of Anna Freud, colleague of Ruth Benedict, Margaret Mead, and Gregory Bateson, and affiliated for a time with the Institute of Child Welfare at the University of California, Berkeley, Erikson played an important role in the popularization of Freudian psychology in the United States, and more particularly in the project of linking the psychological with the social and cultural via the child.[26] Erikson also corresponded with Spock, who arranged a teaching position for him at the University of Pittsburgh after Erikson resigned from the University of California, refusing to sign its McCarthyite loyalty oath.[27]

In his influential *Childhood and Society*, Erikson described what he termed a "composite boy," who, born in the late 1930s, exhibited the baseline American personality:

> The family is Anglo-Saxon, mildly Protestant, of the white-collar class. This type of boy is. . . . shy, especially with women, and emotionally retentive. . . . His mother is somewhat of a "Mom." She can be harsh, loud-voiced, and punitive. More likely than not she is sexually frigid. His father . . . is shy in his intimate relationships and does not expect to be treated with much consideration at home. Such parents in our case his-

tories are still noted down as pathogenic, while it is quite clear that they represent a cultural pattern. (1950, 267)

One component in a broader description of the genealogy of American identity, this imagined boy embodied the latest in a series of missteps in the evolution of that identity. The product of a weak or absent father and an overprotective mother, this 1930s-era composite boy had suffered from his mother's decision to apply behaviorist child-rearing techniques to her children, which she hoped would lead to "automatic compliance and maximum efficiency, with a minimum of friction." Erikson considered this method appropriate for dogs, which were "trained to serve and die," but not for children (269). The purpose of this "mechanical child-rearing" he argued, was to "adjust the human organism from the very start to clocklike punctuality in order to make it a standardized appendix of the industrial world." The product of this approach followed orders better than he gave them, and the democracy he engendered was one of interest groups and compromise. A bit of a milquetoast, he would be a fine middle manager but a poor executive, and "strangely disinterested in the running of the nation" (280).

According to Erikson, the American myth of the self-made man (so crucial to the rise of Walt Disney), had been reinvented in 1920s and 1930s child-rearing as a form of marginal differentiation. Like Walt Disney, the composite boy was expected to mold from a uniformly mundane existence a unique and superior persona—not in spite of that existence, but *because of it*. He was expected to perform a uniqueness that pointed back toward regularity, that mimicked brotherhood. This permitted him to shine if he could and to get by if he couldn't. The composite boy was the result of a mistaken democratic impulse, an idea that efficiency delivered the gift of equality. Adopting the techniques of scientific management, "American mothers (especially of the middle class) found themselves standardizing and overadjusting children who later were expected to personify that very virile individuality which in the past had been one of the outstanding characteristics of the American" (Erikson 1950, 253–54).

In the end, this composite boy, himself mass-produced, would find a mass-produced society in which he was encouraged to imagine that his desires were his own, not simply those provided him by the forces of mass persuasion:

> Thus standardized, he found chances, in his later childhood, to develop autonomy initiative, and industry, with the implied promise that decency in human relations, skill in technical details, and knowledge of facts would permit him freedom of choice in his pursuits, that the identity of free

> choice would balance his self-coercion. As an adolescent and man, however, he finds himself confronted with superior machines, complicated, incomprehensible, and impersonally dictatorial in their power to standardize his pursuits and tastes. These machines do their powerful best to convert him into a consumer idiot, a fun egotist, and an efficiency slave—and this by offering him what he seems to demand. (Erikson 1950, 281–82)

Ultimately, though, the fault for this situation lay not in the conditions of mass society, but in the lack of internal resources the boy had to meet that society—resources that his mother had failed to provide. The solution to this evolutionary deviation, then, was not to be found in a critique of mass culture, nor in a restructuring of industrial relations, as much as it was in the reconfiguration of relations between parent and child.

Like David Riesman's other-directed Americans, the (white), middle-class family that Erikson described—and its "mom" in particular—was the result of a convergence of character traits and complex historical forces. In a chapter in *Childhood and Society* titled "Reflections on American Identity," paraphrasing Freud, Erikson depicted the typical American ego as a quasi-natural adaptation to rapidly and violently changing social conditions, standing like "a cautious and sometimes shrewd patrician, not only between the anarchy of primeval instincts and the fury of the archaic conscience, but also between the pressure of upper-class convention and the anarchy of mob spirit" (Erikson 1950, 241). The American ego, nothing less than the representative ego of the mid-twentieth century, was also its bourgeois zeitgeist, the very essence of the middle class (246). This creature, properly tended and defended, was most likely to navigate the social and political extremes of the moment. To best aid this process, Erikson imagined the psychoanalyst, sociologist, and the historian working hand in hand, developing a psychohistorical picture of the progress of American culture to use as a template for understanding the behavior of parent and child, and envisioning potential outcomes for various interventions in those behaviors (250–51).

As the mother was the parent with whom the child had most contact, it was with her that this work was to begin. Erikson devoted a significant portion of *Childhood and Society* to explaining the psychohistorical roots of "momism" and its place in the ongoing development of an American identity. Momism described the American mother as a domineering, sexually unresponsive narcissist who repressed her children's sensual and sexual instincts and sacrificed their development as individuals to her need for their attention (249). The concept of momism derived not from clinical observation, but from a work of popular fiction, *Generation of Vipers* (Wylie 1942). A hostile reaction to the increased importance of women in the workforce and in managing the domestic economy during the Depression and World War II, momism was widely imagined as a psychosocial disease responsible for male homosexuality, neuroses, and aggressive, domineering female children. The fictional "mom" in this supposed complex was a sort of vampire psychically feeding on her own children, recreating herself in her daughters and creating future submissive husbands in her sons.

For Erikson, though, this largely literary creation described a cultural and historical reality. "Mom" wasn't located in any one individual, yet she existed as an archetype present to some degree in every American woman (Erikson 1950, 248–49). He argued that modern American motherhood derived from social, cultural, and historical circumstances that dated back first to the Puritans and later to the American frontier, and which had originally served the positive function of constraining sexual excess in a society whose limited membership required circumspection for the sake of harmony (251–52). The mother in this society was required to entrain and enforce this repression in her children. As American society grew, the mother became the symbol of proper public decorum and repression: "mom" was the Public Mother, the visible feminine social conscience that would, by the end of the nineteenth century, become the commonplace image of the progressive reformer.

As Euroamericans began pushing westward out of New England, they created a perpetual frontier into which the children of this proto-"mom" fled in search of social and sensual freedom. As each successive frontier settled, however, women arrived and served as the contradictory objects of intense sexual desire and as representatives of the repressive culture that men had just escaped. Converting desire into repression, these women became mothers who exerted a control over their sons that they could not exert over their husbands (250–51). And so on. Since the frontier father was perpetually absent, Erikson suggested, the mother was forced to usurp his role in the family and to demand her children's undivided attention, for their own good: "Momism is only displaced paternalism. . . . The post-revolutionary descendants of the Founding Fathers forced their women to be mothers *and* fathers, while they continued to cultivate the role of freeborn sons" (254).

In this psychohistorical frontier fantasy, the father's absence from the Oedipal triangle created an unwholesome tension between mother and son in which her unspent libidinal energy found its outlet in excessively regulating him. Lacking a strong masculine role model with whom to identify and against whom to rebel, the son became sullen and resentful—overcompensating for a lack of internalized masculinity with a bluff and bravado that masked a feminized dependency on the mother and a desire for a strong external authority. For the daughter, the absence of a father meant that she lacked a proper object of desire over which she could compete with her mother. As a result, she would become narcissistic and demanding, assuming that she was capable of capturing the attention of anyone she desired, yet unable to believe with any certainty that she could hold it. In time the son became the Absent Father, fleeing the demands of the "mom" that the daughter had learned to become. The challenge for 1950s parents was to recognize that this frontier dynamic had outlived its psychohistorical usefulness, and that by remaking themselves they were in a position to reconfigure it. The father had to learn to become a palpable masculine presence in the home, while the mother had to step back and understand that she was no longer solely responsible for the production, regulation, and transmission of culture. And the suburbs became the new frontier where this reconfiguration could take place.[28]

Erikson's composite boy would have reached his twenties by the 1950s. At this age, he would become the 1950s parent whom Erikson believed lacked the balance of individuality and sociability that his children would require to face the demands of the day. Nor was Erikson alone in that sentiment. In "Differential Patterns of Social Outlook and Personality in Family and Children" (1955, 388), by Else Frenkel-Brunswik, a mother hoping to raise her children in a liberal household expressed fears to an investigator that she had been "too much influenced by [the behaviorist] Watson" in her own childhood, and that the experience would inevitably lead her to raise her children under the same model. Based on survey work done in the 1940s by the Institute of Child Welfare at the University of California, Berkeley, on home interviews, and on personality testing, the study attempted "to probe into the underlying patterns of motivation and emotions" in order to determine to what degree parents' social and political beliefs—as expressed in child-rearing choices—shaped those of their children (371).

A boy in Frenkel-Brunswik's study ("Karl") who had grown up in an authoritarian home was in many ways the son of Erikson's composite boy. His parents were depicted as thoughtlessly reproducing the mistakes of the previous generation, demanding blind obedience from their children without regard to their thoughts and feelings. The father had little initiative and the mother was domineering. Although the couple aspired to the middle class, the father apparently lacked the follow-through to succeed. The children, in turn, performed a hollow show of obedience to their parents and to external authorities, under which the researchers detected undercurrents of anger, hostility, and fear of being punished or ostracized. The child raised in an authoritarian home became a reflexive conformist at both the conscious and the unconscious level as he compulsively worked to avoid the apparently irrational and equally reflexive regulation of his environment and behavior. "In the context of American culture, Karl and his family are deviants," Frenkel-Brunswick warned her readers (1955, 400). "Fat, fearful Karl is certainly the opposite of the ideal American boy. . . . [and the whole family adheres] rigidly to some absolute status values which oversimplify the social and cultural realities of our civilization. This renders them helpless and perverts their view of the social scene, making them susceptible to totalitarian propaganda." This rigidly managed family modeled social engineering under the pretense of efficiency, the streamlining of human behavior as an outgrowth of modernization. Against this outmoded and antidemocratic force, a new generation of experts in child development, and their popular counterparts, were frontline agents in a movement to reinsert the natural and human into the process of producing citizens, helping parents to avoid "the compulsive type of conformity" and to encourage "genuine and constructive conformity" (400).[29]

"Psychiatric enlightenment as begun to debunk the superstition that to manage a machine you must become a machine," Erikson argued in 1950 (282–83), "and that to raise masters of the machine you must mechanize the impulses of childhood." New child-rearing experts, he claimed, would plant the seeds for a more durable, natural democratic capitalist society, doing work that would be supported by efforts to rewrite the political landscape into which those children would move. Erikson and his colleagues continued the discursive production of the child as homunculus of the future, offering (unwittingly, perhaps) a means of deferring more concerted social and political action. A signal difference in this new child-homunculus, though, was that, while its predecessor had been imagined as a tabula rasa onto which proper social codes could be imprinted, the 1950s version was imagined as a protosocial animal which already contained the necessary information in primitive form. Were it raised naturally, that information would unfold properly; were it raised like a machine, that information would be perverted. Yet this did not mean that the child was free to grow however it wanted. Rather, it was to be guided instead of managed, a soft hand replacing the hard. Achieving this balance of permission and discipline would prove difficult and produce both anxiety and instruction.

Nature, Not Anarchy

> *The idea has been promoted . . . that, in order to avoid authoritarianism, all authority must be forsworn. Against this excessive view it must be held that total permissiveness would verge upon anarchy. Respect for the authority of outstanding individuals and institutions is an essential aspect of a healthy home and society. It does not as such lead to total surrender to, or an absolute glorification of, the given authorities. . . . Rather than authoritarianism or else anarchy, there must be "guidance," especially when this is combined with acceptance and thus strengthens the moral functions of the child and helps him to overcome the impulses toward selfishness and aggression. By guidance . . . we mean the encouragement of the child to work out his instinctual problems rather than repress them, thus avoiding their later break-through.*
>
> —FRENKEL-BRUNSWIK 1955, 387

Essential to the process of guided enculturation, through which the child became human, was the idea of learning self-control—the notion that the child first had to learn to *recognize* its human feelings, and then to *control* and *channel* them. Self-control had also been a significant concept in the previous generation's child-rearing literature, but in the postwar period it underwent an important change. Previously, self-control had been understood as a pattern of responses imprinted on the child through the repetition of proper stimuli, through which external regulation became internalized. By the 1950s, self-control was more often described as deriving from a process in which the child gained control by first developing an understanding of its own feelings, then learning how to express those feelings in a socially acceptable manner. In effect, this model reversed the vector for the development of self-control, imagining it as proceeding from the child's interior world into the larger social realm. Proper self-control was meant to give the 1930s-era child a competitive edge by providing it with the tools needed to respond independently and correctly to any situation. The 1950s child, however, experienced self-control as engendering a harmonious relationship with its peer group, and success as getting along more than winning. This was the other-directedness about which David Riesman worried, or the Social Ethic that concerned William Whyte, and although the child-centered approach was meant to serve as a corrective to the authoritarian impulse, its detractors saw in it an equal potential for the production of excessive conformity through slavish attention to group norms.

In the 1950s child-rearing ideal, the proper boundary between the natural and the cultural occurred midway between the authoritarian and the anarchic. A child raised too strictly might become susceptible to arbitrary authority; one raised too laxly would be anarchic and rebellious and might contribute to conditions conducive to revolution. The child whose natural impulses were respected but who experienced sensible restraint would be best prepared for democratic capitalism: able to compete, but mindful of the needs of the larger community. Yet for critics of child-centered practices, Spock's brand of "permissiveness" signified a refusal to impart to the child universal and standardized codes of behavior and to give it the necessary tools for its individual agency. The concept was nature run amok, a willingness to allow the child, a precultural being, to dictate the nature of social relations—in the family, and by extension within the larger culture. Within that critique, the blame for the paradigm's excesses and failures circulated between Spock, the overzealous and undereducated parent, and the disobedient child. Indeed, it seemed as if the laxity of the theory itself made everyone somewhat culpable: "Since 1940, horrible excesses have been committed in the name of [permissiveness]. . . . There were no difficult children, it seemed, only difficult parents. One 'problem mother' complained: 'My child won't sleep; he won't eat; he may take what doesn't belong to him. He tells me he hates me, and he hates his baby sister, too. He tears up books, messes his food, and kicks his grandmother' " ("Bringing Up Baby on Books" 1956, 66).

This interpretation derived in part from overly enthusiastic readings of Spock by parents, well-meaning pediatricians, and psychologists, and in part from an uneasiness on the part of some social critics toward an approach to child-rearing that seemed designed more to reduce the parent to the child's level than to introduce the child to the adult world of self-regulation. The tendency to hold Spock responsible for the excesses of his enthusiasts led him to offer a series of disclaimers, including repeated qualifications in the third edition of his book. What mattered more than strictness or permissiveness was that the parent's approach was genuine. "Good hearted parents who aren't afraid to be firm when it is necessary can get good results with either moderate strictness or moderate permissiveness," he counseled. "On the other hand, a strictness that comes from harsh feelings or a permissiveness that is timid or vacillating can each lead to poor results. The real issue is what spirit the parent puts into managing the child and what attitude is engendered in the child as a result" (1957, 46).

Behind the parody of the pampered child lay a real anxiety about how to properly socialize a child without impinging upon its natural aptitudes and desires. The profound desire on the part of parents to do right by their children, to offer them a better life, had not disappeared with the modal change in child-rearing, nor had the basic rhetorical strategy of child-rearing magazines such as *Parents'* in trying to meet that desire. The formula for addressing the practical problems of child-rearing still followed a recognizable pattern: (a) describe the problem, (b) discuss the long-term negative impact—to both the child and society—of not properly addressing said problem, and (c) suggest a means for correcting it. This allowed the parent to identify (with) the problem, to develop anxiety about it, and to find comfort in the solution offered. Even as it involved parents in a matrix of interpretation and consumption that regulated their actions, this strategy—common also to child-rearing texts such as Spock's—still placed primary responsibility or failure of its application squarely on them, particularly on the mother.

For adherents of Spock, being "child-centered" didn't mean allowing the child free rein. Rather, it meant basing one's actions around one's child (especially discipline) on a close examination of its behaviors, instead of on a timetable of developmental stimuli.[30] While parents of the 1920s and 1930s were expected to compare their child to charts, graphs, and photographs to determine whether it was behaving within acceptable parameters, the naturalist-mother of the 1950s was expected to treat each child as a unique case study, a creature bound in its development to its environment and meant to shape that environment even as it was shaped by it. As another child-rearing expert put it, discipline "aims at bringing the child into harmony with the growing demands of his surroundings upon his maturing desires and responsibilities. Permissiveness means accepting . . . the child's impulses and desires at the moment as the basis for guiding him in his further development" (Gruenberg 1956, 82).

To do this necessitated more than simple measurement and correlation. It also required a language and a set of practices enumerated by Spock and applied to the details of daily living laid out in women's magazines. In *Parents' Magazine* in particular, Spock's advice was tested in the field, in articles that recounted the experience of new mothers. In large part, they counseled patient observation. "What comes more slowly, requires more thoughtful understanding, is learning to know the kind of person your baby is," suggested Maja Bernath, author of "How Baby Care Has Changed" (1956, 108). A parent gained this knowledge by reading beneath the child's surface, to the inner drives and instincts that dictated its actions. "With an understanding of your baby's development," Bernath counseled, "you'll see all sorts of behavior in clearer focus. You won't try to buck nature, as mothers were in effect instructed to do in the past, when habit 'training' and habit 'breaking' were the laws of the day" (113).[31]

It is difficult, in retrospect, to determine to what degree popular 1950s child-rearing literatures were reporting on a change, and to what degree they were creating that change to tap into a booming market. What is certain is that they outlined a significant shift in child-rearing, reported an overreaction to previous modes of child care, and attempted to illuminate a middle way between rigid discipline and anarchic "permissiveness."[32] Indeed, locating a healthy middle ground would be one of the major themes in child-rearing throughout the decade. *Parents'*, for instance, would trade on its former association with the masters of discipline, such as John B. Watson, by suggesting that its involvement with discredited methods and practitioners, and its more recent conversion, afforded it a special perspective valuable for avoiding excess. In the magazine's thirty-year anniversary issue, in October 1956, Sidonie Masters Gruenberg (1956, 47), one of the original members of its advisory board and long-time president of the Child Study Association, offered an apologia, suggesting that perhaps it was not so much the experts who had erred in their thinking as overenthusiastic mothers: "Another element in the anti-expert swing is the fact that in every period of change there are bound to be some excesses. When doctors were advising regularity in a child's routine, some mothers took the advice too literally and watched the clock instead of the baby. Similarly, when doctors subsequently found that over-rigid schedules are harmful to a child, some mothers went all-out on their own idea of 'self-demand.'"

In general, *Parents'* anniversary issue was devoted to explaining to parents how they were to make that transition properly. The author of "How Baby Care Has Changed," for instance, laid out a comparison between two brothers, one easy going and the other difficult:

> Johnny is a lucky boy to be spending his babyhood in the 1950's, instead of the 20's or early '30s. His brother Jim would have made out all right in those days—when babies were raised on strict schedules right from the beginning. The directives set up by authorities were based on physical averages, and by those standards Jim was an average baby. . . . A mother was told to fit her baby to the ready-made pattern—never to vary the pattern to fit her baby. Hungry at the "wrong" times, slow to adjust to regularity, Johnny would have been miserable, frustrated, rebellious. His perfectly normal individuality would have fought the authoritarian regime—almost certainly with unhappy effects on his personality. (Bernath 1956, 36)

Jim, the older of the two, fit well within the statistical and behavioral norms being developed in the 1920s and 1930s. Johnny, on the other hand, was just naturally different. The "authoritarian regime" of management-oriented child-rearing (in which *Parents'* had a hand) allowed no room for natural difference and would have turned him into a frustrated rebel, a social problem. The parent who thwarted the child's natural rhythms, acting perhaps on training inherited in the previous generation, who sought tighter control over the child's environment, ran the risk of stunting the child's natural development from the animal toward the social. The result was likely to be a child who demonstrated a "discontinuity between the manifest and the latent," who outwardly seemed willing to submit to authority but inwardly seethed with antisocial anger and resentment apparent perhaps only during personality testing (Frenkel-Brunswik 1955, 397).

Although this rhetoric exaggerated the distance between the previous paradigm and the new child-centered approach, it signaled the importance imputed to that change in thinking and practice in child-rearing. And though World War II had slowed that shift, the postwar boom was creating a bumper crop of new parents willing to associate the rigors of their own upbringing with their recent experience with fascism and with the rise of Stalinism.[33] In a 1950 *Parents'* article titled "Children Need Sensible Parents," Benjamin Spock claimed: "Twentieth-century America has no stable tradition about how children should be reared. In fact, it has a tradition against traditions. Parents in a quandary do not ask themselves what their parents or grandparents would have done under the circumstances. They ask what is the latest theory. Twenty years ago, strictness and regulation were the psychologic and pediatric laws of the land. Now we are in the midst of a strong, even violent, swing in the opposite direction" (Spock 1950, 41). *Parents'* sounded this theme repeatedly in the years to come, gently hinting that the mothers of the previous generation, who had been asked to act as middle managers, assistants, and informants in a national project to standardize child-rearing, had gone too far. In addition, it argued, in overzealously adopting the role of manager, those mothers may have engendered in their daughters an unhealthy need to meddle in their own children's development, or perhaps a too-violent rejection of the maternal role. *Parents'* would act as midwife to the new paradigm—neither fully amateur nor professional—translating the experts' advice into practical suggestions for parents, while offering tips on how to undo the advice it had offered to *their* mothers. What *Parents'* cautioned against was not expert opinion, but a parent's overdependence on that information. The magazine offered to replace expert information with tangible examples and potential solutions, to teach the parent how to translate relatively abstract ideas such as "naturalness" into daily practice. Beginning in the 1940s, the magazine shifted its terms of address so that it appeared less a journal of expert opinion stated simply, and more a forum where mothers could discuss practical issues around applying the child-centered paradigm. Much more than before, it described its female authors as both experts and mothers, adopting a formal scenario in its articles that imagined those mother/experts confronted with a child-rearing problem they came to understand and solve by grappling with the details of the new regime.

To develop this new understanding of her child, the parent would first, of course, have to overcome the very habit-training that her own parents had inflicted upon her. A woman raised within a stimulus-response model of child-rearing had to learn the roots and meaning of her response when her child became upset, or angry, or cried for no apparent reason. "We are not to blame our distrust of strong feelings. We were raised by a generation whose parents taught them that emotions were not to be displayed in public," *Parents'* counseled gently (Wensberg and Northrop 1955, 41). The magazine suggested that the mother's impulse to quell a child's outburst would not only limit her ability to understand the source of that outburst but would also perpetuate an unhealthy tradition of avoidance and repression.

Ironically, though, this failure by the parent derived not from some inherent flaw in her character, but from her condition as the adult product of the previous mode of child-rearing. The assumption was that people raised within the previous regime were damaged goods who had become too dependent on external standards and would either raise their children to be conformists like themselves or—abandoning any attempt to control their children—create anarchists with no sense of proper social behavior. As critics and proponents argued whether "permissive" child-rearing was the solution to the excesses of the previous generation's parents, *Parents'* offered counsel to young postwar parents on how to move beyond the strict regimens of the 1920s and 1930s without ceding responsibility for regulating their children's behavior: "Many parents . . . can't say 'No.' The most susceptible are the well-intentioned parents who want so desperately to bring up well-adjusted, useful children. . . . 'I don't want to be authoritarian,' [a mother] said. 'I'd like them to develop inner discipline.' And so would most intelligent parents. But it's important not to get confused. To gain self-discipline, a child wants to learn how far he can go" (Newman 1950, 24). For the 1950s parent, so desperate to do the right thing, for the good of her child and the human race, the challenge was enormous: to shed her "authoritarian" upbringing, to allow her child to express itself naturally, yet to ensure that her child was not so natural that it was wild. The parent's near-impossible task was to bring her child into culture, but not into the culture from which she derived. This made child-rearing in the 1950s a process of cultural revision in which the parent had as much work to do as the child, and in which she had to learn to let go of the standards and norms which had been so much a part her own upbringing (and which continued to be a part of her child's experience in school). The child of the 1950s, more than just the gradually resolving embodiment of the future, was also an avenue into and means for correcting the past.

If improved self-awareness and a greater sense of inner harmony weren't adequate inducements to enter into the new regime, parents were also reminded that they were already being watched—by their own children. Moving beyond behaviorism's theory of stimulus and response, child-centered models posited the infant as an intensely aware and perceptive creature able to read its parents' moods from a very young age: "When the baby gets older, he becomes aware of the mother's facial expressions and of her voice. He will know how to read his mother's face when she approves or disapproves and will understand what she means whether it is expressed in words, gestures, or facial expression. This will be the case even when the mother consciously tries to suppress her real feelings" (Buxbaum 1951, 52). The problem for the parent wasn't solved simply by putting on a happy face. The child was a perceptive animal, able to read past her attempts to mask her feelings. The domestic environment—more than a laboratory for raising normal children or a blind from which to observe their behavior—was actually a place in which the child studied the parent as much as the parent studied the child. The parent was both the naturalist observing the child and a significant environmental factor in its development. Like a naturalist, she had to avoid assiduously any act that might startle the child or produce in it unnatural behaviors. Her self-understanding was her contribution to an environment in which the child would inevitably read her behavior as one element in his instinctive drive toward enculturation.

In return, the child provided the parent with an alienated vantage point from which to reconsider her day-to-day behavior. Many of the articles in *Parents'* that explored the meaning and purposes of discipline framed the problem with a discussion of the author's own experience of it as a child. These began with a confessional in which the author described an incident in which her child acted out and she responded in an excessively violent or angry way. With the release of that anger, typically, came a memory of her own mother behaving similarly, which then recalled the unpleasant child-rearing techniques of the previous generation. The 1950s mother/author, who had vowed never to do what had been done to her, began a voyage of self-discovery in which she learned to understand her child's moods and behaviors by looking at her reactions to them and to where those reactions came from. Once she learned to read herself correctly, she would be free to see her child for what it was.[34]

In "I Stopped Spanking . . . When I Found Out Why I Did It" (P. Meek 1955, 44), a "farm mother" confessed, "As the mother of four children I've never been entirely sure whether I believed in spanking or whether I didn't. I have had a strong suspicion that there must be wiser ways to discipline a child." The author's solution was not to consult child-rearing experts, nor to do as many poor rural mothers had done since the early part of the century and write to the U.S. Children's Bureau.[35] Instead, she decided to turn her gaze inward. "I resolved to check myself for a period to figure out just why I spanked," she wrote, "and to make an honest appraisal of my reasons" (44). That appraisal took the form of careful self-observation while tending to her youngest child. The result of this investigation was not that her son was acting improperly, but that *she* was projecting her guilt and anger for not paying enough attention to the child onto him: "Gradually it dawned on me that actually I had spanked him because . . . I was cross with myself for being so careless" (45). The result: her small son received more love and attention, and discipline that was appropriately motivated, and she gained further insight into her actions and feelings.

In another example from the same year, an author offered a more detailed analysis of her behavior around her child, one that had all the markings of the new cultural constellation that so troubled social theorists such as Riesman and Whyte. As a young mother in a newly developed suburb, she found herself in the middle of a panoptic nightmare in which she heard a pack of mothers braying at their children: "Through the quiet of the morning I was startled to hear a . . . mother . . . yelling at the top of her lungs at her child, 'Come here! Don't talk back to me!' I had made a mental note to avoid any entangling relations with that woman when I heard another voice from across the street, similar in volume and inflection, scolding another child. Almost before that voice stopped, other mothers joined in the chorus" (M. Peterson 1955, 66). Seeing her own child playing in some mud, she shouted at him—and discovered that her own voice was one of the mob's. This realization led to an analysis of the problem, and then to a renewed appreciation for the child as a natural creature, and a greater openness to self-improvement: "A little introspection revealed that cupboard explorations, wandering from the yard or generally getting in Mother's way were the most likely to create an unpleasant scene. Actually none of these activities is undesirable behavior in a child who is quite naturally learning about his environment. Was the answer, then, more patience? Yes, but more than that. I needed better understanding and a more positive approach to my child, his interests and his activities" (46). For each of these mother/authors, discipline, far from being an unpleasant necessity or simply a parental responsibility, became an opportunity for personal growth, a chance to redress wrongs engendered in an authoritarian past, and to avoid their eventual repetition in the next generation. The suburban frontier was more than a boundary between the urban and the rural or the natural and the cultural; it also represented a temporal boundary between a past in need of redemption and a future in search of perfection.

Having gained experience and insight through introspection, the parent's next task was to turn her gaze back outward, toward her child. A parental advice columnist from the *New York Times Magazine* urged, "parents must try to understand what a child is trying to say by his behavior" (Barclay 1950, 17). The parent turning to Spock, or to another advisor, was no longer simply looking for reassurance that her child's behavior was within the normative bounds for its age. Rather, she was beginning a learning process wherein she would develop a facility for reading the latent meanings inherent in her child's acts. Even the wordless cries of the smallest infant could be understood by a parent patient and calm enough to listen and observe. As the child grew older, it would give more elaborate clues, not necessarily via language, but through gestures, its choice of clothing, or even painting: "Far from being the meaningless smears so many grownups see, a youngster's art is, in a sense, more meaningful than a great many message-bearing adult creations. For what he does is completely spontaneous. . . . [Children] tend to think in pictures. Even adults dream in pictures. This follows the dim dawn pattern of the human species and foreshadows the development of written language" (Deiss 1955, 86; see figure 27). Like the cave paintings of their aboriginal ancestors, children's paintings described the first attempts to formulate a language from the primal urges and basic instincts from which culture would flow over time. Every child was a new beginning to history, and the mistakes of the previous generation didn't need to be passed on to (and through) it, if the parent were careful and read closely the signs being offered.

Nor was it only artwork that offered insights into the child's emerging psyche. Consumable items—clothing, toys, books, movies, games, and so on—formed the environment in which the child developed. While the importance of consumption habits had not lessened (and had in fact increased), the meaning of the environment constituted in that consumption did change. Previously, the environment had primarily been a stimulus—positive or negative—that would affect the developing child and play a significant role in its eventual success or failure as an adult. In the postwar period, the child ceased to be a monadic creature consuming alone, and the environment became a richer semiotic tapestry, loaded with information that affected not only the child, but its parents as well. Parents read their children, children read their parents; parents learned from their children to read themselves, and children learned from their parents to read themselves and others. In what was essentially an annotated toy catalog in *Parents'* (see figure 28), Roma Gans (1955, 46–48), a professor at Teachers' College, Columbia University, advised parents that "play helps youngsters be part of the group . . . teaches teamwork . . . [and] provides a chance to test out ideas. There is learning—actual knowledge—that youngsters acquire through play." Through play, toys, and consumption, children could locate their natural aptitudes, begin to determine their course in life, and practice social behaviors.

Toys and play also provided an important vehicle for the parent's and the child's developing observational skills. A parent could gain important insight into her child's aptitudes and preferences and, by surrounding the child with well-chosen toys, could improve the child's chances for self-knowledge by providing a rich environment from which the child could choose those things that best suited its latent self: "Certain toys have special vocational significance. By choosing them wisely you can see to it that your child's play has an important role in this enlightening process you have initiated. Material provided by Parents' Magazine, publications by the Toy Guidance Council, schoolteachers and often those in charge of toy departments or toy store can advise you in your selection" (Davenel 1956, 49). The properly constituted play environment, the author argued, revealed the child to itself, doing naturally for the child the work that the various aptitude and personality tests it would take in school would do for its teachers and employers. In this light, toys and play became a form of home testing by which parents could "measure, evaluate and rate [personality] against job requirements" so that the child could "get specialized knowledge about himself" to increase "his" odds of "getting a better job and succeeding in it" (Davenel 1956, 111). As the child emerged from the haze of its prehistorical infancy, it made its way along a predetermined evolutionary arc that, if it were properly guided, would end at the job and social role that were a natural extension of that development.

Although both parent and child were meant to benefit from child-centered child-rearing, the child provided the possibility of that therapeutic or remedial action. As a creature entering into culture from nature, the child presented nature to the parent, even as the parent represented culture to the child. Researchers such as Mead or Erikson, and popular translators such as Spock or Edith

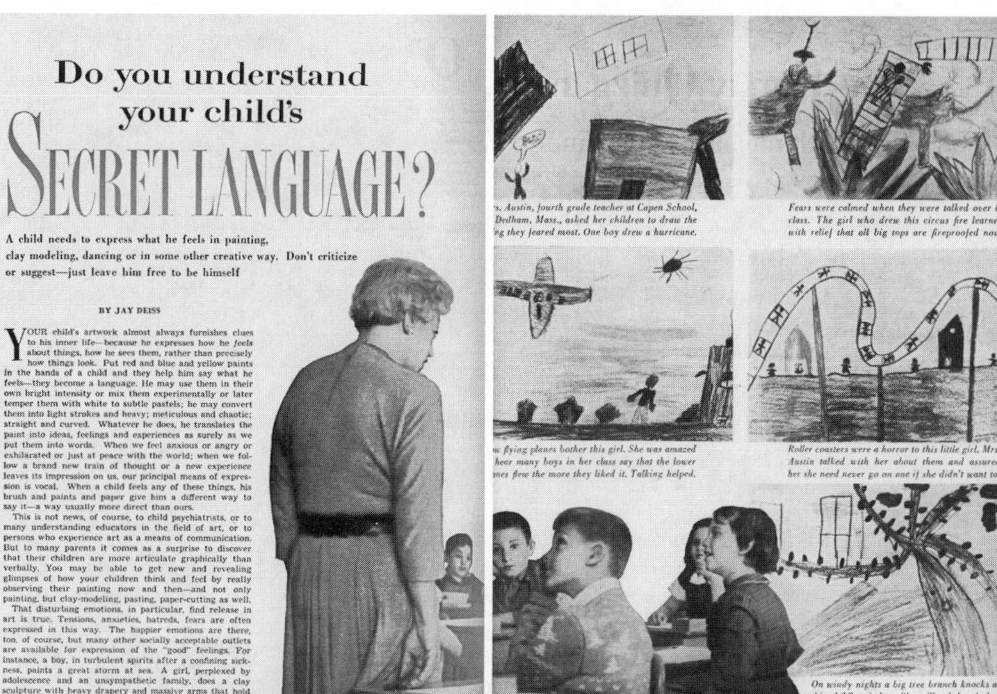

Do you understand your child's SECRET LANGUAGE?

A child needs to express what he feels in painting, clay modeling, dancing or in some other creative way. Don't criticize or suggest—just leave him free to be himself

BY JAY DEISS

YOUR child's artwork almost always furnishes clues to his inner life—because he expresses how he *feels* about things, how he sees them, rather than precisely how things look. Put red and blue and yellow paints in the hands of a child and they help him say what he feels—they become a language. He may use them in their own bright intensity or mix them experimentally or later temper them with white to subtle pastels; he may convert them into light strokes and heavy; meticulous and chaotic; straight and curved. Whatever he does, he translates the paint into ideas, feelings and experiences as surely as we put them into words. When we feel anxious or angry or exhilarated or just at peace with the world; when we follow a brand new train of thought or a new experience leaves its impression on us, our principal means of expression is vocal. When a child feels any of these things, his brush and paints and paper give him a different way to say it—a way usually more direct than ours.

This is not news, of course, to child psychiatrists, or to many understanding educators in the field of art, or to persons who experience art as a means of communication. But to many parents it comes as a surprise to discover that their children are more articulate graphically than verbally. You may be able to get new and revealing glimpses of how your children think and feel by really observing their painting now and then—and not only painting, but clay-modeling, pasting, paper-cutting as well.

That disturbing emotions, in particular, find release in art is true. Tensions, anxieties, hatreds, fears are often expressed in this way. The happier emotions are there, too, of course, but many other socially acceptable outlets are available for expression of the "good" feelings. For instance, a boy, in turbulent spirits after a confining sickness, paints a great storm at sea. A girl, perplexed by adolescence and an unsympathetic family, does a clay sculpture with heavy drapery and massive arms that hold the figure earthbound. She calls it "Despair." A boy living in the slums paints a city street that expresses in its somber grays and dark shadows his (*Continued on page 86*)

52

...s. Austin, fourth grade teacher at Capen School, Dedham, Mass., asked her children to draw the ...ng they feared most. One boy drew a hurricane.

Fears were calmed when they were talked over in class. The girl who drew this circus fire learned with relief that all big tops are fireproofed now.

...w flying planes bother this girl. She was amazed ... hear many boys in her class say that the lower ...nes flew the more they liked it. Talking helped.

Roller coasters were a horror to this little girl. Mrs. Austin talked with her about them and assured her she need never go on one if she didn't want to.

On windy nights a big tree branch knocks at this child's window. She will ask her father to cut it off so it won't scare her again.

Thus fear is released in art. So too are anger, joy, love. Give your child this outlet.

53

27. An article from a 1955 issue of *Parents' Magazine* offers tools to parents for reading the deeper and more primitive meanings in their children's artwork, suggesting that it is a window onto their psyches, and onto human prehistory.

Buxbaum, promised to help sort out what was natural from what was cultural, to help the parent understand what she was seeing when she looked at her child. The promise in this research was not simply of a net increase in knowledge. "If we study primitive cultures," suggested Buxbaum (1951, 194), "they may teach us to look upon our own culture more objectively." This meant understanding better which of baby's behaviors were inherent and which were imprinted, and adjusting one's behavior so that the child encountered the best of one's culture: "Attitudes which we were inclined to consider universal are not universally accepted; they are culturally determined. Methods of childrearing are geared to bring about in the child what is considered the cultural ideal. In as far as parents are the administrators of education, they are the representatives of culture for their children" (192).

Every child's development was to its parents simultaneously a personal

What a thrill for a youngster to find this gleaming Good Humor truck beneath the tree Christmas morning! This new wheel toy is play value; features chain drive, ball bearing wheels. Built-in rear compartment holds White enamel; blue, red trim. $28.95.

Eight Important Things Children Learn From Play

Play is fun, of course. It also teaches children about living and getting along with others. Here a well-known authority explains what child's play is all about

BY ROMA GANS
Professor of Education, Teachers College, Columbia University

GROWNUPS are beginning to realize that children's play is more than a means for keeping them out from under foot or a time killer to reduce boredom. Play can be a powerful educator in many important ways which we've formerly overlooked. What are some of the things play actually teaches children?

Play helps youngsters to be part of the group. Watch the youngster of three, four and five who wants to join a group of other children. Perhaps he offers a child a toy, or asks about a fancy gadget dangling from another child's belt. Sometimes he asks directly, "Can I play with you?" Such interchange helps him to belong. And the most comfortable age to learn how to become a joiner is at three, four and five.

Play teaches teamwork. Good play requires give and take, sharing, waiting and a sense of honest exchange. "Three swings and a jump" were the turn-taking orders agreed on by the group. When George took four he met a vigorous reprimand. "You took more than your share," the other children shouted.

Many such rules are made up and enforced within a group of children at play. Instead of having grownups tell them how to manage and why rules are needed, they sense a need of regulation, make rules and often rigorously enforce them. What a force for the development of good law-abiding citizens!

As children grow older and play organized games with standard rules these early learnings are reinforced. To a play-experienced youngster, rules make sense and are accepted—no fussing, complaining or cheating. "Good sports" in the play sense (*Continued on page* 48)

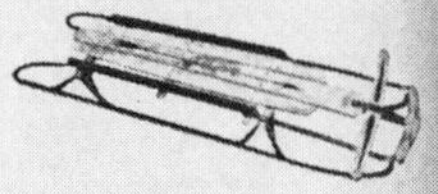

More streamlined than ever! Sure to come in for its share of the winter fun is this new Flexible Flyer sled that features trim, tapered lines, a chrome-finished front bumper and black runners. Equipped with super steering for sharp turns. America's Aristrocrat model, $14.50. S. L. Allen.

Whether singing dolly to sleep, watching a TV or just daydreaming, boys and girls will enjoy this new Cosco rocker. Combines sturdy with attractive styling. All steel frame in black or sand color; choice of colored upholstery. Overall height, 20". $6.45. Hamilton Mfg. Corp.

An exciting mountain climbing game that can be played by two to four players. Magnetic mountain climbing figures "climb" toward the top, try to overcome difficult passes, obstacles. The one who reaches the top of Mt. Everest first wins the game. $3.00. Sam'l Gabriel Sons & Co.

28. *Parents' Magazine* also offered parents guides for buying toys that would both elicit and amplify their children's natural aptitudes. Essentially a toy catalog, this article framed the purchase of toys as an exercise in observation and application.

...ders in your family, whether young or ...re to be thrilled with the action of ...Depot. Top of the car opens; little man ...and pushes ice cakes down chute into ...h closes, then ice comes out through side ...by remote control. $15.95. Lionel Corp.

Lots of action and fun on the Yardbird! Unusual new riding toy runs on its own miniature railroad track that can be set up in area 12 feet square or more. Hand car is crank-operated, chain driven; will hold one or two children and moves forward or backward. With 40 ft. of track, $34.95. Doepke.

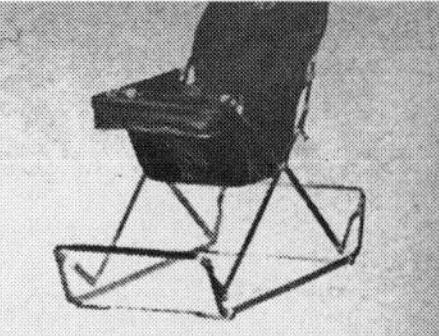

Now dolly has a glider chair, too. Baby's Playmate Glider chair has been copied almost to a "T". They can both rock and jump and have lots of fun together. Chair stands about 8" high, comes in red, yellow or green plastic fabric with aluminum painted frame, play tray, beads. $2.98. Welsh Co.

...um's Revere Ware! These new miniatures ...plicas of the full size copper-clad ...el utensils. And they can be used for ...ng! Five-piece set shown includes tea ...e pans, skillet, sauce pot. Box turns ...me play stove. $9.95. Revere.

It's possible to build an entire community of houses, stores, parks, etc. with Littletown units. New Dow Styron plastic model-building toy consists of structures and accessories which are available individually or in boxed sets. Business Unit shown, $4.98. Banner Plastics.

Gigi is a charming little doll who walks, sits and sleeps. She's 8" tall, has a moving head and her hair can be set. Dressed in this dainty pastel organdy dress with matching bonnet and purse, $1.98. Other costumes available include skating outfit, majorette, nurse's uniform, at $1.00 ea. A & H Doll.

...en about 3 years of age will enjoy ...he elevator go up and down as they turn ...on top. There are colorful doors to ...a ramp to lower and raise to the ...ber." Hardwood construction, stands ...high. $5.00. Childhood Interests.

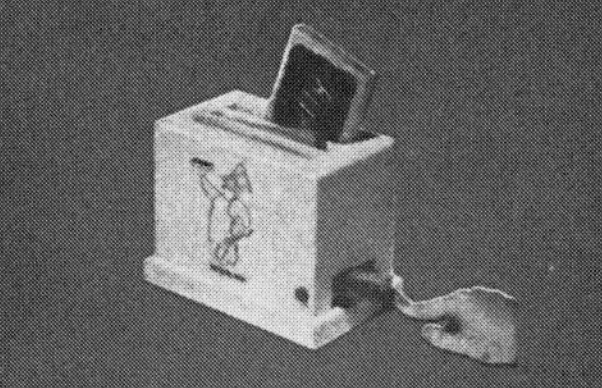

Up pops the toast in this wood Color Toaster! Three vari-colored wood slices fit into their own slots, pop up when matching lever is depressed. Helps child learn to match colors. Junior cooks may want to keep it near Mother's grown-up toaster. White and red, about 7" long. $2.50. Holgate.

The Toddler's Special sounds "choo-choo" as it chugs across the floor to the delight of the children. Wooden train has five gayly colored cars that wobble as it is pulled or pushed along; steel connectors. And see the cow waving from the boxcar! About 17" long. $1.69. Fisher-Price Toys.

...tine, ruffled vanity for little ...ant to be pretty like Mother. Of break- ...ricately shaped plastic, it measures ...14" high. Has real metal mirror, picture ...ther side. Fittings include perfume ...lay cosmetics. $3.98. Transogram.

This bike really has a portable radio built right into the tank! Streamlined, 26" boy's bicycle features a radio complete with station selector, volume control, speaker, antenna. Bicycle is also equipped with Bendix Multi-Speed power brake to facilitate riding. $97.50. Huffman Mfg. Co.

Experiments in electricity and magnetism are fascinating to boys and girls who like to tinker. They can make a buzzer telegraph system, electric light plant, magic cork, even a magnetic suspension with the equipment included in the Fun with Electricity set. $9.95. A. C. Gilbert.

TOYS GENERALLY AVAILABLE IN STORES
ALL PRICES APPROXIMATE

experience and a historical event. The parent wasn't merely witnessing the child's emergence from nature into culture; she was viewing the onward march of human evolution. "He's repeating the whole history of the human race," Benjamin Spock reminded parents (1957, 223–24). "You may think of it as 'learning tricks.' But it's really more complicated and full of meaning than that. Each child as he develops is retracing the whole history of mankind, physically and spiritually, step by step."

In passages such as these, child-rearing experts were at cross-purposes. They professed to want to ease the tension and worry surrounding child-rearing, to reduce the attendant anxieties that they feared might warp the child. At the same time, however, they often felt it necessary to impress upon the parent the absolute importance of proper child-rearing to the future of the species. It was like the classic movie scenario in which one criminal whispers to another to "act natural" to avoid being caught. It had been difficult enough, in the previous generation, when parents were warned that their home, voice, and manner could affect the child (and the nation) for better or worse. Now, parents were being told that it wasn't simply a matter of *proper* behavior on their part, but *natural* behavior—and that the fate of the whole world hung in the balance. As David Riesman (1950, 51) put it in a comment on "permissive" child-rearing:

> In their uneasiness as to how to bring up children [parents] turn increasingly to books, magazines, government pamphlets, and radio programs. These tell the already anxious mother to accept her children. She learns that there are no problem children, only problem parents; and she learns to look into her own psyche whenever she is moved to deny the children anything, including an uninterrupted flow of affection. . . . And while these tutors also tell the mother to "relax" and to "enjoy her children," even this becomes an additional injunction to be anxiously followed.

Ultimately, the invocation of an evolutionary imperative was one element in a push to locate a viable rationale for social control clearly distinguishable from more "authoritarian" approaches. The perceived need to direct practices of introspection, retrospection, and mutual observation operated in tension with a fear of inculcating middle-class parents (and by extension, their children) into regimes of mass specularity that pretended at cultural evolution but were actually socially, politically, and culturally regressive. At the level of the individual (child), the group, and the species, the discursive and practical move to the natural suggested an extracultural logic relatively immune to quasi-historical forces such as communism. In the cultural-historical moment in which the American middle class was asked to imagine itself in the 1950s, the nature made manifest in American culture represented the forward edge of the evolution of the species as a whole.[36] Here, the True-Life Adventures offered a mass-mediated product through which the child could consume representations of natural gender roles, and which parents could also view for clues on how to observe natural behaviors without interfering with them.

Disney's Natural Gender

In its True-Life Adventures, Disney represented a prehistory that had determined the shape of human history and delivered to Americans a means by which they could read the natural world around them to better understand their own social relations. Although Disney's nature documentaries subsumed the class and racial dynamics so present in its animated features under the sign of nature, the gendering of its animal world was central to its storytelling process, both on the screen and off.[37] Like the child-rearing literature of the day, from Erikson to Spock, the illumination of natural gender roles played a significant part in each Disney nature film, as well as in its public relations. Like their suburban human counterparts, Disney's animals entered into good-natured and innocent romantic play almost from birth, frolicking suggestively before settling down to a preordained domesticity. For example, describing the behavior of young female seals, the narrator of *Seal Island* (1948) jovially speculated that "perhaps they're just playing 'hard to get'—taking their time—looking over the prospects, having a final fling of single blessedness. Eventually, however . . . they must make their choice, for better or for worse."

One can almost imagine the young girl seals at the malt shoppe, idly swinging their saddle-shoed flippers and sizing up their prospects. Once the female seals "married," the film explained, they entered into polygamous arrangements that Disney called "harems." Although the term suggested a certain exoticism, Disney contained it by representing that polygamy as a sort of plural monogamy in which the female seals behaved like ordinary suburban American housewives who just happened to share a husband. After marriage, the female seals would settle into normal female pursuits, such as jockeying for superior status and badgering their complacent "husbands" to take a more active role in child care. The narrative carefully managed difference and similarity, assigning an exoticism to those terms that could not easily be incorporated into American life and describing those that could in terms more mundane. Disney's press-release description of the seals' annual mating on an island above the Arctic Circle neatly captured this delicate balance while valorizing its own work in capturing the spectacle: "The patient cameras were trained on this great rendezvous for three months to capture the animals in live action—their swift courtship, plural mating, fierce jealous battles, rearing of cute youngsters, playful antics of the brides and young mothers, and the final balm of instincts satisfied" (Walt Disney Productions 1948).

As much as Disney's management of gender identities and relations was apparent in more commonplace domestic narratives such as that of the kangaroo rat (see chapter 4), the company's performance of mastery over gender was most evident in its willingness to incorporate the seeming exceptions, to turn what seemed to be an unflinching eye toward apparent anomalies, and to discursively constrain them, as in this public-relations promotion for *Secrets of Life* (1956): "The story shows that the Stickleback fish is the counterpart of all henpecked human males. He not only has to lure a reluctant bride to his house, but also has to perform all parental duties in caring for his numerous offsprings [*sic*] before they follow their vagrant mother out among the other loose ladies of the swamp" (Walt Disney Productions 1956b). Deploying a charming verbal reversal (a "henpecked" fish), Disney coyly policed masculinity and femininity in both humans and nonhumans by suggesting that in this instance, males who were in charge of child-rearing weren't truly masculine, and women who abrogated that responsibility weren't truly feminine.

That didn't mean, however, that the father was absent from child-rearing. In 1953, alongside *The Living Desert*, Walt Disney published an article in *American Magazine*, "What I've Learned from the Animals." Yet this piece—which laid out the parallels between animal and human behaviors—was preceded by another piece that Walt Disney ostensibly wrote for *Parents' Magazine* in 1949, "What I Know about Girls" (Disney and Alvin 1949). Even then the naturalist expert, Disney revealed to his audience that his knowledge about girls came from close observation during the performance of his fatherly duties: "What I know about women I learned in no small degree from a close family life together," he confided. "As I look back on my life with Mrs. Disney before the girls came, and since, the thing that stands out is the fact that it's been a lot of fun. I think that's because we've tried to get along with a minimum of rules" (78). Echoing the guidelines for his "naturalist-cameramen," Disney advocated a hands-off approach to child-rearing and performed for his readers the model behavior of a parent who did his best to allow his children to discover in themselves and their environment (rather than in arbitrary and excessive external rules) models for proper comportment: "One of the most serious problems I find confronts parents is how to make children obey. For some reason this has never been much of a problem around our home. Maybe it's because we started very early to have the girls do things through a sense of fair play, rather than responsibility to parents or fear of them" (ibid).

Yet as in the dens and burrows of his nature documentaries (and in popular child-rearing texts of the day), the process of natural child-rearing included the inevitable process of gendering as the young moved from childhood into adolescence. Confronted by his daughters' emerging feminine sexuality, Walt reacted with the detached amusement of a naturalist rather than the anger and dismay of a threatened patriarch. Disney learned by observing his wife and daughters that, whatever outward show they might affect, women's nature was far from gentle and retiring—at least when the search for a proper mate was on. "I never knew females could be so aggressive and predatory!" the astonished Walt informed *Parents'* readers as he recounted his daughters' discussions of prospective beaux (Disney and Alvin 1949, 22). Four years and several True-Life Adventures later, in "What I've Learned from the Animals," Disney would complete the cycle by explaining the nature of mating to his daughter, Diane. When she complained to him about the sexual inequality of the polygamous mating habits of the seals he had depicted in *Seal Island* (1948), he gently replied: "This is sometimes Nature's way in the animal kingdom and among primitive people, although it may seem cruel and even immoral to us. Since only the biggest and strongest bull seals are able to win mates, this means that only the best of the race breeds. Nature considers the race rather than the individual in the battle for survival" (Disney 1953, 108). Higher-order animals (such as the Disney daughters) or lower-order animals (such as seals and primitives) all obeyed the same laws, and all ultimately served their respective race. When one stripped away the extraneous layers of culture and peered through civilization, one found the common behaviors of which properly regulated culture was simply an elaboration. In its products, Disney provided the map for reading the natural landscape over which culture was written, and in its public relations it provided directions for reading the map. The nature Disney provided was "red in tooth and claw"—representing life, death, and procreation as an eternal struggle—but far from anarchic. This was nature that was wild and impulsive, but which always ultimately yielded to the dictates of evolutionarily imperatives, particularly around the natural ordering of gender.

Gender and Natural Conformity

> *Before a child can begin to develop much self-control, he must first accept and understand his natural human feelings. As a parent you can help him to do this.*
>
> —WENSBERG AND NORTHROP 1955, 41

This brief passage from "Children Need to Understand Their Feelings," a how-to article on discipline in *Parents' Magazine*, frames a set of assumptions about the relationship between the parent and child and the natural origin of human feelings and actions. In a rhetoric typical for the period, the authors suggested that the child could best learn to control its behavior if it were taught that its feelings were a natural response to its situation and that it was to control its *expression* of those feelings, not the feelings themselves. The parent was not expected to *instruct* the child in understanding its feelings as natural, but to *guide*; her role had shifted from manager to facilitator. In its cover story on new regimes in child-rearing in May of 1956, *Newsweek* offered a succinct history of this shift and described a troubled power relationship between child-rearing experts and parents: "The new Freudians charged that the old-fashioned, strait-jacket type of upbringing was turning out neurotics. Discipline of this nature, they said, tended to 'scar the child's psyche.' By 1935, child experts were demanding a more relaxed form of training called 'permissiveness' [and urging] that the child should be 'understood' rather than 'managed' " ("Bringing Up Baby on Books" 1956, 66). *Newsweek*'s reference to "new Freudians" was an unusually direct nod to the theoretical underpinnings of child-centered discourses. Popular proponents of the child-centered approach, though the principles they espoused were clearly Freudian, rarely described specifically Freudian concepts such as penis envy, the Oedipus complex, and the like by name, referring instead to expressions of the child's natural development as a sensual creature.[38] As much as they might have indicated otherwise, it wasn't that these "new Freudians" had suddenly inserted the natural into a previously sterile child-rearing discourse, but that they had radically altered the meaning of "nature" in that matrix. Management-based theories had imagined the infant and young child as essentially neuter beings that expressed an inherent nature in predictable responses to external stimuli, developing gendered behaviors only later in their socialization. In the child-centered model, the infant was gendered from birth, and its proper development depended on its parents' ability to guide it to a harmonious relationship between its biological sex and its corresponding social role.[39]

Child-centered discourses directed parents' attention to nature as it became manifest in the child's body and in its interaction with the world through that body. As Anna Freud put it in her introduction to Edith Buxbaum's *Your Child Makes Sense* (1951):

> Childhood is not a period of undisturbed growth and development, lived in an atmosphere of happy, care-free unconcern. On the contrary: from birth onwards, children feel the pressure of urgent body needs and powerful instinctive urges (such as hunger, sex, aggression) which clamor for satisfaction. Soon afterwards, the child encounters the demands of restraint, and the prohibitions on unlimited wish-fulfillment, which come from parents whose task it is to turn their children from unrestrained, greedy and cruel little savages into well-behaved, socially adapted, civilised beings. (Buxbaum 1951, vii)

Freud recast the Victorian sentimental image of childhood prelapsarian innocence as a primeval scene in which the child was wracked by drives so powerful that it could scarcely contain them. As the child went through the necessary and painful process of becoming civilized, its parents took on the role of colonial administrators in a domestic recapitulation of the white man's burden, guiding the child toward the light.

While Freud's version of events was perhaps a bit harsher than most, it captured the notion of the child as a human animal entering into an evolving process of enculturation. By the 1950s, this idea had become a commonplace in discussions of everything from playground fights to dreams, as in "When Children Have Bad Dreams," from the April 1950 *Parents' Magazine*:

> Generally, animals, wild beasts and nature in the raw play predominant parts in their dreams. There is a certain primitive quality in the child's dreams which is lost later in life. . . . Some believe that it is the child's unconscious memory of life in the jungle, of man's struggle with primitive beasts which is relieved in these dreams. In his sleep the child recreates a state which existed for his forefathers; he fights their battles, shares their adventures. As he grows up he sheds these memories and loses them completely along with other primitive traits. (Thrope 1950, 38)

As the child crept out of the jungle of infancy, it had to encounter an orderly and sensible civilization, one in which the proper avenues for channeling its natural impulses were clear. According to an article in the June 1950 *Parents'*, gender was key to this encounter. "Children growing up under feminine domination are often unable to feel as kindly toward the female sex as they should," one author warned (English 1950,86). "This makes boys too passive when they grow up or unconsciously hostile toward their wives. . . . It makes girls too aggressive and keeps them in continual protest against their feminine role."

In the anecdotal and prescriptive form of popular child-rearing discourse, however, articles such as this did not try to explain the political and economic forces, the psychohistorical roots, or the Oedipal complications behind the problem of the father's absence from an increasingly gendered household.[40] Rather, they sought to outline for the father (or the mother reading to the father) methods for performing a form of masculinity readable by his children in the short space of family time allotted him on evenings and weekends. In the increasingly complex depiction of the significance of the parent-child relationship in the child's development, the interplay of latent and manifest elements suggested not only that parents could read the child's physical activities for the root expressions of its emerging character, but that children read their parents' bodies for conscious and unconscious clues as to how they were to perform their own genders. The world imagined in the 1950s neo-Freudian cosmology was intensely panoptic, a feedback circuit in which the interplay between the biological and the cultural produced social meanings and practices with consequences that extended through the domestic and immediate to the national and international.

The important distinction in this regime was between a performed but unconvincing masculinity or femininity and a genuine, natural gender performance. Like the idea of "genuine conformity," a natural gender occurred in a child when its biological sex, its ego, and its social role were all properly integrated (Erikson 1950, 30–32). In unintegrated children like Frenkel-Brunswik's Karl, excessive expressions of masculinity, such as uncontained aggression or precocious desire, were considered to mask a latent feminine passivity, an unease with one's gender expressed as an "overcompensation" in the opposite direction.

At the level of popular advice, these imperatives translated into a simple primer in Oedipal conflict resolution in which parents were taught to understand their children as natural creatures entering into a gendered culture, to see their children's experience of desire and identification as natural, and to present themselves to their children for reading. "A boy needs a friendly, accepting father," Dr. Spock cautioned parents (1957, 314–15).

> A boy doesn't grow spiritually to be a man just because he's born with a male body. The thing that makes him feel and act like a man is being able to . . . pattern himself after . . . men and older boys with whom he feels

> friendly. He can't pattern himself after a person unless he feels that this person likes him and approves of him. If a father is always impatient or irritated with him, the boy is likely to feel uncomfortable not only when he's around his father but when he's around other men and boys, too. He is apt to draw closer to his mother and take on her manners and interests.

Of course, a father who chummed around with his son was expected to evince a very different set of behaviors with his daughter:

> [A girl] doesn't exactly pattern herself after [her father], but she gains confidence in herself as a girl and a woman from feeling his approval. . . . like complimenting her on her dress, or hair-do, or the cookies she's made. When she is older, he can show her that he's interested in her opinions and let her in on some of his. . . . By learning to enjoy the qualities in her father that are particularly masculine, a girl is getting ready for her adult life in a world that is half made up of men. The way she makes friendships with boys and men later, the kind of man she eventually falls in love with, the kind of married life she makes, are all influenced strongly by the kind of relationship she has had with her father.

As one might expect, less space was spent directing mothers in how to perform *their* gender for their children. (Some of the most extensive comments come in Spock's advice to mothers [357–61] on how to negotiate Oedipal desire and hostility.) If gender as a problem in 1950s discourses centered on the lack of contact with a healthy masculinity and the overexposure of children to femininity, none of the literature surveyed suggested absenting the mother from the home more often, through, for instance, employment or civic work—or collective child-rearing—as a means of redressing that imbalance.

Beyond performing his or her gender properly for the child, a parent was expected to have some awareness of how the child might be experiencing its own body at a given moment—that is, orally, anally, genitally, and so on—and to properly facilitate that understanding. A parent had to understand that from infancy the child related to itself sensually, and she had to avoid fostering repression that could create negative associations. A child improperly fed or weaned in its oral stage might well experience this as a trauma that could reassert itself later in life as withdrawal or an inability to speak (Erikson 1950, 70). A child too rigidly and strictly toilet-trained might feel a loss of free will that would later impinge upon its ability to act democratically (270). The parent, of course, didn't need to understand the minutiae of oral-incorporative or anal-expulsive economies, but she was expected to follow the suggestion not to meddle too much in the child's interaction with the world via its various orifices. The parent was to observe—both herself and her child—but to intercede only as circumstances required. Any effort to impose her will, above and beyond the standards of her community, was likely to be an act of repression counter to the general trend of human evolution culminating in the middle-American ego.

This regulation of gendering formed one response to concerns that relying too much on nature in the child's upbringing might lead to anarchic outcomes in character formation in which the child so escaped the bounds of cultural norms that it produced in itself an anarchic discontinuity disruptive to the harmonious historical evolution of the species (Frenkel-Brunswik 1955, 387). A normativity deriving not from the willful imposition of neurological, physiological, or behavioral data on the child, but from guiding the child's natural, biological response to its gender, had the advantage of seeming to free the child to vary the expression of that gender through its particular interests and aptitudes.[41] For boys, this meant encouraging the development of latent aptitudes that would turn into careers; for girls, it meant accommodating those aptitudes to the ultimate task of child-rearing and fending off the "feminine protest" that signaled a refusal to accept the natural correlation between biological function and social role.[42]

For example, the September 1956 issue of *Parents'* ran two interlocking articles, titled "A Mother of Girls Says: Raise Your Boy to Be a Husband" (Denny 1956), and "A Mother of Boys Says: Raise Your Girl to Be a Wife" (Foster 1956), in which the two authors translated Spock's admonitions into more concrete concerns. "The mothers of girl children seem to be more matrimony-minded for them than the mothers of boys," declared the "mother of boys" (43). "This is only natural. For much as our society has changed in the past fifty years, one thing remains the same. The criterion for success for the female, as for the Mountie, is whether she gets her man. Careers for women have merely been added to that goal. For a woman, they are 'something extra,' not a substitute for marriage."

As much as one might hope that the "mother of girls" would have raised an objection to this rather deterministic depiction of female destiny, she was inclined to agree, albeit with a reservation, complaining that "if you have a son around the house, one who can't take it, can't face it, can't share it, can't give, can't bend . . . keep him away from my girls! If he's accustomed to coming home to cry on Mama's shoulder, let Mama get herself a waterproof cape. . . . My girls want to keep their shoulders free for burping babies. Besides, they may want to cry on *his* shoulder, and someone has to be watching the road" (Denny 1956, 44).

The articles repeated, in simple terms, the potential for a multigenerational pathology laid out by Erikson and Frenkel-Brunswik: the son of a domineering or overly permissive mother would present an unacceptable weakness that would threaten the procreative process for which women were designed, and would be unable to properly direct the course of their married life. Echoing Spock, the "mother of boys" warned that similar problems would arise in a daughter not properly gendered by her father:

> Your daughter is born a female, but she has to learn how to be feminine. And that's a big order in our present society where male and female roles are somewhat confused. . . . To me the one essential qualification for a satisfactory daughter-in-law is the ability to be a real woman and like it. For such a girl having children is the most natural thing in the world because it's what everything is all about. . . . Parents of a girl child have a powerful determining influence on whether or not their daughter develops these inner patterns of femininity. I hope my daughters-in-law are lucky enough to have Dads who rave over their first fumbling attempts to bake a cake and make dresses for their dolls. (Foster 1956, 44)

The telling turn in this discourse is the instability of the terms *female* and *feminine*. The notion of a "female" role suggests that while masculinity was a path forward to a career as the cultural realization of natural aptitudes, femininity was a cultural path back to being female, a wife and mother—particularly for those women who had mistaken a career for the means of identity integration in their lives, which was, of course, motherhood. What was distinctive in both gender formulations, or in a concern with developing a naturalistic schema within which to police them, was the apparent concern that both men and women of the previous generation were lacking in some basic instruction in how to be real men and women, hence fathers and mothers. The fathers were absent and the mothers were overbearing. And while the apparent historical cause for this situation might have been World War II, for experts in child development, the actual cause was the previous generation's mode of child-rearing.

The parent's role in the facilitation of the child's transition from its naturally determined sex to its culturally prescribed gender thus had more than one motivation. For the individual child, it was a means of insuring that it would have the best chance to be "well-adjusted" and hence to succeed, both socially and economically. At the same time, it laid at their feet responsibility for the well-being of American culture and society. Discourses of "natural" child-rearing were meant to assure parents that both the child itself and the culture into which it was entering were relatively plastic and durable, and that a parent who remained relaxed and self-assured was unlikely to do damage to either—as long as he or she was properly performing his or her gender. This was the field in which publications such as *Parents'* worked, raising anxieties about common child-rearing problems, framing their larger significance, and offering concrete practical suggestions for their correction. In like fashion, Disney's nature films (and their public relations) framed simple animal behaviors as the evolutionary antecedents to suburban American culture and constructed a through line from human prehistory to the current day, mobilizing a similar trope of anxiety and release. Here was the anxiety-producing evolutionary imperative on display, comfortingly framed within a narrative that promised to illuminate the natural roots of human behavior.

Conclusion

> *Special displays of books and stories dealing with such personalities as Daniel Boone, Kit Carson, George Rogers Clark and other American heroes, can be effectively surrounded with stills from "The Vanishing Prairie." A placard reading: "Before any of these adventures took place, the vast plains of America offered great sagas of tense and dramatic excitement. See the powerful story the grasslands before man ever lived! See Walt Disney's 'THE VANISHING PRAIRIE'!"*
>
> —WALT DISNEY PRODUCTIONS 1954B, 9

The year 1954 marked a watershed in Disney's reconquest of the American frontier. In August of that year, Disney released *The Vanishing Prairie*, a nature documentary about the central plains of the United States. In October, the "Disneyland" television program premiered, and November and December featured three Davy Crockett episodes that would become a feature film the following year, opening two months before the park. Disney's resettling of the West did not begin with Davy Crockett and Frontierland, however. As would be the case for *The Vanishing Prairie* (1954), the press book for *Beaver Valley* (1950) positioned the subjects of the film as preceding, yet providing a (properly American) template for subsequent waves of human incursion into the landscape. "The beaver, whose pelts lured pioneers into the West long before gold and land stampeded the emigrant horde," it announced, "is the leading character in this dramatic presentation of American animal life cycles. . . . A great provider and family man, the beaver is shown in home-and-dam building and in battle with enemies" (Walt Disney Productions 1950c). The rhetoric of this description is almost transparent. The beaver, a "great provider and family man," is an "American animal" whose pelt attracted the "pioneers" into the landscape long before the greedy "emigrant horde" arrived in search of gold and land. Between the denizens of the real landscape and the first pioneers there existed a real bond, which contrasted with the atavistic desires of subsequent arrivals. Disney invited its audience to gaze back through the complex struggle of many *arriviste* cultures to a purer version of America that derived not from any particular previous national culture (not even from Anglo settler culture), but from *the landscape itself.*

Yet this second conquest of North America entailed much more than a couple of television programs, a few coonskin caps, and some cute animal tricks. For Disney, laying claim to the American landscape began with a complex process of erasure and reinscription of the boundary between the human and the animal. The opening sequence of *The Vanishing Prairie* (1954) is a perfect example of this process. As with every True-Life Adventure, the film moves between animation and live action as a narrative voice-over eliminates from the landscape any vestige of human presence. In this case, it begins with that impossible object, the map of the territory before it was discovered. "On the map of North America," the narrator explains, "the Mississippi River and the Rocky Mountains roughly divide the continent into three parts. Before civilization made its mark on the land, all the territory east of the great river was virgin forest and rolling meadow. West of the Rockies lay pine woods, rugged peaks, and barren deserts." In the midst of this blank natural map, he continues, lay an inland sea of grass, across which "white-topped prairie schooners" (suggesting pilgrim ships) made their way. As the animation cross-fades to live action, the narrator suggests a link between past and present, in which "here and there, deep grooved in the face of the prairie, some of the old wagon trails . . . still remain to mark the passing of an era."

Yet this is not the beginning of the history of the American plains. The live-action images of the prairie cross-fade back into animation, and we are told that "long before the wagon trains rolled west toward the setting sun, it was the red man who claimed this vast domain as his own. To him it was a land of plenty and in his primitive way he kept a record of the abundance nature gave him. . . . For this was his paradise to use as he chose . . . his happy hunting ground created on earth." The narrator gives us a sample of this record, a roll call of (unspecified) "Indian" names for plants and animals. Then, in a classic stroke from the rhetoric of natural history that compresses the lives and struggles of various peoples under the master sign of temporally and spatially advancing "civilization" by contrasting the immensity of a geologic time with human history, the voiceover further erases human presence from the landscape, claiming, "But this was only yesterday. There was an earlier time . . . a time without record or remembrance when nature alone held dominion over the prairie realm."

In this earlier time, we are told, nature was unimpeded by civilization, and the interplay of animal habits unambiguously prefigured the origins of natural human culture. And though this epoch seems utterly inaccessible, there is an avenue to that unpolluted past. As the last remnants of animation fade, the narrator intones, "Of the teeming millions . . . of wild creatures that thrived in that by-gone day, only a few scattered remnants survive . . . still. . . . It's enough for us to gain a glimpse of the past and for a little while in this True-Life Adventure . . . re-create the wondrous pageant that . . . was nature's prairie."

Of course, Disney didn't produce the metaphor of the frontier from whole cloth. Since Frederick Jackson Turner's seminal work on the subject at the dawn of the twentieth century, the frontier had operated as a master trope in any number of discussions about the American psyche.[43] Since film's beginnings, the western had been a perennial Hollywood product, from Edwin S. Porter's groundbreaking *The Great Train Robbery* (1903), to the spate of back-lot oaters by favorites such as Tom Mix and William S. Hart, to the classic productions of John Ford and Howard Hawks. But the conflation of the American frontier with the burgeoning suburban landscape, and of American postwar social organization with that of the early American West, were very much creations of the 1950s.[44] As David Riesman imagined it in the same year that *The Vanishing Prairie* and "Disneyland" opened, the growth of the American suburbs recapitulated the frontier experience, both in its familiarity and in its strangeness. "Whereas the explorers of the last century moved to the frontiers of production and opened fisheries, mines, and mills," he told his readers (1954, 211–12), "the explorers of this century seem . . . to be moving to the frontiers of consumption. . . . The move to the suburb, as it occurs in contemporary America, is emotionally, if not geographically, something almost unprecedented historically; and those who move to any new frontier are likely to pay a price, in loneliness and discomfort."

Indeed, by 1954, the image of the frontier had become common. It was used to describe people's relationship not only to a new external landscape, but also to a landscape latent in the American ethos, one now evincing itself as an emerging common American culture. As sociologist and sometime demographer Lyman Bryson put it in *The Next America* (1952, 179–80):

> The women of the pioneer West took the love of gentleness and beauty with them into the scrub and sand, the heat and blizzards, and were not defeated. The struggle they began goes on today, nearer to triumph. They and their building men did not wait for institutions to grow. . . . they made flexible and open institutions which have survived the transformations of industrial life. . . . [This leadership] is latent in American life [and]. . . . that we can accomplish . . . our deep ambition to make our culture common to nearly everyone. . . . These leaders are a natural product of our time.

For theorists such as Bryson or Riesman, the 1950s were inherently a frontier moment, a period the novelty of which naturally evoked dormant qualities forged in the tumult of the previous century. Even William Whyte, whose skepticism set him apart from many other chroniclers of the period, found it necessary to address the concept (1956, 396): "When the suburbanites speak of re-establishing the spirit of the frontier communities, there is a truth in their analogy. Our country was born as a series of highly communal enterprises, and though the individualist may have opened the frontier, it was the co-operative who settled it."

Though brief, Whyte's observation speaks directly to the key contradictions embodied in the figure of the frontier. Evoked as a time and a place that produced rugged individuals, the frontier was imagined as an antidote to a tendency toward excessive mass behavior and the regimentation of daily life in the new managerial middle class and in the suburbs. At the same time, though, the frontier was reimagined as an environment in which people pulled together into collective organizations, not out of compulsion, but in order to confront a hostile environment. This narrative served to naturalize the nation's postwar (and post-Depression) social and economic integration as deriving from the land (as opposed to the state, as was the case in the Soviet Union) and to suggest a prophylactic against the internalization of authoritarian impulses in the newly integrated mass culture and society.

This was the environment Disney offered in True-Life Adventures such as *The Vanishing Prairie* and *White Wilderness*, one in which nature provided a redemptive moment in which parents could imagine correcting the errors generated by historical necessity on the previous frontier—those of the absent father and domineering mother—by witnessing the effects of natural parenting. The elimination of "Momism" was necessary to secure a new frontier, and Disney's nature films made visible the natural order and evolutionary path from which parents had purportedly strayed while inadvertently producing it, offering a way out of that collective pathology. This frontier became important not because it tempered the overbearing individualism of the Victorian father, but because it attenuated the threat of the domineering mother. Providing balance and adjustment, this was a new ecology of gender.

The trope of the frontier, then, embodied a desperate optimism, a need to see American mass culture as originating in a natural landscape and able to successfully assimilate later cultural incursions into that landscape. Beyond a sociologist's metaphor for a new social formation, though, fascination with the frontier was a mass phenomenon, a popular explanation for a seemingly new era. Indeed, as Whyte indicates, the popularity of the term—and the resonance it created between a consuming public and its producers—compelled scholarly commentaries on the phenomenon that in themselves confirmed to a literate, middle-class public the validity of the metaphor.

As its appearance in popular sociological descriptions of American society should suggest, the metaphor of the frontier was far more than a tidy shorthand description. It formed a response to a widely held concern about the need to attenuate the excesses of rapidly rationalizing and interwoven social and economic systems, to avoid a totalitarian state and citizens willing to participate in it. Disney's claim to an expertise in delivering an unadulterated nature resonated in a discursive environment in which the naturally raised child was considered essential to the future well-being of democratic capitalism, and in which parents in particular were considered (unreliable) arbiters of the difference between the natural and the cultural. The natural animal families that preceded and (seemingly) informed Disney's popular frontier human characters were templates for their human suburban counterparts. The company promised an unbroken line of sight from the new suburban landscape back toward an unpeopled frontier in which proper social relations naturally obtained. This depopulated vista required, of course, the unwriting of a very human history, the erasure not only of the "emigrant horde," but also of indigenous peoples, and the reinscription of the American landscape of *The Vanishing Prairie*.[45] "Buffalo, antelope, Bighorn sheep, mountain lion, coyote, badger, and prairie dogs," the narrator intoned, "all these breeds in remnant bands of the once great herds and flocks that roved the prairie are here related in a common factual drama. They are truly vanishing Americans fighting hard for existence" (Walt Disney Productions 1954b). In this history, animals replaced indigenous people as threatened, and represented not so much an ecosystem, but a symbolic order that could teach each generation what it meant to be naturally American. Disney promised access to that dying order, an absolutely "factual" record of natural families, environments, and behaviors in the face of an alienating, rationalized society.

But parents and children lived both in that rationalized society and in the symbolic order. The clearing where they met was the center of the Disney cosmos, where "animal behavior often reveals the instinctive beginnings of the deepest, most basic human emotions" (Disney 1953).[46] The 1950s saw the rebirth of Walt Disney Productions after a rather fallow 1940s (Smoodin 1993). Walt the man metamorphosed from the ultimate industrial manager into the benign human face of science and the gentle and wise translator of the natural into the cultural. His eponymous corporation changed, too, from a Fordist animation factory to an international organization dedicated to articulating relationships between nature and culture, past and future, real and fantastic—in films, on television, and in its new theme park. If the suburbs represented a cold-war "fact on the ground," then Disneyland (as the name of both the place and the television show) was a means by which that global fact became local—the crystallization of the fantasy that the generic child's body represented. So, let's all go to Disneyland . . .

6 DISNEY MAPS THE FRONTIER

The Suburban Frontier as Contact Zone

Disneyland's Main Street, U.S.A., offers a staging area for understanding the Disney cosmos, circa 1955. Spatially linking Disneyland's four zones, it represents an ideal of American life, genteel and placid, a picture of small-town living circa 1901 (the year of Walt's birth), Middletown in the moments before it became the epitome of the tensions of a modernizing American society. (See figure 29.) Main Street, U.S.A., links the natural world (Adventureland), to the historical (Frontierland), to the child's imaginative life (Fantasyland), to the realization of that imagination in the technology of the future (Tomorrowland).

From its inception, this fantastic encapsulation of American social and cultural life in the Disney cosmos was predicated on two distinct tropes—one static, one dynamic—operating in tension with each other. Main Street, U.S.A., existed as a place out of time: the eternal present of Walt's childhood. The four lands that surrounded that still center represented an active evolutionary fantasy—from the animal, to the cultural, to the technological—predicated on Walt's complement, the generic child. Hence, an active arc extending from an ideal prehistoric past to an ideal future wheeled around a still hub, modeling the evolution of American social and cultural life embodied in the imagined child as both changing and changeless, the naturalization and recapitulation of a fantasy of an ideal middle America repeated as theme and variation in every iteration.

The iteration contemporary with Disneyland's opening was the new American suburb, home to the newest evolutionary adaptation to modernization: the natural child at the center of the nuclear family. This child was both a bellwether for conditions prevailing at the time and a set of potentials for a future yet to be realized; it was a conduit from the past into the present and on into the future, and from the domestic, through the local, to the national and international. Just as Disneyland compressed a complex set of relations between nature, culture, and the rationalizing forces of modernization, so the child's

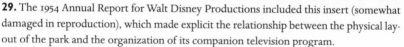

29. The 1954 Annual Report for Walt Disney Productions included this insert (somewhat damaged in reproduction), which made explicit the relationship between the physical layout of the park and the organization of its companion television program.

small body was imagined as the point at which to temper the onward rush of mass culture with humane and natural principles. Like Disneyland, the burgeoning new suburbs were a symbolic contact zone—a new American frontier—within which that process would take place. Disney would use theming—the creation and regulation of boundaries between nature, culture, and a rapidly approaching technological future—to further integrate itself into a landscape that was both symbolic and actual. Like other media producers, it would rely on the press in this process. But, unlike others, it would also develop a campaign to integrate itself into local civic organizations and schools, and it would play upon fears of the socially disruptive introduction of television into the home to position itself as a prophylactic against TV's negative effects—the benign face (Walt's) of mass mediation that maintained a link to nature and to America's historical past. Just as the Disneyland of the 1950s existed both as a television program and as a physical place, so "the child" existed both as a complex of hopes, fears, and desires—an ideal set of social relations realized in its development—and in the millions of bodies that made up the Baby Boom.

This less managed child, resilient through self-knowledge and self-paced development, was imagined as a corrective to the regimes of efficiency to which its parents had been subjected. At the same time, the suburban landscape in which more and more of these children were growing up came to signify a frontier, a liminal zone in which meanings were tested, produced, and consumed. Just as the frontier served as both historical referent and as metaphor, so the suburbs of the 1950s were actual spaces—growing at unprecedented rates—and polysemous signifiers. While social theorists such as David Riesman or William H. Whyte could locate in the new physical and social organization of the suburbs the etiology of an expanding (and troubling) mass consciousness, popular novelists such as Philip Wylie, author of *Tomorrow* (1957), or Sloan Wilson, author of the best-selling *The Man in the Gray Flannel Suit* (1955), depicted the suburbs as environments so new that their rawness inspired in their inhabitants an alienation that allowed them to experience and correct social behaviors previously woven into the fabric of daily life. Members of social policy bodies such as the White House Conference on Children and Youth described suburbs in almost fatalistic terms, as if the newly built environments were springing from a simultaneously physical and historical landscape, rather than deriving from governmental and economic activity:[1]

> Carefully graded according to economic and social status . . . embodying all the features of the technological revolution, suburbs are more and more setting the standards and establishing the mores of our civilization. . . . The new real estate developments, whether vast housing projects for factory workers or more expensive, restricted middle-class subdivisions . . . are more uniform . . . than the towns and villages that grew up gradually in the past. . . . The suburbs are highly organized, for both adults and children, and present a pattern of living to which almost everyone is under heavy pressure to conform. (Dulles 1960, 19–21)

It is a quick, though not necessarily wise, jump from the historical record to an assumption that the suburbs were an actual physical locus of conformist pressures and an excessively panoptic society. Rapid mass construction of whole communities, and architectural and landscape features that seemed to invite mutual observation—such as bay windows and set-off building lots—encouraged the popular discursive construction of the suburbs and their inhabitants as trading freedom for security.[2] While this certainly describes the concerns of contemporary liberal elites and may well offer a meaningful analysis of the social and material relations obtaining there, an emphasis on the dystopian runs the risk of underplaying the utopian potentials projected onto the suburban landscape. Even if many of those potentials were first articulated in a space created between a developer's pitch and a sociologist's fatalistic curiosity, they resonated within a matrix of anxiety and desire that required a different relationship between a people and their society. The 1950s child and the suburbs were locations where the unstoppable march of American rationalization was meant to confront a humanizing nature. Since the suburbs experienced the largest demographic increase in children, the two vectors met and joined in the suburban child, where an encapsulated human evolution combined with a recapitulated American frontier to form a natural environmental laboratory in which the business of observation and (self-)regulation could continue without the suggestion of dislocation and confinement that had characterized the work of the previous generation. In its nature films, Disney would model relationships in the wild as prefiguring social relations in those suburbs, and in *Disneyland* and *The Mickey Mouse Club*, and through its public relations, it would in turn circulate a version of childhood and family life that provided a foundation for arguments for the natural child as an evolutionary necessity.

Disney in Circulation

Just as popular child-rearing discourse shifted from the clinical to the anthropological in the postwar period—changing the home from a laboratory extension into a domestic fieldwork site—so Walt Disney Productions shifted its self-presentation from an emphasis on the industrial efficiency of its operations to a celebration of its skill in translating the natural and scientific into human terms. However, while changes in child-rearing discourse expressed a reaction to the threat of dehumanization inherent in the previous regime, Disney's shift in public relations flowed more from economic circumstances than from a change in philosophy. Disney's rapidly diversifying postwar operations no longer fit easily under the umbrella of one master narrative. During the war years, it had invested heavily in the development of a tone of scientific expertise in its industrial and propaganda work, the calm, assured voice of knowledgeable authority that would surface later in its educational films and television programs, such as *Our Friend the Atom* (1957) or *Magic Highway U.S.A* (1958). This voice did not exactly sync with Walt Disney's small-town, aw-shucks persona, nor with Seven Dwarf–like images of the studios as a happy Fordist family, and for some time the company and its proponents had some trouble deciding how to represent it. In one moment popular depictions of the company emphasized its free and easy nature: "Most Hollywood studios look like storage warehouses: Disney's . . . layout is more of a cross between a country club and a sanitarium. It has a baseball diamond, a battery of ping-pong tables, a couple of horseshoe-pitching lanes and a penthouse sun-deck where the male employees acquire an all-over tan. The workaday buildings are air-conditioned and reasonably dustproof" (Nugent 1947, 22). At others, its representations reverted to celebrations of its Fordist techniques: "There is little in common between the assembly-line methods of producing a Mickey Mouse short and hoity-toity art," crowed one journalist in an odd evocation of populism. "At the 51-acre Disney Studios . . . over 500 highly trained employees grind out the cartoons" (Wallace 1949, 36). As late as 1950 *Newsweek* continued to celebrate Disney's industrial processes, declaring that to "put out a feature-length cartoon film like 'Cinderella,' the Disney studios require the services of at least 750 artists who may discard more than a million drawings before their finished job (nineteen final celluloid drawings per film foot) is complete. At least twice that number of employees are required to handle three-dimensional backgrounds, research, camera work, and administrative details" ("Money from Mice" 1950, 38).

Nor were these contradictory representations limited to the company and the reporters who recycled its public-relations releases. Disney also contended with a diverse public that had come to equate its name with sentiment and innocence, and which expected it never to diverge from that meaning. After declaring Disney's *Treasure Island* (1950) too violent for young children, the reviewer for *The Rotarian* reassured readers that *Cinderella* (1950) was "in all ways, but particularly in the animal sequences, a *delight*. Parents will be glad to know that such 'horror' sequences as have marred some of the full-length Disney features are absent from this one" (Lockhart 1950, 40, emphasis original).

Indeed, a review of *Cinderella* by *Parents' Magazine* suggested not only that forces outside the studio were actively shaping its public presence, but that Disney was at least feigning an open-door policy in which representatives of its public took part in story conferences:

> When we visited the Disney studio some months ago the working synopsis of the story called for one scene where Cinderella was to be shown with so much work to do that she wished for seven Cinderellas to help her—and these seven figures were to appear, and then seven more to make a whole ballet of busy hands and feet. But in the final version this was dropped in favor of more scenes showing the mice and birds helping their adored friend with her heavy tasks. (C. Edwards 1950, 15)

Though it is more likely that Disney opted for one scene over the other because the former was too reminiscent of the sorcerer's apprentice scene in

Fantasia (1940), the review gives the impression that the company invited the input of at least one child-rearing publication (the "we" in the review is never clarified). Perhaps more significantly, though, the choice discussed once again symbolically recapitulated the general trend of the studio, if not of conceptions of childhood in general: The Fordist scene in which exact copies of Cinderella are produced to do manual labor was rewritten in favor of a beneficent nature coming to Cinderella's aid.[3]

This choice marks an early stage in Disney's efforts to thematically separate its familiarity with nature from its industrial expertise. The master narrative the company had developed before the war—that of benign but firm control, a happy voluntary Fordism that directly informed its products—would continue as the guiding principle that knit together Disney's different enterprises, just as it would provide coherence to the physical environment of Disneyland in years to come. But just as the park would be made up of different regions, so that narrative would frame a set of secondary narratives. The company's apparent access to nature found its physical corollary in Adventureland, its access to American history in Frontierland, its ability to translate science in Tomorrowland, and so on. While an idea of mastery and control could hold these elements together, the pretense of theming eased the contradictions between, say, a nature untouched by human hands and very human technologies such as atomic power or interstate highways.[4]

Much more than had been the case when Disney's stock in trade was animated fairy-tale features and cartoon shorts, in the 1950s the mastery of nature played an increasingly important role in the Disney cosmos. On the *Disneyland* television program, Walt introduced minidramas in which the protagonists were animals, as well as segments from its growing library of nature footage. At the same time, the company released public-relation stories in which Walt expounded on the intimate relationship between the behavior of animals and that of humans, and how that informed his parenting. As "nature" became a structuring metaphor in American child-rearing, and in suburban homes imagined as part of a new social and cultural frontier, Disney provided a vision not simply of the natural world, but of its exact relationship to the historical and the technological.

Yet the company did not propagate its version of the natural world solely through theatrical exhibition. Through the press, prescreenings, and promotions, the company provided a frame for the reception of its films. In this, it was simply following standard movie industry practice, creating buzz about its product by making it appear to be newsworthy and a part of "current events."[5] Disney's version of this practice was unique and significant for several reasons, however. While most of the studios generated publicity through the glamour and star quality of their hottest properties, Disney traded on the mundane, the ordinary, and the down-to-earth.[6] Rather than play upon romance and intrigue, creating a sense of abstract separation between Hollywood and the quotidian, Disney sought to narrow the distance between its products and its audience, to suggest to its consumers that the company had insights into their daily lives and the inner workings of their world. And, as the company became more diversified in the 1950s, its efforts to maintain a coherent public persona (for "Walt Disney" the man and for the corporation) required a level of self-explanation that few other media producers felt compelled to deliver.

One of the most important elements in this process was the rearticulation of Walt Disney's public persona and his relationship to his staff and products. Before the war Walt had been cast as the perfect paternal manager overseeing a highly tuned industrial operation; in the 1950s, the company presented him as a sort of folk scientist, an intermediary between the realm of experts and that of everyday life. In the story that the company wove in its public relations, Walt Disney's expertise with science flowed out of his experience as an industrial manager, from his work on industrial shorts for the government and heavy industry, and in the case of his nature films, directly from his work in animation. "I've studied real animals as models for Mickey Mouse, Donald Duck, Pluto the dog, Bambi the deer, Dumbo the elephant, and all the others," Disney stated in the *American Magazine* (Disney 1953, 23). Previously, Disney had used this sort of observation to demonstrate its ability to capture animal actions and behaviors in order to reproduce them in its (or his) animated characters. By the 1950s, however, this skill was remobilized as expert knowledge that wasn't translated but instead was delivered directly to Disney's viewers—knowledge through which those viewers could gain insight into the natural world and into themselves. "As I have observed the behavior of bird, beast, and insect in the field and on film," Walt told his readers, "I've become convinced that they all do a lot more thinking than we give them credit for. And I mean, calculated thought leading to planned action, rather than instinctive reactions. . . . In many ways animals behave just like humans, and the more human they are the funnier they seem to us, and the better we'll understand them" (Disney 1953, 107). No longer studied merely for its entertainment value, this animal world became intelligible through Walt Disney's eyes, revealing itself as far more intelligent and organized than it appeared on the surface—and in that organization, ultimately more human.

In press releases distributed to syndicated columnists and made available to smaller newspapers in need of content, Disney explained the process through which Walt gained his expertise in reading the natural world as one of personal and institutional growth in which he and his staff learned about the differences between real animals and their animated representations:

> "Well," said Walt, "in the entertainment world we have two distinct kinds of critters: genuine living animals and their cartoon relatives. Animals of fable are entirely distinct from the creatures of field, forest and seashore. Just how wide the difference is, we ourselves have just been vividly reminded in making the first few short features of our new True Life Adventure series, factual pictures thus far confined to dramatic camera reports of wild life in its natural color and state." ("Creator Explains 'Disneyland' "1954, 18)[7]

Although the company had made much of its ability to realistically portray animals—and in fact had been criticized for its inability to do the same with humans—during the 1950s Disney discursively repositioned that limitation as a positive example of the company's aesthetic and historical knowledge, and of its central place in promulgating a traditional American culture.[8]

By 1954 Disney had erected a wall between the fantastic and the realistic, just as it had cordoned them off into different areas of its new park, and described its theming as a change in Walt's understanding of the world, not a change in business strategy:

> "A moment's thought will confirm the difference in appearance and behavior between, say, a genuine porker and our Three Little Pigs; between our Thumper and a living rabbit; between Br'er Fox of the Remus tales, as we pictured him in our 'Song of the South,' and Mister Reynard himself in real life. It always amazes me when people are surprised by the obvious fact that our cartoon animals are not in any sense, except a most superficial feature or two, like their namesake in nature." ("Creator Explains 'Disneyland' " 1954, 18)

Like the border between Adventureland and Fantasyland, the porous boundary that Disney maintained between its live and its animated animals served to differentiate product lines and to regulate the frontier between nature and culture. Intentionally or not, its changing characterization of animals paralleled changes in the conception of nature in American child-rearing, moving from a notion of animals as a complex of predictable behaviors to one in which they engaged with their environment as intelligent social actors. This depiction of a shift in Disney's expertise, from one in which he charted and cataloged the movement and behaviors of animals to create an inventory of ideal (animated) forms to one in which he and his employees merely observed animal actions for what they were—unadulterated templates for proper social relations—allowed the company to lay claim to two distinct realms of cultural production, and in doing so, to create and regulate relations between them.

In the True-Life Adventures, Disney the folk naturalist met Disney the Hollywood producer, and animals became the stars in "nature's unending drama." In "Walt Disney Pays Tribute to the Animal Actor Kingdom," the company (speaking through Walt) converted the entire natural world into a performance:

> The most outstanding performers on the screen today, as far as we are concerned, are wild animals. . . . By "best" I mean the most sincere, the most natural, the most convincing in any given situation. They have to be themselves to keep from getting the hook; to stay in the act Nature cast them for in her grand drama and they have to be always in character to survive. . . . Every actor here learns his part from birth. Motives are never obscure. The script is authentic and realistic as life and death. . . . And in its primitive passions and behavior and parallels with human concerns, the play has unfailing interest to all of us, man, woman, and child. (Disney 1952)

In contrast to the average Hollywood performer, Disney's "actors" were naturally sincere and believable, not because Disney had coached them, but because Darwin had. Staying in character was a matter of survival, and rehearsals began at birth. The company's rhetoric (ostensibly Walt's) linked maturation in the wild to human child-rearing and suggested that, to the properly trained eye (such as Walt's), what was latent behind the surface behaviors the company had formerly mastered became self-evident, just as a child's natural behaviors became clear to a parent in tune with his or her own nature.

And like the children of the 1950s, the animals whose dramas Disney "captured" could not be coerced or managed, could not have their environment controlled in any fashion. Any undue influence, any sense that they were acting for anyone but themselves, could ruin their performance. Recapitulating its guide for amateur cinematographers, Disney encouraged its audience to imagine unmediated access to unregulated nature. "They take no bows, these actors. Cameras catch them by stealth. . . . They play to no human audience. They don't even know their performances are being observed or recorded," the company reassured readers. "The naturalist-cameramen and women who contribute to the recording of life cycles and events in the animal kingdom can never know in advance just what they will see." Like 1950s parents, they "must always be ready and vigilant. This calls for vast patience as well as knowledge of the creatures they are stalking" (Disney 1952).

These lurking "cinematographers" were important to Disney's reinscription as the director of a vast observational network. Disney's camera crews (sometimes husband-and-wife teams) were presented as "naturalists," a vague term that suggested the scientific, but without the antiseptic scent of the laboratory. They were Walt's eyes and ears, bringing back the rare footage he had requested, acting as prosthetic extensions of his benign gaze. Although the crews journeyed out into places so distant as to seem inaccessible and prehistoric, they remained as much part of Walt as did his workers in Burbank, California, and this point was repeated in the press kits for each of the True-Life Adventures, as in this release for *Secrets of Life* (1956): "Walt Disney invades some of Nature's most closely guarded hiding places. . . . To bring this great production to the screen . . . Disney co-ordinated the scientific and technical talents of eighteen of the most prominent naturalist-photographers, in addition to working with his own eminent True-Life Adventure staff" (Walt Disney Productions 1956b).

Ironically, even as this discourse worked to produce the sense that the nature in Disney's films was absolutely spontaneous and unrehearsed—and that Walt Disney was a master naturalist—the discourse itself was anything but spontaneous. The circuit that ran from Disney's press releases to its readers via columnists and reviewers was abbreviated enough to guarantee a minimum of interpretive noise, ordered enough in its discursive practices that information delivered into the system would emerge with its intended meaning largely unadulterated. In its press books, Disney distributed ready-made stories that required only minor alterations and the addition of a byline before publication. In the case of *Nature's Half Acre* (1951), it released material that described the making of the film as involving "fifteen expert naturalist cameramen" who "cooperated on the intimate studies of insect, bird, animal and plant life . . . in wilderness where a patch of weeds is a gigantic forest. Before one's eyes the interplay of insects and birds and plants struggling for survival takes on the dimension of ceaseless and thrilling drama" (Walt Disney Productions 1951b), confident that columnists and feature pages would transmit the ideas, if not the very words, faithfully: "Fifteen naturalist-cameramen are said to have co-ordinated intimate studies of this little known realm in which a patch of weeds is a gigantic 'forest.' . . . Under the cameras of Disney's naturalist collaborators, the interplay of insect and bird and living plants struggling for survival and place in nature's order of things takes on the dimension of great and thrilling drama" (Ranney 1951, 20). While Disney may have achieved a remarkable degree of internal consistency regarding the representation of its founder and of its products, its ability depended upon the continuity of external networks of criticism and representation. Omar Ranney, the writer quoted above, was valuable to Disney (as well as to other producers) because he wrote a syndicated column, as did the widely read Jimmy Fidler, who declared of *Nature's Half Acre*, "Educational? Certainly, it's educational as few pictures ever have been. It's the full equivalent of a year's study in zoology, biology, botany, and philosophy. But . . . this is a picture that's rich in drama, loaded with comedy, saturated with visual beauty; in short, it's as completely absorbing as any movie you've ever seen" (Fidler 1951).

The examples above were cut from the *Cleveland Press* and the *Davenport (Iowa) Democrat and Leader*, but since both columns appeared nationally, they might have come from any number of small or medium-sized newspapers.[9] (In some cases the Disney archives clippings files hold identical copies of such columns from different newspapers.) Smaller organs such as these often couldn't afford their own reviewers or counted on nationally syndicated columnists to add a sense of prestige to their reporting. For Disney, one benefit of this system was that it allowed the company substantial control over the representation of Walt Disney and "his" products, as well as wide distribution of those representations in smaller markets. Another was that it virtually guaranteed that Disney's public persona would remain relatively stable in the local suburban and rural markets referred to in the version of the American landscape recapitulated in the vast majority of the corporation's products.

In larger, more diverse markets, Disney was more likely to run into more critical reviews, such as *Time Magazine*'s take on *The Living Desert* (1953):

> Despite all the efforts to Disneyfy what the ages have dignified, *The Living Desert* remains a triumphantly beautiful film. . . . [although more] information could have been presented in a more gracious flow of frames if the editors had not obliged to juice it up at every turn with violence. . . . [and] the beauty is too often vitiated with cuteness [and gags that] . . . reduce the picture sometimes to the level of recent Donald Duck cartoons. . . . Yet all in all, Producer Disney deserves credit for bringing the movie going millions back . . . for a few minutes at a time, to a sense of intimate participation in the vast natural order of life. ("Review—The New Pictures," *Time* 1953)

Though ultimately positive, *Time*'s anonymous review suggested that nature was so pure and powerful that efforts to "Disneyfy" it (to reproduce it as a cartoon event, which was exactly what Disney intended) ultimately could not diminish either its beauty nor its inherent connection to the daily lives of Disney's viewers. If other reviewers uncritically accepted Disney's claim to presenting an unscripted nature, even this sort of criticism granted the man and the company access to that nature and suggested that there were at least moments in which he delivered it. It was almost as if the reviewer were calling for more careful theming on Disney's part, a clearer division between its realms of fantasy and of reality.

The review also points out what Eric Smoodin (1993) has demonstrated: Disney may have done extensive work in producing, maintaining, and limiting the discursive boundaries of Walt and the company, but by the 1950s both had become public commodities, and at times Walt Disney productions had to negotiate with its consuming public the meaning of "Disney." At some points (as above) that work could police Disney for apparent excesses that violated a shared sense of what the company was and what it ought to be.[10] Other reviews, as the *Christian Century*'s coverage of *Beaver Valley* (1950), seemed to do Disney's work for it, declaring that "instead of cartoon animals, he presents real ones . . . at work and play. . . . Without doubt *one of the most remarkable nature films ever made*; your reaction is amazement that such candid shots could have been obtained. In many scenes, the personalities of the animals are as vivid and humorous as those of Disney's famous cartoon characters" ("Current Feature Films" 1950, 1007; emphasis original).[11]

Far from alienating viewers from the constructed quality of Disney's nature, reviews such as this supported Disney's claim to the accurate revelation of animal behavior through their uncritical acceptance—as did the *Time* review for the same film, which gushed that "Skillful editing, scoring and commentary combine to humanize the animals almost as if they sprang from the Disney drawing board, and produce an engaging little story in which Hero Beaver and his friends outwit Villain Coyote while some frivolous otters and baby ducks supply the comic relief" (82). While the review acknowledged that the amazingly anthropomorphic qualities of Disney's animals derived in some part from cinematic technique (particularly expertise in cartooning), it still managed to further the company's claim that it offered access to pure nature—as when it referred to the film as capturing the animals in "unguarded moments," and as "both an informative nature study and a delightful example of moviemaking magic" (82). While the magazine would scold Disney a few years later for tending too far toward the cartoonish, at that moment it willingly participated in a discursive operation in which the very celebration of Disney's expertise as the producer of both cartoons and nature documentaries helped to reconcile the apparent stylistic conflict between the two.

But the circulation of discussion, commentary, and praise of Disney in newspapers and magazines did more than reconcile contradictions and reinforce a sense of the man's mastery over disparate subjects. As the above examples illustrate, it suggested that what Disney offered was not so much overt pedagogy as the salutary influence of a natural philosophy delivered not by humans but by animals themselves. And although Disney promoted this notion very aggressively, the networks of distribution and consumption through which it circulated were also highly receptive to it. Quite simply, Disney could not have engineered its (and his) expertise around the natural and the scientific without a civic infrastructure for doing so, and without a significant public need to reconcile relationships between nature and culture, especially as they related to child-rearing and the family.

Disney in the Community

> *In addition to your regular list [of preview contacts] include the following: . . . Curator of local museum. . . . Editors of school pages, photographic pages and science pages of local newspapers. . . . Officers of* PTA, *Women's Clubs. . . . Lions, Rotary, Elks. . . . President of the Garden Club. . . . Adult Advisors of Girl and Boy Scouts.*
>
> —WALT DISNEY PRODUCTIONS 1953B, 4

These instructions to exhibitors of *The Living Desert* (1953), included in the movie's advance press book, were standard for the True-Life Adventures. Part of a larger campaign strategy, they illustrate the thoroughness of Disney's plans for creating a presence in local communities.[12] While Disney's attempts to convince its exhibitors to reach out to the community met with varying degrees of success, it is clear that the company sought to associate itself with those parts of the local civic infrastructure associated with children and with parenting, as well as those organizations that formed a local bridge between culture and nature. The company urged its exhibitors to contact "wildlife conservation sections of local Department of Agriculture chapters, Future Farmers of America, 4-H clubs, Farm Granges, Homemakers . . . and private clubs dedicated to natural science" to set up group screenings and suggested they send "posters and color reproductions for display on bulletin boards of their Community Halls, for use as decoration during meetings" (Walt Disney Productions 1953b, 4).

Not only did Disney seek to create an aura of expertise through local print media, it also used local leaders and educators whose needs for materials to further their own agendas made them more than willing to work with the company. As a letter from the director of the Buffalo Museum of Science makes clear, the institution was happy to preview Disney products: "I had the pleasure of attending a preview of your feature-length film, 'The Living Desert.' . . . we feel you have not only given us an interesting and colorful story that should be most attractive to any audience, but you have reached an extremely high level in teaching the public some ecology. . . . We have used your past natural history films in our museum education work and we look forward to seeing many more" (F. Hall 1954). More than simply a fan or a satisfied customer, the writer was part of a network of civic and institutional leaders whose opinions carried weight in the community, and whose positions offered access to important institutional resources.[13] In this case, the museum functioned as a site for authorizing Disney's public persona and as a secondary market for the company's backlist.[14] This situation was not lost on Disney, which the year before had announced to its stockholders the formation of an educational film department that would distribute "certain of our motion pictures in the 16 millimeter, non-theatrical field," for use in "churches, schools, clubs, youth groups, industrial establishments and other non-theatrical . . . [venues] . . . throughout the United States" (Walt Disney Productions 1953a).

The educational mission of this department was somewhat vague. By the mid-1950s, Disney offered (through regional distribution companies) everything from segments of *Fantasia* (1940) to film versions of its Little Golden Books, driver-education films, and science featurettes, including its True-Life Adventures. The term *educational* may have referred to a common mid-1950s perception (or Disney's hope) that everything Disney produced was educational, or that the company had developed its most lucrative rental market in a sector that loosely could be described as such. In its campaign for *Secrets of Life* (1956), the company assured distributors that the department could guarantee widespread circulation of publicity for the film because "the Walt Disney educational film division . . . has the finest contacts, long established in this field because they have been selling pictures to schools, libraries, colleges, churches, and private organizations" (Walt Disney Productions 1956b). This approach dovetailed neatly with Disney's ongoing efforts to use syndicated columnists to disseminate an image of Walt Disney's vision and Disney products as inherently educationally valuable, as in this review of *Nature's Half Acre* (1951) from the *Baltimore Sun*: "Patient and skillful photographers and scientists spent many long hours in snaring for the screen, much magnified, these insect, bird, floral, and reptilian actors. . . . Mr. Disney has produced herein a memorable picture, not only for its enduring beauty and high skill in a difficult field, but also for its permanent worth in the schools" (Kirkley 1951).

Before the company had an official arm for dealing with schools and other ostensibly educational institutions, it was encouraging local distributors to develop promotional practices that integrated school administrators and facilities: "Be sure that local school bulletin boards and the student publications carry publicity notices and ads on your showing of 'Water Birds' and suggest the high school principal announce the show to the student body. Offer special rates to Natural History classes" (Walt Disney Productions 1952). The company clearly understood schools and similar institutions not merely as individual promotional sites, but as nodes in an extensive institutional network, the common practices of which could be harnessed in the service of both the immediate goal of movie attendance and the longer-term goal of generating an enduring public presence. In promising its distributors that posters for *Secrets of Life* would appear in schools and libraries nationwide, Disney suggested that "aside from their show-boosting display value, these posters . . . can be used as the basis for camera contests, essay contests, nature exhibits, store window displays, science club discussions and lectures, editorials in school papers and scholastic magazines" (Walt Disney Productions 1956b). As prizes for these contests and other promotions, the company suggested the *Secrets of Life* book, record, and comic book it released as ancillary products. In this way, it extended its presence in the community while increasing market share, using institutional avenues as a means to promote those products that created a durable Disney presence in the home.

At the same time, as it had with other local civic leaders, the company targeted educators through prerelease screenings. An enthusiastic teacher was likely to encourage his or her students to attend a film, and might even be counted upon to develop activities such as those described above. At the very least, a teacher could amplify prerelease publicity. "Yesterday I was one of the teachers of Los Angeles County privileged to attend a special screening of your new True-Life Adventure film, 'The Living Desert,'" one teacher crowed (Knight 1953):

> I was thrilled beyond words with what I saw. . . . Whatever words your Publicity staff uses to describe this picture in forthcoming advertisements will not be adequate. . . . I'm wasting no time in letting my boys and girls and fellow teachers know about this picture. This is just to let you know how much your work is being appreciated by members of the teaching

> profession. I'll be among the first in line when the regular showing begins next month. . . . THANKS!

Teacher-designed exercises or contests around a given film promised a large captive audience and provided opportunities for the distribution and promotion of ancillary products. This encouraged ongoing relationships between Disney distributors and local institutions. And, if the company made a positive contact with the proper administrator, as was the case with the director of the audiovisual department of the Oakland public school system, it opened up the possibility of a long-term rental relationship that kept the company in the public eye year after year:

> We are very certainly grateful to you for making it possible for a selected group of school superintendents, principals, supervisors and teachers from various schools in Oakland and Alameda County to preview your new film THE LIVING DESERT. Once each year, for the past three years, we have been having an educational group preview and evaluate various films from your TRUE LIFE SERIES. These have included BEAR COUNTRY, NATURE'S HALF ACRE, SEAL ISLAND, and BEAVER VALLEY . . . It was also very kind of you not only to make the film available, but to also have Mr. Reddy and Mr. Sherman assist in the presentation. Mr. Sherman gave a talk before the showing of the film, at which time he discussed various aspects of the TRUE LIFE SERIES films and told of some of the productions which you have planned for the future. (Hart 1953)

More than simply targeting those groups, however, Disney's strategies attempted to create an impression that the corporation was integral to community practices, playing a significant role in important civic institutions. The company also understood that its most important character was not Donald Duck, but Walt Disney himself: his presence as the human embodiment of the corporation's expertise was essential to its efforts to appear interested in community values. By constantly referring back to Walt, to his vision, to his understanding of the world, as the guiding principle behind the actions of each of Disney's employees—and by suggesting that Disney's own life and career had been informed by his intimate relationship to nature—the corporation reinscribed Walt's managerial expertise and the studios' industrial image in more organic terms. At the same time, though, because Walt had manifested himself almost entirely in print, he always threatened to become a disembodied consciousness, something that every Disney worker had internalized, hence everywhere and nowhere. Television would change that, bringing a representation of Walt's body, and his defining consciousness—not merely into the community, but into the home. Disney could appear in every home that had a television, furthering the company's attempt to associate itself with the local and the immediate.

Yet if the Disney of the 1950s continued a set of practices that placed it in a spatial matrix that linked the national with the local, it also developed practices and discourses that placed it more firmly in a temporal matrix linking world prehistory to American history to the present day. Like the layout of Disneyland, the company's public relations located Disney the man on the boundary between a prehistoric past and an idealized future, a scout at the edge of a new frontier. "Opening up new horizons of adventure," the company declared, "Producer Disney tells a story as big as America itself, as lavish as the wealth of the great rolling plains, as heart-stirring as the gigantic wilderness which wooed, won and was in turn conquered by the hardy pioneer in one of the most stirring sagas of all time" (Walt Disney Productions, 1954b, 1).

For Disney, as for the rest of the country, the frontier—imagined as the boundary between primitive nature and modern culture—became a central metaphor not only in its theme park, but in many of its other products as well. This entailed a move from cartoons to live action to its audio-animatronic theme-park environments, from reproducing landscapes to revealing and creating them. It also meant reproducing that address as an element both in the content of its media products and in their marketing. And while that address may have been built on the ground in Disneyland, it was regularly delivered directly to American communities and homes through the company's True-Life Adventures and its *Disneyland* and *Mickey Mouse Club* television programs.

Disneyland: *Delivering the Frontier to the Home*

Disneyland did not begin simply as a theme park. The name also referred to a Wednesday-evening ABC television program that Disney had designed to sell the park. To speak of "Disneyland" in the 1950s, then, was to speak simultaneously of a parcel of land in Anaheim, California, and of a central component in the then new public/private ritual of family television watching.[15] Premiering on October 27, 1954, the program actually preceded the park by nine months: Disney televised the park's dedication in a live special on July 17, 1955. Yet before the park became a blueprint for the proper parsing of the middle-American psyche, Disneyland was already an integral part of an increasingly suburban middle-American landscape, a central component in the new domestic practice of prime-time family entertainment.

Though criticized for plugging the theme park and upcoming Disney theatrical releases, and for shamelessly recycling old Disney footage, the television show was extremely popular. Just as *The Mickey Mouse Club* was a masterful vehicle for promoting licensed products (see below), the *Disneyland* television program was designed to pitch the park, not only through outright promotion but also through a repetition of the park's spatial thematic divisions in the program itself. (See figure 30.) The viewing public came back week after week, in record numbers, to watch frontier stories, nature documentaries and dramas, and old cartoons. In short, "Disneyland" was a place where the American public could repeatedly watch the formation of a basic American humanity at the border between the natural and the cultural. The park may have anchored that experience, but first and foremost it happened in the American home.[16]

From its first foray into television in 1950, Walt Disney Productions posed a problem for any popular critic or researcher concerned with children's ability to discern between reality and fantasy, or more specifically, between advertising and creative content. Already masterful at presenting self-promotion as entertainment (consider its 1942 tour film *The Reluctant Dragon*), Disney had few compunctions about producing what were some of television's first infomercials. In a move that continued its practice of timing releases with significant American holidays, Disney arrived on the airwaves on Christmas Day, 1950, with *One Hour in Wonderland*, a preview special on NBC for the company's most recent release, *Alice in Wonderland* (1951)—and on which Walt Disney was joined by his daughters, Diane and Sharon. By Disney's own estimate, the show drew 20 million viewers, providing a willingly captive audience for other Disney products, and Roy Disney assured the company's stockholders that "the telecasting of 'One Hour in Wonderland' commanded the attention of top motion picture as well as television executives and one noted film leader summed up his reaction publicly in these words: 'That telecast should be worth $1,000,000 at the box office to ALICE IN WONDERLAND. I think Disney has found the answer to using television both to entertain and to sell his product' " (Roy Disney, in Walt Disney Productions 1951a, 1). In the same document, Walt Disney elaborated on that observation, bluntly characterizing television as "one of our most important channels for the development of a new motion picture audience." The company would follow up this first special with the *Walt Disney Christmas Show* (a promotion for the 1953 film *Peter Pan*) in 1951, and with a brief promotion for *Peter Pan* on the *Ford Omnibus* program in 1952, during each of which, the company estimated, millions of viewers tuned in.[17]

Each of these programs was a prelude to *Disneyland*, which ran on ABC for four years (until it was replaced by *Walt Disney Presents*). Disney and ABC had

The Legend of Sleepy Hollow

Another literary classic, this one from the capable pen of Washington Irving, is presented in full animation. Ichabod Crane, the Headless Horseman and the other characters of this well-known story come alive once again. This program includes an accurate biography, also in animation, of the author, one of our first important American writers.

Man and the Moon

Last year's television program, "Man in Space," set the stage for this picturization of one of man's long-standing dreams. The earlier program detailed the establishment of a man-made satellite. This program goes on from there to show man fully accomplishing the dream—a visit to the Moon. These programs are known as "Science-Factual" productions for the subject matter is based upon the most accurate research available.

Uncle Remus

Another great American literary figure and highlights from his best known works will make this program a memorable one. An animated biography of Joel Chandler Harris serves to introduce some of his marvelous fables as told by Uncle Remus. The years go by and the activities of Brer Rabbit, Brer Fox and the others become oft-told tales, but never have the basic morals of these stories been more apt or more current than they are today.

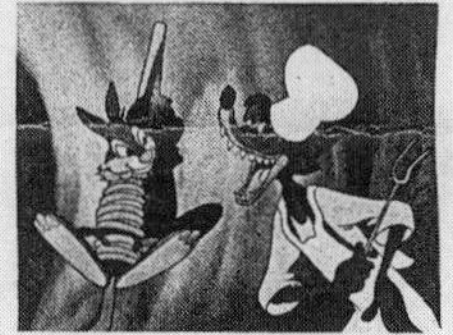

The Olympic Elk

The mist shrouded high country of the Olympic Peninsula in Washington is the setting for this Academy Award winning True Life Adventure nature drama. Here is the home of the majestic Olympic Elk and here is his story. Certainly few creatures of nature enjoy the respect of man as do these handsome animals. Their annual hazardous trek to the high country in search of food is the key sequence to this nature drama.

Robin Hood

Another literary adventure classic—itself a collection of near-legends about a near-legendary figure—serves as the basis of two programs. Filmed in the original Sherwood Forest with English players, many native to the area, Robin Hood once again is afoot to right the wrongs of a cruel, conniving English king. The Disney production crew drew heavily upon British archives to insure accurate reference material about the times and customs of Robin's day.

30. A page from the *Disneyland on Television* classroom guide from 1956—designed for teachers and interested parents—repeats the thematic layout of the park, reinforcing the relationship between an idealized natural prehistory, frontier fantasy, the fairy-tale world, and imaginary future around which Disney structured its diversification.

chosen each other in a reciprocal relationship through which the network contributed substantially to funding the new park, in return for which it gained a one-third stake in it, as well as the network presence of the very bankable figure of Walt Disney, and (regulated) access to the studios' extensive library of popular family fare.[18] Disney retained creative control over the program, a fact it made clear to the public in an extensive promotional campaign that preceded its airing. In Hedda Hopper's nationally syndicated "Hollywood" column in April of 1954, Walt Disney introduced his audience-to-be to the concept of theming, as well as to the notion that he would proudly recycle old and shamelessly promote new material in his first series:

> I asked what kind of shows he would do. "I have four different kinds," said Walt. "One, I'll show the best of our past cartoons, plus a bit of those to come. Then I'll have a nature series, telling stories behind the making of the films which are almost as fascinating as nature itself. Three, we'll show the world of tomorrow. I'm working with scientists now on a film to explain in layman's terms the atom, and how it can be used for good. And four, a series called "Frontierland," yarns of America about exciting, fabled characters, giants of men like Paul Bunyan. We have men big as that today. It will be pure Americana and show America at its best. Like it?" (Hopper 1954)

Over a year before it opened the world's first "theme park," the company presented the concept of theming as a means of locating and managing its diversification within a coherent narrative. At the same time, Disney traded heavily on its public's acceptance of its tradition of self-promotion, one that hinged on a celebration of its eponymous founder's genius, and on the sense of inclusion in a semi-mystical production process that its "behind the scenes" promotions allowed.

Much of the company's public image derived from a repetitive narrative of revelation, with Walt as the public's avuncular Virgil, gladly guiding viewers through different hidden worlds—from the secrets of the atom, to the mating habits of the seal, to the making of an animated cartoon. In a public-relations sleight of hand, Disney appeared to celebrate the productive processes behind its commodities rather than masking them. By placing an emphasis on the creative process behind its shorts and features while downplaying the repetitive labor of animation (as well as its extensive operations involving licensed products and the mundane administrative and support services that are part of any industrial operation), the company reinforced an idea of Disney as a sort of magical entertainment factory, much like the workshop of its Seven Dwarfs.

With only a few complaints, Disney's public had for some time quite willingly participated in this self-aggrandizement, which blurred the line not only between its animated characters and the conditions of their making, but also between the characters'—and Walt's—dual roles as figures of entertainment and company spokescreatures.

Even though Walt and Mickey co-hosted the opening of *Disneyland*, the program wasn't everything Walt had promised. A reviewer for the *Radio and Television Daily* announced that although the nature segments were captivating, "the program needs drastic revision" ("Television Pre-View" 1954) and *The Hollywood Reporter* warned that "the first Disneyland, most disappointing opener of the season after all that ballyhoo, grabbed more than half of the potential audience. But if the second chapter isn't better, viewers will switch back to Liberace" ("Review: Disneyland" 1954). Another review described the first episode as little more than a "50-cent tour" ("Mickey's Night" 1954). Walt Disney was labeled a huckster (albeit a loveable one), and the amount of recycled material in the program was rated a disappointment. The audience statistic nested within the *Reporter*'s pan, however, described the split between critical skepticism over Disney's move to television and the public's willingness to countenance the company's excesses. The *Chicago Tribune* accurately predicted that the program would become a central feature in a new American domestic ritual, the TV dinner: "Something is going to have to be done about the dinner hour of millions of youngsters now that Walt Disney & Co. have arrived on TV," a reviewer giddily warned (Wolters 1954). "Small fry will insist on watching this show regularly and who can say what that will do to eating habits on Wednesdays."

The following week's episode featured an abridged version of *Alice in Wonderland*. During the 1954 Christmas season, Disney released *20,000 Leagues Under the Sea* and simultaneously aired a "making of" episode on *Disneyland*. As the theme park's opening day approached, the program devoted more time to pitching its namesake, so much so that one journalist complained, "We love Disneyland dearly, but feel that Professor Walt should know that we, in company with many other televiewers, do not love him so blindly as to overlook the commercials he's been dishing out disguised as regular programs. . . . Walt has been getting away with murder—and if you want to see the body, take a look at the television code of the National Association of Radio and Television Broadcasters" (B. Williams 1955).[19] Echoing concerns about television's address to children, the reviewer offered anecdotal evidence of the effect of Disney's blurring of the line between advertising and entertainment in *Disneyland*: "The nine-year-old Junior Dialer, unwise to the ways of the hucksters and pitch men, took the bait hook and all. 'Take me there, Daddy,' was the precise quote, long before the program was over."

In spite of these criticisms, the reviewer praised Disney, claiming that the company's infomercials were "better television entertainment than half of the untainted stuff that spills onto our screen" (B. Williams 1955). Like many reviews critical of Disney, both before and after the company came to television, the author's overall tone was far from condemning, and very far from suggesting that the company be investigated or penalized for violating broadcasting codes. Rather, it offered a plaintive plea directed to Walt himself, a request that the producer remember his better self and not abuse his considerable talents in the pursuit of shameless hucksterism—or excessive sentimentalism, or the egregious mixing of live action and animation, or any of the other behaviors for which his public had previously disciplined him.[20] Just as Disney's animators had complained about the constraints placed on Mickey Mouse by his increased popularity, so it was with Walt: he—and by extension everything he made—was expected to behave consistently as "Walt."

Very much like the children for whom he produced amusements—who were disciplined to develop a consonance between their inner desires and their outward behaviors—Walt Disney's public expected him to demonstrate a harmony between his private self and the external, public persona that took shape in the interplay between the company's public-relations organs and its audiences. With his entry into television, Walt Disney performed as the embodied voice of the corporation even more than he had in print. As the company emphasized his role as interlocutor between its audience and an unspecified community of "scientists" and "naturalists"—as well as between the audience and the company's own "backstage" areas in its rituals of revelation—Walt Disney was expected to balance an honest desire for profit with the public service of entertaining and educating. Any behaviors that suggested dissonance between the private and the public Disney, such as any hint that profit was the primary motive behind the enterprise, were punished. Just as a child's ultimate success in life was meant to derive from the fulfillment of its inner desires, so the net gain of Walt Disney Productions was meant to always be a happy byproduct of the dream that Walt Disney followed.

Performances that harmonized the inner Walt with the outer Walt, on the other hand, were richly rewarded. Once *Disneyland* moved beyond brazen pitches for the park, its critics were more willing to countenance the recycling of old material and the promotion of upcoming features. In 1955, the program's first year out, Disney reported to its stockholders, *Disneyland* had exceeded expectations:

A total of 152 stations, including 15 in Canada, now are airing Walt Disney's DISNEYLAND series for ABC-TV. . . . DISNEYLAND is also reaching over 40 million viewers weekly, according to . . . [the] American Research Bureau, Nielsen, Trendex, and other[s]. . . . While we expect to make a profit directly from television sales, such profit will not be great. Our real gain will be in the marketing value to our motion pictures which are still our primary business. (Walt Disney Productions 1955, 1–4)

Appearing in roughly 20 million homes every week and incorporating itself into the dinner hour, Disney was warmly received.[21] This strategy appeared to be effective. In July of 1955 (only a week before the park's preview opening), *Business Week* reported that "the mass audience of the Disneyland show—starting at around 25-million and working up to 50-million—made [*20,000 Leagues Under the Sea*] a smash hit. The estimated box office gross now is set at $12.5 million" ("The Mouse That Turned to Gold" 1955, 74).

Yet the program quickly moved beyond advertising and behind-the-scenes promotional tours. As Disney's pitch to Hedda Hopper suggests, the show's format was set before it aired, and Disney stayed true to its word, presenting material that recapitulated the thematic structure of the park. Each episode opened with an introduction by Walt, a framing device in which he not only announced the evening's fare but usually offered a homily relating it to experiences in his own life, at either the beginning, the end, or both.[22] Individual episodes were to feature one or more of Disney's short cartoons, a segment from one of its True-Life Adventure nature films, one of the "science factual" short features it was developing for its educational market—such as *Our Friend the Atom* (1957) or *Mars and Beyond* (1957)—a frontier adventure story, or mini-dramas in which animal protagonists struggled to find their place in the natural world.

In addition to marketing Walt Disney himself, the program thus served as a clearinghouse for Disney, allowing it to recycle old shorts and features while generating an aura of nostalgia around them (and enhancing Disney's claim as an integral part of American history), as well as to develop stories for theatrical release: "Television, and the changes it has brought about in the motion picture industry, has provided an exciting new stimulus to our creative efforts. We are now able to work closer to the entertainment appetite of the public—much closer than when most of our production was animation and had to be planned in anticipation of the public's moods and market conditions well in the future" (Walt Disney, in Walt Disney Productions 1957, 2).[23] The program offered a feedback loop between Disney and its audiences in which weekly

31. Ad copy for Blue Bell Davy Crockett–themed clothing offers one small example of Disney's effort to extend its presence to the home through, in this case, cross-licensed products. Ayers Collection, Archives Center, National Museum of American History, Smithsonian Institution.

ratings and viewer responses indicated which products, characters, and actors might be successfully spun into successive ventures, as was the case with *Davy Crockett*, which Disney successfully converted from a television program into a hit movie through simple recutting, and which ultimately grossed $300 million for the company and for licensees of coonskin caps, leather-fringe jackets, and other merchandise (see figure 31).[24]

While Disney represented itself to its audiences as a concerned and responsible partner in the child's experience of the world, internally it imagined those concerns as a set of preferences to tap into. To do so, a significant part of the company's activity went beyond the making of television programs and films to the promulgation of the company's name and its trademark characters through the mass marketing of myriad licensed products—practices dating back to the company's origins. Beyond the immensely popular Davy Crockett clothing, the company licensed everything from watches, to pajamas, to chalkboards, art supplies, dolls, and games. These products (like many other toys) were advertised in national women's magazines—which at least one toy company, Trans-o-gram, promised retailers would "pre-sell" products—as good for children. The Walco toy company, for instance, described its Mickey Mouse Blackboard as one of many toys that "teach and sell anytime."[25] In some cases, the beneficial nature of these products was reinforced through positive reviews, such as those for Disney's collections of songs and melodies from its movies and television programs in *Parents' Magazine*'s regular column, "Records for Your Children and You" (Sheehy 1955)—or for the many children's books Disney produced in conjunction with its film and television releases, such as *The Adventures of Ichabod and Mr. Toad* (1949) and *The Living Desert* (1953)—both of which received top mention by the librarian/reviewer for *Parents'* "Book List for Child TV Fans," who placed *Disneyland* at the top of her recommended list (Koenig 1955).

Walt Disney's position as interlocutor was one of the most significant elements in this system of address: standing on the boundary between nature and culture, between science and its subjects, and between Walt Disney Productions and its audiences, Disney's weekly homily—patient, amused, informative—offered a narrative frame that captured the increasingly disparate elements of the Disney enterprise and bound them together through his direct address to the camera and his audience.[26] While the main thrust of the company's offscreen public relations stressed the capability and power of the man and the corporation—to render nature visible (Adventureland), to create lifelike cartoon creatures (Fantasyland), to render science understandable (Tomorrowland), to bring an essential American past into the present (Frontierland)—the body and voice of Walt Disney, which were seen and heard weekly in millions of American homes between 1954 and 1966 (and continuing on in reruns after his death), performed that mastery as the apparently simple and natural act of humanizing the vast social and material forces of the moment. Properly disciplined to avoid the excesses of the hard sell, Walt Disney spoke as native informant, sharing with his audience the wisdom he brought to (and gained from) the production process, all of which derived from the inherent nature of a simple man possessed by a childlike wonder at the world and a simple desire to bring joy to his fellow creatures.

For example, while Walt spoke with a voice of calm authority from the television screen, the studios issued a viewer's guide for teachers, titled *Disney on Television: A Supplementary Materials Guide for Classroom Use in Connection with 2 Television Programs Produced by Walt Disney: Disneyland and Mickey Mouse Club* (Walt Disney Productions 1956a). The guide provided a viewing schedule for the upcoming season, as well as capsule synopses of the programs, and suggested classroom activities (see figure 32). Its introduction, capped with a picture of Walt Disney and ending with a reproduction of his trademark sig-

Tele-Guiding by the Teacher

The "Tele-Digests" enclosed, contain the content upon which the individual programs are based. This information will permit teachers to discuss the programs with their classes before the TV presentation as well as afterwards.

Teachers will see many different ways in which the programs can serve the interests and needs of their classes. However, each class and situation is unique so the suggestions made here are designed to be idea-provoking rather than specifically applicable to an age level or a subject field.

Suggestions For Class Discussion

Before Seeing the Program:

Because teachers, through the content in the tele-digests, have advance information on what the programs are going to be, they should be careful not to take the edge of interest off by letting their classes know the program plan. However, a general discussion of the particular program can be carried on which will direct class viewing, sharpen attention and appreciation, and upgrade evaluation of TV programs. Put the name of the program, the station and time for showing on the chalk board.

- ***What do you know about this subject now?***
- ***What content do you think the program will contain?***
- ***How do you think the presentation will be worked out? Live action, camera reporting of real incidents, animation,—how—?***
- ***Watch for new ideas and information. If there are things you don't understand remember what they are and perhaps we can clarify them tomorrow.***

This Tele-Guide has been prepared by Mrs. Margaret Divizia, Supervisor in Charge, Audio-Visual Section, Los Angeles City Schools.

32. A page from Disney's guide for teachers to incorporate the *Disneyland* and *Mickey Mouse Club* television programs into the curriculum explained how to structure a lesson around a segment in such a way that students would talk about Disney before and after seeing the program.

nature, explained the rationale behind the guide. "This publication," Disney declared, "has been designed to be of direct help to our many friends in the field of education who have told us they find educational values in our programs. Our mail has been heavy with requests from teachers who seek additional supplementary materials which relate to the programs and which can be used in the classroom" (Walt Disney, in Walt Disney Productions 1956a).

Seemingly in response to spontaneous requests for expert assistance caused by the inherently educational nature of Disney's programs, the company purportedly produced thousands of the guides for distribution in the schools, and by extension (since they were meant to augment home viewing), in the home.[27] Using the guide as an announcement for his company's new *Mickey Mouse Club* television program, Disney positioned *Disneyland* (and Walt himself) as a sort of generative principle that had moved the company to more fully acknowledge its responsibility as a member of a simultaneously national and local community:[28]

> From the very first we have been aware of the privilege, as well as the responsibility which we assume, when we enter so many millions of homes each week with our DISNEYLAND program. We feel this even more deeply as we prepare to offer additional programs each day when the majority of our viewing audience will be composed of younger people. . . . We hope all of our programs will provide entertainment, for that is our business. But even beyond this, as we strive to reach our goals, we shall endeavor to place emphasis on the constructive aspects, which can logically be part of "entertainment." (Walt Disney, in Walt Disney Productions 1956a)

The guide thus described a discursive circuit that traveled from "Disneyland," through teachers, back to Walt Disney Productions, and out again into its expanding slate of television programs. Disney encouraged the sense that the company was immediately responsive to its audiences, and that its response was a refinement of an inherent relationship between entertainment and education. Walt's picture and signature signaled that this feedback circuit did not end on the desk of an anonymous public-relations officer but extended all the way up to the organization's founder and formative principle. Since Walt Disney informed everything his company made and his company and its consumers informed Disney, the circuit was alive.

The guide itself also allowed for a more complex framing of each *Disneyland* episode than Walt's televisual introductions allowed. An explicitly educational guide aimed at a narrower demographic of teachers and parents permitted a further refinement of address that demonstrated the company's sensitivity to contemporary thinking about children and its ability to occupy a place in that discourse. Allowing "nature" to frame a lesson for teachers and parents, for instance, Disney described its short film and television segment *Stormy the Thoroughbred* (1954) as "a factual story about a horse who 'didn't belong.' Foaled, by a trick of nature, at the wrong time of the year, this little thoroughbred was denied the glory of the racetrack but proved his worth and breeding as a polo pony. This is the story of a colt who overcame his inferiority complex and the understanding people who recognized his true worth" (Walt Disney Productions 1956a).[29]

Policing the porous border between the natural and the cultural, Disney borrowed a page from Spock in describing a horse's very human alienation and sense of inferiority as deriving from a set of natural circumstances and correctable through a close reading of his latent traumas and abilities. Disney reinforced its claim to an expert understanding of the natural world by framing this tale (among others in the guide) with several of its True-Life Adventures, and with the short nature feature *Survival in Nature* (1956), which was constructed from segments of those films. Recycling material that had not caught the public imagination or wasn't appropriate for theatrical release, the guide promised an episode from Disney's failed People and Places travelogue series, *The Seri Indians* (which was never released), as well as one of its Science-Factual series, *Man and the Moon* (1955). And, touting its *Davy Crockett and the River Pilots* episode, the company carefully turned a phrase to lay claim to a piece of American history without claiming actual historical knowledge: "Sometimes it's difficult for even students of history to know for sure when 'history' stops and the legends begin where such a beloved character as Davy Crockett is concerned. This is not the case here, however. Davy and his amazing exploits as he cleans out the river pirates along the Ohio, is a most satisfying tale" (Walt Disney Productions 1956a).[30] Apparently, it was up to the teacher or parent to clarify whether this "most satisfying tale" ultimately qualified as history or legend.

This guide was important not simply because it stood as an example of Disney's place in the child's educational experience, but because it did so by offering a substantial link between the child's formation in two distinct environments: the home and school. To a certain extent, those worlds were antipathetic: school was a regulated, structuring organ more or less associated with the state, and particularly by the 1950s, the middle-class home was imagined as a haven from the excesses of that rationalization, a space where more natural social relations obtained. Yet the figure of the child and the discourse of media effects — the competing ideas that television might adversely or positively affect a child's abilities, or that the child properly raised and educated might better use television to its own ends—linked both worlds through a set of parental hopes and anxieties. The themed experience of "Disneyland," with "Professor Walt" as narrator, seemed to bridge these two realms through "educational entertainment." Although Disney's theming may have arisen as a mechanism for imposing a commodifiable order on its diversification, it also formally replicated the topical division of a child's education, ostensibly separating the natural sciences from technological studies and history from creative fictions, then linking them through Walt's body and voice just as their counterparts were linked through the child's teacher. Yet perhaps unlike the teacher, Walt Disney performed for his family audience an apparently instinctive understanding of the relationship between nature and culture, and a sense of having mastery over technology rather than being mastered by it. In a sociocultural moment in which a properly policed border between the natural and the cultural in the bodies and behaviors of children was of extreme import, *Disneyland*—the immediate instantiation of Walt Disney's vision of the order of things—walked that border weekly in American homes and inscribed it on the ground at the park.

Although there is little evidence that Disney's guides were widely used in the schools, they apparently were distributed for several years and represent the beginnings of the company's current extensive ventures in education.[31] More significantly, though, they are artifacts of an imaginary working relationship (though by no means an equal one) between the company and its audiences. In this colloquy, Disney constructed its audience as interested in the version of nature outlined above, as concerned about the effects of television on children, and as responsive to approaches that addressed those interests and concerns. And although the company represented its interests in the matter as a gesture of responsible corporate citizenship, it assured its stockholders that these techniques were a reasoned response to the needs of the new mass middle class, a meeting of "mass audience preferences and proved production practices" (Walt Disney Productions 1957, 2).[32]

Although institutions such as Disney had a relative advantage over parents in their degree of organization, and thus were better positioned to channel and shape discourse, they did not generate it independently.[33] Drawing from child-rearing experts such as Spock—who themselves drew from Freud, and from popular social theorists such as Erikson and Mead—middle-class parents (and parents aspiring to the middle class) brought to their consumption a concept of the child as a creature whose natural development needed protection from an excess of social regulation (see chapter 5). The attractiveness of Disney's version of the boundary between the natural and the cultural was not just that it reproduced a recognizable simulacrum of suburban America in the lives of lower orders, but that it suggested through its products and public relations that in those animals parents could locate their proper and natural behaviors and those of their children.[34] For parents concerned about encouraging natural behavior in their children and uncertain about their own understanding of what was natural, Disney and its distributors provided a location for working out that anxiety. Many of these negotiations would find physical and practical expression as a burgeoning American middle class sought a more stable boundary between nature and culture in the suburbs. That they would take place around the new and still somewhat strange technology of television, increasingly a fixture in the suburbs, is both ironic and understandable.

The Effect of Television

> *We have said something about television. Now, what is a child? A child is a young animal learning to be a human. Then he is a young human, being socialized by his elders so that he may assume a place among them. . . . He has barely learned the role of a child when he finds himself no longer a child and having to play the role of an adolescent, a courtship role, or a pre-occupational role.*
>
> —SCHRAMM, LYLE, AND PARKER 1961, 142

The 1950s were properly (though not technically) the decade in which television was born as a mass medium, as well as the decade in which the study of the effects of media on children became firmly institutionalized. In *Television in the Lives of Our Children* (Schramm, Lyle, and Parker 1961), a three-year study on television effects, Wilbur Schramm, of Stanford University's Institution for Communication Research, detailed the expansion of both the medium and its study. In the course of ten years, he asserted, television had grown from a minor phenomenon in the cultural landscape to a central fact in American daily life. "At the beginning of 1948," Schramm stated, "there were barely 100,000 television receiving sets in use in the United States. In 1949, there were a million; at the end of 1959, 50 million. At the beginning of the 1950's, about one out of 15 U.S. homes had television. At the end of the 1950's, seven out of eight homes had it" (11). During the same period, arguments about the effects of television had changed, from personal opinion pieces that bemoaned television as yet one more assault by the forces of mass culture against decency, to (rather vague) studies of the effects of television on family togetherness, to detailed and rigorous research that attempted to isolate exactly television's effect on the minds, bodies, and social relationships of children and adults alike.[35]

The net result of this research, Schramm suggested, was as yet uncertain. Speaking to the effect of television on children in particular, he warned his readers,

> The term "effect" is misleading because it suggests that television "does something" to children. The connotation is that television is the actor; the children are acted upon. Children are thus made to seem relatively inert; television, relatively active. Children are sitting victims; television bites them. . . . Nothing could be further from the fact. . . . It is the children who are most active in this relationship. It is they who use television, rather than television that uses them. (Schramm, Lyle, and Parker 1961, 1)

Accepting television as a social fact, Schramm offered a thorough review of the literature on the subject, presented the relatively inconclusive findings of his own study, and suggested, rather sensibly, that what television did to children depended largely on what those children did with television. Indeed, Schramm had made much the same point in 1949, speaking more of radio than of television:

> The large amount of escape and entertainment material on mass media does not change people's interests or behavior patterns, but is rather used in accordance with existing interests and behavior patterns. (That is, persons who have a great deal of social awareness ordinarily select more of that kind of material, less escape material, from mass media. Persons who have less social awareness select more escape material. Whether the escapist content of mass media encourages social apathy is not known.) (quoted in Shayon 1951, 23)

The congruity of these two statements begs some questions. If mass media in general (and television in particular) had no significant effect on people (and on children in particular), then why had Schramm spent twelve years studying the question further, contributing to the formation of an institutional network that grew rapidly around the question during the 1950s? While an institutional history might go a long way to answering that basic question, explaining the persistence of researchers in exploring what seemed a moot point, it would answer neither why funders continued to support the research, nor why it continues today as a central element in popular debates about the social formation of childhood. For Schramm's observation about the lack of television effects on children came not in the conclusion to his text, but on the first page. What followed that initial observation—in a text that placed quantitative analyses in appendices and a more generally readable summary up front—was a detailed discussion of how television *might* affect children as *one* factor in relation to a number of other factors in their lives, as well as a discussion of what parents could do to minimize television's negative effects on their children's lives.[36]

Like many other texts in the history of media-effects research, Schramm's book effectively shifted the onus of social action from the regulation of the medium itself to the regulation of the social and material relations of its consumers.[37] Given the long prior history of this phenomenon (consider the work of the MPPDA in the 1920s and 1930s, and its offshoot MPAA in later decades), the rhetorical shift from a focus on industrial regulation to the consumption practices of individual consumers is hardly unusual. Yet in terms of the behaviors and social practices it isolated in television viewers, and in terms of those it prescribed as an antidote to the excesses of the medium, Schramm's work offers a historically valuable outline of the social and cultural landscape forming around American media consumption at the time.

While Schramm's text ostensibly addressed itself to parents concerned about understanding television's effects on their children, as well as the appropriate response to those effects, it also offered hints of another focus embedded in the work. "The effect of television," he wrote (Schramm, Lyle, and Parker 1961, 143), "is an interaction between characteristics of television and characteristics of its users. The question now is what is the minimum number of television variables and user variables that will let us understand and predict this interaction." This brief passage points to the generally divided nature of effects research in the 1950s. Given that it was the rare parent who would be able to track a limited set of television variables against a second set of "user variables," the text suggests uses for the data gathered other than that of optimizing the child's development through a refinement of its viewing experience. Research on media effects might have applied equally well to the refinement of advertising techniques, or of programming. Drawing in part from a long history of federal government propaganda research, in part from market research techniques, and, to a lesser degree, from research on film and children, television effects research often threatened to operate at cross-purposes, serving two seemingly opposed sides of the debate—the advertisers and broadcasters who purportedly affected children, and the (parents of) children affected by TV.

A moment's description will make these connections clearer. Early work on propaganda during both world wars had proceeded on the assumption that the American people had to be mobilized to support the war effort. This research had two elements: one that analyzed how people received and worked with information, and another that studied the most effective means of delivering that information.[38] As has been the case with many technologies developed during wartime, the results of that research and the people who had done that work were transferred to the private sector after each war—and effective communication was reconceived as the mobilization of support for products rather than policies. As sociologist Robert Merton, one of the most prominent figures in the emerging field of communication research, put it in 1946, shortly before the rise of Joseph McCarthy:

> Never before the present day has the quick persuasion of masses of people occurred on such a vast scale. The trivial and the large decisions alike are made the object of deliberate control. Large populations are brought to prefer a given brand of soap or hair tonic or laxative. Or, predisposed by their conditions of life, large masses are persuaded to follow a political leader who means many things to many men. Loyalties are captured and control of mass behavior temporarily ensured. Masses of men move in paths laid down for them by those who persuade. (1)

More simply put, the effective distance between patriotism and brand loyalty was perhaps not so wide as one might imagine, and the soapbox served an important function in both arenas. This model of communication—which was first applied primarily to radio and print advertising—assumed that there were always competitive forces at work, struggling for the eyes and ears of the public. During wartime, the government's (or individual politician's) aim was to persuade its public of the moral rectitude of its policies; during peacetime each advertiser's aim was to convince its public of the desirability of its products. This led, of course, to a slight moral queasiness on the part of researchers (as well as the public): given effective techniques, couldn't a people (or, perhaps, children) be persuaded just as easily to do the wrong thing as the right? This uncertainty expressed itself in contradictory impulses in the tenor of effects research: on the one hand, the media were increasingly viewed as an indispensable tool in any large campaign to win the hearts and minds of a public; on the other, communication researchers reassured the public that people in general, and even children, could rarely be influenced *directly* by media. The ever more refined models of communication research—from the "hypodermic" model to the "two-step flow" model, to the "uses and gratifications" model, and so on—presented an ever more attenuated picture of media effects in which technology itself became less and less directly implicated in the process of persuasion, and social relations played a greater and greater role in the final determination of whether individuals were susceptible to media manipulation. While an ongoing public fascination and unease with television's purported powers of persuasion created a conducive atmosphere for funding studies that provided definitive answers as to its ability to control the hearts and minds of Americans, the most common assumption among researchers was that the best inoculant against persuasion was a proper moral and behavioral upbringing. And, as had been the case in the previous generation, susceptibility to media manipulation became a marker of poor socialization or inferior cultural formation—in short, an indicator of failed assimilation into an essentially American middle class.

In addition, the United States in the 1950s *was* at war, not only on the ground with Korea in the early part of the decade, but also in an ideological war with the Soviet Union. In this context, concerns (and skills) around mass persuasion in the media sometimes dovetailed with those of political persuasion. The two even intersected in the persons of researchers: Schramm, for instance, worked in the Office of War Information during World War II and also served as "a consultant on psychological warfare with the Air Force and on educational services with the War, Navy, and Defense Departments" (Schramm 1959, 1). Another early communication researcher, Carl Hovland, brought many film-effects research techniques—such as the use of polygraphs and before/after questionnaires—to his work for the Information and Education Division of the United States Army. In that work, Hovland and his associates attempted to ascertain the effectiveness of Frank Capra's *Why We Fight* films and fully expected that their research would yield "principles which would apply more generally to any mass communication medium" (Hovland, Lumsdaine, and Sheffield 1949, 3–4). In a 1953 textbook on persuasion techniques, Hovland made explicit the promise and the threat of cold-war communication research:

> In the sphere of international relations, numerous practical communication problems are posed by the "cold war," particularly for government policy makers who wish to increase our "influence" on the people of foreign countries and to counteract potentially disruptive foreign propaganda. Also a major concern of agencies such as UNESCO is in developing mass educational programs that will be effective in breaking down psychological barriers which prevent mutual understanding between nations. A similar need has long been apparent to leaders within our own country who have worked to counteract racial, ethnic, and religious prejudices interfering with the consistent operation of democratic values. (Hovland, Janis, and Kelly 1953, 1)

The promise of such research was that it would yield effective means of promoting democratic capitalism both at home and abroad. The threat was that the techniques developed in pursuit of an ideological victory could also serve less noble purposes, and a populace primed to accept the ministrations of mass persuasion could also be manipulated for less than democratic ends. Even though researchers such as Hovland or Schramm went to great lengths to specify that their work could not, in and of itself, be used to generate opinion, at the same time they did claim that the tools they developed could be used to normalize or channel popular taste and opinions that were widely held but not yet fully articulated.[39] In this model, mass media did not create opinion or taste; rather, it crystallized latent sentiments and ideas, providing a vehicle through which disparate individuals and groups could develop an awareness of a shared community of beliefs or values. This recapitulated the linked ideas of the threat of bad media and the promise of good media—such as that which Disney offered.

As had been the case with film, the people considered most at risk of outright manipulation were those who lacked a significantly robust and articulated architecture of opinions and behaviors—in particular, children. If there were a soft spot in the culture at which television might actually significantly influence behaviors and ideas—rather than simply focusing them—its location coincided with this most potentially lucrative and fastest-growing segment of Baby Boom America. Summing up concerns raised at the 1960 White House Conference on Children and Youth, historian Foster Dulles warned that a "danger that is often pointed out, for both adults and children, is the part both radio and television have had in impressing uniformity upon American life. It is charged that the omnipresent commercials tend to force upon society patterns of behavior that are destroying the individuality of an earlier age, and that herein lies one of the greatest changes in American society since the days still symbolized by the frontier" (Dulles 1960, 15).

The uniformity to which Dulles referred (in opposition to the implicit individualism of the frontier) had several aspects. It first referred to family viewing habits, in which the complex interpersonal relations that made up family life were reduced (in principle) to the leveling practice of silent sitting and watching.[40] It also had to do with the uniformity of mass consumption, in which family after family was encouraged, in a simultaneous fashion never before possible, to buy the same products. And, finally, for children it had to do with status issues surrounding the ownership of televisions and the relative freedom to watch programs and to buy products associated with them. In this final point there was a tacit acknowledgment of the emergence of what is now often referred to as a "children's culture" that was based heavily around consumption and associated status rituals:[41]

> In the case of children, who are particularly susceptible to all influences making for conformity, television does often appear to spell out attitudes from which the child departs at his peril. The first of these is the compulsion to watch television. And then there are all the behavior patterns which television suggests as the accepted norm for well-adjusted boys and girls. Somewhat ironically, in the light of complaints that the freedom and individualism of frontier days have been lost, it might be noted that the popularity of Westerns remains one of the most intriguing features of television programming. Witness how the child world can be swept by such a craze as the Davy Crockett fad! (Dulles 1960, 15)

Television and its child viewers represented a strange confluence of conflicting interests and a need to generate some sort of coherent response to the immense social fact of television. By the end of the decade, with a set in almost every American home, the medium was largely a commercial venture funded through advertising, and it was the most prominent node in a mass cultural system that promised prosperity and national unity on a scale never before imagined. At the same time, though, it signified the threat of a totalitarian conformity in the surrender of American individuality to an essentially uniform technology and social practice.[42] Thus, most communication researchers could produce data useful both to parents and to advertisers, and Dulles could find strange comfort in children's mass consumption of the frontier individualism of Davy Crockett (a Disney character) as somehow compensating for the standardization of behavior that television seemed capable of producing. If mass consumption were an inevitable component in television watching, at least its potential damage might be ameliorated by offering up symbols of idealized individualism.

On the other side of the coin, Wilbur Schramm suggested that what mattered was not so much what children consumed via television as what they did with that material. Although it was important to demand quality programming, it was far more important to supply the child with the tools necessary to face the programming that existed in the moment. This was, of course, largely the parent's responsibility. In a list of social and behavioral attributes as useful to advertisers attempting to access the youth market as to parents trying to moderate television's effects, Schramm detailed the significant dependent and independent variables resident within the child (as opposed to within television) as: mental ability, social norms, social relationships, age, and sex. Although mental ability, age, and sex were considered immutable, social norms and relationships weren't. There, Schramm specified that the norms a child would bring to its side of the television screen would be "chiefly the degree to which [it] has internalized the middle-class norm of activity, self betterment, and deferred gratification" (Schramm, Lyle, and Parker 1961, 144). The social relationships the child would bring to television would be those developed between itself and its family and peer group(s). The greater the child's mental ability, he suggested, and the better it was socialized, the more likely it would be to understand television as a form of entertainment and not a lens through which to view reality, and the less likely it would be to internalize socially destructive inputs.

Several significant assumptions were passed on through this formulation. First and foremost, it further naturalized the middle class as the location of norms necessary for a child's success in the world (its ability to fend off television's deleterious effects). More particularly, it continued an intellectual trajectory begun by white, Protestant, progressive reformers in discourses of assimilation developed two generations earlier—once again reinscribing a self-reflexive definition of the middle-class as both natural and necessary to a child's well-being (see chapter 2). Finally—and paradoxically—it suggested a set of middle-class norms to which the child would have to conform if it were to avoid the conformist impulses that television might otherwise amplify. This contradictory prescription—conform to avoid conformity—produced anxieties that found their popular expression in less judicious warnings about television's effects in popular periodicals, and which expanded the list of perpetrators to include not only the producers of popular entertainments but also their abettors—advertisers. And, as had been the case with film, this discussion of negative effects and products created a space for the marketing of products that promised positive effects.

Television: The Two-Way Mirror

Although television-effects research inherited some theoretical concerns and approaches from earlier work on film effects, it differed from that earlier research (and was more similar to research on the effects of radio) for an important reason: advertising. Like radio, television delivered the advertiser into individual homes and, by interweaving commercials within programming, better insured an audience for those commercials. Or, as Dallas Smythe (1977) put it, television was a device for delivering audiences to advertisers. Also like radio, television promised a limited range of settings and social practices into which advertising was delivered—generally within the home, in a room designated as family common space (the living room or den), and often as part of family social life—as well as demographically divided viewing times when more specific audiences—particularly children and women—were likely to be watching.

Unlike radio, of course, television had the added impact of visual representation. It could actually show people enjoying products in their daily lives. While this was considered a negligible effect for adults, who were assumed to be able to tell the difference between reality and fantasy, there existed among popular critics (much more so than researchers) a concern that this distinction was lost on children—particularly those then being raised under new "permissive" regimes that encouraged them not to repress their own desires. In a study often cited in popular articles on television effects, "What Effect Does TV Advertising Have on Children?" (Brumbaugh 1954), Florence Brumbaugh asserted that children showed alarming recall when asked to list the products they had seen on television, and that "when asked reasons for liking or disliking commercials, many of the children gave slogans verbatim . . . [such as] 'It is good for the teeth and body building; the man said so' " and that in many cases, "the spelling of trade names was correct in almost every case even to capitalization and hyphenated words although many of them were nonphonetic, had several syllables, and were far more difficult than words in spelling lists" (33). Although Brumbaugh later cautioned that "the degree to which televised advertising is conditioning children is difficult to determine, since the same articles are usually advertised on radio and in newspapers and magazines," the image of children mindlessly and precisely spouting advertising slogans from television was frightening. In *Television and Our Children*, a series of articles originally written for the *Christian Science Monitor* and later compiled in book form, Robert Shayon (1951) warned parents that advertisers controlled television, that a survey of businessmen in advertising, marketing, and public relations revealed that those very men were themselves concerned about television's effects on children, and that a "heavy majority (67 per cent) believes that viewing cuts into children's reading and study time sufficiently to be detrimental to their education. One states bitterly that he must eat dinner in the dark so the family can watch TV. Another hails the medium as a great boon to manufacturers of cowboy suits and toy guns, but denies it any other virtue" (19–20).

Unsurprisingly, the survey, from *Tide* magazine, an advertising industry organ, focused less on advertising's ability to control young minds, and more on another aspect of television of concern to parents: its ability to distract young viewers from other activities such as homework and outdoor play. In narratives reminiscent of those used to describe the victims of totalitarian brainwashing, popular critics (and some effects researchers) conjured up images of mesmerized children unable to tear themselves away from TV.[43] Even Wilbur Schramm acknowledged its uncanny attraction, warning,

> One of the distinguishing characteristics of television is its absorbing quality. This is innate in the medium. It commands both eyes and ears. It focuses attention on movement within a small space. It puts this small space into one's living room, or beside the dining table, or wherever one finds it most convenient. A user does not have to go out, or buy tickets. Without rising from his chair, he can connect his vision and hearing to studios, stages, and new cameras in distant places. All the conditions for attention and absorption are therefore built into the medium. (Schramm, Lyle, and Parker 1961, 135)

Television's narcotizing quality was often described in lurid detail, in rhetoric that suggested that its critics were not only carefully observing and cataloging its effects but were shocked by what they witnessed, as was one teacher whose distressed observations Shayon quoted at length:

> "The children are tired nervously, physically, emotionally, and mentally; they show the effects of eye-strain; they have acquired erroneous ideas; and their minds are so completely engrossed by television, that they have no capacity for learning. . . . They have no sense of values, no feeling of wonder, no sustained interest. Their shallowness of thought and feeling is markedly apparent, and they display a lack of cooperation and an inability to finish a task. Could this be the result of passively sitting and watching? Or are minds and bodies alike, too tired?" (Shayon 1951, 20)

One researcher was so convinced that these effects were caused by the medium itself that he was quite comfortable extrapolating to the general population from observations of the viewing behaviors of institutionalized schizophrenics, and arguing that television fostered in children "traits of passivity, receptiveness . . . absorbing what is offered." While adults were merely hypnotized by the medium, children were actually damaged:

> Activity, self-reliance, and aggression are notably absent. A great deal of activity and aggression may be present, but they are deceptive, for the demands and even rages are not to be doing but to be getting. . . . Typical, too, of this character structure are the intensity with which needs are felt,

> the poor tolerance of frustration and delay, the demand for immediate satisfaction. The television set is easily and agreeably a mother to whom the child readily turns without the same expectations as to her. (Glynn 1956, quoted in Schramm, Lyle, and Parker 1961, 159–60)

Although Schramm took exception to the extent of Glynn's conclusion—which suggested that in healthy viewers the medium might even *inspire* aggression—he supported one implicit critique of television, albeit one that focused on the practices surrounding reception rather than on any facet of the technology itself. He agreed that if the child were denied other outlets for its inherent need for and love of activity, it would passively accept television as a substitute, just as it would accept the medium as a replacement for its parents' attentions (159).

As Ellen Seiter (1993) has argued, it wasn't just any parent who bore the brunt of responsibility for leaving children to the mercies of television—it was mothers in particular. In terms that have become more racialized than they were in the 1950s, cautionary tales were built around the figure of the mother who dared to use the technology as a substitute for one-to-one contact in child care. "Let's Get Rid of Tele-Violence" (Wharton 1956), an article in *Parents' Magazine* that blamed television for an increase in juvenile violence, drifted easily from a specific statistic into an imagined scenario in which an ignorant mother inadvertently neglected her children through well-meaning inattention: "Surveys show that youngsters average 22 to 27 hours a week in front of TV sets. Television is used by many a mother as a 'baby-sitter.' She leaves her children with the set, and while she is in the kitchen, trying to get a pure, balanced diet for their stomachs, their minds and emotions are being fed with huge hunks of cheap brutality" (54).

Not every contributor to *Parents'* shared this position, though. In an article that surveyed the problem of hostility in children, an author who worked in Yale's Child-Study Center offered insights that echo more contemporary debates about media effects. "Between the ages of six and eleven," she acknowledged, "children are avid comic book readers, moviegoers, and television watchers. Parents and teachers are often disturbed by the content of these media, which seem to be concerned mainly with shooting, killing, fighting and with threatening, evil forces" (Escalona 1955, 64). Yet (perhaps echoing Bruno Bettleheim), she suggested that historically this sort of violence had long been part of children's entertainment, and that "victory of the good over evil through violence and bloodshed has always been a favorite theme for young children. Robin Hood, the Knights of the Round Table . . . and the Old

Testament excited the imagination of young children long before TV, movies, and comic books existed."[44]

This should not suggest that the 1950s saw a balanced debate between those who thought that television directly caused behavioral changes in children and those who believed that children were not affected by television, with the outcome decided by who marshaled the most convincing objective evidence. Rather, most effects research escaped the bind of its divided loyalty between advertisers and parents by augmenting the baby-sitter argument to suggest that any child could be negatively affected by bad television as part of a larger pattern of parental neglect. "I have been in homes in San Francisco during our large television study there," Wilbur Schramm told his readers, "in which the baby's crib was pushed up in front of the television set, and the young fellow was turning his head, wide-eyed, from side to side to follow the horses dashing across the screen." Here, TV fit into a pattern of larger parental neglect:

> Television, in other words, was serving almost from the beginning as a built-in baby sitter. By the age of three, about a third of all children are already seeing television fairly regularly. By school age, it is about 80 per cent; by the end of first grade 90 per cent; By the sixth grade 75 per cent of all children are seeing television *on any given day*. The corresponding figure for other media was in no case above 25 per cent. (Schramm 1959, 5; emphasis original)

This sort of argument was meant to counter more hysterical calls for industry reform, while acknowledging the seriousness of the issue, and to convince parents to participate in the difficult work of regulating their children's viewing, yet it created a trope in which bad parenting seemed a matter of mere inattention.[45] The moment a mother let her guard down, television was there, waiting like a stranger with candy, and children would find it. "Television is the shortest cut yet devised, the most accessible backdoor to the grownup world," Robert Shayon warned (1951, 37). "Television is never too busy to talk to our children. It never shuts them off because it has to prepare dinner. Television plays with them, shares its work with them. Television wants their attention, goes to any length to get it."

In essence, effects theorists and social critics of television expected parents (i.e., mothers) to stand between two virtually uncontrollable forces—television and their children. Television's tendency was to seek an audience by whatever means necessary. Children were naturally drawn to television's narcotizing influence. The best hope a parent had—better than trying to alter television production or broadcasting, which could take years—was to develop an intimate relationship with each child, understanding it as an individual and inspiring in it a sense of equilibrium with its environment that a mere technology couldn't shake.[46] As one contributor to *Parents' Magazine* put it, a failure to do so wasn't necessarily a horrible personal catastrophe, but it did require attention:

> What happens as he grows and civilization tames his spontaneity and instincts? Well, to hear the saddest of our Jeremiahs at the peak of their lamentations, these same babies, six, seven, eight years later, are to be found glued to television sets, comic books in hand, radios blaring behind them, immobile except for the rhythmic chomping of their jaws on outsize wads of gum. . . . Exaggerated? Of course. But not so exaggerated that a sizable group of sensible parents hasn't become seriously alarmed over what they consider to be a cultural crisis. (Puner 1955, 40, 89)

For this author, identified as a mother, the appropriate response to that crisis was to improve the intimate bond of mutual discovery between parent and child through shared activity, a bond facilitated by contact with nature—even (or particularly) nature as presented by Disney. "The feeling of beauty and being a part of beauty and artistry can come in the simplest, homiest activities and sights," she suggested. "It can come in a spring and sunlit back yard as a mother and child plant bulbs together. . . . In the solemnity of a church, the beauty of a wedding, the wonder and mystery of a kaleidoscope or a peacock spreading its tail in the sun at the zoo. In the flight of a gull or an aerialist at the circus, a Disney nature film" (84).

The price for failing to develop this intimate relationship, for some, was an unbalanced child who would find in television satisfaction for and amplification of unwholesome desires and feelings. Summarizing the findings of "child psychologists," Robert Shayon warned parents that if

> a child's basic needs are not satisfied, and the resultant aggression is met with more discipline of the wrong sort [authoritarian and unreasonable], and even parental aggression, a vicious cycle is set in motion which feeds upon itself, creating an "excessive" reservoir of aggression in the child. Such a child, whether he rebels openly or becomes deceptively obedient, develops a craving for violence and fantasy which drives him continually to the mass media, particularly TV. There the child finds unlimited fare but no wholesome satisfaction for an abnormal appetite. (1951, 35)

This is not to say, however, that there was widespread agreement as to how exactly a parent was to provide a proper social environment for her child. For social critics outside of effects research, such as David Riesman, child-centered approaches were far from a solution to the potentially negative effects of television. In Riesman's view, they were just another abnegation of parental responsibility and actually prepared the child to accept mass media uncritically. Permissive parents, Riesman argued (1950, 22), had left the development of the child largely to itself, its peer group, and its schools, and "the pressures of the school and the peer-group are reinforced and continued . . . by the mass media: movies, radio, comics, and popular culture media generally." For Riesman, "permissive" child-rearing techniques leveled relations between parent and child such that the parent was no longer a proper authority figure. Far from the prophylactic against authoritarianism that their adherents imagined, child-centered approaches short-circuited the process by which the child gained autonomy through internalizing and resisting the directions of its parents and replaced it with a slavish attention to external sources such as friends or the mass media.[47] Thus, the media weren't responsible for social problems as much as were parents who trusted in them too much: "The media are blamed for all of our ills because by chance they have developed at the historical moment when the philosophy about bringing up children has been to leave them to their own devices. 'Their own devices' have been the media, and parents have begun to beat a retreat from laissez-faire, without as yet arriving at a well-administered domestic economy" (Riesman 1954, 197–98).

For the parent raising children in this "new-media" environment, the proper course of action was far from clear. For some popular experts, child-centered approaches were the solution; for others, they were the problem. The only consistent point throughout seemed to be that the onus fell on the parent: if things went well, it was because the parent created the proper environment for the child; if things went poorly, that was due to the parent's negligence. In short, the child was a symptomatic marker for parental behaviors, an indicator of how well integrated into middle-class society a family was. As was the case with many child-rearing manuals, arguments about limiting the effects of media on children were ultimately about regulating not children's behaviors, but those of their parents.[48] "Every time a parent finds himself using television as a baby sitter," Wilbur Schramm suggested, "he could well examine his practice and ask whether it is really necessary. Every time a parent finds his child viewing more than two and half hours of television a day, staying inside with the television set when other children are playing outside, he might well ask himself whether there is anything wrong with the child's relationships to his family or with his peer group" (Schramm, Lyle, and Parker 1961, 181–82).

The parent finding "himself" using television as a babysitter was, of course, most likely a woman. Whether tending toward discipline or "permissiveness," the parent who regulated her own media consumption, who monitored her own interpersonal relations with her child, and who made sure that she represented the middle-class norms upon which her child's socialization depended was one that had a fighting chance of producing a child resistant to television's negative influences. Conversely, if a child evinced problematic behaviors *and* watched television, it was reasonable to assume that the parent had not properly prepared her child for its relationship with the medium. Paradoxically, part of that preparation seemed to involve television itself. Just as television effects arguments were caught between parents and advertisers, so television itself (within the mainstream of effects theory) served alternately as symptom and as part of the inoculant process. "As parents," Schramm suggested, "we can try to make our children secure in their interpersonal relationships, and maximize their reality experiences both on television and in real life, so that they will perceive alternatives to the hyperthyroid part of television" (150–51). Since television was becoming an unavoidable part of daily life, the best a parent could do was to develop the child's watching skills, and to make sure that it viewed the best fare available.

Like the Web today, television in the 1950s was a new medium, and its novelty bred speculation, hope, and anxiety among pundits, professionals, and parents alike. And like the Web, it was a medium that children understood better than their parents. Like film before it, the medium was for many a focal point for hope and anxiety—though more of the latter than the former. And like film, television was imagined as a significant force (or tool) in the reconfiguration of social relations and the spaces in which they occurred. Yet while film's imaginary force had been attenuated through the reformation and regulation of public entertainment spaces, television played a role in changing social relations in private domestic spaces, particularly in the suburban home.[49] Not only did television represent a reconfiguration of interpersonal relations in the home by an external force, it also represented an extension of the intrusion of public commercial entities, begun by radio, into the personal and private lives of people henceforth to be known as "viewers" or "the viewing public." Although the relative scarcity of sets in the early days of the medium may have encouraged collective public viewing, as its popularity grew television's use became more monadic and located inside the nuclear family, and the very term *viewing public* became an oxymoron in which a public was constituted in reception rather than in dialog, and in private rather than public spaces.[50] At a time when discourses surrounding observation, privacy, and the state control of private lives circulated widely, the epistemological significance of this change was profound. As the examples above suggest, it made viewing an act that was simultaneously public and private, potentially beneficial or detrimental, and fraught with uncertainty as to its ultimate social meaning. This was the discursive matrix within which notions of childhood, child-rearing, and media consumption circulated when Walt Disney Productions moved beyond the "family entertainment" of its *Disneyland* evening program into the lucrative and contentious realm of children's programming with its *Mickey Mouse Club*.

See You Real Soon: The Mickey Mouse Club *and the Natural Child*

Disney's *Mickey Mouse Club* television program premiered on October 3, 1955, almost exactly one year after the premiere of *Disneyland* and shortly after the eponymous park had opened to the public. Making good on Disney's promise to provide entertaining and ostensibly educational television fare to children, the program ran in the after-school time slot, during which mothers were supposed to be occupied preparing dinner, cleaning, or shopping; fathers were still at work; and school-age children were left to their own devices. Children's television watching during this time period troubled social critics concerned with media effects because it lacked parental supervision, because it could cut into children's homework, and because it could keep them from more salubrious outdoor play. At the same time, for advertisers the slot was considered a gold mine in which they could pitch directly to children with less concern about accommodating other demographics. Children's programming, then, had to respond to a variety of social and institutional forces: it had to deliver youthful audiences to advertisers without appearing too intent on obtaining that market; it had to entertain an increasingly critically adept market segment without threatening or alienating their parents; and to some small degree it had to appear to address concerns about media effects on children. For the most part, broadcasters responded to these conflicting forces by airing exciting and melodramatic programming—particularly westerns, such as *The Roy Rogers Show* (1951–57) or *Cheyenne* (1955–63) or more generic adventure programming such as *Lassie* (1954–71)—interspersed with advertising restrained enough to pass muster as not overly manipulative of children's suggestible natures, but still targeting a youth audience.[51] Some broadcasters offered ostensibly educational "advertainment" such as *Winky Dink and You* (1953–57), or children's variety programming such as *Howdy Doody* (1948–60).

This was the niche that Disney moved into and helped shape with *The Mickey Mouse Club*. Like *Disneyland*, the children's program was highly themed.

Each day had its own motif: Monday was Fun with Music Day, Tuesday was Guest Star Day, Wednesday was Anything Can Happen Day, Thursday was Circus Day, and Friday was Talent Roundup Day.[52] Each program was further subdivided and regulated: it began with a sing-along anthem (the "Mickey Mouse March") and accompanying cartoon, then continued with segments that repeated day to day and week to week, including newsreels, serial stories, nature segments, and other special reports on nature and science. All of the performers, adults and children alike, wore uniform mouse-ear hats and name sweaters and presented themselves at the beginning of each program in military roll-call fashion. Although the program focused on play, creativity, and the exploration of the natural and social worlds, with its uniforms, anthems, drilling, and roll calls, it maintained a strangely military ambiance, as if to offset the exuberance and enthusiasm of its child actors (and audience) with a readily recognizable regimen that could contain and direct their natural energies.

Walt Disney, who always wore a very adult suit coat and tie for his introductions to *Disneyland*, was absent from *The Mickey Mouse Club*. The two men who took his place as masters of ceremony, Jimmy and Roy, dressed as oversized boys in their own mouse-ear hats and name sweaters and joined in with the other children in the roll call. Although Walt participated in some talent contests held to recruit Mouseketeers (as the child performers and their audiences were known), his distance from the program itself suggests that the company didn't find his reassuring, avuncular presence as necessary for children as it did for its family audiences. In fact, *The Mickey Mouse Club* presented a world in which adults behaved more like larger and older children than like authority figures. Although Jimmy and Roy narrated the unfolding of each program and directed the child Mouseketeers in their games, crafts, and musical numbers, they did so dressed in their pseudochildren's uniforms and in a form of verbal address meant to suggest a relative degree of equality with their charges on both sides of the screen. Unlike *Disneyland*—which crafted a world that repeated, over and over, tales of family life across species and historical epochs—*The Mickey Mouse Club* was meant to read as a relatively adult-free zone, a clubhouse for kids in which the grownups attenuated their maturity. This was the leveling of relations between adults and children that David Riesman worried would undermine children's understanding of adult authority, and the sort of false democracy that irritated William Whyte.

On its surface, the show appeared an uncertain candidate for delivering positive media effects to children. Read through the lens of popular child-rearing discourses and arguments about media effects of the time, though, *The Mickey Mouse Club* provided exactly what parents were told they needed to raise their children properly. In a social imaginary in which children were meant to locate themselves comfortably between the poles of rebellion and rigid conformity, the program presented an environment in which Mouseketeers onscreen and off learned songs, dance routines, crafts, and other skills in an environment charged with their own desire to learn and grow, rather than with the force of external authority. Jimmy's and Roy's presentation as oversized children reinforced this conceit: it allowed for the illusion of a symbolic space populated by children—hence unpolluted by the compulsion of adult authority—yet not wholly devoid of the responsible limitation and observation that fended off the potential anarchy of the natural unmodulated by the cultural. If television were to serve as babysitter, this was as good a babysitter as one could expect—one that offered a space for locating and developing skills and interests through free play, monitored by adults whose masquerade as children permitted the illusion of the absence of a constraining cultural authority that might unduly influence a child's exploration of its natural talents and inclinations.

The program's oddly martial format also operated as a counterweight to its emphasis on individual expression and the child's exploration of its own natural talents and aptitudes. Whatever its developmental consequences, the regimentation of the children's dress and their ritual incantations were meant to invoke a "clubhouse" environment in which conformity followed naturally from the child's desire to belong to its peer group. At the same time, activities designed to encourage the child's own creativity and its expression of its personal abilities—from talent shows upon which children at home were encouraged to model their own events to arts and crafts demonstrations—suggested the production of an individualism that offset the desire to belong. This was reinforced through the presentation of the Mouseketeers, each of whom had at least one special talent that complemented those of his or her peers. The program resolved the contradiction between individualism and conformity by placing that individualism in the service of the club as a whole, channeling innate personal talent and drive into collective projects.

As had been the case with *Disneyland* and with its True-Life Adventures, Disney modeled the relations it presented in *The Mickey Mouse Club* on this idea of a constrained, orderly, and purposeful nature. In Disney's universe, the contradictions between nature and culture that bedeviled parents in the 1950s—that is, the difficult task of enculturating their children without inhibiting the trajectory of their natural development—resolved themselves in a shared project of fulfilling evolutionary imperatives. To aid in this project, *The Mickey Mouse Club* recycled segments from True-Life Adventures, offering instructive examples from the animal kingdom. The company further framed this task by suggesting that these lessons in natural history could be incorporated into school activities, as was the case with its description of *Water Birds* (1952) in its teachers' guide:

> Since the beginning of time, the bird has been an inspiration to the artist, the scientist and the poet. . . . Each specie [*sic*] has an interesting history, but none more fascinating than the story to be found in the habits and customs of the water birds. "Free as a bird" is a familiar expression and yet a bird isn't really free at all. He rarely makes a flight without a definite purpose, and he has but one full time job—simply to stay alive. . . . Nature, however, lends a helping hand, and in this True-Life Adventure we will discover how she's adapted the water bird to meet the problems of survival. (Walt Disney Productions 1956a)

This notion of an evolutionary determinism in which all creatures were free to naturally follow their destiny was a central tenet in Disney's conception of nature, and it coincided with the evolutionary inflection of child-centered child-rearing. In this version—theorized by Mead, Erikson, and others, and promulgated by Spock, Buxbaum, and publications such as *Parents'*—a child raised in harmony with its natural instincts, desires, and aptitudes would naturally gravitate toward its proper place in society, facilitating the gradual progress of that society toward an idyll of democratic capitalism in which potential excesses of conformity were properly channeled into the struggle for personal fulfillment.

Whether by conscious design or as a byproduct of its thematic approach to its diverse properties, Disney recapitulated this fantasy in *The Mickey Mouse Club* and in its public positioning of the program. According to the company's public relations, beyond cartoons, sing-alongs, and arts and crafts, "Portions of the MICKEY MOUSE CLUB will touch on travel, science, health, vocational planning, sports, literature and many other things" (Walt Disney Productions 1956a). This translated into a series of regular segments meant to reflect back to children an understanding of the natural world and their place in it. Beyond pieces of its True-Life Adventures, Disney also promised a weekly "International Newsreel" about children in foreign countries shot by Disney's nature-film crews, which was meant to "increase our children's understanding of children in other parts of the world" (Walt Disney Productions 1956a). The program also promised two segments narrated by Jiminy Cricket (continuing his role as the conscience of small children)—"The Nature of Things" and "This Is You"—which were meant to tie the child's understanding of the natural world to its understanding of itself (see figure 33). Combining animation and live action, "The Nature of Things" was meant to reveal to children the underlying logic of natural adaptation. In "This Is You," children were encouraged to understand their bodies as natural organisms like those of other creatures.[53] Finally, moving from "This Is You" to "What I Want to Be," the program worked to link children's knowledge of themselves as natural creatures to carefully gendered career narratives. In the first "What I Want to Be," a boy and a girl were granted the chance to pretend to be their adult selves working in their chosen careers:[54]

> THE AIRLINE PILOT AND THE HOSTESS: Our pilot and hostess are a boy and a girl, each twelve years old, who have the rare opportunity to experience every phase in the operation of a modern airline. The girl goes through "hostess training" school—the boy learns the many responsibilities of being a pilot. Ten episodes, each filling a 15-minute period, are used to tell all aspects of this story. It represents the first in a series of "CAREER" stories we call "WHAT I WANT TO BE." (Walt Disney Productions 1956a)

Thus, Disney offered a framing narrative that moved from the timelessness of the animal world, into the child's body, and on into the future through the enactment of fantasies in which that body was projected into adult roles. Like the *Disneyland* TV dinner, the daily repetition of that cycle was presented as a ritual of identification through which the child might imagine itself as a natural creature exploring itself and its environment and deriving pleasure from a process in which it gradually located its naturally destined place in society.

If that were the intended purpose for the program, it would be difficult to prove that it achieved its effect. While middle-class parents were concerned about the effect of television on their children, the children themselves were interested in entertainment. If, however, the purpose of *The Mickey Mouse Club*, and of other Disney ventures, was to further involve the corporation and its myriad products in the practices of American everyday life, to create an impression that Disney was involved in the national project of helping children discover themselves as natural beings, and by that impression to increase its market penetration without arousing undue suspicion or hostility, then the company was quite successful. Disney reported to its stockholders in 1958, that "the Mickey Mouse Club, now in its third season, continues to dominate the national audience ratings for daytime programs. Latest Nielsen survey discloses that the weekday daytime half-hour TV presentation reaches 7,045,000 homes daily and is watched by audiences totaling 21,000,000" (1).

For Disney, this translated into a guaranteed audience for as many product placements as it could safely work into each program, as well as for the

"MICKEY MOUSE CLUB" HIGHLIGHTS

I'm No Fool

Jiminy Cricket, who was rather proud of his work as Pinocchio's conscience, plays an active part in several portions of the MICKEY MOUSE CLUB. In this series he plays the leading role in five new units dealing with different aspects of safety.

Each unit is in full animation and utilizes humor and a catchy song with varying lyrics to fit the situation. Subjects covered are (a) Bicycle Safety, (b) Fire Safety, (c) Pedestrian Safety, (d) Water Safety, and (e) Safety during Recreation.

As the title of the series (also the title for the song) implies, Jiminy believes it's smart not to be foolish.

The Nature of Things

In this series Jiminy Cricket again assumes a major role, this time somewhat as a moderator or master of ceremonies, as he discusses and sings about a number of things which interest him. Specifically, he is fascinated with the "case histories" of some of our most popular animal friends.

With animation, real photography and a special song he delves into the background, the characteristics and the special qualities of the Horse, the Beaver, the Elephant, the Giraffe and the Camel. He shares with his audience the realization that many of the things associated with these animals which appear strange are really just "THE NATURE OF THINGS."

"This is You"

Our friend, the Cricket, in this series turns to a subject close to every viewer—"YOU." Jiminy finds a discussion of the human body and how it works to be not only a rich source for his particular brand of humor, but a subject full of never-ending marvels.

He limits himself in this series to spotlighting the five senses of man and the relative degrees to which each has been developed. The first unit is introductory to the series titled "The Human Animal." This is followed by one on "The Five Senses." Successively, each of the senses is dealt with.

33. In Disney's teachers' guide, Jiminy Cricket (Pinocchio's conscience) detailed relationships between a child's play, its body, and the natural world in, respectively, "I'm No Fool," "This Is You," and "The Nature of Things."

program's many sponsors.[55] In addition to screening segments from the True-Life Adventures and old cartoons, Disney also promised a "book review" segment through which to create awareness about films available through its "educational" rental service and reprised in licensed Little Golden Books or Dell paperbacks, such as those based on Disney's version of Joel Chandler Harris's work in *Song of the South* (1946), or *The Littlest Outlaw* (1955), which Disney described as "typical of real books, presented as books on the MICKEY MOUSE CLUB BOOK CLUB" (Walt Disney Productions 1956a). This was in addition, of course, to the uniform hats and clothing that offscreen Mouseketeers could purchase, all of which were licensed to Disney (see figure 34), as well as to the myriad Mickey Mouse products already on the market, such as "bath towels, wrist watches, Belgian candy, fruit juices, British milk of magnesia and weather vanes," which in 1949, even before the television program, grossed "upward of $100,000,000 a year for manufacturers using Disney labels" (Wallace 1949, 21).

Occupying a prime spot in children's programming and backed by an almost thirty-year reputation for being beneficial for children, *The Mickey Mouse Club* permitted Disney to pitch its wares with an impunity available to few other producers and to offer to its advertisers the umbrella of that reputation from under which to market their own products. Describing the savvy advertiser in *Advertising and Marketing to Young People* (1957), Eugene Gilbert suggested that, "were he to aim at the 6 to 9 year old market, his logical choice of program would be something on the order of the Mickey Mouse Club" (102).[56]

The Mickey Mouse Club provided a form of absolution to parents (i.e., mothers) who found in television an extremely useful device for occupying their children while they attended to the requirements of the domestic economy. Since popular and professional arguments about television effects on children often constructed this practice negatively as leaving children in the care of a potentially abusive babysitter, programming ostensibly designed to benefit the child formed a potential response to this looming social critique. In addition, the idea of a "club" allowed for the construction of a semiprivate space accessible through "membership," which offset the very new and very real sense of an unbridled televisual public sphere taking root in the privacy of the home. Disney's character-identified and program-identified merchandise became (directly or indirectly) tokens of membership in a society of viewers and extended to activities and rituals outside of viewing, suggesting the building of a community of practice among children left in the care of the television. Thus it was no surprise that *Parents' Magazine* carried a positive review for a collection of sing-along records from Disney, recommending the "Official Mickey Mouse

34. A trade publication ad for Blue Bell Jeans urged local shop owners to contact the company for the full line of cross-licensed Mickey Mouse products. This line, for much younger children, allowed Disney to create another link between its products and child development. Ayers Collection, Archives Center, National Museum of American History, Smithsonian Institution.

Club March and Song; Mickey Mouse Club Pledge and Sho-Jo-Ji; You and The Mickey Mouse Club Book Club Song; Mickey Mouse Picture Book Song and When I Grow Up." These records, which *Parents'* described as a "good buy," all carried "the official Mickey Mouse Club Seal and [were] based on the TV show for children" (Sheehy 1956a, 32).[57]

Records, books, games, and crafts created simultaneously valuable product identification for Disney and a network of practices that, in the case of the "Mickey Mouse Club," were specifically designed to suggest the facilitation of the child's natural development. The imprimatur of child-rearing publications such as *Parents'* reinforced this association in reviews, in references to Disney in child-rearing articles, and in awards such as the medal the magazine awarded to Walt Disney (and eight other Americans, including Jonas Salk, the inventor of polio vaccine) for their work in improving the lives of children. The award went to Disney for "his two fine TV shows, beloved by children, 'Disneyland' and 'The Mickey Mouse Club,' for Disneyland, his imaginative amusement park for children; and for his extraordinary nature studies in the True Life Adventure film series, including the current one, 'The African Lion' " ("Books for Parents" 1956).[58]

Disney's efforts to weave its products and programs into the fabric of daily life, precisely the practice that has so troubled its severest critics, were what endeared it to parents and child-rearing experts alike. *The Mickey Mouse Club* was more than a television program: it was a central node in a matrix of production, distribution, and consumption that offered to regulate difficult relations between the natural and the cultural in the new suburban frontier. The company's rigid control of meaning in its programming, its imprimatur on myriad products for home and school, its certification by authorities, and its concerted efforts to insert itself into local social networks reconfigured media consumption as a complement to proper social interaction, rather than its replacement. *The Mickey Mouse Club* provided a symbolic location for practicing techniques for working Disney products into the daily practices of communities and homes that it had refined over the previous two decades. In its teachers' guide, for instance, the company promised that children would be so stimulated by its television programming that teachers "should be prepared to guide them to undertake further interesting activities such as reading, writing songs, poetry, stories, plays, programs, modeling in clay, painting, dramatizing, making models, experimenting." Not only that, they should do as Disney and "invite a specialist such as a fireman, nurse or scientist, to talk to them." Finally, completing the circuit between living room and school room, teachers could send kids home to "check their own homes for fire hazards, etc." (Walt

Disney Productions 1956a). All of this activity would spring, of course, from the seemingly passive activity of television watching.

It is important to note that Disney folded up *The Mickey Mouse Club* in 1959, when its contractual obligation with ABC expired, and that its viewing guides did not become a stable part of educational or domestic practice. Yet for the few years the show aired, it represented to parents (and to teachers) a countervailing example to other television that was considered either too exciting, or too deadening, or which enticed children into self-destructive consumption patterns.[59] Just as it had done in its public relations work around film, Disney located a point of parental anxiety—the potential for television to destabilize and denaturalize children's lives through unhealthy cultural influences—and created alternatives meant to address and correct the sources of that anxiety.

By September 1958, over 10 million people had passed through Disneyland's gates, the park was well established, and Walt Disney Productions changed the name of its evening television program from *Disneyland* to *Walt Disney Presents*. Under one name or another, the show continued long after Walt's death in 1966. Well into the 1960s, the program(s) maintained a focus on wildlife dramas, the exploits of domesticated animals, and tales from the American historical west. Disney continued to maintain its hold on the dinner hour, offering a collective family viewing moment in an increasingly fragmented and demographically specialized broadcast environment. One ritual of consumption joined with another in direct opposition to the monadic experience of the disposable "TV dinner," first introduced in 1954.[60] The extremely popular weekly appearance of "Professor Walt" (successor to the 1930s' "Uncle Walt") and his gentle homilies became a weekly illustrated lecture series on the proper relationships between nature and culture, and on the benign practice of observation.

Although critics of Disney would argue that the corporation has, over the years, attempted to produce and distribute an American landscape that looks like Disneyland,[61] it would be more accurate to say that Disney mapped Disneyland onto an extant terrain. What Disney did in the 1950s (as well as in the 1930s and 1940s) was to remark on the landscape, to produce a map that middle-class Americans (and those aspiring to the middle class) could recognize as a valuable navigational tool. Constant in this equation was a common need to see children not simply as the precious wards of doting parents, but as repositories of a nascent American future. Also contiguous from one generation to the next was the practice of obtaining a language and a praxis for child-rearing from popular sources that paraphrased and applied scholarly research on American childhood for an audience of practicing parents (particularly mothers). Though it is impossible to determine whether Walt Disney read professional or popular child-rearing literatures (the company's archivist has said he did not), it is clear that the company participated in a national discursive matrix that created an ideal type of child and a set of practices for producing it. The map that Disney offered was one that filled in details where only broad contours had existed. In the 1930s, it offered models of a humanized industrial efficiency that addressed parental desires to produce uniquely normal children. In the 1950s, Disney delivered to parents a frontier in which nature and culture illuminated and reinforced each other. But it could do so only because the need existed for such a model, and for a rudimentary language and a set of practices for attempting to realize it. If child-rearing texts and parenting magazines of the late 1940s and 1950s offered practical advice on how to manage the difficult task of domesticating that wild animal known as the child, Disney offered a map and tools for properly situating that child in local social matrices and in mass-mediated American culture. Disney's thematic reinscription of the American landscape—with Adventureland (Nature), Frontierland (the Old West), Fantasyland (the Fairy Tale), and Tomorrowland (the Technological Future) all separate yet contiguous, and all meeting on Main Street, U.S.A.—crystallized and constellated popular and professional understandings of the delicate operation of socializing the individual without subjugating its spirit to the inexorable forces of rationalization. The metaphor of the frontier, of escape into a forbidding wilderness to avoid the excesses of a decadent civilization, of the reinvestment of culture through encounters with the natural, of the growth of a new America from the roots of its past, was a popular trope Disney converted into apparently instructive and prophylactic entertainment.

Conclusion: Engineering a Better Tomorrowland

Criticized on the right by the likes of Dwight MacDonald and on the left by Theodor Adorno, the producer of mass entertainments in the postwar United States was often depicted as particularly responsible for the drift toward a totalitarian society. The wonders of mass production and consumption became less wonderful when it came to the efficient reproduction and distribution of ideology on a mass scale. In 1946, writing about propaganda (and by extension, entertainment and advertising), Robert Merton suggested that, as a communicator and a member of society, the media producer who wanted to use the most effective and current means of persuasion faced an ethical dilemma:

> He must choose between being a less than fully effective technician and a scrupulous human being or an effective technician and a less than scrupu-

lous human being. The pressure of the immediate objective tends to push him toward the first of these alternatives. For when effective mass persuasion is sought, and when "effectiveness" is measured solely by the number of people who can be brought to the desired action or the desired frame of mind, then the choice of techniques of persuasion will be governed by a narrowly technical and amoral criterion. And this criterion exacts a price of the prevailing morality, for it expresses a manipulative attitude toward man and society. It inevitably pushes toward the use of whatsoever techniques "work." (185)

Disney appeared to circumvent this dilemma by laying claim to an ingenuous understanding of the boundary that divided nature and culture, and by suggesting that it was motivated only by a desire to produce entertainments for parents and children that were informative and beneficial because of that very will to truth. Ironically, what made this effective was the very idea that media could harm children. Without the complex discursive matrix that had produced both arguments about media effects and contemporary thought about the nature of childhood—and which linked child development to larger discourses about national and international development (to the well-being of the species)—Disney could never have occupied the privileged position in which its pursuit of profit and its salutary effect on childhood and society were not at odds. Disney's genius lay in its ability to recognize in discourses about media effects not a potential stumbling block to its operations, but an enduring cultural phenomenon, a node at which the contradictory imperatives of democratic capitalism—to create individuals in whom standard values inhered—produced anxieties and desires that could be temporarily assuaged through consumption. In a paean to Walt Disney written shortly before his death, science-fiction author Ray Bradbury explained, in effect, why Disney deserved an exemption from Merton's rule:

> we live in an age of one billion robot devices that surround, bully, change and sometimes destroy us. The metal-and-plastic machines are all amoral. But by their design and function they lure us to be better or worse than we might otherwise be. . . . In such an age it would be foolhardy to ignore the one man who is building human qualities into robots—robots whose influence will be ricocheting off social and political institutions ten thousand afternoons from today. (1965, 100)

In the ideal world of American child-rearing, those robots could just as easily have been the children of mass society, and in this fatalistic logic, only Walt

Disney could ensure humanization in the midst of intractable rationalization.[62] Every child was a homunculus of the American future, and Disney was a homunculus of its past, the embodiment of an essential America before America, a nation derived not from its people but from its soil. Walt Disney was embodied in each of his products, and the consumption of those products was the consumption of the man. Through this chain of being, an ideal American past made its inexorable and necessary journey toward an ideal American future. Walt Disney worked only for the children, and children existed not for themselves, but for the future.

> *"We require conformity," said a [Disneyland] official. "We tell them right from the start, 'You are not an employee but a performer, on stage at all times. Walt Disney presents you. Leave your worries and cares outside—put on a smile."*
>
> —"TINKER BELL, MARY POPPINS, COLD CASH" 1965, 75

Conclusion THE CHILD AS VICTIM OF COMMODITIES

Many view Walt Disney Productions as a media enterprise cleverly manipulating the intense affect that surrounds childhood for its own gain. Yet others see Disney's profit motive as secondary to its profound social benefit and assume that any critical analysis of the company is necessarily malignant. For example, when I shared some of this work with a person in the banking industry, he was puzzled. Where was the condemnation? I seemed merely to be describing the standard business practices of a healthy, aggressive corporation addressing a well-defined market. His (mis)understanding was based on some apparently standard assumptions. He took for granted that any academic writing about Disney was necessarily hostile to the company, and that I would therefore attempt to demonstrate that Disney's practices were excessively predatory and secretly without regard for the well-being of children. In short, he assumed that any criticism of Disney would attempt to show that the company is evil.

Given the slant of the bulk of critical scholarship on Disney, these assumptions were reasonable. Much critical work on Disney operates from the position that, for the sake of its own profits, the company cynically trades on notions of childhood and Americanness that thinking people ought to recognize as false and ultimately detrimental to society. Yet one doesn't have to agree with Disney's obvious ideological slant to find the implicit notion that its audiences exist in a fantasyland of false consciousness ultimately insulting to those audiences. In the preceding chapters I have critically examined the history of arguments about the role of media in producing antisocial or socially constructive behaviors in children, and the same logic obtains in arguments that accuse Disney of conservative ideological programming. Critical media scholars cannot pick and choose where media have effects and where they do not. Ironically, nowhere is this clearer than in the recent emergence of right-wing critiques of Disney products as delivering encoded pro-homosexual, pedophilic, and anti-Christian messages to American children.[1] Both sides of the American ideological binary undervalue the role of a complex and variegated mainstream culture in providing a substrate within which Disney has been able to anchor its products, and to which the company must always attend in crafting its merchandise and its public image. Furthermore, this type of critique undervalues the potential agency of members of this culture, assuming (with a contempt born of midcentury modernist critiques of popular culture) that the consumer is by definition defenseless, and that none are more defenseless than are child consumers.

This profoundly durable idea—that people in general, and children in particular, can and do permanently absorb values and behaviors directly from the media they consume—offers the comfort of identifiable villains (or heroes) and an easy framework within which to imagine programs of social correction and control. It is a commonplace circuit that, in a single day in a single section of the *New York Times*, can accommodate an article that considers whether playing Mozart to fetuses will make them into more intelligent children (Goode 1999), a piece warning parents too concerned with their children's accomplishments that they may induce stress-related illnesses in those children (S. Gilbert 1999), and one continuing a half-century debate over whether early or late toilet training produces a more well-adjusted child (Brody 1999). It is the same circuit that, following the tragedies involving gun-wielding children in Arkansas and in Colorado, led to legislation mandating the posting of the Ten Commandments in public schools (Mitchell and Bruni 1999), lawsuits against game makers and movie studios by the victims of those shootings ("Media Companies Are Sued" 1999), and, finally (the day after the Mozart debate), a call by the American Academy of Pediatrics for parents to deny their children television entirely until after age two (Mifflin 1999). Here, the hope that Mozart is good for the child's brain comes full circle to meet the fear that violent, sexual, aggressive media (excluding, perhaps, *Don Giovanni*) may contribute to the malformation of the child's psyche, laying seeds for its development into a potentially sociopathic adult. Where the circle closes, powerful assumptions about the nature of childhood, and about the social and material relations that do or should obtain around the child, circulate and take form in arguments about the proper relationship of childhood to adulthood, and in practices derived from those arguments.

One such assumption is that the child's plasticity makes it the natural site at which parents and educators may enact adjustments to immediate social and political problems as deferred solutions resolving in an imagined future. Another is that the influence of complex social and material forces—including the built environment, class relations, gender regulation, voluntary and involuntary regimes of governmentality, and so on—reduce to a single cause ("the media"), or to various technologies designed to regulate and correct those media, from the V-chip and various Internet filters to the rating of movies, television programs, games, and music. And in this regard perhaps the most significant social technology is the insistence that the parent—usually a code word for the mother—is solely responsible for regulating the child's access to those media, as well as for any antisocial acts by the child. (This is now so much the case that in several U.S. cities, a parent may be jailed for her child's crimes.) Thus, as Jacques Donzelot (1979) has pointed out, the child becomes a tool by which adults—constituted as parents—are regulated by the state. More specifically, as Ellen Seiter (1993) has argued, the child as media consumer becomes the vehicle for the social and political regulation of women constituted as mothers.

Built into all of the examples listed above is the explicit or implicit idea that mass media have definite, discernible, and controllable effects on children. In the case of the call to forbid TV to toddlers, which appeared on the *Times'* front page, its author asserted: "Violence in movies and television has been linked to aggressive behavior in young people in studies by the American Medical Association, the American Psychological Association, the American Academy of Child and Adolescent Psychiatry, and the National Institute of Mental Health" (Mifflin 1999). Hidden behind this impressive list of institutional actors is a discursive tradition of vague, imprecise, and passive language that offers the appearance of causality where none definitively exists.[2] Yes, studies by a variety of institutions at different times during the twentieth century have linked media effects to childhood behaviors, but always within a web of provisional clauses under which one finds a common conclusion that determines little more than that violence is common both to media and to the society in which those media are produced. From the Payne Fund Studies on movie effects in the 1930s to Wilbur Schramm's 1950s studies of television effects, George Gerbner and Larry Gross's 1970s study on violence and television, and the most recent longitudinal media-violence study (Huesmann et al. 2003), the most conclusive and verifiable statement that researchers have ever been able to make is that media may have *some* effect on children, but only in conjunction with a host of other influences in their environment.

Yet the studies continue, as do news reports that exaggerate and simplify their findings to suggest that media are the primary causal agents in the production of childhood behaviors. One explanation for this is simply institutional inertia: the network of financial and cultural capital circulating through research facilities, commercial enterprises, and news media is so substantial and well integrated that it continues to be productive in the face of well-reasoned critique. While there is some evidence for this view, it does not, however, explain the ongoing enthusiasm with which the general public greets this particular narrative, especially at moments of tragedy such as those surrounding the Columbine shootings. Discourses on media effects provide a comforting fantasy in which a society apparently out of control is reordered to accommodate the desires of those who envision the possibility of a better world. It is a reasonable desire that leads to a reasonable expectation that produces an unreasonable solution. There may be many good reasons that a society may choose to regulate the content and distribution of its media—such as a desire to set a common representational standard for public venues such as broadcast frequencies, or to make a wide range of social and political ideas available to citizens—but the idea that it can control the behavior and actions of its citizens through that regulation is not one of them.

There is no doubt, however, that the discursive circuits constructed around and through media-effects arguments sell products and build careers. Parents concerned about their children's well-being will not only spend money on products designed to address that concern but will also seek out the opinions of professionals as to how best to use them. As parents press their needs and as companies, institutions, and individuals move to meet those needs, however, the idea of the generic child susceptible to media maintains its currency simply by circulating. What I have attempted to demonstrate here is that this notion has retained its cultural currency in the face of decades of inconclusive evidence and critique, not simply because of institutional inertia, but because it smoothes over some unpleasant contradictions in the construction of personhood and identity in democratic capitalist society. Quite simply: the child as susceptible to commodities stands in for the child as commodity-in-the-making, the child preparing for (and being prepared for) membership in a culture the primary social metaphor of which is the marketplace, a culture in which persons must be simultaneously and impossibly unique individuals *and* known quantities.

The Child as a Commodity

> *In capitalist culture . . . [the] . . . blindness to the social basis of essential categories makes a social reading of supposedly natural things deeply perplexing. This is due to the peculiar character of the abstractions associated with the market organization of human affairs: essential qualities in human beings and their products are converted into commodities, into things for buying and selling on the market.*
>
> —TAUSSIG 1980, 4

The very commodity nature of the child and its active denial inform the notion of the generic child as a homunculus for a better American future. To say that a child represents a future as yet unrealized, and that its future social, economic, and political life may be determined by its media consumption today, is to peg it with the very definition of the commodity, what Marx called "the embodiment of abstract human labor"—in this case, as a proto-adult accumulating its future value through acts of consumption. The twentieth-century generic American child, created as actual children were removed from labor markets, had the new task of self-making, a personalized labor process in which even its leisure time was taken up with productive activity. The same remains true today. Everything in the child's life is imagined as contributing to its eventual cumulative value as an adult, the exchange value it will bring to a labor market in which the term *labor* suggests only manual labor (which connotes a certain evolutionary failing, an inability to attain a higher order such as that of a "knowledge worker"), and in which more and more workers enter into employment under the rubric of "at will," which imagines the employer and the worker as two equal individuals who meet and determine a rate of exchange based strictly upon services bought and rendered. In an increasingly rationalized and competitive labor market, the productivity of one's childhood consumption is imagined as providing the potential edge necessary to marginally differentiate one's self over one's competitors in this supposedly free exchange. Although beyond the scope of this particular study, this is perhaps most apparent in a realm ostensibly outside of the child's leisure activity: school. In school, the child is evaluated regularly, and from that evaluation it begins to accrue forms of accreditation for its emergence into adulthood. Diplomas, grade-point averages, conduct reports, athletic awards, and so on contribute to a profile that the child develops and will trade on in subsequent interactions in its life. The degree to which such accreditation is associated with the accumulation of personal capital was recently neatly captured in scandals in which million-dollar bribes were offered to New York preschools to secure admissions for toddlers taking their first steps on a road that necessarily leads to Harvard.[3]

In the democratic capitalist social imaginary, however, the idea that anyone is or will be a commodity is ontologically irreconcilable with concepts of personal freedom and individual integrity. It is useful to conceive of children as *affected by* commodities rather than as occupying the same systems of exchange as those commodities, because this maintains the illusion of a humanity separate from and vulnerable to the social and material practices and discourses embedded in the things they consume. If there are elements of capitalist culture and society that are contestable, the child's apparent outsider status allows for the possibility of picking and choosing only those elements that should properly continue into the next generation. The durability of the notion of the child affected by media derives not only from the requirements of producers and institutions invested in the verity of that condition (such as Disney), but from a larger social formation predicated upon a generic American child that begins its life outside the inherently unequal and competitive social and material relations of the adult world. This child is understood to gain advantage (or disadvantage) not from extant sociocultural traits such as race, class, gender, or sexual orientation, but from the consumption practices it engages in, first under the supervision of its parents and later independently. The production and maintenance of this child in discourses of psychology and sociology as a natural creature entering the process of enculturation, and the circulation of this idea in popular periodicals and books, converts a cultural metaphysics of being into a natural fact. The notion that the child begins life as a human animal is not in question here. Rather, it is that the child is denatured through enculturation, and that this denaturing has very particular outlines, that is important.

In the 1920s and 1930s, this idea of the child as a highly plastic medium upon which adults could impress engrams for a better future took the form of rigorous child-rearing that would erase the severe social inequities of the time by imprinting within the child notions of efficiency, deferred gratification, and discipline that would allow it to succeed and to contribute to a more efficient and orderly society that better used its limited resources. Although the New Deal and World War II seemed more significant factors in reordering the United States' economic and social order, scientific child-rearing provided members of the middle class (and aspirants to that class) with a means to imagine a personal investment in the reordering of society through the actions of the individual.

In the 1950s, this idea took the form of a suburban child naturally resistant to the very excesses of social and economic rationalization that had been engendered by the New Deal and the war. A response to fears that a mass culture and society were leading the United States toward an authoritarianism similar to that of the Nazis it had just defeated, or a totalitarianism like that of the Soviet Union it opposed, the natural child of the 1950s was meant to resist the rationalization of American culture and society (without sacrificing its own economic future) by developing skill sets derived from the channeling of its natural instincts and aptitudes. In both periods, the ideal of the child resolved the contradiction between the opportunity for personal success in a competitive economy and the need to maintain social order in a centralized democratic capitalist society.

The child susceptible to the enticements of commodities, then, has stood in for the commodified child because it embodies a régime of social control and organization that appears to devolve both power and responsibility to the most basic units of American society: the family and the individual. Rather than imagining the child as a mere repository of value entering a market culture peopled by other units embodying varying quantities of necessarily anonymous and transferable value, the homunculus figure of the child affected by commodities provides motive force to a conception of social relations in which personal gain (or loss) and social cohesion (or dissolution) are at least partially reconciled through the regulation of acts of consumption by individual proto-persons (i.e., children). The possible conflict between economic self-interest and democratic action is smoothed over in a metaphysics of self-realization in which the inherent inequality of life in capitalist society (the very difference that is mobilized to create and circulate value) is, as a social problem, indefinitely deferred until a relatively unspecified future.

It is this seemingly natural motive force that cultural anthropologist Michael Taussig has characterized—in his gloss on Durkheimian sociology—as always leaning away from the material and toward the ideal, enacting a Hegelian dumb show of transubstantiation in which ideas and values briefly visit the material world so that they may be taken up again in the act of consumption. Here, the social and material relations from which the child is created, and into which it will enter, lose their specific relations of power and the sense that they are made, becoming merely "society," a virtually living entity unto itself (Taussig 1993, 236). The subtle relationship between the child and the things it consumes is one in which the child appears natural in relation to the culture it absorbs through media commodities, so that the values it imbibes may appear in its adult future relatively unadulterated by rational apprehension. It is the child's very innocence, its lack of understanding of society, that makes it available for imprinting. Viewed in this light, both the child and its media are commodity fetishes, mystified tokens of powerful social forces, deployed in a common metaphysical operation of "social construction"—the production of a future society through the dispersion of germs of social behavior, belief, and attitude in the natural medium of the as-yet-unenculturated child.[4] Children are our future.

Commodification: From Walt to the Child and Back

Throughout this text I have referred to Walt Disney less as a historical personage and more as what Michel Foucault (1984, 107–13) described as an "author function." In Foucault's formulation, a person is not an author simply because she has written something, but because she has willingly entered a complex discursive matrix by which authority is assigned in accordance with the dictates of various systems governing the production, evaluation, criticism, and taxonomy of texts:

> the author function is linked to the juridical and institutional system that encompasses, determines, and articulates the universe of discourses . . . it does not affect all discourses in the same way at all time and in all types of civilization . . . it is not defined by the spontaneous attribution of a discourse to its producer, but rather by a series of specific and complex operations . . . it does not refer purely and simply to a real individual, since it can give rise simultaneously to several selves, to several subjects—positions that can be occupied by different classes of individuals. (113)

Although Foucault intended the author function to apply primarily to writing, it is easily adaptable to the case of the producer of cartoons and films for children. In its most basic form, the author function merely points out that what Foucault calls "the writing subject" is distinct from the person who writes by virtue of the complex of discursive practices involved in authoring texts. For instance, it is understood that the author produces with an audience in mind, one limited by a set of discursive boundaries such as those that govern genre or discipline. This "writing subject" is very different from the same person writing a letter to a friend or contesting a telephone charge, even though each act properly involves writing. From the perspective of reception, Foucault understands the author function to limit and define which works an audience will accept as properly attributable to the author. Provided that the author's letters to a friend conform to the rules governing the epistolary form, they might fall within the category of the author's works. However, if they diverge stylistically from the bulk of that work, or reveal details that are deemed to add nothing to understanding it, they may be excluded (108). The important point in this instance, however, is not whether the quality of the work determines its place in the author function, but that this determination is made by persons other than the author. The writing subject consciously aware of the liminal operations of her author function might write even the smallest notes with posterity in mind, but she cannot fully control the ultimate determination of the deposition of those works in relation to her function.

Thus, for example, Walt Disney was scolded in the 1940s for *Song of the South* (1946) and *Saludos Amigos* (1942), because the company mixed live action with animation, and because of Donald Duck's expression of explicit sexuality in the latter film (Smoodin 1993).[5] When the company, which was built around the idea that each of its products issued ultimately from the mind of one man, attempted to move in directions its public and its critics felt were not appropriate, the language used to discipline it was personal: Walt Disney the man was in error, and it was he who had to rectify the situation. The meaning of Walt Disney the producer thus followed a circuit that began in the studio and extended through the public to include audiences (in theaters, schools, the military, and in industrial workplaces as the company expanded its production to include instructional films), critics, and exhibitors, finally returning to the company in the form of reviews and letters. In this way, Walt Disney was discursively disciplined not as a private individual, but as a producer, the author of a wide range of texts.

Walt Disney Productions also participated in the discursive construction of Walt Disney as the ultimate author of an incredibly vast array of merchandise by creating a complex public rhetoric that described Disney's spirit as invested in each of his workers, and through them in his products. To a degree unimaginable in conventions of literary authorship (indeed, antithetical to the stereotype of the lone author), the company celebrated the production process, throwing open its doors to journalists and producing films and television programs about that process. In these many spectacles of production, the company freely admitted that Walt Disney spent little to no time actually drawing the creations that bore his name, writing the stories, filming, or engaging in many of the other operations involved in the production of large-scale animation projects. Rather, it celebrated the production of its cartoons as an industrial process, detailing the many steps involved from the initial storyboards to the final product.[6] At the same time, however, it posited Walt, the voice of Mickey, as the organizing principle of the entire operation, the constant inspiration behind every single industrial process and its eventual product. Even when employees invented a new process, credit for the invention largely went to Walt.

Within these narratives of genius and inspiration, the company wove the biography of its founder as leitmotif. The repetition of the details of Walt's career—childhood in the Midwest, lack of excessive formal education, lower-middle-class, white roots, enthusiasm for the natural world—in conjunction with narrative celebrations of production, formed a counterpoint to reformist critiques of the movie industry that (in terms implicit and explicit) suggested that the ethnic, working-class, metropolitan roots of most movie producers were transmitted to the middle-class consumer through their products. Walt Disney represented the antithesis of the stereotypical Hollywood producer, and his ethos became available to the consumer through the magic of animation, in which the dilution of that essence by other human agents was minimized and distilled in a fantasy of industrial control. This performance brings new meaning to Foucault's claim that "using all the contrivances that he sets up between himself and what he writes, the writing subject cancels out the signs of his particular individuality" (1984, 102). Through the celebration of industrial management and control, Walt Disney became an amalgamated being, a uniquely average American distributed throughout a productive network of bodies and machines, disappearing as an individual and reappearing as an archetype.

This version of Walt Disney acted in a fashion nearly identical to that of the generic child because it was invested with the same sort of transformative power the child was (and is) imagined to contain. To some degree this condition derived from the company's consistent efforts to associate the man with beneficial developmental processes. It also occurred, however, because of the specific operation that Disney professed to perform for that child. In Disney's representations of itself and its founder, the company presented a facility with the distillation, reinvention, and redistribution of an idealized American experience. More specifically, it claimed to take the essence of Walt Disney's turn-of-the-century, small-town origins (Disney was born in Chicago in 1901 but soon moved to Marceline, Missouri) and convert it into products from which children could draw useful tools for a process of self-production that would incorporate that idealized American culture in their eventual adult bodies and behaviors. Disney was represented as interceding between an ideal past and an unrealized ideal future, distilling the best impulses of that past into a digestible form that would reappear as the present corrected in that future. This function was analogous to the child's imagined purpose, the conversion of an embodied primitive human past into a better American future through the incorporation of programming designed to correct perceived shortcomings in the social and material relations of the moment. In short, Walt Disney performed the successful result of the child's symbolic function, and promised the recirculation of that success through a miracle of transmogrified consumption in which his life force and experience became available through his products—the commodified and dispersed presence of his self in the world. In a miracle of capitalist transubstantiation, the more Walt Disney became commodified, the more he became himself; the more he appeared to be the product of ideally American circumstances, the more he seemed self-made.

It is not difficult to hear in Foucault's author function the distant echoes of Marx's conception of the commodity.[7] Foucault describes the author function as "characteristic of the mode of existence, circulation, and functioning of certain discourses within a society" (1984, 108). In other words, the means by which a person (such as Walt Disney) disappears as an individual and reappears as an author depends on the specific social and historical understandings that pertain to writing, to publishing, to criticism, to disciplinarity, to "intellectual property," and so on, at the moment when she undertakes authorship. When Foucault states that the author function "does not refer purely and simply to a real individual, since it can give rise simultaneously to several selves, to several subjects," he describes the self as commodity, determined not by a bourgeois fantasy of self-making but by the discursive requirements of authorship (113). According to Marx (1961, 72), the commodity is "a mysterious thing, simply because in it the social character of men's labour appears to them as an objective character stamped upon the product of that labour: because the relations of the producers to the sum total of their own labour is presented to them as a social relation, existing not between themselves, but between the products of labour become commodities." This holds true whether we are speaking of a book or movie, or of a producer's public persona.

Whether in regard to becoming an author or to becoming an archetypal movie producer, the act of positioning one's self within disciplinary boundaries and discursive networks is inherently a productive and practical activity. More so than in the social representation of manual labor, in which individual workers are described as interchangeable units, machines made of flesh, in professional practices, vast matrices of training and valorization are encapsulated in one's title. In a culture in which networks of affiliation, marriage, and civil intercourse trade in professional status, the self produced through the labor of professional education, though it appears a creature of one's own "self-making," becomes a commodity that circulates widely and variously, obtaining different values in relation to the other selves it encounters and the social situations in which those encounters occur.[8] Although Walt Disney projected an image of a self-taught and self-made man, and although he earned no accredited title, networks of public relations, awards, and honorary degrees conferred on him a value not entirely of his own making.

Following this, the idea that Walt Disney was more commodity than man seems reasonable. But it is wrong. Disney was not *more* commodity than man; rather, in his widespread circulation as a public figure he was readily *apprehended* as a commodity. Through the celebratory discourse of Disney's public relations, his commodity nature was more apparent than it might be for most people, but it was no more substantial. That commodity nature is something all members of a capitalist society share, and something that we work to erase or obscure through discourses of individuation and of self-making. This is not merely because as a working people we exchange our labor on a supposedly open market, or because we want to imagine that even though this exchange occupies the majority of our waking hours, it does not represent the totality of who we are. Rather, our notions of individuation, if not the very ability to sell our own labor—and to deliver ourselves in other arenas of exchange—require that we see ourselves not as embodying the complex matrices of social and material relations that support our existence, but as wholly independent, self-possessed beings. To acknowledge our commodity nature is to deny our individuality, to suggest that who we are derives not from personal initiative or inner essence, but from the complex of determinations by which our individuality becomes hyphenated—classically, by race, gender, class, and sexual orientation. Marx stated this quite bluntly in the *Grundrisse* (1858, 247): "Society does not consist of individuals, but expresses the sum of interrelations, the relations within which these individuals stand." One cannot be an individual except in relation to other individuals, and in relation to social, political, and economic understandings of the meaning of individuality. Nowhere has this been more evident than in the "culture wars," in which the struggle to define the proper relationship between the individual, the state, society, and different classes has come into sharp conflict.[9]

Although the idea that the individual does not exist appears on its surface absurd, apprehended as it most likely is by a reading subject who experiences herself as an individual, it expresses an understanding of consciousness as a social act, not as the isolated experience of the Cartesian subject. It follows from a view of life and of the experiencing subject as engaged not in the abstracted act of contemplation, but in "sensuous activity" in "practice" (Marx 1845, 143). It is an indication, finally, that Marx's critique of capital is not simply a detailed exposition of the relations of economic power in capitalism, but also an attempt to explain capitalist ontology—the experience of being in the world in capitalist society. Commodity nature is a sense-making tool. This is evident in that class of objects to which we easily assign values, the things we make, buy, and sell. To call these things commodities is to admit that they have a value—that they represent a "use-value" (one or more purported functions useful to their possessor) and an "exchange-value" (the cost of obtaining them)—comprised of a complex set of economic and social determinants (Marx 1867, 302–19). It is less evident when we turn to classes of objects—such as ourselves—that appear free and self-determining. We may be willing to confer a limited commodity status on these objects, bracketing off (as Marx does) our labor from the rest of our activity and admitting that it has value in the same fashion that products do. Yet Marx's heavy emphasis on relations as economic, and some vulgar interpretations that have followed, make it harder for us to admit the philosophical and metaphysical aspects of his work, to see that to name ourselves commodities would be to admit the possibility that our identity points to the complex of social and material relations—the "sum of interrelations"—that the commodity form obscures. To class ourselves as commodities would call into question the boundaries between our personal life—our family names, homes, intimate relationships, and so on—and our public personae as workers, mothers, teachers—seemingly leading us ultimately to a Stalinist parody of equality in which we could address each other dutifully only as "comrade." But even our names have a public and social history, and our intimate relations remain intimate only as long we respect certain social and cultural understandings of the proper bounds of that behavior—as recent debates in the United States over the regulation of sodomy and marriage have certainly revealed.

This refusal to name our commodity nature is not what is sometimes called "false consciousness," but simply the consciousness necessary to function effectively in a capitalist society. This is true at the level of day-to-day interaction, just as it is in the organization of our analyses of those interactions. As Bruno Latour (1993) has pointed out, for example, divisions between psychology, anthropology, politics, and economics—different modes of describing practical existence—are not natural, but the boundary work that establishes them as separate disciplines does naturalize understandings of the organization of our social and material life. Marx tells us that we come to this understanding not through collusion or coercion, but as a matter of course:

> Man's reflections on the forms of social life, and . . . his scientific analysis of those forms, take a course directly opposite to that of their actual historical development. He begins . . . with the results of the process of development ready to hand before him. The characters that stamp products as commodities, and whose establishment is a necessary preliminary to the circulation of commodities, have already acquired the stability of natural, self-understood forms of social life, before man seeks to decipher,

> not their historical character, for in his eyes they are immutable, but their meaning. (1867, 323–24)

The commodity form—the idea that a thing (or identity) embodies the social and material relations that go into its making—serves as the means by which we mediate between the ideal form of things and our immediate material and practical experience of them.

Confronted with an actual child—in child-rearing, education, or simply passing one on the street—we invoke the concept of "child," with all of its varied and complex relations to different discursive realms—such as developmental theory, marketing, or family life—without calling to mind all of those relations. We have to diaper the child, or teach it addition, or cross the street to avoid it, and in that practical activity all of those socially and historically produced understandings of what this small thing, this "child," is, are present yet relatively unarticulated. To call this child a commodity is to point out that the people who deal with children, or even with the abstraction of "children," do so through the mediation of the commodity form—through the production, limitation, and circulation of meanings that may obtain around the sign of "the child." The child is commodified, for instance, in the belief, commonly (and stubbornly) held since before the beginning of the last century, that its development recapitulates that of the entire species, from its animal prehistory to its arrival in present-day civilization. It is commodified in Freud's (1924) description of the oral, anal, and pregenital stages of development, or in Piaget's (1928) delineation of the stages entailing the child's arrival at abstract, rational thought. These are sense-making operations by which we reconcile ideal notions of the child with the physical creature in front of us, or with a representation of that child in the media. Here the abstract concept of the child is made manifest through the immediate social and historical understandings of its instantiation. In his discussion of commodity fetishism, William Pietz (1993, 147) describes this process as "the historical production of universal forms." Arising as "the real representation of material social relations," he explains, "these exist as material objects; they are fetishes insofar as they have become necessary functional parts that are privileged command-control points of a working system of social reproduction." "The child" is such a historically specific universal form, a real representation of social and material relations, and, as I have suggested above, one that is extremely important in the regulation of social reproduction. From the moment the child is born (if not before), it—and everyone associated with its care—is bound in a complex and highly codified matrix of social regulation that depends very much upon its metaphysical function as a link between an ideal natural prehistory and a future in which the missteps of the present society have been corrected. To say what a child (or Walt Disney) is, then, is to invoke a set of specific social and historical understandings that make it useful to us but bring us no closer to its ideal form.

The commodity form is a compromise we broker with the world, foreclosing on certain meanings and determinations in order to render an object useful and cognizable. Neither wholly ideal nor wholly material, the commodity form is an oscillation between the two, an acknowledgment that the material world is obtainable only through the ideal, and that the ideal cannot exist except as grounded in the material. The values we assign to that object do not sit lightly on it, like shrink-wrap on a new CD; they *are* that object as we use it at a given moment. The object per se does not exist except as we apprehend it as having value to us in a given social and material operation. In doing so, we simultaneously make that object knowable and mystify it. "Value," Marx tells us (1961, 74), "does not stalk about with a label describing what it is. It is value, rather, that converts every product into a social hieroglyphic. Later on, we try to decipher the hieroglyphic, to get behind the secret of our own social products; for to stamp an object of utility as a value, is just as much a social product as language." As Marxist philosopher Evald Ilyenkov puts it, "The ideal form is the form of a thing created by social human labour. Or, conversely, it is the form of labour realized . . . in the substance of nature, 'embodied' in it, 'alienated' in it, 'realized' . . . in it, and thereby confronting its very creator as the form of a thing or as a relation between things, which are placed in this relation . . . by human beings, by their labour" (quoted in Bakhurst 1991, 182).

Similar to Lukács's idea of reification, this understanding of the relation between the material and the ideal appreciates commodification, not as the act of pejorative diminution that it is usually understood to be in capitalist society—the cheapening of a thing—but a necessary part of human activity.[10] Yrjo Engestrom (1990) has further refined this definition, arguing that, as an organizing principle in that activity, the commodity also embodies the limitations and contradictions inherent in its making—in the act of limiting the number of determinations that describe it—and that as the commodity is deployed in human activity the participants in that activity will eventually encounter, and be required to deal with, those limitations and contradictions. This, Engestrom argues, is the engine of cultural activity in capitalist societies, ever moving us to adjust the values we assign to commodities and to make sense of those reevaluations. For example, we cannot keep Walt Disney the self-made man and Walt Disney the product of public relations in mind together, so we resolve this contradiction by imagining that he is the prime cause behind the corporation that issues the public relations that reproduce us for him, and so on.

Commodification and the "Death" of Childhood

The negative connotation that is attached to the concept of commodification in the United States is particularly relevant when we speak of the child. Here, the term is synonymous with "commercialization," the process by which a seemingly inviolate natural object is forced against its will (or that of its producers) into the market. It points to a fantastic realm that is ideal by virtue of being removed by the process of evaluation associated with the market, a prelapsarian, precapitalist location where all are pure, all are equal. "Commodification" is bound up with a sense of the loss of an inherently unique quality in the object, its entry into a set of relations that undermine that authenticity by assigning to the object a value that by definition is in relation to other objects. For the child, this process is palpable. It enters the world an ostensibly unique being, wholly and utterly itself. Within a few years, however, it has begun the inevitable descent into culture, a process that entails evaluation—in relation to its peers, in schooling, even in relation to its earlier and later selves.[11] The teleology of this process is inexorable: the child accrues value in competition with its peers—at first playful, and gradually more serious—in its march toward adulthood and relative exchange value in labor markets, marriage markets, and so on.

Since this trajectory is inevitable, and since it is taboo to speak of humans as commodified in this culture, the child is often depicted as the (potential) *victim* of commodities—its inherent purity polluted by contact with the adult desires and attitudes they contain, in what has been referred to as the "death of childhood."[12] In a mass-market culture, the child's progress into the world is marked by the consumption of cultural artifacts described as either adding to its eventual value when it fully enters its commodity status, or detracting from that value. In short, the commonly held belief is that the child produces its future self through acts of consumption.[13] It is in this latter sense of the meaning of the term that the commodification of the child becomes truly important. For it is in this sense that real children may be imagined as transhistorical objects able to accept programming designed to correct immediate social and material problems in an imagined future in which that programming becomes active. By imagining the child as initially standing outside of and susceptible to commodity relations, we assume the fantasy of regulating the process by which meaning accretes in the child through the values it obtains through acts of consumption. This makes the child at any specific moment in history and in any particular cultural location a unique and valuable object for understanding how social and material relations are imagined at that moment, both through how they are described in relation to the child, and in what changes the proper regulation of that child would engender in its adult future.

Although this ontological function may obtain across the entire history of the United States, it is particularly pronounced in the twentieth century because of signal changes in the status of the child that are specific to the century—the containment of child labor and the spread of mass media, including compulsory public education.[14] The former is important because it ostensibly freed the working-class child from labor, creating conditions within which it appeared categorically equal to its middle-class counterparts, helping to pave the way for the generic American child. The latter is important for similar reasons: with the advent of mass culture, children of different classes were more likely to mix, requiring a model of the child entering that culture that bridged class lines. Together, these two changes contributed to a condition in which the ideal American child increasingly appeared a natural creature outside of class (as well as race), one which took shape as a person in acts of consumption during its leisure time and its schooling.[15] This sounds remarkably similar to the terms Marx uses in the *Grundrisse* to describe the development of the liberal, bourgeois subject in capitalist society: "Free time—which is both idle time and time for higher activity—has naturally transformed its possessor into a different subject, and he then enters into the direct production process as this different subject. This process is then both discipline, as regards the human being in the process of becoming; and, at the same time, practice, experimental science, materially creative and objectifying science, as regards the human being who has become, in whose head exists the accumulated knowledge of society" (1858, 290).[16]

This is what makes Walt Disney the proper complementary object in the study of the commodified child. In the repetitive retelling of the man's life story we find a trajectory in which his will is multiplied into the productive activity of the many bodies of his workers, and their labors are returned to him in the form of products that bear his name, and, according to the company's public relations, his very spirit. Alongside the tales told in Disney's products, we experience a narrative of triumphant containment, in which Walt Disney is made to embody the social and material relations of an industrial plant and to emerge more himself as a result. This experience is then made directly available to the child, who may partake of the commodified man by consuming the products imbued with his spirit. In the discourse of media commodities, this has a positive effect on the child, enhancing its value in the process of its inevitable commodification, and, more important, supplying it with indirect experience of a life made more, not less, authentic through that process. For rather than decrying his commodification, Walt Disney appeared to celebrate it, and to suggest that it made him more who he truly was, the embodiment of an ideal American culture.

The Nature of Culture

Here, the word *culture* revisits its agrarian roots as a medium for growth. What I have suggested throughout this work is that the figure of the child has served as a tool in the process of describing American democratic capitalist culture as grounded in the natural environment. Certainly, part of the reason for this derives from the Enlightenment notion of the child, embodied in Rousseau's Emile or in the Wild Boy of Aveyron, which conceived of it as a wild animal to be domesticated into the adult domain of reason.[17] As Viviana Zelizer (1985) has pointed out, in this century the distance between a natural (and animal) childhood and a cultured and rational adult realm has increased significantly. For Zelizer, childhood became "sacralized" when children began to lose their exchange value as they were excluded from the labor markets of American industrial society in the late nineteenth and early twentieth centuries.[18] At roughly the same time, neo-Darwinian American social scientists imagined that these sacralized, sentimentalized children embodied in their development an encapsulated version of the progress of a human civilization that expressed its evolutionary pinnacle in twentieth-century white, middle-class, Protestant American society. In emerging discourses of professional child-rearing, the relationship between parent and child recapitulated the tensions of the colonial "encounter." The child was depicted as a sort of noble savage, the adult as bearing the white man's burden of bringing civilization to the child and the child into civilization. In the rhetoric of the Progressive Era of the early twentieth century (and in the neocolonial discourse of 1950s postwar internationalism), every parent/child dyad was a reenactment of a contact zone, an opportunity for the parent to experience in miniature the sociocultural evolution of the species as a biological fact, and, it was suggested, to correct for the excesses of civilization, to steer the child away from the evolutionary cul-de-sacs into which other cultures and races had wandered.[19]

In this discursive formation, the child appears as a link between a rapidly modernizing culture and its roots in human prehistory, signifying the grounding of that culture in the natural world. This notion informed the impulse behind Teddy Roosevelt's enthusiasm for the Boy Scouts, if not the physical culture movement in general.[20] Later, it would underpin the imagined frontier ethos of 1950s suburban America, the idea of balancing the encounter of the natural and the cultural in the child's experience so that it could resist the dehumanizing excesses of rationalization. In Judeo-Christian terms, the child represented access to a prelapsarian world, and nature a form of partial (though ultimately ineffective) redemption for the necessary capitulation to the requirements of capitalist culture, that one strive against one's fellow citizens.

The 1930s and the 1950s represent two important moments in twentieth-century American popular culture in which the child as a natural, precultural being was mobilized to act as a governor on the relentless machine of first industrial and later post-Fordist capitalism. In the language of scientific management of the 1920s and 1930s, the regulation of the child's development through the rigorous control of its environment was an attempt to program corrections into an emerging national socioeconomic system through its individual components. In this version, the child was a sort of laboratory animal, and the home and nursery its testing ground. In the 1950s, the recourse to the child was one of securing a (neo-Freudian) animal humanity in the child flexible enough to adapt to rapid technological change by assisting it to properly incorporate into the process of its enculturation its evolutionary imperatives toward survival. By encouraging in the child a harmony between its own instincts and aptitudes and its social environment, parents could better help it locate a career that represented a balance between its natural self and the demands of a highly technological and rationalized society. This equilibrium between instinct/aptitude and career was to become the guarantee that American democratic capitalist society would be populated by citizens whose lives were freely chosen, uncoerced, and deriving from a culture homologous to and contiguous with the natural landscape from which it arose. Parents of the 1920s and 1930s and then the 1950s were to focus upon this negotiation between the natural and the cultural through the figure of the child—albeit in very different ways—because both periods witnessed rapid shifts in the organization of everyday life, and because they were encouraged to understand those changes as a potential threat to an inherently American mode of existence. At those moments of tension, anxiety, and seemingly irrevocable social change, the child acted as a natural touchstone in a culture suddenly alien and potentially alienating.[21]

To approximate the terms of historical materialism, this comforting, prelapsarian child could also be described as a precapitalist creature learning its way into democratic capitalist culture. The child offered the appearance of access to a life and a world from which adults were otherwise barred by the irreversible condition of their own enculturation. In this apparent opening, the romanticism that often informed the anthropological gaze into primitive societies extended to the vision of the child as a creature as yet unsullied by the vicissitudes of capitalist life. Michael Taussig's (1980, 7) description of the problematic of this gaze in the study of persons entering into capitalist social relations (in this case, peasants and workers in South America) applies remarkably well to the generic "American" child in the process of enculturation: "Set against the images that capitalist society presents of itself, precapitalist life can appeal (or frighten) on account of its apparent idealism and the enchantment of its universe by spirits and phantoms that display the course of the world and its salvation. Furthermore, precapitalist societies acquire the burden of having to satisfy our alienated longings for a lost Golden Age." If the child's recapitulation of the history of human civilization offered to the society at large the opportunity to adjust its evolutionary trajectory, it also presented to the middle-class parent the daunting prospect of offering up this sacred object, this thing outside of culture, this ideal of human prehistory, to that society and its markets. The figure of the child simultaneously evoked hope and fear, anxiety and envy in the parent/citizen. Having escaped capitalist labor markets, the child lived a life of if not boundless leisure, certainly more ease than its parents. Rather than encouraging the child to revel in this exceptional status, the parent was granted the bittersweet task of managing the child's departure from its edenic, ludic green world and its necessary sacrifice to the dictates of responsible adult life. In 1914, Sigmund Freud framed this very specific historical phenomenon in terms that both universalized its experience and particularized and personalized the social and material forces at work in it:

> If we look at the attitude of fond parents towards their children, we cannot but perceive it as a revival and reproduction of their own, long since abandoned narcissism. . . . they are impelled to ascribe to the child all manner of perfections which sober observation would not confirm, to gloss over and forget all his shortcomings. . . . and to renew in his person the claims for privileges which were long ago given up by themselves. The child shall have all things better than his parents; he shall not be subject to the necessities which they have recognized as dominating life. . . . the laws of nature, like those of society, are to be abrogated in his favour; he is really to be the centre and heart of creation, "His Majesty the Baby," as

> once we fancied ourselves to be. He is to fulfil those dreams and wishes of his parents which they never carried out, to become a great man and a hero in his father's stead, or to marry a prince as a tardy compensation to the mother. (72–73)

Although Freud would not become widely popular with the American middle class until the arrival of Dr. Spock, his description of the etiology of bourgeois narcissism is an apt example of the process by which the experience of the middle-class (male) child (one cannot help but envision "him" marrying a prince) was mapped onto a generic version of childhood slowly taking form in the United States during the early part of this century.[22] Beyond that example, however, it also describes nicely the compression of a complex of social and material forces into the parent/child relationship, and the sense of the inevitable blending of hope, fear, and betrayal in that relationship as the parent leads the child out to take its place in the marketplace.

Only a fictional stereotype such as Disney's Gepetto could escape the feelings of envy and shame that Freud ascribed to the universally middle-class parent. Yet even he must perform the anxiety of devolved solitary parental responsibility during Pinocchio's long walk from home to school and from inanimate insensibility to animate humanity. What makes *Pinocchio* (1940) an apt metaphor for the metaphysics of midcentury American child-rearing, though, is not merely Gepetto's performance of parental anxiety in the face of Pinocchio's first encounter with human society, but also the film's depiction of public space and leisure time as locations in which civilization is lost or found. As I suggested in chapter 1, Disney's *Pinocchio* is ultimately an assimilationist fable, one that hints that membership in the middle class was (and is) not a birthright but the endpoint of a very specific process of enculturation: the abandonment of a set of pleasures associated both with the working class and with childhood, and the adoption of the lifelong project of self-making and self-improvement, the accumulation of value in one's person. The reason that Pinocchio must make it to school in the end is not only to receive the imprimatur of the state to obtain full citizenship, but also to organize and validate his experiences into recognizable and exchangeable values. In the post-Enlightenment notion of personhood beginning with the precapitalist and prelapsarian child, leisure time gradually ceases to exist. All is self-making, all is accumulation—of knowledge, of experience, and ultimately, of value. As David Lloyd and Paul Thomas (1998, 67) make clear in their analysis of the mobilization of the idea of culture in the service of the state in eighteenth- and nineteenth-century Europe, culture as a concept has long served in the production and regulation of class relations, both as the marker of social distinction and as a means of regulating the meaning of leisure activity:

> Culture designates not a discursive formation in opposition to society but rather a set of institutions within society at the point of its intersection with the state. The oppositional relation between culture and society can only be maintained ideally; in practice, the very formulation of the space of culture demands . . . its actualization in pedagogical institutions whose function is to transform the individual of civil society into the subject of the state. That naturalization of the often violent production of citizens overlaps with the universal historical narrative of the evolution of humanity from animal or savage to civilized being.

Yet even before the child can take its place in the citizen-making operation of schooling, it must accumulate the tools that will allow it to emerge from that process as both a productive citizen and an individual capable of maximizing its own advantage. In the middle-class culture of early- and mid-twentieth-century America—which derived much of its authority and definition from the traditions Lloyd and Thomas discuss—culture was culture only if it edified and improved upon the person. All else was folly. Pinocchio is animated at the film's beginning, not its end, and is told quite specifically that to be animate does not mean to be human. His adventures throughout the film form an object lesson in which he (and perhaps his audience) learns that living for the moment imperils one's self and those one loves (as well as threatens devolution into a lower form of life, a donkey), while hard work, deferred gratification, and self-denial deliver one into full humanity, the full possession of one's person through its constant deferral. (This makes Jiminy Cricket's "When You Wish upon a Star" just a bit ironic.) In terms of the movies, if the middle class could not stop the juggernaut of mass culture, it could at least maintain a taxonomy that evaluated amusements for their net contribution to the child's personal ledger.

The obverse side of this arrangement found Disney's (ostensibly) human cartoon characters always aided and abetted by animal characters and eventually found the suburbs reproduced in the landscape of Disney's nature films (though the company might have argued that the generative order was reversed). Here, the natural, precapitalist world from which the child departed remained present as an anchor, lest the process of enculturation alienate the child from its own humanity, so much so that it would become, like a failed Pinocchio, simply an animate object adrift in capitalist culture, an embarrassing reminder of the crass essentials—the bottom line—of capitalist ontology (that is, a commodity). The trope of nature and its association with the child served the dual purpose of assuaging parental guilt at the prospect of guiding the child out of its edenic youth (its "kindergarten") and maintaining a fantasy in which the habits and behaviors in which the child had to be entrained appeared as part of its natural landscape and not an external imposition. This is, of course, contradictory, and the contradiction moves the process forward: the child's recapitulation of the evolution of human culture provides the adult with access to nature, which may be enlisted to attenuate the excesses of a culture that derives from (yet is alienated from) that same natural landscape . . . and so on. The situation is not unlike Taussig's (1980, 3) description of the alienation caused by studying the interpretation of capitalism by precapitalist peasants: "Those of us who are long accustomed to capitalist culture have arrived at the point at which this familiarity persuades us that our cultural form is not historical, not social, not human, but natural—'thing-like' and physical. In other words, it is an attempt forced upon us by confrontation with precapitalist cultures to account for the phantom objectivity with which capitalist culture enshrouds its social creations." For Taussig, this moment of encounter represents an opportunity for the progressive, leftist intellectual to strip away the veil of mystification that daily living places over the social and discursive construction of relations in his or her own capitalist culture.[23] For the middle-class American adult confronting the child, however, it describes a device through which to adjust the operations of that culture such that they better align with the evolutionary imperatives of the species, apparently accommodating the needs of the individual to those of the society at large. A precapitalist peasant reading of the operations of capitalism as a mystical metaphysics, or fetishism, has the potential to denaturalize a set of social and material relations for its participants, revealing their constructed nature.[24] In a similar (if more limited) fashion, the understanding of the child as offering its adult caretakers access to the prehistory of their own culture allows for the fantasy of attenuating or altering the flow of that culture. While one may be conceived of as an ideological operation and the other a natural one, they imagine a similar end: the humanization of a society that tends perpetually toward the inhuman (so understood), using the master's tools of capitalist metaphysics. The difference between the two scenarios, however, is that it has been the task of popular child-rearing discourse to erase the alienated understanding provided by the child, renaturalizing the social for the anxious parent.

Humanity

I have suggested that the child is a relatively unique ontological object in American democratic capitalist culture, operating as a fetish or homunculus in which complexes of social and material relations are distilled and then deployed when the child reaches adulthood. Strangely, though, Walt Disney was (and remains) a remarkably similar object. Through his company's public relations, Disney performed and celebrated his commodified condition in a complex ritual of signification in which his values and behaviors appeared to pass from his person into his company's products via a somewhat mystical operation in which all of his hundreds of employees were invested with his spirit and in turn invested that spirit in their productive output. This operation began with the compulsive retelling of Disney's life story and continued in the equally repetitive revelation and celebration of the company's productive processes, which made it clear to Disney's audiences that Walt appeared regularly in every corner of the operation, investing, inspiring, adjusting, and controlling. Thus Walt Disney's personal attributes, his fading ethnicity and his class mobility, as well as his embodiment of industry, integrity, and deferred gratification, appeared fused into the company's media and material products and made available to the child as the added value it needed to marginally differentiate itself from its peers—as the culture revisited at its protocapitalist, nineteenth-century middle-American roots, untainted by twentieth-century rationalist excess, or by the complications of an emergent multicultural society.

Walt Disney's performance in his company's public relations was a masterpiece of signification. Rising from an amalgam of northern European ethnicities and a poverty the company chose to describe as "middle class," Disney enacted a passion of assimilation that flowed from virtues natural to his geographical origins in the American Midwest, manifesting the Weberian Protestant work ethic, which was merely the inherent quality that predestined him to be the epitome of middle-class sensibility. His entry into an industry coded as "ethnic" and "working class" by its detractors, and as representing the dregs of a decadent (southern and eastern) European civilization and East Coast cosmopolitanism, was presented as answering the call of the inventor (such as Thomas Edison or Henry Ford) rather than that of the showman or vaudevillian. His success was described as deriving not from the cynical manipulation of his audience, but from a combination of dogged determination and homespun genius. The company blurred the line between the man and his eponymous corporation, between the body of Walt Disney—who was driven to channel all of the profits from his films back into the operation—the factories that produced his films and ancillary products, and the films themselves. All became Walt (as Walt became them), and all became a celebration of a natural and uncompelled commodification, the performance of a humanity magnified by capitalism rather than diminished by it. The figure of Walt Disney performed the mastery of his own capital, the multiplication of that capital into myriad forms, and its distillation into media products for children.

In his gloss on Karl Marx's description of the function of the commodity in capitalist society, Pietz (1993, 141) characterizes the idea of commodity fetishism in Marx's writing as one in which the bourgeois capitalist treats capital as a fetish, one which "is believed by its deluded cultists to embody *(super)natural causal powers of value formation*, but which is recognized by the savage, expropriated through 'primitive accumulation,' and by the worker, exploited through the capitalist accumulation process proper, as having no real power outside its *social power to command* the labor activity of real individuals" (emphasis original). Marx's sarcasm aside, this was exactly the operation performed by Disney and its proponents. Walt Disney Productions recognized that the "social power to command the labor activity of real individuals" constituted a compelling performance in itself, and that the fetishistic performance of the multiplication of Walt's self in the persons and particulars of its industrial cinematic operation, right down to Mickey Mouse (for whom Walt had supplied the voice), appealed to an audience of equally "deluded cultists" who could witness the mystical operation by which Walt was multiplied and fragmented, only to become even more himself. The means by which Disney appeared to make his ideal qualities available to his audience were, ironically, derived from the very industry from which his company sought to differentiate itself. Suggesting that the inferior class and ethnic positions of Hollywood producers could actually pollute susceptible middle-class audiences (of children) with their values, proponents of the idea of movie effects had for some time established the idea that the person of the producer could infect the consumer in the act of consumption. If this were true, so was its obverse: children just as easily equally consume the good as the bad. Walt Disney's enactment of essential American-ness, and of commodification mastered and transformed into capital, thus entered the system as an inoculant by the same route as the contagion it was designed to dispel.

Both Disney and the generic American child, then, represent an effort to embody the ideal qualities of a democratic capitalist culture, a fantasy through which contradictions in the social and material relations of a given moment are resolved by the reinscription of those relations in a hiatus between a determining past and an indeterminate future. Disney and the child represent the moment at which American culture is apprehended and worked upon before it rushes on into an ideal future that never arrives. Whether Disney understood this when it designed the public-relations narrative it has enacted for over seventy years matters less than how Walt Disney and the child express a common understanding of the metaphysics of personhood in a capitalist society.

Agency

> *The real inculcation of voluntary acceptance of capitalism occurs not so much through the ideological indoctrination of the means of communication, as in the invisible diffusion of commodity fetishism through the market of the instinctual habits of submission induced by the work-routines of factories and offices. . . . Yet whether the primary emphasis is given to the effect of cultural or economic apparatuses, the analytic conclusion is the same. It is the strategic nexus of civil society which is believed to maintain capitalist hegemony within a political democracy, whose State institutions do not directly debar or repress the masses. The system is maintained by consent, not coercion.*
>
> —P. ANDERSON 1977, 27

Once one accepts that there exists no solid body of evidence to support the notion of media effects—or at the very least that there is no proof of media effects of the order that are suggested in the news media during times of national tragedy—one is left with a number of questions. Why it is that these discourses have remained so durable, and why do they continue to evoke such affect? How, in the absence of conclusive evidence, can we lay the blame for schoolyard massacres at the feet of musicians, filmmakers, or computer programmers? How do people circulate widely popular arguments that Walt Disney Productions plays a significant role in shaping the minds and values of children? If one believes the Christian Right, Disney is seducing children into godless liberalism through the allure of immoral sexual practices subliminally encoded into its cartoons. If one believes a wide range of leftist social critics, the company is training children (and adults) to become mindless walking advertisements who understand citizenship (local, national, or global) only in terms of consumption. The comfort in such constructions of social relations is that they generate regimes of agency: if media producers are responsible for inducing excessive violence or sexuality in children, then regulating their production will limit the expression of those excesses in children. If the lifelong behavioral profiles of persons are indeed set through their childhood consumption habits, then regulating that consumption becomes an effective means of distributing the labor of changing society across an extended network of semi-autonomous production units (families). What seems diffuse, unmanageable, and threatening becomes localized and manageable.

If, however, the assumptions underpinning this model of social action are unsupported by hard data of a direct causal relationship, then one is left with the task of suggesting a more reasonable explanation. Most often the social critic (of any stripe) resorts to an argument of mystification. The real social relations are merely masked by a layer of false consciousness that needs only to be stripped away to reveal the delusional quality of life under its regime. This is often the implicit idea behind arguments for "social construction"—that there is a place outside of ideology in which true social relations obtain. What I have attempted to demonstrate here is that the social construction of a generic American child susceptible to media effects persists not merely because of the investment of a variety of institutions and individuals in its verity, not merely because it provides an illusion of (eventual) personal control over large and impersonal social forces, but because it speaks very directly to understandings of personhood and agency in a democratic capitalist society. Were these understandings not widely accepted as describing real life, no amount of cynical manipulation on the part of global concerns such as Disney could sway the population to believe them. As Lloyd and Thomas (1998, 19) put it, "Hegemony depends exactly, not on direct control (domination), but on dispersion. It is not a mode of mystification, producing not 'false consciousness' as opposed to scientific and political knowledge, but a disseminated form of self-evidence or 'common sense' that regulates subjects across differentiated domains of modern society."

The logical error in placing the blame (or credit) for social conditions at the foot of Disney, or Time Warner, or Fox, is that it presupposes a certain kind of intent (other than to dominate a market), and in doing so, imagines another form of purer intent outside of the rough-and-tumble of capitalist social and material relations. Bluntly put, it is the fantasy that there exists a benign regime of capital that will replace or correct the current inhumane regime, a gentler ontology for the next generation. It is born of a widely shared will to improve on society that finds its outlet in available forms of social action. As I have suggested, the child plays a crucial role in this fantasy precisely because it appears to exist, initially, outside of culture, hence outside of ideology, and appears able to keep that culture anchored in an evolutionary moral order and to bring adjustments to the social order through the perceptual and behavioral matrix it develops during the course of its development.

If we reveal this idea of agency as socially constructed, does this then doom us to a fatalistic acceptance of the contingent nature of social change, of its subjugation to a pervasive capitalist ontology? This continues to be a matter of productive debate in Marxist philosophy, media studies, critical legal theory, and feminist political and epistemological theory.[25] The answer would seem to be, yes and no. What is at stake seems to hinge, ultimately, on a sort of realpolitik: the attribution of "false consciousness" to an individual or group of individuals can easily constitute a negation of experience and of networks of affiliation. The stripping away of "mystification" that does not properly acknowledge the immediate value of the constructions revealed may also fail to give proper credit to the amount of labor invested in those constructions by individuals and social groups. For example, if one mounts a criticism of "family values" with the ultimate purpose of expanding the definition of "family" to include marginalized social formations, one ought to be prepared to address with sensitivity the incredible circulation of affect that occurs around the term for those who are most likely to use it uncritically. A set of values may be socially constructed, but that does not mean that it isn't fervently held.

This is certainly true in the case of the figure of the child. No matter how correct one is in pointing out the function of this figure in foreclosing or limiting the immediate claims of the working class, racial or ideological minorities, or women in political and social discourse, that truth may be easily swept aside in the intense affect that the figure of the child inspires. It does not matter whether or to what degree that affect has its source in natural disposition or ideological indoctrination. Thus, the purpose of this work is not to reveal how the social construction of the relationship between nature and culture embodied in the child masks a truer form of nature located elsewhere. Nor is it to reveal a "truer" Walt Disney lurking under the discursive production of the man by his eponymous company, his chroniclers, and his fans. Nor is it to suggest that merely revealing the social construction of nature in the child divests it of its ideological power. Rather, it is to suggest that, while some sort of relationship between nature and culture must always obtain in our understanding of the child, we may exert a limited and contingent, yet meaningful, agency in seeing all of the terms in the equation—"nature," "culture," and "the child"—not as fixed in some immutable order (such as evolution or predestination) but as open to interrogation and local interpretation.[26] In a case of nature versus nurture, for example, we would understand that, as important as the question of determining the causal weight of the two terms might be, of equal importance would be the question of why the two terms were presented as oppositional, and who that opposition might serve. In the case of media producers such as Walt Disney Productions, and of their semiautonomous creations (such as Walt Disney) it involves seeing them not as affecting a social fabric of which they are not a part, but as arising from and contributing to that fabric as (very powerful) nodes in the circulation of social and discursive formations. Media producers change social relations not through representations, but through business practices—such as by limiting access through monopoly practices to the means of producing media. This line of questioning does not attempt to answer whether children are permanently affected by media. Instead, it points to the social power that is lost by pegging social change on appeals for more humane business practices by media producers.

Finally, if we agree with Lloyd and Thomas (1998, 21) that "the subject of ideology is formed not in 'wholeness,' but in the displacement of its multiple possibilities," then we would also happily accept that there is no subject *except* through ideology, and that the displacement of possibility is necessary to that act of formation. But we would also accept that this displacement occurs by choice rather than by some sort of biocultural form of natural selection. Nature would no longer be available as an indulgence granted in the face of the necessity of social choice, and the child's life no longer an IOU written on the deferral of that choice. These are steps well worth taking, if only for the sake of the children.

Notes

Introduction

1 Perhaps these children did grow up on Disney, but if so, their apparent choice to turn away from it would merely confirm arguments about the pernicious effect of violent media for those who subscribe to them.

2 Disney does make media products that deal with sex and violence but does so under other labels, such as Touchstone and Hollywood Pictures. This fact isn't lost on conservative critics such as the Southern Baptist Convention, which organized a (largely failed) boycott of Disney to protest its gay-positive employment practices and its seeming promotion of sex and violence under its other names.

3 This is not to suggest that identities formed around class, race, or gender are devoid of social construction. This is exactly the point of Wendy Brown's (1993) argument, that the construction of an identity around the concept of rights (to be won from the state in contention with other identities) places one in a subordinate position that even in victory retains its clientist origins. While one can never claim total mastery over the construction of one's position in a liberal society, in this instance Brown is attempting to locate a means of understanding that position other than that of a "wounded identity" in need of redress.

4 There are some excellent histories of childhood that do explore the place of children in social systems. See, for instance Cunningham 1995 or Orme 2001 for recent work on the subject. On the twentieth-century United States, see Fass 1979 and Fass and Mason 2000.

5 One could argue that Rousseau's *Emile* (1762) marks the beginnings of the scientific study of childhood—an almost proto-behaviorism—as it posits raising a child in strictly controlled conditions to better regulate and shape its habits. Yet *Emile* was a thought experiment, not an actual one, and was in part written in response to Locke's *Some Thoughts Concerning the Education of Children* (1693), which built on Montaigne's "Concerning the Education of Children" (1580), which referred to Seneca, who pointed back to Aristotle and Plato. For a discussion of the role of classical thought in theories of childhood, see Cunningham 1995. For a discussion of child-rearing in ancient Greece, see Golden 1990, and in ancient Rome, Evans 1991. For a related discussion of pederasty as an educational tool, see Foucault 1988.

6 For a discussion of the rise of the child consumer, see Cook 2000a and 2000b. For

a discussion of children's media consumption during the period, see, for instance, Nasaw 1992 and 1993, or Fuller 1996.

7 For a discussion of the study of childhood in the Progressive Era, see Cravens 1985 and Hardyment 1983. See also Howard 2001 and LaRossa 1997.

8 See, for instance, Addams 1926 as an example of class-specific values naturalized in science and practice.

9 Child-rearing manuals have been a part of literate life in the United States since before the revolution, and many may be read as manuals for engendering middle-class behaviors. See Youcha 1995 or Wishy 1968. What I am concerned with here, however, is the rise of the child as a generic, natural object and the normalization of middle-class behaviors as natural human behaviors.

10 See, for instance, S. Turner and J. Turner 1990 and D. Ross 1991. Although similar efforts were made on the behalf of African Americans, these rarely extended to assimilation, a point that Gunnar Myrdal would make much of in his groundbreaking *An American Dilemma* (1944). For an example of a parallel sociology of African Americans, see Du Bois 1899.

11 Members of the Catholic Church were active in early efforts to reform and censor the movies, but it would not be until the promulgation of the Production Code in the 1930s that Catholics would play a leading role. See Maltby 1995 and Couvares 1996.

12 This operation is always gendered, and the strictures and benefits imposed upon the parent will vary according to the meanings assigned to "mother" and "father," "single mother" (the apposite term does not properly exist), and so on.

13 This piece in particular has provided a valuable template for developing the concept of the child as commodity. Although not directly related to the topic at hand, Mukerji's *Territorial Ambitions and the Gardens of Versailles* (1997b) also provides a model for understanding the material instanciation of historically specific social relations.

14 For a sharply critical discussion of Aries, see Pollock 1983; for a more generous and detailed discussion of the text, see Cunningham 1995. For another approach, see DeMause 1974. (For a discussion of the psychohistorical analysis of childhood, see chapter 5.) Other sources more closely related to the topic at hand are Ellen Seiter's *Sold Separately* (1993), a study of the relationship between arguments about media, consumption, and class construction in the United States; Carmen Luke's *Constructing the Child Viewer* (1990), a study of the discursive construction of children via arguments about the effects of television in the 1950s; and *In Front of the Children* (Bazalgette and Buckingham 1995), a collection of essays on children and media. See also Buckingham 2000. For an overview of discussions about childhood in the twentieth century from a cultural-studies perspective, see the collection *The Children's Culture Reader* (Jenkins 1998). For a work that examines the social, cultural, and historical underpinnings constructing the child's subjectivity in modern schooling, see Walkerdine's *The Mastery of Reason* (1988). This list is

meant to be representative of a rich and varied literature and is by no means exhaustive.

15 In many of these features the protagonist (whether human or animal) is usually assisted by a network of animal helpers. These creatures are drawn to the protagonist because of its inner qualities and act merely as extensions of its own abilities.

16 See Dysinger and Ruckmick 1933.

17 This arrangement was further complicated in the 1950s, when both popular and professional discourses of child-rearing positioned themselves in opposition to the management-oriented philosophies of the previous generation. For popular child-rearing periodicals and manuals, this sometimes meant the repudiation of the notion of one kind of expert and the valorization of another. See chapter 5.

18 See, for instance, Schickel 1968 or Giroux 1999 for examples of this critique in Disney.

19 "Discourse," de Certeau has suggested (1988, 13), "is doubtless a form of capital, invested in symbols; it can be transmitted, displaced, accrued, or lost." This was certainly the case with Disney, which, having invested heavily in associations between its founder and childhood, lost its way for almost twenty years following Walt's death. During the 1960s, however, the concepts of the generation gap and of the youth revolution complicated notions of the child as carrier of American culture and may have created discursive problems for Disney even if Walt had lived longer. These shifts in the meaning of childhood are outside of the scope of this investigation.

20 See Foucault 1972, 21–49.

21 For a succinct discussion of this shift, see Strathman 1984.

22 For a similar analysis of the social and economic functions of aesthetics and cultural consumption, see Bourdieu 1984. Obviously, this emphasis on the child as a vehicle of social change also forecloses on larger questions of whether the family is the most equitable and sensible basic unit of social organization—and upon the social claims of those who choose to organize their fundamental living functions in alternate social groups.

23 In attempting to chart large-scale epistemic shifts around the figure of the child, I am aware of the admonition Michel de Certeau offered in *The Writing of History* (1988, 28): "Attempts have been made to identify overall mentalities of periods of history, for example in the *Weltanshauung* in Max Weber . . . the scientific 'paradigm' in Thomas Kuhn's work, the 'unit idea' of A. O. Lovejoy, and so on. These standards of measure refer to what Lévi-Strauss called the society that is *thought* in opposition to the society that is *lived*. They tend to make coherences 'sanctioned' by a period spring forth—that is, the received coherences implied by what can be 'perceived' or 'thought' in a given time, the cultural systems that might provide the basis for periodization of temporal distinction." De Certeau goes on to warn his readers that such actions are inherently ideological, the imposition of an order through the act of interpretation that ultimately reveals more about the researcher

than the topic: "This approach declares that it is impossible to eliminate from the labor of historiography the ideologies that inform it. But in awarding them the place of an object, in isolating them from socioeconomic structures, or in supposing, furthermore, that 'ideas' function in the same fashion as these structures, parallel to them and on another level, the 'history of ideas' can only find in the form of an 'unconscious' this inconsistent reality in which it dreams of discovering *autonomous* coherence. What it manifests is in fact the unconscious of historians, or rather, that of the group to which they belong. The will to define history ideologically is the concern of a social elite" (28–29). If, as de Certeau argues, the will to define even a corner of history is "the concern of a social elite," then the production of a cultural history of childhood is even more so, for the child offers the fantasy of control over the future, over a history not yet written, and the attempt to isolate and explain that child ultimately derives from a desire to share in that control. At best, one can claim to alloy that desire with the will to distribute that control more broadly, to participate more knowingly in the democratic capitalist imaginary, the will of which is always to disappear.

Chapter 1 Disney Makes Disney

1 On Retlaw, see Lewis 1994.
2 For different analyses of the man and the corporation, compare Waller 1980, K. Merritt 1988, and Fjellman 1992.
3 See Crafton 1982 or Klein 1993 for a discussion of early animation.
4 Compare Schickel 1968 and Watts 1997 on Disney's biography.
5 See Forgacs 1992 for a discussion of early Disney business practices and childhood.
6 For example, Disney-licensed products provided $7 million in gross sales in 1933, for gross income of $300,000 to Disney, slightly less than what it earned on its films ("The Big Bad Wolf" 1934).
7 Compare Zelizer 1985, F. Gilbreth and Carey 1963, Watson 1928 on the sentimentalization of childhood.
8 See R. Sklar 1975 and Nasaw 1993. As Nasaw points out, after 1930 the regulation of the physical space of movie theaters (mainly by owners) continued only in the area of segregation. Since the 1920s, movie palaces had been touted as havens of democratic mixing (L. May 1980), even as African Americans were excluded or had their access limited and circumscribed. See also Regester 1996.
9 Many histories of the formative years of the movies focus on conditions in major metropolitan areas, particularly New York. For a discussion of the rise of movies outside of the New York metropolitan area, see Morey 1996. For an excellent discussion of exhibition practices in Pittsburgh, see Aronson 2002.
10 See Nasaw 1992 and 1993, Peiss 1986, Horne 2001, and Hansen 1991 for discussions of labor and entertainment.
11 For histories of early film censorship, see Czitrom 1996 and Couvares 1996. For a survey of early arguments about movie effects, see Luke 1990.

12 In 1915, the National Board of Censorship was made up of 125 representatives from a variety of civic organizations. It censored 167,000 feet of film in that year and made 1,197 changes to films (McConoughey 1915).

13 For a critical analysis of the study of early film audiences and exhibition practices, see R. Allen 1998.

14 See Koszarski 1990 and Wasko 1982. For a more detailed accounting of early distribution and exhibition practices, as well as attempts to regulate them, see, for instance, R. Allen 1980 and 1983, J. Allen 1983, Hollyman 1983, and Jowett 1983.

15 For an excellent discussion of the progressive cinema and working-class women, see Stamp 2004.

16 Strangely, the pamphlet did not list those films, although it did offer a list of producers who had "educational film" departments.

17 Although John Burnham (1977) suggests that the progressives, never a completely coherent movement, had their share of eugenicists, their overall tone was more cautious than that of hardened eugenics believers. Robert Park, for example, expressed both interest in and concern for blacks but adhered to the segregationalist thinking of the time (D. Ross 1991). In general, progressives argued for social policies that recognized both heredity and environment as factors in individual and social development. See Haraway 1989.

18 This is not to say that there could have been a system by which racial difference could have been swept away through the application of reason. Indeed that was, and has been, the progressive program. Rather, it is to suggest (with Omi and Winant [1994], as well as many others) that every program that attempts to ameliorate social conditions around race and ethnicity must in some fashion produce its own racial effects.

19 The "origins" of stars such as Valentino or Bara were, of course, open secrets with their fans, but the impulse to conform to divisions of ethnicity and whiteness operated nonetheless. The circulation of concepts of racial otherness and Americanness in the star system is too complex to be accurately summarized here. To be sure, there were "American" stars such as Mary Pickford and Douglas Fairbanks alongside the remade exotics, as there were "genuine" exotics such as Pola Negri. Ultimately, such distinctions tend to erase the production of ethnic, racial, and national boundaries that circulate through them. See, for instance, Hansen 1991, 245–68.

20 See Rogin 1996 or Lott 1993 for discussions of minstrelsy.

21 Compare Gabler 1988 and Maltby 1995 on anti-Semitism and the movies.

22 It is perfectly reasonable that Hollywood producers, who were after all businessmen, would tend to produce and distribute movies that looked favorably on capitalism and unfavorably on labor unrest. One need only consider the efforts of a number of producers to undermine Upton Sinclair's 1934 candidacy for governor of California for an example of conservative advocacy that played on issues of race and ethnicity for reasons relatively removed from ethnic or racial passing.

23 Moley's book, *The Hays Office* (1945), was less a disinterested history than a lauda-

tory retrospective designed as an argument for industry self-regulation over political censorship.

24 For an excellent discussion of *Photoplay*, and of moviegoing practices in the early part of the century, see Fuller 1996. For a discussion of female fans in the silent period, see Stamp 2000.

25 See Seiter 1993 on the use of children to regulate women's behavior.

26 It is important to note that both of these letters were written in response to contests that offered money for the best commentary of the month (both won $25), and as such were written to the imagined expectations of the editors. Far from discrediting their content, this detail indicates the willingness of fans to participate in arguments about movie effects and, more significantly, the availability and free circulation of the terms of that debate, in particular the idea that children in general (rather than the working-class and immigrant children of previous generations' debates) were susceptible to both positive and negative movie effects. As Richard Maltby put it (1995, 41), discussing the MPPDA's Production Code, "The institution of censorship in Hollywood was not primarily about controlling the content of movies at the level of forbidden words or actions or inhibiting the freedom of expression of individual producers. Rather, it was about the cultural function of entertainment and the possession of cultural power."

27 Besides these reasons, a number of reformers were concerned about industry distribution policies and their effects on the small exhibitor, particularly the practice of block booking, in which an exhibitor was required to accept a large lot of films regardless of their acceptability to the exhibitor or her audiences. Space does not permit a full treatment of this subject. See Maltby 1995 or Jowett, Jarvie, and Fuller 1996.

28 As Maltby (1995) points out, appealing to outside reviewers also placed the MPPDA in the position of bending to outside pressure to accommodate those groups, as in the case of its efforts to include members of the Episcopal Church who felt marginalized by the central role played by Catholic groups.

29 Compare Maltby 1995 and Moley 1945 for histories of the Code.

30 An undercurrent of anti-Semitism ran through much of the rhetoric produced around the regulation of the movies and seemed to suggest that one of the reasons that movies were potentially corrupting was racial (see Maltby 1995, Gabler 1988). For Disney, who was Protestant, this would further serve to distinguish him from other Hollywood producers as being more wholly "American."

31 See, for example, Adler 1937. For a discussion of struggles between historicism and empiricism in the social sciences of the early twentieth century, see D. Ross 1991 and J. Mills 1998. For a detailed history of the Payne Fund, see Jowett, Jarvie, and Fuller 1996.

32 This was the desired outcome for William Short, the primary instigator of the series, though not for W. W. Charters, the man behind the Motion Picture Research Council and the principal architect and coordinator of the studies. For a full history of the politics behind the studies, see Jowett, Jarvie, and Fuller 1996.

33 Although Forman uses psychoanalytic language in this passage, the overall tone of the series avoided Freudianism, which would not become widely popular in child-rearing until after World War II. See chapters 4 and 5.

34 Forman's tone would prove too much even for Short, who with Charters would work to tone down Forman's prose in *Our Movie Made Children* (1934) in the hopes of preserving a sense of scientific objectivity (Jowett, Jarvie, and Fuller 1996).

35 One study, *Movies, Delinquency, and Crime* (Blumer and Hauser 1933), focused on the effects movies had on delinquent children, but the purpose of the study was to determine if movies could be considered a significant factor in the development of *all* children's delinquency. The answer was yes.

36 In recruiting researchers for the studies, Short went to major child-study universities, including Yale, Iowa, Minnesota, and Columbia (Jowett, Jarvie, and Fuller 1996, 60). Each of these institutions maintained child-research laboratories. See chapter 2.

37 Correspondence filed in the United States National Archives indicates that although Grace Abbot, head of the federal Children's Bureau in the 1920s and 1930s, refused to officially become a member of the advisory board to the MPRC and Payne Fund studies, the bureau did recommend the studies to individuals and organizations interested in the relationship of children to the movies.

38 For a discussion of Renshaw and Miller, see Jowett, Jarvie, and Fuller 1996, 70, 348.

39 In *Motion Pictures and the Social Attitudes of Children* (Peterson and Thurstone 1933), Payne Fund investigators attempted to quantify changes in attitudes toward violence, crime, race, and war caused by movie-viewing. The researchers had students in public schools in the Chicago area fill out questionnaires detailing their feelings about certain social issues, showed films relating to those issues, then tested them again. In spite of a large and varied sample (comprising a range of Chicago-area schools), rigorous statistical analysis, and a plethora of tables, charts, and graphs, the authors concluded that there was a rather slight, though nonetheless demonstrable, effect on attitudes, which faded somewhat over time. And, although the effect reported in their data was so slight as to be criticized as negligible (see Adler 1937; Jowett, Jarvie, and Fuller 1996), they concluded that "the experiments we conducted show that motion pictures have definite, lasting effects on the social attitudes of children" (Peterson and Thurstone 1933, xv).

40 Indeed, Mark May was so uncertain about the meaning of the study's findings that he felt obligated to correct reporting by Forman and others that made the study appear to confirm movies' negative effects on children. In 1933, he wrote to the *Christian Science Monitor*: "I regret very much that the [New York] Times quotes only the aspect of our study which appears unfavorable to the movies. The entire study, as a matter of fact, reveals conditions which were about one-third unfavorable to the movies, about one-third favorable, and about one-third neutral. Our conclusion was that it is impossible to say from our data whether or not the movies are a causal factor in moral conditions, or whether or not they are a concomitant factor."

41 See Adler 1937; Moley 1938; Jowett, Jarvie, and Fuller 1996. Beyond encouraging results that reflected poorly on the movies, Short even went so far as to tell Blumer to avoid any positive results that could be used by the industry as public relations against the studies.

42 Jowett, Jarvie, and Fuller (1996, 91) suggest that overall, the studies cautiously suggested that any effects the movies had on children were filtered through the specific conditions in their social environments. While this may be true, the design of most of the studies, and their public presentation, attempted the obverse: to eliminate individual and local social conditions in the pursuit of broadly applicable data.

43 For industry reaction to the studies, see also Moley 1938 and *The Movies on Trial* (1936).

44 Although Jowett, Jarvie, and Fuller (1996, 107) suggest that Rorty was hostile to Forman's summary of the Payne Fund studies (for being too biased), his own articles in *Parents'* are remarkably similar to Forman's. The most discernible difference, perhaps, is in Rorty's relatively greater insistence on the potential of beneficial fare to positively influence children.

45 The MPPDA had taken up that suggestion a decade earlier, only to be accused of attempting to attract children to moviegoing. One may assume that the library in this case would have been collected by another party. William Short favored some sort of regulation of motion picture production outside of the purview of the industry; William Seabury, another of the studies' founders, wanted to bring an end to block-booking practices that forced exhibitors to take desirable and undesirable films alike; W. W. Charters, the coordinating investigator of the series, worked to further both his career and the discipline of educational research through the successful execution of the first large-scale examination of movie effects. And so on, for the investigators themselves.

46 Space does not permit a discussion of Disney's positioning and reception in international markets, which would require an examination of Disney's public relations in those markets, and of the social and cultural discourses into which those public relations campaigns fit.

Chapter 2 Making a Manageable Child

1 While the problem of urban poverty in the late nineteenth and early twentieth centuries extended well beyond the cities of the Northeast and Midwest, and beyond immigrants of European origin, most progressive efforts centered in these regions, and the intersection of race and class in the rhetoric generated around those efforts shaped national discourse on the issue. See also Roediger 1991 and Chambers 2000.

2 As Burnham (1977) has pointed out, the term *progressive* is somewhat vague, sometimes referring to politicians such as Teddy Roosevelt, at other times to reformers and social workers such as Jane Addams or Florence Kelly. Although the term is

unspecific, its use here refers throughout to individuals and collectives who espoused a social philosophy that dedicated its members to the improvement of social and material conditions of the poor through programs of practical support and moral and behavioral uplift. Underneath this philosophy operated a neo-Darwinist (if not Lamarckian) assumption that the evolution of the species was necessary to its survival, and that it was the duty of more advanced members of the race (the middle class) to bring along its less fortunate members, who would otherwise retard the species' necessary evolution. See Haller 1963, Bellomy 1984, and Bannister 1979.

3 This advertisement appears in the files of the N. W. Ayers collection in the archives of the National Museum of American History of the Smithsonian Institution. Although not explicitly dated, its location in the files indicates that it was produced sometime between 1935 and 1940.

4 *Youth in the Depression* actually held up the Soviet Union as a model of a nation providing meaningful instruction to its youth as part of a larger plan for its future, and suggested that the Civilian Conservation Corps (CCC) were a measure of like kind, in which a set of core values could be instilled in youth that would serve them, and the nation, in better times.

5 Here, I refer to the work of the Child Study Association and like groups, and not to the mental hygiene movement. For a detailed analysis of that movement, see Horn 1989.

6 See also Nasaw 1985 and 1992 and Macleod 1982 and 1983. Although girls also found associational groups to join in the early twentieth century, much of the public discourse focused on the socialization of boys, particularly because women did not receive the vote until the 1920s.

7 The description of the Protestant middle class as "white" unfortunately elides the complex interplay of racial and class discourses that linked class position with relative whiteness. This ruling class was white more by virtue of its class position than due to some absolute genetic condition. For a more detailed discussion of these issues, see Roediger 1991, Lott 1993, and Levine 1991.

8 Significant differences exist between the writings and work of progressive reformers such as Gilman, Addams, or Kelley, and the purpose of this work is not to suggest that this diverse group of thinkers and social activists was always in accord in either social theory or methods. However, there remain significant resonances in their address to their public audiences, a meeting and recirculation of common terms surrounding assimilation and Americanization.

9 For a discussion of progressive values and ideology, see O'Conner 2001, 39–54; Roediger 1991; Burnham 1977; and Hofstadter 1963.

10 Although progressive work marks a particularly stark example of the translation of ideology into practice, this analysis is not intended to disparage the hard work and sincere efforts of many progressive social workers. Settlement houses such as Hull House provided incredibly valuable services to poor families (particularly poor mothers), and the fact that this work stood in for more extensive state action,

or for a more radical redistribution of wealth and productive capital, should not diminish the real human good accomplished in those centers.

11 In short, the child was to develop a middle-class, Protestant interior self that would monitor the behavior of its working-class, social and material self. This idea prefigured the work of George Herbert Mead, which appeared in the decades that followed.

12 See Roosevelt 1895, 293–317; Haraway 1989; and Joas 1980. This attitude was by no means always logical. At the same time that they argued for American society as the pinnacle of human evolution, many middle-class progressives lionized European high culture as superior to American popular culture, and a necessary component in the education of American elites (see Levine 1991). Space does not permit a full discussion of this contradiction. For one approach to this question, see Sammond and Mukerji 2001.

13 See Youcha 1995, Appel 1971, and Bennett 1988. Such was the tenor of the time that Roosevelt, supposedly a moderate, could himself claim, "It is urgently necessary to check and regulate our immigration, by much more drastic laws than now exist; and this should be done both to keep out laborers who tend to depress the labor market, and to keep out races which do not assimilate readily with our own, and unworthy individuals of all races—not only criminals, idiots, and paupers, but anarchists" (Roosevelt 1895, 27). This mild program of eugenics—which focused on the genetic makeup of families and smaller collectives and avoided passing judgment on whole races—marked the progressive response to more severe nativist condemnations of whole nationalities and ethnic/racial groups (see Haller 1963 and Bellomy 1984).

14 For a similar argument about the transformative power of the United States, see Roosevelt 1927, quoted in Mink 1990, 104.

15 One wag (quoted in a 1912 child-rearing manual) responded to Boas's report with the observation, "The real deduction from all this work, if indeed it should be confirmed, is that it is easier to modify a bone than it is a brain" (F. A. Woods quoted in Swift 1912, 88).

16 While one might easily dismiss Gilman's, Ellwood's, or even Boas's statements as simply racist, such a quick dismissal today obscures the construction of race at the time. As George Stocking (1968) has pointed out, that seemingly liberal persons at the turn of the century should espouse apparently racist views is not a contradiction of their liberalism, but a facet of it. In each case, the author's expression of race indicated a teleology designed to correct the racial imbalance it constructed through its discourse.

17 See D. Ross 1991, Cravens 1985, Bellomy 1984, Burnham 1977, Stocking 1968, and Hofstadter 1963. Hamilton Cravens sees a more significant shift in philosophy and temperament from the era of progressive reformers to that of professional developmental theorists. While certainly there was a shift, much of the progressive values espoused by reformers were carried forward as developmental traits in the professional period.

18 One should also remark on a trend of the United States in the twentieth century to export unpleasant labor relations, such as child labor, to other countries.

19 As Geraldine Youcha reports (1995, 131–32), "The revolutionary idea that childhood was a sacred time, and that children had rights, formed the moral basis for a reform movement that gradually reduced the involvement of children in the labor force. . . . by the 1920s the number of children from ten to fourteen years old in nonagricultural jobs had dropped by two-thirds. . . . [But it was not until] 1938 and the Fair Labor Standards Act . . . that child labor was really outlawed nationwide." According to Youcha, when Roosevelt's NRA outlawed home labor, "the middle-class ideal of the sacred family with the father its sole support became the ideal for all Americans" (132). See also Zelizer 1985.

20 Zelizer describes the sacralization of childhood as the extension of Victorian-era sentimental depictions of childhood from the upper classes into the lower. The status of women also underwent a significant change at the turn of the century. Following the *Bradwell* (1873) and *Muller* (1908) Supreme Court decisions, women received special protections under the law predicated on bifurcation of their roles as mothers and workers. The domestic sphere became even more a protected realm of women and children, distinct from the public sphere where men operated. In this light, municipal reform efforts may be described as acts of domestication. Progressive feminists in the early 1900s played upon this, arguing that women were well-suited to participating in local and state government, which were more domestic, while men were suited to the more public role of federal and international governance (Mink 1990 and Jenson 1990).

21 For a discussion of eugenics, see Haller 1963. For discussions of "social Darwinism," see Bellomy 1984 and Bannister 1979.

22 For a history of late-nineteenth-century discussions on problems in the apprehension of sense and mental data in experimental psychology, see Cole 1996 and D. Ross 1991. Notions of discursive policing and disciplinary boundaries refer to Foucault 1980.

23 See Goddard 1919 as an example of the sometimes blurry line between eugenics and progressivism.

24 See Bannister 1979 and 1987, Haraway 1989, and Freeman 1983. Here, as elsewhere, I cite Freeman with trepidation. I concur with the genealogy he traces from Boas through Mead, which presumes the articulation of a theory of sociocultural evolution based on Darwinian theories of biological evolution. I do not agree with the sociobiological critique Freeman offers in rebuttal. The notion of "selfish genes" driving social policy is ultimately no more satisfying than an idea of somatic evolution generated through behavioral or cultural regulation.

25 For a survey of early child-study texts and researchers, see Wishy 1968.

26 Acknowledgments for the monograph thanked Wilhelm Wundt and William T. Preyer.

27 The idea of child as animal owes much to the celebrated Wild Boy of Aveyron, circa 1800 (Shattuck 1980, Newton 2002).

28 For a brief discussion of early attempts to quantify the child's development in the home, such as Anna Noyes's *How I Kept My Baby Well* (1913), see Beekman 1977, 126–28.

29 One may easily trace this idea back to Rousseau (1762), who in turn relies heavily upon Locke (1693 [1989]) and may reasonably be called the founder of modern child psychology. Yet while Rousseau, and every thinker before him back to Plato, based arguments for the regulation of childhood upon moral or philosophical considerations, the twentieth century was unique in its emphasis on the physiological and sociological underpinnings of enculturation.

30 As with "behavioral genetics" today, the tentative investigations and arguments of researchers, when themselves not implicated in larger reform programs, were often translated into popular arguments for social and political policies (for a contemporary example, see Herrnstein and Murray 1994).

31 This is not to say that Hall, or other progressives, completely eschewed eugenic arguments. At the time the belief persisted that eugenics were important for identifying sub- and abnormal children and removing them from the gene pool. Consider, for example, Hall's comments in a 1915 issue of *Woman's World*: "I do not wish to dwell here upon eugenics in any detail. Everyone knows that there are weeds in the human garden, and the many institutions for subnormal children are taking very diverse measures . . . to prevent the multiplication of degenerate families which are a burden to every community and state. . . . We must fully realize that the future of nations depends . . . upon their ability to produce healthy and abundant offspring. On this topic we already have innumerable special studies which have already laid down a great many very useful laws concerning the best age for effective parenthood, [and] the favorable and unfavorable race mixtures" (5).

32 For a discussion of the use of photography and cinema as devices in the regulation of criminals and the insane, see Gunning 1995.

33 Strangely, Gilbreth's publisher reissued *Living with Our Children*, her argument for efficiency in child-rearing, in 1951, when efficiency and management had been officially repudiated in child-rearing circles (see Strathman 1984), and she published a book on efficiency in housekeeping in 1954 (see chapter 3). While these books indicate Gilbreth's commitment to the cause of efficiency, they do not signal an ongoing public fascination with the topic. One may speculate that an increased interest in Gilbreth might have followed the popular biographical movie of her family life, *Cheaper by the Dozen* (Lang 1950).

34 Although Thom was a psychiatrist, he would not explore explicitly Freudian themes in his child-rearing texts until the mid-1930s, when the shift to Freudian approaches realized after World War II began.

35 As in the workplace, however, the state maintained at least marginal regulatory oversight over domestic relations (Gordon 1990).

36 *Parents'* exceeded its publisher's expectations from the beginning, selling 100,000 copies a month within its first year, and 500,000 copies a month several years later.

In 1929, the Rockefeller Memorial, as it withdrew support from child study, purchased stock in *Parents'* and donated it to Columbia, Yale, and the Universities of Minnesota and Iowa, thus further cementing the relationship between those institutions and the popular child-rearing media (Cravens 1985; 441, 451).

37 Seen in this light, progressive efforts toward assimilation form a part of a set of discursive operations dating to the early nineteenth century in which European ethnics were gradually drawn into the category of white, while blacks, Latinos, and Asians were excluded. See Lott 1993, Roediger 1991, and Omi and Winant 1994.

38 Space does not permit a discussion of radio-effects arguments. See Czitrom 1982 and Tuttle 1992.

39 The magazine also offered a group-study program with Lasch's article.

40 In 1935, for instance, the bureau replied to a parent, "We do not have for distribution any literature relating to motion pictures suitable for children. In the Parents Magazine each month there is a section entitled 'Family Movie Guide' which gives reliable appraisals of movies as to their suitability for adults, young folks and children" (Oppenheimer 1935). Records at the United States National Archive indicate a steady stream of correspondence between the bureau and *Parents'*. In 1936, when the magazine celebrated its tenth anniversary, it solicited and was gladly granted this endorsement from the bureau's director, Katherine Lenroot: "Each year it is more than ever clear that parents are eager for authoritative information and suggestions concerning the best that scientific developments and practical experience can offer regarding methods of caring for and training children. Evidence of this interest is the fact that the Children's Bureau publications for parents steadily rate among the Government's 'best sellers.' Another indication is the steadily growing circulation of Parents' Magazine, and its use as basis for systematic study throughout the year by groups devoted to child study" (Lenroot 1936).

41 In this Disney was no different from a number of other animation concerns, which, beginning around 1915, began to organize their operations on a Taylorist model (see Crafton 1982). What differentiated Disney was its willingness to celebrate this organization.

42 Initially, the departments were divided almost exclusively by gender, with men producing stories and drawings, and women inking, painting, bookkeeping, and doing domestic chores: "Not until a set of drawings is approved by Walt and the director does it go to the inking and painting department, where over 150 nimble-fingered girls trace the sketches" ("Mouse and Man" 1937, 20).

43 Consider also this description of Disney's facilities: "The creation of a cartoon film is purely mechanical. Two unchanging things form the foundation on which the film is built: The sixty-cycle electric impulse in the power line and the speed of the film through the projection machine, which is ninety feet a minute, or twenty-four frames, or pictures, a second. The story department prepares a work sheet. The picture shall be 630 feet long, showing seven minutes on the screen, which means that 10,080 composite cartoons must be created" (Churchill 1934, 21).

44 The public presentation of Disney's labor practices didn't necessarily jibe with the perceptions of its workers. Maltin (1980, 69) notes that by the late 1930s "short subjects became a specialty, and . . . there was very little cross-breeding of talent from the feature-film staff. The shorts had their own directors, animators, writers, and artists. 'Walt would get you into a position where the wheels were going smoothly where you were, and he was very reluctant to break up that situation,' one employee recalls. This caused some resentment among talented people who had the ambition to move on to other things, and it also created a caste system within the studio."

45 This is not to suggest that Addams or her colleagues disappeared in the late 1920s. Although they continued their important work, their discourse ceded its dominance to scientistic and abstract discourses about childhood in the popular sphere.

46 See Haber 1964, Beekman 1977, Cravens 1985, and Ladd-Taylor 1986.

47 See Becker 1982 or Baumann 2001 for a discussion of the film industry as a highly rationalized social organization.

48 See Farber 1942. Smoodin (1993, 125–29) reports that in 1943 Disney artists were referred to as "scientists." Not too much later, Disney would coin the term *imagineer* to describe the function of workers responsible for developing "animatronic" figures.

49 One might argue that cinema, animation, and scientific management share a common root in the works of Muybridge and Marey, both of whom analyzed work and play, and who de- and reanimated human and animal figures. What makes this work significant, however, is that Disney made a point of publicizing it as an indication of its commitment to reproducing reality in animation. Waller (1980, 57) points out that Disney was criticized by some reviewers who felt that the company was limiting the fantastic and highly plastic nature of animation through its focus on realism.

50 See Andrus 1928, Waller 1980.

51 The twentieth century has witnessed the rise of ever more refined diagnostic devices for the interpellation of individuals into hierarchies of intelligence, aptitude, and behavior, and these devices have been applied to ever larger portions of the population as the century has progressed. Developed at the turn of the century, the Stanford-Binet "IQ" test had been widely used since at least 1916. Standardized achievement tests appeared in the late 1930s, were consolidated during the 1940s, and the Educational Testing Service, provider of the Scholastic Aptitude Test, formed in 1947. Multiple-aptitude batteries began after World War II (Anastasi 1976).

52 Although the progressive paradigm was superseded by that of professionalism as the dominant trope for speaking about childhood, progressive ideas and programs continued to operate in social work, and public education. See, for instance, Dewey 1938.

Chapter 3 In Middletown

1 Strathman (1984, 6–8) notes that by the mid-1930s, a transition from management-oriented discourses of childrearing toward more humanistic, "child-centered" discourses was under way. This transition would not be complete until the World War II encounter with Nazi Germany and the cold war.

2 For discussions of the American consumer at the beginning of the twentieth century, see Strasser, McGovern, and Judt 1998; Ewen 1976 and 1988; Marchand 1985; Strasser 1989; and Fox and Lears 1983. For more general discussions of advertising and consumers, see Schudson 1984, Bronner 1989, and Tedlow 1990.

3 Graham (1997, 11–12) argues that one purpose of scientific management was the internalization of management by workers, and that the next and more difficult stage in this process was to encourage the same sort of internalization in consumers, by which they would find in efficiency the presence of an implicit management in their lives.

4 In *The Theory of the Leisure Class* (1899), Thorstein Veblen referred to this tendency as "invidious distinction," the compulsive need to compare one's self with others.

5 In regard to the public's willingness to yield information, Graham (1997, 539–66) suggests, "In tandem with the new consumer 'freedom' granted to women came a finer articulation of their family 'responsibilities' including the obligation to study the physical and psychological needs of themselves as well as other family members and to purchase those products and services that would meet those needs. . . . A dual responsibility for surveillance and confession . . . contributed toward the rise of a consumer society where middle-class women are politically free but economically quite predictable: without coercion or brainwashing, many now willingly buy virtually the same consumer goods and services as their neighbors in part to fulfill their responsibilities as wives and/or mothers."

6 This was not entirely accurate. See, for instance, George Kenngott's *The Record of a City: A Social Survey of Lowell Massachusetts* (1912).

7 See also *Middletown Families* (Caplow 1982), an attempt to reproduce the original study in the 1970s, and *Middletown Jews* (Rottenberg 1997), an oral history of Muncie's Jewish community. Also consider one of the originary texts of communication studies, *Personal Influence* (Katz and Lazarsfeld 1955), usually referred to as the "Decatur study."

8 The Lynds mentioned in particular the work of W. H. R. Rivers, Bronislaw Malinowski, William Ogburn, and Radcliffe Brown (Lynd and Lynd 1937, Hoover 1990).

9 Compare this to the introduction to Margaret Mead's *Coming of Age in Samoa* (1928), published one year before *Middletown*. See chapter 5.

10 One high-school student even contacted the researchers to correct an error in self-reporting: "One boy said, 'I think I answered one question wrong. I put "true" after "nine out of every ten boys and girls of high school age have petting parties," and I really don't believe its more than three out of four' " (Lynd and Lynd 1929, 138n).

11 At the beginning of *Middletown*, for instance, the authors declared, "Had this study sought simply to observe the institution of the home under extreme urban conditions, the recreational life of industrial workers, or any one of dozens of other special 'social problems,' a far more spectacular city than Middletown might readily have been found. But although it was its characteristic rather than its exceptional features which led to the selection of Middletown, no claim is made that it is a 'typical' city, and the findings of this study can, naturally, only with caution be applied to other cities or to American life in general" (Lynd and Lynd 1929, 9).

12 See Chase 1948 and Hoover 1990.

13 At least as far as the Jewish population was concerned, these demographics were accurate. Indiana in general, and Muncie in particular, had a lower percentage of Jews per capita than other states in the Midwest or nationally (Rottenberg 1997).

14 In a lengthy catalog of those truisms so widely accepted as to be almost subconscious, titled "The Middletown Spirit," the second volume included: "That people should have community spirit. . . . That 'American ways' are better than 'foreign ways.' . . . That most foreigners are 'inferior.' There is something to this Japanese menace. Let's have no argument about it, but just send those Japs back where they came from. . . . That Negroes are inferior. . . . That individual Jews may be all right but that as a race one doesn't care to mix too much with them" (Lynd and Lynd 1937, 401–8).

15 This choice followed a suggestion by John Dewey in an article titled "The American Intellectual Frontier" (1922) that because of its commitment to moderation, the Midwest represented the vanguard of American social and political thought.

16 Hoover (1990) suggests that *Middletown in Transition* is colored by Robert Lynd's reading of Marx during the late 1920s and early 1930s. In this light, allusions to the Middletown worker's isolation from immigrant workers and class consciousness may be read as ironic. However, the Lynds' possible intent is not reflected in either the popular reception of the work or the lack of direct class critique in the text itself.

17 Even contemporary socialists argued for the primacy of the middle class in determining America's future. In *Crisis of the Middle Class* (1935), Lewis Corey argued that the traditional middle class of small merchants and craftspeople was being superseded by a new middle class of corporate middle managers that undermined the "rugged individualism" essential to the transition from capitalism to socialism. The Lynds located that Capra-esque quality in the rapidly vanishing pastoral family, quoting F. Stuart Chapin's lionization of that family at length: "The family was an economic institution as well as a biological and affectional. It possessed recreational, educational, and protective, as well as economic functions . . . [and] afforded a place where boys learned their trade, and where girls were trained to be skilled housewives" (Chapin, quoted in Lynd and Lynd 1929, 176). See also Fisher 1936.

18 In *Middletown*, the Lynds indicated that the State Manual for Elementary Schools for 1921 directed history teachers to inform students that "the right of revolution

does not exist in America. . . . Americanism . . . emphatically means . . . that we have repudiated old European methods of settling domestic questions, and have evolved for ourselves machinery by which revolution as a method of changing our life is outgrown, abandoned, outlawed" (198).

19 Two decades later, explaining cultural evolution to a popular audience, Stuart Chase (1948, 68) would find that American culture even predated colonial settlement, claiming that "our own American culture . . . can be viewed as a continuum extending back unbroken through written history, through archeological time, through the unrecorded dark, to the very dawn of the race."

20 For earlier examples of scientific management applied to the home, particularly in relation to the design of domestic workspaces, see Frederick 1913 and 1920. Space does not permit a detailed discussion of the literature, and for argument's sake, Gilbreth's text is taken as representative. For a detailed and insightful discussion of Gilbreth's application of scientific management to the home, particularly to consumption, see Graham 1997, and see Gilbreth 1928.

21 Graham (1997, 22) reports that in 1927 Lillian Gilbreth "organized the Teachers College Conference on Homemaking for 240 New York homemakers and home economics students. . . . To prepare for the conference, Gilbreth studied a profile of the typical American home and family gleaned from the 1920 U.S. census. This gave her the basic information necessary for devising a series of questionnaires inquiring about women's aims in homemaking, their principal causes of difficulty and fatigue, family relationships, daily work schedules, and which organizations provided them with the most help in their daily work. . . . Over the course of eight weekly meetings, participants became accustomed to filling out surveys and taking psychological tests."

22 Not surprisingly, 61 percent of the "business class" and 51 percent of the working class scored in the "normal" category in the test, placing Middletown's white children solidly in the mean for intelligence.

23 See, for instance, Lerner's (1958) argument for the disadvantages of traditional society to regulated social organization.

24 By the late 1930s, the Lynds informed their readers that "as this is being written, the Federal Bureau of Labor Statistics is making an elaborate study of family income and expenditure on all income levels in Middletown as part of a series of comparable studies in all sections of the country. When these materials are available one will have a better basis than ever before for appraising the balance of income and possessions in Middletown families" (Lynd and Lynd 1937, 62n).

25 It would be a mistake to imagine that the Lynds were reporting a social fact. As other parts of both texts reveal, local social and governmental institutions remained healthy and active during the Depression. Yet the popularity of the texts, particularly the first, and the willingness for a variety of different organs and persons to accept them as accurate, would argue that this conception of social life carried a significant amount of popular weight.

26 See Anastasi 1976, Lunbeck 1994, and Pfister and Schnog 1997.

27 Graham (1997) reports that Herbert Hoover actually worked with Lillian Gilbreth during the early years of the Depression to encourage efficiency in the home as a means of encouraging consumption, hence production.

28 For a discussion of progressive feminist arguments that the domestic environment, school, and local government were homologous entities and ought to be in the control of women, see Hayden 1981.

29 For a discussion of the relationship of scientific management to progressive uplift, see Haber 1964.

30 For historical perspective on the relationship between habit training and social harmony, see Locke 1693.

31 The Lynds seemed unaware that *The Care and Feeding of Infants* was itself written in 1894. They did, however, list more recent texts, such as Hardy Clark's *A System of Character Training for Children* (1923).

32 See Stearns 2003 for a discussion of parental anxiety.

33 Even in the 1930s, the Lynds reported, children were more likely than adults to experience class mixing in the movies: "Middletown is probably representative of other localities in the fact that, especially in the better class houses, adult females predominate heavily in the audiences and, as one producer remarked, 'set the type of picture that will "go."' In one of Middletown's better theaters, the audiences during the depression are estimated . . . to have consisted of 60 per cent women over sixteen, 30 per cent males over sixteen, and 10 per cent children. The Middletown theater specializing in 'thrill stuff for the farmers and working class,' according to a local exhibitor, 'draws mostly children'" (Lynd and Lynd 1937, 261n).

34 Maltby (1995, 63) also points out that the MPPDA used the classics to convert appeasement into demand: "The MPPDA's long-term policy of co-operation with teachers' organizations as a way to 'improve the quality of demand' came to fruition in the 1934–35 production season, with the regular use of study guides sponsored by the National Council of Teachers of English. The guides became a regular attachment to the prestige productions of 1934–35 and subsequent seasons; they were widely circulated, with print runs of several hundred thousand." Twenty years later, Disney would use teachers' guides to weave its television programs into daily scholastic and domestic practices; see chapter 6.

35 Disney claims the club had as many as five hundred chapters, with at least a million members.

36 In one issue, Disney announced, "Last month I said I would award MICKEY MOUSE WATCHES to the six boys and girls who sent in the best drawings, poems or compositions about milk. Well, I never dreamed we'd get so MANY! *Thousands* came in!" (Disney 1933–34).

37 See deCordova 1983 for a discussion of the MPPDA and children's matinees.

38 See Lynd and Lynd 1929, 268–69.

39 For Benjamin's musings on Mickey Mouse, see Benjamin 1931.

40 In *The Human Problems of an Industrial Civilization* (1933, 130), Mayo invoked Plant's

study of a New York suburb, which described how children raised in an unstable and under-regulated community suffered from its lack of planning, arguing that "in a surrounding such as this, one cannot expect children to grow up with the same capacity of self control, as children brought up in an environment of greater stability and more obvious collaborative function."

41 In the conclusion to *The Home-Maker and Her Job*, for instance, Gilbreth cautioned her middle-class readers that the application of scientific management principles to the home and child did not require the imposition of draconian regimes. "There is no hard-and-fast behavior pattern here outlined that can be pressed ruthlessly down on a child," Gilbreth warned (1927, 151–52). "We do not want Mary to be like Ethel or Johnny or even like our ideal of a perfect child. We want her to be the best that is in her, and to have every chance to use her likenesses to others to help her work better with them, and her differences to make her more interesting and worth working with herself."

42 See Merritt and Kaufman 1993 on Disney's Alice shorts.

43 This scene prefigured Disney's *Victory Through Airpower* (1943), as did the final scene in which Dumbo became a dive-bomber.

44 Disney would repeat this form of compression in its True-Life Adventure series. See chapters 5 and 6.

45 The casual mention of psychoanalysis points to the shift in popular discourse away from behaviorism and toward more individualized and "human" regimes in child-rearing specifically and popular psychology generally. See Strathman 1984.

46 Disney also received a Silver Medal of Honor from the Pennsylvania Women's Society for the Prevention of Cruelty to Animals in February 1943.

47 See note 51 to chapter 2 above.

48 In spite of this disclaimer, the author cites a range of authorities on child development and favors Buhler and Piaget.

49 See Piaget 1928.

50 Estimates by Disney and by journalists at the time place the amount of the company's output that was directly war-related at between 70 and 90 percent. See Disney 1944, Wanger 1943, Lewis 1994.

51 See also Homan 1944.

52 Dixon's book (1942, 18) also discussed at length the management of human difference and racial tolerance as necessary to the future of world peace, arguing, "We must keep in mind that every time his toy gun kills a Jap or his submarine sinks a Nazi boat he has deepened in his character by way of his muscles and his ears and his eyes and his sharp heart beat and his quick breathing that the surest way out of difficulty is to destroy the thing you fear. . . . In twenty years he will make a good soldier for a Third World War. And so will millions of other children, both white and black and yellow." As part of this discourse, Dixon reproduced a version of the black child disturbingly similar to that of Gilman, as closer to nature, hence more resilient.

Chapter 4 America's True-Life Adventure

1 In November 1953, *Film Daily* reported that *The Living Desert* broke the record for the most business in one week at New York's Sutton Theater ("$23,402").

2 This reasoning had operated during the Depression as well. See chapter 3.

3 See Foner 1980, 360–94; Herman 1995, 48–81; Gatlin 1987, 1–49 for a discussion of women and regulation in the 1930s and 1940s.

4 As early as 1910, advertising agencies such as N. W. Ayer and J. Walter Thompson were making tentative steps toward developing demographic techniques (McGovern 1993). By the teens, magazines such as *Photoplay* were describing their target audiences to advertisers, promising the delivery of a guaranteed market segment whose tastes had been sounded out by the magazine's staff (Fuller 1996). In the 1920s and 1930s, the relationship between the media, advertisers, and consumers began to formalize, and trade publications such as *Printers' Ink* were soon running ads that described to manufacturers the habits and tastes of young boys and girls in great detail ("Importance of Youth Market" 1947). Data on everyday consumption practices did more than reveal patterns of social behavior; they were useful for developing strategies for influencing those behaviors on a long-term basis.

5 Like a crass version of Rousseau, marketers considered the child a tabula rasa upon which desires to consume could be written: "Just look at youth! No established pattern. No backlog of items. . . . Youth, from the time he is carried proudly down the hospital steps to the time he marries and renews the cycle, is the greatest growing force in the community. His physical needs alone constitute a continuing and growing requirement in food, clothes, entertainment, etc. It has definitely been established that because he is open-minded and desires to learn, he is often the first to accept new and forward-looking products" (E. Gilbert 1957, 4).

6 Ultimately, self-reporting could provide only retrospective information: that which children had seen, had liked, had bought at the time they were surveyed. And, as time went on, the possibility arose that children could become *too* familiar with survey techniques and could develop "a tendency to give to researchers querying young people about their product preferences all kinds of twisted answers. . . [such as] . . . exactly the answer they thought the interviewers wanted to hear . . . [and] . . . an extreme of what the interviewer did not want to hear" (E. Gilbert 1957, vii). As they grew up, children became aware of their value as observational subjects and became potentially less useful as either sources of marketing data or as a means of influencing the habits of the domestic economy. Eugene Gilbert's book, *Advertising and Marketing to Young People*, was about how to overcome youth resistance to market analysis and was devoted to a psychological understanding of childhood, for which he relied heavily upon Gesell.

7 While it may have seemed to men in the new postwar middle class that American society had suddenly become extremely self-reflexive, for the working classes and immigrants, and for middle-class women and children, this had been true for

quite some time. From before the turn of the century, immigrants and members of the urban working class had been the objects of probing questions and observing gazes by settlement workers, social workers, industrial psychologists, and sociologists, all of whom, for various reasons, needed to understand the means by which the lives of poorer folk were conducted. Children in particular had been the objects of observation for quite some time.

8 For discussions of scientific management and labor, see Lipsitz 1981, 87–99; Montgomery 1987; and Whyte 1956.

9 For a discussion of the rise of market research, see Lears 1994, particularly 211 and 244.

10 See Wrong 1956.

11 The final True-Life Adventure, *Jungle Cat*, appeared in 1960. See Smith 1996, 3, 542.

12 The score for *White Wilderness* was written by Oliver Wallace, who began scoring for Disney in 1936, and who may then be said to be responsible for the company's practice of "Mickey Mousing," the literal syncing of beats in the music to actions on the screen. The score was conducted by Clifford Vaughan, a composer and conductor with credits for many movie westerns.

13 Both the development of the interstate highway system and the introduction of television played a role in the disruption of urban social networks and the isolation of an emerging white middle class from other ethnic and racial groups. Space does not permit a detailed discussion of the negative consequences of these changes. See, for instance, Lipsitz 1981, 1995.

14 First published in *Diogenes* magazine in 1953, the essay was later collected in the volume *Mass Culture* in 1957 and reissued in MacDonald's own collected essays, *Against the American Grain*, in 1962.

15 For a discussion of the emergence of the high art/mass art split, see Levine 1991.

16 For discussions of the intellectual pedigree of "A Theory of Mass Culture," see Seaton 1996 and Wreszin 1994.

17 While it could be argued that *Diogenes* did not have a mass middle-class circulation and would be a poor place to locate exhortations to that class, MacDonald's work, like that of several other influential scholars of the period (see Erikson 1961), began in *Diogenes* but quickly gained currency in intellectual and then popular discourses.

18 This work was one part in a trilogy of treatises on the relation of industrial psychology to larger social organization; the other works are Mayo 1945 and 1947. Space does not permit a detailed discussion of the apparent anti-Semitism in Mayo's description of Freud, nor of his confusing use of Piaget (1928) in modeling workplace relations as derivative of both child development and larger sociohistorical phenomena (see Mayo 1933, 152–58). Further analysis of Mayo would discuss his use of a study of female workers, psychoanalysis, and developmental psychology to make claims about a worker that he genders male in his broader theoretical discussion. The link between feminization and infantilization—so consistent in the history

of childhood—may relate to organized labor's rejection of human relations. As William Whyte points out in his critique of Mayo (see 1956, 33–38), resistance by industrial unions following World War II to management intervention into the lives of workers sharply curtailed the application of "human relations" to the rank and file. Instead, industrial psychology increasingly focused on the lives of middle management.

19 Both Bryson and Mayo had links to Lillian Gilbreth (see chapter 3). From the late 1920s, all three were involved, severally and together, in projects to join consumption, production, and the domestic to produce more social harmony. Gilbreth worked with Bryson to promote rationales of efficient consumption and domestic management in the 1920s and early 1930s. She worked with Mayo on the issue of humanizing industrial management, and of integrating domestic and industrial life. See also Bryson 1939.

20 One could certainly place this trend in the larger frame of "American exceptionalism" that extends back at least as far as Tocqueville (1835, 1840) and Crèvecoeur (1782). For a discussion of the range of character studies, see Wilkinson 1988. Although each of these works offers a fascinating glimpse into midcentury understandings of ideal social and material relations, and of ideal American character, and although there are important institutional and theoretical links between a number of the authors, space permits an analysis of only a few of these works, specifically those that garnered significant popular exposure and reviews.

21 Implicit in Mead's argument was a notion that parents could call upon dormant qualities in American character such as thrift and self-reliance, that had developed in earlier moments of the culture's formation. This argument both recapitulated progressive assumptions that nineteenth-century white Protestant values marked the American culture into which immigrants were to assimilate, and both Riesman's and Whyte's invocations of the Protestant ethic in confronting excessive conformity in 1950s culture. See below.

22 Although Gorer described the American character as male, he identified an "American conscience" that was inherently female (1948, 56–69). This conscience operated to regulate that character through its civic institutions, which were controlled by increasingly powerful women's groups.

23 Although the whole of the American people is taken up with this psychoanalytic explanation, see particularly Gorer 1948, 23–69.

24 The student of the social theory of the period may be surprised at the absence of key texts such as *The Authoritarian Personality* (Adorno et al., 1950), Horkheimer and Adorno's *The Dialectic of Enlightenment* (1944), or the works of C. Wright Mills. To a certain extent, the influence of Fromm and the Frankfurt School will be addressed in chapters 5 and 6. Mills does not appear more prominently here because the hostility to his work outside of critical left circles requires a discussion beyond the scope of this work.

25 While *Individualism Reconsidered* (Riesman 1954) offered a more nuanced and thoughtful deliberation on the terms set out in *The Lonely Crowd*, it did not re-

fute its key positions and is treated here as roughly contiguous with the earlier work.

26 Although the Reader's Subscription Book Club's subscription rolls peaked at 40,000, it provided a valuable point of dissemination for *The Lonely Crowd*. If *Middletown* had its greatest impact with the middle class of the metropolitan east coast, *The Lonely Crowd* approached a metropolitanism developing in other parts of the country. As such, it might prove an interesting case study in relation to Katz and Lazarsfeld's "opinion leader" theory (compare Rubin 1992, Menand 2001).

27 While not as specifically Freudian in his approach as was Gorer, Riesman relied heavily upon Freudian theory, and upon the work of Erich Fromm (who had analyzed him) and Erik Erikson, to model the individual in its relation to society (Riesman 1950, 3–11).

28 For a contemporary discussion of mobility and capitalist development, see Lerner 1958.

29 The elaboration of his first model was based on a wide variety of works, including the biometrician Raymond Pearl, Malthus, and more contemporary demographic theorists (Riesman, Denny, and Glazer 1961, 420–21).

30 See Lipset and Lowenthal 1961 and Riesman, Denny, and Glazer 1961, 420–43.

31 Compare Riesman to Whyte 1956 and Tyler May 1988.

32 See Riesman 1954, 32, 94–98, 414–25.

33 See also Riesman, Denney, and Glazer 1950, 304, and Riesman 1954, 187.

34 Compare to Riesman and Glazer 1961, 423–28.

35 Riesman's formulation avoided a common popular trope, particularly but not exclusively in the South, that linked civil rights organizing to communist subversion.

36 To some extent, this gloss simplifies the differences between *The Lonely Crowd* and *Individualism Reconsidered*. In the latter, Riesman made a concerted effort to distinguish between critiques of Nazi Germany and those of the Soviet Union, and to critique the elitist tendencies of social-engineering advocates such as Elton Mayo.

37 See Lipset and Lowenthal 1961.

38 This idea builds on Lazarsfeld's and Merton's notion of "opinion leaders" (cf. Riesman 1950, 77n).

39 See also Riesman 1954, 183–93.

40 Compare Riesman's discussion of individualism to that of Bryson 1952.

41 Here, I compress a complex discussion of the relationship between adjustment, autonomy, and anomie, which attempts to apply Durkheim's concept of the *anomique*, and which, although intellectually dense and interesting, is somewhat tangential to the points made here (see Riesman 1950, 286–306).

42 Following the war, many high schools offered educational film programs that featured not only movies on hygiene and rudimentary sex education, but works on social integration. In films such as *Shy Guy* (Coronet Instructional Films, 1947), students were offered narratives of belonging on which they could model their own behavior, further adjusting to group norms and "fitting in." The Prelinger Archives (www.archive.org) maintains an extensive catalogue of these films.

43 On a grander (and somewhat stranger) scale—and speaking more to the central role that consumption played in the enculturation of 1950s children—Riesman imagined an "everyday world's fair" for children at which producers, advertisers, and market researchers would come together to create a sort of consumption camp where children could practice buying luxury items. The camp would provide market researchers with free data, while encouraging each child to explore its personal tastes, "released from ethnic and class and peer group limitations" (1950, 338–40). In this fantasy of beneficial consumption, children would somehow discover those tastes that derived from their own desires and impulses, not from status pressures and preconceived models of who they should be. From this more autonomous mode of consumption, perhaps, would spring a more autonomous individual, a leader rather than a follower.

44 This was a double-bind: to encourage autonomous behavior in others required yet another level of self-observation, and of self-evaluation, if one was to determine if one (or one's children) were actually breaking off from the herd or merely following instructions.

45 See Rosenberg and White 1971, Tyler May 1988, and Marling 1994.

46 A reviewer in *The Reporter* described Whyte's book as "a serious study of the contrasts between American assumptions about ourselves handed down from yesteryear and our realities today." He concluded his positive review by urging everyone to memorize the appendix in which Whyte outlined how to cheat on personality tests, suggesting, "If enough of us memorize these points, and also don't do something foolish such as painting our garage doors an antisocial color, we may yet frustrate our American collectivizers" (E. Edwards 1956, 35–37).

47 In 1945, the birth rate was 2.7 million per year. By 1956, it was over 4 million per year. While urban populations increased by 14 percent, outlying suburban areas increased by 47 percent (Gould 1956, 50–51; see also "Suburbia" 1957).

48 It is perhaps no accident that the term *filarchy* recalls Freud's "His Majesty the Baby" (Freud 1914, 72; see conclusion). The concept referred to projected parental expectations that the child would achieve those things the parent could not. In this way, the idea of the child as placeholder of future social and material relations became naturalized as a component of bourgeois psycho-social development.

49 Given the current emphasis in public schooling on aptitudes necessary for gainful employment, and the evacuation or elimination of discussions of the rights and responsibilities of citizenship (often portrayed as an incursion into the regulatory rights of parents), one might reasonably ask whether Whyte neglected to consider the importance of this sort of socialization in the maintenance of a democratic society.

50 Rather than treating schools as social institutions mandated by state or federal law, thus as an extension of a set of nationalizing operations, Whyte focuses on their local aspect. He describes them as mandated by school boards, funded by local appropriations, and directed by the PTA. This would, of course, become part

of his perceived national middle class as it networked with other school systems and hired professionals (see Whyte 1956, 391).

51 For example, Whyte quoted and critically analyzed one executive's claim that "I generally warn the younger men . . . of this danger of their wives not keeping up with them. I suggest to them that they encourage their wives to join things, to play golf, to go on business trips with them occasionally." Whyte noted that "many have been grateful for the advice" (1951b, 210).

52 Thomas Frank (1997) raises a similar point, arguing that the very notion of rebellion (which was to arise, in part, from the growing public awareness of and concern with conformity) was popularized by the advertising industry. While Frank tends follow his Frankfurt School predecessors by slighting local cultural practices in favor of the political economy of the culture industry, his analysis offers an important recontextualization of the ideas of conformity and rebellion.

53 Compare Packard 1959, Goodman 1960, and Frank 1997 on the notion of a Social Ethic for tropes of science in postwar material culture.

54 See, for instance, Tyler May 1988, Marling 1994, and Spigel 1992.

55 Although Disney would refine its process slightly by the mid-1950s, on the whole it kept its questions vague, asking only how different staff members liked or disliked different segments.

56 One could hardly expect that parents could find in the buffoonish and ineffective adult figures in Disney's animated features a personality with which they could identify. While this explanation of the affective hook of these films is speculative, it avoids the fallacy of effects arguments, which would view as more accurate the self-reports of adult viewers than a correlation between plot, public relations, and consumption. For a discussion of the problems of mobilizing self-reporting in the construction of a historical record, see, for instance, Scott 1992.

57 See Merton 1946.

58 Compare Bernays 1952 and Ewen 1976 and 1996 on the social role of marketing.

59 This became physically true with the opening of Disneyland in 1955.

60 See also Mitman 1999 or Chris forthcoming.

61 See, for example, Wylie 1954 for a fictional account of 1950's suburban civil defense.

Chapter 5 Raising the Natural Child

1 Disney's restructuring and diversification during and after the war flowed out of necessity, as did the company's move into nature documentaries. "To speed up production," *Business Week* informed its readers in 1955, "Disney experimented with combination live action and cartoons, and in 1949 [*sic*] started his True Life Adventure series" ("The Mouse That Turned to Gold" 72). The first seven of these were half-hour opening shorts, but in 1953 Disney began producing full-length nature features with *The Living Desert*, which the magazine touted as "rivaling Gone With the Wind at European box offices, and [making] as much money, at less cost,

as any of Disney's cartoons" (72). Roy Disney—Walt's brother and the president of the company—explained to Disney's shareholders that its plan to restructure production around "a variety of short subjects and special material, three basic kinds of feature-length pictures—All Cartoon, Live Action and Nature Pictures" would free the company from the risk of relying on "a few high-cost, all-cartoon features" (Walt Disney Productions 1954a, 5).

2 According to Disney archivist Dave Smith, the company began using demographic techniques in the 1940s. Where other producers used Gallup's Audience Research Institute (ARI) to preview films, Disney conducted this work in-house for fear of giving away trade secrets or story lines, but referred to its survey work as "ARIS" (personal conversation, 1996). In the 1950s, the company would "preview" its nature films with school boards and museum societies, but this was done more to promote essentially finished work than to gain input.

3 Disney made no Mickey Mouse movies between 1942 and 1947; it made two a year from 1948 to 1953, with the exception of 1950, then did not make another until 1983.

4 Spock also sat on the advisory board for *Parents' Magazine*.

5 See M. Mead 1955, 3–18; Maier 1998; see also Wilkinson 1988 and Foerstel and Gilliam 1992.

6 Although the reading of Mead I offer here is fairly critical, particularly regarding her perhaps unintended role in reinforcing profoundly damaging norms of gender and sexuality, and in her valorization of the white middle class in that process, in no way do I wish to diminish the very real and valuable contributions that she made to the study of anthropology and to liberal social discourse in general. Mead and Benedict both advanced the validity of the study of women in culture, and Mead in particular continued the project begun by Boas and continued by Benedict, arguing persuasively for the importance of respecting cultural difference in American liberal discourse.

7 For a discussion of the literary conceits employed in this anthropological moment, see Clifford 1986a and 1986b. For a broader discussion of the function of othering in American anthropology, see Marcus and Fischer 1986.

8 The figure of the child as a natural creature in modern thought dates back at least as far as Rousseau (1762) and is present in Darwin's (1840) study of his own infant son. See Jenkins 1998. The specific importance of the idea here is that it occurs in reaction to behaviorism's version of the child as primitive organism, and in that it is articulated as part of a larger project of aligning child-rearing with national well-being.

9 The book contained essays by Mead, Erik Erikson, David Riesman, and others. The institutional network mentioned in its acknowledgments is worth noting: "This book grew out of Columbia University Research in Contemporary Cultures, inaugurated by Ruth Benedict in 1947; it also includes research done under the American Museum of Natural History Studies in Contemporary Culture. Both of these projects were conducted under grants from the Human Resources Division of the Office of Naval Research" (M. Mead and Wolfenstein 1955, vii).

10 A corollary to the idea of child as ideological prophylactic was that children not properly raised would more easily fall victim to communist propaganda. In 1948, Harry Gideonse, president of Brooklyn College and a member of *Parents' Magazine*'s board of advisory editors warned that "thousands of boys and girls are being exposed to Communism every year in our schools and colleges, and a good many of them are catching the virus. . . . clever and unscrupulous Communists have infiltrated our educational system. . . . They are throwing everything they have into a drive to convert our young people to their doctrines because they know, as Hitler did, that if they can get our youth of today, they will have the nation tomorrow" (Gideonse 1948, 19).

11 There is an extensive literature on the history of concepts of nature, too broad and contested to be meaningfully discussed here. See, for instance, Merchant 1980 or Leiss 1994. For an approach to the topic more germane to this analysis, see Haraway 1989. Much of this literature is concerned with the relative meanings of "nature" and "culture" in the history of scientific knowledge and practice. My concern is in the working out of the relationship in popular science and culture.

12 See also Mead 1951b.

13 Although some of the excesses described may have occurred, Soviet developmental theory was not as monolithic as Mead and Calas described it. See, for instance, Wertsch 1985, Vygotsky 1978, or Bakhurst 1991. See also Bauer 1952 for a surprisingly even-handed cold-war-era analysis of Soviet psychology. If conditions in the Soviet Union were as Mead and Calas described them, it would by no means negate perceived or actual similarities in the United States, or American anxieties around them.

14 In this light, the frequent confusion of the term *mass society* with *mass culture* was a means of displacing anxieties about the development of a coordinated federal government/economy that appeared homologous to the Soviet Union through the assumption that the social, governmental, and cultural were autonomous but mutually determining realms.

15 For an example of this Cold War postcolonial struggle, see, for instance, Lerner 1958.

16 The transition between one paradigm and the next was best described in Gesell's later works (1940, Gesell and Ilg 1946)—in which he moderated gestures toward management with an acknowledgment of natural difference—and in Piaget 1953, all of which attempted to balance the idea of the child's individual development against normative parameters and timetables.

17 As early as 1941, five years before he published *The Pocket Book of Baby and Child Care* (Spock 1946), Spock wrote in *Parents'*: "A few decades ago we were fascinated by standards. A child of a certain age should weigh so much. Weaning to a cup should take place by such an age. We now see that each child has its own pattern of growth, intellectual and emotional as well as physical. The job of physicians and parents is to provide the child with care that is right for its own stage of development" ("Benjamin Spock, M.D." 1956, 109).

18 By 1956, the book had sold 70,000 hardcover copies and 3,247,588 paperbacks ("Bringing Up Baby on Books" 1956, 64).

19 Although the father was also encouraged to observe his children's behaviors, the mother (generally assumed to be at home) had the advantage of being able to study the child while engaged in the daily activities of housework. Her normal domestic workload ostensibly afforded a perfect cover from which to watch the child.

20 This is not to say that Spock was the first or only person to espouse this approach. See, for instance, Buxbaum 1951 or Aldrich and Aldrich 1938. Rather, Spock became synonymous with "natural" child-rearing, and eventually with the concept of child-rearing in general. As *Newsweek* put it in 1956: "In the last 25 years, to boot, some 7,500 volumes on child care have been published. While a quarter century ago, the American home had on the shelf a home remedy or 'doctor book' emphasizing first aid and how to recognize the rash of a contagious disease, today there is a copy of Spock or Gesell" ("Bringing Up Baby on Books" 1956, 64).

21 In 1948, the United Nations ratified the Declaration of Universal Human Rights, which in its preamble described humanity as one large family, and which further stated: "The family is the natural and fundamental group unit of society and is entitled to protection by society and the State [and] Motherhood and childhood are entitled to special care and assistance" (United Nations 1951, 39–40).

22 An obvious distinction between Adorno or Mills and Riesman, Mead, or Erikson is that the latter group avoided a sustained critique of capitalism. In 1956, *Newsweek* negatively reviewed *The Power Elite*, questioning whether Mills could rightly be called a sociologist and claiming "he is a moralist, and an angry one at that." (*Newsweek* 1956, 101–102).

23 Spock and Mead studied together intermittently at the New York Psychoanalytic Institute in the mid-1930s. Spock and Erikson worked together in Pittsburgh in the 1950s (see Maier 1998).

24 Note that the article shifts from a discussion of "parents" to ridicule of the mother. This was in line with the general misogyny common in depictions of mothers at the time.

25 See Jenkins 1998b.

26 In the forward to *Childhood and Society* (1950), Erikson states that "it would be impossible to itemize my overall indebtedness to Margaret Mead" (13). Space does not permit a detailed discussion of the evolution of Erikson's thought into the contested subfield of psychohistory.

27 This oath remains in place.

28 For an example of wartime discourse on the father's absence and its pathological effect on boys' enculturation, hence American character, see M. Mead 1942, 138–57.

29 See also Lindner 1948 and 1956 for discussions of positive and negative conformity.

30 Although Spock used the term *management*, more commonly associated with the previous mode of child-rearing, the term here did not carry the discursive weight that it had in the 1920s and 1930s. By the 1950s, management—in child care and in

business—had taken on a meaning much more aligned with adjustment to group expectations than with strict regulation. See chapter 4.

31 This is not to say that the systematic gathering of data about children's bodies and behaviors ceased in the 1950s. What changed was the meaning of those data: instead of underpinning strict norms against which children's bodies and behaviors were to be constantly measured, the data were meant to support claims for the natural fundament of children's entry into culture.

32 Summing up advances in the study of childhood, *Newsweek* described the pioneering laboratory work of Arnold Gesell in the 1920s and 1930s as historically necessary but ultimately sterile and outdated, and the data collected by Gesell became reconfigured as a surface beneath which another layer of information operated: "Dr. Milton Senn, Gesell's successor at Yale, prefers to examine the environment of the child, plus the physical, metabolic, and psychological forces that determine his growth. Besides recording child behavior, Dr. Senn and his group want to know what behavior means, or why children do as they do" ("Bringing Up Baby on Books" 1956, 66). (Senn served on the advisory board of the 1960 White House Conference on Children and Youth. Benjamin Spock was an associate of Senn's during their residency at New York Hospital in the 1930s.) Although in this instance, Gesell was presented as a representative of outmoded child-rearing regimes, he continued to publish well into the 1950s. See, for example, Gesell, Ilg, and Ames 1956. Indeed, it is somewhat unfair to portray Gesell's long career (which spanned five decades) in the same light as more extreme work by figures such as Watson or Skinner. Gesell's efforts to understand child behavior, though focused on clinical observation, were neither as rigidly deterministic as those of the behaviorists nor bound to a specific theoretical moment. Rather, he adjusted his thought and rhetoric (if not his research) according to prevailing arguments of the moment.

33 See also Mead 1955, 11–12.

34 This model assumed that the mother was at home with the child, and that she had sufficient time to observe the child and herself, or that she could structure her domestic work to include these observational strategies. It assumed membership in the middle class.

35 The U.S. Children's Bureau, a division of the Department of Labor, was intended to provide a coordinated federal response to problems of child-rearing. It did so by organizing conferences, coordinating research, distributing informational pamphlets, and answering mothers' queries. See, for instance, Ladd-Taylor 1986 for a history of the Children's Bureau.

36 In a sense an antecedent to Bourdieu's notion of *habitus* (loosely, a set of structuring structures), this constituted a reciprocal relationship between nature and culture in which nature directed the development of the culture that instantiated it. See Bourdieu 1977.

37 This is not to say, of course, that Disney's animated features did not pay as much attention to the proper performance of gender. The relative absence of positive

maternal figures (or *any* maternal figures) and of strong or positive paternal figures in Disney features has long been noted, as has been the stereotypical gendering of both human and animal animated characters. The difference here is in Disney's claim to representation of the real.

38 Space does not allow a thorough examination of why child-centered proponents adopted such circumspection around the name "Freud." It may be that they feared offending the post-Victorian, progressive sensibility that had previously occupied the center of child-rearing discourse, or that they wished to avoid association with a 1920s-era popularization of Freud that seemed to celebrate libidinal excess.

39 This is not to say that management-based theories of child-rearing, or particularly their popularizations, ignored gender. Although management-based theories acknowledged gender, they did so only in relation to the older child and tended to focus on social aspects of gendered behavior as inflecting work done by parents in earlier stages. For a discussion of the emergence of Freudian discourse in Spock and others, see Jenkins 1998.

40 Although it is usually assumed that women left the workplace for the home following World War II, recent scholarship has suggested that female participation in the workplace actually continued to increase after the war. See Hartmann 1994, Foner 1980, Ehrenreich 1983, and Tyler May 1988. For examples of domestic/workplace tensions from popular fiction, see Himes 1947 and Wilson 1955.

41 One could argue, also, that as race and ethnicity became publicly less acceptable means of marking differentiation, gender became a more acceptable location for natural difference. Ironically, efforts by post-progressive social theorists such as Mead to remove distinctions based on ethnic origins as explanations for social inequality, or as justifications for the construction of an exclusive American culture, turned to gender as the significant category for understanding difference in child-rearing. Though this allowed for a discussion of gender difference in American culture that has been incredibly important in subsequent articulations of gender in everyday life and in the social sciences, it also reduced gender difference to a set of essential markers that played into contemporary misogyny. As had been the case in the previous generation, race (referring to those not subsumed under the category of "ethnicity") continued to be largely ignored in mainstream discussions of child-rearing. The importance of Kenneth Clark's analysis of the effects of racism and discrimination on black children to the successful prosecution of *Brown v. Board of Education*, and the debate that followed, would play a role in changing this dynamic, but the effects of that change would not reach significant popular attention until the 1960s. For examples of brief, tentative, and ultimately unsuccessful attempts to integrate race into problems of child-rearing in the 1950s, see, for example, Riesman 1950 and Erikson 1950.

42 For two contemporary and opposed arguments about feminine protest, see de Beauvoir 1953 and Lundberg and Farnham 1947.

43 See F. Turner 1893, 1920 for a foundational discussion of the frontier.

44 Inexpensive to produce and popular with children, westerns were also essential to the early days of television.

45 The image is contemporaneous with Disney's offensive caricature of "Indians" in *Peter Pan* (1953).

46 Indeed, one passed down Disneyland's Main Street, U.S.A., to reach the junction where the rational and symbolic realms met.

Chapter 6 Disney Maps the Frontier

1 For a discussion of the politics of suburbanization, see Lipsitz 1993 or Tyler May 1988.

2 For gender, domesticity, and the suburbs, see Tyler May 1988 and Spigel 1992.

3 The difference between *Cinderella* (1950) and *Snow White* (1937) is worth mentioning. While Snow White was aided both by a beneficent nature (the creatures that helped her clean the dwarfs' house) and by the industrious efficiency of the dwarfs themselves, Cinderella's own industriousness was part of what kept her in servitude and was ameliorated by a magically enhanced nature.

4 One of the ways the company accomplished this was by putting distance between science and the bodies affected by it by increasingly invoking terminology such as "imagineering" and "animatronics" to describe its industrial practices. For example, in a promotional film about the construction of the park (one that the company recycled for a television special celebrating the park's fortieth anniversary), Walt Disney takes viewers on a walking tour of the construction site. As he speaks about each attraction, it rises magically from the ground through time-lapse photography, the workers a blur of labor that masks the individual bodies involved. The only body visible, the only voice audible, is that of Walt Disney, and it is as if the landscape "animatronically" responds to the "imagineering" power of that voice, arranging itself at his command. On Disney and Gilbreth, see Graham 1998.

5 Many of these practices had consolidated during the implementation of the Motion Picture Conduct Code in the late 1920s and early 1930s, when the Hays Office sought to standardize reporting on Hollywood by channeling news through press agents and correspondents. See Maltby 1995 and Jowett, Jarvie, and Fuller 1996.

6 According to Denise Mann (1992, 41–67), there was a trend toward the domestication of stardom in early television, but this traded upon an uneasy tension between the celebrity aura and mundane domesticity.

7 This quote and those that follow are from a small-town newspaper in West Virginia, saved in Disney's archives, a record of the circulation of those press releases. Disney's archives have no apparent consistent practice for retaining clippings of these releases. In some cases, the archives hold copies of the same release from several different sources; in others, only one copy exists. These three quotes, drawn from the same source, were most likely distributed widely, but no record of that distribution was available.

8 See, for example, J. Brown 1945 or "The Mouse That Turned to Gold" 1955.

9 Compare also Walt Disney Productions 1951b and Peach 1951.

10 See also Brown 1950 and Smoodin 1993 for the discursive regulation of "Disney."

11 In words remarkably similar, the reviewer for the *Rotarian* described *Beaver Valley* as "certainly *one of the most excellent Nature records* ever made" (Lockhart 1950; emphasis original). Although study of the press book for *Beaver Valley* did not turn up these lines, a more thorough investigation might.

12 Disney would repeat these instructions in its press book for *The Vanishing Prairie* (1954): "Such groups as The Child Welfare League, The Community Chest, The American Legion, University Clubs, The Kiwanis, Rotarians, Lions, and Police Benefit Leagues are always anxious to place their 'seal of approval' on motion pictures with the wide community appeal that 'The Vanishing Prairie' possesses" (Walt Disney Productions 1954b).

13 Indeed, one could scarcely find a better example of the Katz and Lazarsfeld's (1955) "two-step" model in action: "100,000 copies of a new brochure on Disney's True-Life Adventures and People and Places series have been mailed to leading educators, motion picture columnists and other opinion makers. This is probably the largest distribution of motion picture promotional material ever made through these channels" (Walt Disney Productions 1954a).

14 Far from simply acting as repositories for artifacts or instructional institutions, museums are a significant component in the youth entertainment market, a fact museum administrators increasingly have embraced in the last two decades.

15 See Spigel 1992 on the introduction of television to the home.

16 Ironically, the park's enormous semiotic weight, its importance as the single largest undertaking by Walt Disney in the 1950s, and its presence as the physical instantiation of the Disney ethos have led to its overdetermination as an object of academic study (see Bryman 1995; Fjellman 1992; Bell, Haas, and Sells 1995; Project on Disney 1995). Lost in that focus has been a detailed examination of Disney's efforts to diversify and integrate its production, to create a matrix of imbrication, of which the park was only one element.

17 See Smith 1996, Walt Disney Productions 1953a.

18 On the ABC-Disney relationship, see Smith 1996 and Marling 1994.

19 This article appeared in an item in Disney's own archives, the name of the newspaper long lost.

20 See Smoodin 1993.

21 Schramm, Lyle, and Parker (1961, 228–29) reported that in San Francisco between 1957 and 1960, the program rated number one for grades 1–5, second for grade 6, and fourth for boys and eighth for girls in grade 8. They offered no statistics for adult preference.

22 As of this writing, Disney has since resurrected this format in its new iteration of *The Wonderful World of Disney*. In this incarnation, Michael Eisner provides the opening frame, often focusing on the technological innovations behind whatever is being shown (usually a Disney movie from a previous season).

23 Disney made the success of that strategy clear to its stockholders, reporting in 1959: "Our material is well diversified to cover the widest audience range . . . [and] . . . please theatre goers and television viewers in every age bracket. . . . I feel we have made good progress in achieving a closer coordination of our theatrical and television interests, particularly in the way we have been able to use talent developed on our television programs in such important theatrical features as OLD YELLER and SHAGGY DOG" (Walt Disney Productions 1959, 2).

24 See Smith 1996, "The Mouse That Turned to Gold" 1955.

25 Both the Trans-o-gram and Walco catalogs are to be found in the Warshaw Collection in the Archives Center at the National Museum of American History at the Smithsonian Institution.

26 See Silverman 1990 for a discussion of voice in visual regimes.

27 Research in the Disney Archives contained some letters from teachers, but none that called for teaching guides or help with the programs, nor did there seem to be any record of such.

28 The guide seems a fitting response to a call from teacher Barbara Alice Wolf in the January 1950 issue of *Journal of the Association for Education by Radio*: "Preferring to turn the enemy's guns to our advantage, we decide to make clear to our students the relationship between the delights of TV and the rewards of study. . . . One can absorb strength and beauty from every element of life, if only the proper associations be made consciously or otherwise. Guidance quickens the process and guidance is our job. . . . Let's make TV a contributing force to the betterment of our work—let's make television a topic of conversation in as well as outside of school. . . . Don't lets depend on someone else for video material of educational value, let's you and I and all of us together make everything on and about video educationally valuable to ourselves and our TV-wise charges!" (Shayon 1951, 85–86).

29 The notion of an "inferiority complex," suggested by Adler in the 1920s, achieved widespread popularity by the mid-1950s.

30 The guide finally laid claim to being part of the educational process by stating, "This 'Tele-Digest' has been prepared by Mrs. Margaret Divizia, Supervisor in Charge, Audio-Visual Section, Los Angeles Schools" (Walt Disney Productions 1956a).

31 Conversation with Dave Smith, 1996.

32 In another instance, the Little Golden Book *Disneyland on the Air* (1955) ostensibly showed Donald Duck learning to control his feelings and practice deferred gratification in waiting for his turn on the program, but an important subtext of the story was the idea that children could write in and express their preferences as to what they would like to see.

33 For example, when Disney proudly declared in its 1958 annual report that "for the third consecutive year 'Disneyland' will receive Look Magazine's TV Award for Best Children's Series" and that "award winners are voted by television editors throughout the country to presentations made on a national television program"

(1), it was describing an elaborate discursive matrix in which authority was generated through its circulation between Disney, *Look Magazine*, the television editors who voted for *Disneyland*, and the television audiences that tuned in for the award ceremony. Disney gained authority by producing the winning program; *Look* by conferring the award; the editors by acting as a professional body with the skills necessary for determining a winner; and the audience by providing the concern about children's programming. For a discussion of the circulation of discursive authority within academic, juridical, and professional disciplines, see Foucault 1984.

34 Although children during this period constituted an increasingly independent market, that market was weighted toward preadolescent and adolescent children. Younger children formed a market only inasmuch as their parents purchased for them. As it is today, this particular demographic derives its economic power from its ability to influence parents directly, or through appeals by producers and distributors to parents' sense of responsibility to their children.

35 The overview offered here is by no means comprehensive. It uses representative figures to sketch a broad outline of the discursive terrain. For an institutional history of effects theory, see McLeod, Kosicki, and Pan 1991. For broader historical overviews, see Luke 1990, 61–114, or Wartella and Reeves 1985. For a thoughtful analysis of effects literature, see Freedman 2002.

36 For instance, Schramm suggested that "There is another reason for expecting that the effects of television may not be so potent as they have sometimes been pictured. This is the fact that television always enters into a pattern of influences that already exist. Actually television may bulk rather small beside these other influences, for they come from the home, the peer group, the school, the church, the culture generally. . . . In any case it is seldom that we can point to any behavior of a child and say that this is due solely to television. Television contributes to it, or catalyzes it, or gives it a particular shape" (Schramm, Lyle, and Parker 1961, 146).

37 Compare, for instance, Merton 1946 to Shayon 1951 or Schramm 1961.

38 For example, see Lasswell 1927, 185–222. For an overview, see Sproule 1987.

39 See, for instance, Hovland, Lumsdaine, and Sheffield 1949, 254.

40 See Spigel 1992 for a discussion of the dynamics of domestic TV viewing.

41 For a popular discussion of status rituals in the 1950s, see Packard 1959.

42 This was brought home most vividly by the role that Edward R. Murrow's *As It Happens* series had in the fall of Senator Joseph McCarthy.

43 Shayon began each chapter of his book with a quote from *The Pied Piper of Hamelin*, and suggested that television was like the title character, stealing children away from unsuspecting parents.

44 These sentiments closely match those of the leading child-rearing expert of the decade, Benjamin Spock (1957, 393): "Do comics, TV, and movies contribute to delinquency . . . ? A great majority of child psychiatrists believe that comics, TV, and movies do not play any important part in delinquency, and I agree with them. They believe that serious delinquency is a manifestation of a fundamental defect in a child's character. This may have been caused by growing up with parents who

had delinquent tendencies themselves or who had no real love for the child. . . . If a judge asks him where he got the idea for his crime, he may answer, 'From a comic book' or 'From a program.' But the impulse to carry it out must have come from deep inside and from way back in his childhood."

45 The quote above is from a reprint of a talk given before the American Association of University Women, funded by the Television Information Office, the public-relations arm of the National Association of Broadcasters, so its emphasis on parental responsibility is understandable.

46 See Shayon 1951, 51–82.

47 Indeed, media theorists were quite aware of the relationship between peer groups and media messages. See, for instance, Katz and Lazarsfeld 1955, or Hovland, Janis, and Kelly 1953. This research suggested that conformists in a group resisted change, while nonconformists embraced it. Consider the following passage, which prefigures Frank's (1997) recent observation that rebellion and youthful mistrust of adults, far from a social problem, were actually advantageous to marketers: "As a result of repeated instances in which they are misled, disappointed, or exploited, children are apt to become highly sensitive to cues to manipulative intent. Sometimes they even receive specific training in this respect from their parents and, later on, from their age-mates (e.g., 'don't be a sucker'). As a result of learning experiences of this kind, most individuals acquire strong motives which incline them to notice signs of communicator intent and to avoid being influenced when they expect that the communicator is attempting to manipulate them. . . . The motives aroused by expectations of manipulative intent seem to be closely linked with feelings of humiliation and with various types of noncompliant behavior that are sometimes described in terms of 'need for autonomy.' Consequently, expectations of manipulative intent are likely to give rise to strong resisting tendencies that extend beyond the motivation to avoid adopting an erroneous belief" (Hovland, Janis, and Kelly 1953, 295).

48 Consider, also, Schramm's comments in 1959: "I can predict with some confidence what kind of media patterns his children would have; and if you could tell me what kind of television the parents watch, what kind of books, if any, they read, what magazines, what music they hear, and so on, then I could predict with almost complete confidence what use their children will make of the media" (6).

49 See Spigel 1992.

50 For an excellent discussion of nondomestic television viewing, see McCarthy 2000.

51 See Spigel 1992, Boddy 1990, and Hendershot 1998.

52 See Smith 1996 for a brief description of the *Mickey Mouse Club*.

53 See Walt Disney Productions 1956a.

54 Disney promised this lineup to parents and teachers in its informational guides, but did not always deliver it as expected.

55 In the guide it distributed to teachers, Disney listed sponsors for *The Mickey Mouse Club*: "Am-Par Record Corp; Armour & Co.; B&B Enterprises, Inc.; Bristol Meyers Co.; Campbell Soup Co.; The Carnation Co.; The Coca Cola Co.; General Mills,

Inc.; S. C. Johnson & Son, Inc.; Lettuce, Inc.; Mars, Inc.; Mattel, Inc.; Miles Laboratories, Inc.; Minnesota Mining & Manufacturing Co; Morton Salt Co; S.O.S. Co.; Vick Chemical Co.; Welch Grape Juice Co" (Walt Disney Productions 1956a). As might be expected, the list reveals a preponderance of food and toy companies.

56 Offering as an example the toy manufacturer Mattel, Gilbert (1957, 54–55) described the power of that association: "Several years ago at the 1955 Toy Fair, prior to signing on the Mickey Mouse Club, Mattel did close to a million dollars worth of advance business. The following year, after appearing on the show for approximately six months, it wrote over two million dollars."

57 See also Sheehy 1956b.

58 This was not the first time that Disney won this award. In its 1950 annual report, Disney announced that "Disney has won more Parent's Magazine [*sic*] medallions than any individual producer in Hollywood" (Walt Disney Productions 1950a, 1). In the 1950s, *Parents'* also awarded Disney medals for *So Dear to My Heart* (1949), *Treasure Island* (1950), *20,000 Leagues under the Sea* (1954), and *Lady and the Tramp* (1955).

59 The program was not alone in winning acclaim as beneficial children's programming. *Ding Dong School* and *Romper Room* were just two of a number of children's programs held up during the 1950s as examples of constructive television.

60 On the TV dinner, see Spigel 1992, 90.

61 See Fjellman 1992 and Schickel 1968.

62 In one of Disney's behind-the-scenes tours of an animatronics lab—another author explained why Walt Disney could do this. Describing an automated elephant, he observed: "The artist who had done this had not followed nature: he had observed it. I was told that the modeling had been done from sketches, and the first sketches had been drawn by Disney. . . . I went behind the half-elephant. It was hollow, and the space was filled the machinery that raised the trunk and flapped its ears. The mechanism had a homemade look. It was like the first working models that inventors make for themselves. I asked who designed such things, and I was told that it was Mr. Disney" (Menen 1963, 70).

Conclusion

1 See Schweizer and Schweizer 1998.

2 For a balanced critique of the science of media effects studies, see Freedman 2002. Although the most recent longitudinal study of media and violence (Huesmann et al. 2003) claims to avoid these defects, cursory examination of its methodology—particularly its designation of dependent and independent variables—suggests otherwise.

3 See Morgenson and McGeehan 2002.

4 For a discussion of commodity fetishism, see Pietz 1993. For a concise definition, see Bottomore et al. 1983, 87.

5 Remarkably, *Song of the South* (1946) received little criticism for its racist representations. In general though, Disney's racist codings—the crows in *Dumbo* (1941) or the "Indians" in *Peter Pan* (1953) are but two examples—generally went unremarked.

6 In many ways, this approach reprised the vaudeville roots of animation, in which the labor-intensive process that yielded relatively short amusements became incorporated into the performance, either as a live demonstration, or as a short live film of the process. See Robinson 1991, Halas 1987, and Canemaker 1987. Disney's interpretation of this trope was significant, however, in that it treated the process not as a feat of legerdemain, but as an industrial process. It celebrated production itself.

7 For a discussion of Foucault's work in relation to Marx, see Fracchia 1998.

8 Marx approached this idea obliquely in *Capital*, claiming at one point, "In a sort of way, it is with man as with commodities. Since he comes into the world neither with a looking glass in his hand, nor as a Fichtian philosopher, to whom 'I am I' is sufficient, man first sees and recognises himself in other men" (Marx 1978, 317n).

9 For a complex and troubling discussion of the relation of the individual to the state and to civil society, see also Marx's "On the Jewish Question" (Marx 1978, 26–52).

10 One should not reduce Lukács's intellectual career to the concept of reification, especially in light of the complex history of the term and of his thinking on it. Space does not permit a full discussion of the problem of reification and Lukács's working and reworking of it. See, for instance, Lukács 1963, 1971, 2000.

11 Zelizer (1985) describes the crisis brought on by this entry into capitalist society as "sacralization." In her account, as more children were excluded from the labor market in the late nineteenth and early twentieth centuries, the question of their value became uncertain. In issues of insurance and wrongful death suits, the child's value as a worker was replaced by its emotional value to its parents. It became more a sacred object as its value became abstracted.

12 See, for example, Postman 1982.

13 In the *Grundrisse*, Marx traces this idea to an extension of the observation that the intake of food is necessary to the production of the person's body: "Consumption is also immediately production, just as in nature the consumption of the elements and chemical substances is the production of the plant. It is clear that in taking in food . . . the human being produces his own body. But this is also true for every kind of consumption which in one way or another produces human beings in some particular aspect" (Marx 1858, 228).

14 See Zelizer 1985 and C. Mills 1957.

15 Since this ideal child was modeled on children of the white middle class, those children would have an edge in marginally differentiating themselves from their working-class peers and feel anxiety about the failure to do so.

16 It is also similar to the way Wendy Brown (1993, 395) describes the idealized middle-class subject position that is the object of arguments for equal rights in identity-based politics: "Poised between the rich and the poor, feeling itself to be protected

from the encroachments of neither, the phantasmatic middle class signifies the natural and the good between the decadent and the corrupt, on the one side, and the aberrant or the decaying, on the other."

17 See Rousseau 1762, Shattuck 1980, and Newton 2002. Locke (1693) also describes the enculturation of the child as a process of domestication. Still, his version of the process is indebted to his own Puritan upbringing and is rooted much more in countering the primal amorality of the child with reason than it is in elevating the child from a state of nature into reason.

18 It bears repeating that, during the course of the twentieth century, the statutory exclusion of children from labor markets has systematically and repeatedly overlooked many children of color. Because these laws, whether at the state or federal level, have consistently excepted children working in agriculture, for instance, this process has not extended to African American, Latino, and Asian American children who engage in tenant and migrant agricultural labor. Though the rationale for the exception has been that it allows family farms to continue, the law has not been adjusted to acknowledge the more widespread labor relations of industrial agriculture.

19 In the assimilationist rhetoric of the progressive movement, the proper enculturation of at least some European ethnic groups into the life ways of white, Protestant, middle-class America permitted the reversal of such evolutionary missteps. See chapter 2. Where discourses of race and culture were more firmly interwoven—as was the case for African Americans, Asian Americans, Native Americans, and certain Latino groups, the possibility of assimilation diminished and the rhetorics of evolutionary hierarchy remained more durable (see Herrnstein and Murray 1994).

20 See Roosevelt 1907 and 1911; see also Macleod 1982, 1983, and 1993.

21 With the stabilization of age-specific youth markets and the concomitant rise of the "generation gap" and "youth rebellion" of the 1960s, the relationship of nature to culture in the child and its role in the health of the social order were called into question. The details of this shift and their ultimate contribution to contemporary understandings of the child are beyond the scope of this study. It would not be an unreasonable generalization to say that American child-rearing has settled into a steady periodicity that moves between the disciplinarian sentiments of Locke and the experiential approach of Rousseau.

22 In 1954, David Riesman would offer a 1950s spin on Freud's figure of "His Majesty the Baby," stating, "This would seem to hang together with the devaluation of the individual we have been discussing: children are a kind of unequivocal good in a world of changing values, and we can lavish on children the care and emotions we would now feel it egotistical to lavish on ourselves" (227).

23 It is important to note that the work cited here represents some of Taussig's earlier material, which has since been superseded by a more nuanced and problematic approach to the issue of mystification.

24 For Marx's version of the alienation of the fetish, see Marx 1978, 163–77, particularly 169–72. For an excellent gloss on the subject, see Pietz 1993.

25 See Harding 1987, MacKinnon 1989; Hartsock 1987, Scott 1988a, Brown 1993 and 2001, and C. Allen and Howard 2000.

26 Here, Haraway's (1991) work on the cyborg is significant.

References

Adams, Grace. 1934. *Your child is normal: The psychology of young childhood.* New York: Covici Friede.

Addams, Jane. 1926. *The spirit of youth and the city streets.* New York: Macmillan.

———. 1930. *Twenty years at Hull House.* New York: Macmillan.

———. 1960. *A centennial reader.* New York: Macmillan.

Adler, Mortimer. 1937. *Art and prudence.* New York: Longmans, Green and Co.

Adorno, Theodor W., Else Frenkel-Brunswik, Daniel J. Levinson, and R. Nevitt Sanford. 1950. *The authoritarian personality.* New York: Harper and Bros.

Aldrich, C. Anderson, and Mary M. Aldrich. 1938. *Babies are human beings: An interpretation of growth.* New York: Macmillan.

Aldridge, John W. 1955. Gray new world. *Nation*, June 25, 585–588.

Alexander, Ruth. "The Only Thing I Wanted Was Freedom": Wayward Girls in New York, 1900–1930. In *Small Worlds*, ed. Elliott West and Paula Petrik. Lawrence: University of Kansas Press, 1992.

Algar, James. 1952. Triumph of patience over nature. In *The story of . . . Walt Disney's True-Life Adventure series.* Burbank, Calif.: Walt Disney Productions.

Algar, James, dir. 1948. *Seal island.* Walt Disney Pictures.

———. 1949. *The adventures of Ichabod and Mr. Toad.* Walt Disney Pictures.

———. 1950. *Beaver valley.* Walt Disney Pictures.

———. 1951. *Nature's half acre.* Walt Disney Pictures.

———. 1952. *The Olympic elk.* Walt Disney Pictures.

———. 1953. *Bear country.* Walt Disney Pictures.

———. 1953. *Prowlers of the Everglades.* Walt Disney Pictures.

———. 1953. *The living desert.* Walt Disney Pictures.

Algar, James, and Ben Sharpsteen, dirs. 1952. *Water birds.* Walt Disney Pictures.

Allen, Carolyn, and Judith A. Howard, eds. 2000. *Provoking feminisms.* Chicago: University of Chicago Press.

Allen, Jeanne. 1983. Copyright and early theater, vaudeville, and film competition. In *Film before Griffith*, ed. John L. Fell, 176–187.

Allen, Robert C. 1980. *Vaudeville and film, 1895–1915: A study in media interaction.* New York: Arno Press.

———. 1983. Motion picture exhibition in Manhattan, 1906–1912: Beyond the nickelodeon. In *Film before Griffith*, ed. John L. Fell, 162–175.

———. 1998. From exhibition to reception: Reflections on the audience in film his-

tory. In *Screen histories: A* Screen *reader*, ed. Annette Kuhn and Jackie Stacey, 13–21. New York: Oxford University Press.
American Youth Commission. 1942. *Youth and the future: The general report of the American Youth Commission*. Washington, D.C.: American Council on Education.
Ames, Louise Bates. 1942. Letter to Walt Disney. New Haven, Conn., September 25. Walt Disney Archives, Burbank, Calif.
Anastasi, Anne. 1976. *Psychological testing*, 4th ed. New York: Macmillan Publishing Co.
Anderson, Perry. 1976. The antinomies of Antonio Gramsci. *New Left Review*, no. 100: 5–77.
Anderson, Sherwood. 1940. *Home town*. New York: Alliance Book Corporation.
Andrus, Ruth. 1928. *An inventory of the habits of children from two to five years of age*. New York: Teachers College, Columbia University.
Anspacher, Carolyn. 1942. "Management—1942 model." In *American women at war*. New York: National Association of Manufacturers.
Appel, John J. 1971. Introduction to *The new immigration*. New York: Jerome S. Ozer.
Arendt, Hannah. 1945. *The origins of totalitarianism*. New York: Meridian, 1958.
Aries, Phillipe. 1965. *Centuries of childhood: A social history of family life*. Trans. Robert Baldick. New York: Random House.
Arnold, Alexander. 1922. Letter to editor. *Photoplay*, November.
Aronson, Michael G. 2002. The wrong kind of nickel madness: Pricing problems for Pittsburgh nickelodeons. *Cinema Journal* 42: 71–96.
Bakhurst, David. 1991. *Consciousness and revolution in Soviet philosophy: From the Bolsheviks to Evald Ilynenkov*. Cambridge: Cambridge University Press.
Bannister, Robert C. 1979. *Social Darwinism: Science and myth in Anglo-American social thought*. Philadelphia: Temple University Press.
———. 1987. *Sociology and scientism*. Chapel Hill: University of North Carolina Press.
Barclay, Dorothy. 1950. Aggressiveness in the very young. *New York Times Magazine*, December 17.
Barrie, J. M. 1950. *Peter Pan*. New York: Scribner.
Baruch, Dorothy. 1942. *You, your children, and war*. New York: D. Appleton-Century.
Bauer, Raymond A. 1952. *The new man in Soviet psychology*. Cambridge, Mass.: Harvard University Press.
Baumann, Shyon. 2001. Intellectualization and art world development: Film in the United States. *American Sociological Review* 66:3, 404–426.
Bayley, Nancy. 1940. *Studies in the development of young children*. Berkeley: University of California Press.
Bazalgette, Cary, and David Buckingham, eds. 1995. *In front of the children: Screen entertainment and young audiences*. London: British Film Institute.
Becker, Howard S. 1982. *Artworlds*. Berkeley: University of California Press.
Beekman, Daniel. 1977. *The mechanical baby: A popular history of the theory and practice of child raising*. Westport, Conn.: Lawrence Hill and Co.
Bell, Elizabeth, Lynda Haas, and Laura Sells, eds. 1995. *From mouse to mermaid: The politics of film, gender, and culture*. Bloomington: Indiana University Press.

Bellomy, Donald. 1984. "Social Darwinism" revisited. In *Perspectives in American History, new series I*. Cambridge: Cambridge University Press.

Benedict, Agnes. 1936. What's ahead in the movies? *Parents' Magazine*, September.

Benjamin, Walter. 1931. Mickey Mouse. In *Selected writings, 1927–1934*, trans. Rodney Livingston et al., ed. Michael Jennings, Howard Eiland, and Garry Smith, 545. Cambridge, Mass.: Harvard University Press, 1999.

Benjamin Spock, M.D., in our June 1941 Issue. 1956. *Parents' Magazine*, October.

Bennett, David H. 1988. *The party of fear*. Chapel Hill: University of North Carolina Press.

Bergheger, Mrs. A. H., and Mrs. J. Morgan Wilson. 1942. Letter to Walt Disney. Madison, Wisconsin, September 17. Walt Disney Archives, Burbank, Calif.

Bernath, Maja. 1956. How baby care has changed. *Parents' Magazine*, October.

Bernays, Edward L. 1952. *Public relations*. Norman: University of Oklahoma Press.

The big bad wolf. 1934. *Fortune*, November.

Billings, Ethel M. Warren. 1922. Letter to editor. *Photoplay*, September.

Blatz, William E., and Helen Bott. 1931. Are you fit to be a father? *Parents' Magazine*, June.

Blumenthal, Albert. 1932. *Small-town stuff*. Chicago: University of Chicago Press.

Blumer, Herbert. 1933. *Movies and conduct*. New York: Macmillan.

Blumer, Howard, and Philip Hauser. 1933. *Movies, delinquency and crime*. New York: Macmillan.

Boas, Franz. 1911. *Changes in bodily form of descendants of immigrants*. Washington, D.C.: United States Government Printing Office.

Bobbink, Billie. 1922. Letter to the editor. *Photoplay*, September, 115.

Boddy, William. 1990. *Fifties television*. Chicago: University of Illinois Press.

Books for parents. 1956. *Parents' Magazine*, August.

Bottomore, Tom, Laurence Harris, V. G. Kiernan, and Ralph Miliband, eds. 1983. *A dictionary of Marxist thought*. Cambridge, Mass.: Harvard University Press.

Bourdieu, Pierre. 1977. *Outline of a theory of practice*. London: Cambridge University Press.

———. 1984. *Distinction*. Cambridge, Mass.: Harvard University Press.

Bourdieu, Pierre, and J. C. Passeron. 1977. *Reproduction in education, society and culture*. Beverly Hills, Calif.: Sage.

Bradbury, Ray. 1965. The machine-tooled happyland. *Holiday*, October.

Bringing up baby on books: Revolution and counterrevolution in child care. 1956. *Newsweek*, May.

Brody, Jane. 1999. How to keep toilet training from being a power struggle. *New York Times*, August 3.

Bronner, Simon, ed. 1989. *Consuming visions: Accumulation and display of goods in America, 1880–1920*. New York: W. W. Norton.

Brown, John Mason. 1945. Mr. Disney's caballeros. *Saturday Review of Literature*, February 24.

Brown, Wendy. 1995. Wounded attachments. In *States of injury: Power and freedom in late modernity*, 52–76. Princeton, N.J.: Princeton University Press.

———. 2001. *Politics out of history*. Princeton, N.J.: Princeton University Press.

Brumbaugh, Florence. 1954. What effect does television advertising have on children? *Education Digest*, April.

Bryman, Alan. 1995. *Disney and his worlds*. New York: Routledge.

Bryson, Lyman. 1939. *Which way America? Communism—Fascism—Democracy*. New York: Macmillan.

———. 1952. *The next America: Prophecy and faith*. New York: Harper and Bros.

Buckingham, David. 2000. *After the death of childhood: Growing up in the age of electronic media*. Cambridge, U.K.: Polity.

Burnham, John. 1977. Essay. In *Progressivism*, by John Buenker, John Burnham, and Robert Crunden, 3–30. Cambridge, Mass.: Schenkman.

Buxbaum, Edith. 1951. *Your child makes sense: A guidebook for parents*. London: Allen and Unwin.

Canemaker, John. 1987. *Winsor McCay, his life and art*. New York: Abbeville.

Caplow, Theodore. 1982. *Middletown families*. Minneapolis: University of Minnesota Press.

Cartwright, Lisa, and Brian Goldfarb. 1994. Cultural contagion: On Disney's health education films for Latin America. In *Disney Discourse*, ed. Eric Smoodin, 169–180. New York: Routledge.

Chambers, John W. 2000. *The tyranny of change: America in the Progressive Era, 1890–1920*. New Brunswick, N.J.: Rutgers University Press.

Chase, Stuart. 1948. *The proper study of mankind*. New York: Harper and Bros.

Chris, Cynthia. Forthcoming. Watching Wildlife. Minneapolis: University of Minnesota Press.

Churchill, Douglas. 1934. Now Mickey Mouse enters art's temple. *New York Times Magazine*, June 3, 12–13, 21.

———. 1938. Disney's "philosophy." *New York Times Magazine*, March 6, 9, 23.

Clark, G. Hardy. 1923. *A system of character training of children*. 4th ed. Long Beach, Calif.: Children's Health Laboratory.

Clement, Priscilla Ferguson. 1985. The city and the child, 1860–1885. In *American childhood: A research guide and historical handbook*, ed. Joseph Hawes and N. Ray Hiner, 235–72. Westport, Conn.: Greenwood.

Clifford, James. 1986a. Introduction: Partial truths. In *Writing culture: The poetics and politics of ethnography*, ed. James Clifford and George Marcus. Berkeley: University of California Press.

———. 1986b. On ethnographic allegory. In *Writing culture: The poetics and politics of ethnography*, ed. James Clifford and George Marcus. Berkeley: University of California Press.

Cole, Michael. 1996. *Cultural psychology: A once and future discipline*. Cambridge, Mass.: Belknap Press of Harvard University Press.

Commager, Henry Steele. 1950. Five great problems of the new century. *New York Times Magazine*, January 1, 3, 28–30.

Congressional Record. 1922. Washington, D.C.: United States Government Printing Office, June 29.

Cook, Daniel T. 2000a. The other "child study": Figuring children as consumers in market research, 1910s–1990s. *Sociological Quarterly* 41:487–507.

———. 2000b. The rise of "the toddler" as subject and as merchandising category in the 1930s. In *New forms of consumption: Consumers, culture, and commodification*, ed. Mark Gottdiener, 111–30. Lanham, Md.: Rowman and Littlefield.

Corey, Lewis. 1935. *The crisis of the middle class*. New York: Covici Friede.

Corken, Charles M. 1942. Letter to Walt Disney Productions. November 14. Walt Disney Archives, Burbank, Calif.

Couvares, Francis G. 1996. Hollywood, Main Street, and the church: Trying to censor the movies before the production code. In *Movie Censorship and American Culture*, ed. Francis Couvares, 129–158. Washington, D.C.: Smithsonian Institution Press.

Crafton, Donald. 1982. *Before Mickey: The animated film, 1898–1928*. Cambridge, Mass.: MIT Press.

Cravens, Hamilton. 1985. Child-saving in the age of professionalism, 1915–1930. In *American childhood: A research guide and historical handbook*, ed. Joseph Hawes and N. Ray Hiner, 415–488. Westport, Conn.: Greenwood.

Creator explains "Disneyland": Walt Disney says Mickey Mouse, Goofy, Donald Duck aren't really animals at all. 1954. *Parkersburg, West Virginia, News*, October 31.

Crèvecoeur, J. Hector St. John de. 1997. *Letters from an American farmer*. Ed. Susan Manning. Oxford: Oxford University Press.

Crowther, Bosley. 1953. The screen. *New York Times*, November 10.

Cunningham, Hugh. 1995. *Children and childhood in Western society since 1500*. New York: Longman.

Current feature films. 1950. *Christian Century*, August 23.

Czitrom, Daniel. 1982. *Media and the American mind: From Morse to McLuhan*. Chapel Hill: University of North Carolina Press.

———. 1996. The politics of performance: Theater licensing and the origins of movie censorship in New York. In *Movie censorship and American culture*, ed. Francis Couvares, 16–42. Washington, D.C.: Smithsonian Institution Press.

Dale, Edgar. 1935. *Children's attendance at motion pictures*. New York: Macmillan.

———. 1938. *How to appreciate motion pictures*. New York: The Macmillan Company.

Darling, Ernest. 1928. Letter to editor. *Photoplay*, October.

Darwin, Charles. 1840. A biographical sketch of an infant. In *Little masterpieces of science: Mind*, ed. George Iles. New York: Doubleday, 1902.

Davenel, George. 1956. Help your child develop career talents. *Parents' Magazine*, March, 46–50, 111–115.

Davis, Allison, Burleigh B. Gardner, and Mary R. Gardner. 1941. *Deep South: A social anthropological study of caste and class*, directed by W. Lloyd Warner. Chicago: University of Chicago Press.

Davis, Kingsley. 1935. *Youth in the Depression*. Chicago: University of Chicago Press.
Dear Reader. 1932. *McCall's Magazine*, September.
de Beauvoir, Simone. 1953. *The second sex*. New York: Knopf.
de Certeau, Michel. 1988. *The writing of history*. Trans. Tom Conley. New York: Columbia University Press.
deCordova, Richard. 1983. Ethnography and exhibition: The child audience, the Hays Office and Saturday matinees. *Camera Obscura*, no. 23:91–107.
———. 1990. *Picture personalities: The emergence of the star system in America*. Urbana: University of Illinois Press.
———. 1994. The Mickey in Macy's window: Childhood, consumerism, and Disney animation. In *Disney Discourse*, ed. Eric Smoodin, 203–213. New York: Routledge.
Deiss, Jay. 1955. Do you understand your child's secret language? *Parents' Magazine*, December.
DeMause, Lloyd, ed. 1974. *The history of childhood*. New York: Psychohistory Press.
Denny, Alma. 1956. A mother of girls says: Raise your boy to be a husband. *Parents' Magazine*, September, 43–44, 113.
De Roos, Robert. 1963. The magic worlds of Walt Disney. *National Geographic*, August, 159–207.
Dewey, John. 1922. The American intellectual frontier. *New Republic*, May 10.
———. 1938. *Experience and education*. New York: Macmillan.
Disney, Walt. 1930. General campaign covering launching and operation of the Mickey Mouse Club, an organization for boys and girls. Walter E. Disney. Walt Disney Archives, Burbank, Calif.
———. 1933. An important message to parents from Mickey Mouse. *Mickey Mouse Magazine*, November, 2.
———. 1934a. Boys will be Boy Scouts. *Mickey Mouse Magazine*, February, 3–5.
———. 1934b. It's great to be a Girl Scout. *Mickey Mouse Magazine*, March.
———. 1952. Walt Disney pays tribute to the animal actor kingdom. *Hollywood Reporter*, November 10.
———. 1953. What I've learned from the animals. *American Magazine*, February, 22–23, 106–109.
Disney, Walt, and Joe Alvin. 1949. What I know about girls. *Parents' Magazine*, January, 22–23, 77–78.
Disney films animal life. 1953. *Oregonian*, September 27.
Disneyland on the Air. 1955. New York: Simon and Schuster.
Dixon, C. Madeleine. 1942. *Keep them human: The young child at home*. New York: John Day.
Donzelot, Jacques. 1979. *The policing of families*. Trans. Robert Hurley. New York: Pantheon Books.
Du Bois, W. E. B. 1899. *The Philadelphia Negro: A social study, by W. E. Burghardt Du Bois. Together with a special report on domestic service by Isabel Eaton*. Philadelphia: University of Pennsylvania.

Dulles, Foster Rhea. 1960. From frontier to suburbia. In *Nation's Children*, ed. Eli Ginzberg, 1–23. New York: Columbia University Press.

Dysinger, Wendell S., and Christian Ruckmick. 1933. *The emotional responses of children to the motion picture situation*. New York: The Macmillan Company.

Eckelberry, Don. 1943. Letter to Walt Disney. January 1. Walt Disney Archives, Burbank, Calif.

Eckert, Charles. 1987. Shirley Temple and the house of Rockefeller. In *American media and mass culture: Left perspectives*. Donald Lazere, ed., 164–177. Berekely: University of California Press.

Edwards, Catherine C. 1950. Family movie guide. *Parents' Magazine*, January, 15.

———. 1955. Family movie guide. *Parents' Magazine*, April, 9.

———. 1956a. Family movie guide. *Parents' Magazine*, March, 11.

———. 1956b. Family movie guide. *Parents' Magazine*, November.

Edwards, E. E. 1956. All together now: Love that system! *Reporter*, December 27, 35–37.

Ehrenreich, Barbara. 1983. *The hearts of men: American dreams and the flight from commitment*. New York: Anchor.

Eichelberger, Clark M. 1950. It's your United Nations. *Parents' Magazine*, May, 26.

Eisner, Michael, with Tony Schwartz. 1998. *Work in progress*. New York: Random House.

Engestrom, Yrjo. 1990. *Learning, working, imagining*. Helsinki: Orienta-Konsultit-Oy.

English, O. Spurgeon. 1950. How to be a good father. *Parents' Magazine*, June, 32.

Erie County Children's Aid Society and Society for Prevention of Cruelty to Children. 1933. Radio talk over WKBW. January 4. U.S. National Archives, Children's Bureau files.

Erikson, Erik. 1950. *Childhood and society*. New York: W. W. Norton.

———. 1955. Sex differences in play configurations of adolescents. In *Childhood in contemporary cultures*, ed. Margaret Mead and Martha Wolfenstein, 324–344.

———, ed. 1961. *The challenge of youth*. Garden City, N.Y.: Anchor, 1965.

Escalona, Sibylle. 1955. Hostility: How it develops in children and how it should be handled. *Parents' Magazine*, January, 33.

Evans, John K. 1991. *War, women, and children in ancient Rome*. London: Routledge.

Ewen, Elizabeth. 1985. *Immigrant women in the land of dollars*. New York: Monthly Review Press.

Ewen, Stuart. 1976. *Captains of consciousness: Advertising and the social roots of the consumer culture*. New York: McGraw-Hill.

———. 1988. *All consuming images*. New York: Basic Books.

———. 1996. *PR! A social history of spin*. New York: Basic Books.

Faegre, Marion, and John Anderson, eds. 1927. *Child care and training: A correspondence course*. Minneapolis: Institute of Child Welfare, University of Minnesota.

Family movie guide: Reliable appraisals for adults, young folks, and children. 1939. *Parents' Magazine*, December.

Farber, Manny. 1942. "Saccharine symphony—*Bambi*." In *The American animated cartoon*, ed. Danny Peary and Gerald Peary, 90–91. New York: E. P. Dutton, 1980.

Fass, Paula S. 1979. *The damned and the beautiful: American youth in the 1920's*. New York: Oxford University Press.

Fass, Paula S., and Mary Ann Mason, eds. 2000. *Childhood in America*. New York: New York University Press.

Fell, John L., ed. 1983. *Film before Griffith*. Berkeley, Calif.: University of California Press.

Ferguson, Norman, and Wilfred Jackson, dirs. 1942. *Saludos amigos*. Walt Disney Pictures.

Fidler, Jimmy. 1951. In Hollywood. *Davenport, Iowa, Democrat and Leader*, July 29.

Fisher, Dorothy Canfield. 1916. *Self reliance*. Ed. M. V. O'Shea. Indianapolis: Bobbs-Merrill.

———. 1922. *What grandmother did not know*. Boston: Pilgrim Press.

Fiske, John. 1902. The part played by infancy in the evolution of man. In *Little masterpieces of science: Mind*, ed. George Iles, 3–20. New York: Doubleday.

Fjellman, Stephen. 1992. *Vinyl leaves: Walt Disney World and America*. San Francisco: Westview.

Fleischer, Richard, dir. 1954. *20,000 leagues under the sea*. Walt Disney Pictures.

Flower, B. O. Letter. 1893. In *Childhood: A monthly magazine for parents of all that concerns the welfare of the child*, ed. George Winterburn, 254–255. New York: A. L. Chatterton.

Foerstel, Lenora, and Angela Gilliam, eds. 1992. *Confronting the Margaret Mead legacy: Scholarship, empire, and the South Pacific*. Philadelphia: Temple University Press.

Foner, Philip S. 1980. *Women and the American labor movement: From World War I to the present*. New York: Free Press.

Forgacs, David. 1992. Disney animation and the business of childhood. *Screen* 33:361–374.

Forman, Henry James. 1932a. Molded by the movies. *McCall's Magazine*, November, 7.

———. 1932b. Movie madness. *McCall's Magazine*, October, 14.

———. 1932c. To the movies—But not to sleep! *McCall's Magazine*, September, 12.

———. 1934. *Our movie made children*. New York: Macmillan.

Foster, Constance. 1956. A mother of boys says: Raise your girl to be a wife. *Parents' Magazine*, September, 43–44, 113.

Foucault, Michel. 1972. *The archaeology of knowledge and the discourse on language*, trans. A. M. Sheriden Smith. New York: Vintage.

———. 1980. *Power/knowledge*. Trans. Colin Gordon, Leo Marshall, John Mepham, and Kate Soper. New York: Pantheon.

———. 1984. What is an author. In *The Foucault reader*, ed. Paul Rabinow, 101–120. New York: Pantheon.

———. 1988. *The history of sexuality: The care of the self*. Vol. 3, trans. Robert Hurley. New York: Vintage.

Fox, Richard W., and T. J. Jackson Lears, eds. 1983. *The culture of consumption: Critical essays in American history, 1880–1980*. New York: Pantheon.

Fracchia, Joseph. 1998. Michel Foucault, Karl Marx, and the historical-materialist horizon. *Intellectual History Newsletter*, December, 1–23.

Frank, Thomas. 1997. *The conquest of cool: Business culture, counterculture, and the rise of hip consumerism*. Chicago: University of Chicago Press.

Frankenheimer, John, dir. 1962. *The Manchurian candidate*. M. C. Productions.

Frederick, Christine. 1913. *The new housekeeping*. New York: Doubleday, Page.

———. 1920. *Household engineering: Scientific management in the home*. Chicago: American School of Home Economics.

Freedman, Jonathan L. 2002. *Media violence and its affect on aggression: Assessing the scientific evidence*. Toronto: University of Toronto Press.

Freeman, Derek. 1983. *Margaret Mead and Samoa: The making and unmaking of an anthropological myth*. London: Harvard University Press.

Frenkel-Brunswik, Else. 1955. Differential patterns of social outlook and personality in family and children. In *Childhood in contemporary cultures*, ed. Margaret Mead and Martha Wolfenstein, 369–404.

Freud, Sigmund. 1914. On narcissism: An introduction. In *General psychological theory*, ed. Philip Rieff, trans. Cecil M. Baines. New York: Macmillan, 1963.

———. 1918. *Totem and taboo: Some points of agreement between the mental lives of savages and neurotics*. Trans. James Strachey. New York: W. W. Norton, 1962.

———. 1924. *Three essays on the theory of sexuality*. Trans. James Strachey. New York: Basic Books, 1962.

———. 1963. *Civilization and its discontents*. Ed. James Strachey. Trans. Joan Riviere. London: Hogarth, 1963.

Friedrich, Carl J., and Zbigniew K. Brzezinski. 1956. *Totalitarian dictatorship and autocracy*. New York: Praeger.

Fromm, Erich. 1955. *The sane society*. New York: Rinehart.

Fuller, Katherine. 1996. *At the picture show: Small-town audiences and the creation of movie-fan culture*. Washington, D.C.: Smithsonian Institution Press.

Gabler, Neal. 1988. *An empire of their own: How the Jews invented Hollywood*. New York: Crown Publishers.

Gans, Roma. 1955. Eight important things children learn from play. *Parents' Magazine*, November, 46.

Gatlin, Rochelle. 1987. *American women since 1945*. Jackson: University Press of Mississippi.

Gerbner, George, and Larry Gross. 1976. Living with television: The violence profile. *Journal of Communication* 26:173–199.

Gesell, Arnold. 1930. *The guidance of mental growth in infant and child*. New York: The Macmillan Company.

———. 1940. *The first five years of life: A guide to the study of the preschool child*. New York: Harpers.

Gesell, Arnold, and Francis L. Ilg. 1946. *The child from five to ten*. New York: Harper and Bros.

Gesell, Arnold, Francis L. Ilg, and Louise Bates Ames. 1956. *Youth: The years from ten to sixteen*. New York: Harper and Bros.

Gideonse, Harry D. 1948. The Reds are after your child. *American Magazine*, July, 19.

Gilbert, Eugene. 1957. *Advertising and marketing to young people*. Pleasantville, N.Y.: Printers' Ink.

Gilbert, Susan. 1999. For some children, it's an after-school pressure cooker. *New York Times*, August 3.

Gilbreth, Frank, Jr., and Elizabeth Gilbreth Carey. 1963. *Cheaper by the dozen*. New York: Thomas Y. Crowell.

Gilbreth, Lillian. 1927. *The home-maker and her job*. New York: D. Appleton and Co.

———. 1928. *Living with our children*. New York: W. W. Norton.

Gilman, Charlotte Perkins. 1900. *Concerning children*. Boston: Small, Maynard and Co.

———. 1913. The waste of private housekeeping. *Annals of the American Academy of Political and Social Science* 48.

Giroux, Henry A. 1999. *The mouse that roared: Disney and the end of innocence*. Lanham, Md.: Rowman and Littlefield.

Glynn, Eugene David. 1956. Television and the American character—A psychiatrist looks at television. In *Television's impact on American culture*, ed. William Y. Elliot, 175–82. East Lansing: Michigan State University Press.

Goddard, Henry Herbert. 1919. *The Kallikak family: A study in the heredity of feeble-mindedness*. New York: Macmillan.

Golden, Mark. 1990. *Children and childhood in classical Athens*. Baltimore: Johns Hopkins University Press.

Goode, Erica. 1999. Mozart for baby? Some say, maybe not. *New York Times*, August 3.

Goodman, Paul. 1960. *Growing up absurd: Problems of youth in the organized system*. New York: Random House.

Gordon, Linda, ed. 1990. *Women, the state, and welfare*. Madison: University of Wisconsin Press.

Gorer, Geoffrey. 1948. *The American people: A study in national character*. New York: W. W. Norton.

Gould, Dr. Jay. 1956. In 1957 . . . what population boom means to you. *Sales Management*, November 10.

Graham, Laurel. 1997. Beyond manipulation: Lillian Gilbreth's industrial psychology and the governmentality of women consumers. *Sociological Quarterly* 38:539–566.

———. 1998. *Managing on her own: Dr. Lillian Gilbreth and women's work in the interwar era*. Norcross, Ga.: Engineering and Management Press.

Greenberg, Clement. 1939. Avant-garde and kitsch. In *Art and culture: Critical essays*. Boston: Beacon Press, 1961.

Gruenberg, Sidonie M. 1956. Do parents need the experts? *Parents' Magazine*, October, 46.

Grundy, Mrs. 1922. Letter to editor. *Photoplay*, November, 17.

Gunning, Tom. 1995. Tracing the individual body: Photography, detectives, and early cinema. In *Cinema and the invention of modern life*, ed. Leo Charney and Vanessa Schwartz, 15–45. Berkeley: University of California Press.

Haber, Samuel. 1964. *Efficiency and uplift: Scientific management in the Progressive Era, 1890–1920*. Chicago: University of Chicago Press.

Hager, Alice Rogers. 1934. Movies reflect our moods: Through twenty varied years styles on the screen have mirrored the national mind. *New York Times Magazine*, April 22.

Halas, John. 1987. *Masters of animation*. London: BBC Books.

Hall, Fred T. 1954. Letter to Walt Disney. January 18. Walt Disney Archives, Burbank, Calif.

Hall, G. Stanley. 1915. Child training. *Woman's World*, May, 5.

———. 1965. *Health, growth, and heredity: G. Stanley Hall on natural education*. Ed. Charles E. Strickland and Charles Burgess. New York: Teachers College Press.

Haller, Mark. 1963. *Eugenics: Hereditarian attitudes in American thought*. New Brunswick, N.J.: Rutgers.

Hamilton Luske, dir. 1955. *Lady and the tramp*. Walt Disney Pictures.

Hanawalt, Barbara. 1993. *Growing up in medieval London: The experience of childhood in history*. New York: Oxford University Press.

Hand, David, dir. 1997 (1942). *Bambi: 55th anniversary limited edition*. Walt Disney Studios.

Hansen, Miriam. 1991. *Babel and Babylon: Spectatorship in American silent film*. Cambridge, Mass.: Harvard University Press.

Haraway, Donna. 1989. *Primate visions*. London: Routledge.

———. 1991. A cyborg manifesto: Science, technology, and socialist-feminism in the late twentieth century. In *Simians, cyborgs, and women: The reinvention of nature*. New York: Routledge.

Harding, Sandra. 1987. Is there a feminist method? In *Feminism and methodology*, ed. Sandra Harding, 1–14. Bloomington: Indiana University Press.

Hardyment, Christina. 1983. *Dream babies: Three centuries of good advice on childcare*. New York: Harper and Row.

Hart, Gardner. 1953. Letter to Walt Disney. December 16. Walt Disney Archives, Burbank, Calif.

Hartmann, Susan M. 1994. Women's employment and the domestic ideal in the early cold war years. In *Not June Cleaver: Women and gender in postwar America*, ed. Joan Meyerowitz. Philadelphia: Temple University Press.

Hartsock, Nancy. 1987. The feminist standpoint: Developing the ground for a specifically feminist historical materialism. In *Feminism and methodology*, ed. Sandra Harding, 283–310. Bloomington: Indiana University Press.

Haskin, Byron, dir. 1950. *Treasure island*. Walt Disney Pictures.

Hayden, Dolores. 1981. *Grand domestic revolution*. Cambridge, Mass.: MIT Press.

Hays, Will H. 1934a. *Annual report to the Motion Picture Producers and Distributors of America, Inc*. New York: MPPDA.

———. 1934b. Why this bulletin? *The motion picture and the family*, October 15, 1.

Hecht, George. 1950. 1950–1960: The decade of the child. *Parents' Magazine*, January, 18.

———. 1956. The coming international brains race. *Parents' Magazine*, November, 35.

H. E. M. 1922. Miscasting—A misdemeanor. *Photoplay*, December.

Hendershot, Heather. 1998. *Saturday morning censors: Television regulation before the V-chip*. Durham, N.C.: Duke University Press.

Herman, Ellen. 1995. *The romance of American psychology: Political culture in the age of experts*. Berkeley: University of California Press.

Herrnstein, Richard J., and Charles Murray. 1994. *The bell curve: Intelligence and class structure in American life*. New York: Free Press.

Hibler, Winston, dir. 1956. *Survival in nature*. Walt Disney Pictures.

Himes, Chester. 1947. *Lonely crusade*. Chatham, N.J.: The Chatham Bookseller.

Hofstadter, Richard. 1963. *The progressive movement*. Englewood Cliffs, N.J.: Prentice Hall.

Hollister, Paul. 1940. Genius at work: Walt Disney. *Atlantic Monthly*, December, 689–701.

Hollyman, Burnes St. Patrick. 1983. Alexander Black's picture plays, 1893–1894. In *Film before Griffith*, ed. John L. Fell, 188–195.

Holt, L. Emmett. 1894. *The care and feeding of children: A catechism for the use of mothers and children's nurses*. New York: Appleton.

Homan, Leslie B. 1944. *As the twig is bent*. New York: Macmillan.

Hoover, Dwight W. 1990. *Middletown revisited*. Muncie, Ind.: Ball State Monograph.

Hopper, Hedda. 1954. Disney planning four kinds of films on TV. *Los Angeles Times*, April 10.

Horkheimer, Max, and Theodor Adorno. 1944. *Dialectic of enlightenment*. San Francisco: HarperCollins, 1975.

Horn, Marilyn. 1989. *Before it's too late: The child guidance movement in the United States, 1922–1945*. Philadelphia: Temple University Press.

Horne, Gerald. 2001. *Class struggle in Hollywood, 1930–1950: Moguls, mobsters, stars, Reds, and trade unionists*. Austin: University of Texas Press.

Hovland, Carl I., Arthur A. Lumsdaine, and Fred D. Sheffield. 1949. *Experiments on mass communication*. New York: John Wiley and Sons.

Hovland, Carl I., Irving L. Janis, and Harold H. Kelly. 1953. *Communication and persuasion: Psychological studies of opinion change*. New Haven, Conn.: Yale University Press.

Howard, June. 2001. *Publishing the family*. Durham, N.C.: Duke University Press.

Huesmann, L. Rowell, Jessica Moise-Titus, Cheryl-Lynn Podolski, and Leonard D. Eron. 2003. Longitudinal relations between children's exposure to television violence and their aggressive and violent behavior in young adulthood: 1977–1992. *Developmental Psychology* 39:200–201.

Hulbert, Anne. 2003. *Raising America: Experts, parents, and a century of advice about children*. New York: Knopf.

Illick, Joseph. 2002. *American childhoods*. Philadelphia: University of Pennsylvania Press.

Importance of youth market shown in three studies. 1947. *Printers' Ink*, April.

Institute of Child Welfare. 1938. *The first Berkeley growth study*. Berkeley: University of California Press.

Jackson, Wilfred, and Harve Foster, dirs. 1946. *Song of the south*. Walt Disney Pictures.

Jenkins, Henry. 1992. *What made pistachio nuts? Early sound comedy and the vaudeville aesthetic*. New York: Columbia University Press.

———, ed. 1998. *The children's culture reader*. New York: New York University Press.

Jenson, Jane. 1990. Representations of gender: Policies to "protect" women workers and infants in France and the United States. In *Women, the state, and welfare*, ed. Linda Gordon, 152–177.

Joas, Hans. 1980. *G. H. Mead: A contemporary re-examination of his thought*. Trans. Raymond Meyer. Cambridge: Polity.

Jowett, Garth S. 1983. The first motion picture audiences. In *Film before Griffith*, ed. John L. Fell, 196–206.

Jowett, Garth S., Ian C. Jarvie, and Kathryn H. Fuller. 1996. *Children and the movies: Media influence and the Payne Fund controversy*. New York: Cambridge University Press.

Julian, Rupert, dir. 1925. *The phantom of the opera*. Universal Pictures.

Katz, Elihu, and Paul Lazarsfeld. 1955. *Personal influence: The part played by people in the flow of mass communication*. Glencoe, Ill.: Free Press.

Kaufman, Michael T. 1999. William H. Whyte, "Organization Man" author and urbanologist, is dead at 81. *New York Times*, January 13.

Kazan, Elia, dir. 1957. *A face in the crowd*. Warner Brothers.

Kenngott, George F. 1912. *The record of a city: A social survey of Lowell Massachusetts*. New York: Macmillan.

Kimball, Ward, dir. 1955. *Man in the moon*. Walt Disney Pictures.

Kirkley, Donald. 1951. Column. *Baltimore Sun*, August 12.

Klein, Norman M. 1993. *Seven minutes: The life and death of the American animated cartoon*. New York: Verso.

Knight, Vick. 1953. Letter to Walt Disney. November 7. Walt Disney Archives, Burbank, Calif.

Koenig, Elizabeth W. 1955. A book list for child television fans. *Parents' Magazine*, November, 112.

Koszarski, Richard. 1990. An evening's entertainment: The age of the silent feature picture, 1915–1928. In *History of the American cinema*, vol. 3, ed. Charles Harpole. New York: Charles Scribner's Sons.

Koury, Phil. 1942. Bambi gets a spanking. *Kansas City Star*. Walt Disney Archives, Burbank, Calif.

Kuhn, Thomas. 1962. *The structure of scientific revolutions*. Chicago: University of Chicago Press.

Ladd-Taylor, Molly, ed. 1986. *Raising a baby the government way: Mothers' letters to the Children's Bureau, 1915–1932*. New Brunswick, N.J.: Rutgers University Press.

Lang, Walter, dir. 1950. *Cheaper by the dozen*. 20th Century Fox.

LaRossa, Ralph. 1997. *The modernization of fatherhood: A social and political history*. Chicago: University of Chicago Press.

Lasch, Fred. 1937. Movie values for boys and girls. *Parents' Magazine*, December, 26.

Lasswell, Harold Dwight. 1927. *Propaganda technique in the World War*. New York, Alfred A. Knopf.

Latour, Bruno. 1993. *We have never been modern*. Trans. Catherine Porter. Cambridge, Mass.: Harvard University Press.

Lears, Jackson. 1994. *Fables of abundance: A cultural history of advertising in America*. New York: Basic Books.

Leiss, William. 1994. *The domination of nature*. London: McGill-Queen's University Press.

Lenroot, Katherine. 1936. Letter to Clara Savage Littledale. September. U.S. National Archives, Children's Bureau files.

Lerner, Daniel. 1958. *The passing of traditional society*. Glencoe, Ill.: Free Press.

Levine, Lawrence. 1991. William Shakespeare and the American people: A study in cultural transformation. In *Rethinking popular culture: Contemporary perspectives in cultural studies*, ed. Chandra Mukerji and Michael Schudson, 157–197. Berkeley: University of California Press.

Lewis, Jon. 1994. Disney after Disney: Family business and the business of family. In *Disney Discourse*, ed. Eric Smoodin. New York: Routledge.

Lindner, Robert M. 1948. *Rebel without a cause: The hypnoanalysis of a criminal psychopath*. New York: Grune and Stratton.

———. 1956. *Must you conform?* New York: Rinehart and Co.

Lipset, Seymour, and Leo Lowenthal, eds. 1961. *Culture and social character: The work of David Riesman reviewed*. New York: The Free Press of Glencoe.

Lipsitz, George. 1981. *Class and culture in Cold War America*. New York: Praeger Publishers.

———. 1995. The possessive investment in whiteness: Racialized social democracy and the "white" problem in American Studies. *American Quarterly* 47:369–387.

Littledale, Clara Savage. 1931. After the conference what? *Parents' Magazine*, January, 1.

———. 1937. The home behind the child. *Parents' Magazine*, November, 11.

Lloyd, David, and Paul Thomas. 1998. *Culture and the state*. New York: Routledge.

Locke, John. 1693. *Some thoughts concerning the education of children*. Ed. John W. and Jean S. Yolton. Oxford: Clarendon Press, 1989.

Lockhart, Jane. 1950. Looking at movies. *Rotarian*, May, 40.

Lott, Eric. 1993. *Love and theft: Blackface minstrelsy and the American working class*. New York: Oxford University Press.

Lukács, György. 1963. *The meaning of contemporary realism*. Trans. John and Necke Mander. London: Merlin.

———. 1971. *History and class consciousness: Studies in Marxist dialectics*. Trans. Rodney Livingstone. Cambridge, Mass.: MIT Press.

———. 2000. *A defense of history and class consciousness*. Trans. John Rees. New York: Verso.

Luke, Carmen. 1990. *Constructing the child viewer: A history of the American discourse on television and children, 1950–1980*. New York: Praeger.

Lunbeck, Elizabeth. 1994. *The psychiatric persuasion: Knowledge, gender, and power in modern America*. Princeton, N.J.: Princeton University Press.

Lundberg, Ferdinand, and Marynia F. Farnham. 1947. *Modern woman: The lost sex*. New York: Harper and Row.

Lynd, Helen Merrell. 1937. Books for parents. *Parents' Magazine*, October, 128.

Lynd, Robert S., and Helen M. Lynd. 1929. *Middletown: A study in American culture*. New York: Harcourt Brace and Co.

———. 1937. *Middletown in transition: A study in cultural conflicts*. New York: Harcourt, Brace and Co.

MacDonald, Dwight. 1953. A theory of mass culture. In *Mass culture: The popular arts in America*, ed. Bernard Rosenberg and David Manning White, 59–73. Glencoe, Ill.: Free Press, 1965.

MacKinnon, Catharine A. 1989. *Toward a feminist theory of the state*. Cambridge, Mass.: Harvard University Press.

Macleod, David. 1982. Act your age: Boyhood, adolescence, and the rise of the Boy Scouts of America. *Journal of Social History* 16.2:3–20.

———. 1983. *Building character in the American boy: The Boy Scouts, YMCA, and their forerunners, 1870–1920*. Madison: University of Wisconsin Press.

———. 1993. *Sons of the empire: The frontier and the Boy Scout Movement, 1890–1918*. Toronto: University of Toronto Press.

Maier, Thomas. 1998. *Dr. Spock: An American life*. New York: Harcourt Brace.

Maltby, Richard. 1995. The Production Code and the Hays Office. In *Grand design: Hollywood as a modern business enterprise*, ed. Tino Balio, 37–72. Berkeley: University of California Press.

Maltin, Leonard. 1980. *Of mice and magic: A history of American animated cartoons*. New York: McGraw Hill.

Mann, Denise. 1992. The spectacularization of everyday life: Recycling Hollywood stars and fans in early television variety shows. In *Private screenings: Television and the female consumer*, ed. Lynn Spigel and Denise Mann, 41–70. Minneapolis: University of Minnesota Press.

Marchand, Roland. 1985. *Advertising the American Dream: Making way for modernity: 1920–1940*. Berkeley: University of California Press.

Marcus, George E. and Michael M. Fischer. 1986. *Anthropology as cultural critique: An experimental moment in the human sciences*. Chicago: University of Chicago Press.

Marling, Karal Ann. 1994. *As seen on television: The visual culture of everyday life in the 1950s*. Cambridge, Mass.: Harvard University Press.

Marshall, Robert. 1933. *Arctic village*. New York: Literary Guild.

Marx, Karl. 1845. *Theses on Fuerbach*. In *The Marx-Engels reader*, ed. John Tucker, 143.

———. 1858. *Grundrisse*. In *The Marx-Engels reader*, ed. John Tucker, 221.

———. 1867. *Capital*. Vol. 1. In *The Marx-Engels reader*, ed. John Tucker, 294.

———. 1961. *Capital*. Vol. 1. Trans. Samuel Moore and Edward Aveling. Moscow: Foreign Languages Publishing House.

———. 1978. *The Marx-Engels reader*. Ed. John Tucker. 2nd ed. New York: W. W. Norton.

May, Lary. 1980. *Screening out the past*. Chicago: University of Chicago Press.

May, Mark. 1933. Movies and morals. *Christian Science Monitor*, January 3, 1.

Mayo, Elton. 1933. *The human problems of an industrial civilization*. New York: Macmillan.

———. 1945. *The social problems of an industrial civilization*. Boston: Division of Research, Graduate School of Business Administration, Harvard University.

———. 1947. *The political problem of industrial civilization*. Boston: Division of Research, Graduate School of Business Administration, Harvard University.

McCardell, Roy L. 1915. Sore heads and slander. *Exhibitor's Bulletin*, January, 13.

McCarthy, Anna. 2001. *Ambient television: Visual culture and public space*. Durham, N.C.: Duke University Press.

McClelland, David C. 1961. *The achieving society*. New York: Van Nostrand Co.

McConoughey, Edward M. 1915. *Motion pictures in religious and educational work*. Boston: Methodist Federation for Social Service.

McGovern, Charles. 1993. Sold American: Inventing the consumer, 1890–1940. Ph.D. diss., Harvard University.

McLeod, Jack M., Gerald M. Kosicki, and Zhongdang Pan. 1991. On understanding and misunderstanding media effects. In *Mass media and society*, ed. James Curran and Michael Gurevitch. London: Edward Arnold.

Mead, G. H. 1956. *The social psychology of George Herbert Mead*. Ed. Anselm Strauss. Chicago: University of Chicago Press.

Mead, Margaret. 1928. *Coming of age in Samoa*. New York: American Museum of Natural History, 1972.

———. 1944. *The American character*. Harmondsworth, Middlesex: Penguin Books.

———. 1951. *Soviet attitudes toward authority: An interdisciplinary approach to problems of Soviet character*. New York: McGraw-Hill.

———. 1955a. Implications of insight—II. In *Childhood in contemporary cultures*, ed. Margaret Mead and Martha Wolfenstein, 449–464.

———. 1955b. Theoretical setting—1954. In *Childhood in contemporary cultures*, ed. Margaret Mead and Martha Wolfenstein, 3–20.

Mead, Margaret, and Elena Calas. 1955. Child-training ideals in a postrevolutionary context: Soviet Russia. In *Childhood in contemporary cultures*, ed. Margaret Mead and Martha Wolfenstein, 179–203.

Mead, Margaret, and Martha Wolfenstein, eds. 1955. *Childhood in contemporary cultures*. Chicago: University of Chicago Press.

Media companies are sued in Kentucky shooting. 1999. *New York Times*, April 13.

Meek, Lois H. 1931. The bird's eye view of parent education. *Parents' Magazine*, April, 19.

———. 1940. *Your child's development and guidance told in pictures*. New York: Lippincott.

Meek, Pauline P. 1955. I stopped spanking . . . when I found out why I did it. *Parents' Magazine*, April.

Menand, Louis. 2001. The culture club. *New Yorker*, October 15, 202.

Menen, Aubrey. 1963. Dazzled in Disneyland. *Holiday*, July, 60–75, 106.

Merchant, Carolyn. 1980. *The death of nature: Women, ecology, and the scientific revolution*. San Francisco: HarperCollins.

Merritt, Karen. 1988. The little girl/little mother transformation: The American evolution of "Snow White and the Seven Dwarfs." In *Storytelling in animation: The art of the animated image*, vol. 2., ed. John Canemaker, 105–121. Los Angeles: American Film Institute.

Merritt, Russell, and J. B. Kaufman. 1993. *Walt in Wonderland: The silent films of Walt Disney*. Baltimore: Johns Hopkins University Press.

Merton, Robert K. 1946. *Mass persuasion: The social psychology of a war bond drive*. Westport, Conn.: Greenwood.

Mickey's night. 1954. *Mirror*. October 27.

Mifflin, Lawrie. 1999. Pediatricians urge limiting television watching. *New York Times*, August 4.

Mills, C. Wright. 1957. *The power elite*. London: Oxford University Press.

Mills, John. A. 1998. *Control: A history of behavioral psychology*. New York: New York University Press.

Mink, Gwendolyn. 1990. The lady and the tramp: Gender, race, and the origins of the American welfare state. In *Women, the state, and welfare*, ed. Linda Gordon, 92–122.

Mitchell, Alison, and Frank Bruni. 1999. Debate sprawls, touching religion and gun control. *New York Times*, June 18.

Mitman, Gregg. 1993. Cinematic nature: Hollywood technology, popular culture, and the American Museum of Natural History. *Isis* 84:637–661.

———. 1999. *Reel nature: America's romance with wildlife on film*. Cambridge, Mass.: Harvard University Press.

Moley, Raymond. 1938. *Are we movie made?* New York: Macy-Masius.

———. 1945. *The Hays Office*. New York: Bobbs-Merrill.

Money from mice. 1950. *Newsweek*, February 13.

Montaigne, Michel. 1580. *Essays*. Trans. J. M. Cohen. London: Penguin, 1993.

Montgomery, David. 1987. *The fall of the house of labor: The workplace, the state, and American labor activism, 1865–1925*. New York: Cambridge University Press.

Moore, Kathleen Carter. 1896. The mental development of a child. *Psychological Review*, October 3, 1–137.

A moralist's view. 1956. *Newsweek*, April.

Morey, Anna. 1996. Early film exhibition in Wilmington, North Carolina, 1897–1915. *Spectator* 17:8–27.

Morgenson, Gretchen, and Patrick McGeehan. 2002. Wall St. and the nursery school: A New York story. *New York Times*, November 14.

Mouse and man. 1937. *Time Magazine*, December 27.

The mouse that turned to gold. 1955. *Business Week*, July 9.

Moving pictures forward. 1922. Atlanta: Better Films Committee.

Mukerji, Chandra. 1997a. Monsters and muppets: The history of childhood and techniques of cultural analysis. In *From sociology to cultural studies: New perspectives*, ed. Elizabeth Long, 155–84. Malden, Mass.: Blackwell.

———. 1997b. *Territorial ambitions and the gardens of Versailles*. Cambridge: Cambridge University Press.

Myrdal, Gunnar. 1944. *An American dilemma: The Negro problem and modern democracy*. New York: Harper and Brothers.

Nasaw, David. 1985. *Children of the city: At work and at play*. Garden City, N.Y.: Anchor Press/Doubleday.

———. 1992. Children and commercial culture: Moving pictures in the early twentieth century. In *Small worlds: Children and adolescents in America, 1850–1950*, ed. Elliot West and Paula Petrik, 14–25. Lawrence: University Press of Kansas.

———. 1993. *Going out: The rise and fall of public amusements*. New York: Basic Books.

National Board of Review of Motion Pictures: Its background, growth, and present status. 1935. New York: National Board of Review.

Nelson, Daniel. 1980. *Frederick W. Taylor and the rise of scientific management*. Madison: University of Wisconsin Press.

Newman, Ruth G. 1950. When and how to say no. *Parents' Magazine*, January, 24.

The new pictures. 1942. *Time Magazine*, February 9.

Newton, Michael. 2002. *Savage girls and wild boys: A history of feral children*. New York: Picador.

Nicholson, Meredith. 1922. Will H. Hays—A real leader. *Photoplay*, May, 30.

Noyes, Anna. 1913. *How I kept my baby well*. Baltimore: Warwick and York.

Nugent, Frank. 1947. That million dollar mouse. *New York Times Magazine*, February 21, 22.

O'Conner, Alice. 2001. *Poverty knowledge: Social science, social policy, and the poor in twentieth-century U.S. history*. Princeton, N.J.: Princeton University Press.

O'Shea. M. V. 1920. *The trend of the teens*. Chicago: Frederick Drake and Co.

———. 1929. *Newer ways with children*. New York: Greenberg.

Omi, Michael, and Howard Winant. 1994. *Racial formation in the United States from the 1960s to the 1990s*. New York: Routledge.

Oppenheimer, Ella, M.D. 1935. Letter to Lula Shelburne. October 15. U.S. National Archives, Children's Bureau files.

Orme, Nicholas. 2001. *Medieval children*. New Haven: Yale University Press.

Packard, Vance. 1957. *The hidden persuaders*. New York: David McKay Co.

———. 1959. *The status seekers: An exploration of class behavior in America and the hidden barriers that affect you, your community, your future*. New York: D. McKay Co.

Patterson, Edwin. 1932. Letter to editor. *Photoplay*, May, 6.

Peach, Gene. 1951. Gene Peach. *San Diego Evening Tribune*, August 22.

Peiss, Kathy. 1986. *Cheap amusements: Working women and leisure at the turn of the century.* Philadelphia: Temple University Press.

Perlman, William J., ed. 1936. *The movies on trial: The views and opinions of outstanding personalities about screen entertainment past and present.* New York: Macmillan.

Perry, Ralph B. 1949. *Characteristically American.* New York: Knopf.

Peters, Charles C. 1933. *Motion pictures and standards of morality.* New York: Macmillan.

Peterson, Marion. 1955. I've stopped yelling. *Parents' Magazine*, December, 46.

Peterson, Ruth C., and L. L. Thurstone. 1933. *Motion pictures and the social attitudes of children.* New York: The Macmillan Company.

Pfister, Joel, and Nancy Schnog, eds. 1997. *Inventing the psychological: Toward a cultural history of emotional life in America.* New Haven, Conn.: Yale University Press.

Piaget, Jean. 1953. *The origin of intelligence in the child.* London: Routledge and Paul.

Piaget, Jean, E. Cartalis, S. Escher, A. Hanhart, L. Hahnloser, O. Matthes, S. Perret, and M. Roud. 1928. *Judgment and reasoning in the child.* New York: Harcourt, Brace.

Pietz, William. 1993. Fetishism and materialism: The limitations of theory in Marx. In *Fetishism as cultural discourse*, ed. Emily Apter and William Pietz, 119–151. Ithaca, N.Y.: Cornell University Press.

Plant, James Stuart. 1937. *Personality and the cultural pattern.* New York: The Commonwealth Fund.

Pollock, Linda A. 1983. *Forgotten children: Parent-child relations from 1500 to 1900.* New York: Cambridge University Press.

Postman, Neil. 1982. *The disappearance of childhood.* New York: Delacorte Press.

Potter, David M. 1954. *People of plenty: Economic abundance and the American character.* Chicago: University of Chicago Press.

Pringle, Henry F. 1932. Mickey Mouse's father. *McCall's Magazine*, August, 7.

Project on Disney. 1995. *Inside the mouse: Work and play at Disney World.* Durham, N.C.: Duke University Press.

Publicity on Walt Disney's Silly Symphony "Grasshopper and the Ants." 1934. Burbank, California: United Artists.

Puner, Helen. 1955. You, your children, and the finer things in life. *Parents' Magazine*, May, 40.

Quigley, Martin. 1937. *Decency in motion pictures.* New York: Macmillan.

Quirk, James. 1922a. Moral house-cleaning in Hollywood: An open letter to Mr. Will Hays. *Photoplay*, April, 53.

———. 1922b. The screen and the child. *Photoplay*, October, 19.

Ranney, Omar. 1951. Stage and screen. *Cleveland Press*, June 6.

Raper, Arthur Franklin. 1936. *Preface to peasantry: A tale of two black belt counties.* Chapel Hill: University of North Carolina Press.

Regester, Charlene. 1996. Black films, white censors. In *Movie censorship and American culture*, ed. Francis Couvares, 159–186. Washington, D.C.: Smithsonian Institution Press.

Renshaw, Samuel, Vernon L. Miller, and Dorothy P. Marquis. 1933. *Children's sleep*. New York: Macmillan.

Review. 1953. *Time Magazine*, November 16.

Review: Disneyland. 1954. *Hollywood Reporter*, October 29.

Richardson, Frank Howard. 1935. How good a father are you? *Parents' Magazine*, June.

Riesman, David. 1954. *Individualism reconsidered*. Glencoe, Ill.: Free Press.

Riesman, David, and Nathan Glazer. 1961. The lonely crowd: A reconsideration in 1960. In *Culture and social character*, ed. Seymour Lipset and Leo Lowenthal.

Riesman, David, Reuel Denney, and Nathan Glazer. 1950. *The lonely crowd: A study of the changing American character*. New Haven, Conn.: Yale University Press.

Ripperger, Henrietta. 1934. Healthier days for our children: To their well-being, emphasized by May Day observance, diet has largely contributed. *New York Times Magazine*, April 29, 16.

Robertson, John S, dir. 1934. *Wednesday's child*. RKO Pictures.

Robinson, David. 1991. *Masterpieces of animation, 1833–1908*. Gemona del Friuli, Italy: La Cineteca del Friuli.

Roediger, David. 1991. *The wages of whiteness: Race and the making of the American working class*. London: Verso.

Rogin, Michael. 1992. Blackface, white noise: The Jewish jazz singer finds his voice. *Critical Inquiry* 18:417–453.

———. 1996. *Blackface, white noise: Jewish immigrants in the Hollywood melting pot*. Berkeley: University of California Press.

Roosevelt, Theodore. 1895. *American ideals*. New York: G. P Putnam's Sons.

———. 1911. *The new nationalism*. New York: Outlook Co.

Rorty, James. 1933a. How the movies harm children. *Parents' Magazine*, August, 18.

———. 1933b. New facts about movies and children. *Parents' Magazine*, July, 18.

Rosenberg, Bernard, and David Manning White, eds. 1971. *Mass culture revisited*. New York: Van Nostrand Reinhold.

Ross, Dorothy. 1991. *The origins of American social science*. Cambridge: Cambridge University Press.

Ross, Steven J. 1990. Cinema and class conflict: Labor, capital, the state, and American silent film. In *Resisting images: Essays on cinema and history*, ed. Robert Sklar and Charles Musser, 68–107. Philadelphia: Temple University Press.

Rottenberg, Dan, ed. 1997. *Middletown Jews: The tenuous survival of an American Jewish community*. Bloomington: Indiana University Press.

Rousseau, Jean-Jacques. 1979. *Emile; or, On education*. Trans. Allan Bloom. New York: Basic Books.

Rubin, Joan S. 1992. *The making of middle-brow culture*. Chapel Hill: University of North Carolina Press.

Sahlins, Marshall. 1991. *La penseé bourgeoise*: Western society as culture. In *Rethinking Popular Culture*, ed. Chandra Mukerji and Michael Schudson, 278–90. Berkeley: University of California Press.

Sammond, Nicholas, and Chandra Mukerji. 2001. "What you are . . . I wouldn't eat":

Ethnicity, whiteness, and performing "the Jew" in Hollywood's Golden Age. In *Classic whiteness*, ed. Daniel Bernardi, 3–30. Minneapolis: University of Minnesota Press.

Sandler, Kevin, ed. 1998. *Reading the rabbit: Explorations in Warner Bros. Animation*. New Brunswick, N.J.: Rutgers University Press.

Schickel, Richard. 1968. *The Disney version: The life, times, art, and commerce of Walt Disney*. New York: Simon and Schuster.

Schramm, Wilbur. 1959. *Children and television: Some advice to parents*. New York: Television Information Office.

Schramm, Wilbur, Jack Lyle, and Edwin B. Parker. 1961. *Television in the lives of our children*. Stanford, Calif.: Stanford University Press.

Schudson, Michael. 1984. Advertising as capitalist realism. *Advertising, the uneasy persuasion*. New York: Basic Books.

Schuster, Harold, dir. 1949. *So dear to my heart*. Walt Disney Pictures.

Schweizer, Peter, and Rochelle Schweizer. 1998. *Disney, the mouse betrayed: Greed, corruption, and children at risk*. Washington, D.C.: Regnery.

Scott, Joan W. 1988a. Deconstructing equality-versus-difference; or, The uses of poststructuralist theory for feminism. *Feminist Studies* 14:33–50.

———. 1988b. Gender: A useful category of historical analysis. In *Gender and the politics of history*. New York: Columbia University Press.

———. 1992. Experience. In *Feminists theorize the political*, ed. Joan Scott and Judith Butler, 22–39. New York: Routledge.

Seaton, James. 1996. *Cultural conservatism, political liberalism: From criticism to cultural studies*. Ann Arbor: University of Michigan Press.

Seiter, Ellen. 1993. *Sold separately: Parents and children in consumer culture*. New Brunswick, N.J.: Rutgers University Press.

Shattuck, Roger. 1980. *The forbidden experiment: The story of the Wild Boy of Aveyron*. New York: Farrar Straus Giroux.

Shayon, Robert Lewis. 1951. *Television and our children*. New York: Longman, Green.

Sheehy, Emma D. 1955. Records for your children and you. *Parents' Magazine*, July, 87.

———. 1956a. Records for your children and you. *Parents' Magazine*, March, 28.

———. 1956b. Records for your children and you. *Parents' Magazine*, October.

Shuttleworth, Frank K., and Mark May. 1933. *The social conduct and attitudes of movie fans*. New York: Macmillan.

Siegel, Don, dir. 1956. *Invasion of the body snatchers*. Allied Artists.

Silverman, Kaja. 1990. Dis-embodying the female voice. In *Issues in feminist film criticism*, ed. Patricia Erens, 309–329. Bloomington: Indiana University Press.

Sklar, Kathryn Kish. 1993. The historical foundations of women's power in the creation of the American welfare state, 1830–1930. In *Mothers of a new world: Maternalist politics and the origins of welfare states*, ed. Seth Koven and Sonya Michel, 43–93. New York: Routledge.

———. 1995. *Florence Kelley and the nation's work: The rise of women's political culture, 1830–1900*. New Haven, Conn.: Yale University Press.

Sklar, Robert. 1975. *Movie-made America: A cultural history of American movies*. New York: Random House.

———. 1980. The making of cultural myths—Walt Disney. In *The American animated cartoon: A critical anthology*, ed. Gerald Peary and Danny Peary, 58–65. New York: E. P. Dutton.

Smith, David. 1987. New dimensions—Beginnings of the multiplane camera. In *Art of the animated image*, ed. Charles Solomon. Vol. 1, 37–51. Los Angeles: American Film Institute.

———. 1996. *Disney A to Z: The official encyclopedia*. New York: Hyperion Press.

Smith, Frederick James. 1922. Foolish censors. *Photoplay*, October, 39.

Smith, Julia Holmes. 1893. First causes of character. In *Childhood*, ed. George Winterburn, 347–352. New York: A. L. Chatterton.

Smoodin, Eric. 1993. *Animating culture: Hollywood cartoons from the sound era*. New Brunswick, N.J.: Rutgers University Press.

Smythe, Dallas. 1977. Communications: Blindspot of Western Marxism. *Canadian Journal of Political and Social Theory* 1:1–27.

Spigel, Lynn. 1992. *Make room for television: Television and the family ideal in postwar America*. Chicago: University of Chicago Press.

Spock, Benjamin. 1950. Children need sensible parents. *Parents' Magazine*, September, 40.

———. 1957. *The common sense book of baby and child care*. 3rd ed. New York: Duell, Sloan, and Pearce.

Sproule, J. Michael. 1987. Propaganda studies and the rise of the critical paradigm. *Quarterly Journal of Speech* 73, 60–78.

Spurr, Dolly. 1922. Children and the movies. *Photoplay*, May, 88.

Stamp, Shelley. 2000. *Movie struck girls: Women and motion picture culture after the nickelodeon*. Princeton, N.J.: Princeton University Press.

———. 2004. Lois Webber, progressive cinema, and the fate of the "Work-a-Day Girl" in *Shoes*. *Camera Obscura* 19, no. 2:56.

Stearns, Peter. 2003. *Anxious parents: A history of modern childrearing in America*. New York: New York University Press.

Stelzle, Charles. 1904. *Boys of the street: How to win them*. New York: Fleming H. Revell.

Stocking, George. 1998. *Race, culture, and evolution: Essays in the history of anthropology*. New York: Free Press, 1968.

Strasser, Susan. 1989. *Satisfaction guaranteed: The making of the American mass market*. New York: Pantheon.

Strasser, Susan, Charles McGovern, and Mattias Judt. 1998. *Getting and spending: European and American consumer societies in the twentieth century*. Cambridge: Cambridge University Press.

Strathman, Terry. 1984. From the quotidian to the utopian: Child rearing literature in America, 1926–1946. *Berkeley Journal of Sociology* 29, 1–33.

Streeter, Coolidge. 1916. Photoplay children at the big studios. *Picture Progress*, December, 10.

Suburbia: The key to market expansion. 1957. *Printers' Ink*, September 27.

Sully, James. 1902. The new study of children. In *Little Masterpieces of Science: Mind.* George Iles, ed., 21–52. New York: Doubleday.

Swift, Edgar James. 1912. *Youth and the race.* New York: Charles Scribner's Sons.

Taussig, Michael. 1980. *The devil and commodity fetishism.* Chapel Hill: University of North Carolina Press.

———. 1993. Maleficium: State fetishism. In *Fetishism as cultural discourse*, ed. Emily Apter and William Pietz. Ithaca: Cornell University Press.

Tedlow, Richard. 1990. *New and improved: The story of mass marketing in America.* New York: Basic Books.

Television pre-view. 1954. *Radio Daily—Television Daily*, October 21.

Thom, Douglas A. 1925. *Child management.* Minneapolis: Institute of Child Welfare, University of Minnesota.

———. 1928. *Everyday problems of the everyday child.* New York: D. Appleton and Co.

Thompson, J. Walter. 1949. 5,000 families under glass! *Sales Management*, September 1.

Thrope, Elsielise. 1950. When children have bad dreams. *Parents' Magazine*, April, 38.

Tinker Bell, Mary Poppins, cold cash. 1965. *Newsweek*, July 12.

Tocqueville, Alexis de. 2000. *Democracy in America.* Ed. Harvey C. Mansfield and Delba Winthrop. Chicago: University of Chicago Press.

Turner, Frederick Jackson. 1893. The significance of the frontier in American history. In *The American studies anthology*, ed. Richard P. Horwitz, 83–96. Wilmington, Del.: SR Books, 2001.

———. 1920. *The frontier in American history.* New York: H. Holt and Company.

Turner, Stephen Park, and Jonathan H. Turner. 1990. *The impossible science: An institutional analysis of American sociology.* London: Sage.

Tuttle, William J. 1992. The homefront children's popular culture: Radio, movies, comics—adventure, patriotism, and sex-typing. In *Small worlds: Children and adolescents in America, 1850–1950*, ed. Elliot West and Paula Petrik, 143–164. Lawrence: University Press of Kansas.

$23,402: The biggest week's business in the history of New York's 575-seat Sutton Theater. 1953. *Film Daily*, November 20.

Tyler May, Elaine. 1988. *Homeward bound: American families in the cold-war era.* New York: Basic Books.

United Nations. 1951. *The impact of the Universal Declaration of Human Rights.* New York: United Nations.

United States Department of Labor, Children's Bureau. 1930. *Child labor: Facts and figures.* Washington, D.C.: United States Printing Office.

Van Doren, Mark. 1938. Review of *Snow White. Nation*, January, 108.

Veblen, Thorstein. 1899. *The theory of the leisure class.* New York: Macmillan.

Vidor, King, dir. 1949. *The fountainhead.* Warner Brothers.

Vygotsky, Lem S. 1978. *Mind in society: The development of higher psychological processes.* London: Harvard University Press.

Walkerdine, Valerie. 1988. *The mastery of reason: Cognitive development and the production of rationality*. London: Routledge.

Wallace, Irving. 1949. Mickey Mouse, and how he grew. *Colliers*, April 9, 20.

Waller, Gregory A. 1980. Mickey, Walt, and film criticism from *Steamboat Willie* to *Bambi*. In *The American animated cartoon: A critical anthology*, ed. Gerald Peary and Danny Peary, 49–57. New York: E. P. Dutton.

Walt Disney Productions. 1932. Manager enlists mothers' interest. *Mickey Mouse Club Bulletin*, April 15.

———. 1934a. Walt Disney's Silly Symphony "The China Shop." Burbank, Calif.: United Artists.

———. 1934b. Publicity on Walt Disney's Mickey Mouse in "Camping Out." Burbank, Calif.: United Artists.

———. 1935. Publicity on Walt Disney's Silly Symphony "Broken Toys." Burbank, Calif.: United Artists.

———. 1938. *Walt Disney's Snow White and the Seven Dwarfs: Press book*. Burbank, Calif.: RKO Radio Pictures.

———. 1940. *Pinocchio campaign book*. Burbank, Calif.: RKO Radio Pictures, Inc.

———. 1944. *1943 annual report*. Burbank, Calif.: Walt Disney Productions.

———. 1948. *Seal Island pressbook*. Burbank, Calif.: RKO Pictures.

———. 1950a. *Annual report*. Burbank, Calif.: Walt Disney Productions.

———. 1950b. Audience reaction survey for *Nature's Half Acre*. Burbank, Calif.: Walt Disney Productions.

———. 1950c. *Beaver Valley pressbook*. Burbank, Calif.: RKO Pictures.

———. 1951a. *Annual report*. Burbank, Calif.: Walt Disney Productions.

———. 1951b. *Nature's Half Acre pressbook*. Burbank, Calif.: Walt Disney Productions.

———. 1952. *The story of . . . Walt Disney's True-Life Adventure series*. Burbank, Calif.: Walt Disney Productions.

———. 1953a. *Annual report*. Burbank, Calif.: Walt Disney Productions.

———. 1953b. *Living Desert pressbook*. Burbank, Calif.: Walt Disney Productions.

———. 1953c. *Walt Disney presents new explorations in true-life adventures and people and places*. Burbank, Calif.: Walt Disney Productions.

———. 1954a. *Annual report*. Burbank, Calif.: Walt Disney Productions.

———. 1954b. *Vanishing Prairie pressbook*. Burbank, Calif.: Walt Disney Productions.

———. 1955. *Annual report*. Burbank, Calif.: Walt Disney Productions.

———. 1956a. *Disney on television: A supplementary materials guide for classroom use in connection with 2 television programs produced by Walt Disney: Disneyland and Mickey Mouse Club*. Burbank, Calif.: Walt Disney Productions.

———. 1956b. *Secrets of Life pressbook*. Burbank, Calif.: Walt Disney Productions.

———. 1957. *Annual report*. Burbank, Calif.: Walt Disney Productions.

———. 1958. *Annual report*. Burbank, Calif.: Walt Disney Productions.

———. 1959. *Annual report*. Burbank, Calif.: Walt Disney Productions.

Wanger, Walter. 1943. Mickey Icarus, 1943: Fusing ideas with the art of the animated cartoon. *Saturday Review of Literature*, September 4.

Warner, W. Lloyd, and Paul Lunt. 1941. *The social life of a modern community*. New Haven, Conn.: Yale University Press.

Wartella, Ellen, and B. Reeves. 1985. Historical trends in research on children and the media, 1900–1960. *Journal of Communication* 35:118–133.

Wasko, Janet. 1982. *Movies and money: Financing the American film industry*. Norwood, N.J.: Ablex Pub. Corp.

Watson, John B. 1912. Instinctive activity in animals: Some recent experiments and observations. *Harper's Magazine*, February, 376–381.

———. 1928. *Psychological care of infant and child*. London: Allen and Unwin.

Watts, Steven. 1997. *The magic kingdom: Walt Disney and the American way of life*. New York: Houghton Mifflin.

Weber, Max. 2001. *The Protestant ethic and the spirit of capitalism*. Trans. Talcott Parsons. London: Routledge.

Wednesday's child. 1934. *The Motion Picture and the Family*, November 15, 3.

Wensberg, Katherine S., and Mary M. Northrop. 1955. Children need to understand their feelings. *Parents' Magazine*, September, 40.

Wertsch, James V. 1985. *Vygotsky and the social formation of mind*. Cambridge, Mass.: Harvard University Press.

Wharton, Don. 1956. Let's get rid of tele-violence. *Parents' Magazine*, April, 54.

Whyte, William H., Jr. 1951a. The corporation and the wife. *Fortune*, November.

———. 1951b. The wives of management. *Fortune*, October.

———. 1956. *The organization man*. New York: Simon and Schuster.

Wilkinson, Rupert. 1988. *The pursuit of American character*. New York: Harper and Row.

Williams, Bob. 1955. Around the dials. [Name of newspaper not known.] Walt Disney Archives, Burbank, Calif.

Williams, Raymond. 1977. *Marxism and literature*. New York: Oxford University Press.

———. 1985. *Keywords: A vocabulary of culture and society*. Rev. ed. New York: Oxford University Press.

Wilson, Sloan. 1955. *The man in the gray flannel suit*. New York: Simon and Schuster.

Winterburn, George, ed. 1893. *Childhood: A monthly magazine for parents of all that concerns the welfare of the child*. New York: A. L. Chatterton.

Wishy, Bernard. 1968. *The child and the republic: The dawn of modern American child nurture*. Philadelphia: University of Pennsylvania Press.

Withers, Carl [pseud. James West]. 1945. *Plainville, U.S.A.* New York, Columbia University Press.

Wolf, Anna. 1937. Children need to be enjoyed. *Parents' Magazine*, September, 20.

Wolfenstein, Martha. Interviews with parents and children: Introduction. In *Childhood in contemporary cultures*, ed. Margaret Mead and Martha Wolfenstein, 345–348.

Wolters, Larry. 1954. Disneyland could cut into dinner. *Chicago Daily Tribune*, October 28.

Wreszin, Michael. 1994. *A rebel in defense of tradition: The life and politics of Dwight Macdonald*. New York: Basic Books.

Wrong, Dennis. 1956. Riesman and the age of sociology. *Commentary* 21:331.

Wylie, Philip. 1942. *Generation of vipers*. New York: Farrar and Rinehart.

———. 1954. *Tomorrow!* New York: Rinehart.

Yerkes, Robert M. 1941. Letter to Walt Disney. New Haven, Conn. Walt Disney Archives, Burbank, Calif.

Youcha, Geraldine. 1995. *Minding the children: Child care in America from colonial times to present*. New York: Scribner.

Zelizer, Viviana. 1985. *Pricing the priceless child: The changing social value of children*. Princeton, N.J.: Princeton University Press.

Filmography

The Adventures of Mr. Ichabod and Mr. Toad. Walt Disney Pictures (U.S.), 1949. James Algar, dir.

Alice in Wonderland. Walt Disney Pictures. (U.S.), 1951. Clyde Geronimi and Wilfred Jackson, dirs.

Babes in the Woods. Walt Disney Pictures (U.S.), 1932. Burt Gillett, dir.

Bambi. Walt Disney Pictures (U.S.), 1942. David Hand, dir.

Bear Country. Walt Disney Pictures (U.S.), 1953. James Algar, dir.

Beaver Valley. Walt Disney Pictures (U.S.), 1950. James Algar, dir.

Broken Toys. Walt Disney Pictures (U.S.), 1935. Ben Sharpsteen, dir.

The China Shop. Walt Disney Pictures (U.S.), 1934. Wilfred Jackson, dir. (uncredited).

Cinderella. Walt Disney Pictures (U.S.), 1950. Clyde Geronimi and Wilfred Jackson, dirs.

Davy Crockett, King of the Wild Frontie.r Walt Disney Pictures (U.S.), 1954. Norman Foster, dir.

Dumbo Walt Disney Pictures. (U.S.), 1941. Ben Sharpsteen, dir.

Fantasia Walt Disney Pictures. (U.S.), 1940. James Algar, Samuel Armstrong, Ford Beebe, Norman Ferguson, Jim Handley, T. Hee, Wilfred Jackson, Hamilton Luske, Bill Roberts, Paul Satterfield, Ben Sharpsteen, dirs.

Flowers and Trees. Walt Disney Pictures (U.S.), 1932. Burt Gillett, dir.

The Great Train Robbery. Edison Manufacturing (U.S.), 1903. Edwin S. Porter, dir.

The Littlest Outlaw. Walt Disney Pictures (U.S.), 1950. Roberto Gavaldón, dir.

The Living Desert. Walt Disney Pictures (U.S.), 1953. James Algar, dir.

Magic Highway U.S.A. Walt Disney Pictures (U.S.), 1958. Ward Kimball, dir.

Man and the Moon. Walt Disney Pictures (U.S.), 1955. Ward Kimball, dir.

Nature's Half Acre. Walt Disney Pictures (U.S.), 1951. James Algar, dir.

The Old Mill. Walt Disney Pictures (U.S.), 1937. Wilfred Jackson, dir.

The Olympic Elk. Walt Disney Pictures (U.S.), 1952. James Algar, dir.

Our Friend the Atom. Walt Disney Pictures (U.S.), 1958. Hamilton Luske, dir.

Peck's Bad Boy. Sol Lesser Productions (U.S.), 1934. Edward F. Cline, dir.

Peter Pan. Walt Disney Pictures (U.S.), 1953. Clyde Geromini, Wilfred Jackson, Hamilton Luske, dirs.

The Phantom of the Opera. Universal Pictures (U.S.), 1925. Rupert Julian, dir.

Pinocchio. Walt Disney Pictures (U.S.), 1940. Hamilton Luske, Ben Sharpsteen, dirs.

Prowlers of the Everglades. Walt Disney Pictures (U.S.), 1953. James Algar, dir.

The Reluctant Dragon. Walt Disney Pictures (U.S.), 1941. Alfred Wirker, Ford Beebe, Jasper Blystone, Jim Handley, Hamilton Luske, Erwin L. Verity, dirs.

Santa's Workshop. Walt Disney Pictures (U.S.), 1932. Wilfred Jackson, dir.

Seal Island. Walt Disney Pictures (U.S.), 1948. James Algar, dir.

Secrets of Life. Walt Disney Pictures (U.S.), 1956. James Algar, dir.

The Seri Indians. Walt Disney Pictures (U.S.), unreleased.

Snow White. Walt Disney Pictures (U.S.), 1937. David Hand, supervising dir.

Song of the South. Walt Disney Pictures (U.S.), 1946. Harve Foster, Wilfred Jackson, dirs.

Steamboat Willie. Walt Disney Pictures (U.S.), 1928. Walt Disney and Ub Iwerks, dirs.

Survival in Nature. Walt Disney Pictures (U.S.), 1956. Winston Hibler, dir.

The Three Caballeros. Walt Disney Pictures (U.S.), 1944. Norman Ferguson, dir.

The Three Little Pigs. Walt Disney Pictures (U.S.), 1933. Burt Gillett, dir.

Treasure Island. RKO British Radio (U.K.) and Walt Disney Pictures (U.S.), 1950. Byron Haskin, dir.

20,000 Leagues Under the Sea. Walt Disney Pictures (U.S.), 1954. Richard Fleischer, dir.

The Vanishing Prairie. Walt Disney Pictures (U.S.), 1954. James Algar, dir.

Water Birds. Walt Disney Pictures (U.S.), 1952. James Algar, Ben Sharpsteen, dirs.

Wednesday's Child. RKO Pictures (U.S.), 1934. John S. Robertson, dir.

White Wilderness. Walt Disney Pictures (U.S.), 1958. James Algar, dir.

Why We Fight (series). U.S. Army Special Services Division (U.S.), 1943–1945. Frank Capra, Anatole Litvak, dirs.

Index

NICHOLAS SAMMOND IS ASSISTANT PROFESSOR OF CINEMA STUDIES AT THE UNIVERSITY OF TORONTO. HE IS THE EDITOR OF *STEEL CHAIR TO THE HEAD: THE PLEASURE AND PAIN OF PROFESSIONAL WRESTLING.*

LIBRARY OF CONGRESS
CATALOGING-IN-PUBLICATION DATA
SAMMOND, NICHOLAS.
BABES IN TOMORROWLAND: WALT DISNEY AND THE
MAKING OF THE AMERICAN CHILD, 1930–1960 /
NICHOLAS SAMMOND.
P. CM.
INCLUDES BIBLIOGRAPHICAL REFERENCES AND
INDEX.
ISBN 0-8223-3451-8 (CLOTH : ALK. PAPER)
ISBN 0-8223-3463-1 (PBK. : ALK. PAPER)
1. CHILDREN—UNITED STATES—HISTORY—20TH
CENTURY. 2. DISNEY, WALT, 1901–1966. 3. CHILDREN
IN MOTION PICTURES. I. TITLE.
HQ792.U5S26 2005
305.23'0973'0904—dc22 2005000325